Introduction to Computer Science

THIRD EDITION

Introduction to Computer Science

THIRD EDITION

Neill Graham

West Publishing Company
St. Paul   New York   San Francisco   Los Angeles

Copyediting:
Deborah Drolen Jones

Interior design:
Biblio Book Design

Artwork:
Editing, Design & Production, Inc.

Composition:
The Clarinda Company

Cover photograph:
Floyd Rollefstad, Laser Fantasy Production

Library of Congress Cataloging in Publication Data

Graham, Neill, 1941–
    Introduction to computer science.

    Bibliography: p.
    Includes index.
    1. Electronic digital computers.   2. Electronic data
processing.   I. Title.
QA76.5.G658   1985   001.64   84-21940
ISBN 0-314-85240-9

Contents

Preface   **xi**

Part I   **Computers, algorithms, and problem solving**   **1**

Chapter 1   **Computers, information, and algorithms**   **3**

1.1   Information, symbols, and data   5
1.2   Examples of information processing   6
1.3   Properties of algorithms   9
1.4   Two algorithms   12

Chapter 2   **Problems, algorithms, and recursion**   **27**

2.1   Problem theory   27
2.2   Polya's four steps for solving a problem   35
2.3   Problem-solving techniques   39
2.4   Recursion   51

Part II   **Computer hardware and software**   **65**

Chapter 3   **Computer hardware**   **67**

3.1   The parts of a computer—an overview   67
3.2   The central processing unit   69

3.3   Computer memory   71
3.4   Input and output devices   74
3.5   Classifications of computers   78

Chapter 4   Information representation   81

4.1   Binary codes   81
4.2   Operations on binary values   87
4.3   Octal and hexadecimal notation   90
4.4   Signed numbers   94
4.5   Floating-point numbers   97
4.6   A simple computer   100

Chapter 5   Computer software   117

5.1   Programming languages   118
5.2   The operating system   123
5.3   Concurrent execution   129

 Part III   Principles of algorithm construction   137

Chapter 6   Values, constants, and expressions   139

6.1   Data types   139
6.2   Output   144
6.3   Identifiers, constants, and algorithms   147
6.4   Arithmetical operations and expressions   151
6.5   Functions   156
      Pascal Supplement   160
         Data types   161
         Output   164
         Identifiers   169
         Constant definitions   170
         Program format   171
         Expressions   173

Chapter 7   Variables, assignment, and input   177

7.1   Variables   177
7.2   Declarations   179
7.3   Assignment   180
7.4   Variables in expressions   182
7.5   Input and output   187
7.6   Interactive and batch processing   190

7.7   Four algorithms   192
        Pascal Supplement   206
                Variables and declarations   206
                Assignment and expressions   207
                Input and output   208
                Prompts and responses   213
                Example programs   213

Chapter 8   Repetition   219

8.1   The **for** construction   220
8.2   Algorithms using the **for** construction   223
8.3   The **while** construction   231
8.4   Algorithms using the **while** construction   235
8.5   The **repeat** construction   241
        Pascal Supplement   248
                *The **for** statement   248*
                Compound statements   249
                *Programs using the **for** statement   251*
                *Conditions, Boolean expressions, and relational
                operators   251*
                *The **while** statement   255*
                *Programs using the **while** statement   257*
                Reading data and the eof predicate   258
                *The **repeat** statement   261*

Chapter 9   Selection   265

9.1   One- and two-way selection   265
9.2   Algorithms using one- and two-way selection   269
9.3   Multiway selection   278
9.4   Compound conditions and Boolean operators   290
9.5   Algorithms using Boolean operators   292
        Pascal Supplement   303
                One- and two-way selection   303
                Multiway selection   309
                Boolean operators   317

Chapter 10   Subalgorithms   321

10.1   Functions   322
10.2   Procedures   328
10.3   Input, output, and input/output parameters   329
10.4   Parameter-passing methods   332
10.5   An algorithm for playing craps   336

10.6   Scope and lifetime   346
10.7   Recursion revisited   371
10.8   Verifying algorithms that use functions and procedures   382
        Pascal Supplement   *389*
            Functions and procedures   389
            Parameters and parameter passing   393
            The program craps   *396*
            Access to variables   400
            Recursion   414

Chapter 11   Software design, coding, and testing   419

11.1   Software engineering   420
11.2   Characteristics of high-quality software   421
11.3   Requirements analysis   423
11.4   Specification   426
11.5   Design   427
11.6   Implementation   439
11.7   Validation, verification, and testing   449
11.8   Maintenance   464
        Pascal Supplement   467

Part IV   Data structures   475

Chapter 12   Types, records, and files   477

12.1   Type definitions   478
12.2   Record types   478
12.3   Files and streams   487
12.4   File types   491
12.5   Sequential file processing   497
12.6   Three examples of sequential file processing   498
        Pascal Supplement   515
            Type definitions   516
            Enumerated types   516
            Subrange types   517
            Operations on values of ordinal types   519
            Set types   520
            Record types   523
            File types   528

Chapter 13   Arrays   547

13.1   One-dimensional arrays   547
13.2   Elements of array processing   550

13.3   Searching arrays   555
13.4   A table-handling module   571
13.5   Sorting   578
13.6   Multidimensional arrays   589
        Pascal Supplement   601
            One-dimensional arrays   601
            Multidimensional arrays   603
            Examples   604

Chapter 14   Stacks and queues   615

14.1   Stacks   616
14.2   Array implementations of stacks   620
14.3   Applications of stacks   631
14.4   Queues   643
14.5   Array implementations of queues   646
14.6   Applications of queues   656
        Pascal Supplement   664

Chapter 15   Strings   673

15.1   Fixed-length strings   674
15.2   Variable-length strings   677
15.3   Operations on variable-length strings   678
15.4   Implementation considerations   684
15.5   A string-processing module   691
15.6   Substitution for parameters   713
        Pascal Supplement   725
            Packed types   725
            String types   727
            The string-processing module   728

Chapter 16   Linked structures   741

16.1   Pointer types   742
16.2   Linked lists   748
16.3   Applications of linked lists   750
16.4   Trees   770
16.5   Notations and traversals   774
16.6   Linked representation of trees   782
16.7   Binary search trees   790
        Pascal Supplement   806
            Pointer types   806
            Summary of type system   822

Part V   Numerical methods   825

Chapter 17   Errors, equations, and areas   827

17.1   Numerical errors   827
17.2   Nonlinear equations   831
17.3   Systems of linear equations   842
17.4   Numerical integration   856
        Pascal Supplement   868

Index   879

Preface

This book is intended for a two-semester introductory course in computer science. No mathematical preparation is required beyond the usual elementary and high school courses. Although high school algebra is desirable, it is not necessary because the concepts that it might contribute—variables, functions, and expression evaluation—are developed in detail in this book. Most of the problems require no mathematical background. The occasional mathematically oriented problem, such as computing binomial coefficients, is intended only for students with sufficient mathematical background for the problem to be meaningful. The chapter on numerical methods requires somewhat greater mathematical sophistication than does the rest of the book.

The book has been completely rewritten for the third edition, with extensive changes in both content and presentation. Although I have not attempted to adhere rigidly to any one set of guidelines, the revision has been influenced by the course descriptions for CS1 and CS2 in the Association for Computing Machinery's Curriculum '78, the course description for the advanced placement test in computer science, currently available textbooks, and the recommendations of those who commented on the second edition. The following are some of the changes made in the third edition.

The first two chapters of the book present several algorithms for solving easily visualized problems such as sorting three names into alphabetical order and solving the Towers-of-Hanoi problem. Many instructors felt that the traditional Euclidean algorithm, with which the previous editions began, was too difficult for students without extensive mathematical backgrounds. These early algorithms are written in an Englishlike pseudolanguage to avoid all problems with the technicalities of an algorithmic language.

A new chapter on problems, problem-solving techniques, and their relation to the principles of algorithm construction has been included. The chapter on software design and testing has been expanded to discuss a number of concepts of modern software engineering, such as the software development life cycle, simulation of specifications, walkthroughs, correctness proofs, and program synthesis.

The use of assertions for understanding and verifying algorithms has been introduced from the outset and is referred to throughout the book. Although algorithm verification is discussed and illustrated, the emphasis is on assertions as an aid to understanding rather than as a tool for producing formal proofs of correctness.

Algorithms and programs are typeset in the boldface-italics form of Algol and Pascal rather than in the uppercase-letters-only form used in previous editions.

Data types, type definitions, and required variable declarations have been introduced into the algorithmic language. In the previous editions, types were treated informally and declarations were usually optional. This approach no longer seems appropriate in view of the importance of types and type checking in modern programming languages such as Pascal and Ada.

The discussion of parameter passing for procedures and functions has been completely revised. Parameters are classified as **in, out,** and **in out.** Parameter transmission by copy and by reference are both discussed. As in the second edition, the call-by-name mechanism is not discussed. Although call by name is of theoretical and historical interest, it plays no role in modern programming languages.

The discussion of global variable access—access to variables declared outside of a function or procedure—is expanded to include three possibilities: (1) **common** declarations as in FORTRAN and some other languages; (2) nested procedure declarations as in Algol and Pascal; and (3) modules encapsulating procedures, functions, and declarations, as in such languages as Modula-2, Ada, and UCSD Pascal. The third alternative is used throughout the remainder of the book to present many data structures as implementations of abstract data types. Emphasis is placed on the principle of information hiding as a guide to dividing a program into modules.

The discussions of data structures have been modified to emphasize depth rather than breadth; instead of trying to survey as many data structures and as many ways of representing a given structure as possible, fewer structures and representations are treated in greater detail.

The elements of algorithm analysis are introduced in the context of comparing the efficiency of different searching and sorting routines.

The two chapters on numerical methods have been combined into a single chapter, which provides sufficient coverage at the level of an introductory computer science course. Numerical integration is now illustrated by finding the area under a curve rather than by solving differential equations. Since it is assumed that students studying this chapter have a background in college algebra and trigonometry, standard mathematical concepts and notations are used more freely than in the other chapters. No previous knowledge of calculus is required; the chapter introduces the derivative as the slope of a tangent line and the definite integral as the area under a curve.

Part I introduces computers, information processing, computer applications, algorithms, and problem solving. Algorithms whose operation can be readily visualized are presented in an Englishlike pseudolanguage. A sequential algorithm and an iterative algorithm are discussed in Chapter 1, and a recursive algorithm is discussed in Chapter 2. Since the recursive algorithm is somewhat more difficult to understand than the other two, some instructors may wish to postpone its discussion until Chapter 10, which also discusses recursion.

Part II covers computer hardware, software, and information representation. Instructors differ as to how deeply they wish to go into the technicalities of information representation. To make it as easy as possible to cover only the material desired, the topics in Chapter 4 are arranged in order of increasing difficulty. Section 4.1 and the discussion of binary addition and subtraction in Section 4.2 are elementary. The rest of Section 4.2 and Sections 4.3 and 4.4 are of intermediate difficulty. Sections 4.5 and 4.6 are somewhat more difficult still. Section 4.5 is not prerequisite to Section 4.6, so one can study the hypothetical computer without taking up floating-point-number representations.

Part III on algorithm construction is the heart of the book. Data types, constants, and variables are introduced, along with the fundamental manipulations of input, output, assignment, and expression evaluation. This part is organized around the basic control structures: sequencing, selection, repetition, and function and procedure invocation. Repetition is taken up before selection since much more interesting and realistic examples can be presented once repetition has been mastered. Part III ends with a chapter on program design and testing. This chapter reviews and systematizes the algorithm construction techniques that have been used so far and discusses the additional problems that arise in large programming projects.

In Part IV the emphasis switches from control structures to data structures. Type definitions and structured types are introduced, and records, files, arrays, strings, and linked structures are explored. Chapter 13 introduces arrays and describes searching and sorting of one-dimensional arrays. Since different searching and sorting algorithms can differ dramatically in efficiency, this chapter seems a good place to introduce the elements of algorithm analysis. Chapter 14, on stacks and queues, introduces these data structures not only for their own interest but as examples of abstract data types defined by means of the operations that can be carried out on their values.

Part V provides a brief introduction to numerical analysis. Included are discussions of roundoff and truncation errors, solving nonlinear equations, solving systems of linear equations, and numerical evaluation of definite integrals.

I wish to thank the following persons for their comments on the second edition and their suggestions for the third edition: Dian Lopez, University of Minnesota (Morris Campus); John Leeson, University of Central Florida; Jean Rogers, University of Oregon; and David Weldon, Winona State University.

Introduction to Computer Science

THIRD EDITION

Part I
Computers, algorithms, and problem solving

1

Computers, information, and algorithms

The idea of the computer can be traced back to the early nineteenth century, when the British mathematician Charles Babbage proposed a mechanical "Analytical Engine" to carry out mathematical calculations under the control of punched cards. The first electronic computers were built in the early 1940s, about a century after Babbage's original proposal.

For many years, the cost, size, and power consumption of computers restricted their use to large organizations, and it was difficult or impossible for individuals to gain access to them. In the mid 1970s, however, progress in microelectronics led to the development of small, low-cost, *microcomputers* or *personal computers.* The same developments gave rise to *embedded computers,* which can be incorporated in consumer products such as microwave ovens, television sets, cameras, automobiles, and video games. Today most people living in developed countries have probably used a computer, although in the case of embedded computers they may not be aware that they have done so.

The first computers were built to carry out the complex numerical calculations of science, engineering, and mathematics. People quickly realized, however, that computers are not limited to numbers, but are general-purpose machines for storing and manipulating information. In principle, any information-processing task can be carried out by a computer if we can code the information to be processed in symbols the computer can manipulate and if we can describe precisely the manipulations to be carried out. In practice, factors such as the memory (information storage) capacity of a computer, the speed with which it operates, and the means by which it communicates with the outside world determine whether a particular computer is suitable for a particular information-processing task.

A computer operates under the control of a set of detailed, step-by-step instructions called a *program*. Program control is responsible for the computer's enormous versatility: by changing the program we can drastically change the information-processing task the computer carries out. With one program a computer might control a robot; with another it might print workers' paychecks; with still another it might play a game with the user. The other side of this coin, however, is that we must write or purchase* a program for every job we want the computer to do for us. The programs, or *software,* for a computer system may cost far more than the computing machinery, or *hardware*.

Programs are to computers what phonograph records are to phonographs. The program determines the behavior the computer will exhibit, just as the record determines the sounds that the phonograph will produce. Changing the program changes the computer's behavior, just as changing the record makes the phonograph play a different tune. What's more, we tend to attribute the behavior exhibited to the program rather than to the computer, just as we attribute the music to the record rather than to the phonograph. For example, we might say that a particular program plays chess and that we enjoy a particular record, instead of making the more precise statements that the computer plays chess under the control of the program and that we enjoy the sounds produced by the phonograph when a particular record is played.

To summarize, no matter how much computers differ in size, cost, and internal construction, they all have the following two characteristics in common:

1. A computer is a general-purpose information processor.

2. A computer works under the control of a program—a set of detailed, step-by-step instructions for the processing to be done.

These two characteristics of computers determine the subject matter of computer science. Since computers process information, computer science studies *data structures*—means for representing information in a form suitable for computer processing. And since a computer works under the control of a detailed set of instructions, computer science studies *algorithms,* sets of instructions for carrying out particular information-processing tasks.

The discipline that we know as computer science in the United States is known in many other countries as *information science* or *informatics*. The well-known Dutch computer scientist E. W. Dijkstra advocates the term *computing science*. These alternate names emphasize that computer science is more concerned with the techniques of information processing than with the technical details of the machines that carry out that processing.

---

*Some programs may be permanently built into a computer, some may be included in the purchase price of the computer, and some may be available through *users' groups*—associations formed by persons who use a particular kind of computer. Mostly, however, computer users must write or buy the programs they need.

1.1 Information, symbols, and data

Information   *Information* means facts and ideas. The facts and ideas are independent of the form in which they are expressed. If you inform me that I am invited to your house at eight o'clock next Thursday, this information will be the same regardless of whether you tell me in person, send me a note, call on the phone, or send a telegram.

Symbols   Information is an abstraction. Yet we do not use abstractions to communicate with one another! We use facial expressions; bodily movements; inarticulate grunts, groans, cries, and laughter; spoken English (and other languages); notes: memos; letters: telegrams; telephone calls; pictures; and many other concrete, physical things.

Before we can manipulate information, or even pass it from one person to another, we must represent it in some concrete, physical form. The physical things we use to represent information are called *symbols*. The letters of the alphabet, the sounds we make when speaking, the electrical currents that travel over telephone lines, and the electromagnetic waves our TV sets pick up are all examples of symbols. Figure 1.1 gives some additional examples of symbols.

Any time we convey, store, or manipulate information, we must actually work with concrete symbols that represent the information. To write a love letter, for instance, you need to make a large number of marks on a piece of paper with pen or pencil. Whatever the emotional content of the letter, the only way you can express that content is by arranging marks on paper in the proper order.

Data   We use the term *data* for information represented by concrete symbols. Computer people often use *data* and *information* almost interchangeably. But to be precise, we should use *data* when we want to emphasize the symbols themselves and *information* when we want to emphasize the facts and ideas that the symbols represent.

Incidentally, there is a curious controversy over whether the word *data* should be singular or plural. In Latin, the word *data* is plural, the singular being *datum*. Most English dictionaries, however, authorize both the singular and plural usages. Those who, like the author, prefer the singular usage, treat *data* as a mass noun, like "grass" or "sand" or "information." We say "the data has been processed" just as we say the "the grass has been cut," "the sand has been shoveled," or "the information has been processed." Those who prefer the plural usage would say "the data have been processed."

Information processing, data processing, and *symbol manipulation* are three terms we can use to describe what a computer does. *Information processing* describes what we are trying to accomplish. *Data processing* and *symbol manipulation* refer more specifically to the manipulations a computer must carry out to process information. *Data processing* is most frequently used in connection with programs that process large files of data, as in business applications; thus we are more likely to

Figure 1.1   Some symbols used in traffic control, chemistry, mathematics, electronics, and music.

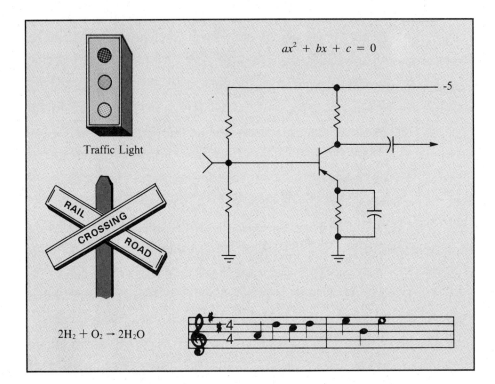

apply *data processing* to a program that prints paychecks for every employee in a company than to one that plays a video game.

Data is stored in a computer as *binary codes,* which are described in detail in Chapter 3. Computers can manipulate any symbols that can be converted into electrical signals representing binary codes. With modern electronics technology, most kinds of symbols can be so converted. Thus in addition to letters, digits, and punctuation marks, computers can process pictures, drawings, speech, music, and electrical sensing and control signals that allow a computer to monitor and control another machine.

1.2

Examples of information processing

The kinds of information processing a computer can perform are so varied that it is impossible to summarize them in a few words. The following examples, however, will give you some feeling for the computer's versatility.

Text processing A *text editor* program allows a computer to be used as an electronic typewriter. Text typed on the keyboard appears on the computer's display screen and is stored in the computer's memory. By giving appropriate commands to the computer, we can display any part of the stored text on the screen and make corrections, insertions, or deletions at any point. Blocks of text can be moved or copied from one part of the stored text to another. When we are satisfied with the stored text, we can print it out in whatever format we desire. The latter job is done by a *text formatter* program, which, in accordance with commands given by the user, might print the stored text in the proper format for a business letter, a legal contract, a student report, or a book manuscript. A *word processor* is a text editor and a text formatter combined into the same program; word processors are among the most popular programs for personal computers.

Simulation and modeling A computer can be programmed to simulate the behavior of such systems as a business, a spacecraft, or a telephone exchange. The computer, together with the simulation program, serves as working model of the simulated system. Studying the model can yield valuable insight into the behavior of the real system. In engineering, computer models are used to predict the performance of such real systems as airplanes and spacecraft before they are actually constructed. Simulation is particularly valuable in education since students can experiment freely with a computer model, something they could never do with such real systems as a large corporation or the economy of a country. Many computer games are simulations although they may simulate imaginary systems, such as space battles or haunted dungeons.

A popular tool for business simulations is a *spreadsheet program,* which causes the computer's display to represent a sheet of paper divided into rows and columns. The intersection of each row and column defines a *cell.* Normally, numerical values are entered for some cells, while for others formulas are entered telling how the values for those cells are to be calculated from the values of other cells. On command, the computer will carry out all the calculations called for by the formulas and display the values (entered directly or calculated) for all the cells.

In a typical application, the rows of the spreadsheet correspond to business data items such as income and expenses, and the columns correspond to months. The formulas describe how the data values for each month are to be calculated from those of the previous months. If values representing the business situation at the beginning of the year are entered in the January column, the program will calculate the corresponding values for the remaining months, thus predicting how the business will operate throughout the remainder of the year. (The accuracy of the prediction will depend, of course, on the validity of the assumptions on which the formulas were based.) Like word processors, spreadsheet programs are extremely popular with users of personal computers.

Data analysis The raw data collected in a survey or a scientific experiment usually needs to be analyzed to extract its meaning. Frequently, one needs to *count* the number of data items satisfying a certain criterion. In processing data collected in a political poll, for example, we would want to count the number of respondents favoring each candidate, the number belonging to each political party, the number considering a particular issue important, and so on.

Measures of central tendency, such as the mean (average), median, and mode, and *measures of dispersion,* such as the standard deviation, help us visualize the way data values are distributed. *Correlation coefficients* help us find relationships among the variables being studied. *Statistical tests* help us determine whether the data collected is meaningful or whether it can be explained by the workings of random chance. Having analyzed our data, we usually wish to display the results graphically—as line graphs, bar graphs, pie charts, and so on. *Statistical software packages* contain programs for analyzing data and displaying the results graphically.

Perhaps the best-known example of data analysis is that carried out on the data collected every ten years during the United States Census. The data on millions of census forms must be tabulated and analyzed to determine facts of great social, political, and economic importance. For example, the population of a city affects the amount of federal aid the city will receive. Census figures are sometimes challenged in court by those who feel that their localities will be adversely affected. The Census Bureau was a pioneer in the use of automatic data processing equipment.

Data management   One of the most widely used applications of computers is for storing and maintaining large data files, such as the files containing data on a company's customers, employees, suppliers, and inventory. Such a collection of files is known as a *data base* (the term *data bank* is also occasionally used).

As the above examples indicate, data management is important in business, but its importance is not limited to that field. The data collected during a complex scientific experiment—say a rocket launch—may be stored in a data base and manipulated with data management programs. Governments maintain many large data bases, such as the one containing the records of all people who file income tax returns. Controversy frequently arises over the ways governments use data bases, such as to locate persons who are not paying child support, to detect persons cheating on welfare, or to ferret out young people who have not registered for the draft.

A data base is maintained by a set of programs called a *data-base management system.* Users who access the data directly as well as programs that use it in their processing all work through the data-base management system. The data-base management system provides a simple logical view of the data regardless of how it is actually stored on such media as tapes and disks. For one type of data base, called a *relational data base,* the data is viewed as if it were arranged in tables. By requesting the data-base management system to combine rows and columns selected from particular tables, the user can specify the data to be retrieved and processed. *Natural language interfaces,* which are still experimental, allow nontechnical users to ask the system questions in English or some other natural language and receive answers based on the contents of the data base.

Like spreadsheet programs and word processors, data-base management systems are popular with users of personal computers.

Games   One of the best-known computer applications is game playing. Computer games come in several forms: arcade games, video games to be attached to home television sets, hand-held video games with their own built-in displays, and game-playing programs for personal computers.

Although computers are best known for video games, they can also play more traditional games, such as chess. The idea of a machine playing chess has fascinated people since the eighteenth century when a (fraudulent) chess-playing machine was widely exhibited. Chess tournaments in which computers play one another are now annual events, and computers sometimes participate in human chess tournaments. The best chess programs play at the expert level, and one program was recently recognized as playing at the master level.

As mentioned earlier, many computer games simulate some real-world situation such as managing a business or flying an airplane. (The best-known simulation game is not a computer game at all but the board game Monopoly, which simulates real-estate invetment.) If the game programs accurately reflect the systems they are supposed to simulate, then simulation games can be as educational as they are entertaining.

1.3 Properties of algorithms

An algorithm is a set of instructions for carrying out a particular task. A program, in contrast, is an algorithm expressed in a form suitable for execution by a computer. Our use of the terms *algorithm* and *program* is analogous to our use of the terms *information* and *data*. The algorithm is the abstract idea; the program is its concrete realization in a form suitable for use with a computer. Like *information* and *data,* the words *algorithm* and *program* are often used interchangeably.

Every correct algorithm comes with a guarantee that, if we faithfully follow its instructions, we will solve a particular problem or accomplish a particular task. This guarantee is essential if we are to use the algorithm with confidence. We probably wouldn't bother learning the multiplication algorithm—the set of rules for multiplication that we learned in grade school—if we weren't sure that it would give the right answer for any pair of numbers we chose to multiply. And we would be even more hesitant to incorporate an unreliable algorithm in our computers, where the results calculated under its direction might not be checked or even seen by human beings.

Frequently, we must place some restrictions on the data an algorithm is to manipulate in order to guarantee correct results. In arithmetic, for example, division by zero is not defined. Therefore, the guarantee for the division algorithm—the familiar rules for long division—has a clause stating that the guarantee holds only if the divisor is not zero.

To assure that algorithms live up to their guarantees—that we can always carry out the instructions in an algorithm, and that doing so will yield the specified results—every correct algorithm must have the following four characteristics.

1. *An algorithm is precise.* Every step of an algorithm must specify precisely what action is to be taken; there is no room for vagueness. Each step has to be given explicitly; none can be "assumed" or "understood." Because it

is almost impossible to achieve the necessary precision in English, people have devised a variety of *algorithmic languages*. These are analogous to the notations used in mathematics, dance, chemistry, knitting, and crocheting to express technical ideas more concisely and precisely than is possible in English.

2. *An algorithm is effective.* No instruction can be impossible for the person or machine executing the algorithm to carry out.

Suppose, for instance, that an algorithm demands that we take the square root of 2 with perfect precision. The square root of 2 is given by

$$\sqrt{2} = 1.4142135623. . .$$

where the dots indicate an infinite sequence of additional digits. This unending sequence of digits could never be written out on a blackboard or a piece of paper, and could never be stored inside any computer. An algorithm that requires us to take the square root of 2 with perfect precision, then, is not effective.

3. *An algorithm must have a fixed, finite number of instructions.* The number of instructions in an algorithm must be finite because we could never finish carrying out an algorithm with an infinite number of instructions and thus the algorithm could never yield the guaranteed results. We further require that the algorithm, and hence the number of instructions in it, remain the same regardless of the data that is processed.

These requirements may seem obvious enough, but consider the following problem. Suppose we are writing an algorithm to make out workers' paychecks. We can suppose that the algorithm will contain a sequence of instructions describing how to make out one paycheck—where to print the date, the name of the payee, the amount, and so on. But if our algorithm is to be useful, it must print many paychecks, not just one.

We might try writing the instructions for printing one paycheck over and over again as many times as required, but that won't work for two reasons. First, if thousands of checks are to be printed, then writing out the same instructions thousands of times would be an enormous waste of labor. Second, and most important, when we write the algorithm we may not know how many paychecks are to be printed. We would like to write the algorithm in such a way that it can be used just as well by a small company with only a few employees as by a large company with many thousands. What's more, for a given company, the number of paychecks to be printed will vary from week to week as workers are hired and fired.

The solution is to write the instructions for making out a paycheck just once, but specify that the instructions are to be carried out as many times as necessary. For example, the instructions for printing one paycheck might be prefaced with the following statement:

Using the following instructions, print a paycheck for each record in the payroll file.

By specifying that some instructions are to be executed repeatedly, we can write an algorithm containing a fixed, finite number of instructions that, nevertheless, can process an arbitrarily large amount of data or solve an arbitrarily complex problem.

4. *The execution of an algorithm must terminate.* When a person or machine executes an algorithm, he, she, or it must eventually reach a point where the task is complete and no more instructions are to be executed. The execution of an algorithm must not go on indefinitely.

If an algorithm can contain only a fixed, finite number of instructions, how can its execution fail to terminate? The answer, of course, is that the algorithm can specify that some instructions are to be executed repeatedly. If the conditions under which the repetition is to terminate are not stated correctly, the repetition may continue indefinitely and the algorithm will fail to terminate.

In our paycheck example, we specified that the instructions for making out one paycheck would be executed once for each record in the payroll file. This is a "safe" repetition because there can be only a finite number of records in the payroll file. Eventually, all of them will be processed, and the repetition will terminate. Likewise, we are safe in specifying that a series of instructions will be carried out a fixed number of times—1,000 times, say—since we can be sure that execution of the instructions will terminate after the one-thousandth repetition.

On the other hand, we sometimes want to specify that a series of instructions will be executed until a certain condition becomes true. Here lurks danger, for if we have made an error in our reasoning, the repeated instructions may not ever cause the terminating condition to become true, no matter how many times they are executed. In that case, the repetition will continue indefinitely.

For example, a recipe might read "Stir the pudding gently over low heat until it comes to a boil." The terminating condition is "the pudding comes to a boil." The fact that the pudding is being heated assures that it will eventually boil and hence that the stirring will eventually terminate. If the recipe had just said, "Stir the pudding gently until it comes to a boil," without saying that it should be heated, then the terminating condition would never occur. Someone who took the recipe literally—a robot, for instance—would stir indefinitely.

Since an algorithm that fails to terminate cannot arrive at any results, correct or otherwise, termination is required by the guarantee that accompanies every correct algorithm. Because devising proper termination conditions and assuring that they will eventually become true is tricky, failure to terminate is one of the most common failings of incorrect algorithms.

Although the four characteristics just described are necessary for an algorithm to fulfill its guarantee, they are not sufficient. An incorrect algorithm might possess all four characteristics, yet still contain erroneous instructions that prevent it from accomplishing the task for which it was designed.

1.4

Two algorithms

Algorithms are built using three basic *control structures: sequencing, selection* (also called *alternation*), and *repetition* (also called *iteration*). With sequencing, instructions are executed one after another in the order in which they appear in the algorithm. With selection, the conditions that prevail when the algorithm is executed determine which instructions will be selected for execution; by allowing different instructions to be executed under different conditions, selection provides computers with their famed decision-making capability. With repetition, as we have seen, a set of instructions is executed a given number of times, while a given condition holds true, or until a given condition becomes true.

Recursion is a technique whereby an algorithm reduces the problem to be solved to a simplified version of the same problem, then calls on itself to solve the simplified version. (That is, the same algorithm that produced the simplification is applied to the simplified version of the problem.) Recursion and repetition are similar in that both cause some instructions of an algorithm to be executed repeatedly. Algorithms using the two methods are organized quite differently, however. The structure of the problem to be solved often determines whether repetition or recursion will be most effective.

Algorithms are sometimes classified as *sequential, iterative,* or *recursive,* according to whether they rely mainly on sequencing, repetition, or recursion. (Many algorithms, of course, make use of two or all three techniques, and so cannot definitely be placed in any one of the three classes.) In this chapter we will look at a sequential algorithm and an iterative algorithm. In Chapter 2 we will look at a recursive algorithm.

We need an algorithmic language in which to state the example algorithms. We could use one of the standard *programming languages,* such as BASIC, FORTRAN, or Pascal. Programming languages, however, are inevitably restricted by the requirement that the language be suitable for computer processing and thus are not necessarily the best languages for describing algorithms. For the latter task, people often use *pseudolanguages*—algorithmic languages not intended for and not suitable for computer processing. A pseudolanguage can be similar to natural language such as English, or it can be similar to a programming language such as Pascal. In this chapter we will use an English-like pseudolanguage; in later chapters we will use one that is much closer to programming languages.

To avoid all technicalities of computers at this point, we will let our algorithms deal with everyday objects, such as cards with names written on them. The algorithms will be written as if they are to be executed by a human being who will manipulate the cards or other objects according to the instructions in the algorithm. This choice of subject matter will make it easy to write our instructions in English, avoiding the more specialized notations necessary to describe operations performed by computers.

A sequential algorithm: placing three cards in alphabetical order   As shown in Figure 1.2, we are given three cards, each containing a person's name. No name

Figure 1.2   The operation of the sorting algorithm. Note that each
arrangement of cards satisfies the corresponding assertion in
the algorithm. Thus, after step 1 the first two cards are in
order, after step 2 the third card follows the other two in
alphabetical order, and after step 3 all three cards are in
alphabetical order.

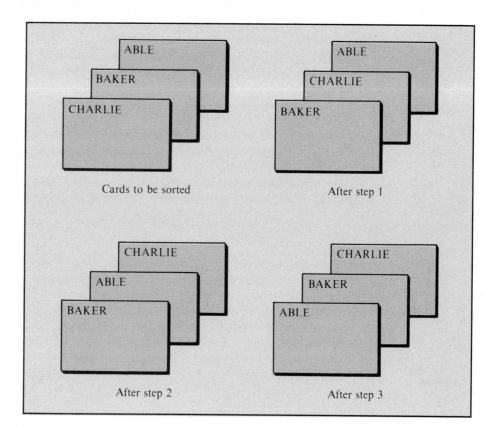

appears on more than one card.* We wish to arrange the three cards so that the
names are in alphabetical order. We assume that, given any two names, we can
recognize which comes first in alphabetical order. Arranging names in alphabetical
order is an example of *sorting,* an operation that computers are frequently called on
to perform.

---

*This assumption simplifies the explanation of the algorithm, since we are relieved from
having to refer continually to the special case in which two cards contain the same name. It is
left as an exercise to show that the algorithm will still work properly when the same name
appears on more than one card.

If somebody handed you three cards and told you to put them in order, you would probably spread them out in your hand, see at a glance which should come first, which second, and which third, and arrange the cards accordingly. But computers cannot see things at a glance, and so this ability cannot be assumed when writing algorithms. To write a sorting algorithm, we must give a definite procedure whereby the names on specific cards will be compared for alphabetical order and the cards will be manipulated as a result of those comparisons. We must convince ourselves by logical reasoning that the procedure we devise will always place the cards in alphabetical order regardless of their initial order.

There are many approaches to sorting. For our example we will use sorting by *exchanges,* in which selected cards are compared and their positions exchanged if they are out of order—that is, if the name on the card that comes first should follow in alphabetical order the name on the card that comes second.

Figure 1.2 illustrates a method of sorting three cards by means of exchanges. An obvious first step is to compare the names on the first two cards (CHARLIE and BAKER) and exchange those cards if they are out of order. After the exchange has been made, the first two cards will be in alphabetical order.

In the pseudolanguage we are using in this section, we will write each step of an algorithm on a separate numbered line. Thus, we write the first step as follows:

1. Compare the names on the first and second cards.
   Exchange the cards if they are out of order.

As we write an algorithm, we must never forget our duty to verify by logical reasoning that the algorithm always produces the correct results. We can aid the reasoning process by interleaving steps of the algorithm with *assertions,* which describe the current state of the objects that the algorithm is manipulating. The *initial assertion,* the one preceding the first step of the algorithm, describes the starting state before the algorithm is executed; the *final assertion,* the one following the last step of the algorithm, describes the desired state that the algorithm is being executed to bring about. To distinguish assertions from steps of the algorithm, we will enclose insertions within braces. The following shows the first step of our algorithm sandwiched between two assertions:

{ The three cards are in arbitrary order }

1. Compare the names on the first and second cards.
   Exchange the cards if they are out of order.

{ The second card follows the first in alphabetical order }

The assertion preceding a step is the *precondition* for that step; the assertion following a step is the *postcondition* for that step. The postcondition for one step of the algorithm is the precondition for the following step.

To verify the correctness of a sequential algorithm, we need to establish for each step that, if the precondition is true before the step is carried out, the postcondition will be true after the step has been carried out. This is certainly true for the first step of our algorithm. The precondition places no restriction on the order of the cards, and the effect of the first step is to place the first two cards in alphabetical order, which is the situation described by the postcondition.

After the first step has been carried out, we can do nothing more with the first two cards, since they are already in alphabetical order. Let's try, then, exchanging the second and third cards. Our algorithm now looks like this:

{ The three cards are in arbitrary order }

1. Compare the names on the first and second cards.
   Exchange the cards if they are out of order.

{ The second card follows the first in alphabetical order }

2. Compare the names on the second and third cards.
   Exchange the cards if they are out of order.

We want the postcondition for step 2 to say as much as can be concluded about the order of the cards after step 2 has been carried out. To be sure, we can say at once that the second and third cards are in alphabetical order, because step 2 would produce that result regardless of the initial order of the cards. But by taking into account the order described in the precondition for step 2, we can follow step 2 with a stronger assertion that will show exactly what must be done to complete the job and get all the cards in order. The assertion we want to be able to make is that, after step 2 is carried out, *the name on the third card follows the names on both of the preceding cards in alphabetical order.*

We know that before step 2 is carried out, the second card follows the first in alphabetical order. To see the effect of the second step, we must consider two cases, which are illustrated in Figure 1.3.

Case 1: The second and third cards are already in order, so step 2 does not carry out an exchange; the situation after step 2 will be the same as it was before. Since the last two cards are in order, the name on the third card follows that on the second. But, by the precondition for step 2, the name on the second card follows that on the first. Consequently, the name on the third card follows those on both the first and second cards, which is the postcondition assertion that we wish to make. (Actually, the three cards are in alphabetical order at this point, but the assertion "The three cards are in alphabetical order" is too strong, since it holds for case 1 but not necessarily for case 2.)

Case 2: The second and third cards are out of order, so step 2 exchanges them. Because step 2 places the second and third cards in order, we know that after step 2 the name on the third card will follow that on the second. What's more, as a result of the exchange, the card in the third position after step 2 is the one that was in the second position before step 2. But from the precondition for step 2, we know that the name on this card follows the name on the first card. Hence, the name on

Figure 1.3   The two cases that arise in analyzing step 2 of the sorting algorithm. In each case, the first and second cards are in order before step 2 is carried out. In case 1, the second and third cards are already in order and so do not have to be exchanged; step 2 takes no action. In case 2, the second and third cards are out of order and are exchanged by step 2. In each case, after step 2 is carried out, the third card follows the other two in alphabetical order.

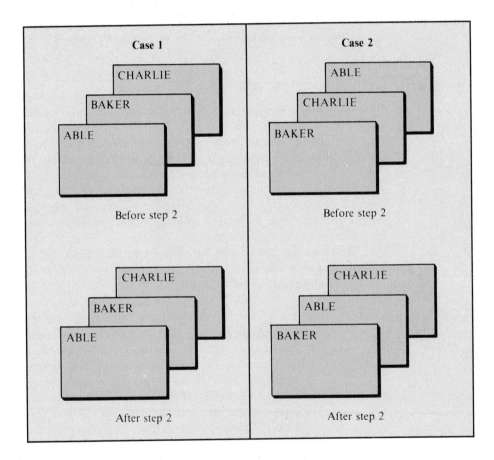

the third card follows the ones on both the preceding cards, which is the assertion we want to make.

Since the desired assertion can be made for each of the two possible cases, we can write it as the postcondition for step 2:

{ The three cards are in arbitrary order }

1. Compare the names on the first and second cards.
   Exchange the cards if they are out of order.

   { The second card follows the first in alphabetical order }

2. Compare the names on the second and third cards.
   Exchange the cards if they are out of order.

   { The third card follows the first and second cards in alphabetical order }

The postcondition for step 2 tells us how to finish the algorithm with one more step. We know that the name on the third card follows those on the first two cards. The first two cards, however, may be out of order; although they were placed in order by step 1, they may have been put out of order by step 2, as Figure 1.2 illustrates. If we can get the first and second cards in order without disturbing the third card (which is already where we want it), all three cards will be in order. We can accomplish this by comparing the first two cards and exchanging them if they are out of order.

These observations give us the third step of our algorithm and the final assertion. Figure 1.4 shows the complete algorithm. A header line, Algorithm Sort, has been

Figure 1.4   The complete algorithm for sorting three cards into alphabetical order.

Algorithm Sort

{ The three cards are in arbitrary order }

1. Compare the names on the first and second cards.
   Exchange the cards if they are out of order.

   { The second card follows the first in alphabetical order }

2. Compare the names on the second and third cards.
   Exchange the cards if they are out of order.

   { The third card follows the first and second cards in alphabetical order }

3. Compare the names on the first and second cards.
   Exchange the cards if they are out of order.

   { The three cards are in alphabetical order }

added to give a name (Sort) to the algorithm. The header line will prove most useful in connection with recursive algorithms, which need to be able to refer to themselves by name.

Each of the three steps in this algorithm is conditional: the action described (exchanging two cards) is carried out only if a certain condition holds (the names on the two cards are out of order). Thus this algorithm makes use of selection (choosing which instructions are to be executed) as well as sequencing (carrying out instructions in the order in which they appear in the algorithm).

The initial assertion of an algorithm describes the state of affairs before the algorithm is executed. Any restrictions necessary for the algorithm to be applicable are given in the initial assertion; for example, the initial assertion for the division algorithm would state that the divisor must not be zero.

The final assertion describes the state the algorithm is to bring about. If the initial assertion holds before the algorithm is executed, the algorithm is guaranteed to bring about the state described in the final assertion.

The remaining assertions serve as stepping stones as we work our way from the intial assertion to the final assertion; they allow us to study the effect of each step of the algorithm separately, instead of having to verify the entire algorithm in a single operation.

An iterative algorithm: merging   Suppose we have several decks* of cards (the exact number of decks does not matter) with a name appearing on each card. The cards in each deck are arranged so that the names are in alphabetical order. As before, we will simplify the explanation slightly by assuming that no two cards contain the same name. We want to combine, or *merge,* the decks into a single deck in which the names are also in alphabetical order (see Figure 1.5). As with sorting, computers are frequently called on to perform merging.

Let's begin by trying to see which card should come first in the merged deck. The first card in the merged deck must precede every other card in alphabetical order. How can we locate this card? Before merging begins, the topmost card of each deck precedes all the other cards in the deck since the cards in each deck are in alphabetical order. Let's compare the topmost cards for alphabetical order and select the topmost card that precedes all the other topmost cards. The selected card certainly precedes every card in its own deck, since that deck is in alphabetical order. The selected card also precedes every card in any other deck, since it precedes the topmost card of the other deck and so precedes all the cards in the other deck (because the other deck is in alphabetical order). Since the selected card precedes every other card, it should be the first card in the merged deck.

To begin merging, then, we compare the topmost cards for alphabetical order. We select the topmost card that precedes all the other topmost cards and make it the first card in the merged deck. Now we have to select the second card in the merged deck. The second card of the merged deck should precede every card except the first.

---

*We follow the terminology of playing cards by referring to a pile or stack of cards as a *deck*.

Figure 1.5   The task to be carried out by the merging algorithm. Each of the original decks is in alphabetical order according to the names written on the cards. The merging algorithm is to combine the three original decks into a single merged deck that is also in alphabetical order. Note that, of the topmost cards of the original decks, the one that precedes the other two in alphabetical order becomes the topmost card of the merged deck.

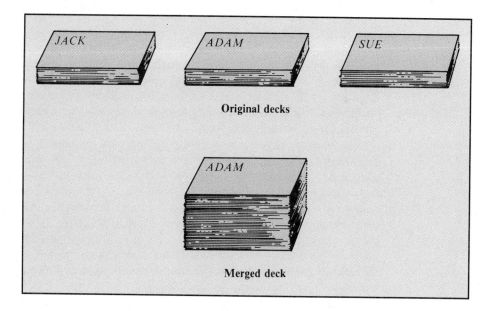

Only the first card has been removed from the original decks and placed in the merged deck. Thus, the second card should precede every other card in the original decks. But we already know how to select such a card—the procedure is the same as the one we used for the first card. To select the second card, then, we compare the current topmost cards of the original decks, select the one that precedes all the others in alphabetical order, and place that card at the end of the merged deck.

It isn't hard to see that the same procedure that worked for the first and second cards will also work for all the remaining cards. Thus, at each step of the algorithm, we compare the current topmost cards of the original decks, select the one that precedes all the others in alphabetical order, and place the selected card at the end of the merged deck. We continue this process until all cards have been transferred to the merged deck. When we have used up all the cards in one of the original decks, we forget about it and concentrate on the remaining decks. Eventually, only one deck will remain, and our selection procedure will always select the topmost card of that deck. Thus all the cards in the last remaining deck are simply transferred one by one to the merged deck.

We can write out the merging algorithm in our pseudolanguage as follows:

Algorithm Merge

1. Repeat the following until all cards have been transferred to the merged deck:

   1.1 Compare the topmost cards of the remaining original decks. Select the topmost card that precedes the other topmost cards (if any) in alphabetical order. Place the selected card at the end of the merged deck.

Although the preceding discussion makes the correctness of this algorithm plausable, we still have to logically prove that it will work as advertised. We must be particularly careful since the algorithm contains a repetition, and repetitions are notorious for failing to terminate. In fact, for every repetition we must prove two things: first, that the repetition terminates, and, second, that when the repetition terminates the desired assertion holds.

In the case at hand, proving that the repetition terminates is straightforward. Each repetition of step 1.1 moves one card from one of the original decks to the merged deck. The repetition terminates when all the cards in the original decks have been transferred to the merged deck. Because the original decks contain only a finite number of cards, and each repetition of step 1.1 transfers one card to the merged deck, eventually all the cards in the original decks will have been transferred to the merged deck, and the repetition will terminate. Most termination proofs work in much the same way. We must show that each repetition "makes some progress" in the task at hand so that a sufficient number of repetitions will complete the task and thus make the termination condition become true.

Having proved that our algorithm terminates, we still need to prove that it produces the desired results—that when the algorithm terminates, all the cards will have been transferred to the merged deck and the cards in the merged deck will be in alphabetical order. We want to use basically the same technique that we used for our sequential algorithm—interleaving the steps of the algorithm with assertions and proving that the assertion following each step follows from the assertion preceding the step and the changes made by the step in question.

But how can we use assertions with repeated steps? We might have one assertion true after the step is carried out the first time, another assertion true after the step is carried out the second time, still another true after the step is carried out the third time, and so on. If the step is to be repeated thousands of times—not at all unusual in computer programs—then we would have to deal with thousands of assertions, which is clearly impossible. What we must do instead is find an assertion that is not changed by executing the repeated step. This so-called *invariant assertion* will hold true both before the repeated statement has been executed and after it has been executed any number of times. Thus we will have to deal with only one assertion for the repeated step, the invariant assertion, instead of a different assertion for each execution of the repeated step. Figure 1.6 shows the complete merging algorithm with assertions inserted.

Figure 1.6   The merging algorithm with assertions inserted.

Algorithm Merge

{ Each of the original decks is in alphabetical order, and there are no cards in the merged deck }

1. Repeat the following until all cards have been transferred to the merged deck:

    { The cards in the merged deck (if any) are in alphabetical order, and the last card of the merged deck (if any) precedes any cards remaining in the original decks }

    1.1. Compare the topmost cards of the remaining original decks. Select the topmost card that precedes the other topmost cards (if any) in alphabetical order. Place the selected card at the end of the merged deck.

{ All cards have been transferred to the merged deck and the cards in the merged deck are in alphabetical order }

Our analysis centers around the invariant assertion, which has been written immediately before the repeated step. The invariant assertion must hold true before the repetition begins; that is, it must follow from the precondition for the repetition construction. By definition, the truth of the invariant assertion must not be changed by the repeated step. When the repetition terminates, we know two things: first, that the termination condition is true, and, second, that the invariant assertion is true. From the termination condition and the invariant assertion, we can deduce the postcondition for the repetition construction.

As usual, the initial assertion of the algorithm gives the state of affairs before the algorithm is executed. Each of the original decks is in alphabetical order and no cards have yet been transferred to the merged deck.

The invariant assertion states that any cards in the merged deck are in alphabetical order, and the last card of the merged deck precedes any cards still in the original decks. The two "if anys" make clear that the invariant assertion holds even if there are no cards in the merged deck.

The invariant assertion must follow from the precondition for the repetition construction, which in this case is the intitial assertion for the entire algorithm. The initial assertion tells us that there are no cards in the merged deck. Since the invariant assertion places restrictions only on cards in the merged deck, it is automatically satisifed when there are no cards in the merged deck. An assertion that is satisfied because none of the elements that it restricts are present is said to be satisfied *vacuously* (from the Latin *vacuum* meaning *empty*).

The crux of the proof is to show that the invariant assertion is indeed left invariant by the repeated step; if the invariant assertion is true before the repeated step is carried out, it will remain true afterwards. Thus, we assume that, before step 1.1 is carried out, any cards in the merged deck are in alphabetical order, and the last card of the merged deck (if any) precedes any cards remaining in the original decks. We have to show that these two statements remain true after step 1.1 has been carried out.

Since the last card of the merged deck (if any) precedes all the cards remaining in the original decks, the merged deck will remain in alphabetical order if any card is selected from the original decks and placed at the end of the merged deck. Thus, regardless of the selection procedure used by step 1.1, the merged deck will still be in alphabetical order after a card has been transferred from one of the original decks to the merged deck. Hence, the first part of the invariant assertion holds true after step 1.1 has been carried out.

In fact, step 1.1 uses the procedure previously described to select the card that precedes all other cards in the original decks. After this card has been transferred to the merged deck, the last card of the merged deck precedes all cards in the remaining original decks. Thus the second part of the invariant assertion also holds true after step 1.1 has been carried out.

When the repetition terminates, we know that the termination condition and the invariant assertion are both true. The termination condition tells us that all cards have been transferred to the merged deck. The invariant assertion tells us that the merged deck is in alphabetical order. These two statements give us the postcondition for the repetition construction, which is also the final assertion for the entire algorithm.

Review questions

1. In what ways do *microcomputers* or *personal computers* differ from the computers that existed before the mid 1970s?

2. What is an *embedded computer?*

3. Distinguish between computer *hardware* and *software*.

4. Give two characteristics common to all computers.

5. What are some alternative names for ''computer science''? How does the emphasis of these alternative names differ from that of ''computer science''?

6. Define *information*.

7. Give ten examples of symbols.

8. Distinguish between *information* and *data*.

9. Give two other terms that can be used in place of *information processing* to describe what a computer does.

10. What is *text processing?*

11. How are computers used in simulation and modeling?

12. What is a *spreadsheet program?*

13. Describe some ways computers are used in *data analysis.*

14. Define *data management.*

15. Describe some of the ways computers are used for playing games. What is a *simulation game?*

16. Distinguish between *algorithms* and *programs.*

17. What is an *algorithmic language?* A *programming language?* A *pseudolanguage?*

18. What guarantee is associated with every correct algorithm?

19. Give four characteristics of all correct algorithms.

20. Define *sequencing, selection, repetition,* and *recursion.*

21. What are *assertions?* How are they used to verify the correctness of algorithms?

22. Define *precondition, postcondition, initial assertion,* and *final assertion.* How is the guarantee of correctness for an algorithm related to the initial and final assertions?

23. What are *invariant assertions?* How are they used to verify the correctness of repetition constructions?

Exercises

1. Prove that the sorting algorithm also works when the same name appears on more than one card. Two cards containing the same name are always considered to be in order and are never exchanged. In giving your proof, you may find the phrases "does not precede" and "does not follow" useful. The name on one card *does not precede* the name on a second card if the name on the first card *follows or is the same as* the name on the second card. Likewise, the name on one card *does not follow* the name on a second card if the name on the first card *precedes or is the same as* the name on the second card.

2. Prove that the merging algorithm also works when the same name appears on more than one card. In the step where one of the topmost cards of the original decks is selected, the name on the selected card must not follow any of the names on the other topmost cards. If more than one topmost card satisfies this criterion, one of the cards satisfying the criterion is arbitrarily selected.

3. We often *count* a series of items by first clearing a counting device (say a mechanical counter, such as those sometimes used in taking inventory) to

zero before beginning and increase the count by 1 for each item counted. Write an algorithm to count the number of cards in a deck. Assume that the current count is written on a blackboard and changed according to the instructions in the algorithm. Use an invariant assertion to prove that, when the algorithm terminates, the count written on the blackboard is the number of cards in the deck that was counted.

4. We often add up a series of numbers with an adding machine or calculator as follows. First, we clear the display of the calculator to zero. Then each of the numbers is added in turn to the value currently on the calculator display. At any time, the calculator displays the running total of all the numbers that have been added so far. Write an algorithm to add up a series of numbers written on cards, one number on each card. Use an invariant assertion to prove that, when the algorithm terminates, the value displayed on the calculator is the sum of all the numbers written on the cards.

5. You are given a deck of 24 cards, each of which contains an hour of the day (such as 1:00 P.M.) and the temperature that was measured at that hour (such as 65°F). Write an algorithm to scan through the deck of cards and find the high and low temperatures for the day and the times at which the high and low occurred. If the high or low occurs on more than one card, the time on the first card bearing the temperature in question should be found. (This will be the time at which the temperature was first recorded if the cards are in ascending order according to times.) Use an invariant assertion to prove the correctness of your algorithm.

Hint: Athletic records provide a helpful analogy for this problem. The first person who attempts a particular feat automatically becomes the record holder. When someone breaks the record, that person's name and performance replace those of the previous record holder. Only the first person to achieve a particular performance is remembered; no notice is taken of others who later achieve the same performance but do not break the old record. In finding the high and low temperatures, assume that one place is set aside on a blackboard for writing the time and temperature of the record high for the day and another place is set aside for the record low. As your algorithm scans through the cards bearing the temperatures it should specify what values are to be entered into the positions for the record high and low in order to keep those records up to date. At any time during the execution of the algorithm, the blackboard should show the record high and low *for all the cards that have been examined so far*.

For further reading

The following are representative of the many books now available on computers, computer applications, and the impact of computers on society.

Evans, Christopher. *The Micro Millennium*. New York: The Viking Press, 1979.

Fedida, Sam, and Malik, Rex. *The Viewdata Revolution*. New York: John Wiley & Sons, 1979.

Graham, Neill. *The Mind Tool*. 3d ed. St. Paul, Minn.: West Publishing Company, 1983.

Laurie, Edward J. *Computers, Automation, and Society*. Homewood, Ill.: Richard D. Irwin, 1979.

Martin, James. *The Wired Society*. Englewood Cliffs, N. J.: Prentice-Hall, 1978.

McCorduck, Pamela. *Machines Who Think*. San Francisco: W. H. Freeman, 1979.

Nelson, Ted. *Computer Lib/Dream Machines*. Swarthmore, Pa: Ted Nelson, Publisher (distributed by The Distributors, 702 S. Michigan, South Bend, Ind., 46618), 1974.

Rothman, Stanley, and Mosmann, Charles. *Computers and Society*. Chicago: Science Research Associates, 1976.

Stern, Nancy, and Stern, Robert A. *Computers in Society*. Englewood Cliffs, N. J.: Prentice-Hall, 1983.

The following article is a good introduction to algorithms by a well-known computer scientist:

Knuth, Donald E. "Algorithms." *Scientific American,* April 1977, pp. 63–80.

2

Problems, algorithms, and recursion

E very algorithm is designed to solve a particular problem, such as the problem of placing three cards in alphabetical order. Given the problem to be solved, our task is first to devise a method for solving the problem and second to incorporate that method into an algorithm. Thus it will help us to look, as we do in this chapter, at some general properties of problems and some general techniques for solving them. Some of these problem-solving techniques can be incorporated directly into our algorithms. Others are better suited to helping us organize our thoughts as we work to devise a method for solving a problem and to construct an algorithm based on that method.

2.1
Problem theory

Most problems have certain common characteristics that are independent of the details of any particular problem. The study of these common characteristics is known as *problem theory*. Since algorithms are designed to solve problems, we won't be surprised to find a direct correspondence between the elements of problem theory and such features of algorithms as instructions and assertions.

Problem state, initial state, and goal state The statement of a problem generally describes certain elements, such as the parts of a puzzle, that must be manipulated to bring about a solution. The configuration of those elements at any particular time is the *problem state*. As we manipulate those elements—as we move the parts of a puzzle, for example—the problem state changes. Solving a problem consists of manipulating the elements of the problem to change the problem state from the given *initial state* to the desired *goal state*. The initial state of a puzzle, for example, is the arrangement of its parts when we begin our attempt to solve it. The goal state is the arrangement we are trying to achieve, the one that corresponds to a solved puzzle.

Consider the sorting problem we looked at in Chapter 1, in which three cards are to be arranged so that the names on the cards are in alphabetical order. Each particular arrangement of the cards is a problem state; there are six possible arrangements for three cards and so six possible problem states. If the names on the cards are ABLE, BAKER, and CHARLIE, the six problem states are as follows:

ABLE	BAKER	CHARLIE
BAKER	ABLE	CHARLIE
ABLE	CHARLIE	BAKER
CHARLIE	BAKER	ABLE
CHARLIE	ABLE	BAKER
BAKER	CHARLIE	ABLE

Any operation that changes the order of the cards, such as exchanging the positions of adjacent cards, changes the problem state.

Since the cards can be in any order initially, each of the problem states is a possible initial state. There is only one goal state, however—the state in which all three cards are in alphabetical order:

ABLE	BAKER	CHARLIE

Likewise, for the merging problem considered in Chapter 1, the problem state consists of the arrangements of cards in the original decks as well as in the merged deck. In the initial state, the original decks are in alphabetical order and the merged deck is empty. In the goal state, the original decks are all empty and the merged deck is in alphabetical order.

Assertions describe problem states. More specifically, an assertion characterizes those problem states that can occur at a given point in the execution of an algorithm. For example, in the sorting algorithm of Chapter 1, the assertion

{ The three cards are in arbitrary order }

applies to all six possible problem states. Hence, any of the states is allowed initially. On the other hand, the assertion

{ The second card follows the first in alphabetical order }

applies only to the three problem states

ABLE	BAKER	CHARLIE
ABLE	CHARLIE	BAKER
BAKER	CHARLIE	ABLE

Only these three states can occur after step 1 of the algorithm has been carried out.

Likewise, the assertion

{ The third card follows the first and second cards in alphabetical order }

applies only to the two problem states

ABLE	BAKER	CHARLIE
BAKER	ABLE	CHARLIE

Only these states are possible after step 2 of the algorithm has been executed. The final assertion of the algorithm

{ The three cards are in alphabetical order }

describes the single goal state

ABLE   BAKER   CHARLIE

Operators   We change the problem state by means of *operators*. Sometimes we are given the set of operators we are allowed to use in solving a problem. In the case of a puzzle, for instance, the instructions that come with the puzzle describe the operators allowed in attempting a solution. Using other operators, such as taking apart a puzzle that is not intended to be taken apart and reassembling it in the goal state, is considered to be cheating.

An algorithm specifies the sequence of operations to be carried out to solve a problem. Each instruction of the algorithm specifies one of the permissible operators. For each initial state, the algorithm specifies a sequence of operators that will transform the initial state into the goal state. In general, the sequence of operators depends on the initial state. That is, a different sequence of operators is required to transform each initial state into the goal state.

In the problem of sorting three cards, for example, we restrict ourselves to operators that exchange adjacent cards. Thus we confine ourselves to the following two operators:

Operator	*Abbreviated Notation*
Exchange the first and second cards.	$1 \leftrightarrow 2$
Exchange the second and third cards.	$2 \leftrightarrow 3$

Other operators are certainly possible, such as exchanging the first and third cards or placing the first card at the end of the deck so that it becomes the third card. If we know that a restricted set of operators is sufficient to solve a problem, however, it may help to confine our attention to the restricted set, which may be easier to understand than the set of all allowable operators.

Rarely are we able to leap from the initial state to the goal state in a single operation. Usually, a *sequence* of operators must be used to transform the initial state into the goal state. We write the operators of a sequence in the order in which the operators are to be applied and use semicolons to separate adjacent operators. Using the abbeviated notation for the operators of the card-sorting problem, we write

$1 \leftrightarrow 2; 2 \leftrightarrow 3$

to represent the operator 1 ↔ 2 followed by the operator 2 ↔ 3. Suppose we apply this sequence to the state

| CHARLIE | BAKER | ABLE |

Applying 1 ↔ 2 gives the state

| BAKER | CHARLIE | ABLE |

Applying 2 ↔ 3 to this state gives

| BAKER | ABLE | CHARLIE |

Thus, the sequence

1 ↔ 2; 2 ↔ 3

transforms the problem state

| CHARLIE | BAKER | ABLE |

into

| BAKER | ABLE | CHARLIE |

Note that we can obtain results with sequences of operators that we cannot obtain with any single operator. For example,

1 ↔ 2; 2 ↔ 3

moves the first card to the end of the deck without changing the order of the other two cards, an effect that cannot be obtained with 1 ↔ 2 or 2 ↔ 3 or indeed with any single exchange.

Also note that, in general, the result of applying two operators in succession depends on the order in which the operators are applied. For example, reversing the order in which 1 ↔ 2 and 2 ↔ 3 are applied gives us the sequence

2 ↔ 3; 1 ↔ 2

This sequence transforms the problem state

| CHARLIE | BAKER | ABLE |

into

| ABLE | CHARLIE | BAKER |

which differs from the state that resulted when

1 ↔ 2; 2 ↔ 3

was applied to the same starting state. The sequence 1 ↔ 2; 2 ↔ 3 moves the first card to the end of the deck; the sequence 2 ↔ 3; 1 ↔ 2 moves the last card to the beginning of the deck.

An algorithm specifies a sequence of operators for transforming the initial state of a problem into the goal state. If the same sequence of operators will work for each initial state, the algorithm can use the sequencing control structure to specify the required sequence directly. In general, however, the required sequence depends on the initial state. The selection and repetition constructions provide the algorithm with the flexibility needed to generate a different sequence of operators for each initial state.

For example, if the initial state of the sorting problem is

BAKER   ABLE   CHARLIE

then the single operation

$1 \leftrightarrow 2$

will transform the initial state into the goal state. On the other hand, if the initial state is

CHARLIE   BAKER   ABLE

the following sequence of three operators

$1 \leftrightarrow 2; 2 \leftrightarrow 3; 1 \leftrightarrow 2$

is required. The following table gives for each possible initial state a sequence of operators that will transform the initial state into the goal state:

Initial State			*Sequence of Operators*
ABLE	BAKER	CHARLIE	no operation
BAKER	ABLE	CHARLIE	$1 \leftrightarrow 2$
ABLE	CHARLIE	BAKER	$2 \leftrightarrow 3$
CHARLIE	BAKER	ABLE	$1 \leftrightarrow 2; 2 \leftrightarrow 3; 1 \leftrightarrow 2$
CHARLIE	ABLE	BAKER	$1 \leftrightarrow 2; 2 \leftrightarrow 3$
BAKER	CHARLIE	ABLE	$2 \leftrightarrow 3; 1 \leftrightarrow 2$

These sequences are not necessarily unique. For example, the sequence

$2 \leftrightarrow 3; 1 \leftrightarrow 2; 2 \leftrightarrow 3$

will also transform

CHARLIE   BAKER   ABLE

into the goal state. The sequences shown are the ones produced by the algorithm given in Chapter 1.

The sorting algorithm uses the *selection* control structure to make the sequence of operators depend on the initial state. A *conditional* instruction can specify that an operator be applied only to certain problem states and not to others, or it can specify different operators for differnt problem states. For example, step 1 of the sorting algorithm

1. Compare the names on the first and second cards.
   Exchange the cards if they are out of order.

causes the operator

$1 \leftrightarrow 2$

to be applied to problem states in which the first two cards are out of order:

BAKER	ABLE	CHARLIE
CHARLIE	BAKER	ABLE
CHARLIE	ABLE	BAKER

No operator is applied, however, to problem states in which the first two names are already in order:

ABLE	BAKER	CHARLIE
ABLE	CHARLIE	BAKER
BAKER	CHARLIE	ABLE

Constraints   There may be restrictions, or *constraints,* on the sequences of operators that can be used to solve a problem. Sometimes these constraints can be taken into account in choosing the set of allowable operators. The allowable operators for solving a puzzle, for example, may include various manipulations of the parts of the puzzle but may not include prying the puzzle apart with a screwdriver. In a game such as chess, the allowable operators are the possible moves of the pieces as defined and constrained by the rules of the game.

Sometimes constraints arise because some operators cannot be applied to some problem states. In using a calculator or a computer to solve mathematical problems, for example, we are not allowed to divide by zero or take the square roots of negative numbers.* Nor can a calculation being done by calculator or computer yield a number too large to be held in the machine's memory registers.

The most subtle kind of constraint arises, however, when a sequence of otherwise legitimate operators nevertheless yields an undesired result. The effect of the constraint is usually to prevent a problem from being solved in the most straightforward way. We cannot go directly to the goal state but must detour as needed to avoid violating the constraint, much as we might have to detour on an automobile trip to avoid the constraints imposed by closed roads.

A famous problem involving a constraint is the *missionaries and cannibals problem.* Three missionaries and three cannibals are to be transported across a river using a boat that holds only two people. The constraint is that on each bank of the river the cannibals may never outnumber the missionaries, for otherwise the outnumbered missionaries would be unable to prevent themselves from being eaten. You may enjoy trying to solve this problem before reading on.

The party is originally on the left bank of the river and wishes to reach the right bank. If there were no constraints, each boat trip from the left bank to the right bank

---

*Most calculators and computer programming languages do not provide the *complex numbers* needed to express the result of taking the square root of a negative number. Hence attempting to take such a square root is treated as an error.

would carry two people to the other bank. But someone has to bring the boat back to the left bank, so each trip except the last is a round trip that has the net effect of moving one person from the left bank to the right bank. The last trip can carry two people, however, since the boat does not have to be brought back. Thus five trips are required: four round trips that move one person each across the river and a fifth trip that carries the two remaining people across. Without the constraint, we can move directly to the solution of the problem in that each round trip, as well as the final one-way trip, decreases the number of people on the left bank and increases the number on the right bank.

Figure 2.1 shows the solution with the constraint. The two one-way trips comprising a round trip are given the same step number. Thus step 1a refers to a trip from the left bank to the right back, and step 1b refers to the return trip from the right bank to the left. We would like for the number of people on the right bank to increase by one for each round trip. But with the constraint, this turns out to be impossible; we must make one "detour"—a round trip that does not increase the number of people on the right bank and so moves us no closer to a solution.

We can reason out the solution like this. The first round trip must move a cannibal to the right bank; if a missionary were moved, the missionaries on the left bank would be outnumbered and eaten. We can send two cannibals across and let a cannibal bring the boat back, or (as in Figure 2.1) we can send a missionary and a cannibal and let the missionary bring the boat back.

The next trip across must carry two cannibals. If we sent a missionary and a cannibal, the cannibal in the boat and the one already on the right bank would eat the missionary when the boat arrived. If we sent two missionaries, the missionary remaining on the left bank with two cannibals would be eaten. Since there are only cannibals on the right bank, a cannibal must bring the boat back. Thus, overall, the second round trip moves another cannibal to the right bank.

Each of the first two round trips has moved one person (a cannibal) to the right bank. But now further progress seems blocked. There is only one cannibal on the left bank so we cannot send two cannibals across. We cannot send a missionary and a cannibal, for the missionary would be eaten when the boat arrived. We can send two missionaries, but who is to bring the boat back? If a missionary brings the boat back, the missionary who remains on the right bank will be eaten. If a cannibal brings the boat back, then there will be two cannibals and one missionary on the left bank.

It is here that we must detour from our steady progress toward a solution and make a round trip that does not increase the number of people on the right bank but changes the arrangement of missionaries and cannibals on the two banks. The new arrangement will allow us to continue toward a solution while still satisfying the constraint. We send two missionaries across and let a missionary and a cannibal bring the boat back, giving us two missionaries and two cannibals on the left bank and one missionary and one cannibal on the right bank. Put another way, the overall effect of the round trip is to carry a missionary across and bring back a cannibal. Realizing the need for this detour is the key to solving the missionaries and cannibals problem.

The next trip carries two missionaries across. Sending two cannibals would result in the missionary on the right bank being eaten, and sending a missionary and a

Figure 2.1 A solution to the missionaries and cannibals problem.

{ Left bank: M = 3, C = 3; Right bank: M = 0, C = 0 }

1a. Missionary and cannibal cross.

{ Left bank: M = 2, C = 2; Right bank: M = 1, C = 1 }

1b. Missionary brings boat back.

{ Left bank: M = 3, C = 2; Right bank: M = 0, C = 1 }

2a Two cannibals cross.

{ Left bank: M = 3, C = 0; Right bank: M = 0, C = 3 }

2b. Cannibal brings boat back.

{ Left bank: M = 3, C = 1; Right bank: M = 0, C = 2 }

3a. Two missionaries cross.

{ Left bank: M = 1, C = 1; Right bank: M = 2, C = 2 }

3b. Cannibal and missionary bring boat back.

{ Left bank: M = 2, C = 2; Right bank: M = 1, C = 1 }

4a. Two missionaries cross.

{ Left bank: M = 0, C = 2; Right bank: M = 3, C = 1 }

4b. Cannibal brings boat back.

{ Left bank: M = 0, C = 3; Right bank: M = 3, C = 0 }

5a. Two cannibals cross.

{ Left bank: M = 0, C = 1; Right bank: M = 3, C = 2 }

5b. Cannibal brings boat back.

{ Left bank: M = 0, C = 2; Right bank: M = 3, C = 1 }

6. Two cannibals cross.

{ Left bank: M = 0, C = 0; Right bank: M = 3, C = 3 }

cannibal would just undo the previous right-to-left trip. A cannibal must bring the boat back since a returning missionary would be met by two cannibals on the left bank.

Now we are home free. All three missionaries are on the right bank where they belong; if they all stay there they can never be outnumbered. It remains only for the three cannibals on the left bank to transport themselves across the river. This they can do with one round trip and a final one-way trip.

2.2

Polya's four steps for solving a problem

The classic book on problem solving, which should be in the library of every computer science student, is *How to Solve It* by mathematician G. Polya. Polya proposes four steps for solving a problem and verifying the solution:

1. Understand the problem

2. Devise a plan

3. Carry out the plan

4. Look back

For us, solving a problem means devising an algorithm for a solution. Let's see how Polya's four steps can be applied to constructing algorithms.

Understanding the problem   A systematic approach to understanding a problem is to identify the elements described in the section on problem theory. How is the problem state described? What are the possible initial states? What is the goal state? What operators are available for manipulating the problem state? Are there any constraints to be satisfied?

In determining how to describe the problem state, we must focus on the essential features of the problem and eliminate whatever is irrelevant. In the card-sorting problem, for example, we describe the problem state by listing the three names in the order in which they occur on the cards. This description corresponds to the realization that only the order of the names is important. Such factors as where the name is written on each card, the size, shape, and color of the cards, and whether they are held in the hand or stacked on a desk, are all immaterial.

Because an algorithm should apply to as wide a range of problems as possible, some features of the problem description and problem state may be deliberately left arbitrary. For example, in the merging problem, the number of decks of cards to be merged and the number of cards in each deck were not specified. Thus we were expected to formulate our algorithm in such a way that it would work regardless of the number of decks or the number of cards in each deck.

Once you see how to describe the problem state, the next thing you want to know is what your algorithm is expected to accomplish. What is the goal state? Can you write an assertion characterizing the goal state? This will be the final assertion of your algorithm.

Once you know where you want to go, it helps to find out where you will be starting from. You need to characterize the initial states to which the algorithm can be applied. You want the algorithm to be as general as possible so that it will apply to as many initial states as possible. However, there may be some initial states for which the problem has no solution or for which the method contemplated for the algorithm does not work, and these initial states must be excluded. For example, division problems with the divisor zero must be excluded for the division algorithm since those problems have no solution. Likewise, because the merging algorithm has no chance of producing a merged deck in alphabetical order unless the original decks are in alphabetical order, this requirement is imposed in the initial states. Once you understand the requirements for the initial states, you should write an assertion characterizing them. This will be the initial assertion of your algorithm.

The operators make up a tool kit for transforming the initial state into an acceptable goal state. Sometimes the allowable operators are given or are known; this is the case for most problems based on games and puzzles. The instructions for a puzzle tell what manipulations are allowed. Sometimes the operators are reasonably obvious; if the problem requires an arithmetic result, the usual arithmetical operators are clearly the ones to use. Sometimes you must use what is available; if you are writing a program in a particular programming language, you are limited to the operators that can be expressed in that language.

Sometimes, however, it is left to you to choose a reasonable set of operators for solving a problem. In this case, you must often draw upon your knowledge of the problem area and of similar problems to select a suitable set of operators. For example, exchanges of adjacent cards were selected for the card-sorting problem based on the author's knowledge that these operators would yield a reasonably straightforward solution.

Constraints often influence the selection of operators. Sometimes it is the constraints that keep the problem from being trivial. For example, in setting the problem of sorting three cards, we might impose the constraint that each operator can affect the positions of at most two cards. This would restrict the allowable operators to those that exchange two (not necessarily adjacent) cards. If this constraint is not imposed, the problem can be "solved" by defining a single operator that places three cards in alphabetical order; if this operator is allowed, the problem becomes trivial.

If you can find a set of operators that all satisfy the constraints, this is the simplest way to take the constraints into account. Once suitable operators have been chosen, the constraints can be forgotten. It may happen, however, that, as in the missionaries and cannibals problem, the constraints restrict the problem states that can occur during a solution, and there is no way to choose operators that will avoid the forbidden states. In that case, you must make sure that every problem state reached during the execution of the algorithm satisfies the constraints.

Often it helps to draw one or more figures depicting the problem situation. For example, Figures 1.2 and 1.3 help us visualize the states that can arise during the card-sorting problem.

It sometimes helps to devise a concise notation for the problem states and the operators. We did this for the operators of the sorting problem when we introduced $1 \leftrightarrow 2$ and $2 \leftrightarrow 3$ to represent the two allowable operators, and when we introduced the semicolon for separating operators in a sequence.

We could also introduce a more concise notation for the states of the sorting problem, since the actual names on the cards are not important, but only their order. Thus we could write A for the name that comes first in alphabetical order, B for the name that comes second, and C for the name that comes last. Then ABC would represent the state in which all three names are in alphabetical order, BAC would represent the state in which the first two names are out of order, ACB would represent the state in which the second and third names are out of order, and so on. The ABC notation was avoided in Chapter 1 since it would have made the problem more abstract and harder to understand; the simplest notation for solving a problem may not always be the best one for presenting it.

The various elements of the problem are rarely independent of one another. For example, there may be more than one way to describe the problem state, and the description chosen can affect the ease with which you define the operators and state the constraints and the conditions to be satisfied by the initial and goal states. Sometimes these elements are obvious from the statement of the problem; sometimes considerable trial and error, study of similar problems, and thought will be needed to arrive at a suitable combination. It often happens that you fully understand a problem only after having made one or more false starts at attempting to solve it.

Devising a plan   Before beginning to write an algorithm you need to devise a plan, method, or procedure for solving the problem. Starting to work on an algorithm before you understand the problem or have planned its solution is likely to lead to a dead end from which you must backtrack and start anew.

In planning the solution, you should draw on your knowledge and experience with similar problems. Is there a similar or related problem that you have seen before? Perhaps the related problem provides only part of the solution to your problem, or perhaps only part of the solution to the related problem is sufficient to solve your problem. Can you generalize the solution of a related problem so that it applies to your problem? Can you specialize the solution of a related problem? (Our algorithm for sorting three cards is the specialization of a well-known algorithm for sorting any number of cards called a *bubble sort*.) Is there some discipline, such as a branch of mathematics, that studies the kind of problem you are trying to solve? Textbooks in that discipline may contain hints, related problems, or even the solution you are looking for.

Always keep in mind the three control structures out of which all algorithms are built: sequencing, selection and repetition. Will a specific sequence of operators move the problem state closer to the goal state? Use sequencing to generate the required sequence. Are different operators, or sequences of operators, needed for different problem states? Use selection to specify the proper operator or sequence for each state. Does a certain operator or sequence of operators need to be repeated until some desired result is obtained? Use a repetition construction to specify the repeated operator applications.

Finally, if you cannot solve the given problem, you might try solving an easier related problem and use the insight you gain to aid you with the original problem. One way to simplify a problem is to relax one or more constraints. For example, by solving the missionaries and cannibals problem without the constraint, we find that the solution consists of a series of round trips, each of which transports one person across the river, followed by a final one-way trip that transports two people. The solution with the constraint has a similar structure, except for the need for one round trip that doesn't increase the number of people on the right bank.

Carrying out the plan   Carrying out the plan means writing an algorithm using the method of solution you have devised. You must transform your plan, which may be only roughly outlined or may exist only in your head, into a series of precisely stated algorithm steps. Selection and repetition must be specified when needed to achieve the purposes of your plan.

As you write the algorithm, make sure that you understand the purpose of each step and that each step accomplishes the desired purpose. Make sure that each repetition will terminate and accomplish the purpose for which it was introduced. If the size and complexity of the algorithm permit, the best way to achieve this understanding is to introduce preconditions, postconditions, and invariant assertions. Check that each step transforms its precondition into its postcondition, that each repetition terminates, and that each invariant assertion is left unchanged by the associated repeated statements. Beyond merely formal reasoning, however, try to let the preconditions, postconditions, and invariant assertions serve as a basis of your intuitive grasp of the operation of the algorithm.

When you attempt to write and verify your algorithm, you may well find that some steps fail to achieve the purposes that you thought they would when you planned the solution. Sometimes alternative steps with the required properties will come immediately to mind, but often there is nothing to do but backtrack to the devise-a-plan or even the understand-the-problem stage. As already mentioned, sometimes full understanding of a problem comes only after one or more false starts at devising a solution.

Looking back   In looking back on a problem you have just solved, you should be concerned with two things. First, you want to make sure that your solution is correct, that your algorithm lives up to its guarantee. Second, you want to learn as much as you can from this problem-solving experience and apply what you have learned to other problems you will be faced with in the future. It is mainly through solving a large number of problems and learning as much as possible from each one that you will eventually be able to solve many problems routinely without wasting a lot of time on false starts and backtracking.

The first step is to check the correctness of your solution. If you supplied preconditions, postconditions, and invariant assertions when you wrote the algorithm, most of the job is already done. Now is the time to make one last check of your reasoning. If the algorithm is too complex for formal verification, try to grasp intuitively the changes in the problem state produced by each step. Think of the kinds of states that can arise at each point in the algorithm and see that each step is appropriate for the states to which it will be applied and the purpose it is to accomplish. Have you overlooked any special cases of the problem state that need to be handled by additional selection constructions? Can you see clearly why every repetition must terminate?

Of course, none of us are immune to slips in logical reasoning; indeed, more than one algorithm that has appeared as an example in a paper on algorithm verification has been found, on closer inspection, to contain embarrassing errors. Therefore, it is wise to test your algorithm by carrying out its instructions for typical initial states and seeing that the goal state results. Sometimes an algorithm can be exhaustively tested. In the three-card-sorting problem, for example, there are only six possible initial states, and the algorithm can be tested for each one. The more usual situation, however, is the one exemplified by the merging algorithm, in which there are many possible initial states and no possibility of testing the algorithm for all of them.

Choose initial states to test any extreme cases of your algorithm. For example, two extreme cases for testing a sorting algorithm are: (1) when the cards are already in order (the sorting algorithm should not disturb them); and (2) when the cards are in reverse order. For each selection construction, be sure that at least one test case makes the condition in the selection true and one makes the condition false. If a repeated instruction can be executed zero times (because the termination condition is already true when the repetition construction is reached) or only once (because the termination condition becomes true after the first execution of the repeated statement), use test cases that produce these extreme situations.

Finally, see what you have learned from this problem that you can apply to other problems that you will be called on to solve in the future. Can the algorithm be generalized to solve a larger class of problems, or specialized (and simplified) to solve a narrower class? Could your algorithm serve as part of some larger algorithm handling a more complex task? (Sorting and merging algorithms are often used as parts of other algorithms.) Does your algorithm employ any operator sequences that accomplish generally useful results and so might be worth remembering for use in other algorithms? Does your experience with this problem illuminate any of your studies in mathematics, computer science, or other disciplines?

2.3 Problem-solving techniques

In this section we will look briefly at some specific problem-solving techniques. Some, such as inference and analogy, will help you with your reasoning but will not appear directly in the algorithm you are constructing. Others, such as case analysis and macros, can be incorporated directly in the algorithm. Further examples of these techniques can be found in the books by Polya and by Wickelgren listed at the end of this chapter.

Inference   Often we can simplify a problem considerably by applying logical inference, or reasoning, to such problem elements as the problem situation, the initial states, the goal states, the operators, and the constraints. Sometimes inference will lead us directly to the solution of the problem, eliminating the need for an algorithmic solution. More often, inference simplifies the problem elements or exposes relationships among them that would not otherwise be obvious, thus aiding us in finding an algorithmic solution and simplifying the resulting algorithm.

Sometimes simple commonsense reasoning provides the key to solving or simplifying a problem. An example of this is the famous *checkerboard and dominos problem* illustrated in Figure 2.2. We are given a notched checkerboard and a supply of dominoes. The two white squares at opposite corners of the checkerboard have been removed; the rest of the checkerboard is intact. Each domino covers exactly two adjacent squares on the checkerboard. Can we arrange the dominoes on the checkerboard so that they cover all the remaining squares, that is, all the squares except the two missing corner squares?

At this point, a student of computing might be tempted to write a program that, using a model of the checkerboard in the computer's memory, would test every possible arrangement of dominoes in search of one that covered all the remaining squares. But a little thought shows that there are a very large number of possible arrangements, so such a program might take a long time to complete its work, even when run on a fast computer. Fortunately, some simple reasoning can save an enormous amount of computer time, a situation that is by no means unusual.

The key observation is that a domino always covers one black square and one white square. This must be true because the squares alternate between black and white both horizontally and vertically, and a domino always covers two adjacent squares. A full checkerboard would contain an equal number of black and white squares. But because two white squares have been removed from our checkerboard, there remain two more black squares than white, and so the remaining squares cannot be completely covered by dominoes. To completely cover the board, one domino would have to cover two black squares, which is impossible.

The checkerboard and dominoes problem calls only for commonsense reasoning about the arrangement of squares on a checkerboard. Frequently, however, inference is based on knowledge drawn from a particular area, such as mathematics, computer science, or the area (such as physics or business) from which the problem was drawn.

For example, here is a problem that actually arises in computer programming and whose solution requires knowledge of some elementary properties of odd and even numbers. Suppose we have a counting device such as a hand-operated mechanical counter) that can only count in steps of 1—1, 2, 3, and so on. We want to use this counter to generate a series of odd numbers, say all the odd numbers from 1 through 999. If the counter could count by twos we would be home free. We could set the counter to 1 and count 1, 3, 5, 7, and so on. But since the counter will only work in steps of 1, and we want to produce an odd number each time the counter is incremented, we need a way of converting counter readings into odd numbers.

Knowledge of the elementary properties of numbers comes to our rescue. To begin with, odd and even numbers alternate. Every odd number is preceded by an even number and followed by an even number. Therefore, every odd number can be expressed as one greater than the preceding even number

$$odd\ number\ =\ even\ number\ +\ 1$$

or as one less than the following even number

$$odd\ number\ =\ even\ number\ -\ 1$$

For example, the odd number 9 can be expressed as either $8 + 1$ or $10 - 1$, where 8 and 10 are even numbers.

Figure 2.2   The checkerboard and domino problem. The domino may be
aligned horizontally or vertically; in either case it covers
exactly two adjacent squares on the checkerboard.

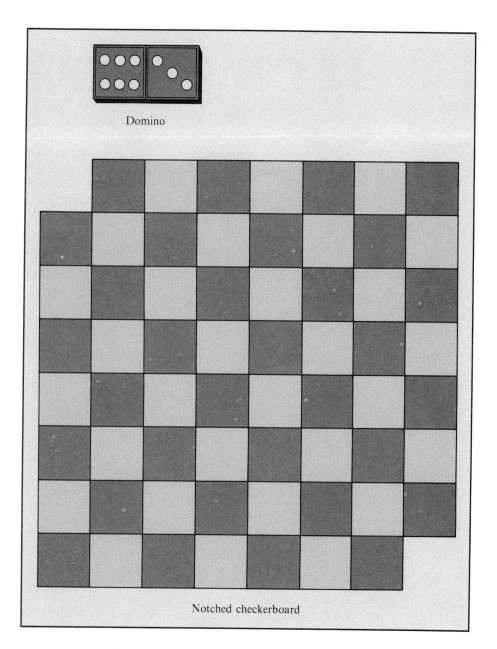

Domino

Notched checkerboard

But an even number is evenly divisible by 2 and so equals 2 times another number. For example, 6 equals 2×3, 8 equals 2×4, 10 equals 2×5, and so on. Thus every even number can be expressed by

even number $= 2n$

where n can be an even or an odd number.

We now begin to get the feeling that we are on the right track. We can express an odd number as

odd number $=$ *even number* $+ 1$
$\qquad\qquad\quad = 2n + 1$

If we let the value of n be 0, 1, 2, and so on, the corresponding values of $2n + 1$ will be 1, 3, 5, and so on—precisely the odd numbers that we want to generate. Initializing the counter to zero before we start results in the first odd number being 1. How high must we count in order to generate all the odd numbers through 999? For the last count, we have

$2n + 1 = 999$

Subtracting 1 from both sides of this equation gives

$2n = 998$

and dividing both sides by 2 gives

$n = 499$

Thus the counter should be stepped from 0 through 449. The following algorithm uses this method to print the odd numbers from 1 through 999:

1. Clear the counter to zero.

2. Repeat the following until the counter reading exceeds 449:

   2.1. Multiply the counter reading by 2, add 1 to the product, and print the result.

   2.2. Increment the counter reading by 1.

Hill climbing   When our goal is nowhere in sight, we need some way to determine if we are on the right track. That is, we need some way of knowing which operators will move the current problem state closer to the goal state and which will move it further away. Sometimes we can assign a numerical value to each problem state in such a way that the value will be either a maximum or a minimum (depending on the problem) for the goal state. If the value for the goal state is a maximum, we will apply operators that increase the value for the current state. If the value for the goal state is a minimum, we will apply operators that decrease the value for the current state. A rule for computing such a value for every problem state is called an *evaluation function*.

The name of this method—"hill climbing"—comes from the following example. Suppose we are somewhere on a hill and are trying to reach the top. Because trees are on the hill, we cannot see the top—our goal is not in sight. But by judging the slope of the land, we can tell which direction is up. We climb always in the upward direction, confident that this course will eventually take us to the top.

More formally, we define an evaluation function whose value for each point on the hillside is the altitude of that point. Because our goal has the highest altitude of any point on the hill, we apply operators that increase the altitude as rapidly as possible. When we observe the slope of the land, we compare the altitude of our current position with that of adjacent positions. We then apply the operator that produces the greatest increase in altitude: we step in the direction of greatest slope. Note that we don't even have to know the altitude of the point we are at or the one to which we are going. We only have to know the *changes* in altitude produced by the available operators.

A practical problem involving hill climbing is planning a trip with a road map. We want to reach our destination by traveling the shortest possible distance. A suitable evaluation function is the distance between our current position and our destination. At each intersection, we will take the road that reduces this distance as rapidly as possible, that is, the one that leads as directly as possible in the direction of our destination. In most cases we will do this by common sense, without actually using the evaluation function. We will choose roads that go in the general direction of our destination, avoiding those that go in the opposite direction or off to the side. But sometimes we will find two routes that carry us to the same destination, and it may not be obvious which is the best. In that case, we may apply the evaluation function directly by using the mileage information on the map to determine which route is the shortest.

Hill climbing is not without its problems. For one thing, hill climbing only finds a *local* maximum or minimum of the evaluation function. Suppose, for example, that we are wandering in a forest in which there are a number of hills of different heights, and we need to reach the highest point in the area. Following the first upward slope we come to will take us to the top of *a* hill, but there is no guarantee that this hill is the highest in the area. What's more, when we have reached the top of one hill, hill climbing can no longer be used unless we backtrack by going back down the hill and seeking out another upward slope.

Hill climbing is also subject to *detours*. If on our road trip we find that a road is blocked, we must follow a detour even if it does not take us any closer to our destination or takes us away from it. In problem solving, constraints often serve as roadblocks. For example, in the missionaries and cannibals problem, a suitable evaluation function is the number of people on the right bank after each round trip. But the constraints for the problem require one detour—a round trip that does not increase the number of people on the right bank. If we are to solve the missionaries and cannibals problem by hill climbing, we must be aware that such a detour can occur.

Finally, hill climbing can simply lead to a dead end. A cartoon that circulated in the artificial intelligence community some years ago showed a robot sitting in the top of a tree and looking at the moon. The robot said, "Since my goal is to reach the moon, I have climbed this tree to reduce the distance between myself and my goal.'' A slightly smarter robot might try airplanes or balloons, which likewise reach dead ends.

Human problem solvers seldom bother to actually work out the values of an evaluation function for each problem state. On the other hand, they may well follow some intuitive notation of changing the problem state in such a way as to bring it closer to the goal. For example, we might manipulate an algebraic equation to try to make it ''look more like'' the equation we are trying to derive. This constitutes hill climbing, with all its possible pitfalls, even though we are not using a precisely defined evaluation function.

On the other hand, computer programs, particularly those that play games, often do attempt to maximize or minimize explicitly defined evaluation functions. Programs that play chess or checkers, for example, use an evaluation function to estimate the desirability of the game positions that can be reached from the current position by particular sequences of moves. By its moves, the program tries to steer the game in the direction of positions with high values for the evaluation function.

Analogy   Two objects are *analogous* if certain similarities between them can be found. The similarities usually reside in the relationships between the parts of each object rather than in the appearance or construction of the objects. If you can set up an analogy between the problem you are trying to solve and one whose solution you know, you may be able to adapt the known solution to the problem at hand. If the differences between the problems are too great to permit a direct adaptation, the solution to the analogous problem should still provide you with useful hints for attacking your problem.

For example, consider the problem of a man who must transport a fox, a goose, and a bushel of corn across a river. The only available boat will hold two of the four entities (man, fox, goose, and corn). Only the man can operate the boat. The man cannot leave the fox and the goose unattended, or the fox will eat the goose, nor can he leave the goose and the corn unattended, lest the goose eat the corn.

This problem is clearly analogous to the missionaries and cannibals problem. Both involve transporting entitites across a river in a boat that will not allow all to make the trip at once. Constraints forbid certain combinations of entities from occurring on either bank. On the other hand, the number and types of entities are different for the two problems, as are the constraints. Also, for the current problem, only one entity, the man, can operate the boat, and so he must go on every trip; no similar restriction applies to the missionaries and cannibals problem.

The differences between the two problems make it unlikely that the solution to the missionaries and cannibals problem can be adapted directly. On the other hand, we can certainly glean some insights from the analogous problem. We know that we should concentrate on round trips of the boat, and the number of entities on the destination bank after each round trip is a good evaluation function. We can use hill climbing with this evaluation function, but we must bear in mind the possibility of a detour, in which the entities on the two banks have to be juggled without increasing the number on the destination bank. With these insights, you should have little difficulty in solving the fox, goose, and corn problem.

Now let's look at an example where the solution of one problem can be readily adapted to solve an analogous problem. Computer files are sometimes compared to locate persons whose names occur in both files. For example, if persons are not allowed to receive payments from two particular government agencies at the same time, we might want to compare the payee files of the two agencies to locate any "double dippers" who are violating the regulations.

To give a simplified version of the problem, suppose we have two decks of cards. Each card contains a person's name, and the cards in each deck are in alphabetical order according to the names. Each name occurs at most once in a given deck, but the same name can occur in different decks. We want to compare the two decks and produce a third deck containing one card for each name that occurs in both of the original decks. The cards in the third deck must also be in alphabetical order.

This problem is clearly analogous to the merging problem* we have already looked at. The difference is that in the merging problem all the cards from the original decks go into the merged deck. In the present problem, one card goes into the merged deck for each card that occurs in both the original decks. All other cards in the original decks are discarded. Can we modify the solution of the merging problem to solve this analogous problem?

We observe for the original merging algorithm that, if the same name occurs in both decks, then eventually the two cards bearing the same name must be on top of their respective decks at the same time. Put another way, if one of the two cards in question is the topmost card of its deck, then all cards must be selected from the other deck until the card bearing the name in question comes to the top in that deck. If this were not so, the two cards bearing the same name would be separated by other cards in the merged deck, and the merged deck would not be in alphabetical order.

What's more, when the two topmost cards bear different names, the name that comes first in alphabetical order cannot occur in the other deck, because the other deck is in alphabetical order. In the original merging algorithm, the topmost card that comes first in alphabetical order is selected and moved to the merged deck. Here, we know that this card has no counterpart in the other deck, so it should be selected and discarded.

With these observations, we can modify the selection step for the merging algorithm as follows.

> Compare the topmost cards of the two decks. If they are the same, place one of the cards in the merged deck and discard the other. If the two topmost cards are different, discard the one that comes first in alphabetical order.

Macros We have seen that a sequence of operators can often accomplish a desired result that cannot be obtained with any single operator. It is worthwhile mem-

---

*Specifically, it is analogous to the version of the merging problem described in Exercise 2 of Chapter 1, in which the same name can occur on more than one card.

orizing sequences that accomplish generally useful results; the memorized sequences join the single operators in our tool kit for solving a particular type of problem. Sequences that are used as if they were single operators are called *macrooperators, macroactions, macroinstructions,* or just *macros.* Some programming languages allow the programmer to define macros and assign them names. Thereafter, wherever the programmer writes the name of a macro, the computer inserts the sequence of instructions given in the macro definition.

A good example of macros is provided by the *cube puzzle* that was the subject of a worldwide fad a few years ago. As shown in Figure 2.3, the puzzle consists of a large cube that is divided into 27 smaller "cubelets" or "cubies." (only 26 cubies are visible on the surface of the cube; the 27th, which theoretically occurs in the center of the cube, is in fact replaced by the working mechanism of the puzzle.) Each of the six outer layers of cubies can be turned independently of the others; Figure 2.3 shows the top layer in the process of being turned. We say that we "turn a face" when we turn the layer of cubies containing that face; thus Figure 2.3 shows the top face being turned. Turns through 90 degrees or multiples thereof preserve the shape of the large cube. When a new cube is taken from its box, each face is a different solid color. Only a few random turns are sufficient to scramble the colors to the extent that it is practically impossible to restore the original solid-colored faces by trial and error.

The operators for the cube puzzle are the turns of the six faces through 90 degrees or multiples thereof. For example, "turn the top face clockwise through 90 degrees" or "turn the left face through 180 degrees" are typical operators. The problem states are the configurations of cubies than can be obtained by starting with

Figure 2.3   (a) A cube puzzle. (b) The top layer of cubies in the process of being turned. The top, bottom, left, right, front, and back layers of cubies each can be turned independently of the others.

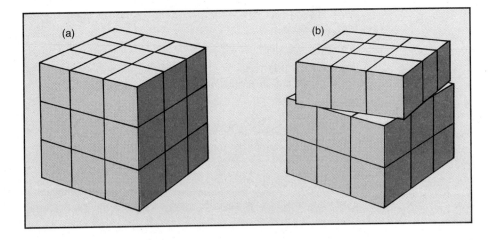

a new cube and applying various sequences of operators. The initial state can be any scrambled state. The goal state is the original state of a new cube—the state in which each face has a solid color.

To solve the cube puzzle a large repertoire of macros is essential to accomplish the various things that need to be done. For example, there are macros for moving an edge cubie (one that occurs on the edge of the large cube) to the proper position, for moving a corner cubie to the proper position, for exchanging the colors on the two visible faces of an edge cubie, for shifting the colors on the three visible faces of a corner cubie, for moving a cubie from one layer to another, for rearranging the cubies visible on any face, and so on. Some of these macros are complex and unobvious, so it is out of the question to make them up on the spur of the moment as you solve the cube. You must either discover them through extensive experimentation with the cube or, more likely, learn them by studying a book on how to solve the cube.

The reason some of the macros are so complex is that they must not only accomplish their intended purposes but must do so without scrambling those cubies that are already in their proper positions. As we begin to work on a solution, we can use simple macros because most of the cube is still scrambled and we don't care if the scrambled parts are changed. But as more and more cubies are moved to their proper positions, it becomes increasingly difficult to position new ones without disturbing the old ones, and so the macros become more and more complex. The parts of the cube that are to be preserved by a macro are temporarily disturbed while the operators of the macro are being applied, but they are restored by the time the macro is completed. If we lose track of what we are doing in the middle of applying a macro, the cube will most likely be hopelessly scrambled, and we will have to restart our solution from the beginning.

Case analysis It frequently happens that at some point in the solution of a problem, the operator that must be applied next depends on the current problem state. Usually the possible problem states can be classified into a small number of *cases* with a different operator for each case—hence the term *case analysis*. Case analysis corresponds directly to selection in algorithms; wherever we must use case analysis to devise a solution to a problem, we incorporate a selection construction at the corresponding point in the algorithm for solving the problem.

Many of the algorithms we have already considered involve case analysis. In the sorting algorithm, for example, each step involves two cases: either the two cards under consideration in that step are in order or they are not. In the case where the two cards are in order, no action is taken. In the case where the two cards are out of order, the cards are exchanged.

Or consider the modified merging algorithm described in this chapter, the one that finds all names that occur in both of two decks of cards. Let's call the two original decks A and B. The step in which we select the next card and decide what to do with it involves three cases:

Case 1: The same name appears on both the topmost card of deck A and the topmost card of deck B.

Case 2:   The topmost card of deck A precedes the topmost card of deck B in alphabetical order.

Case 3:   The topmost card of deck B precedes the topmost card of deck A in alphabetical order.

The action to be taken depends on which case occurs. For case 1, one of the topmost cards is discarded and the other is moved to the merged deck. For case 2, the topmost card of deck A is discarded. For case 3, the topmost card of deck B is discarded.

Case analysis is crucial to *weighing problems* such as the following. Suppose we have 27 apparently identical coins, one of which, however, is heavier than the rest. We have a balance that we can use to determine which of two piles of coins is heavier. We want to locate the heavy coin with as few weighings as possible.

The basic insight for solving this problem is that we can use the balance to make a three-way decision, not just a two-way decision as you might at first suppose. Suppose we divide the 27 coints into three piles of nine coins each. We place one pile in the left pan of the balance and one in the right pan; the remaining pile is not weighed. Three cases can occur:

Case 1:   The pile in the left pan is heavier; this pile contains the heavy coin.

Case 2:   The pile in the right pan is heavier; this pile contains the heavy coin.

Case 3:   The piles in the left and right pans weigh the same; the pile that was not weighed contains the heavy coin.

We select the pile that contains the heavy coin and divide it into three piles of three coins each. The same weighing procedure is used to select the pile containing the heavy coin. This pile is divided into three "piles" of one coin each. A final weighing determines which of these three coins is the heavy one.

Instructions for solving cube puzzles often involve case analysis. For example, we may be instructed to note the pattern of colors on a particular face of the cube and determine which of several different cases occur. We are then instructed to apply a particular macro for each case. Sometimes we will be told to orient the cube in a manner depending on the colors on one or more faces; for example, the instructions may say to position the cube so that a particular edge cubie is at the intersection of the top and front faces. After performing the orientation, we are told to apply a particular operator such as "turn the right face clockwise by 90 degrees." The orientation of the cube determines which face is the right face and hence to which face the operator will actually be applied. Thus we have an implicit case analysis: the patterns on one or more faces of the cube determine, via the orientation of the cube, which operator will be applied next.

Subgoals and subproblems   One of the most useful problem-solving techniques is to devise a series of intermediate goals, or *subgoals,* to serve as stepping stones between the initial state and the goal state. The original problem is then replaced by the *subproblems* of getting from the initial state to the first subgoal, from the first subgoal to the second, and so on. We try to choose the subgoals in such a way that all the subproblems are substantially easier to solve than the original problem.

We have already seen the importance of planning the solution of a problem before actually solving it or writing an algorithm to solve it. One way to plan a solution is to give a series of subgoals with subproblems that can be solved routinely.

For example, in planning a road trip, we might make a list of the major cities we intend to pass through, confident that we can find our way from one city to the next by using road signs or asking directions. The cities are the subgoals, and the list of cities constitutes the plan for the trip. We carry out our plan on the road as we solve the subproblems of getting from one city to the next.

Cubists—cube puzzle enthusiasts—work by achieving subgoals according to a systematic plan. One plan, for example, is to first get correct the edge cubies on the top layer, then the corner cubies on the top layer, then the middle layer, then the corner cubies on the bottom layer, and finally the edge cubies on the bottom layer. The cubiest knows a specific set of macros suitable for achieving each subgoal. Other cubists may prefer to achieve the subgoals in a different order—to get the top and bottom layers correct, for example, before beginning to work on the middle layer— but all follow some methodical plan. In fact, a systematic plan for achieving subgoals together with macros appropriate to each subgoal are the keys to quickly solving this puzzle that is almost impossible to solve by trial and error or commonsense reasoning.

It may happen that the subproblems that arise from our first set of subgoals are still too difficult to solve directly. We can then *refine* our plan by choosing subgoals for each subproblem, thus breaking each subproblem down into still smaller subproblems. The process can be repeated until we eventually arrive at subproblems that are simple enough to solve directly. This approach to problem solving is known as *stepwise refinement*.

We can illustrate stepwise refinement by the problem of writing a book. The author might start by deciding on a title for each chapter and writing a brief description of its contents. The original problem of writing the book has now been broken down into the subproblems of writing the chapters. The author might now break down each chapter into sections, writing a title and brief description of each section. The problem of writing each chapter has been reduced to the subproblems of writing the sections. If the book is extremely complex, the sections might be broken down into subsections, subsubsections, and so on.

Of all the problem-solving methods described in this chapter, subgoals, subproblems, plans, and stepwise refinement are the ones that will be used most often in the rest of the book.

Working backward In trying to solve a problem, our normal impulse is to try to work forward from the initial state to the goal state considering the operators in the order in which they will be applied when the solution is carried out. Sometimes, however, it helps to start with the goal state and work backward, first considering states that can be transformed into the goal state by the application of a single operator, then those that can be transformed into the goal state by the application of two operators and so on. While it is possible to work backward all the way from the goal state to the initial state, it is often most convenient to use a combination of working backward and working forward. We work backward from the goal state to find subgoals that we can easily reach from the initial state by working forward.

The *water-jar problem* is often used to illustrate working backwards. Suppose we have a 9-quart jar and a 4-quart jar, and we need to measure out 6 quarts of water. How can we do so using only the given jars? We can fill or empty a jar and pour water from one jar to another as often as we wish.

Let's start with the goal state and work backward. In the goal state we have 6 quarts of water, which must be in the 9-quart jar, since the 4-quart jar will not hold 6 quarts. We want to try to guess the state that immediately precedes the goal state in the solution. That is, we are looking for states from which the goal state could be obtained in a single step.

There are a number of possibilities. For example, if we have 3 quarts in the 9-quart jar and 3 quarts in the 4-quart jar, then pouring the contents of the 4-quart jar into the 9-quart jar would give the desired 6 quarts in the 9-quart jar. But we suspect that a state in which there is a specific amount in each jar will not be very useful as a subgoal, since it might be harder to attain than the goal state, in which there is a specific amount of water in only one jar. Thus, let's concentrate on next-to-last states in which only one jar contains a specific amount of water, the other jar being full or empty.

After a little thought, two such possibilities present themselves. Suppose we have 1 quart of water in the 4-quart jar. Then we can fill the 9-quart jar and pour water into the 4-quart jar until the latter is full. Since we started with 1 quart in the 4-quart jar, we will have poured 3 quarts out of the 9-quart jar, leaving 6 quarts, the desired amount.

The other possibility is to have 2 quarts in the 9-quart jar. If we now fill the 4-quart jar and empty it into the 9-quart jar, the 9-quart jar will contain the desired 6 quarts.

Thus we have found two states from which the goal state can be reached. Let's try each of these states as a subgoal. Since water can always be poured from one jar to another, it doesn't matter which jar contains the 1 quart or the 2 quarts. Our possible subgoals, then, are 1 quart or 2 quarts in either jar.

Now let's start with the initial state (both jars empty) and try to reach either subgoal. No way of getting 2 quarts immediately presents itself, but a way of getting 1 quart does if we look at the arithmetical relationship between the sizes of the two jars. The size of the 9-quart jar is related to that of the 4-quart jar by

$$9 = 4 + 4 + 1$$

The 1 is significant because getting 1 quart is one of our possible subgoals. We can reach this subgoal by filling the 9-quart jar, pouring out 4 quarts into the 4-quart jar, then emptying the 4-quart jar and filling it again from the 9-quart jar, leaving 1 quart in the 9-quart jar. Piecing together the results we obtained by working backward and working forward, we obtain the complete solution, as shown in Figure 2.4.

Figure 2.4   A solution to the water-jar problem.

{ Both jars are empty }

1. Fill 4-quart jar from 9-quart jar. Empty 4-quart jar.

{ 5 quarts in 9-quart jar; 4-quart jar is empty }

2. Fill 4-quart jar from 9-quart jar. Empty 4-quart jar.

{ 1 quart in 9-quart jar; 4-quart jar is empty }

3. Pour contents of 9-quart jar into 4-quart jar; fill 9-quart jar.

{ 9 quarts in 9-quart jar; 1 quart in 4-quart jar }

4. Fill 4-quart jar from 9-quart jar.

{ 6 quarts in 9-quart jar }

2.4

Recursion

When we apply the method of subgoals and subproblems, it may happen that the subproblems are simplified versions of the original problem. We then may be able to use the same algorithm to solve the subproblems as we use to solve the original problem. We can think of the algorithm for the original problem as calling on, or *invoking* itself to solve each subproblem, a process known as *recursion*. When an algorithm invokes itself, we speak of a *recursive call* or a *recursive invocation*.

Two requirements must hold if recursion is to work:

1. The subproblems must be *simplified* versions of the original problem. If they were of the same difficulty, or if they were more difficult, it would be easier to solve the original problem directly rather than breaking it down into sub-problems.

2. Applying the subdivision process repeatedly (the original problem is divided into subproblems, the subproblems are divided into subsubproblems, and so on) must eventually yield trivial versions of the problem that can be solved without any further subdivision. If this were not the case, the process of division into subproblems would continue indefinitely, and the algorithm for the original problem would not terminate.

The Towers of Hanoi   The *Towers of Hanoi* problem is often used to illustrate subgoals, subproblems, and recursion. As shown in Figure 2.5, we have three pegs labeled A, B, and C. In the initial state, peg A contains a certain number of disks. We denote the number of disks by n and speak of an n-disk problem. In Figure 2.5, for example, six disks are shown; thus the value of n is 6, and we have a 6-disk problem. The disks are numbered from 1 through n in order of increasing size. Thus the disks in Figure 2.5 are numbered 1 through 6, with disk 1 being the smallest disk and disk 6 being the largest.

Figure 2.5   The 6-disk Towers of Hanoi problem. The disks are to be moved from peg A to peg C. Only one disk can be moved at a time, and a larger disk can never be stacked above a smaller one.

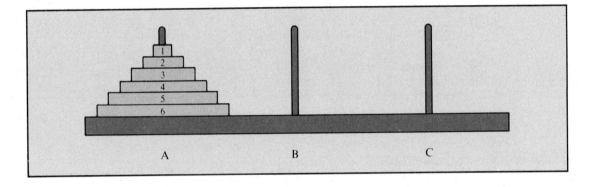

The problem is to move all the disks from peg A to peg C, using peg B as needed, subject to the following two constraints:

1. We can only move one disk at a time.

2. We can never stack a larger disk above a smaller disk.

Thus the disks on each peg must always be stacked in order of their sizes, with the smallest disk on top and the largest on the bottom.

Let's try to find some subgoals that will lead to simplified subproblems. We might reason as follows. Why can't we move the bottommost disk, disk n, from peg A to peg C? The answer is that, since only one disk can be moved at a time, we must somehow remove the $n - 1$ disks stacked above disk n before we can move disk n. Since disk n is to be moved to peg C and must be the bottommost disk on peg C, none of the disks to be removed can be moved to peg C. Hence, disks 1 through $n - 1$ must be moved to peg B, after which disk n can be moved to peg C. At this point, disk n is in its final position; if disks 1 through $n - 1$ can be moved from peg B to peg C, where they will be stacked atop disk n, we will have solved the problem.

The following list gives the subgoals and subproblems, which are illustrated in Figure 2.6:*

{ Initial state: disks 1 through n on peg A }

1. Subproblem: move disks 1 through $n - 1$ from peg A to peg B.

{ Subgoal: disk n on peg A; disks 1 through $n - 1$ on peg B }

2. Subproblem: move disk n from peg A to peg C.

{ Subgoal: disk n on peg C; disks 1 through $n - 1$ on peg B }

3. Subproblem: Move disks 1 through $n - 1$ from peg B to peg C.

{ Goal state: disks 1 through n on peg C }

The subproblem in step 2 can be solved by applying a single operator. The subproblems in steps 1 and 3, however, call for moving more than one disk (when n is greater than 2) and so must be broken down into still simpler subproblems.

The important point is that, when we solve the n-disk problem, both subproblems are $(n - 1)$-disk problems. That is, both have the same form as the original problem, except there is one less disk to be moved. What's more, if this division into subproblems is applied repeatedly, each time we pass from a problem to its subproblems the number of disks decreases by 1. Eventually we are left with only 1-disk subproblems, which can be solved without any further divisions into subproblems, since we can move one disk in a single operation.

Figure 2.7 illustrates the original problem and all the subproblems that occur in solving the 3-disk Towers of Hanoi problem. The original problem and each subproblem is enclosed in a box. When a problem is divided into subproblems, lines drawn from the bottom of the box containing the problem connect it to the boxes containing the subproblems. When there are no lines from the bottom of the box for a subproblem, the subproblem can be solved by applying a single operator, so no further subdivision into subproblems is needed. The bottommost subproblems—the ones that are not further subdivided—represent the operators that are used to manipulate the disks. Reading these from left to right, we get the actual disk manipulations needed to solve the 3-disk Towers of Hanoi problem:

1. Move disk 1 from peg A to peg C.   5. Move disk 1 from peg B to peg A.

2. Move disk 2 from peg A to peg B.   6. Move disk 2 from peg B to peg C.

3. Move disk 1 from peg C to peg B.   7. Move disk 1 from peg A to peg C.

4. Move disk 3 from peg A to peg C.

---

*For brevity, the assertions, and subproblem statements do not state that the disks on each peg must be in order of decreasing size, with the smallest disk on top.

Figure 2.6   Two subgoals for the Towers of Hanoi problem: (a) Disks 1
through 5 have been moved to peg B; disk 6 remains on peg
A. (b) Disks 1 through 5 have been moved to peg B; disk 6
has been moved from peg A to peg C. Moving disks 1
through 5 from peg B to peg C will achieve the goal state
and hence solve the problem.

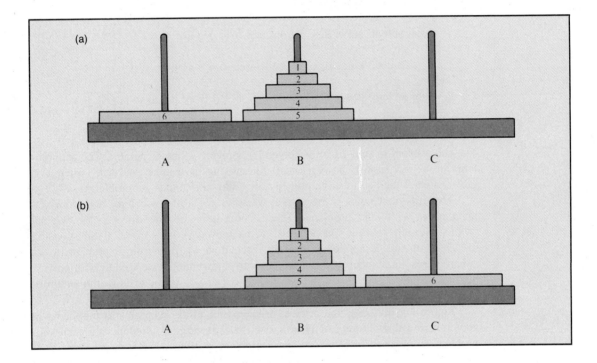

A recursive algorithm   We want to write a recursive algorithm for solving the
n-disk problem. If the value of *n* is 1, this algorithm will solve the 1-disk problem
in a single move. Otherwise, the algorithm will invoke itself twice, each time to
solve an ($n - 1$)-disk problem. To allow the algorithm for the original problem to
also be used for the subproblems, the algorithm must be made independent of some
details that vary from one problem or subproblem to another, such as the number of
disks to be moved, the source peg (the peg from which the disks are to be moved),
and the destination peg (the peg to which the disks are to be moved).

We can make the algorithm independent of these details with the aid of *parameters*. Each parameter is an italicized word that is listed in the heading of the
algorithm and appears throughout the text of the algorithm. Whenever we invoke the
algorithm, we must supply a value for each parameter. Before executing the algorithm, we make a new copy of the algorithm in which every parameter is replaced
by its value. The new copy, in which the parameters have been replaced by their

Figure 2.7   The solution of the 3-disk Towers of Hanoi problem by repeated division into subproblems. Each problem and subproblem is enclosed in a box. The top-level box shows the original problem; the bottom-level boxes show the problems that are not further divided into subproblems but are solved by actually manipulating the disks. When a problem is divided into subproblems, lines drawn from the bottom of the box containing the problem connect it to the boxes containing the subproblems.

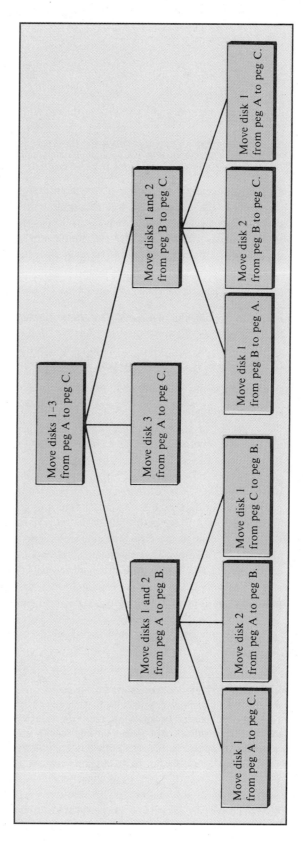

values, is then executed.* In this way we can customize the algorithm to handle different numbers of disks and different source and destination pegs on each invocation.

The heading for the algorithm for the Towers of Hanoi is as follows:

Algorithm Towers of Hanoi (*n, source, dest, aux*)

Towers of Hanoi is the name of the algorithm; *n, source, dest,* and *aux* are the parameters. The parameter *n* represents the number of disks to be moved;† *source* and *dest* represent the source and destination pegs, respectively; *aux* is the remaining auxiliary peg, which is neither the source nor the destination peg but is used as needed as the disks are moved from source to destination.

The instruction

Invoke Towers of Hanoi (6, A, C, B)

means to execute the algorithm Towers of Hanoi with 6 substituted for *n*, A substituted for *source*, C substituted for *destination*, and B substituted for *aux*. Thus this invocation of the algorithm solves the problem of moving 6 disks from peg A to peg C using peg B as the auxiliary peg. Likewise,

Invoke Towers of Hanoi (5, A, B, C)

solves the problem of moving 5 disks from peg A to peg B, using peg C as needed.

A recursive algorithm must always deal with two cases: the trivial case, which can be solved without recourse to recursion, and the nontrivial case which is solved by one or more recursive invocations of the algorithm. For our problem, the 1-disk problem (in which the value of *n* is 1) is the trivial case, and the *n*-disk problem (in which the value of *n* is greater than 1) is the nontrivial case. Figure 2.8 shows the complete algorithm for the Towers of Hanoi problem.

Steps 1 and 2 are both conditional; step 1 handles the trivial case (*n* equals 1) and step 2 handles the case that requires recursive invocations (*n* greater than 1). Only one of these two steps is executed, depending on the value of *n*; never are both executed. For this reason, the precondition and postcondition are the same for both step 1 and step 2; the common precondition is written before step 1 and the common postcondition is written following step 2.

Figure 2.9 shows the instructions that are carried out when the algorithm is invoked to solve the 3-disk problem. Each instruction is enclosed in a box. When

---

*This "copy rule" for parameter passing has the advantage of being easy to describe and understand. But for computer programs, making a new copy of the program each time it is invoked is usually not practical because of the time required to make the copies and the memory space they use. The methods of parameter passing actually used for computer programs are described in detail in Chapters 10: one such method is described briefly in Excercise 4.

†Note that we are using *n* in two slightly different ways. In algorithms, *n* is a parameter; in general discussions it is just a letter representing the number of disks that have to be moved. Since these two uses do not conflict with each other (in each case the value of *n* is the number of disks to be moved), we will not always bother to distinguish between the two.

Figure 2.8   A recursive algorithm for solving the Towers of Hanoi problem. Parameter *n* is the number of disks to be moved; *source* is the peg from which the disks are to be moved; *dest* is the peg to which the disks will be moved; and *aux* is the auxiliary peg that will hold disks temporarily while they are being moved.

Algorithm Towers of Hanoi (*n, source, dest, aux*)

{ Disks 1 through *n* on peg *source; source, dest,* and *aux* are distinct pegs }

1. If *n* is equal to 1, do the following:

   1.1. Move disk 1 from peg *source* to peg *destination*.

2. If *n* is greater than 1, do the following:

   2.1. Invoke Towers of Hanoi (*n* − 1, *source, aux, dest*).

   { Disks 1 through *n* − 1, on peg *aux*; disk *n* on peg *source* }

   2.2 Move disk *n* from peg *source* to peg *dest*.

   { Disks 1 through *n* − 1 on peg *aux*; disk *n* on peg *dest* }

   2.3 Invoke Towers of Hanoi (*n* − 1, *aux, dest, source*).

{ Disks 1 through *n* on peg *dest* }

---

the instruction in a box invokes the algorithm recursively, the instructions carried out by the recursive invocation are placed below the box and connected to it by lines. Note the similarity of Figures 2.7 and 2.9; subproblems in Figure 2.7 correspond to instructions in Figure 2.9. Subproblems that are broken down into still smaller subproblems correspond to instructions that recursively invoke the algorithm. As in Figure 2.7, reading from left to right the bottommost instruction on each path gives the instructions actually used to manipulate the disks.

Let's work through part of Figure 2.9. The instruction

Invoke Towers of Hanoi (3, A, C, B)

causes the algorithm to be executed with *n* replaced by 3, *source* replaced by A. *dest* replaced by C, and *aux* replaced by B. Step 1 is not executed, since *n* is replaced by

Figure 2.9 The execution of the recursive algorithm Towers of Hanoi (abbreviated "T of H" in the diagram) when it is invoked to solve the 3-disk problem. Each instruction, including the original and recursive invocations of the algorithm, is enclosed in a box. A box containing an instruction to invoke the algorithm is connected by lines to the boxes containing the instructions executed by the invoked algorithm. The boxes that do not invoke the algorithm contain the instructions that are actually used to manipulate the disks.

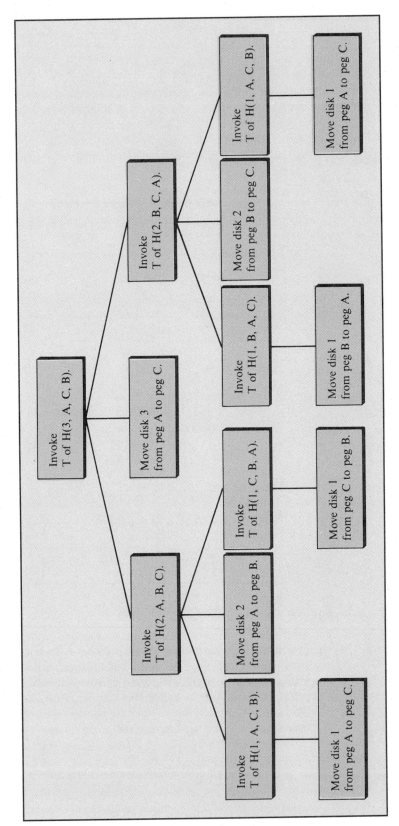

3, and 3 is not equal to 1. Step 2 *is* executed, however, and causes the following operations to be carried out:

2.1 Invoke Towers of Hanoi (3 − 1, A, B, C)
2.2 Move disk 3 from peg A to peg C
2.3 Invoke Towers of Hanoi (3 − 1, B, C, A)

Steps 2.1 and 2.3 each recursively invokes the Towers of Hanoi algorithm. Note that 3 − 1 comes from $n − 1$ when n is replaced by 3. When an arithmetical expression such as 3 − 1 is given for the value of a parameter, the value is worked out before the algorithm is invoked. Thus step 2.1 is equivalent to

2.1 Invoke Towers of Hanoi (2, A, B, C)

Thus the algorithm is invoked with n replaced by 2, *source* replaced by A, *dest* replaced by B, and *aux* replaced by C. Again, step 1 is not executed, since 2 is not equal to 1. Step 2 causes the following operations to be carried out:

2.1 Invoke Towers of Hanoi (2 − 1, A, C, B)
2.2 Move disk 2 from peg A to peg B
2.3 Invoke Towers of Hanoi (2 − 1, C, B, A)

Again steps 2.1 and 2.3 invoke the algorithm Towers of Hanoi recursively. This time, however, n is replaced by 1 (the value of 2 − 1), so step 1 rather than step 2 is executed, and no more recursive invocations take place. Instead,

Invoke Towers of Hanoi (1, A, C, B)

causes the operation

Move disk 1 from peg A to peg C

to be carried out, and

Invoke Towers of Hanoi (1, C, B, A)

causes the operation

Move disk 1 from peg C to peg B

to be carried out.

Verifying a recursive algorithm How can we prove that a recursive algorithm is correct? If we begin to work through the algorithm step by step, we immediately encounter invocations of the algorithm we are supposed to be proving. We find ourselves in the position of being able to prove the algorithm correct only if we assume that it is already correct. We need some technique to avoid this apparently circular reasoning.

The tool we need for proving the correctness of recursive algorithms is called *mathematical induction*. Let us use the abbreviation $S(n)$ for the statement we wish to prove true. The n in parentheses indicates that n appears in the statement. For example, the statement we wish to prove for the Towers of Hanoi problem is

> S(n): If *source, aux,* and *dest* represent distinct pegs, then
>> Invoke Towers of Hanoi (*n, source, dest, aux*)
>> solves the *n*-disk Towers of Hanoi problem with the given source, destination, and auxilary pegs.

If some other value or expression appears in parentheses, that value or expression replaces *n* in the statement. For example, S(1) is given by

> S(1): If *source, aux,* and *dest* represent distinct pegs, then
>> Invoke Towers of Hanoi (1, *source, dest, aux*)
>> solves the 1-disk Towers of Hanoi problem with the given source, destination, and auxilary pegs.

and S(n − 1) is given by

> S(n − 1): If *source, aux,* and *dest* represent distinct pegs, then
>> Invoke Towers of Hanoi (*n* − 1, *source, dest, aux*)
>> solves the (*n* − 1)-disk Towers of Hanoi problem with the given source, destination and auxilary pegs.

We wish to prove that S(n) is true for any integer *n* greater than or equal to 1. That is, we want to prove that the statements S(1), S(2), S(3), and so on are all true. The principle of mathematical induction allows us to draw this conclusion if we can prove the following two statements:

1. *Base Case:* S(1) is true.

2. *Induction Step:* For all *n* greater than 1, if S(n − 1) is true, then S(n) is true. That is, if we assume that S(n − 1) is true, we can prove that S(n) is true.

It's easy to see why the principle of mathematical induction is valid. The base case tells us that S(1) is true. But if S(1) is true, the induction step allows us to conclude that S(2) is true, since S(2 − 1) is S(1). In the same way, if S(2) is true, the induction step allows us to conclude that S(3) is true, since S(3 − 1) is S(2). Continuing in the same way, we prove that S(4), S(5), S(6), and so on are also true. The principle of mathematical induction summarizes this reasoning by stating that, if we can prove the base case and the induction step, we can conclude the S(n) is true for every integer *n* greater than or equal to 1.

For the Towers of Hanoi algorithm, the base case corresponds to the invocation of the algoarithm with *n* replaced by 1; in this case only step 1 is executed. Step 1 solves the Towers of Hanoi problem by moving the single disk from peg *source* to peg *dest*. Thus the algorithm works when *n* is equal to 1, and the base case is proved.

To prove the induction step, we are allowed to assume that S(n − 1) is true; on that assumption, we must prove that S(n) is true. The proof must be good for any value of *n* greater than 1. Since the value of *n* is greater than 1, step 2 of the algorithm is executed. Step 2 invokes the algorithm being proved twice, each time with *n* − 1 for the value of the first parameter. But since we can assume that S(n − 1) is true, we can assume that Towers of Hanoi works when called with *n* − 1 for its first parameter. Thus in proving the invocation with parameter value *n*, we can assume that the recursive invocations solve the corresponding $(n - 1)$-disk problems. Under this assumption, we readily convince ourselves that step 2 does indeed solve the n-disk problem.

Note the requirement in S(n) that the values of *source, dest,* and *aux* be distinct. We cannot invoke the algorithm with the same value for more than one parameter, because then we would not have the three distinct pegs that we know are needed to solve the problem.

Review questions

1. What is *problem theory?*

2. Define the following terms: *problem state, initial state, goal state, operator,* and *constraint.*

3. What features of an algorithm correspond to the initial state, the goal state, and the operators for a problem?

4. We can think of an algorithm as giving a sequence of operators for transforming the initial state of a problem into the goal state. On what does this sequence of operators depend?

5. Since an algorithm always yields a sequence of operators, why is the sequencing control structure alone not sufficient? Why are selection and repetition needed?

6. Give the four steps recommended by Polya for solving problems.

7. What are some of the elements of a problem that we should try to identify when we are trying to understand the problem?

8. What might be one result of trying to write an algorithm to solve a problem without having thoroughly understood the problem and planned a solution in advance?

9. Give some of the insights we might hope to gain by looking back on a problem we have already solved.

10. How can *inference* be applied to problem solving?

11. What is *hill climbing?* What are some of the pitfalls of this approach to problem solving?

12. Why are we usually ahead of the game if we know of a previously solved problem analogous to the one we are trying to solve?

13. Why are *macros* often helpful? Give an example of a problem where a well-chosen repertoire of macros is almost essential for finding a solution.

14. *Case analysis* in problem solving corresponds to what control structure in algorithms?

15. What are *subgoals? Subproblems?* How might an author writing a book use *stepwise refinement?*

16. Describe the method of *working backward.* How is working backward related to the method of subgoals?

17. Define *recursion.*

18. What two requirements must be met for recursion to be used successfully?

19. What does it mean to *invoke* an algorithm? What is a *recursive invocation?* What are *parameters?*

20. State the principle of *mathematical induction.* What is the *base case?* The *induction step?*

Exercises

1. Solve the fox, goose, and corn problem. Try to identify the ways in which you were helped by the analogy between this problem and the missionaries and cannibals problem.

2. Write the algorithm for the modified merge problem described in this chapter, including appropriate assertions, and prove that the algorithm is correct.

3. Show that the solution to the water-jar problem that we derived for 9-quart and 4-quart jars with 6 quarts of water needed can be applied unchanged to the following related problems:

Jars Available	*Amount of Water Needed*
7 quart and 3 quart	5 quarts
11 quart and 5 quart	7 quarts

   What relationships must hold between the sizes of the two jars and the amount of water needed in order for the solution to be applicable? Give some additional related problems that have the same solution.

4. Use the Towers of Hanoi algorithm to solve the 4-disk problem. To save yourself the trouble of making copies of the algorithm with values substituted for parameters, you can use the following procedure, which is similar to that used in many computer languages. At the beginning of each invocation, make out a card (called an *activation record*) which gives the parameter values for this invocation (or activation) of the algorithm. For example, if the algorithm is invoked with

   Invoke Tower of Hanoi (5, A, B, C)

   the activation record is

n	5
source	A
dest	B
aux	C

Each time you encounter a parameter while executing the algorithm, you can determine the value of the parameter by consulting the activation record.

The activation records for different invocations can be kept as a stack of cards, one record on each card. Whenever we invoke the algorithm, we write an activation record for the new invocation on a card and place it on top of the stack. When we are through executing the invoked algorithm, we remove its activation record from the top of the stack, exposing the activation record for the invocation that was in progress before the just concluded invocation took place.

When we invoke an algorithm, we must make note of the step with which the invocation now in progress is to continue after the new invocation has terminated. For example, when we execute step 2.1 of the Towers of Hanoi algorithm, we must note that the current invocation is to continue with step 2.2 after the recursive invocation has been completed. When we execute step 2.3, we must note that the current invocation is to be terminated (since step 2.3 is the last step of the algorithm) after the recursive invocation has been completed. A good place to note this continuation point is on the activation record for the new invocation. For example, when executing step 2.1, the activation record for the new invocation might look like this:

n	5
source	A
dest	B
aux	C

Resume invoking algorithm at step 2.2

5. The *factorial* of an integer greater than or equal to 1 is defined as the product of all integers from 1 through the integer in question. For example, the factorial of 3 is $1 \times 2 \times 3$ which equals 6, and the factorial of 4 is $1 \times 2 \times 3 \times 4$, which equals 24. The following is a recursive algorithm for computing the factorial of *n* on a pocket calculator:

Algorithm Factorial(*n*)

1. If *n* is equal to 1, enter 1 on the calculator display.

2. If *n* is greater than 1, do the following:

   2.1 Invoke Factorial($n - 1$)

   2.2 Multiply the number displayed on the calculator by *n* and leave the result on the calculator display.

Use mathematical induction to prove that this algorithm computes the factorial of n for every integer n greater than or equal to 1.

For further reading

The following are two good books on problem solving. Polya's book is *the* classic work on the subject.

Polya, G. *How to Solve It*. Princeton, N.J.: Princeton University Press, 1945.

Wickelgren, Wayne A. *How to Solve Problems*. San Francisco: W. H. Freeman and Co., 1974.

Fascinating and offbeat examples of recursion, as well as many other topics in computer science, can be found in Douglas Hofstadter's Pulizer-Prize-winning best seller.

Hofstadter, Douglas R. *Godel, Escher, and Bach: an Eternal Gold Braid*. New York: Basic Books, 1979.

Further information on cube puzzles can be found in

Hofstadter, Douglas R. ''Metamagical Themas.'' *Scientific American,* March 1981, pp. 20–39.

Singmaster, David. *Notes on Rubik's Magic Cube*. Hillside N.J.: Enslow Publishers, 1981.

Part II
Computer hardware and software

3

Computer hardware

A *computer system* is made up of *hardware* and *software*. The hardware consists of the physical components that make up the computer system: transistors, integrated circuits, microprocessors, tape decks, disk drives, card readers, printers, computer terminals, and the like. The software consists of the programs that the computer executes.

In this chapter we will look at computer hardware, and in Chapter 4 we will explore a closely related topic—the way in which information is represented inside the computer. Computer software will be discussed Chapter 5.

3.1
The parts of a computer—an overview

Figure 3.1 shows the components of a typical computer: the *central processing unit, main memory, input and output devices,* and *auxiliary memory.*

The *central processing unit* (also called the *CPU* or *central processor*) is the heart of the computer. Some of the other parts are optional, but without a central processor, we don't have a computer. The central processor executes the user's program by fetching instructions from memory one by one and carrying out the operations that they request. Arithmetical and similar data-manipulating operations are carried out by the central processor itself. For other operations, the central processor sends the necessary command to the devices whose services are required. A computer can have more than one central processor: in that case we refer to the computer's *processors,* since no one processor is more central than the others.

Figure 3.1   The hardware components of a typical computer system.
There can be any number of peripherals—input, output, and
auxiliary memory devices.

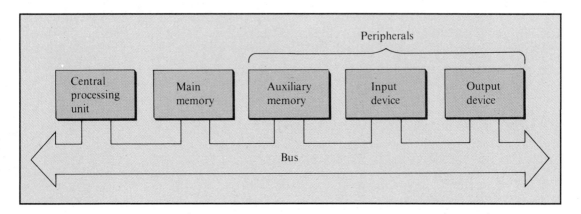

Memory refers to any component used to store information. (Some people prefer the term *storage* to *memory*.) The computer's *main memory* stores the program that the computer is executing and the data it is manipulating. We can think of main memory as the computer's blackboard or scratch pad because during a calculation it is used for temporary storage of intermediate results that will be needed later in the calculation.

Peripheral devices include input devices, output devices, and auxiliary memory. *Input and output (I/O) devices* let the computer communicate with the outside world. They convert data between the forms useful to people (text, pictures, and sounds) and the codes that computers use to store data internally. *Auxiliary memory* is used for long-term storage of data and programs. If main memory is the computer's scratch pad, auxiliary memory is its library and filing cabinets.

Many computers are organized around a group of 50–100 wires called a *bus,* over which the components can communicate with one another. Frequently, the various components are constructed on *circuit boards,* which plug into *slots,* or sockets, installed along the bus. For larger components, such as printers, a *device-controller* board plugs into the bus. A cable, which is not part of the bus, connects the device controller to the device itself.

We can think of the bus as an electronic highway along which the different units can send data to one another. Most of the "traffic" on the bus is between the central processor and main memory, with a lesser amount between the central processor and the peripheral devices. Some peripheral devices can transfer data directly to or from main memory, without going through the central processor, so there is also traffic between main memory and peripheral devices. Rarely is there any direct communication between different peripheral devices. *Bus contention*—the need for each unit to wait until the bus is not in use before sending its data—can limit the performance of the system; this is particularly true if the system has more than one processor.

3.2 The central processing unit

The central processing unit is the most complex part of the computer. This isn't surprising, since the central processor has to interpret each instruction in the program and either carry it out or see that it is carried out by other components of the computer. In early computers, the central processor often occupied a large cabinet and cost tens or hundreds of thousands of dollars.

In the early 1970s, engineers learned how to construct a complete central processor on a tiny chip of silicon. The result is known as a *microprocessor*. Removed from its protective package, a microprocessor will fit on the end of your finger; inside its package, it will fit in the palm of your hand. Because microprocessors can be produced in large quantities at low cost, computers now can be used in applications that once would have been out of the question, such as in household appliances and electronic games. These drastic changes in the ways people use computers is often called the *microprocessor revolution*.

The central processor itself is made up of two components: the *arithmetic/logic unit*, which does the calculations, and the *control unit*, which coordinates the activities of the entire computer. (For microprocessors, both units usually occupy the same chip, although for particularly complex designs more than one chip might be used.)

The arithmetic/logic unit We can think of the arithmetic/logic unit as the computer's calculator; it performs many of the same jobs for a computer that a pocket-calculator performs for a person. The following are some of the jobs of the arithmetic/logic unit:

- *Arithmetical Operations.* The arithmetic/logic unit adds, subtracts, multiplies, and divides. The arithmetic/logic units for some computers do not include multiplication or division; for such machines, it is necessary to program multiplications and divisions in terms of repeated additions and subtractions.

- *Logical Operations.* Logical operations require some explanation. Suppose we have a compound sentence made up of simple sentences joined with *and* and *or*. For example:

    It is raining *and* I am indoors *or* it is sunny *and* I am out playing.

    Given whether each of the simple sentences is true or false, the arithmetic/logic unit can compute (under the control of a program) whether the entire compound sentence is true or false.

- *Comparisons.* The arithmetic/logic unit can determine such things as whether two alphabetic characters are the same or whether one number is less than, equal to, or greater than another. This information is passed to the control unit, which uses it to determine which instruction will be executed next. This feature of the central processor allows us to implement *selection*—to program the computer to make decisions depending on the conditions that hold when the program is executed. Comparisons are also important for implementing *repetition* because they allow the termination condition to be tested.

The control unit   When an instruction is fetched from memory, it goes to the control unit, which decodes the instruction and generates the control signals that cause the other parts of the computer to carry out the instruction. In particular, the control unit determines which arithmetical, logical, or comparison operation the arithmetic/logic unit should carry out. If we think of the arithmetic/logic unit as the computer's calculator, we can think of the control unit as "punching the keys" of this calculator.

The control unit oversees the movement of data back and forth between the arithmetic/logic unit and main memory. It also oversees the movement of data between the arithmetic/logic unit and some peripheral devices. (Other peripheral devices transfer data directly to and from main memory without going through the arithmetic/logic unit.)

The control unit also fetches program instructions from main memory. Normally the control unit takes instructions from successive memory locations, just as a person might start at the top of a list of instructions and work through the list instruction by instruction. This step-by-step execution implements the sequencing control structure.

But sometimes an instruction will direct the control unit to jump to another part of the program rather than to fetch the next instruction in sequence. Usually the jump is to take place only if a certain condition is true. The control unit has the arithmetic/logic unit check whether or not the specified condition is true. If it is, the control unit jumps to the designated part of the program for its next instruction and continues execution from there. Otherwise the control unit just fetches the next instruction in sequence.

Jumps are important for implementing both selection and repetition. For selection, the computer jumps to the appropriate part of the program depending on the conditions that hold when the program is executed. For repetition, a jump from the end back to the beginning of a sequence of instructions causes the sequence to be executed repeatedly. Another jump causes the computer to leave the repeated sequence and continue with the rest of the program when the termination condition for the repetition becomes true.

The control unit operates in a *fetch-execute* cycle. Instructions are fetched from memory and executed one after another. No matter how complex the task that the computer is carrying out, the control unit is always just fetching and executing instructions, one after another.

The central processor is driven by a circuit called a *clock,* which produces electrical pulses ("ticks") at regular intervals. Computer clocks usually tick millions or tens of millions of times a second. The interval from one tick to the next is called a *clock cycle.* Normally, a fetch-execute cycle requires more than one clock cycle (five-to-ten clock cycles are typical).

Regardless of whether we consider clock cycles or fetch-execute cycles, we can think of *cycles* as the basic commodity of computation. A certain number of cycles are required to execute a program; the faster the computer can go through those cycles, the faster the program will be executed. (However, the time required to execute a program that does large amounts of input and output may depend more on the speed of the input and output devices than on that of the central processor. Such a program is said to be *input-output bound*.) In *time sharing,* where many people work on the same computer system at the same time, we can think of the available cycles as being divided among the various users. Adding more processors to such a system, or speeding up the existing ones, can make more cycles available per unit time and so speed up the execution of all programs that are not input-output bound.

3.3 Computer memory

Most computers have both *main memory* and *auxiliary memory.* (Main memory is sometimes referred to as *primary memory* or *primary storage.* It is also sometimes called *core memory* because in older computers main memory is made up of a large number of tiny magnetic rings called *cores.* Auxiliary memory is sometimes called *secondary memory, secondary storage, mass memory,* or *mass storage.*)

Main memory is very fast. The computer can store or recall the contents of a main memory location in less than one millionth of a second. Unfortunately, one has to pay for such performance; main memory is more expensive than auxiliary memory with the same capacity. Also, some forms of main memory are *volatile:* data stored in them is lost when the computer is turned off.

Therefore, most computers also make use of auxiliary memory, which is about a thousand times slower than main memory but costs correspondingly less. And auxiliary memory isn't volatile, so it can be used to store program libraries and permanent data files.

Main memory   A computer's main memory is divided into a number of individual *memory locations,* each of which can hold a certain amount of data. Each location has an *address,* which other parts of the computer can use to refer to that location. We can think of a computer's memory as being like an array of post office boxes, each having an address and containing a piece of data.

Main memory is *random-access memory.* This means that the speed at which the computer can gain access to individual memory locations doesn't depend on the order in which the locations are referred to. A series of locations can be accessed in some random order just as rapidly as if they were accessed in order of increasing or decreasing addresses. We will see that this statement isn't always true for auxiliary memory.

There are two types of main memory: *read-only memory* and *read-write memory.* The contents of read-only memory are fixed when the memory chips are manufactured and cannot be changed during normal operation of the computer. The outstanding advantage of read-only memory is that it is *nonvolatile:* because its contents are permanent, they are retained when the computer is turned off. Read-only memory is often used for the programs for computers embedded in consumer products, such as automobiles and cameras, since the user has no reason to change these programs and the program must be present whenever the device is turned on. Some of the software for a computer may be placed in read-only memory; software in read-only memory is sometimes referred to as *firmware*. Read-only memory is frequently referred to by the acronym ROM.

As its name implies, read-write memory allows data to be both retrieved (read) and stored (written). Read-write memory is usually volatile. Read-write memory is usually designated by the acronym RAM, which actually stands for *random-access memory*. This is a poor choice of terms since ROM also has the property of random access.

Main memory devices, like microprocessors, can be built on silicon chips that can be produced in large quantities at low cost. These low-cost memory chips have contributed almost as much to the microprocessor revolution as the microprocessors themselves.

Auxiliary memory   Auxiliary memory is used for large permanent files such as those holding the accounts of a corporation. Program libraries stored in auxiliary memory allow a person to use the computer without writing a program, if a program for the desired job is already on file in the library. If the computer's "scratch pad" becomes too large to fit in main memory, part of it can be stored in auxiliary memory until needed.

We will look at three kinds of auxiliary memory: magnetic tape, magnetic disks, and magnetic bubbles.

- *Magnetic Tape.*   The magnetic tape that computers use is similar to the tape used by home sound and video recorders. The main drawback of magnetic tape is familiar to anyone who has ever used a tape recorder. Suppose you have a number of musical selections recorded on the same tape. If you want to play the selections in the same order in which they were recorded, you have no problem. You just put the tape on and let it play. But if you want to play a selection at the beginning of the tape first, then one near the end, then one near the middle, and so on, you will waste a lot of time using the rewind and fast-forward controls to position the tape for the next selection.

  In short, tape is a *sequential access* medium: items recorded on tape can be retrived most rapidly when they are played back in the same order in which they were recorded. To play back the items in some other order requires excessive winding and rewinding of the tape. This behavior is in marked contrast to that of main memory, which provides random access: the speed with which stored items are recalled is independent of the order in which they were stored.

  Magnetic tape is the lowest cost form of data storage and so is favored for long-term storage of massive amounts of data. The tape library of a large organization may contain many thousands of reels.

- *Magnetic Disks.*   Magnetic disks (usually just called disks) resemble phonograph records but work on the same principle as magnetic tape; the data is recorded as patterns of magnetization rather than in grooves.

  To understand how a disk works, imagine the phonograph-record-like disk attached to a *spindle*—a spinning rod. An *access arm* comes in from the side and points toward the center of the spinning disk. The access arm is shaped like a two-pronged fork, with one prong going above the disk and the other below it. At the end of each prong is a *read-write* head that records and plays back the data. The head on the top prong records and plays back from the top surface; the head on the bottom prong does the same for the bottom surface. Depending on the design of the disk, the heads may actually touch the surface, or they may be separated from it by a small gap.

The access arm can move the read-write heads either in toward the center of the disk or out toward the edge. When a read-write head is in a particular position, the portion of the disk that moves past the read-write head is in a particular position, the portion of the disk that moves past the read-write head as the disk spins is called a *track*. Unlike the grooves of a phonograph record, the tracks on a disk cannot be seen by looking at the disk; they are just the paths along which data is recorded. Also, each track on a disk is a circle, whereas the grooves of phonograph record form one gigantic spiral running from the edge of the record to its center.

In operation, the access arm positions the read-write head over the track on which data is to be written or from which data is to be read. The actual read or write takes place when the rotation of the disk carries the desired part of the track past the read-write head.

Disks are often called random-access media, because the access arm can position the read-write head over any track, and any data on the track can be accessed during one revolution of the disk. Still, the access time isn't completely independent of the location of the data. Obviously, access will be faster if the read-write head happens to be positioned over the track containing the requested data than if it must be moved to a distant track. And if the read-write head is on the correct track, access will be fastest if the desired data is just about to move past the read-write head when it is requested and slowest if the desired data has just finished moving past the read-write head (so that we must wait for almost a full revolution of the disk to get another chance at it).

■ *Magnetic Bubbles*. Both magnetic tape and magnetic disks involve mechanical devices with moving parts. Mechanical devices are slower, less reliable, and usually bulkier and more expensive than electronic ones. Magnetic bubbles provide a completely electronic form of auxiliary memory.

Magnetic bubbles are magnetized regions on a thin film of an appropriate material, such as garnet. Although they are not actually bubbles, they behave in some ways like bubbles in a liquid: the individual regions retain their identity and can be moved around on the film. New bubbles can be created when needed, and old ones can be destroyed.

In operation, an external magnetic field causes bubbles to circulate around a loop, like cars driving around a traffic circle. There can be any number of loops on a given chip, and each loop corresponds to one track on a disk. The data is recorded in the pattern formed by the bubbles and the gaps between them. Special components on the chip detect the presence of bubbles and so serve as a read head. Other components that create and destroy bubbles serve as a write head.

Magnetic bubble storage has been touted for some years as the technology that will replace disks. So far, this replacement has not come about; magnetic bubble storage is substantially more expensive than disk storage and is not nearly so widely used. Magnetic bubble storage *is* being used in some of the highly portable "notebook size" computers, which are too small to contain disk drives: the first extensive use of magnetic bubbles undoubtedly will be in this area.

3.4 Input and output devices

The input and output devices, frequently called I/O devices, serve to get data into and out of the computer.

Displays   A display presents computer output in a form in which it can be read by the user. A *text display* can display only letters, digits, and various special characters such as punctuation marks; a *graphics display* can also display drawings and pictures.

The most popular and widely used display device is the *video display,* which is similar in appearance to a television set or a video monitor. In fact, a television set or a video monitor can be used as a video display although neither is as good as a display designed especially for computer use. A monochrome display produces output in black and white only, whereas a color display allows other colors as well. For a black-and-white display, "white" is frequently green or amber, which is more restful for the eyes than the white produced by a black-and-white television set.

Liquid crystal displays (LCDs), similar to those found in calculators and digital watches, are widely used in "notebook size" and "pocket size" computers. Strong demand for portable computers is leading to rapid improvements in LCDs, which currently do not provide the resolution and contrast of video displays. Several other display technologies are under development but have not seen widespread use.

Keyboards   Computer keyboards are usually similar to the standard typewriter keyboard with the addition of a few special signs and mathematical symbols. A keyboard may have a *numeric keypad,* similar to that of a calculator, to simplify entering large amounts of numeric data. It also might have a *Ctrl (control) key,* which works somewhat like the shift keys on a typewriter. When the control key is held down and another key—usually a letter of the alphabet—is pressed, a special control character is transmitted. Many computer systems interpret control characters as commands; for example, Ctrl-C (the C key pressed while the Ctrl key is held down) is often used to interrupt a program and demand the computer's attention. Some keyboards have more than one control key; holding down the proper control keys for a particular command can require considerable finger gymnastics. Many keyboards also have one or more rows of special *function keys,* each of which transmits a command to the computer. A good supply of function keys can reduce the need for the Ctrl key and hence the amount of finger gymnastics needed to send commands to the computer.

The point at which the next character typed will appear on a display is usually indicated by a flashing line or block called a *cursor*. Computer keyboards often contain a set of four *cursor control keys* for moving the cursor left, right, up, or down. An arrow on the top of each cursor control key shows the direction in which it moves the cursor.

Many keyboards are designed so that the keys will automatically repeat if held down; holding down the space bar, for example, will type a series of spaces. This feature is particularly useful with the cursor control keys; to move the cursor in a particular direction we press the corresponding key and hold it down until the cursor has moved as far as desired.

Computer terminals and modems A computer terminal is used to communicate with a distant computer. A terminal consists of a keyboard and a display; the latter is usually a video display, but some portable terminals use the more compact liquid crystal display. Sometimes a printer is provided in place of or in addition to the display.

A terminal can communicate with the distant computer over ordinary telephone lines with the aid of a *modem (modulator-demodulator),* which converts between the electrical signals used by computers and those that can be transmitted over telephone lines. The more elaborate modems serve as a telephone set for a terminal or computer, dialing numbers on request, alerting the computer or terminal when a ringing signal is received on the telephone line, and answering incoming calls. Some terminals have built-in modems so that the terminal can be plugged directly into a telephone jack. (Otherwise, an external modem must be connected between the terminal and the telephone line.) Most desktop and portable computers also can be used as terminals; some even have built-in modems.

Pointing devices The need frequently arises for a computer user to point out something on the display to the computer—for example, to point to a word to be erased by a word-processing program. The computer may display a *menu* of available commands and allow the user to point to the command to be executed. Most users find this method easier than having to remember which control key or function key correspnds to each command.

One of the earliest pointing devices was the *light pen,* which can be used only with video displays. A video display is produced by an electron beam which repeatedly scans the display screen from left to right and from top to bottom. Because of this scanning action, which is too fast for the eye to follow, each point on the display is illuminated at a slightly different time. The light pen, a penlike device with a light-sensitive cell in its tip, is connected by wire to the computer. The user places the tip of the light pen over the point he or she wishes to designate; when that point is scanned, the light-sensitive cell sends an electrical pulse to the computer. By noting the time at which the pulse arrives, the computer can determine the point over which the light pen is positioned. Light pens allow the user to draw on the face of the display (computer software tracks the motion of the light pen and fills in the line the user is drawing). Light pens are not so popular for more mundane tasks such as selecting items from command menus.

A display can be made *touch sensitive:* the user need only touch the appropriate point on the display to point out an item to the computer. Some touch-sensitive displays have a screen that is coated with an electrically conductive film; touching the coating changes its electrical properties and allows the computer to determine the point at which the screen was touched. Other touch-sensitive displays have a grid of invisible infrared light beams immediately in front of the screen. Touching the screen breaks two light beams, one in the horizontal direction and one in the vertical direction, allowing the computer to locate the point that was touched. A *touch pad* is a touch-sensitive pad with the same shape as the display but separate from it. Touching a particular point on the pad designates the corresponding point on the screen.

Currently, the most popular pointing device is the *mouse,* a small boxlike object that is connected to the computer by a wire and can be rolled around on a desk. A pointer on the screen follows the movements of the mouse; rolling the mouse left moves the pointer left by an equivalent amount, rolling the mouse right moves the pointer right, and so on. The user presses a button on the mouse when the pointer is at the desired position, such as on the command that is to be selected. Mice work well for such undemanding jobs as selecting commands but not as well for more delicate jobs such as drawing on the screen.

Card readers   Card readers transfer to the computer data that has been recorded in the form of holes punched in cards. The cards themselves are variously known as *punched cards, tab cards, IBM cards,* and *Hollerith cards.* The last name honors Herman Hollerith, who first used punched cards for data processing.

The most common type of punched card is divided into 80 columns. One character can be punched into each column, so a card can hold a maximum of 80 characters. The cards are punched by a machine called a *card punch.* Some card punches, called *keypunches,* are designed to be operated by a person using a typewriterlike keyboard. Other card punches serve as output devices for computers, punching on cards data transmitted by computers.

In addition to the 80-column punched card, there is a 96-column card that holds 96 characters. The 96-column card uses a more efficient method of coding characters than does the 80-column card, so the 96-column card is the smaller of the two, even though it can hold 16 more characters than the 80-column card.

Optical character readers   Optical character readers read handwritten, typed, or printed characters directly from source documents, such as filled out forms. With other types of data entry, a person must read the source document and strike keys on a keyboard. In these cases mistakes are inevitable; in fact, most ''computer errors'' can be traced to erroneously entered data. Optical character recognition allows us to bypass the error-prone typing process and have the computer read source documents directly.

Unfortunately, present optical character readers cannot cope with most human handwriting or even with most ordinary typing and printing. The characters must be carefully hand printed according to certain rules, or they must be typed or printed using special typefaces designed for optical character recognition. Research in optical character recognition continues, however, so no doubt some of these restrictions will disappear in time.

Printers   Printers are usually used when a permanent record of computer output is required. High-speed printers can print hundreds, thousands, or even tens of thousands of lines per minute. Printer technology runs the gamut from typewriterlike impact printers to those that use such exotic techniques as laser beams and electrically controlled ink jets to form the characters.

The most popular type of printer for small computers is the *dot matrix printer,* which forms characters as arrays of dots. Dot matrix printers are compact, reliable, and relatively fast and quiet; some people, however, dislike the appearance of the printout they produce. An enormous advantage of dot matrix printers is that they can print graphics as well as text; in fact, anything that can appear on a black-and-white display device can be printed by a suitable dot matrix printer. (For example, the *computer portraits* often sold in shopping malls and on boardwalks are produced by dot matrix printers.) Dot matrix printers that can print in three or four colors are also available.

Personal computer users who are dissatisfied with the printout produced by dot matrix printers use typewriterlike *letter quality* printers. The output from a letter quality printer appears to have been typed with a high quality typewriter. On the other hand, letter quality printers are more expensive than dot matrix printers, operate more slowly, and can print only text, not graphics.

Plotters   Plotters allow computers to make drawings. They are often used to plot graphs, draw maps, and produce engineering drawings. They are also used to draw the patterns from which microprocessors, memory chips, and other integrated circuits are manufactured. Plotters are used when the highest quality and greatest accuracy are required. For less demanding tasks, a dot matrix printer with graphics capabilities will often serve just as well.

Speech synthesizers   Computers can speak as well as print. Consumer products that use computer-generated speech include educational toys that pronounce and spell words, electronic phrase books that pronounce phrases in a foreign language, calculators for the blind, and countless electronic games.

How does speech synthesis work? A program looks up the words in a dictionary that shows how each word is to be pronounced and stressed. Using this information, the computer sends codes representing the sounds to the speech synthesizer, an electronic device that actually produces the sounds.

With current hardware and software, the result is not perfect; the computer seems to speak with an accent. But people who really need a talking computer, such as blind persons, have little trouble learning to follow the machine's accent. And tests have shown that children would rather have their toys speak with a computer accent than have them imitate natural speech more closely.

Much of the computer's accent can be eliminated if the machine only has to utter stock phrases rather than be able to read any text. A programmer chooses the codes to be sent to the synthesizer for each phrase, experimenting with the codes until each phrase sounds as natural as possible. The codes for each phrase are stored in the computer's memory and recalled when needed. Consumer products that use speech synthesis normally use this method.

Equipment that allows a computer to recognize spoken words is under development, and some is actually in use. At present, however, speech recognition is not as highly developed as speech synthesis.

3.5 Classifications of computers

Computers can be roughly classified as *embedded computers, microcomputers, minicomputers, main frames,* and *supercomputers.* Although there is some overlap between the classifications, machines in different categories generally differ in price, memory capacity, speed of operation, and intended use. We will not try to pin down these details for each category since the rapid change in computer technology would quickly make any such enumeration obsolete. Instead, we will look at some of the general characteristics and applications of machines in each category.

Embedded computers   Embedded computers are incorporated as parts of other machines, such as automobiles, television sets, kitchen appliances, and cameras. These machines are all built around microprocessors. The program for the microprocessor is permanently installed in read-only memory, so the user never has to worry about programming or even be aware that a program exists. A small amount of read-write memory is present for use as a scratch pad for calculations and to store user requests, such as the time at which a microwave oven should turn on. Embedded computers are of necessity quite inexpensive since products containing embedded computers are unlikely to sell if they cost too much more than their noncomputerized counterparts.

Microcomputers   Microcomputers are computers that are built around microprocessors. Unlike embedded computers, which are used to enhance the performance of other products, microcomputers are used as computers. Alternate names for microcomputers are *personal computers, desktop computers, portable computers, notebook-size computers,* and *pocket computers.* As a general rule, microcomputers offer less processing capability than minicomputers. However, the best microcomputers do match or exceed the performance of some minicomputers, and in the future they may reach the performance level of main frames.

Minicomputers   Minicomputers are small computers that are *not* built around microprocessors. Minicomputers stand between microcomputers and main frames in size, cost, and processing capability. Some of the more advanced minicomputers, called *superminis,* offer capabilities similar to those of main frames. Minicomputers are often sold to *original equipment manufacturers,* who install them in other equipment, such as scientific apparatus. Minicomputers are often operated in a *time-sharing mode,* in which a number of terminals are connected to one computer, allowing a number of people to use the computer at the same time. Microcomputers, in contrast, are usually used by only one person at a time.

Main frames   Main frames are the large-scale computers found in the computer rooms of corporations, universities, and government agencies. A main frame is capable of meeting all, or a substantial part of, the information processing requirements of a large organization. Main frames often use time sharing to allow simultaneous access to the computer from terminals placed throughout the organization. Because main frames cost hundreds of thousands or millions of dollars, they are definitely for organizations, not individuals.

Supercomputers   Very powerful, very fast, and very expensive, supercomputers are generally used for scientific problems requiring massive amounts of computation. Some applications are weather prediction, cryptography (attempting to decipher secret messages sent by foreign governments), and producing high quality computer graphics for special effects in motion pictures.

Review questions

1. What are the two main components of a computer system?

2. What are the three main hardware components of a computer?

3. What is the function of the *central processing unit?*

4. What is the function of *main memory?*

5. Give two functions performed by *peripherals.*

6. What is the *bus* and what is its function?

7. What is the function of *device controllers?*

8. What are *microprocessors?* Why are they important?

9. What are the two parts of the *central processing unit?*

10. Describe three functions of the *arithmetic/logic* unit. What capability of the arithmetic/logic unit supports *selection* and *repetition?*

11. Describe the operation of the *control unit.* What characteristic of the control unit supports *sequencing?* What characteristics support *selection* and *repetition?*

12. What is a *fetch-execute* cycle? A *clock cycle?* Why can we say, somewhat loosely, that *cycles* are the basic commodity of computation?

13. Contrast *main memory* and *auxiliary memory* in terms of access time and cost.

14. What does *volatile* mean in reference to computer memory? Distinguish between *read-only memory* and *read-write memory.*

15. Describe three kinds of auxiliary memory.

16. Distinguish between random and sequential access.

17. Describe two types of display devices.

18. Describe some keys usually found on a computer keyboard but not on a typewriter keyboard.

19. Describe three kinds of *pointing devices*.

20. Describe two kinds of output devices that can be used to print drawings.

21. Describe briefly five categories into which computers can be classified.

For further reading

Computers and Computation. San Francisco: W. H. Freeman and Co., 1971.

Mandell, Steven L. *Computers and Data Processing: Concepts and Applications.* St. Paul, Minn.: West Publishing Company, 1979.

Scientific American (special issue on microelectronics), September 1977.

Vacroux, Andre G. "Microcomputers." *Scientific American,* May 1975.

White, Robert M. "Disk Storage Technology." *Scientific American,* August 1980, pp. 138–148.

4

Information representation

4.1

Binary codes

hat is the simplest and most natural way to represent information inside a machine? This depends on the kinds of parts of which the machine is made. A mechanical desk calculator, for example, is made of gears and other mechanical components. Each digit that is stored in the machine is represented by a gear with ten teeth and ten possible positions. One possible position represents a 0, the next possible position represents a 1, the next a 2, and so on through 9.

Computers, on the other hand, are made of electrical circuits, each of which can be switched on or off. Whereas a gear in a desk calculator can have ten different positions, or states, a circuit in a computer can have only two. Either a current is flowing in the circuit, in which case it is on, or no current is flowing, in which case it is off. Yet we can represent information with these two-state circuits just as well as we can with gears or any other mechanism. Let's look at some examples.

Suppose we have only one circuit. We can represent two alternatives, one by the state in which the circuit is off and the other by the state in which the circuit is on. For example, we could use the circuit to represent the answer to a yes-or-no question by representing ''yes'' by the state in which the circuit is on and ''no'' by the state in which the circuit is off. We can present our method of representing, or coding, the answer in a table:

Data	Representation
no	off
yes	on

Now suppose we have two circuits instead of one. With two circuits we have four states:

off-off	on-off
off-on	on-on

With two circuits we can represent four alternatives. For example, we can represent the four seasons of the year as follows:

Data	Representation
Fall	off-off
Winter	off-on
Spring	on-off
Summer	on-on

Obviously, the particular correspondence we chose (off-off for fall, off-on for winter, and so on) is completely arbitrary. There are, in fact, 24 different ways of representing the four seasons with two circuits, and all these ways are equally satisfactory.

With three circuits we have eight states:

off-off-off	on-off-off
off-off-on	on-off-on
off-on-off	on-on-off
off-on-on	on-on-on

There are enough states to represent the seven days of the week, with one state left over:

Data	Representation
Sunday	off-off-off
Monday	off-off-on
Tuesday	off-on-off
Wednesday	off-on-on
Thursday	on-off-off
Friday	on-off-on
Saturday	on-on-off
(unused)	on-on-on

Whenever we add another circuit, we double the number of alternatives we can represent. This is because we can now use all the states we had before in two different ways—once with the newly added circuit off and once with the newly added circuit on. Thus we don't actually have to write down all the possible states to say that four circuits will give 16 (2 × 8) alternatives, five circuits will give 32 (2 × 16) alternatives, six circuits will give 64 alternatives, and so on.

We use the term *binary code* for any method of representing information with two-state circuits. The word *binary* refers to *two*—in this case, the two possible states of each circuit. When we talk about binary codes, we don't want to bother writing the words *off* and *on* in such complicated combinations as:

off-on-off-off-on-on-off-on

To avoid this, we use 0 to stand for *off* and 1 to stand for *on*. With 0s and 1s, the eight-circuit state just given can be written more simply as:

01001101

What's more, we can use the 0s and 1s in ways that have nothing to do with circuits or currents. For instance, we can represent a 1 by a hole punched in a particular position of a card and a 0 by the absence of a hole in that position. Or we can represent a 0 by a particular area on a magnetic tape being magnetized in one direction and a 1 by that area being magnetized in the opposite direction.

When 0 and 1 are used in this way, we refer to them as *binary digits* or *bits*. A *binary code* is a method of representing information using combinations of bits. Our two previous examples each defines a binary code, as we can see by replacing *off* and *on* by 0 and 1. To represent the four seasons, we need two bits:

Data	Representation
Fall	00
Winter	01
Spring	10
Summer	11

For the seven days of the week, we need three bits:

Data	Representation
Sunday	000
Monday	001
Tuesday	010
Wednesday	011
Thursday	100
Friday	101
Saturday	110
(unused)	111

The number of bits we need to represent a given number of alternatives is the same as the number of two-state circuits. Thus, with one bit we can represent 2 alternatives, with two bits we can represent 2×2 or four alternatives, with three bits we can represent $2 \times 2 \times 2$ or eight alternatives, and so on.

Repeated products of a number with itself are called the *powers* of that number. Mathematicians have a special shorthand for powers called *exponential notation*. In exponential notation, 2×2 is written 2^2, $2 \times 2 \times 2$ is written 2^3, $2 \times 2 \times 2 \times 2$ is written 2^4, and so on. By convention, 2^0 represents 1, and 2^1 represents 2. The raised number, which represents the number of 2s to be multiplied together, is called the *exponent,* from which exponential notation gets its name.

Thus we can say that with one bit we can represent 2^1 alternatives, with two bits we can represent 2^2 alternatives, and so on. With n bits we can represent 2^n alternatives.

Character codes   The most common way to communicate information to a computer is to represent it using the letters, digits, and punctuation marks with which we are all familiar. An input device such as a keyboard converts these characters into binary codes that the computer can manipulate. An output device such as a video display or a printer converts the computer's binary codes into symbols meaningful to people.

For this approach to work, we need a *character code*—a standard scheme for representing characters by combinations of bits. The most widely used character code is the *American Standard Code for Information Interchange,* usually abbreviated to ASCII, which is pronounced *as' key*. The ASCII code uses seven bits to represent each character. Seven bits gives 2^7 or 128 alternatives, so ASCII can represent 128 characters. This is enough to represent the upper- and lower-case letters, the digits, the punctuation marks, and a small number of special signs.

In addition, ASCII has 32 nonprinting *control characters* that can be used to control video displays and printers and to make it easier for different pieces of equipment to exchange messages with one another. Some programs, particularly word processors, use control characters for commands. When the word processor receives printing characters (that is, noncontrol characters) from the keyboard, it assumes that the user is typing text to be processed and stores the corresponding character codes in memory. When the program receives a control character, however, it carries out the command defined for that particular control character.

Figure 4.1 illustrates the ASCII code. To find the code for any character, note the row and column containing the character in question. The three bits at the head of the column containing the character are the leftmost three bits of the code. The four bits to the left of the row containing the character are the rightmost four bits of the code. Thus, the code for A is 1000001, the code for B is 1000010, and so on.

The two- and three-letter abbreviations represent control characters. We won't go through all of them since many are used for specialized technical purposes. The following three are commonly used: CR, *carriage return,* returns the typing mechanism to the left margin; LF, *line feed,* advances the paper by one line; BEL, *bell,* causes a bell or other alarm device to sound.

Most computer keyboards have a *Ctrl* key for typing control characters. To type a control character, you hold down the Ctrl key and type the corresponding key in

Figure 4.1 The ASCII character code. The two-and three-letter abbreviations represent control characters. Examples are CR (carriage return), LF (line feed), and BEL (bell).

			Leftmost Three Bits					
		000	001	010	011	100	101	110	111
	0000	NUL	DLE	Space	0	@	P	`	p
	0001	SOH	DC1	!	1	A	Q	a	q
	0010	STX	DC2	"	2	B	R	b	r
	0011	ETX	DC3	#	3	C	S	c	s
	0100	EOT	DC4	$	4	D	T	d	t
	0101	ENQ	NAK	%	5	E	U	e	u
	0110	ACK	SYN	&	6	F	V	f	v
Rightmost	0111	BEL	ETB	'	7	G	W	g	w
Four	1000	BS	CAN	(	8	H	X	h	x
Bits	1001	HT	EM	)	9	I	Y	i	y
	1010	LF	SUB	*	:	J	Z	j	z
	1011	VT	ESC	+	;	K	[	k	{
	1100	FF	FS	,	<	L	\	l		
	1101	CR	GS	-	=	M	]	m	}
	1110	SO	RS	.	>	N	^	n	~
	1111	SI	US	/	?	O	_	o	DEL

the 100 or 101 column of Figure 4.1. Thus, you can type the control character NUL by holding down the Ctrl key and typing @; this key combination is usually written Ctrl-@. Likewise, SOH is Ctrl-A, STX is Ctrl-B, DC1 is Ctrl-Q,and so on. CR is Ctrl-M, LF is Ctrl-J, and BEL is Ctrl-G.

Binary notation   The system for representing numbers that we use in everyday life uses the ten digits 0 through 9. We call it the *base-10* or *decimal system*, and we say that a number represented in this system is in *decimal notation*.

In a computer, we have only the two symbols 0 and 1 at our disposal. The most natural way to represent numbers, then, is to take 0 and 1 as our digits and use the *base-2* or *binary number system*. Numbers represented in the binary system are said to be in *binary notation*.

The easiest way to understand the binary system is to compare it with the already familiar decimal system. Let's begin, then, by reviewing some properties of decimal notation. The number 10 enters the base-10 system in two ways:

1. Every number is represented by a combination of the ten digits 0, 1, 2, 3, 4, 5, 6, 7, 8, 9.

2. The digits of a decimal number, taken from right to left, represent units, tens, hundreds, thousands, and so on. The numbers 1, 10, 100, 1000, and so on are just the powers of 10—10^0, 10^1, 10^2, 10^3, in exponential notation—that we get by starting with 1 and multiplying repeatedly by 10.

For example, the decimal number 8,274 can be analyzed as:

Thousands	Hundreds	Tens	Units
8	2	7	4

That is, 8,274 represents eight thousands, two hundreds, seven tens, and four units. Arithmetically, we can express this as:

$$8{,}274 = 8 \times 1000 + 2 \times 100 + 7 \times 10 + 4 \times 1$$

or, using exponential notation for the powers of 10, as

$$8{,}274 = 8 \times 10^3 + 2 \times 10^2 + 7 \times 10^1 + 4 \times 10^0$$

The number two plays exactly the same role in the binary system that 10 does in the decimal system. Thus, 2 enters the binary system in the following two ways:

1. Every number is represented by a combination of the two digits 0 and 1.

2. The digits of a binary number, taken from right to left, represent units, twos, fours, eights, and so on. The numbers 1, 2, 4, 8, and so on are the powers of two—2^0, 2^1, 2^2, 2^3, in exponential notation—that we get by starting with 1 and multiplying repeatedly by 2.

For example, the binary number 1101 can be analyzed as:

Eights	Fours	Twos	Units
1	1	0	1

That is, 1101 represents one eight, one four, zero twos, and one unit. Arithmetically, we can express this as:

$$1101 = 1 \times 8 + 1 \times 4 + 0 \times 2 + 1 \times 1 = 13$$

or, using exponential notation for the powers of 2, as:

$$1101 = 1 \times 2^3 + 1 \times 2^2 + 0 \times 2^1 + 1 \times 2^0 = 13$$

These equations could be confusing since we might not realize that 1101 is in the binary system and wonder how one thousand, one hundred and one can equal 13. When the possibility of confusion exists, we can write the equations more clearly as:

$$1101_2 = 1 \times 8 + 1 \times 4 + 0 \times 2 + 1 \times 1 = 13$$

and

$$1101_2 = 1 \times 2^3 + 1 \times 2^2 + 0 \times 2^1 + 1 \times 2^0 = 13$$

The subscript 2 in 1101_2 indicates that 1101 is in the binary, or base-2, system.

We can see how to count in binary notation by imagining a counter, such as the mileage indicator on a car. Suppose, however, that each dial of the counter has only two digits, 0 and 1, instead of the usual 0 through 9. What's more, whenever a dial turns from 1 back to 0, it causes the dial to the left to advance one place, just as happens with an ordinary counter when a dial turns from 9 back to 0.

Suppose the counter has four dials. Its initial reading is 0000, and the first count causes it to advance to 0001. The next count causes the rightmost dial to turn from 1 back to 0. This, in turn, causes the next dial to the left to advance one position. So after two counts the counter reads 0010, after three counts it reads 0011, after four counts it reads 0100 (why?), after five counts it reads 0101, and so on.

4.2 Operations on binary values

The arithmetical operations   Let's start with addition. The addition table for binary numbers is as follows:

$$0 + 0 = 0$$
$$0 + 1 = 1$$
$$1 + 0 = 1$$
$$1 + 1 = 10_2 \qquad \textit{(that is, 0 with 1 to carry)}$$

Notice how simple this is compared to the addition table for the decimal system that we all had to learn as schoolchildren. The simplicity of the addition table leads to a corresponding simplicity in the electrical circuits that do the addition in a computer.

With the help of the addition table, we can easily work out a binary addition. Throughout this section, we will use four-bit binary numbers as examples. To help you follow the examples, the decimal value of each binary number will be written in parentheses beside the binary value:

$$
\begin{array}{rl}
1001 & (9) \\
+\underline{0101} & (5) \\
1110 & (14)
\end{array}
$$

Note that the addition in the rightmost column produces a carry.

As in decimal notation, the addition table also provides us with the information we need to do subtractions:

$$
\begin{array}{rl}
1001 & (9) \\
-\underline{0101} & (5) \\
0100 & (4)
\end{array}
$$

Note that the subtraction in the second column from the left requires a borrow.

The binary system uses the following multiplication table:

$$0 \times 0 = 0$$
$$0 \times 1 = 0$$
$$1 \times 0 = 0$$
$$1 \times 1 = 1$$

This is even simpler than the addition table because no carries are involved. We arrange our work for a binary multiplication much as we do in the decimal system:

```
    1010    (10)
  × 1101    (13)
    1010
    0000
    1010
    1010
  10000010  (130)
```

Of course, we usually don't bother to write out a row of zeros when doing a multiplication. The reason for writing out the row of zeros here is to make the overall pattern of the multiplication as clear as possible.

Like multiplication, division is done much as in the decimal system, but using the binary addition and multiplication tables:

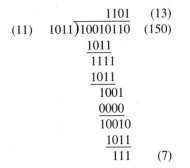

The logical and shift operations The arithmetical operations all assume that the binary values being operated on represent numbers. Sometimes, however, we need to engage in what programmers call "bit twiddling"—manipulating the individual bits of binary codes. The logical and shift operations provide us with the means for doing this.

The logical operator OR gives a result of 1 if either or both of the operands are 1. We can define the OR operator by means of a table similar to the ones used for addition and multiplication:

```
0 OR 0 = 0
0 OR 1 = 1
1 OR 0 = 1
1 OR 1 = 1
```

One application of OR is to set any particular bits of a binary value to 1. For instance, by ORing a four-bit binary value with 0010, we can set the second bit from the right to 1 while leaving the remaining three bits unchanged:

```
     1001           0111
OR   0010      OR   0010
     1011           0111
```

In each case, the second bit from the right is set to 1, regardless of whether it was 0 or 1 initially.

The *exclusive or* operation, XOR, is similar to OR except that it gives 0 when both its operands are 1:

0 XOR 0 = 0
0 XOR 1 = 1
1 XOR 0 = 1
1 XOR 1 = 0

We can use the XOR operation to flip particular bits from 0 to 1 or from 1 to 0. For example, XORing a binary value with 0010 will change the second bit from the right to 1 if it was originally 0 and to 0 if it was originally 1. The other three bits remain unchanged:

```
        1001              0111
XOR 0010          XOR 0010
        1011              0101
```

If we XOR a four-bit value with 1111, we flip all four bits:

```
        1010
XOR 1111
        0101
```

This bit-flipping operation is so important that we define a separate operator, NOT, for it:

NOT 0 = 1
NOT 1 = 0

We can then use NOT to change 1010 to 0101:

```
NOT 1010
        0101
```

The operator AND yields 1 only if both its operands are 1:

0 AND 0 = 0
0 AND 1 = 0
1 AND 0 = 0
1 AND 1 = 1

We can use AND to set any particular bits to 0. For instance, ANDing a four-bit value with 1001 sets the two middle bits to zero and leaves the two outer bits unchanged:

```
        1101              0111
AND 1001          AND 1001
        1001              0001
```

The logical operations allow us to change particular bits, but they don't provide any means for changing the positions of the bits. The shift operations remedy this by allowing us to shift all of the bits to the left or right. For example, the *shift left* operation, SHL, shifts each bit one place to the left. A 0 is shifted into the rightmost position:

SHL <u>1101</u>
1010

The *shift right* operation, SHR, shifts each bit one place to the right. A 0 is shifted into the leftmost position:

SHR <u>1011</u>
0101

Here is a typical application of shifting. Suppose we have 2 four-bit values, 1011 and 0110. We want to isolate the rightmost two bits of each and combine them into a single four-bit value, 1110.

We begin by getting the rightmost two bits of 1011 into the leftmost two bit positions—the positions those two bits will occupy in the final value. We shift 1011 left:

SHL <u>1011</u>
0110

and then shift left once again:

SHL <u>0110</u>
1100

Next we take the second value, 0110, and set its two leftmost bits to 00 to make room for the two bits to be inserted from the first value:

0110
AND <u>0011</u>
0010

Finally, we use the OR operation to combine our two intermediate results, 1100 and 0010, to get the final desired result, 1110:

1100
OR <u>0010</u>
1110

The logical operations allow us to change the values of bits without changing their positions; the shift operations allow us to change the positions of bits without changing their values. We can always find some combination of logical and shift operations to carry out any bit manipulations that we wish.

4.3 Octal and hexadecimal notation

As suitable as binary numbers are for us inside a computer, they give people trouble. For example, consider the following 24-bit binary number:

110000100011101001001011

Can you copy this number without making a mistake? Can you look at it and then copy it from memory? Can you call it out for someone else to write? Try comparing it with:

110000100011101001011011

Are the two numbers the same? If not, where do they differ?

Chances are that you found these tasks difficult or impossible to carry out. Human beings find long strings of 0s and 1s tedious or impossible to work with.

To avoid the problem of working with binary numbers, programmers usually use one of two alternative notations, *octal* and *hexadecimal*. Each is so closely related to binary notation that we can convert between octal and binary or between hexadecimal and binary at a glance. Yet each is enormously easier than binary notation for people to work with.

Octal notation   One way to make long binary numbers easier to deal with is to mark off the digits in groups of three, the way we do with decimal numbers. Let's try this with the first 24-bit binary number that we looked at earlier:

110,000,100,011,101,001,001,011

This helps some, but we can go even further. Let's replace each group of three bits by the single digit that has the same numerical value. Thus, we replace 000 by 0, 001 by 1, 010 by 2, and so on. The digits that replace the three-bit groups are called *octal digits*. Figure 4.2 shows the correspondence betwen octal digits and three-bit groups.

Replacing each three-bit group in the example by the corresponding octal digit, we get:

60435113

This is certainly easier to deal with than the original binary number. You should have no trouble copying it either while looking at it or from memory, or in calling it

Figure 4.2   The correspondence between three-bit groups and octal digits.

Three-Bit Group	Octal Digit
0 0 0	0
0 0 1	1
0 1 0	2
0 1 1	3
1 0 0	4
1 0 1	5
1 1 0	6
1 1 1	7

out to someone else. You were asked to compare the first binary number with a second one; if we transcribe the second binary number into octal, we get:

60435133

Now you should have no difficulty in seeing not only that the two numbers are different but exactly where the difference lies.

We can work the process just described in reverse, of course. That is, given an octal number, we can convert it to binary by substituting the proper three-bit group for each octal digit. For example, to convert the octal number 5743 to binary, we substitute 101 for 5, 111 for 7, and so on. This gives us:

101,111,100,011

or, after removing the commas,

101111100011

The octal number system represents numbers using the eight digits 0, 1, 2, 3, 4, 5, 6, and 7. Octal notation is a *base-8* number system for the same reasons that binary notation is a base-2 number system and decimal notation is a base-10 system. Where confusion might result, we can use the subscript 8 to indicate that a number is in octal notation:

$$5743_8 = 101111100011_2$$

Hexadecimal notation   Instead of marking off binary digits in groups of three, we can mark them off in groups of four instead. Let's try this with the first of the 24-bit binary numbers we have been using as examples:

1100,0010,0011,1010,0100,1011

Following the same path as we did for octal notation, we would like to replace each four-bit group by a single digit.

This idea runs into trouble at once. There are 16 possible four-bit binary numbers. But we have only the ten digits 0 through 9 at our disposal. To put our plan into effect, we have to come up with six more digits from somewhere. The solution is to use the digits 0 through 9 for the four-bit groups 0000 through 1001 and the letters A through F for the remaining four-bit groups 1010 through 1111.

Figure 4.3 shows the correspondence between the four-bit groups and the hexadecimal digits 0 through 9 and A through F. For each of the digits A through F, we have to bear in mind two things—the bit pattern it represents and the corresponding numerical value. Thus we should think of A as representing 1010 and ten, of B as representing 1011 and eleven, and so on. The need to learn both the bit patterns and the numerical values of A through F makes hexadecimal notation slightly more difficult than octal for beginners.

Replacing the four-bit groups in our example by hexadecimal digits, we get:

C23A4B

As in the case of octal notation, you should have no trouble copying or remembering this number. If we write our second 24-bit binary number in hexadecimal, we get:

Figure 4.3   The correspondence between four-bit groups and
hexadecimal digits.

Four-Bit Group	Hexadecimal Digit
0 0 0 0	0
0 0 0 1	1
0 0 1 0	2
0 0 1 1	3
0 1 0 0	4
0 1 0 1	5
0 1 1 0	6
0 1 1 1	7
1 0 0 0	8
1 0 0 1	9
1 0 1 0	A
1 0 1 1	B
1 1 0 0	C
1 1 0 1	D
1 1 1 0	E
1 1 1 1	F

C23A5B

Again, you should have no trouble seeing that the two numbers differ and exactly where they differ.

By using Figure 4.3 in reverse, we can easily convert from hexadecimal to binary. To convert AC9F to binary, for example, we first replace each hexadecimal digit by the corresponding four-bit group:

1010,1100,1001,1111

Omitting the commas gives the corresponding binary value:

1010110010011111

The hexadecimal system represents numbers using the 16 digits 0 through 9 and A through F. Thus, hexadecimal is a base-16 number system. To avoid confusion, we can use a subscript of 16 to indicate that a number is written in hexadecimal notation:

$$AC9F_{16} = 1010110010011111_2$$

4.4
Signed numbers

So far we have only seen how to represent unsigned numbers in binary notation—numbers that do not have an algebraic sign. Signed numbers are often required in computing, so we must see how to represent both positive and negative numbers as binary codes. There are several schemes for doing this, the most popular of which are the *sign-magnitude representation* and the *twos-complement representation*.

The sign-magnitude representation   In the sign-magnitude representation, the leftmost bit of a binary code represents the sign of the value (0 for positive, 1 for negative); the remaining bits represent the magnitude (the value with the sign ignored) in ordinary binary notation. Let's use four-bit binary codes as examples. In 0011, the leftmost 0 is the *sign bit* and tells us that the number is positive. The remaining three bits, 011, represent the magnitude of the number in ordinary binary notation. Since 011 represents 3, 0011 represents $+3$ in the sign-magnitude representation. Likewise, 1011 represents -3; the magnitude is the same, but the sign bit is 1, telling us that a negative number is represented. Here are all the numbers that can be represented with four bits using the sign-magnitude representation:

Sign-Magnitude Representation

Value	Representation	Value	Representation
$+0$	0000	-0	1000
$+1$	0001	-1	1001
$+2$	0010	-2	1010
$+3$	0011	-3	1011
$+4$	0100	-4	1100
$+5$	0101	-5	1101
$+6$	0110	-6	1110
$+7$	0111	-7	1111

The sign-magnitude representation is easy for people to understand and work with. Unfortunately, it has some drawbacks for computers. Before adding two sign-magnitude numbers, the computer must examine their signs. If the two have the same sign, their magnitudes are to be added; if they have opposite signs, however, the smaller magnitude is to be subtracted from the larger. If the two numbers have the same sign, that sign will also be the sign of the result. If the two have opposite signs, the sign of the result will be the sign of the larger number. All this comparing of signs, deciding what operation to perform, and determining the sign of the result slows the computer down. We would prefer a method whereby the computer could do a simple binary addition without having to take into account the signs of the numbers being added.

Another drawback to the sign-magnitude representation is that $+0$ and -0 are represented by different codes. In arithmetic, $+0$ and -0 are equal, so the computer must not make any distinction between $+0$ and -0. One way to accomplish this is to change -0 to $+0$ whenever the former occurs as the result of an arithmetical operation, which gives the computer one more thing to check on each operation.

Because of these drawbacks, the sign-magnitude representation is rarely used for binary integers although, as described in Section 4.5, it is often used for floating point numbers—numbers written in scientific notation. For binary integers, most computers use the *twos-complement* system, which avoids the problems of the sign-magnitude representation.

The twos-complement representation The following table shows the values that can be represented by four-bit binary codes using the twos-complement representation:

Twos-Complement Representation

Value	Representation	Value	Representation
$+0$	0000	-1	1111
$+1$	0001	-2	1110
$+2$	0010	-3	1101
$+3$	0011	-4	1100
$+4$	0100	-5	1011
$+5$	0101	-6	1010
$+6$	0110	-7	1001
$+7$	0111	-8	1000

As in the sign-magnitude representation, the leftmost bit serves as a sign bit: codes with the leftmost bit equal to 0 represent positive numbers; those with the leftmost bit equal to 1 represent negative numbers. The two columns on the left, which give the representations for positive numbers, are the same for the twos-complement and the sign-magnitude representation; positive numbers are represented the same way in each representation. The two columns on the right, which give the representations for negative numbers, are not the same however. The -0 is missing (good riddance!) and an additional negative number, -8, is present. The representation column has simply been turned upside down, so that now 1000 is at the bottom (representing -8 instead of -0) and 1111 is at the top (representing -1 instead of -7).

To change the sign of a number, we subtract its twos-complement representation from 2^n, where n is the number of bits in the binary codes. For four-bit codes, we change the sign of a number by subtracting it from 2^4, which equals 16 or 10000_2. For example, to change $+5$ to -5, we subtract the code for $+5$, 0101, from 10000:

$$
\begin{array}{rl}
10000 & (16) \\
-\ 0101 & (+5) \\
\hline
1011 & (-5)
\end{array}
$$

The result, 1011, is the code for -5, as we confirm from our table. Likewise, to change -2 to $+2$, we subtract the code for -2, 1110, from 10000:

$$
\begin{array}{rl}
10000 & (16) \\
-\ 1110 & (-2) \\
\hline
0010 & (+2)
\end{array}
$$

The result, 0010, is the code for $+2$. The operation of subtracting from 2^n is referred to as taking the *twos complement* of a number. The twos-complement system is so named because each negative number is represented by the twos complement of the code for the corresponding positive number.

The most important characteristic of the twos-complement system is that the binary codes can be added and subtracted as if they were unsigned binary numbers, without regard to the signs of the numbers they actually represent. Any carry from or borrow by the leftmost column is ignored. For example, to add $+4$ and -3, we simply add the corresponding binary codes, 0100 and 1101:

$$
\begin{array}{rl}
0100 & (+4) \\
+1101 & (-3) \\
\hline
0001 & (+1)
\end{array}
$$

A carry from the leftmost column has been ignored. The result, 0001, is the code for $+1$, the sum of $+4$ and -3. Likewise, to subtract $+7$ from $+3$, we subtract the code for $+7$, 0111, from that for $+3$, 0011:

$$
\begin{array}{rl}
0011 & (+3) \\
-0111 & (+7) \\
\hline
1100 & (-4)
\end{array}
$$

A borrow by the leftmost column has been ignored. The result, 1100, is the code for -4, the result of subtracting $+7$ from $+3$.

Not only is addition and subtraction simplified in the twos-complement system, the bothersome -0 is eliminated. In its place we get -8, a negative number for which there is no corresponding positive number. (In general, with n bits the twos-complement system represents values ranging from -2^{n-1} through $2^{n-1}-1$; -2^{n-1} is the negative number having no positive counterpart.) Although this extra negative number can occasionally prove troublesome, it is not nearly so troublesome as -0 in the sign-magnitude representation.

The twos-complement system offers no particular advantages for multiplication and division; in fact, many computers convert twos-complement numbers to the sign-magnitude representation before multiplying or dividing them, then convert the results back to the twos-complement representation. Addition and subtraction, however, are by far the most frequent operations performed on binary integers, so any system that speeds up addition and subtraction is well worthwhile even if it makes multiplication and division slightly more complicated.

4.5

Floating-point numbers

So far, we have seen how to represent only integers in binary notation. To represent numbers with fractional parts, we can follow the method familiar to us from the decimal system. The integer and fractional parts of a number are separated by a "decimal point," hereafter called a *radix point* since its use is not limited to the decimal number system.

In the decimal system, the digits to the right of the radix point, read from left to right, represent tenths, hundredths, thousandths, and so on. For example, we can analyze 27.45 as:

Tens	Units	Tenths	Hundredths
2	7	4	5

Thus, 27.45 represents two tens, seven units, four tenths, and five hundredths. Arithmetically, we can express this as:

$$27.45 = 2 \times 10 + 7 \times 1 + 4 \times 1/10 + 5 \times 1/100$$

We can represent the powers of ten in exponential notation by using the convention that a number with a negative exponent is one over the number with the corresponding positive exponent—in symbols, $a^{-n} = 1/a^n$. Thus we can write 1/10 as 10^{-1} and 1/100 as 10^{-2}:

$$27.45 = 2 \times 10^1 + 7 \times 10^0 + 4 \times 10^{-1} + 5 \times 10^{-2}$$

In binary notation, the digits to the right of the radix point, taken from left to right, represent halves, quarters, eighths, and so on. For example, we can analyze 10.11_2 as:

Twos	Units	Halves	Quarters
1	0	1	1

Thus, 10.11_2 represents one two, zero units, one half, and one quarter. Arithmetically, we can express this as:

$$10.11_2 = 1 \times 2 + 0 \times 1 + 1 \times 1/2 + 1 \times 1/4$$
$$= 2 + 0 + .5 + .25$$
$$= 2.75$$

Using exponential notation for the powers of two gives:

$$10.11_2 = 1 \times 2^1 + 0 \times 2^0 + 1 \times 2^{-1} + 1 \times 2^{-2}$$

In the decimal system, we often write numbers in *scientific* or *floating-point notation*. The significant digits of a number are always written with the radix point between the first and second digits; this part of the number is called the *significand*. The significand is multiplied by a power of 10 to move the radix point to the desired position. For example, 1,250,000 is written:

$$1.25 \times 10^6$$

The significand is 1.25. Since multiplying a number by 10 moves the radix point one place to the right, multiplying by 10^6—multiplying by 10 six times—moves the radix point six places to the right, giving 1,250,000.

In the same way, 0.0000352 can be written in floating-point notation as:

$$3.52 \times 10^{-5}$$

The significand is 3.52. Since multiplying a number by 1/10 moves the radix point one place to the left, multiplying by 10^{-5}—multiplying by 1/10 five times—moves the radix point five places to the left, giving 0.0000352.

The advantage of floating-point notation is that nonsignificant zeros—zeros that serve only to show the position of the radix point—do not have to be written. This is particularly important in computing, for we usually have only a fixed number of digits with which to represent a number inside a computer. If some of those digits are wasted on nonsignificant zeros, fewer digits are available to represent the significant part of the number, and the accuracy with which the number can be represented is reduced.

Binary numbers can also be written in floating-point notation in much the same way as decimal numbers, except that powers of two rather than powers of ten are used to shift the radix point. For example, 11010000 can be written as:

$$1.101_2 \times 2^7$$

and 0.0000111 can be written as:

$$1.11_2 \times 2^{-5}$$

For ease of reading, the exponents (7 and -5) are written in decimal notation, although they must, of course, be coded in binary notation before being stored in the computer.

Let's look at one way of representing floating-point numbers by binary codes. A floating-point number has three parts, or *fields*, that must be coded and stored: the *sign*, the *exponent*, and the *significand*. The sign-magnitude representation is often used for floating-point numbers; floating-point arithmetic involves so much processing that any additional work occasioned by the sign-magnitude representation is negligible. Also, some frequently performed manipulations, such as rounding off to a given number of digits, are easier to perform in the sign-magnitude representation. Thus, the first field of our floating-point representation will be the sign bit, which will be 0 for a positive number and 1 for a negative number.

The second field of a floating-point number is its exponent. We must be able to represent both positive and negative exponents. Rather than using the sign-magnitude or the twos-complement representation for the exponent, it turns out to be the most convenient to add a constant value, or *bias*, to the exponent, so that negative numbers are converted into positive ones. For example, suppose we choose a bias of 127; we add 127 to the value of each exponent before storing it. Thus an exponent of 5 is stored as $127 + 5$ or 132, and an exponent of -5 is stored as $127 + (-5)$ or 122. If the actual exponent ranges from -127 through 128, the *biased exponent*—

the value actually stored—will range from 0 through 255. This is the range of values that can be represented by 8-bit, unsigned binary numbers. Thus we will store biased exponents as unsigned binary numbers in an 8-bit field.

The significand is said to be *normalized* when the digit to the left of the radix point is 1. Every significand, *except the one corresponding to the number zero*, can be normalized by choosing the exponent so that the radix point falls to the right of the leftmost 1 bit. Ignoring zero for the moment, we will assume that every significand is normalized. Since the digit to the left of the radix point is 1, we don't actually have to store it; only the bits to the right of the radix point need be stored. The significand is often stored in 23-bit field, and we will use this size field for our representation. Thus the significand field will consist of the 23 bits to the right of the radix point in the significand.

Now let's see how

$$1.101_2 \times 2^7$$

would be stored. The sign bit is 0, and the biased exponent is $7 + 127 = 134 = 10000110_2$. The bits to the right of the radix point in the significand are 101 followed by enough 0s to fill out the 23-bit signigicand field:

Sign	Biased Exponent	Significand
0	10000110	10100000000000000000000

Likewise,

$$-1.11_2 \times 2^{-5}$$

is represented as:

Sign	Biased Exponent	Significand
1	01111010	11000000000000000000000

The biased exponent is $-5 + 127 = 122 = 1111010_2$. The entire floating-point number takes up 32 bits. Many computers store 8, 16, or 32 bits in a memory location; on these machines, one floating-point number would take up, respectively, 4, 2, or 1 memory locations.

We still have to find a way to represent zero, which cannot be normalized and so does not fit into the representation just given. The simplest method is to specify that, as a special case, a floating-point number consisting of all 0s represents zero. Thus,

Sign	Biased Exponent	Significand
0	00000000	00000000000000000000000

represents 0 instead of 2^{-127}, which it would represent if we had not made it a special case.

A slightly more general approach is to treat a biased exponent of zero as a special case. When the biased exponent is zero, then: (1) the bit to the left of the radix point is assumed to be 0, and (2) the exponent is assumed to be -126. Put another way, when the biased exponent is zero, the significand is assumed to be an *unnormalized* binary fraction, which is to be multiplied by 2^{-126}. For example,

Sign	Biased Exponent	Significand
0	00000000	00000110000000000000000

represents

$$0.0000011_2 \times 2^{-126}$$

which equals

$$1.1_2 \times 2^{-132}$$

This value could not be represented in our system without the provision for unnormalized significands.

Again, zero is represented by

Sign	Biased Exponent	Significand
0	00000000	00000000000000000000000

since

$$0.0 \times 2^{-126} = 0$$

4.6
A simple computer

In this section we will look at a very simple computer. The computer will be a hypothetical one since we can make a hypothetical computer much simpler and easier to understand than a real one. In spite of this computer's simplicity, however, its overall structure will be similar to that of real computers, and it will serve as a good introduction to real machines.

Words   A computer normally works not with individual bits but with groups of bits called *words*. The number of bits in a word varies from one computer to another; typical word sizes are 8, 12, 16, 32, 36, and 60 bits. Some computers allow words of several different sizes; others have only one word size.

Our computer will use only one word size, 16 bits. All the data and instructions that the computer works with must fit into 16-bit words. Figure 4.4 illustrates the 16-bit word of our computer.

We can represent a 16-bit word conveniently by means of four hexadecimal digits. Figure 4.5 shows several words of data with their hexadecimal representations. Note that, if the number of bits in a word had been a multiple of three instead of four, we would probably have used octal notation instead of hexadecimal notation. Why?

Figure 4.4   A 16-bit word.

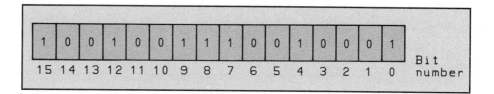

Figure 4.5   Three examples of how we can represent the contents of a 16-bit word by four hexadecimal digits.

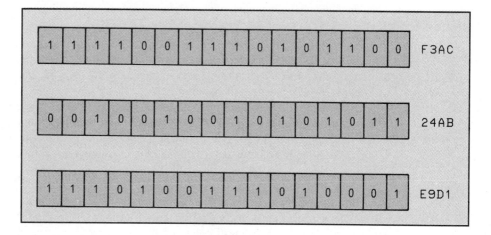

Data and instruction formats   To keep our computer simple, we will allow it to manipulate only one kind of data—signed integers. We can use either the sign-magnitude or the twos-complement representation. The sign-magnitude representation is easiest for people to work with; on the other hand, the twos-complement representation is more typical of real computers. For the sign-magnitude representation, each word can hold an integer in the range -32767 through 32767 ($-(2^{15}-1)$ through $2^{15}-1$). For the twos-complement representation, the range is -32768 through 32767 (-2^{15} through $2^{15}-1$). Regardless of which representation is used, the leftmost bit (bit 15) serves as a sign bit, as illustrated in Figure 4.6. Bit 15 is 0 for a positive number and 1 for a negative number.

Not only do we have to represent the data the computer is going to manipulate, we have to represent the computer's instructions as well. Each instruction consists of an *operation code* and an *address*. The operation code specifies the operation the computer will carry out. The address part allows the instruction to refer to a location in main memory. If a particular instruction doesn't need to refer to any main-memory location, its address part isn't used.

Figure 4.6 We can use either the sign-magnitude or the twos-complement representation for signed numbers. In either case, bit 15, the leftmost bit of the word, serves as a sign bit, which is 0 for positive numbers and 1 for negative numbers.

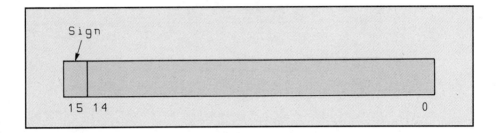

Figure 4.7 shows the format for instructions. As with data items, each instruction fits into one word. The leftmost four bits of a word give the operation code; the rightmost twelve bits give the address.

This subdivision works nicely with hexadecimal notation. When an instruction is written in hexadecimal, the leftmost hexadecimal digit gives the operation code. The remaining three digits give the main-memory address. For example, the operation code of the instruction 2C0E is 2, and the instruction refers to the main-memory address C0E.

Main-memory organization As Figure 4.8 shows, the main memory of our computer is made up of individual memory locations, each of which holds one 16-bit word. Each memory location has an address, which consists of 12 bits or three

Figure 4.7 The instruction format. The leftmost four bits of a word hold the operation code, which tells the computer what operation to carry out. The rightmost 12 bits usually hold the address of a memory location that the computer will have to refer to in order to carry out the requested operation.

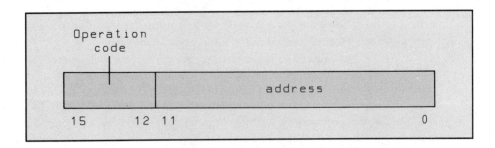

Figure 4.8   Main memory. Each memory location holds one word. The
address of each location is represented by 12 bits or three
hexadecimal digits. The addresses, expressed in
hexadecimal, range from 000 through FFF.

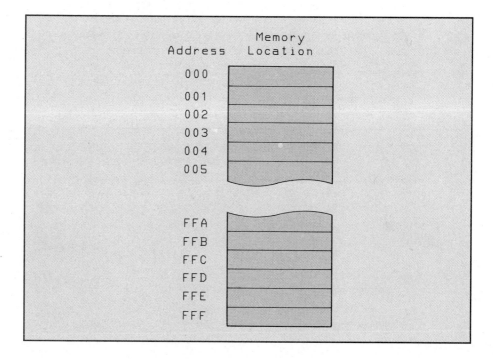

hexadecimal digits. (Remember that the address part of an instruction occupies 12
bits or three hexadecimal digits.) With 12 bits we can represent 2^{12} or 4096 alternatives. Thus our computer's memory can consist of, at most, 4,096 words. In hexadecimal notation the address of the first word is 000, and the address of the last word
is FFF.

   The central processing unit   The central processor of a computer contains a
small number of memory locations called *registers*. Some of these hold the data that
the central processor is currently manipulating. Others help the central processor keep
track of such crucial information as its place in the program and the results of the
tests it has carried out.

   Figure 4.9 shows the registers of our hypothetical computer that the programmer
can manipulate directly. A description of these registers and their uses is sometimes
called a *programming model*, since it represents what one must know about the structure of the central processor to program the computer. The central processor has other
registers for its own internal use, but since these are not accessible to the programmer, they are not part of the programming model.

Figure 4.9   The central processing unit consists of three registers that the programmer can manipulate directly. The *accumulator*, which serves somewhat the same purpose as the display register on a calculator, holds the data currently being manipulated. The *condition code register* records the result of comparing the contents of the accumulator with the contents of a main memory location. The table at the bottom of the figure shows how the contents of the condition code register depend on the outcome of the comparison. The *instruction address register* contains the address of the next instruction to be executed.

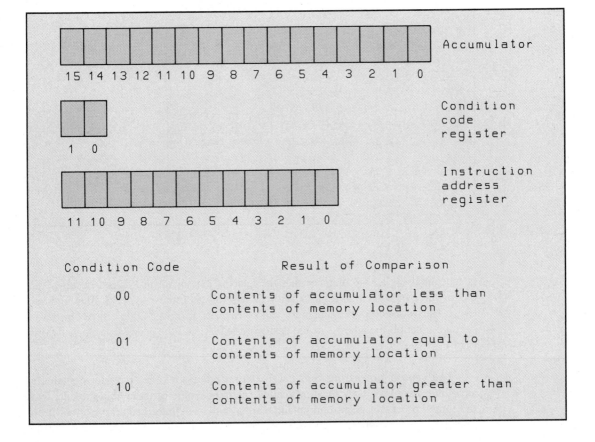

As we see from Figure 4.9, the central processor of our computer contains exactly three registers accessible to the programmer: the *accumulator*, the *condition code register*, and the *instruction address register*.

The *accumulator* is analogous to the display register of a calculator. It holds one of the operands for each arithmetic operation, one of the values on which the operation will be performed. The other operand is in main memory at the address given in the instruction for the arithmetic operation. After the operation has been carried out, the result is stored in the accumulator. Since the accumulator must be able to hold any data item the computer can manipulate, it holds one word or 16 bits. We say that it is "16 bits wide."

The computer has a *compare* instruction that compares the contents of the accumulator with those of a designated main-memory location. The comparison can have three possible outcomes: (1) the contents of the accumulator are less than those of the main-memory location: (2) the contents of the two locations are equal; and (3) the contents of the accumulator are greater than those of the main-memory location.

The *condition code register* is a two-bit register that stores the outcome of a comparison. The outcomes are coded as follows: 00 if the contents of the accumulator are less than those of the main memory location; 01 if the contents of the two are the same; and 10 if the contents of the accumulator are greater. The code 11 isn't used. The condition codes are summarized in Figure 4.9.

The *instruction address register* contains the address of the next instruction the computer is to execute. During the fetch part of the fetch-execute cycle, the central processor fetches the next instruction from the address contained in the instruction address register.

As soon as an instruction is fetched, the central processor adds 1 to the contents of the instruction address register. Therefore, successive instructions will normally come from successive memory locations. However, certain instructions called *jump* instructions change the contents of the instruction address register to a value specified in the instruction, thus causing the computer to jump to some other part of the program and continue execution from there.

Since the instruction address register holds an address, and an address occupies 12 bits, the instruction address register is 12 bits wide.

The instructions   The most imporant part of the description of any computer is the description of its *instruction set*. Figure 4.10 shows the instruction set for our hypothetical computer. For each instruction, the figure gives the operation code, which is a single hexadecimal digit, and an abbreviation call a *mnemonic*, which is easier to remember than the operation code. (In general, a mnemonic is anything that serves as a memory aid.)

The load and store instructions   These are the instructions that load values from main memory into the accumulator and store values from the accumulator into main memory.

In our examples, we will write each instruction in two ways: once as it is actually stored in the computer, and once in an easier-to-read form with the mnemonic in place of the hexadecimal operation code.

The *load accumulator* instruction, LDA, copies the contents of the addressed location into the accumulator. The contents of the addressed location does not change. Thus,

     1074   LDA 074

Figure 4.10 The instruction set. We will usually refer to instructions by their mnemonics, which are easier to remember than the operation codes.

Operation Code	Mnemonic	Instruction
1	LDA	load accumulator
2	STA	store accumulator
3	ADD	add
4	SUB	subtract
5	MUL	multiply
6	DIV	divide yielding integer quotient
7	MOD	divide yielding remainder
8	CMP	compare
9	JMP	unconditional jump
A	JLT	jump if less than
B	JEQ	jump if equal to
C	JGT	jump if greater than
D	IN	input
E	OUT	output
F	HALT	halt

loads the contents of main-memory location 074 into the accumulator. The contents of location 074 remain unchanged.

The *store accumulator* instruction, STA, copies the contents of the accumulator into the addressed location. The contents of the accumulator remain unchanged. Thus,

        213F   STA 13F

stores the contents of the accumlator into location 13F.

The arithmetic instructions The arithmetic instructions are ADD, SUB, MUL, DIV, and MOD. There are two division instructions, DIV and MOD. DIV yields the integer quotient of a division, and MOD yields the remainder.

For each instruction, one of the numbers on which the operation is to be carried out is in the accumulator; the other is in the memory location specified in the instruction. The result of the operation is always stored in the accumulator; the contents of the memory location always remain unchanged.

For subtraction, the contents of the memory location are subtracted from the contents of the accumulator. For division, the contents of the memory location are divided into the contents of the accumulator.

For example, the instruction

```
3402     ADD 402
```

adds the contents of location 402 to the contents of the accumulator. The sum is stored in the accumulator; the contents of location 402 remain unchanged.

The instruction

```
43CD     SUB 3CD
```

subtracts the contents of location 3CD from the contents of the accumulator. The result goes into the accumulator; the contents of location 3CD remain unchanged.

The instruction

```
613F     DIV 13F
```

divides the contents of location 13F into the contents of the accumulator. The quotient goes into the accumulator; the contents of location 13F remain unchanged.

Finally, the instruction

```
713F     MOD 13F
```

also divides the contents of location 13F into the contents of the accumulator. For MOD, however, it is the remainder of the division that is stored in the accumulator, rather than the quotient as was the case for DIV. As with DIV, the contents of location 13F remain unchanged.

Real computers can carry out many data-manipulating operations besides arithmetic. At a minimum, they can do the logical and shift operations described earlier. For simplicity, however, the data manipulations that our hypothetical computer can carry out were restricted to the arithmetical operations.

The compare instruction   The compare instruction and the jump instructions are crucial for implementing selection and repetition. The compare instruction, CMP compares the contents of the accumulator with that of the designated memory location; it records in the condition code register whether the contents of the accumulator were less than, equal to, or greater than the contents of the main-memory location.

Thus, the instruction

```
8314     CMP 134
```

compares the contents of the accumulator with the contents of location 134; it records in the condition code register whether the contents of the accumulator are less than, equal to, or greater than the contents of location 134.

The jump instructions   The unconditonal jump instruction, JMP, loads its address part into the instruction address register. This causes the computer to take its next instruction from the specified address. The computer jumps to the point in the program specified in the jump instruction and continues execution from that point. Thus,

```
9431     JMP 431
```

causes the computer to jump to location 431 and continue execution from there. In the absence of further jump instructions, the computer will execute the instructions in locations 431, 432, 433, and so on.

JLT, JEG, and JGT are the *conditional jump* instructions. For each one, the jump takes place only if the contents of the condition code register have a particular value. If the contents of the condition code register do not have the required value, the jump does not take place and the computer continues execution with the instruction in the memory location following the one containing the jump instruction.

JLT jumps only if the contents of the condition code register are 00 (less than); JEQ jumps only if the contents are 01 (equal to); and JGT jumps only if the contents are 10 (greater than). Thus,

```
A305      JLT 305
```

causes the computer to jump to location 305 in the program only if the contents of the condition code register are 00 (less than). If the condition code is 01 or 10, the computer continues with the instruction in the memory location following the one containing the jump instruction.

The input and output instructions   The input instruction, IN, transfers data from the computer's single input device to main memory; the output instruction, OUT, transfers data from main memory to the computer's single output device. Thus,

```
D205      IN 205
```

reads one number from the input device and stored it in location 205. The instruction

```
E157      OUT 157
```

sends the number in location 157 to the computer's output device. The contents of location 157 remain unchanged.

The halt instruction   The halt instruction, HALT, causes the CPU to stop fetching and executing instructions and go into a standby mode. The address part of the instruction is ignored. Thus,

```
F000      HALT
```

brings instruction execution to a stop.

A sample program   The instruction codes we have been discussing are known as *machine language*, and a program expressed in terms of such codes is called a *machine-language* program. Let's look at a machine-language program for our hypothetical computer that will cause it to input and add a series of numbers. Simple as this task is, it is typical of the kinds of processing that computers are often called upon to perform.

Specifically, we will enter a series of numbers to be added, say by typing them on a keyboard. All the numbers to be added will be positive—greater than or equal to zero. To let the computer know when we have finished entering numbers to be added, we will enter a negative number, which will serve only to mark the end of the data. (A value that serves to mark the end of a series of data items is called a *sentinel*.) When we enter the sentinel value, the computer will display the sum of all the values that preceded the sentinel. For example, suppose we enter

        1 0 0   2 5 0   3 0 0   2 5   − 1

The sentinel is − 1. When the sentinel value is entered, the computer should display 675, the sum of all the numbers preceding the sentinel.

Our program will need to use three memory locations for data storage. Just as we found it convenient to use mnemonics such as LDA instead of operation codes for instructions, we also find it helpful to assign names to memory locations instead of just referring to them by their addresses. We name the three locations our program will use as follows:

Name	Address
VALUE	000C
TOTAL	000D
ZERO	000E

VALUE serves as temporary storage for each value entered by the user. TOTAL is used to store the running total of all the values that have been entered so far; TOTAL plays a role analogous to that of the display register of a calculator. ZERO contains the constant 0, which is used in comparisons and for clearing the contents of TOTAL to zero before any numbers are added.

Let's write an algorithm to add a series of numbers terminated by a negative sentinel. The idea of the algorithm is to clear the contents of TOTAL to zero, then add each value (other than the sentinel) to the contents of TOTAL. At any time, then, TOTAL contains the sum of all the numbers added so far. When the sentinel is encountered, the program displays the contents of TOTAL, which is the sum of all the numbers that preceded the sentinel. Figure 4.11 shows the complete algorithm.

Step 1 clears the contents of TOTAL to zero, just as we clear the display of a calculator before we begin entering numbers to be added. Step 2 gets the first value to be processed and stores it in VALUE. Steps 3.1 and 3.2 are repeated as long as the contents of VALUE are greater than or equal to zero—as long as VALUE does not contain the sentinel value. Step 3.1 adds the contents of VALUE to the running total being maintained in TOTAL, and step 3.2 inputs the next value to be processed. Note the invariant assertion, whose truth is established by steps 1 and 2 and is maintained by steps 3.1 and 3.2

Figure 4.12 shows the machine-language program corresponding to this algorithm. The contents of ZERO are shown as 0000, indicating that this value will be stored in ZERO when the program is loaded into the computer's memory, so ZERO will contain the value zero when the program begins execution. The contents of VALUE and TOTAL are represented by question marks, indicating that no particular values are placed in these locations when the program is loaded and their contents are unknown when execution of the program begins.

Figure 4.11   An algorithm for adding a series of nonnegative numbers
terminated by a negative sentinel value. Note that the truth
of the invariant assertion is established by steps 1 and 2 and
is preserved by steps 3.1 and 3.2.

Algorithm Sum

{ The data to be processed consists of a series of integers terminated by a
negative sentinel. The contents of ZERO is the constant 0 }

1. Copy the contents of ZERO into TOTAL.

{ TOTAL contains 0, the sum of all the numbers (none) which have been
added so far }

2. Input a value and store it in VALUE.

{ VALUE contains the first value to be processed—either the sentinel value
or the first value to be added }

3. While the contents of VALUE are greater than or equal to zero, execute
the following:

   { Invariant assertion: TOTAL contains all values previously added and
      VALUE contains the next input value to be processed }

   3.1 Add the contents of VALUE to the contents of TOTAL and store
       the sum back into TOTAL.
   3.2 Input another value and store it in VALUE.

{ TOTAL contains the sum of all the numbers preceding the sentinel value }

4. Output the contents of TOTAL.

Step 1 of the algorithm clears TOTAL by copying the contents of ZERO into
TOTAL. We do this by *loading* the contents of ZERO into the accumulator and
storing them in TOTAL:

```
100E      LDA ZERO
200D      STA TOTAL
```

Step 2 inputs the first value to be processed and stores it in location VALUE. In
machine language, this job is done with single IN instruction:

```
D00C      IN VALUE
```

Figure 4.12   A machine-language program using the algorithm of Figure 4.11 to compute the sum of a series of nonnegative numbers terminated by a negative sentinel value. The *Address* column gives the addresses of the memory locations holding the program and data, and the *Contents* column gives the contents of the locations. Locations with addresses 000 through 00B hold instructions; locations with addresses 00C through 00E hold data. The *Mnemonic* and *Explanation* columns are not part of the machine-language program but are to help you understand the program.

Address	Contents	Mnemonic	Explanation
000	100E	LDA ZERO	Initialize TOTAL to 0
001	200D	STA TOTAL	
002	D00C	IN VALUE	Input first value
003	100C	LDA VALUE	Compare VALUE . . .
004	800E	CMP ZERO	. . . with ZERO . . .
005	A00A	JLT 00A	. . . exit loop if less than
006	300D	ADD TOTAL	Add TOTAL to VALUE
007	200D	STA TOTAL	Store sum in TOTAL
008	D00C	IN VALUE	Input next value
009	9003	JMP 003	Jump back to start of loop
00A	E00D	OUT TOTAL	Output total
00B	F000	HALT	Terminate execution
00C	?	VALUE	Storage for VALUE
00D	?	TOTAL	Storage for TOTAL
00E	0000	ZERO	Storage for constant 0

Steps 3.1 and 3.2 are to be repeated only so long as the contents of VALUE are greater than or equal to zero. Before executing these steps, the computer must compare the the contents of VALUE with those of ZERO. If the contents of VALUE are less than the contents of ZERO (VALUE contains the sentinel), the computer is to jump around steps 3.1 and 3.2 and go directly to step 4. If the contents of VALUE are greater than or equal to zero, however, the computer is to continue with steps 3.1 and 3.2

The program loads the contents of VALUE into the accumulator

        100C   LDA VALUE

and compares the contents of the accumulator with the contents of ZERO:

        800E   CMP ZERO

If the contents of VALUE are less than the contents of ZERO, the computer should jump to step 4, the instructions for which begin at memory location 000A:

```
A00A     JLT 00A
```

If the contents of VALUE were greater than or equal to zero, the JLT instruction has no effect, and the computer goes on to the instructions for steps 3.1 and 3.2. Step 3.1 adds the contents of VALUE to the contents of TOTAL and stores the result back into TOTAL. The contents of VALUE have already been loaded into the accumulator; thus we use an ADD instruction to add the contents of the accumulator to the contents of TOTAL

```
300D     ADD TOTAL
```

and an STA instruction to store the sum back into TOTAL:

```
200D     STA TOTAL
```

Step 3.2 obtains the next value to be processed and stores it in VALUE:

```
D00C     IN VALUE
```

Steps 3.1 and 3.2 are to be repeated while the contents of VALUE are greater than or equal to zero. This means that, when step 3.2 has been executed, the computer must jump back to the beginning of step 3. Step 3 will once again check for the sentinel value, jumping to step 4 if the contents of VALUE are negative and continuing with steps 3.1 and 3.2 otherwise. When steps 3.1 and 3.2 have been executed, the computer will again jump back to the beginning of step 3, where the sentinel value will be checked for again, and so on. An unconditional jump instruction causes the computer to jump back to the beginning of step 3:

```
9003     JMP 003
```

Step 4 outputs the contents of TOTAL and terminates the program:

```
E00D     OUT TOTAL
F000     HALT
```

Review questions

1. Give two examples showing how the parts of which a computing device is made influence the way the machine represents information.

2. What is a *bit*?

3. What is a *binary code*? Give two examples of binary codes.

4. What is ASCII? How are the characters X, 5, $, +, and the blank space coded in ASCII?

5. Give two statements that characterize the decimal number system.

6. Give the two corresponding statements that characterize the binary number system.

7. How can we indicate whether 101 is the binary representation of five or the decimal representation of one hundred and one?

8. Contrast the addition and multiplication tables for the binary system with those for the decimal system.

9. Describe the four logical operations and give one application of each.

10. Describe the two shift operations discussed in this chapter.

11. Describe the octal and hexadecimal systems. What advantages do these systems have over binary notation?

12. Contrast the *sign-magnitude* and the *twos-complement* representations for signed numbers. Give two disadvantages of the sign-magnitude representation and show how they are overcome in the twos-complement representation.

13. Describe the operation of taking the *twos complement* of a number. Why is the twos-complement system named after this operation?

14. Describe how numbers containing a radix point can be represented in binary notation.

15. What is *floating-point* notation? Illustrate floating-point representations for both binary and decimal numbers.

16. What is a *biased exponent*? Why are exponents often stored in biased form?

17. What is a *word*?

18. For the computer described in this chapter, what is the purpose of the *accumulator*? The *condition code register*? The *instruction address register*?

19. Describe the instruction format for the computer described in this chapter.

20. Which instruction changes the contents of the condition code register? What instructions make use of its contents?

Exercises

1. Using the table for the ASCII code given in this chapter, show how a short message would be coded in ASCII. Remember to code the punctuation marks and blank spaces as well as the letters and numbers.

2. Find the decimal value corresonding to each of the following binary numbers:
   (a) 110   (b) 1101
   (c) 110011   (d) 10101101

3. Work each of the following problems in binary arithmetic:
   (a) 0101 + 1010
   (b) 0111 + 0110
   (c) 0111 − 0101
   (d) 1000 − 0011
   (e) 1010 × 0110
   (f) 1111 × 1111
   (g) 11001000 ÷ 1101
   (h) 10001100 ÷ 1111

4. Convert each of the following binary values to hexadecimal:
   (a) 10011110   (b) 100111000001
   (c) 001100011101   (d) 1110100111011100

5. Convert each of the following hexadecimal values to binary:
   (a) AB   (b) F3D
   (c) 2EB   (d) 5A3C

6. What signed decimal number is represented by each of the following codes in the four-bit, twos-complement representation?
   (a) 0110   (b) 1011
   (c) 1111   (d) 1000

7. Carry out the following operations in the four-bit, twos-complement representation. Give the signed decimal number represented by each code:
   (a) 0011 + 0010   (b) 0110 + 1110
   (c) 0001 + 1111   (d) 1101 + 1110

8. What decimal value is represented by the following binary floating-point number coded in the representation described in this chapter?

Sign	Exponent	Significand
1	10000001	00010000000000000000000

9. Prove that the algorithm for adding a series of numbers terminated by a sentinel is correct. Why might the program fail in spite of the algorithm having been proved correct?

   Hint: Consider the range of values that can be stored in the accumulator and the memory locations.

10. Illustrate how compare and jump instructions are used to implement repetition in the example machine-language program.

For further reading

American National Standard Code for Information Interchange. New York: American National Standards Institute, 1977.

Asimov, Isaac. "One, Ten, Buckle My Shoe." in *Adding a Dimension*. New York: Doubleday, 1964.

Chu, Yaohan. *Introduction to Computer Organization*. Englewood Cliffs, N. J.: Prentice-Hall, 1970.

Communications of the ACM (special issue on computer architecture), January 1978.

Katzen, Harry. *Computer Systems and Organization*. Science Research Associates, 1976.

Tannenbaum, Andrew S. *Structured Computer Organization*. Englewood Cliffs, N. J.: Prentice-Hall, 1976.

5

Computer software

oftware, we recall, consists of the programs a computer system executes. There are two kinds of software: *system software* and *applications software*. System software consists of programs that help people write and execute other programs. Programs that translate other programs from one computer language to another are examples of system software, as are programs that supervise the execution of other programs on a computer. Applications software, on the other hand, does the jobs that we bought the computer to handle in the first place, jobs that usually have nothing to do with the operation of the computer system. Programs that play games, design machinery, make up payrolls, guide spacecraft, do word processing, and simulate spreadsheets are examples of applications software.

Applications software is as varied as the applications of computers themselves. Each of the computer applications described in Chapter 1, such as word processing and spreadsheet simulation, requires the use of an appropriate applications software program. In the remaining chapters of this book, we will see many examples of programs for various applications. Since applications programs are discussed throughout the remainder of the book, we will concentrate on system software in this chapter.

Computers can be classified as *general purpose* or *special purpose*. A general-purpose computer is intended to do many different jobs, such as meeting all the computational needs of an individual or a business. A special-purpose computer is devoted to a single job, such as controlling a microwave oven or regulating an automobile engine.

General-purpose computer systems are designed to change from one program to another as quickly as possible when we want the computer to do a different job. In fact, much system software is concerned with making such changes as quickly as possible. For special-purpose computers, however, we usually want to install programs permanently in read-only memory so the user won't have to bother putting them in memory and so they can't be erased accidentally. We recall that programs installed permanently in read-only memory are called *firmware*. The only difference between software and firmware is that software is easy to change and firmware isn't. Therefore, we usually won't have to distinguish between the two.

General-purpose computers, particularly personal computers, may also contain some commonly used programs in read-only memory; these programs are available as soon as the computer is turned on, saving the user the trouble of loading them from tape or disk. For example, many personal computers contain an interpreter program for the BASIC programming language in read-only memory, allowing BASIC to be used as soon as the computer is turned on. Some recent personal computers have frequently used applications programs such as word processors in read-only memory.

5.1 Programming languages

Machine language   As we saw in Chapter 4, the instructions a computer executes are stored in binary-coded form. These binary codes are called *machine code* or *machine language*. The central processor can only execute programs coded in machine language. The *Contents* column of Figure 4.12 contains the binary codes (expressed in hexadecimal notation) of a machine-language program. The remaining columns of Figure 4.12 are there to help you understand the program but are not part of the program itself.

A machine-language programmer has to know the operation code for each operation the computer can carry out. Since most computers have hundreds of operation codes, a machine-language programmer must memorize many obscure codes or, more likely, carry around a reference card giving the code for each operation. Machine-language programmers must also be familiar with the internal organization of the computer, such as the central-processor registers and the layout of main memory, even though these machine-oriented details have nothing to do with the problem the programmer wants the computer to solve.

A machine-language programmer must also keep track of all the addresses of main-memory locations that are referred to in the program. These may number in the hundreds or thousands. With only the addresses to go by, it is difficult to remember the significance of the data stored in each location. It is easy to make a slip and write an instruction that causes the machine to refer to the wrong memory location.

Still another problem with machine language is that, if we modify a program, we will probably have to change the addresses of some of the memory locations the program uses. For example, if we insert another instruction in the program, all the instructions and data items following the point of insertion must be moved forward by one location to make room for the new instruction. When instructions and data items are moved, their addresses change, and so the address parts of any instructions referring to them must be changed. Therefore, inserting one new instruction in the program may require us to modify the address parts of many instruction codes.

Thousands, tens of thousands, or hundreds of thousands of machine-language instructions are required to make a computer do useful jobs. If you found the machine-language program in Chapter 4 hard to follow, imagine being faced with hundreds of pages of machine code.

For these reasons, machine-language programming is extremely tedious. A programmer might write a few machine-language instructions for some special purpose, such as making corrections to an existing machine-language program, but few would write a program of any size in machine language.

Assembly language　　Assembly language allows us to use convenient abbreviations (called *mnemonics*) for operations and memory locations.

Figure 5.1 shows an assembly-language program corresponding to the machine-language program in Figure 4.12. With the exception of LOOP, FINISH, DW, DC,

Figure 5.1　　An assembly-language program corresponding to the machine-language program in Figure 4.12. Labels appear in the leftmost column; each label represents the address of the memory location whose contents are given on the same line as the label. The middle column gives the instructions and data items that will appear in memory. The rightmost column contains comments intended to help human readers follow the program. The comments are ignored by the assembler.

```
        LDA ZERO        INITIALIZE TOTAL TO 0
        STA TOTAL
        IN VALUE        INPUT FIRST VALUE
LOOP    LDA VALUE       COMPARE VALUE . . .
        CMP ZERO        . . . WITH ZERO . . .
        JLT FINISH      . . . EXIT LOOP IF LESS THAN
        ADD TOTAL       ADD TOTAL TO VALUE
        STA TOTAL       STORE SUM IN TOTAL
        IN VALUE        INPUT NEXT VALUE
        JMP LOOP        JUMP BACK TO START OF LOOP
FINISH  OUT TOTAL       OUTPUT TOTAL
        HALT            TERMINATE EXECUTION
VALUE   DW  1           STORAGE FOR VALUE
TOTAL   DW  1           STORAGE FOR TOTAL
ZERO    DC  0           STORAGE FOR CONSTANT 0
        END
```

and END, the mnemonics are the same as used in our discussions in Chapter 4. LDA stands for operation code 1, STA for operation code 2, and so on. Each line of the assembly-language program represents a memory location containing either an instruction or a data item. The leftmost column of the assembly-language program is the *label* column; when a mnemonic appears in the label column, it is defined to represent the address of the memory location whose contents are given on that line. Thus, noting the addresses of the various instructions and data items as given in Figure 4.12, we see that LOOP, FINISH, VALUE, TOTAL, and ZERO stand, respectively, for the addresses 003, 00A, 00C, 00D, and 00E. Mnemonics representing addresses are used to give the address parts of instructions. Thus, the assembly-language instruction

LDA VALUE

is equivalent to the machine-language instruction

100C   LDA 00C

and the assembly-language instruction

JMP LOOP

is equivalent to the machine-language instruction

9003   JMP 003

The central processor cannot understand assembly language, of course; it can only execute programs in machine code. Before an assembly-language program can be executed, it must be translated into machine language. Fortunately, we can program the computer to do the translation. The program that tells the computer how to do the translation is called an *assembler*. The assembler program is our first example of a *language processor*. Language processors allow computer systems to execute programs written in languages other than machine language.

The assembly-language program in Figure 5.1 contains several mnemonics for *pseudooperations*—operations to be carried out by the assembler program rather than to be translated into machine code. DW (define word) tells the assembler to reserve the specified number of words of memory (one in this case) to hold data; no particular value is stored in words reserved by DW, so the contents of these memory locations when the program begins execution are unknown. DC (define constant) tells the assembler to reserve a memory location and place a particular value in it (zero in this case). When the program begins execution, the location in question will contain the value specified in the DC pseudooperation. END informs the assembler that it has reached the end of the assembly-language program.

Assembly language, then, makes it possible for programmers to use convenient mnemonics rather than obscure codes for operations and memory locations. Also, since memory locations are referred to by name rather than by address, the programmer can modify a program without worrying that the modifications will change some addresses and thus require still more modifications. Addresses are assigned by the assembler, which does the job anew each time that it translates a modified version of the program.

On the other hand, the assembly-language programmer must still write a line of assembly language for each machine instruction,* so assembly-language programs that do significant jobs are many thousands of lines long. Assembly-language programmers must also be concerned with the technical details of the computer, such as how the central-processor registers are to be used, how much data will fit into a memory location, and what operations are available for manipulating the data. Thus, although assembly language is vastly superior to machine language and is far more widely used, programming in it is still tedious and requires knowledge of the internal workings of the computer.

Higher-level languages   We need languages that hide the internal details of computer operation, allowing programmers to phrase a program in the same terms that would be used to describe to a colleague the procedure being carried out. Since procedures are stated in different ways in different subject areas and by different groups of programmers, more than one higher-level language is required. Currently, there are about 170 higher-level languages in use, although the number in reasonably widespread use is closer to 20 than to 170. The following table lists six popular programming languages and gives the principal application area of each:

Language	*Application Area*
BASIC	education, personal computing
COBOL	business data processing
FORTRAN	science, engineering, and mathematics
LISP	artificial intelligence, robot control
Logo	education
Pascal	education, personal computing, computer science research

We recall that adding the contents of memory location VALUE to the contents of memory location TOTAL requires three assembly-language or machine-language instructions:

```
LDA VALUE
ADD TOTAL
STA TOTAL
```

The same addition can be expressed as a single line in each of the six higher-level languages:

---

*This is not strictly true because most assemblers allow programmers to define *macroinstructions* or *macros,* each of which can represent a (perhaps lengthy) sequence of assembly-language instructions. A line containing a macro instruction can cause many machine-language instructions to be produced. Convenient as macros can be, however, they rarely affect the magnitude of the task of writing a substantial assembly-language program.

BASIC	`LET T = T + V`
COBOL	`ADD VALUE TO TOTAL.`
FORTRAN	`TOTAL = TOTAL + VALUE`
LISP	`(SETQ TOTAL (PLUS TOTAL VALUE))`
Logo	`MAKE "TOTAL :TOTAL + :VALUE`
Pascal	*total := total + value*

None of the higher-level language statements refer to any machine components (such as central-processor registers) or machine operations. The business programmer who prefers Englishlike sentences to algebralike formulas can have them with COBOL. The scientific programmer who prefers the formulas gets them with FORTRAN. The personal computer user who is willing to trade drastic abbreviations (such as T for TOTAL) for the ability to use the language on a small computer will be happy with BASIC. And the student who would rather program the computer to draw pictures than program it to do arithmetic will enjoy Logo.

Higher-level language programs are much shorter than machine-language or assembly-language programs. A single line in a higher-level language program may translate into five, ten, or even hundreds of machine-language instructions.

Language processors   The program that translates other programs from a given computer language into machine language is called a *translator*. A translator program for assembly language is usually called an assembler; translators for higher-level languages are often called *compilers*. Translators, assemblers, and compilers are all examples of *language processors*. The result of the translation process is always a machine-language program that can be executed by the computer just as if it had been coded by hand. As far as the computer is concerned, there is no distinction between hand-coded machine-language programs and those produced by translator programs. The program to be translated is called the *source program;* the program produced by the translator is called the *object program.*

In practice, an additional step called *linking* must often be taken before a translated program can be executed. The object program produced by the translator may call, or invoke, *subprograms* stored in auxiliary memory. (A subprogram is a program that is called by another program rather than directly by the user.) The object program contains references to these subprograms but does not contain the subprograms themselves. Another software program, called a *linker,* must be used to combine the object program with the subprograms it calls. The linker produces an *executable program* that contains not only the object program but all the subprograms that it calls.

Interpreters are another widely used type of language processor. Instead of translating the statements of the source program into machine language, the interpreter program carries out the operations called for by each statement. Thus the source program is executed when it is processed by the interpreter, instead of being translated into machine language for later execution by the central processor. Put another way, the interpreter fetches and executes statements of the source program just as the central processor fetches and executes machine-language instructions; an interpreter program is to a higher-level language program as the central processor is to a machine-language program.

It can take much longer to execute an interpreted program than a translated one. The reason is that most programs use repetition constructions to specify that some statements will be executed many times. Such repeated statements need to be analyzed only once by a translator. But an interpreter must analyze a repeated statement every time it is executed. And every time the interpreter analyzes a statement, it may have to search a table to find which memory locations are referred to by mnemonics such as TOTAL and VALUE. A translator converts mnemonics into memory addresses that can be used to access the corresponding memory locations directly.

In spite of this drawback, interpreters often provide the most convenient way to develop programs in a higher-level language. The interpreter makes it easy to intermix execution and editing (correcting and modifying a program). (Most interpreters also contain a text editor for entering and changing the source program.) We can execute a few lines of the program, check the results, make some changes, execute the same few lines again, and so on. With a translator, we would have to go through the entire process of translating and linking after each change. When testing an interpreted program, we can use mnemonics such as TOTAL and VALUE to refer to memory locations whose contents we wish to examine. For a translated program, we would probably have to use hexadecimal memory addresses to specify the locations to be examined. When an error occurs, as when the program requests an impossible operation, the interpreter can tell us which statement in the higher-level language program caused the problem; for a translated program, we may only be given the hexadecimal address of the machine-language instruction that produced the error.

Finally, interpreters relieve us of the need to worry about translation, linking, and execution. As mentioned earlier, an interpreter for BASIC is often permanently installed in the firmware of personal computers. As far as the user is concerned, the computer understands BASIC. The user never has to worry about machine language.

Note that translation and interpretation can be combined. Instead of producing machine language, the translator can produce an intermediate code that is then processed by an interpreter. The translator and the interpreter each benefit from the existence of the other: the translator can produce the intermediate code more easily than it could produce machine language, and the partial translation relieves the interpeter of some time-consuming chores, such as analyzing complex statements and looking up mnemonics. Pascal programs are often processed by both a translator and an interpreter.

5.2

The operating system

The operating system is the program that supervises the execution of other programs. It is also known as the *supervisor, monitor, master control program,* or *disk operating system (DOS).* (The last name comes from the fact that one of the main functions of an operating system is to transfer programs and data between main memory and disks.) By means of *system commands,* the user requests the operating system to execute particular programs and give those programs access to particular data. The operating system takes care of all the details necessary to comply with the user's requests. The following are some of the functions that a modern operating system performs.

Program loading   Most computer systems maintain program libraries in auxiliary memory. Upon request by the user, the operating system will load a program for auxiliary memory into main memory and arrange for the computer to execute it. The user who has written a program in a higher-level language can request that the program be translated into machine code and that the machine code be executed. The operating system handles all the details of loading the translator, executing the translator with the source program as data, storing the object program on disk, loading the linker, providing it with the object program as input, locating the subprograms called for by the linker, storing the executable program on disk, loading the executable program into main memory, and executing the machine code. When a program finishes executing, it returns control to the operating system. Thus on a modern computer system, the HALT instruction in Figures 4.12 and 5.1 would not actually halt the computer, but would terminate execution of the program and return control to the operating system.

Operating system macros   Many operating systems allow the user to define *macrocommands,* each of which represents a sequence of system commands. Giving the macrocommand causes every command in the sequence to be carried out. For example, translation, linking, and execution of a program are often handled by a macrocommand. Macrocommands go by a variety of names including *batch files, submit files,* and *procs* (procedures).

Control of peripherals   Peripheral devices often require complex, hard-to-write programs to control the transfer of data between the device and the computer. Writing such a *device handler* program calls for detailed technical knowledge about the operation of the device. For this reason, device handlers are usually written once and for all and included in the operating system. A user's program transfers information to or from a device by making the appropriate request to the operating system. The form of the request is the same for all devices, even though the coded commands that actually have to be sent to the devices vary widely from one device to another. Often there are provisions for adding new device handler programs to the operating system when new types of peripheral devices are installed.

Data management   Not only do computer systems maintain program libraries in auxiliary memory, they store data files there as well. Typical data files would be the accounts of the customers of a company or the data collected in a scientific experiment.

When a program needs data from one of these files, it requests it from the operating system. The operating system must first find the desired file in auxiliary memory. It must then find the particular data requested and pass it on to the program. Data that a program wishes to be stored in a file is handled in much the same way.

Many operating systems handle files and I/O devices in exactly the same way. A programmer can write a program to take data from certain files, process it, and store the results in other files. Only when it's time to execute the program does the user have to specify which of these "files" are files in auxiliary memory and which are I/O devices. This specification can be changed each time the program is executed; what was a disk file on one execution of the program can be a printer on the next.

Concurrency   Concurrency refers to more than one program running on the computer at the same time; the techniques by which concurrent execution can be achieved are described in Section 5.3.

Concurrency can increase the utilization of the central processor. If one of the programs sharing the processor has to wait for a slow input or output device, the processor can devote all of its time to the remaining programs, ignoring the waiting program until it is ready to continue. If the computer executed only one program at a time, the central processor would have nothing to do while that program was waiting for an input or output operation. *Time sharing* allows a large number of people to access the computer from remote terminals at the same time. Time sharing is usually used with minicomputers or main frames; it is used less frequently with microcomputers.

Even though microcomputers are usually used by only one person at a time, we can still find applications for concurrency. For example, we may want one program to produce printed output while we are working with another program. We might, for example, want to run two "incarnations" of a word processor program at the same time; one would be printing a previously edited text file while we are using the other to enter or edit a new file.

Even if we don't want programs to execute simultaneously, having them simultaneously *ready* for execution can be useful. To start a program, we must request the operating system to load and execute the program, tell the program what files it is to process, and perhaps provide additional information. To terminate a program, we may have to tell it to save in auxiliary memory the data that we wish to retain from one session to the next. Changing from one program to another, then, can be annoyingly time consuming. With concurrency, we can keep several programs in main memory at the same time, each with the data it is currently working on and the knowledge of what files it is supposed to be processing. With a single system command, we can switch the computer's keyboard and display from one program to another, thus moving from program to program as needed without going to the trouble of terminating one program and starting another each time. Some personal-computer operating systems provide concurrency for just this purpose.

Concurrency provides challenges for the operating system that go beyond the basic one of sharing the processor's time among a number of programs. For example, if more than one program requests use of the printer, the operating system must give exclusive use of the device to one program until it finishes its printout, then let another program takes its turn, and so on. It must not (as an operating system of the author's acquaintance was notorious for doing) print one line of one program's output, then a line of still another program's output, and so on. The users are guaranteed to be unhappy with their joint printout!

On the other hand, accesses to a disk by different programs can often be interleaved. In this case, the program must schedule the movement of the disk's read-write heads so as to satisfy each program's request as rapidly as possible. In one approach, called the *elevator algorithm,* the read-write heads move inward toward the center of the disk, like an elevator going up. Just as the elevator stops at each floor for which service has been requested, the read-write heads stop at each track for which an access has been requested. When the innermost track for which an access has been requested is reached, the read-write heads reverse direction and begin moving outwards, like an elevator that has reached the top floor for which service has been requested and has switched from "going up" to "going down."

Simultaneous access by programs to a data base can present problems. Suppose one program is to make two changes to a record in a data base—say it is to change a person's birthdate and the person's age (presumably to correct previous errors). Suppose that, after the first program changes the birthdate, but before it changes the age, a second program accesses the record. The second program will obtain an inconsistent record, since the birthdate and the age will not agree. The operating system must provide means whereby one program can lock out accesses to a record by other programs until all changes have been completed.

Granting programs exclusive use of system resources, such as peripheral devices, can lead to a problem called *deadlock*. Suppose a system has two tape drives, and two programs each need two tape drives. Each program requests and is granted one tape drive. Now each program requests a second tape drive. The second request from each program will never be granted, however. Neither program will get the second tape drive that it needs, and so it will never release the tape drive that it already has and which the other program is waiting for. Neither program can proceed; both are deadlocked. Also, both tape drives are permanently tied up, although neither is being used. The operating system needs to be able to detect deadlock and take remedial action.

Virtual memory   Often a program and the data it is manipulating are too large to fit into main memory at one time. Therefore, only the parts of the program and data that are being used at the moment are kept in main memory. The remaining parts reside in auxiliary memory until needed. During execution of the program, parts of the program and data must be swapped back and forth between main and auxiliary memory.

It is tedious for the programmer to have to divide the program in parts and worry about making sure that the needed parts are always in main memory. We would like to free the programmer to concentrate on the problem being solved without having to worry about computer-oriented technicalities such as main and auxiliary memory.

With a technique known as *virtual memory,* the operating system takes over the task of dividing the program into parts and juggling the parts between main and auxiliary memory. The programmer writes the program as though the computer had a very large main memory. The operating system takes care of the rest. Typically, the program and data are divided into blocks called *pages*. The pages that the program is currently using—that it has referred to recently—are part of the program's *working set* and are kept in main memory. When a page isn't referred to for a while, it falls out of the program's working set and becomes a candidate for being "swapped out" to auxiliary memory. If the program refers to a page that is not in main memory, this page becomes part of the working set and is "swapped in" to main memory, preferably replacing a page that has fallen out of the working set and so has become a candidate for being swapped out. If a program refers to many different pages in rapid succession, a phenomenon called *thrashing* takes place, in which the computer spends more time swapping pages than doing useful work.

We speak of a *virtual* memory since the computer appears to have a very large main memory that doesn't actually exist. Any part of a computer system that appears to be present as a result of programming but doesn't actually exit is said to be *virtual*. For example, we can think of language processors as implementing *virtual machines,* imaginary computers that accept higher-level languages as their machine languages. Sometimes people use terms such as BASIC machine or Pascal machine to refer to these virtual machines.

User-friendly systems   System commands can be rather cryptic. For example, to edit a file with a word processor, we might issue the system command:

```
WORDPROC A:REPORT.TXT
```

Here WORDPROC is the name of the word processor program, that is, the name under which the program is stored in auxiliary memory. REPORT is the name of the file to be edited, which can be found on the disk in disk drive A; the extension TXT, which is given to all files produced by the word processor, distinguishes them from files with the same names produced by other programs. All this is confusing to those who are using a computer for the first time or who do not use the computer regularly. Nor does it help that the very details one is likely to have trouble remembering—where the colon and period must be used, the symbols for designating disk drives, and the name of the word processor program—are likely to vary from one computer system to another.

As a result of the microprocessor revolution, computers have fallen into the hands of many people who want to use them for particular jobs, such as word processing or spreadsheet analysis, without bothering to master the commands and technical details of a particular operating system. They gladly leave the beauties of computer technology to computer science students; they just want to get the mail out, get their reports written, and get next year's budget planned. They demand *user-friendly systems* whose operation is sufficiently obvious that it can be mastered with brief instruction, a bit of experimentation, and common sense.

One way to make a system user-friendly is to employ a *metaphor*—to make the operation of the system similar to some process with which the user is already familiar. A currently popular metaphor is the *desktop metaphor,* in which the display simulates the top of the desk. Various papers appear to lie on the desk; these papers are actually *windows*—areas of the display in which programs present their output. The user can adjust the size of each window, so that several windows can occupy the desktop simultaneously or one window can be expanded to fill the entire desk, temporarily covering up the others. If the system supports concurrent execution, programs can be run simultaneously, presenting their output in different windows. Data can be transferred between windows maintained by different programs. For example, a chart produced with a graphics program can be inserted into a report being created with a word processor.

Icons—small pictures along one side of the desktop—represent sources and destinations for data. For example, a picture of a disk represents a particular disk drive; a picture of a printer represents that output device; a picture of a trash can represents a destination for data that is to be discarded. Sources or destinations for data can be selected by using a mouse to position a pointer over the desired icon and pressing the button on the mouse.

The mouse is also used to give commands to the operating system and to the various applications programs. A bar across the top of the display lists the types of commands that are currently available. For example, "edit" symbolizes all commands that can be used to edit a program. If the user positions the mouse over the word "edit" and presses the button on the mouse, a menu of all editing commands is "pulled down" (appears in a temporary window below the word "edit"). The user then moves the mouse until the pointer is over the desired editing command and releases the button.

Commands for use by programs In addition to carrying out commands entered directly by the user, the operating system will also carry out commands for other programs. As mentioned in connection with peripheral devices, all access by programs to input devices, output devices, and files in auxiliary memory is through commands to the operating system. This is particularly important when concurrent execution is allowed, since only if all devices are accessed through the operating system can the system meet such responsibilities as granting exclusive use of some peripherals, arranging for efficient simultaneous use of others, and detecting deadlock.

The operating system can help different applications present a consistent *user interface,* so that it will seem to the user that all the applications operate according to similar principles. For example, in a system using the desktop metaphor, the operating system can provide commands by which applications programs can create, delete, and change the size of windows, send output to particular windows, create pull-down menus, determine which menu items or icons have been selected by the user, and so on.

Accounting In many organizations, it is necessary to keep track of computing resources (such as computation time and memory space) that each job uses so that each department in the organization can be charged for the resources it consumes. Some companies, by letting other people use their computers, make a business of selling computer resources. Like other utilities, they must prepare monthly bills for their customers. In either case, the job of accounting for who uses how much of what resources falls on the operating system.

Security You may have gotten the impression that the operating system will try its best to honor any request made by any user. But on large systems with many users, there are usually some requests that should be denied. For example, some files might contain confidential data to which only authorized persons should have access.

Others might contain records that someone could benefit from changing, such as bank accounts, student grades, or payroll information. In defense industries, some data and programs might be military secrets. Even in an academic environment, programs and data files must be protected against malicious mischief.

Recent developments in computer technology and use have made security particularly important. Many computers can now be accessed by "dial up" telephone lines; if you know the computer's telephone number, you can call it. Such computers can be located by systematically dialing telephone numbers (a computer can be programmed to do this) and noting which numbers answer with the characteristic whine of a data signal. Microcomputers and the modems that allow computers to communicate over telephone lines are now widely available, and, alas, a number of (usually) young people make a hobby of using their microcomputers to gain unauthorized access to other computer systems. Since security is a weak point with many current operating systems, such attempts at unauthorized access are often successful. Although these young computer enthusiasts usually do not have any criminal intent, their unauthorized meddling can destroy valuable data files or even "crash" the system—interrupt its operation until the computer operator can restart it from scratch by reloading the operating system and performing the system startup procedure.

5.3 Concurrent execution

The original motivation for concurrent execution came from the enormous disparity between the speed of the central processor and that of most peripheral devices. For example, many computer terminals send and receive characters at the rate of 30 per second. (For sending, this rate is purely theoretical, since nobody can type that fast.) On the other hand, a fast computer can carry out millions of instructions each second. While the computer is waiting for the terminal to send or accept another character, it could have executed at least 30,000 instructions. If the computer is made to wait for the terminal, most of the central processor's time will be wasted.

There are two solutions to this problem. One, made possible by the microprocessor revolution, is to use an inexpensive computer so that the wasted time doesn't really matter. The other, more interesting solution is to arrange for the computer to work on other programs while one program is waiting for a peripheral device. Execution of the program that is waiting is not resumed until the request to the peripheral device has been fulfilled.

Multiprogramming *Multiprogramming* refers to the situation in which a single central processor seems to execute a number of programs at the same time. Actually, the central processor is switched rapidly from one program to another. Each program is executed for a short time, called a *time slice* or a *time quantum*. Before the operating system gives a particular program control of the computer, it sets an electronic timer to interrupt the computer when the time slice has expired. When the timer interrupts, control of the computer is returned automatically to the operating system. The operating system then moves on to the next program awaiting execution, sets the timer again, and gives that program temporary control of the computer.

In this way, control of the computer passes from program to program in round-robin fashion. Each program is executed briefly, after which the operating system passes on to the next program. Since it is the central processor that executes the programs, we can think of various programs as taking turns at the central processor.

When a program has to wait for a peripheral device, it loses its turns at the central processor until the request to the peripheral device has been satisfied. But while that program is waiting, other programs are busy taking their turns at the central processor, so the central processor does not remain idle.

Processes and interrupts   We have spoken loosely about programs sharing the central processor, but it is more precise to speak of *processes* rather than of *programs*. As shown in Figure 5.2, a process has three components:

1. A program;

2. The data the program is manipulating; and

3. The address of the next program instruction to be executed. Because the address designates, or points out, the next instruction, it is called the *pointer* to the next instruction.

Note that the data component includes not only data stored in main memory but that stored in the registers of the central processor, such as the accumulator and the condition code register. (The address of the next program instruction is just the contents of the instruction address register.) Also, the data component contains descriptions of any files in auxiliary memory that the program is processing.

The most important property of a process is that its execution can be stopped at any time and restarted later as if nothing had happened. We say that a process is *active* when it is actually being executed and *inactive* or *suspended* when it is not. The components of an active process reside in the central-processor registers, in main memory, and perhaps partially in auxiliary memory. An inactive process resides in either main memory or auxiliary memory, or partially in both.

A process leads an independent existence, interacting with users through input and output devices and perhaps exchanging messages with other processes. A process can even create offspring that carry out their assigned tasks and report back to the parent process. With tongue only slightly in cheek, people have referred to a process as "an organism that lives in a computer system."

Although each process must have its own individual instruction-pointer and data components, a single program can be shared by many processes. Thus a frequently used program, such as a particular language processor, can be placed in memory once and shared by many processes. The only requirement is that the program must never change itself; changes can only be made in the data and instruction-pointer components of the processes, never in the program component. A program that satisfies this requirement is said to be *reentrant*. Translators for modern programming languages such as Pascal generally produce reentrant programs.

A process can be in one of three states: *running, ready,* and *blocked.* A process that is *running* is currently being executed by the central processor. In a system with only one processor, only one process can be running at one time. Only a process that

Figure 5.2   The three components of a process: the program, the data
the program is processing, and a pointer to the next
instruction to be executed. The data component includes the
contents of central-processor registers such as the
accumulator and the condition code register. When the
process is active, the pointer to the next instruction resides
in the instruction address register.

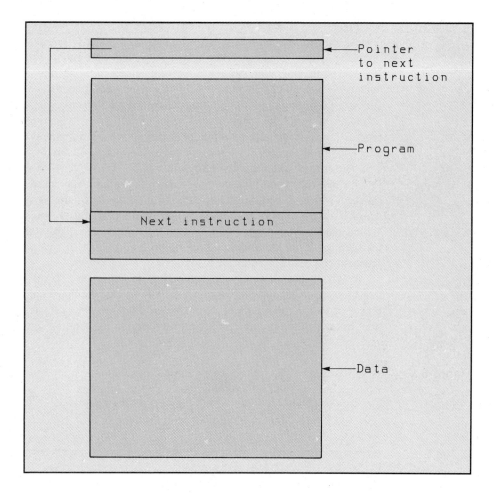

is running is active. A process is *ready* when it is waiting its turn at the central
processor. It is inactive but will become active when its turn comes up. A process is
blocked when it is waiting for a request to the operating system to be satisfied. While
the process is blocked, it loses its turns at the central processor. Usually a blocked
process is waiting for a peripheral device, but other situations are possible. For example, some systems allow a process that does not need to run continually to request
the operating system to "put it to sleep" (block it) for a certain period of time.

An *interrupt* is a signal indicating that a peripheral device needs attention—that it has data for the computer or that it is ready to accept data from the computer. The system timer also produces an interrupt when a process's time slice has expired. We can compare an interrupt to the ringing of a telephone, doorbell, or alarm clock. When an interrupt is received, the central processor is automatically switched from the process it is currently executing to an *interrupt handler* process that is part of the operating system. Thus, an interrupt always forces control of the computer to return to the operating system.

Figure. 5.3 shows how the running-ready-blocked state of a process can change. Once a process is running, it will continue to run until control is returned to the operating system. This can occur in two ways. First, the running process can explicitly request the operating system to perform some action, such as an input or output operation; the process is blocked until the requested operation can be carried out. Second, an interrupt can force a transfer of control from the running process to the operating system. The interrupt can be from the timer, indicating that the running process has used up its time slice, or it can be from a peripheral device that needs attention. In either case, the running process is placed in the ready state so that it will be run again when its turn next comes up.

An interrupt often indicates that a request made by a blocked process has been satisfied—either a peripheral has data for the process or the peripheral can accept data from the process. After carrying out the requested data transfer, the operating system places the process that was waiting in the ready state so that it can resume taking turns at the central processor. Thus an interrupt often results in a blocked process being transferred to the ready state.

When all interrupts have been handled for the moment, the operating system activates the ready process whose turn it is to run. Giving control of the central processor to a particular process is called *dispatching;* thus dispatching is the operation that switches a process from the ready state to the running state.

Figure 5.3 How processes make transitions among the three states *running, ready,* and *blocked*. Note that the same interrupt can both move the currently running process to the ready state and move a blocked process to the ready state.

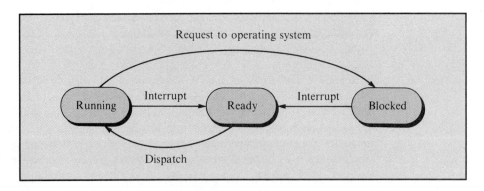

Operating systems are usually organized so that only a small part of the system, called the *kernel,* is responsible for dispatching processes and handling interrupts. The remaining parts of the operating system are processes that are executed in much the same way as user's processes. Thus only the kernel must deal with the rather chaotic situation in which the central processor is rapidly switched from one unrelated process to another, often by interrupts occurring at unpredictable times. Outside of the kernel, we can simply consider all processes as being executed concurrently, without having to worry about how the central processor is switched from one process to another.

Time sharing   Time sharing is a form of multiprogramming in which users can communicate with their programs while the programs are being executed. (More precisely, users communicate with the processes created when their programs are executed.) Each user seems to have the entire computer to himself or herself and need not be concerned with the fact that the computer is serving many other users at the same time.

What distinguishes time sharing from other forms of multiprogramming is the need for fast response. When a user makes a request of a process, the process should respond promptly—a second or two is the longest tolerable delay. This means that every process must get a turn at the central processor often enough to respond to its user without undue delay. If the number of users and processes is large, the time slice must be short.

Another characteristic of time sharing is that, if the number of users is large, all their processes will not fit into main memory at one time. As a result, the operating system must continually swap processes between main and auxiliary memory so that each process will be in main memory when its turn at the central processor next comes up. Note that only ready processes need be swapped; a blocked process can be left in auxiliary memory until it becomes unblocked. At any given time, many of the processes on a time-sharing system will be blocked because they are waiting for users who are sitting at their terminals thinking.

Multiprocessing and distributed processing   In the past, because of the cost of central processors, each computer system had only one. (If there were others, they probably had specialized functions, such as communicating with peripheral devices.) Now, the microprocessor revolution has drastically reduced the cost of processors, and computer systems with many processors are beginning to appear.

We use two terms to describe such systems; which term we choose depends on the organization of the processors and main memory. If all the processors share the same main memory, we speak of *multiprocessing*. If each processor has its own private memory (but the processors are able to send messages to one another), we speak of *distributed processing*. With multiprocessing, all the processors must be in one geographical location—the same location as the shared memory. With distributed processing, the processors with their private memories can be in different cities, states, or countries. Combinations of distributed processing and multiprocessing are also possible, with each processor having access to both private and shared memory.

Multiprocessing and distributed processing are new, and not nearly so much is known about them as about multiprogramming. Discovering ways of using multiple processors effectively is a subject of continuing research. In everyday life, we know that there are some jobs in which several people helping make the work go faster, and others in which the extra people just get in one another's way. We now have to gain the same wisdom about the jobs that computers do.

Review questions

1. Distinguish between *system software* and *applications software*.

2. What is *firmware?* How is it related to software?

3. What is *machine language?* What are some of its disadvantages?

4. What is *assembly language?*

5. How is assembly language related to machine language?

6. What is an assembler?

7. Why is assembly language, despite its advantages over machine language, still not convenient for many users?

8. Give two advantages of higher-level languages over assembly language.

9. Name six widely used higher-level languages, and give the areas in which each is most likely to be used.

10. What is a *language processor?*

11. Distinguish between *translators* and *interpreters*.

12. What is an operating system?

13. Give ten functions that an operating system performs.

14. What is *concurrent execution?*

15. Describe multiprogramming and time sharing.

16. What is a *time slice?*

17. What is a *process?* Distinguish between active and inactive processes.

18. Describe the circumstances under which the running-ready-blocked state of a process changes.

19. What distinguishes multiprogramming from multiprocessing and distributed processing?

20. What is the difference between multiprocessing and distributed processing? How are combinations of the two possible?

For further reading

Denning, Peter J. "Third Generation Computer Systems." *Computing Surveys,* December 1971, pp. 175–216.

Donovan, John H. *Systems Programming.* New York: McGraw-Hill Book Company, 1972.

Holt, R. C. et al. *Structured Concurrent Programming with Operating Systems Applications.* Reading, Mass: Addison-Wesley Publishing Company, 1978.

Kernighan, Brian W., and Plauger, P. J. *Software Tools.* Reading, Mass: Addison-Wesley Publishing Company, 1976.

Sammet, Jean E. *Programming Languages: History and Fundamentals.* Englewood Cliffs, N.J.: Prentice-Hall, 1969.

Tannenbaum, Andrew S. *Structured Computer Organization.* Englewood Cliffs, N.J.: Prentice-Hall, 1976.

Part III
Principles of algorithm construction

6

Values, constants, and expressions

n this chapter, we turn to the main object of this book, which is learning how to construct algorithms and write computer programs.

As always, we need some language or notation in which to express our algorithms. The Englishlike pseudolanguage we used in previous chapters is neither precise nor concise enough for the needs of this and succeeding chapters. Thus, in this chapter, we will begin to develop a new pseudolanguage that is much closer to programming languages than to English. We will usually refer to this pseudolanguage as our *algorithmic language* or *algorithmic notation*.

Like all pseudolanguages, this one is informal, and you should feel free to modify it to suit your own needs and preferences. On the other hand, while taking a computer science course, you will probably need to keep your algorithmic language reasonably close to the one in the book so that your algorithms can be understood by your instructors and fellow students.

6.1
Data types

Computers can process many different kinds of data. The different kinds of data are coded differently inside the computer and are manipulated using different operations. For example, we might wish to carry out arithmetical operations on a set of numbers and arrange a list of names in alphabetical order. Attempting to do arithmetic on people's names is clearly inappropriate, and although we can arrange numbers in alphabetical order, there is usually no point in doing so.

To make it easier to deal with this diversity of data, and to help us avoid silly mistakes like trying to multiply and divide people's names, we classify data into different *data types*. Items belonging to the same data type are manipulated using the same operations and are represented in similar ways both in our programs and inside the computer. The data items belonging to a particular data type are called *values* of that type. For example, one data type consists of integers, so ten, twelve, and fifteen are values of type *integer*. We represent ten, twelve, and fifteen in the algorithmic language by the usual symbols 10, 12, and 15. We refer to 10, 12, and 15 as *integer literals,* since they represent integer values directly, or "literally," rather than being names whose definitions must be consulted to determine the values that they represent.

For now, we will look at five data types: *integer, real, Boolean, char* (character), and *string*. We can consider these as being predefined in our algorithmic language, in that we can use them without having to include definitions of them in our algorithms. In later chapters we will see how to define many additional data types.

Type integer   Integers are whole numbers that do not contain decimal points. The following are examples of integer literals:

25   100   75   1000   523

An integer literal can be preceded by a plus or minus sign:

+25   −100   +75   −1000   +523

When the sign is omitted, plus is assumed. Thus +25 and 25 represent the same value.

Integer (and other numeric) literals cannot contain commas. Commas are used to separate items in lists, and allowing them to appear in numbers as well would cause confusion. Thus, the following are not valid integer literals:

1,000   12,340   2,500

Instead, we must write

1000   12340   2500

In practice, there is always a smallest and a largest value of type *integer*. For example, if integers are stored as 16-bit codes using the twos-complement representation, the smallest possible integer is −32768 and the largest is 32767. Since algorithms are independent of particular computer hardware, we will not worry about these limits when writing in the algorithmic language. We must definitely be concerned about them, however, when writing programs to be run on a particular computer system.

Type real   For historical reasons, numbers that can have fractional parts (that is, whose literals can contain decimal points) are called *real numbers* and belong to type *real*. The following are examples of real literals:

3.5   −2.75   7.943   8.25

As was the case with integer literals, commas may not be used in real literals. Thus,

1,349.25

is invalid; instead, we must write

1349.25

Real literals can also be written in *floating-point* or *exponential* notation. The number following the letter E is called the *exponent* and tells how many places the decimal point is to be moved to the right or left. If the exponent is positive, the decimal point is moved to the right; if the exponent is negative, the decimal point is moved to the left. For example, in

1.25E+9

the exponent, +9, indicates that the decimal point should be moved nine places to the right. Thus 1.25E+9 is equivalent to

1250000000.

Likewise, in

1.75E−7

the exponent, −7, indicates that the decimal point should be moved seven places to the left. Thus, 1.75E−7 is equivalent to

0.000000175

This floating-point notation is the same as that introduced in Chapter 4 except that, for brevity, we indicate the exponent with the letter E instead of writing out 10 raised to the power of the exponent. Thus, 1.25E+9 is equivalent to 1.25×10^9 and 1.75E−7 is equivalent to 1.75×10^{-7}.

The type *real* provided by any computer system can at most approximate the mathematicians' real number system. As with integers, only a limited range of values can belong to type real, although the real number system contains arbitrarily large and arbitrarily small numbers. Even more important, there is a limit to the precision with which real numbers can be represented. For example, if numbers can only be represented with a precision of six significant digits,* then

1.9876524

cannot be represented exactly. The best we can do is represent it approximately by

1.98765

This is the value of type *real* that is closest to the value we wish to represent.

---

*The term *significant digits* excludes leading and trailing zeros used only as place holders. Thus, 135247000 and 0.00000698234 each has six significant digits.

Arithmetical operations applied to values of type *real* may yield values that do not belong to type *real* and so can only be represented approximately. For example, if values of type *real* can be represented with six significant digits, then 9.73691 and 8.96723 both belong to type *real*. If we multiply these numbers, however,

$$9.73691 \times 8.96723 = 87.3131114593$$

the result, 87.3131114593, does not belong to type *real* since it contains 12 significant digits. The best result the computer can give is 87.3131, the value of type *real* that is closest to the exact result. Arithmetical operations on type *real*, then, are only approximate, since the value of type *real* given as a result may only be an approximation to the exact result.

We can roughly characterize the type *real* offered by a particular computer system by giving the range of allowable exponents (when numbers are written in floating-point notation) and the number of significant digits that can be represented. For example, the floating-point representation described in Chapter 4 provides seven significant digits and allows exponents to range from -38 through 38. Thus, the smallest positive number different from zero is approximately $1.0E-38$, and the largest positive number is approximately $1.0E+38$.

Since type *real* contains whole numbers such as 235.0 and -300.0, why do we need both type *integer* and type *real*? Integers can be stored more compactly than real numbers, operations can be carried out on them more rapidly, and operations on integers always yield exact results. When we are only going to deal with whole numbers, therefore, we can often improve the performance of our program by using type *integer* rather than type *real*.

Note that, although 235 and 235.0 correspond to the same numerical value, the values they represent belong to different data types and so are represented quite differently inside the computer. For example, 235 might be represented using the 16-bit twos-complement representation described in Chapter 4, whereas 235.0 might be represented using the 32-bit floating-point representation also described in Chapter 4. Some of the operations that are defined for integers are not defined for real numbers. In general, integer and real literals cannot be used interchangeably; even in places where either an integer or a real number may be used, one of the two will usually be the better choice.

Type Boolean   Both the selection and repetition control structures require the computer to test conditions to determine whether they are true or false. To represent the results of such tests, we use a data type which has only two values:

true   *false*

This type is usually known as type *Boolean*, after the English mathematician George Boole who was the first to develop an algebra of logic. The two values of type *Boolean, true* and *false*, are referred to as *Boolean values*.

Type char   The type *char* consists of the letters of the alphabet, the numerals 0 through 9, the usual punctuation marks, and a small number of special signs such as @, + and −. Exactly which characters are available on a particular computer system depends on which character code is being used. If the ASCII code is used, then the available characters will be those shown in the table in Figure 4.1.

A character literal consists of a character enclosed in single quote marks (apostrophes):

'A'   'a'   '@'   '+'   '−'   '5'

The quote marks distinguish character literals from other elements of the language that are similar in appearance:

'+'   *character literal*

+   *addition sign*

'5'   *character literal*

5   *integer literal*

Type string   A series of characters, such as a word or sentence, is known as a *string*. The characters making up a string must all be of type *char*. Like a character literal, a string literal is enclosed in single quote marks:

'Computer programming is fun'

'Enter your move, please'

'The system has crashed'

'All your files have been erased'

'!@#$%&*'

A problem occurs when representing the single quote mark itself in a character or string literal, since the quote mark that is part of the literal may get confused with the quote marks that enclose the literal. The most commonly used solution is to require that the quote mark be written twice in succession when it occurs in a character or string literal. The two quote marks in the literal represent one quote mark in the character or string. The two quote marks are produced by striking the single quote mark key twice; they are not the same as the double quote mark, which is an entirely different character. Thus,

'Don''t go near the water'

'Why aren''t you in school today?'

''''

represent

Don't go near the water

Why aren't you in school today?

'

The first two literals are string literals; the third is a character literal.

As with character literals, the quote marks around string literals prevent them from being confused with other elements of the language:

'750'	*string literal*
750	*integer literal*
'3.1416'	*string literal*
3.1416	*real literal*

6.2 Output

The instructions in an algorithmic or programming language are usually called *statements*. Other names, such as *command, instruction,* or *order,* would probably be better, but *statement* is traditional. We should bear in mind, however, that the statements are *imperative statements*—each directs the person or machine executing the algorithm to take some action. The first statement of our algorithmic language that we will look at is the **output** statement, which allows an algorithm to produce printed output.

We will speak of the output as being printed, although in practice it may be displayed on a screen instead of printed on paper. Also, although algorithms in our algorithmic language cannot be directly executed by any computer, we assume that they will eventually be so executed after translation into a programming language. Ignoring this translation step, we will often speak of the computer as taking some action in response to a statement of the algorithmic language—printing a given value in response to an **output** statement, for example.

Most statements of the algorithmic language begin with a boldface keyword, such as **output,** which tells what action the statement accomplishes. Following the keyword is additional information that the computer needs to carry out the operation specified by the keyword. For the **output** statement, the keyword **output** is followed by the data items to be printed. For example,

output 3.1416

causes the computer to print

```
3.1416
```

and

output 'Computer programming is fun'

causes the computer to print

```
Computer programming is fun
```

Note that

output 'Don''t go near the water'

causes the computer to print

```
Don't go near the water
```

since the two single quote marks in succession in the string literal represent one quote mark in the string.

We can print more than one value with a single **output** statement by listing the values to be printed following the word **output.** The items in the list are separated by commas. The listed values are printed one after another, without any intervening spaces. Thus,

output 1, 2, 3, 4, 5

produces the output

```
12345
```

and

output 'A', 'B', 'C', 'D', 'E'

produces the output

```
ABCDE
```

To provide spacing between printed items, we can include spaces in character or string literals. Thus,

output 'The answer is ', 25

prints

```
The answer is 25
```

The space between "is" and "25" comes from the last space of the string literal. Likewise,

output 'The answers are: ', 25, ' ', 30, ' ', 50

prints

```
The answers are: 25 30 50
```

All the spaces are provided between the character and string literals.

More and tab Normally, each **output** statement prints on a separate line. Thus, the two statements

output 'The answer is '
output 25

print

```
The answer is
25
```

We can force two **output** statements to print on the same line by ending the first with the special command **more**, which indicates that there is more to come on the same line. Thus,

> **output** 'The answer is ', **more**
> **output** 25

prints

```
The answer is 25
```

A sequence of **output** statements ending in **more** all print on the same line. After an **output** statement not ending in **more**, a new line is started. Thus, the statements

> **output** 'a', **more**
> **output** 'b', **more**
> **output** 'c'
> **output** 'd', **more**
> **output** 'e', **more**
> **output** 'f'

cause the computer to print

```
abc
def
```

By allowing special formatting commands, such as **more**, to be listed along with items to be printed, we can produce printout in complex formats. Since our aim is simplicity rather than complexity, however, we will have occasion to use only one other formatting command, **tab**(*n*). We assume that the character positions on a printed line are numbered from left to right, with the leftmost character numbered 1. **tab**(*n*) instructs the computer to begin printing the next item in character position *n*. We can use **tab**(*n*) to arrange printed output in columns. For example,

> **output** 'Name', **tab**(10), 'Grade'
> **output** 'John', **tab**(12), 'A'
> **output** 'Karen', **tab**(12), 'C'
> **output** 'Larry' **tab**(12), 'B'
> **output** 'Sue', **tab**(12), 'F'

produces the printout

```
Name      Grade
John        A
Karen       C
Larry       B
Sue         F
```

An **output** statement without any data items or formatting commands causes the computer to go to the next line. Thus,

> **output** 'Name', **tab**(10), 'Grade'
> **output**
> **output** 'John', **tab**(12), 'A'
> **output** 'Karen', **tab**(12), 'C'
> **output** 'Larry' **tab**(12), 'B'
> **output** 'Sue', **tab**(12), 'F'

produces the printout

```
Name       Grade

John        A
Karen       C
Larry       B
Sue         F
```

6.3

Identifiers, constants, and algorithms

Identifiers   We often need to assign names to the various elements with which an algorithm works so that the same element can be referred to from different parts of the algorithm; such names are called *identifiers*. We must place some restrictions on identifiers to make sure that they can be distinguished from other elements of the language. For example, if 25 and 'computer' were allowed as identifiers, there would be no way to distinguish them from the integer constant 25 and the string 'computer'. Thus, we require that identifiers be formed according to the following two rules:

1. An identifer must be composed of the letters of the alphabet (upper case or lowercase) and the numerals 0 through 9. No other characters, such as spaces or hyphens, are allowed.

2. An identifier must begin with a letter of the alphabet.

According to these rules,

taxRate

Module25

SortThreeNumbers

itemCount

are all valid. Each of the following is invalid:

tax rate	space not allowed
employee#	# not allowed
Sort-three-numbers	hyphen not allowed
3rdFile	must start with letter

In this book we will follow the common practice of printing identifiers in italics.

Arbitrary names such as Tom, Dick, and Mary would be of little help to someone reading an algorithm and trying to determine the role played by each named
element. The names we choose, therefore, will usually be English *phrases*—several
English words describing the item in question, such as *SortThreeNumbers* for the
name of an algorithm and *taxRate* for the name of a real number.

The problem is how to combine several English words into a valid identifier and
yet allow the individual words to be easily read. One might allow spaces in identifiers, but then spaces could not be used to separate adjacent identifiers. Some languages allow hyphens in identifiers; however, in most computer character sets, the
hyphen and the minus sign are the same character, and it is difficult to prevent the
two from getting confused.

A method that has recently become popular, and which you have already noticed
in the examples, it is to capitalize each word except possibly the first. Thus, we can
easily pick out the three words making up *SortThreeNumbers,* which would be much
more difficult to do if the identifier had been written *Sortthreenumbers*. This is the
method that will be used in this book. We will capitalize the initial letter of the
names of major constructions such as algorithms and use lowercase for the first letter
otherwise. The word *Boolean* is an exception; it is usually capitalized since it is
derived from a person's name.

Another possibility, used in some languages, is to relax rule 1 to allow the
underscore character, _, in identifiers. Underscores are then used to separate the
words making up the identifier. Unlike hyphens and spaces, underscores do not cause
any problems with other parts of the language. With this convention, *SortThree-
Numbers* could be written *Sort_Three_Numbers* or *Sort_three_numbers*. You can use
this alternative method in your own algorithms, if you prefer it.

The algorithmic language contains some *predefined identifiers* that we can use
without providing definitions for them. The names of the predefined types, *integer,
real, Boolean, char,* and *string,* are predefined identifiers, as are the identifiers representing the two Boolean values, *true* and *false*.

Constants   *Constants* represent values that remain the same throughout the execution of an algorithm. They are in contrast to *variables* (introduced in Chapter 7),
whose values normally change during the execution of the algorithm. Literals are
examples of constants, since 25 will always represent twenty-five and 50 will always
represent fifty, regardless of what actions an algorithm might take.

We can also represent constants by identifiers, which are known as *constant
identifiers*. Using constant identifiers instead of literals can make an algorithm easier
to read. For example, if we encounter 0.045 in the middle of an algorithm, we might
be puzzled as to its significance. We need not puzzle over the significance of
salesTaxRate, however, although we will have to locate its definition to determine
its numerical value. Also, if 0.045 appears many times in an algorithm, and we need
to modify the algorithm to use a new sales tax rate, we must locate and change every
occurrence of 0.045. If *salesTaxRate* appears throughout an algorithm, however, we
need only to change its definition (which appears only once) to change the value
represented by each occurrence of *salesTaxRate*.

Constant definitions are preceded by the keyword **const**:

const *salesTaxRate* = 0.045

const *message* = 'Invalid input. Please try again'

Everywhere that *salesTaxRate* appears in the algorithm containing these definitions, the effect will be the same as if 0.045 had been written; everywhere that *message* appears the effect will be the same as if 'Invalid input. Please try again' had been written. We refer to *salesTaxRate* and *message* as *constant identifiers*. By the definition of constants, the values associated with *salesTaxRate* and *message* remain the same throughout the algorithm containing the definitions. An algorithm can no more change the value of *salesTaxRate* than it can change the value of 0.045.

Algorithms Now let's see what a complete algorithm looks like in our algorithmic language. An algorithm has the following general form:

algorithm name
declare
      definitions and declarations
execute
      statements to be executed
end name

The name of the algorithm, which is an identifier made up by the programmer, appears after the keyword **algorithm** that begins the algorithm and also after the keyword **end** that ends the algorithm. The algorithm itself consists of two major sections. The section introduced by **declare** contains definitions and other descriptive information that the computer needs to execute the algorithm. The only thing we have looked at so far that would go into the **declare** section is constant definitions. The section introduced by **execute** contains the imperative statements that the computer is to execute. The **output** statement that we looked at earlier in this chapter would go in the **execute** section.

Figure 6.1 is an example of a complete, if not very useful, algorithm. When this algorithm is executed, it produces the output

```
The sales tax rate used to be 0.045
Now it's 0.06
That's too high
```

The name of the algorithm is *ConstantsAndOutput;* note that this name appears on both the first and last line of the algorithm.

The braces { and } are used to enclose *comments*. Comments are for the sake of someone trying to understand the algorithm; they are ignored when the algorithm is executed. Comments can be inserted between lines or at any point on a line where a blank space could go. Comments are used for two purposes: (1) as here, to describe the purpose and operation of the algorithm or some part of it; and (2) to exhibit assertions that will be used to prove the correctness of the algorithm.

Figure 6.1   Algorithm illustrating algorithm format, constant definitions,
and the **output** statement. Note the heading line (beginning
with **algorithm**), the comment, the **declare** section, the
constant definitions, the **execute** section, the **output**
statements, and the terminating line (beginning with **end**).

---

algorithm *ConstantsAndOutput*

{ Illustrate constant definitions and output }

declare
    const *oldSalesTaxRate* = 0.045
    const *newSalesTax Rate* = 0.06
    const *complaint* = 'That''s too high'
execute
    output 'The sales tax rate used to be ', *oldSalesTaxRate*
    output 'Now, it''s ', *newSalesTaxRate*
    output *complaint*
end *ConstantsAndOutput*

The **declare** section defines three constant identifiers: *oldSalesTaxRate, new-SalesTaxRate,* and *complaint*. The first two represent real constants and the third represents a string constant.

The **execute** section contains three **output** statements, which are executed in the order in which they appear in the algorithm. The statement-by-statement execution of an algorithm is an example of the *sequencing* control structure. As expected, each **output** statement prints the data items following the keyword. Note that constant identifiers are treated as if they were replaced by their defined values. Thus, when *oldSalesTaxRate* occurs in an **output** statement, 0.045 is printed; when *newSales-TaxRate* occurs, 0.06 is printed, and so on.

Note that, aside from comments, the algorithm is made up of three kinds of symbols:

1. *Keywords,* which are printed in boldface and have predefined meanings in the algorithmic language. The keywords in the example algorithm are **algorithm, declare, const, execute, output,** and **end.**

2. *Identifiers,* such as *ConstantsAndOutput,* which are printed in italics.

3. *Literals,* such as 0.045 and 'That''s too high', which are printed in roman letters (neither boldface nor italics).

In writing algorithms by hand, it is customary to underline keywords but otherwise to use ordinary handwriting for all parts of the algorithm.

6.4 Arithmetical operations and expressions

Any sequence of characters that designates a value is called an *expression*. An expression designating an integer or real value is an *arithmetical expression;* an expression designating a Boolean value is a *Boolean expression,* and so on. Literals and constant identifiers both denote values, so both are special cases of expressions.

A common way of designating a value is to describe how it can be computed. The result of the computation is the value of the expression. For example, $3 + 5$ designates the integer value 8, and $25.7 - 14.2$ designates the real value 11.5. In this section we will look at expressions describing the computations of integer and real values. Expressions for computing values of other types, such as Boolean values, will be discussed in later chapters.

The value designated by an expression is called the *value of the expression.* We *evaluate* an expression when we compute its value.

Arithmetical operators An *operator* is a symbol representing an operation that is carried out on values and yields another value as a result. The symbols $+$ and $-$ are familiar arithmetical operators, corresponding to the operations of addition and subtraction. The values operated on by an operator are called its *operands.* The following are the arithmetical operators in the algorithmic language:

$+$	addition
$-$	subtraction
$*$	multiplication
/, **div**, and **mod**	division
$**$	exponentiation

Addition and subtraction are represented by the usual signs $+$ and $-$. The usual signs for multiplication and division are not available on most computer keyboards, so $*$ and / are used instead. **Div** and **mod**, which are represented by keywords rather than signs, are used for quotient-remainder division of integers, which yields an integer quotient and an integer remainder instead of a real quotient.

Exponentiation is the operation of raising a number to a power, which is usually symbolized by a raised exponent, as in 2^3 and 10^4. The second operand of $**$ is the exponent, which tells how many instances of the first operand are to be multiplied together. Thus, $2 ** 3$ represents the same value as $2 * 2 * 2$ or 8, and $10 ** 4$ represents the same value as $10 * 10 * 10 * 10$ or 10000. Noninteger exponents such as 1.5 are also allowed; however, we will not go into the meaning of noninteger exponents, which are taken up in algebra and other mathematics courses. We will have little need for exponentiation in studying computer science; indeed, Pascal, the most popular programming language for teaching computer science, does not provide exponentiation. Since many languages do provide an exponentiation operator, however, it is included here for completeness.

The arithmetical operators can be applied to both integer and real operands. For $+$, $-$, $*$, and $**$, if both operands are integers, the result is an integer. If either or both operands are real numbers, however, the result is a real number. The following expressions illustrate this rule for $+$:

Expression	Value	Type
3 + 5	8	*integer*
3.0 + 5	8.0	*real*
3 + 5.0	8.0	*real*
3.0 + 5.0	8.0	*real*

This rule is not satisfactory for division, however, since even when two integers are divided the result may be a real number. For example, dividing 3 by 2 yields 1.5. Nor may it be possible to represent the result of the division exactly. For example, dividing 1 by 3 yields the repeating decimal 0.33333333. . . . Since this result contains an infinite number of digits, it cannot be represented in the type *real* available on any actual computer system. If the type *real* that is available allows six significant digits, then the best we can do is approximate the value of 1 / 3 by 0.333333. For these reasons, the division operator / gives a real result regardless of whether its operands are integers or real numbers:

Expression	Value	Type
3 / 2	1.5	*real*
3.0 / 2	1.5	*real*
3 / 2.0	1.5	*real*
3.0 / 2.0	1.5	*real*

There is, however, a way of dividing two integers and obtaining exact, integer results. This is the *quotient-remainder* division often taught in grade school before fractions and decimals are taken up. With quotient-remainder division, we compute an integer quotient and an integer remainder instead of a single real quotient:

$$
\begin{array}{r}
4 \\
3\overline{)14} \\
12 \\
\hline
2
\end{array}
$$

(quotient)

(remainder)

In the algorithmic language, the **div** operator computes the integer quotient, and the **mod** operator computes the integer remainder:

Expression	Value
14 **div** 3	4
14 **mod** 3	2

Since expressions represent values, we can use them to specify the values to be printed by an **output** statement. The algorithm in Figure 6.2 illustrates the use of

Figure 6.2   Algorithm illustrating the use of expressions in the **output** statement. Since no definitions or declarations are needed, the **declare** section is empty. This is a rare occurrence; only the most trivial of algorithms can get by without any definitions or declarations. In the **output** statements, be careful to distinguish between string literals such as $'3 + 5 = '$ and expressions such as $3 + 5$.

---

algorithm *Expressions*

{ Illustrate use of expressions in output statement }

declare

   { Nothing to declare }

execute
   output $'3 + 5 = '$, $3 + 5$
   output $'3 - 5 = '$, $3 - 5$
   output $'3 * 5 = '$, $3 * 5$
   output $'3 / 5 = '$, $3 / 5$
   output $'10$ div $3 = '$, 10 **div** 3
   output $'10$ mod $3 = '$, 10 **mod** 3
   output $'3 ** 2 = '$, $3 ** 2$
end *Expressions*

---

expressions in an **output** statement. When executed, this algorithm produces the following output:

```
3 + 5 = 8
3 - 5 = -2
3 * 5 = 15
3 / 5 = 0.6
10 div 3 = 3
10 mod 3 = 1
3 ** 2 = 9
```

Note carefully that $'3 + 5 = '$ is a string literal, *not* an arithmetical expression, and it is simply printed as is when it is encountered in an **output** statement. When the expression $3 + 5$ is encountered, however, it is evaluated—the addition is done—and its value, 8, is printed.

More complex arithmetical expressions It is often convenient to specify more than one arithmetical operation in an expression. For example, the expression

3 + 2 + 9 + 8

specifies that the values of 3, 2, 9, and 8 are to be added, and

3 * 2 * 9 * 8

specifies that the same values are to be multiplied.

When we use different operators in the same expression, we must be concerned about the order in which the operators will be applied—the order in which the corresponding operations will be carried out—since different orders will cause the computation to have different results. For example,

2 + 3 * 4

has different values depending on whether the addition or the multiplication is done first. If the addition is done first, we get

2 + 3 * 4 =
   5 * 4 =
    20

On the other hand, if the multiplication is done first, we get

2 + 3 * 4 =
2 + 12 =
14

To determine the order in which operators are to be applied, we assign a *priority* to each operator. Operators with higher priority are applied before operators with lower priority. Operators with the same priority are applied in left-to-right order as they occur in the expression. The following are the priorities of the arithmetical operators:

**	*highest priority*
*, /, **div**, and **mod**	
+ and −	*lowest priority*

Operators listed on the same line, such as + and −, have the same priority. To evaluate an expression, all the exponentiations are carried out, then all the multiplications and divisions, and finally all the additions and subtractions.

Here are some examples of expression evaluation using operator priorities:

Example 1:   2 + 3 * 4 =
    2 + 12 =   *Multiplication first . . .*
    14   *. . . then addition*

Example 2:   2 * 3 ** 4 =
    2 * 81 =   *Exponentiation first . . .*
    162   *. . . then multiplication*

Example 3: $4 + 3 ** 2 =$

$4 + 9 =$ *Exponentiation first . . .*

13 *. . . then addition*

Example 4: $2 + 9 \textbf{ mod } 2 ** 3 =$

$2 + 9 \textbf{ mod } 8 =$ *Exponentiation first . . .*

$2 + 1 =$ *. . . then division . . .*

3 *. . . and then addition*

Operators with the same priority are evaluated in left-to-right order:

Example 5: $3 + 4 - 2 =$

$7 - 2 =$ *Leftmost operator first . . .*

5 *. . . then next operator to the right*

Example 6: $12 / 4 * 3 =$

$3.0 * 3 =$ *Leftmost operator first . . .*

9.0 *. . . then next operator to right*

Warning: Because of the way built-up fractions like

$$\frac{12}{4 * 3} = \frac{12}{12} = 1$$

are treated in arithmetic and algebra, people sometimes expect the multiplication to be done before the division in Example 6. But this is incorrect: multiplication and division have the same priority and are evaluated in left-to-right order as they occur in the expression.

Parentheses   Sometimes we want the operators in an expression to be applied in some other order than the one dictated by the priorities. We can enforce the order we want by enclosing part of the expression in parentheses. The part of the expression in parentheses is evaluated first, regardless of the priorities:

Example 7: $(2 + 3) * 4 =$

$5 * 4 =$ *Parenthesized part first . . .*

20 *. . . then rest of expression*

Example 8: $(4 + 3) ** 2 =$

$7 ** 2 =$ *Parenthesized part first . . .*

49 *. . . then rest of expression*

Sets of parentheses can be nested one inside the other. When this occurs, the part of the expression in the innermost set of nested parentheses is evaluated first, then the part in the next outermost set, and so on.

Example 9:

((2 + 3) * 4) ** 2 =
(5 * 4) ** 2 =   *Inner parentheses first . . .*
20 ** 2 =   *. . . then outer ones . . .*
400   *. . . and then rest of expression*

6.5

Functions

Abs   Not all operations are represented by signs, at least by signs that are available on computer printers and display devices. Consider, for example the *absolute value* operation, which leaves a positive number unchanged but changes a negative number into the corresponding positive number. We can indicate this operation as follows:

$abs(5) = 5$

$abs(-5) = 5$

$abs(3.1416) = 3.1416$

$abs(-3.1416) = 3.1416$

We call *abs* a *function*. The parenthesized value following *abs* is the *argument* of the function. The function, together with its argument, forms an expression whose value is the result of applying the function to its argument. We sometimes speak of this value as the value *returned* by the function. The value returned by *abs* is of type *integer* if the argument is of type *integer* and is of type *real* if the argument is of type *real*.

The argument of the function may itself be an expression. Since the argument is in parentheses, it is evaluated before the function is applied:

Example 10:

$abs(5 - 6 * 3) =$
$abs(5 - 18) =$ *Evaluate argument . . .*
$abs(-13) =$
13   *. . . then apply function*

A function with its argument can be used as part of another expression:

Example 11:

$3 + 2 * abs(7 - 50)$
$3 + 2 * abs(-43)$ *Evaluate argument . . .*
$3 + 2 * 43$ *. . . then apply function . . .*
$3 + 86$ *. . . multiplication next . . .*
89   *. . . and then addition*

Trunc   The function *trunc* converts a real number into an integer by discarding all digits to the right of the radix point (truncation). The argument of *trunc* must be a real number; the value returned is an integer:

$trunc(3.1416) = 3$

$trunc(25.0) = 25$

$trunc(4.75) = 4$

$trunc(-3.1416) = -3$

$trunc(-4.75) = -4$

Round   Like *trunc*, round converts a real number to an integer. *Round*, however, rounds the real number to the nearest integer, instead of just discarding the digits to the right of the radix point:

$round(3.1416) = 3$

$round(25.0) = 25$

$round(4.75) = 5$

$round(-3.1416) = -3$

$round(-4.75) = -5$

As with *trunc*, the argument of *round* must always be a real number, and an integer result is always returned. *Trunc* and *round* are sometimes called *type transfer functions*, since they convert, or transfer, values from one type *(integer)* to another *(real)*.

Sqrt   The *sqrt* function takes the square root of its argument. The argument can be either an integer or a real number; in either case, a real result is returned:

$sqrt(25) = 5.0$

$sqrt(9) = 3.0$

$sqrt(2.25) = 1.5$

The function names *abs, trunc, round,* and *sqrt* are examples of predefined identifiers.

Review questions

1. What is the basis for classifying data into different types?

2. What is a *value?*

3. Describe briefly each of the five data types discussed in this chapter.

4. Contrast the types *real* and *integer*.

5. Which of the data types described in this chapter has only two values? What is this data type used for?

6. Distinguish between 3.1416 and '3.1416'. Between '3 + 5' and 3 + 5.

7. Any character that indicates the beginning or end of a particular language construction is called a *delimiter*. What is the delimiter for character literals and strings?

8. What are *identifiers?* Give the two rules according to which identifiers are formed.

9. What are *constants?* Give two language constructions that can represent constants.

10. Give the general format for writing an algorithm. What parts of an algorithm are printed in boldface? In italics? What are the functions of keywords, identifiers, and literals?

11. What is an *expression?* Give three different constructions discussed in this chapter that serve as expressions.

12. Give the seven arithmetical operators described in this chapter. Give the types allowed for the operands of each and state how the type of the result depends on the types of the operands.

13. What is *quotient-remainder division?* What arithmetical operators are used for quotient-remainder division?

14. Explain the use of *operator priorities* to determine the order in which operators are applied in arithmetical expressions.

15. State in words the order of operator application implied by the operator priorities.

16. Algebra students use the catch phrase ''my dear Aunt Sally'' to remember that multiplications and divisions are done before additions and subtractions. Extend the phrase to take exponentiation into account.

17. What is the *argument* of a function? The *result returned by the function?*

18. Describe briefly the four functions discussed in this chapter.

19. What two *type transfer functions* are described in this chapter?

20. When a function occurs in an expression, which is evaluated first, the argument of the function or the rest of the expression?

Exercises

1. Write each of the following in floating-point notation:
   (a) 1000.0
   (b) 254000.0
   (c) 345600000.0
   (d) 1000000000.0

    (e) 0.01

    (f) 0.00015

    (g) 0.00234

    (h) 0.0000054

2. Write each of the following in conventional notation:

    (a) 1E5

    (b) 1.25E+4

    (c) 6.02E23

    (d) 7.549E+2

    (e) 3.5E−1

    (f) 6.43E−2

    (g) 7.05E−5

    (h) 1.0E−1

3. Evaluate the following expressions:

    (a) 3 + 12 − 4

    (b) 3 + 4 * 12

    (c) 4 + 12 / 4

    (d) 12 **div** 4 − 3

    (e) 24 / 6 * 4

    (f) 3 * 3 ** 3

    (g) 3 + 2 * 5 + 7

    (h) 2 * 5 − 3 * 4 + 7 **mod** 2

    (i) 4 ** 3 / 8

    (j) 12 / 4 / 3

4. Compare the results of evaluating the parenthesized and unparenthesized expressions:

    (a) 10 / 5 * 2   10 / (5 * 2)

    (b) 12 − 4 * 3   (12 − 4) * 3

    (c) 3 * 4 ** 2   (3 * 4) **2

    (d) 3 − 4 + 12   3 − (4 + 12)

    (e) 7 − 4 − 3   7 − (4 − 3)

    (f) 16 / 4 / 2   16 / (4 / 2)

5. Which of the following are invalid?

    (a) 6.5 **div** 3

    (b) 9.2 **mod** 4

    (c) 9 **mod** 5 / 2

    (d) 13 / 5 **mod** 2

    (e) 13 / (5 **mod** 2)

    (f) 10.0 **div** 5.0

    (g) (9 / 2) **div** 6

    (h) (13 **mod** 4) / 2

6. What will be printed by each of the following sets of **output** statements?

    (a) **output** 'pi = ', 3.1416

      (b) **output** 'pi = '
          output 3.1416
      (c) **output** 'pi = ', **more**
          output 3.1416
      (d) **output** '7∗5 − 6∗3 = ', 7∗5 − 6∗3

7. Evaluate each of the following expressions and give the type of the value
   obtained:
   (a) *abs*(− 100)
   (b) *abs*(3.45)
   (c) *trunc*(6.93)
   (d) *trunc*(9.32)
   (e) *round*(6.93)
   (f) *round*(9.32)
   (g) *sqrt*(16)
   (h) *sqrt*(16.0)

8. Which of the following identifiers are invalid?
   (c) *lineCounter*
   (b) *Scan Game Board*
   (c) *employee#*
   (d) *Part100*
   (e) *10sCounter*
   (f) *$Amount*
   (g) *section12Count*
   (h) *Print.Final.Report*

9. Write an algorithm to compute and output the volume of a box 73 centimeters long, 47 centimeters wide, and 29 centimeters high.

10. A field is 39 meters wide and 67 meters long. Write an algorithm to com-
    pute and output how many meters of fence wire will be required to enclose
    the field.

Pascal Supplement

Pascal is now the most widely used programming language for teaching computer
science, having largely supplanted FORTRAN, which once enjoyed that distinction,
and PL/I, which once aspired to it. Many of the chapters of this book are accompanied by Pascal supplements, such as this one, which describe the Pascal language
and show how to translate the algorithms studied in the chapter into Pascal.

    Some constructions in Pascal are similar or identical to the corresponding ones
in the algorithmic language, and these similarities are pointed out when they exist.
Such constructions are fully described in the Pascal supplements, however, even at
the expense of repeating some of the material in the main text, so that you do not
have to turn back to discussions of the algorithmic language in order to learn Pascal.
On the other hand, the definitions, concepts, and programming principles discussed

in the main text are not repeated in the supplements. For example, the Pascal data types *integer, real, Boolean,* and *char* are described fully in this supplement, even though they are the same as the corresponding types introduced in the main text for the algorithmic language. On the other hand, the discussion of what data types are and why we need them is included only in the main text.

In short, although the Pascal supplements are complete as far as the details of Pascal are concerned, you will need to read the corresponding chapters in the main text first for the concepts and principles needed to understand the discussion of Pascal.

The supplements describe ANSI/IEEE standard Pascal, the version of Pascal standardized by the American National Standards Institute and the Institute for Electrical and Electronics Engineers. Since this standard only recently went into effect, deviations from it will be found in many existing Pascal systems. Some of the most common deviations will be mentioned to warn you of the variations likely to be encountered among actual Pascal systems. A few extensions to Pascal, which go beyond the standard, are discussed because of their inherent interest.

Data types

Pascal provides the predefined data types *integer, real, Boolean,* and *char,* each of which is identical to the corresponding type in the algorithmic language. Pascal does not provide a predefined type *string;* however, string literals are allowed.

Type integer   Type *integer* consists of the positive and negative whole numbers lying in a particular range, which can vary from one system to another. Integer literals are written in conventional decimal notation:

$$300 \qquad -25 \qquad +65 \qquad 9000 \qquad -825$$

Commas are not allowed in integer literals, so the following are invalid:

$$3,000 \qquad 25,700 \qquad -8,325$$

Instead, we must write:

$$3000 \qquad 25700 \qquad -8325$$

Pascal provides a predefined identifier* *maxint* representing the largest value of type *integer*. Values of type *integer* range from $-maxint$ through *maxint*. For example, if the value of *maxint* is 32767, then type *integer* consists of all whole numbers in the range -32767 through 32767. A Pascal program can refer to the value of *maxint* to determine the range of integer values available for the Pascal system on which the program is being executed.

---

*Identifiers in Pascal are described in the next section.

Type real   Type *real* consists of numbers that can contain decimal points. When real literals are written in conventional (not floating-point) notation, the decimal point must be present:

    123.45   0.457 -96.35 250.0

Commas are not allowed, so the following are invalid:

    1,234.79   123,762.23 $-45,221.0$

Instead, they must be written as

    1234.79   123762.23 -45221.0

Pascal requires that a decimal point be preceded by and followed by at least one digit; that is, a number cannot begin or end with a decimal point. Thus, the following are invalid:

    .35   .01   25. $-1000.$

Instead, we must write

    0.35   0.01   25.0 -1000.0

Real numbers can also be written in floating-point notation, such as 3.5E4. As in the algorithmic language, the number following the letter E is the *exponent,* which tells how many places to the left or right the decimal point should be moved. If the exponent is positive, the decimal point is to be moved to the right; if the exponent is negative, the decimal point is to be moved to the left. Thus, $3.5E+4$ represents the same value as 35000.0, and $2.9E-3$ represents the same value as 0.0029.

Since only values of type *real* can be written in floating-point notation, the decimal point that signals real values can be omitted. When the decimal point is omitted, it is assumed to immediately precede the letter E. Thus, in the following examples, each set of three literals represents the same value:

$3E+5$	$3.0E+5$	300000.0
$25E+2$	$25.0E+2$	2500.0
$5E-3$	$5.0E-3$	0.005
$30E-4$	$30.0E-4$	0.003

If a decimal point is present in a floating-point literal, it must still be preceded and followed by at least one digit. Thus, the following are invalid:

    $.35E+4$ $7.E-3$

Instead, we must write

    $0.35E+4$ $7.0E-3$ (or $7E-3$)

Type Boolean   Type *Boolean* contains two values, which are represented by the predefined identifiers *true* and *false*.

Type char   Type *char* consists of the characters available on a particular Pascal system. The available characters will vary from one system to another, and the *graphics*—the printed symbols that represent the characters—may vary from one output device to another. Character literals are enclosed in single quote marks (apostrophes):

    'a'   'C'   '3'   '@'

Don't confuse the apostrophe with the grave accent, `, which is also present on many computer keyboards. A single quote mark is represented by a pair of single quote marks enclosed in single quotes, giving four single quote marks in all:

    ''''

This is typed by pressing the single quote key four times. Don't confuse two single quotes in succession with the double quote, which is an entirely different character.

String literals   Pascal does not provide a predefined type *string;* types containing strings must be defined by the programmer using techniques that will be described in later chapters. Predefined string literals *are* provided, however, and can be used for such purposes as printing messages to the user. As in the algorithmic language, string literals are enclosed in single quote marks:

    'Pascal'

    'computer science'

    '325'

    '$$$$'

A single quote mark is represented in a string literal by two single quote marks in succession. Thus the string literal

    'We''re going home this weekend'

represents the string:

    We're going home this weekend

Again, don't confuse the two single quotes in succession with the double-quote-mark character.

Ordinal types   Types *integer, Boolean,* and *char* are known as *ordinal* types. Ordinal types have a variety of uses other than the specific purpose for which each type was designed. Values of ordinal types can be used for counting, for designating entries in lists or tables, and for selecting which statement is to be executed in a particular situation. In describing what types may be used for a particular purpose, the expression "any ordinal type" will be frequently used. Note particularly that type *real* is *not* an ordinal type; real numbers can be used only for arithmetical calculations.

Output

Output in Pascal is done by *procedures,* which are parts of a program that can be called by name to do a particular job. Procedures can be predefined or defined by the programmer. The Pascal output procedures *write* and *writeln* (''write line'') are predefined.

A procedure is called with a *procedure statement,* which consists of the name of the procedure followed by a list of *parameters* giving the procedure the information it needs to do its job. The list of parameters is enclosed in parentheses. For both *write* and *writeln,* the parameters give the data values that are to be printed.

For example, the procedure statement

writeln(20, 35, 90)

calls the *writeln* procedure to print three integer values. The computer prints

```
20      35      90
```

The spacing between the printed values will vary from one Pascal system to another. Likewise,

writeln('The answer is ', 100)

calls *writeln* to print a string and an integer:

```
The answer is     100
```

Again, the spacing is system dependent.

We will often find it convenient to refer to a procedure statement by the name of the procedure that the statement calls. Thus, we will refer to a procedure statement that calls *write* as a *write statement* and to a procedure statement that calls *writeln* as a *writeln statement.*

When *writeln* finishes printing the values of its parameters, it goes to a new print line on the display or printed page. Thus when a sequence of *writeln* statements is executed, the output from each statement appears on a separate line. For example, the statements

writeln('abc');
writeln('def');
writeln('ghi')

produce the printout:

```
abc
def
ghi
```

A *writeln* statement without any parameters causes the display or printer to go to a new line. For example, the statements

writeln('abc');
writeln;

```
writeln('ghi')
```

produce the printout

```
abc
```
                    (this line is skipped)
```
ghi
```

Write, on the other hand, does not go to a new line after printing the values of its parameters. Thus when a sequence of *write* statements is executed, the output from all the statements appears on the same line. For example, the statements

> *write*('abc');
> *write*('def');
> *write*('ghi')

produce the printout:

```
abcdefghi
```

What's more, since the last statement in the sequence is a *write* statement, the printing device remains on the line on which the output was printed, and the next output statement *(write* or *writeln)* will print its output on the same line.

In terms of the algorithmic language, *writeln* is equivalent to the normal **output** statement, which goes to a new line after printing the requested output. *Write* is equivalent to an **output** statement ending with the **more** command, which specifies that the print device is to remain on the same line after the output has been printed.

In the preceding examples, note that the statements in each sequence are separated by semicolons. The semicolons occur only between statements; there is no semicolon before the first statement of the sequence and none following the last statement. The role of the semicolons as statement separators is more evident if the statements are all written on one line:

> *writeln*('abc'); *writeln*('def'); *writeln*('ghi')

Field-width parameters A *field* is the area on a printed line in which a particular data value is printed. *Write* and *writeln* allow us to specify the size of the field in which each value will be printed by means of a *field-width parameter.* The printed value is *right-justified* in the field: it is positioned as far to the right in the field as possible. Any unused positions of the field are filled with blanks. For example, in

> *writeln*('abc':10)

the field-width parameter 10 specifies that the value of 'abc' will be printed in a field 10 characters wide. Since the printed value is right-justified in the field, the value of 'abc' is preceded by seven blank spaces to fill out the 10-character field. The field-width parameter follows the value to be printed and is separated from it by a colon.

To make blanks visible in example printouts, we will represent each blank by a number sign, #. With this convention, we can represent the printout produced by the *writeln* statement as follows:

```
#######abc
```

Likewise, the statement

writeln('abc':10, 'def':8, 'ghi':15)

produces the printout

#######abc#####def############ghi

or, as it would actually appear, with the #s replaced by the blanks they represent

       abc   def   ghi

When the field width is less than the number of characters in the string to be printed, the string is *truncated* on the right—that is, as many characters as necessary are discarded from the right end of the string so that the string will fit the field. For example,

writeln('supervisor':4)

prints

super

When no field-width parameter is supplied, a default field width is used. For string and character values, the default field width is simply the number of characters making up the value to be printed. Thus,

writeln('abc')

prints three characters

abc

without any additional blanks, and

writeln('abc', 'def', 'ghi')

prints each value in a three-character field:

abcdefghi

Note that a field width equal to the number of characters to be printed is often exactly what we want for strings, so we frequently do not use field-width parameters when printing strings.

For integer, real, and Boolean values, the default field widths are implementation defined—they vary from one Pascal system to another. Thus,

writeln(10, 200, 3000)

would print

######10#####200####3000

on a system where the default field width is eight characters and would print

102003000

on a system where the default field width is the number of digits to be printed. Because we cannot rely on all systems to have the same default field widths, and because the default field widths provided by a particular system may not be convenient for our purposes, we usually use field-width parameters when printing integer, real, and Boolean values.

Like strings, integers are printed right-justified in their fields, with any unused positions filled with blanks. Thus,

writeln(10:6, −200:6, 3000:6)

prints

####10##−200##3000

or as the printout would actually appear

10   −200   3000

For real values, if we specify only the field widths, the values are printed in floating-point notation. Thus,

writeln(105.25:15, −73.5:15, 1000.0:15)

prints

####1.05250E+02###−7.35000E+01####1.00000E+03

or as the printout would actually appear

1.05250E+02   −7.35000E+01   1.00000E+03

Some details of the floating-point representation, such as the number of decimal places and the number of digits in the exponent, are implementation defined.

To get real numbers printed in conventional fixed-point notation, we must follow the field-width parameter with another parameter giving the number of decimal places to be printed. For example,

writeln(105.25:15:2, −73.5:15:2, 1000.0:15:2)

specifies that each value is to be printed in fixed-point notation with two decimal places:

#########105.25#########−73.50#########1000.00

or, as it would actually appear

105.25   −73.50   1000.00

For integers and real numbers, if the specified field width makes the field too small to hold the value to be printed, the field-width parameter is ignored and the field is made as large as needed to hold the printed value. Integer and real values are *not* truncated as string values are. For example,

writeln('Please pay $', 125.95:1:2, ' on your account')

causes the computer to print

```
Please pay $125.95 on your account
```

By specifying a field width of 1, which we know to be too small, we leave it to the computer to choose a field just large enough to contain the printed value, without any additional blanks. This technique is useful when we wish to insert a numerical value in running text and so do not want any unnecessary blanks to be printed*.

The Boolean values *true* and *false* are printed as if they were the character strings 'true' and 'false', except that the default field width is implementation defined. Because the values are printed as if they were strings, they can be truncated to *t* or *f*, which may be convenient when many Boolean values are to be printed. For example,

writeln(*true*:1, *false*:1, *true*:1, *true*:1)

prints

```
t f t t
```

Pascal does not provide an equivalent of the **tab** command that we use in the algorithmic language for lining up printed values in columns. However, we can get much the same effect by specifying the same field width for each item in a column, including the column headings. Different field widths can be used for different columns. For example, the statements

writeln('Name':5, 'Grade':10);
writeln;
writeln('John':5, 'A':10);
writeln('Karen':5, 'C':10);
writeln('Larry':5, 'B':10);
writeln('Sue':5, 'F':10)

produce the printout

```
Name    Grade

John        A
Karen       C
Larry       B
  Sue       F
```

---

*According to the Pascal standard, no blanks should be printed before an integer or a real number in fixed-point notation when the specified field width makes the field too small to hold the number. However, some existing systems deviate from the standard by always preceding a positive number with at least one blank space (the blank space occupies the same position that would be occupied by the sign of a negative number). On such systems it is impossible to print a dollar sign (or any other character) immediately to the left of a number.

Identifiers

The following three rules govern the formation of identifiers in Pascal:

1. Identifiers are made up of the letters of the alphabet and the numerals 0 through 9.

2. An identifier must begin with a letter.

3. An identifier must not have the same spelling as any of the following *reserved words:*

and	**downto**	**if**	**or**	**then**
array	**else**	**in**	**packed**	**to**
begin	**end**	**label**	**procedure**	**type**
case	**file**	**mod**	**program**	**until**
const	**for**	**nil**	**record**	**var**
div	**function**	**not**	**repeat**	**while**
do	**goto**	**of**	**set**	**with**

As in the algorithmic language, identifiers will be printed in italics and reserved words (keywords, operators, and one constant) will be printed in boldface. When a program is entered into a computer, however, the distinction between italics and boldface is usually lost, so we cannot rely on typeface to distinguish reserved words from identifiers. Hence we require rule 3, which prevents any identifier from having the same spelling as a reserved word.

An identifier can be of any length—that is, it can contain any number of characters. In standard Pascal, all the characters of an identifier are significant: all are taken into account in distinguishing one identifier from another. However, existing Pascal language processors frequently do place a limit on the number of significant characters, a common choice being to let only the first eight characters be significant. If only the first eight characters are significant. *SubtractExpenses* and *Subtract-Returns* represent the same identifier, since both begin with the same eight characters. In standard Pascal, however, they would represent different identifiers, since, in comparing the two, standard Pascal would take all the characters into account.

As in the algorithmic language, capital letters can be used to make the individual words forming an identifier stand out, as in *SubtractExpenses, interestRate, high-Score,* and *FindNextMove.* Some versions of Pascal allow the underscore character in identifiers, so that identifiers such as *interest_rate* and *Find_next_move* are allowed. Identifiers containing underscores are not valid in standard Pascal, however.

Pascal provides a number of *predefined identifiers*—identifiers for which definitions have already been given. We have already encountered the predefined identifiers *integer, real, Boolean,* and *char* for data types, *maxint* for the largest value of type *integer, true* and *false* for the two values of type *Boolean,* and *write* and *writeln* for the output procedures. Unlike the case with reserved words, you can redefine a predefined identifier. Your definition will replace the one built into Pascal. Redefining predefined identifiers is not recommended for two reasons: (1) You lose access to the Pascal feature designated by the predefined identifier; if you provide new definitions for *write* and *writeln,* you will have no way to call the standard output procedures. (2) You confuse people reading your program, who will expect the standard definitions for predefined identifiers and may overlook the fact that you have redefined some of them.

The following are some examples of valid, invalid, and poorly chosen programmer-defined identifiers:

errorCount	valid
x35	valid but poor—does not describe the item to which it refers
WriteMasterFile	valid
pay rate	invalid—space not allowed
%interest	invalid—% not allowed
30DayTotal	invalid—must start with letter
real	poor—redefines predefined identifier
begin	invalid—same spelling as reserved word

Constant definitions

Like the algorithmic language, Pascal allows constants to be represented by identifiers as well as literals. Three predefined identifiers with which we are already familiar, *maxint, true,* and *false,* represent constant values. Programmers can define identifiers to represent constant values in the *constant definition part* of a Pascal program, which is introduced with the reserved word **const**:

const
    seatingCapacity = 2500;
    discountRate = 0.075;
    request = 'Insert your data disk in drive B';

The reserved word **const** is followed by a series of *constant definitions*. Each constant definition consists of the identifier being defined, an equal sign, and a constant representing the value to be given to the identifier. Each constant definition ends with a semicolon. Constant identifiers can be defined to represent integers, real numbers, characters, and strings.

A constant identifier can also be defined in terms of another, previously defined constant identifier. If the previously defined identifier represents a number, it can be preceded by a plus or minus sign:

const
    rangeUpperlimit = 5000;
    rangeLowerLimit = −*rangeUpperLimit*;

The constant identifier *rangeLowerLimit* represents the integer value -5000.

Note that the term *literal* is not a part of standard Pascal terminology. Pascal uses the word *constant* both for constants represented by literals and those represented by constant identifiers.

Program format

A Pascal program has the following general form:

program program-name(parameters);
definition and declaration parts
begin
    sequence of statements to be executed
end.

Figure 6.3 shows a complete Pascal program, the Pascal translation of the algorithm in Figure 6.1. The first line of the program

program *ConstantsAndOutput(output)*;

Figure 6.3 The Pascal translation of the algorithm in Figure 6.1. Note the program heading, the file parameter *output,* the comment, the constant definition part, the constant definitions, the compound statement, the *writeln* statements, and the period that terminates the program. Also note that the program heading and the constant definitions are each *terminated* by a semicolon, whereas the statements making up the compound statement are *separated* by semicolons.

```
program ConstantsAndOutput(output);

{ Illustrate constant definitions and output }

const
    oldSalesTaxRate = 0.045;
    newSalesTaxRate = 0.06;
    complaint = 'That''s too high';
begin
    writeln('The sales tax rate used to be ', oldSalesTaxRate:5:3);
    writeln('Now it''s ', newSalesTaxRate:4:2);
    writeln(complaint)
end.
```

is the *program heading*. The reserved word **program** is followed by the name of the program, which is a programmer-defined identifier. Thus the name of the program in Figure 6.3 is *ConstantsAndOutput*.

In Pascal, a *file* is any source from which data can be obtained or any destination to which data can be sent. Input and output devices, such as keyboards and displays, are considered as much files as are sets of data stored in auxiliary memory. The heading of a Pascal program must list as parameters the names of all files that the program will use. Two standard files are represented by predefined identifiers: *input* is the standard input file, usually the user's keyboard, and *output* is the standard output file, usually the user's display. Unless we specify otherwise, *write* and *writeln* send their output to the standard output file. Since *ConstantsAndOutput* uses the standard output file, *output* must be included as a parameter in the program heading. For a program that uses both the standard input and standard output files, we would need to list both *input* and *output* as parameters in the program heading:

> **program** *Conversation*(*input, output*);

Note that the list of parameters is enclosed in parentheses, the individual parameters are separated by commas, and the program heading is terminated with a semicolon.

Following the program heading is a *comment* describing the purpose of the program. As in the algorithmic language, comments in Pascal are enclosed by braces { and }. Since braces do not appear on all computer keyboards, Pascal allows the symbols (* and *) to be used instead. Thus, the comment in *ConstantsAndOutput* could also be written

> (* Illustrate constant definitions and output *)

As in the algorithmic language, a comment can be placed on a line by itself or anywhere that a space would be allowed.

Next come any definitions and declarations needed by the program. Unlike the algorithmic language, Pascal does not use a single keyword, such as **declare**, to introduce definitions and declarations. Instead, each kind of definition and declaration has its own definition part introduced with its own keyword. Thus **const** introduces the constant definition part, **type** introduces the type definition part, and so on. *ConstantsAndOutput* contains a constant definition part that defines three constants:

> **const**
>
> > *oldSalesTaxRate* = 0.045;
> >
> > *newSalesTaxRate* = 0.06;
> >
> > *complaint* = 'That''s too high';

OldSalesTaxRate and *newSalesTaxRate* are defined as real constants and *complaint* is defined as a string constant. Note that each constant definition is terminated by a semicolon.

The statements to be executed are enclosed by the reserved words **begin** and **end**. A sequence of statements enclosed by **begin** and **end** is called a *compound statement*. As mentioned earlier, the statements in a sequence are *separated* by semicolons; note that there is no semicolon between **begin** and the first statement of the sequence or between the last statement and **end**. The statements in the sequence are indented with respect to **begin** and **end**, making it easy to see at a glance which statements belong to the compound statement. When the compound statement is executed, the statements of the sequence are executed one after another in the order in which they appear in the compound statement.

The end of the program is marked by a period following the **end** of the compound statement.

When the program is executed, the three *writeln* statements are carried out in the order in which they appear in the program. Each statement produces a separate line of output. Note the use of literals, constant identifiers, and field-width parameters in the *writeln* statements. When the program is executed, it produces the following output:

```
The sales tax rate used to be 0.045
Now it's 0.06
That's too high
```

Expressions

Arithmetical operators   The arithmetical operators in Pascal are:

+	*addition*
−	*subtraction*
*	*multiplication*
/, **div**, and **mod**	*division*

These are the same as in the algorithmic language except for the exponentiation operator, which is not present in Pascal. As in the algorithmic language, +, −, and * can take either integer, real, or mixed integer and real operands. The result of the operation is an integer if both operands are integers; otherwise, the result is a real number. The operator / can take integer, real, or mixed integer and real operands, but the result is always real, regardless of the types of the operands. **Div** and **mod** are used for quotient-remainder division of integers; **div** yields the integer quotient and **mod** yields the integer remainder. Both **div** and **mod** take only integer operands and yield integer results.

The operator priorities are the same as in the algorithmic language. In the absence of exponentiation, there are only two levels of priority:

*, /, **div**, and **mod**	*high priority*
+ and −	*low priority*

The priorities are easily summarized by stating that multiplications and divisions are done before additions and subtractions. As in the algorithmic language, parentheses can be used to override the operator priorities.

Functions   Pascal provides ten predefined arithmetical functions—functions that take numerical arguments and yield numerical results. These functions can be divided into five general-purpose functions, which have uses in many areas of computer science, and five scientific functions, which are mainly used in scientific, engineering, and mathematical programs. The five general-purpose functions are:

abs   Returns the absolute value of its argument. Thus, *abs*(5) = 5 and *abs*(−7) = 7. The argument can be an integer or real number; the value returned has the same type as the argument.

sqr   Returns the square of its argument. Thus, *sqr*(5) = 25 and *sqr*(1.3) = 1.69. The argument can be an integer or a real number; the value returned has the same type as the argument. This function makes up somewhat for the lack of exponentiation in Pascal, since the most frequent use of exponentiation is for squaring.

sqrt   Returns the square root of its argument. Thus, *sqrt*(25) = 5.0 and *sqrt*(1.69) = 1.3. The argument can be an integer or a real number, but the result returned is always real. It is an error to attempt to take the square root of a negative number.

trunc   Converts its argument from a real number to an integer by discarding all digits to the right of the decimal point. Thus, *trunc*(3.2) = 3 and *trunc*(4.9) = 4.

round   Converts its argument from a real number to an integer by rounding the argument to the nearest integer. Thus, *round*(3.2) = 3 and *round*(4.9) = 5.

The scientific functions all take integers or real numbers as arguments and return real numbers as results:

sin   Returns the sin of its argument. The argument must be in radians.

cos   Returns the cosine of its argument. The argument must be in radians.

arctan   Returns the arctangent of its argument. The result is in radians.

exp   Returns e^x where x is the argument and e is the base of natural logarithms.

ln   Returns the natural logarithm of the argument. It is an error if the argument is negative.

The functions *exp* and *ln* can be used to replace the missing exponentiation operation. For nonnegative values of x, the value of $x ** y$ can be computed using the expression:

$$exp(y * ln(x))$$

This expression cannot be used for negative values of x, since the function *ln* is not defined for negative arguments.

Expressions can be used in *write* and *writeln* statements to specify values to be printed. The program in Figure 6.4, which is a translation into Pascal of the algorithm in Figure 6.2, illustrates the use of expressions in *writeln* statements. Since

Figure 6.4   The Pascal translation of the algorithm in Figure 6.2. Note that each field-width parameter applies to the value of the preceding expression. Thus, 3 / 5:3:1 indicates that the value of 3 / 5, which is 0.6, is to be printed in a three-character field with one digit to the right of the decimal point.

```
program Expressions(output);

{ Illustrate use of expressions in writeln statement }

begin
    writeln('3 + 5 = ', 3 + 5:1);
    writeln('3 - 5 = ', 3 - 5:1);
    writeln('3 * 5 = ', 3 * 5:2);
    writeln('3 / 5 = ', 3 / 5:3:1);
    writeln('10 div 3 = ', 10 div 3:1);
    writeln('10 mod 3 = ', 10 mod 3:1);
    writeln('sqr(3) = ', sqr(3):1)
end.
```

this program does not contain any definitions or declarations, the compound statement containing the statements to be executed immediately follows the program heading.

In *writeln* statements such as

$$writeln('3 + 5 = ', 3 + 5:1)$$

note two things. First,

$$'3 + 5 = '$$

is a string literal and is printed as is. Second, in

$$3 + 5:1$$

the field-width parameter 1 applies to the entire preceding expression. That is, the result of evaluating the expression $3 + 5$ is to be printed with a field-width parameter of 1.

Since Pascal does not provide exponentiation, the *sqr* function is used to compute the square of 3 in the last *writeln* statement. When the program is executed, the following printout results:

```
3 + 5 = 8
3 - 5 = -2
3 * 5 = 15
3 / 5 = 0.6
10 div 3 = 3
10 mod 3 = 1
sqr(3) = 9
```

7

Variables, assignment, and input

I n Chapter 6 we saw how to use expressions to instruct the computer to carry out arithmetical calculations. But all we could do with the results of the calculations was to print them with **output** statements. No way was provided for saving the results of one calculation for use in later calculations, or for accepting input data from the user and saving it until it is needed in the calculations. In this chapter we will see how to use the computer's main memory to store input data and the results of calculations for later use.

7.1 Variables

A computer's main memory, you recall, is divided into many separate *memory locations,* each of which can hold a certain number of bits of data. Each memory location has a unique *address,* which can be used to designate the location for storing data in it or retrieving data from it. We can think of main memory as a set of post office boxes, the boxes corresponding to memory locations and the box numbers corresponding to addresses.

We could refer to memory locations by their addresses, as machine-language programmers do. But hexadecimal addresses such as 3F6 and C2E are hard to remember and give us no clue as to the significance of the data stored in each location. Fortunately, higher-level languages (and pseudolanguages) allow us to designate memory locations by identifiers. We can choose identifiers so that they describe the contents of the memory locations they name; this makes the identifiers easy to remember and provides substantial aid to someone trying to read and understand our algorithm.

A *variable* is a memory location named by an identifier. The identifier is called the *variable name;* the value stored in the memory location is called the *value of the variable.* Since different values can be stored in a memory location during the course of a computation, the value of a variable can change, or vary, as the computation progresses—hence the name ''variable.'' Variables, whose values can change as an algorithm is executed, are in contrast to constants, whose values are never changed by the execution of an algorithm.

Figure 7.1 shows two ways of visualizing variables and their values. The diagram at the top shows the memory locations together with their names and the values they contain. Each memory location establishes a correspondence between a variable name (the name of the location) and a value (the contents of the location). We can display this correspondence in a *variable-value table,* such as the one at the bottom of Figure 7.1, by listing the variable names in one column and the values of the

Figure 7.1   Two ways of visualizing variables and their values: at top, a
diagram showing memory locations, their names, and their
contents; at bottom, a table showing variables and their
values.

Name	Memory location
employeeName	'Mary Jones'
hoursWorked	40
hourlyRate	3.25
grossWages	130.0

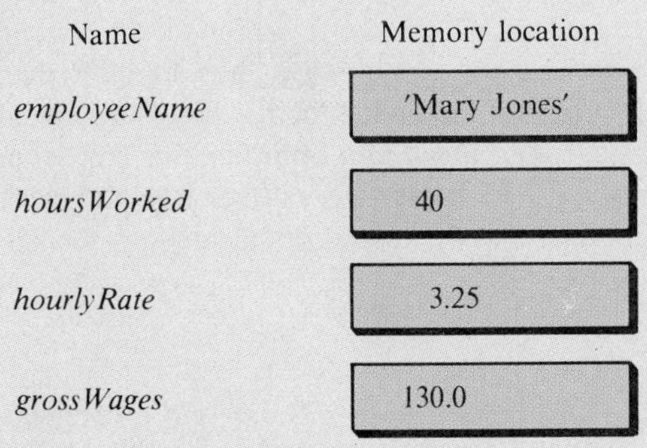

Variable-value table

Variable	Value
employeeName	'Mary Jones'
hoursWorked	40
hourlyRate	3.25
grossWages	130.0

variables in the other. The table at the bottom of Figure 7.1 conveys the same information as the diagram at the top. Using either one, we can determine that the value of *employeeName* is 'Mary Jones', the value of *hoursWorked* is 40, the value of *hourlyRate* is 3.25, and the value of *grossWages* is 130.0.

7.2 Declarations

Before we can use an identifier as a variable name, we must *declare* the identifier as a variable and state the data type to which the values of the variable will belong. There are several reasons for this requirement. First, declaring an identifier as a variable prevents it from being confused with other identifiers, such as those naming constants, types, and algorithms. Second, stating the type to which the values of a variable must belong allows the language processor to reserve a memory location of the proper size to hold the values of the variable. Finally, by knowing the type of the values of each variable, the language processor can catch some of our mistakes. For example, the language processor would report an error if it came upon a statement instructing the computer to multiply the values of two variables whose values were of type *string*.

The *type of a variable* is the type declared for its values. Thus a *string variable* is a variable declared as having string values, an *integer variable* is a variable declared as having integer values, a *real variable* is a variable declared as having real values, and so on.

Variable declarations are given in the **declare** section of an algorithm. Each variable name is followed by a colon and the type of the variable. No keyword, such as the **const** used for constant definitions, is required; the colon is sufficient to signify a variable declaration:

declare

    employeeName: *string*
    hoursWorked: *real*
    hourlyRate: *integer*
    grossWages: *real*

This **declare** section declares *employeeName* as a string variable, *hoursWorked* as a real variable, and so on. That is, *employeeName* can only have string values, *hoursWorked* can only have real values, and so on. When several variables have the same type, we can combine their declarations by listing them all to the left of a single colon and type identifier:

declare

    employeeName: *string*
    hoursWorked, grossWages: *real*
    hourlyRate: *integer*

Both *hoursWorked* and *grossWages* are declared as real variables.

7.3 Assignment

Assignment is the operation that stores a value in a memory location. The newly stored value replaces the previous contents of the memory location. Since the new value stored in the memory location becomes the new value of the corresponding variable, the assignment operation gives the variable a new value. We say that it *assigns* a new value to the variable—hence the term "assignment."

The assignment operator in the algorithmic language is the left-pointing arrow ←. The *assignment statement* has the following form:

variable ← expression

When an assignment statement is executed, the expression is evaluated and its value is assigned to the variable. The assignment operator was chosen as a left arrow to suggest graphically that the value of the expression is to be stored in the memory location named by the variable. The assignment operator can be read as "becomes," indicating that the value of the variable becomes equal to the value of the expression.

For example, in the assignment statement

employeeName ← 'Mary Jones'

the variable is *employeeName* and the expression is the string literal 'Mary Jones'. When the assignment statement is executed, the string 'Mary Jones' is stored in the memory location designated by *employeeName*. Likewise, when

hoursWorked ← 15 + 30

is executed, the value of the expression, 45, is stored in the memory location named *hoursWorked*.

The value assigned to a variable must belong to the type of the variable. If *employeeName* is a string variable, *hoursWorked* is an integer variable, and *hourlyRate* is a real variable, the assignments

employeeName ← 'Larry Jones'
hoursWorked ← 35
hourlyRate ← 10.55

are all valid. On the other hand,

employeeName ← 35
hoursWorked ← 10.55
hourlyRate ← 'Larry Jones'

are all invalid. We cannot assign an integer to a string variable, a real number to an integer variable, or a string to a real variable.

For convenience, however, we are allowed, as a special exception, to assign integer values to real variables. For every integer there is a corresponding real number: 10.0 corresponds to 10, 25.0 corresponds to 25, 100.0 corresponds to 100, and so on. When an integer is assigned to a real variable, the integer is automatically converted to the corresponding real number. Thus the assignment

$hourlyRate \leftarrow 15$

is valid and assigns 15.0 to *hourlyRate*.

The reverse conversion, from real numbers to integers, is *not* done automatically. Instead, we must use the functions *trunc* and *round* to convert real numbers to integers when needed. Which function we choose determines whether the real number will be truncated or rounded by the conversion. Thus,

$hoursWorked \leftarrow 41.7$

is invalid. Instead, we must write

$hoursWorked \leftarrow trunc(41.7)$

or

$hoursWorked \leftarrow round(41.7)$

The value assigned to *hoursWorked* will be 41 when *trunc* is used and 42 when *round* is used.

We can think of the assignment operator in terms of the effect it has on the values of variables. For example, suppose *employeeName, hoursWorked,* and *hourlyRate* have the values shown:

Variable	Value
employeeName	'Bob Smith'
hoursWorked	45
hourlyRate	4.25

After the assignment statements

$employeeName \leftarrow$ 'Jane Lee'
$hoursWorked \leftarrow 41$
$hourlyRate \leftarrow 5.15$

are executed, the variables have the following values:

Variable	Value
employeeName	'Jane Lee'
hoursWorked	41
hourlyRate	5.15

Figure 7.2 illustrates these assignments in terms of memory locations.

Figure 7.2   The effect of assignment statements is to change the
contents of memory locations.

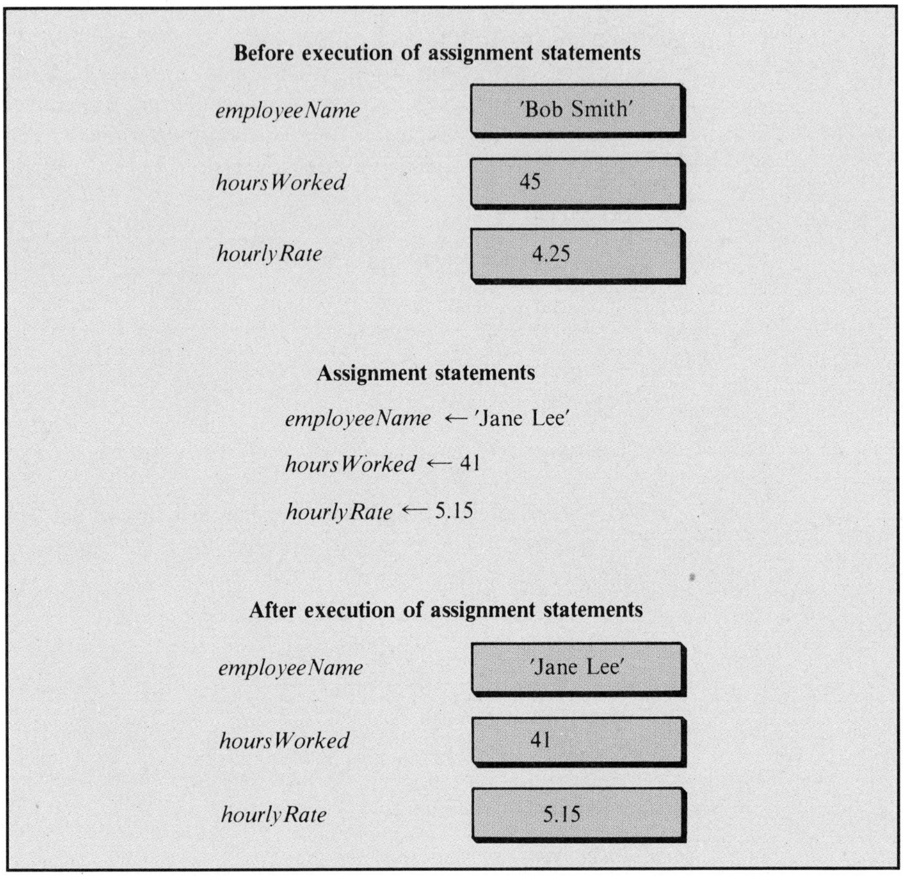

Before execution of assignment statements

employeeName   'Bob Smith'

hoursWorked   45

hourlyRate   4.25

Assignment statements

employeeName ← 'Jane Lee'

hoursWorked ← 41

hourlyRate ← 5.15

After execution of assignment statements

employeeName   'Jane Lee'

hoursWorked   41

hourlyRate   5.15

7.4

Variables in expressions

An expression, we recall, is any construction that represents a value. Variables represent values—the values stored in the corresponding memory locations—so variables can be used as expressions or as parts of expressions. When an expression containing variables is evaluated, the variables are replaced by their values before the operators are applied. The operation of replacing variables by their values is called *dereferencing:* each variable is replaced by the value to which it refers.

For example, consider the expression

hoursWorked ∗ *hourlyRate*

Before this expression can be evaluated, *hoursWorked* and *hourlyRate* must be de-referenced—replaced by their values. If the values of the two variables are given by

Variable	Value
hoursWorked	41
hourlyRate	5.15

then after dereferencing the expression becomes

41 * 5.15

Carrying out the multiplication gives 211.15 as the value of the expression.

Expressions—including, of course, those containing variables—can appear to the right of the assignment operator in an assignment statement. The simplest case occurs when the expression consists of a single variable. For example, suppose that *source* and *destination* are integer variables with values given by

Variable	Value
source	50
destination	75

and consider the assignment statement

destination ← *source*

The expression to the right of the assignment operator is evaluated by dereferencing *source*—replacing it by its value, 50. Thus the assignment statement is equivalent to

destination ← 50

The value of 50 is assigned to *destination,* so that after the assignment statement is executed the two variables have the following values:

Variable	Value
source	50
destination	50

Figure 7.3 illustrates the role of dereferencing in carrying out this assignment statement.

Note that the value of *source* was not changed. Using a variable in an expression never changes its value. The only variable whose value is changed by an assignment statement is the one that appears to the left of the assignment operator.

The overall effect of the assignment statement

destination ← *source*

is to make a copy of the contents of memory location *source* and store that copy in memory location *destination*. The contents of *source* remain unchanged; the previous

Figure 7.3   The operation of dereferencing replaces a variable by its
value. Dereferencing is carried out automatically for any
variable appearing to the right of an assignment operator.
On the other hand, the variable to the left of the assignment
operator is *not* dereferenced; it represents a memory location
rather than a value.

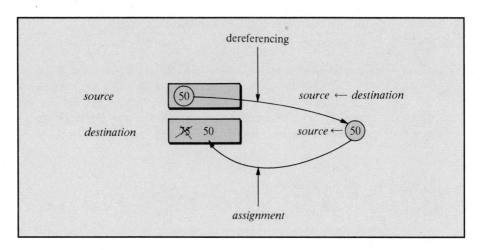

contents of *destination* are replaced by the copy of the contents of *source*. Figure 7.4
illustrates this copying operation.

Now let's consider an assignment statement with a more complex expression to
the right of the assignment operator. Suppose that *a, b, c,* and *d* are integer variables
with the values

Variable	Value
a	5
b	10
c	15
d	20

and the following assignment statement is executed:

$$d \leftarrow a + b * c$$

This statement is executed as follows:

$d \leftarrow a + b * c$
$d \leftarrow 5 + 10 * 15$ *Dereference variables in expression . . .*
$d \leftarrow 5 + 150$ *. . . multiplication next . . .*
$d \leftarrow 155$ *. . . addition next . . .*
. . . and assign 155 to d

Figure 7.4   An assignment statement with a single variable to the right of the assignment operator can be thought of as copying the contents of one memory location into another memory location.

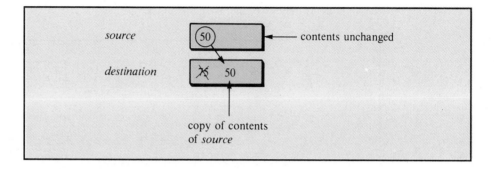

After the assignment has been executed, the variable-value table is:

Variable	Value
a	5
b	10
c	15
d	155

Only the value of *d* was changed by the assignment statement. Figure 7.5 illustrates this assignment.

Sometimes the same variable appears on both the left and the right sides of the assignment operator. Since the expression on the right is evaluated before the assignment takes place, the old value of the variable—its value before the assignment statement was executed—is used in evaluating the expression. The result of evaluating the expression becomes the new value of the variable. For example, suppose the value of *a* is 5 before the assignment statement

$$a \leftarrow a + 1$$

is executed. Execution proceeds as follows:

$a \leftarrow a + 1$
$a \leftarrow 5 + 1$ *Dereference a in expression . . .*
$a \leftarrow 6$ *. . . do addition . . .*
            . . . and assign 6 to a

After the assignment has been executed, the value of *a* is 6. The effect of the assignment statement was to add 1 to the value of *a*. This assignment statement is illustrated in Figure 7.6.

Figure 7.5 To execute an assignment statement with an expression to the right of the assignment operator, the variables in the expression are first dereferenced. The expression is then evaluated—the calculation called for by the expression is carried out—and the value of the expression is assigned to the variable to the left of the assignment operator.

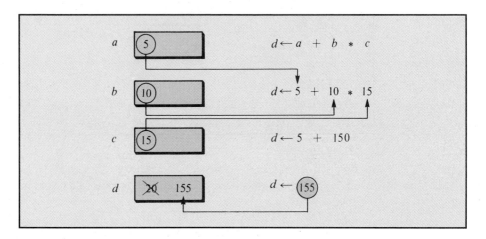

Figure 7.6 Adding 1 to the contents of a memory location. This operation is frequently carried out for the purpose of counting; the memory location holds a running count, which is increased by 1 each time an item is counted.

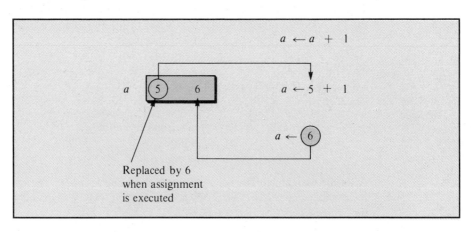

Assignment statements such as this one are often used for counting. For example, if the integer variable *recordCount* is used to keep count of the number of file records a program has processed, then the program can use the statement

$$recordCount \leftarrow recordCount + 1$$

to increase the value of *recordCount* by 1 each time a new record is processed.

Note that the meaning of a variable name depends on the context in which it occurs. When a variable name occurs where an expression is expected, as to the right of the assignment operator, the variable name represents a value. On the other hand, when a variable name occurs where the name of a memory location is expected, as to the left of the assignment operator, the variable name represents a memory location in which a value can be stored. For example, in

$$destination \leftarrow source$$

source represents a value whereas *destination* represents a memory location. And in

$$recordCount \leftarrow recordCount + 1$$

the occurrence of *recordCount* to the right of the assignment operator represents a value and the occurrence of *recordCount* to the left of the assignment operator represents a memory location.

In conversation and in explanations, we often use variable names to represent values. Thus we might say *"destination* equals 50," *"recordCount* is greater than 100," and *"a* is less than *b"* instead of making the more precise but longer statements, "the value of *destination* is 50," "the value of *recordCount* is greater than 100," and "the value of *a* is less than the value of *b."* In the shorter statements, we are using the variable names to represent the values of the corresponding variables.

7.5 Input and output

Output statement The **output** statement, we know, contains a list of *expressions* whose values are to be printed. When a variable name appears where an expression is expected, the variable name represents the value of the variable. Thus, variables appearing in the list of expressions represent their values, and it is the values of the variables that are printed. For example, if *length* and *width* are integer variables, the statements

length ← 7
width ← 5
output *length*, ' ', *width*

produce the printout

7 5

As usual, variables may appear as parts of more complex expressions, in which case the variables are replaced by their values before the expressions are evaluated.

For example, the statements

$$length \leftarrow 7$$
$$width \leftarrow 5$$
output $length * width$, $'\ '$, $2 * (length + width)$

produce the printout

```
35   24
```

The expressions are evaluated just as if they appeared to the right of assignment operators. Indeed, we would get exactly the same results if we assigned the values of the expressions to variables and used the variables in the **output** statement:

$$length \leftarrow 7$$
$$width \leftarrow 5$$
$$area \leftarrow length * width$$
$$perimeter \leftarrow 2 * (length + width)$$
output $area$, $'\ '$, $perimeter$

We can think of an **output** statement as equivalent, in a certain sense, to the right-hand side of an assignment statement—the part that is to the right of the assignment operator. Each expression in the **output** statement is evaluated exactly as if it appeared to the right of an assignment operator. The value of the expression is sent to an output device, however, instead of being assigned to a variable.

Input statement   In an **input** statement, the keyword **input** is followed by a list of variables for which values are to be obtained. The **input** statement reads a line of input, such as a line typed by the user, and assigns the values on the line to the variables in the **input** statement. For example,

input $length$, $width$

causes **input** to read a line of input and obtain two values from it. If the line entered by the user is

```
9   2
```

the value 9 is assigned to *length* and the value 2 is assigned to *width*.

If the **output** statement is equivalent to the right-hand side of an assignment statement, then the **input** statement is equivalent to the left-hand side. The variables in the **input** statement *do not* represent their values but instead represent memory locations in which the input values will be stored. Only variables can appear in the **input** statement, never expressions. Each variable is assigned a value just as if it appeared to the left of an assignment operator. The assigned value, however, is not the value of an expression but comes from the line of input typed by the user.

On the line of input entered by the user, adjacent numeric values are separated by a comma, one or more spaces, or both. Thus, in response to

input $length$, $width$

the user could enter any of the following

```
9,2
9, 2
9   2
9               2
```

but not

```
92
```

No separators are needed or allowed for character values. Any blanks or commas in the input line will be taken as characters to be read. For example, suppose that *c*, *d*, and *e* are character variables. If the user responds to

input *c*, *d*, *e*

with the input line

```
o   k
```

c, *d*, and *e* receive the following values:

Variable	Value
c	'o'
d	' '
e	'k'

The blank between o and k was read as a character value and assigned to *d*. Likewise, the input

```
o , k
```

would assign the comma character to *d*.

There is no way to separate string values, because any spaces or commas will be taken as characters to be read, not as separators. Thus when a string variable is encountered in an **input** statement, the entire rest of the input line is made into a string and assigned to the string variable. For example, suppose *height* and *weight* are integer variables and *nameAndAge* is a string variable. If the user responds to

input *height*, *weight*, *nameAndAge*

with

```
72, 200, J. Random User, 25
```

then 72 will be assigned to *height* and 200 will be assigned to *weight*. However, the entire rest of the input line, 'J. Random User, 25', will be assigned to *nameAndAge*.

Each value entered by the user must have the same type as the variable to which it is to be assigned. Thus entering 25.0 for the value of an integer variable is an error, since real values cannot be assigned to integer variables. On the other hand, as with the assignment statement, an integer will be converted to the corresponding real number if need be. Thus if the user enters 25 for the value of a real variable, 25 will be converted to 25.0, which will be assigned to the real variable.

7.6 Interactive and batch processing

There are two different methods by which a computer system can process a program and its input data. In *batch processing,* the program and its input data are prepared in advance and submitted to the computer system as a deck of punched cards or as a disk file prepared from a terminal. When the computer system gets around to executing the program, it will print the output the program produces or store the output in a disk file where it can be examined from a terminal.

With batch processing, then, you cannot interact with your program while it is being executed. Therefore, all the data the program is to process must be prepared in advance. Since the file containing the input data may not be conveniently available when you are examining your program's output, it is a good idea for the program to print its input data as well as the output it produces.

With *interactive processing,* in contrast, you can exchange data with your program while it is executing. The program can request input, produce output, request more input, produce more output, and so on. The input you provide may well be based on previous output produced by the program. For example, if you are playing a game with the program, your next move (input) will be based on the program's previous moves (output).

Both batch processing and interactive processing have their places. If a program is to process a large data file, say print monthly statements for all of a company's customers, there is little need for interaction. Assuming that the program and the file to be processed are already in auxiliary memory, you need only submit a few commands telling the computer system what program to execute, from what file the program's input is to come, and to what device the output from the program is to be sent. On the other hand, many modern computer applications, such as word processing, information retrieval, spreadsheet analysis, computer-assisted instruction, and computer games call for extensive interaction between the user and the program that is being executed.

Input for an interactive program is typed in by the user at the program's request. It is up to the program to *prompt* the user for each needed item of input. For example, a program might use the following statements to obtain a user's name and assign it to the string variable *name*:

> **output** 'Enter your name'
> **input** *name*
> **output** 'Hi, ', *name*

The exchange with the user would go like this:

```
Enter your name
Angela
Hi, Angela
```

The middle line was typed by the user; the first and last lines were typed by the program.

If we want the user's response to appear on the same line as the prompt, we can end the **output** statement with **more,** preventing the output device from going to a new line after printing the prompt:

> **output** 'What's your name? ', **more**
> **input** *name*
> **output** 'Hi, ', *name*

Now the exchange with the user looks like this:

```
What's your name? Angela
Hi, Angela
```

The name following the question mark was typed by the user; everything else was typed by the computer.

The following statements illustrate the interaction between the user and a program computing the area and perimeter of a rectangle:

> **output** 'Length and width of rectangle? ', **more**
> **input** *length, width*
> *area* ← *length* ∗ *width*
> *perimeter* ← 2 ∗ (*length* + *width*)
> **output** 'Area = ', *area*
> **output** 'Perimeter = ', *perimeter*

When these statements are executed, the exchange with the user goes like this:

```
Length and width of rectangle? 4, 3
Area = 12
Perimeter = 14
```

How should these statements be modified for use with batch processing? First, no prompt is needed, since all the input data must be prepared in advance. Second, the input data as well as the calculated output should be printed, since the cards or disk file containing the input may not be handy when you are trying to decipher the output:

> **input** *length, width*
> *area* ← *length* ∗ *width*
> *perimeter* ← 2 ∗ (*length* + *width*)
> **output** 'Length = ', *length*
> **output** 'Width = ', *width*
> **output** 'Area = ', *area*
> **output** 'Perimeter = ', *perimeter*

If the input data file contains the line

4 3

these statements produce the following output:

```
Length = 4
Width = 3
Area = 12
Perimeter = 14
```

Most of the algorithms in this book are in a form suitable for interactive processing. Most are easily adapted to batch processing by making the changes just described.

7.7 Four algorithms

In this section we will examine four algorithms, each of which does a simple arithmetical calculation. Each uses only the *sequencing* control structure: the statements are executed one after another in the order in which they appear in the algorithm. Each algorithm first obtains the input data it needs from the user, then does its calculations, and finally prints the results. We can outline the statement part of such an algorithm as follows:

"Obtain data from user"
"Calculate desired results"
"Output results of calculations"

When outlining algorithms, we will use double quote marks to enclose the steps that the algorithm must take. Essentially, the double quote marks enclose statements in an Englishlike pseudolanguage. To go from the outline to the algorithm, we *refine* the statements in the outline by replacing each by one or more statements in the algorithmic language.

For complex algorithms, the refinement might be done in several steps, with the original outline replaced with a more detailed one, the more detailed outline replaced with a still more detailed one, and so on until the statements in the outline can be translated into statements of the algorithmic language. An algorithm arrived at through this process is said to have been developed by *stepwise refinement*.

Discounts Given the regular price of an item of merchandise and the percentage by which its price is discounted, we want to compute the amount of the discount and the discounted price the customer must pay.

The input data for the algorithm consists of the regular price and the percent discount. The data might be obtained through an interactive exchange such as the following:

```
Regular price and percent discount? 49.50, 10
```

The response indicates that the regular price is $49.50 and the discount rate is 10%. The output should have the form:

```
Amount of discount is $4.95
Discounted price is $44.55
```

where the numbers are the results calculated from the given input data.

Before the percentage discount can be used in any calculations, it must be converted to a decimal, which is done by dividing it by 100 or, alternatively, moving the decimal point two places to the left. Thus a 5% discount corresponds to a discount rate of 0.05, and a 10% discount corresponds to a discount rate of 0.10 (or just 0.1), and so on. We compute the amount of the discount by multiplying the regular price by the discount rate. For example, if the regular price is 49.95 and the discount rate is 0.1, the amount of the discount is $49.50 \times 0.1 = 4.95$. Finally, we compute the amount that the customer must pay by subtracting the amount of the discount from the regular price: $49.50 - 4.95 = 44.55$

The basic outline for the algorithm is the one given previously: the algorithm must get its input data, carry out the calculations, and print the results. Refining the previous outline slightly for the case at hand, we get:

"Prompt user for regular price and percentage discount"

"Input regular price and percentage discount"

"Convert percentage discount to decimal"

"Compute amount of discount"

"Compute discounted price"

"Output amount of discount"

"Output discounted price"

With our algorithm outlined, we can see what variables are needed and the types that should be declared for them. We can use *regularPrice* and *percentDiscount* to hold the data obtained from the user. The decimal discount rate, obtained by converting the value of *percentDiscount* to a decimal, can be stored in *discountRate*. Finally, we need storage for the two computed results, *amountOfDiscount* and *discountedPrice*. Since all the numbers we are working with can contain decimal points, all six variables will be declared as *real* variables:

declare

   regularPrice, percentDiscount, discountRate, amountOfDiscount,
   discountedPrice: *real*

(Note that in the algorithmic language a list of items, such as the list of variable names above, can stretch over as many lines as needed. If one line ends with a comma, it is assumed that the list is continued on the next line.)

With the declarations and outline at hand, we have little trouble writing the statements of the algorithm:

execute

   output ′Regular price and percentage discount? ′, **more**
   input *regularPrice, percentDiscount*
   discountRate ← *percentDiscount* / 100.0
   amountOfDiscount ← *regularPrice* ∗ *discountRate*
   discountedPrice ← *regularPrice* − *amountOfDiscount*
   output ′Amount of discount is $′, *amountOfDiscount*
   output ′Discounted price is $′, *discountedPrice*

Figure 7.7 shows the complete algorithm *Discounts*. When the algorithm is executed, the ensuing dialogue with the user looks something like this:

```
Regular price and percent discount? 49.50, 10
Amount of discount is $4.95
Discounted price is $44.55
```

We have discussed the reasoning behind this algorithm in considerable detail to illustrate the process of developing a simple algorithm. To summarize: first determine what the input data will be and what output is required. Then determine how the output values can be calculated from the given data; remember that you must know how to solve a problem before you have any hopes of programming a computer to solve it. Decide what variables are needed to hold the input data and the results of calculations; this is often most easily done while you are considering how the calculations will be carried out. Outline your algorithm and translate your outline into the algorithmic language, either directly or through a series of more refined outlines.

Batting averages We wish to write an algorithm to compute a baseball player's batting average, given the number of times the player was at bat, the number of times the player walked, and the number of hits the player got. The input data, for which the user should be prompted, consists of three integers: the number of times the player came to bat, the number of times the player walked, and the number of

Figure 7.7 Algorithm for computing the amount of discount and the discounted price for an item of merchandise.

---

algorithm *Discounts*

{ Compute amount of discount and discounted price from regular price and percentage discount }

declare
    regularPrice, percentDiscount, discountRate,
    amountOfDiscount, discountedPrice: *real*
execute
    output 'Regular price and percentage discount? ', **more**
    input *regularPrice, percentDiscount*
    discountRate ← *percentDiscount* / 100.0
    amountOfDiscount ← *regularPrice* ∗ *discountRate*
    discountedPrice ← *regularPrice* − *amountOfDiscount*
    output 'Amount of discount is $', *amountOfDiscount*
    output 'Discounted price is $', *discountedPrice*
end *Discounts*

hits the player got. The output should be the batting average computed from the input data.

To see how to calculate the results from the given data, we must determine how such calculations are traditionally done in baseball. Frequently a programmer must delve into some specialized field, be it baseball or accounting or a branch of science, to determine how the calculations called for in a program are to be done. Investigation shows that a batting average is calculated by subtracting the number of times walked from the number of times at bat (so that the times a player is walked are not counted against him) and dividing the result into the number of hits. Using the integer variables *timesAtBat, timesWalked,* and *hits* for the input data items, and the real variable *battingAverage* for the calculated result, we can express the calculation in the following assignment statement:

battingAverage ← *hits* / (*timesAtBat* − *timesWalked*)

We can outline the algorithm as follows:

"Prompt for and input number of times at bat"
"Prompt for and input number of times walked"
"Prompt for and input number of hits"
"Calculate batting average"
"Output batting average"

We have already chosen variable names for the data and the result. *Hits, timesAtBat,* and *timesWalked* can all be integer variables, since their values must be whole numbers. *BattingAverage* must be a real variable, however, for two reasons. Logically, a batting average is usually less than one and so must be represented by a real number. In terms of the algorithmic language, the batting average is computed with the operator /, which always returns a real result. These considerations give us the algorithm in Figure. 7.8. When the algorithm is executed, the dialogue with the user looks like this:

```
Number of times at bat? 40
Number of times walked? 7
Number of hits? 10
Batting average is 0.303030
```

Batting averages are normally given to three decimal places, so the player's batting average is .303.

Note that this algorithm would fail if the player was walked every time he came to bat, since the second operand of the division operator would have the value zero. Division by zero is not defined in arithmetic and so cannot be carried out by any computer.

Units conversion We wish to write an algorithm that will accept a length in feet and inches and convert it to centimeters. The input will be two integers: the number of feet and and the number of inches in the length to be converted. The output will be the length in centimeters.

Figure 7.8   Algorithm for computing a baseball player's batting average.
The algorithm fails if the number of times at bat is the same
as the number of times walked.

---

algorithm *ComputeBattingAverage*

{ Compute baseball player's batting average from number of times at bat,
number of times walked, and number of hits }

declare
    hits, *timesAtBat*, *timesWalked*: *integer*
    battingAverage: *real*
execute
    output 'Number of times at bat? ', **more**
    input *timesAtBat*
    output 'Number of times walked? ', **more**
    input *timesWalked*
    output 'Number of hits? ', **more**
    input *hits*
    battingAverage ← *hits* / (*timesAtBat* − *timesWalked*)
    output 'Batting average is ', *battingAverage*
end *ComputeBattingAverage*

For the calculation we will need two conversion factors: 12, the number of inches in a foot, and 2.54, the number of centimeters in an inch. Rather than letting 12 and 2.54 be "magic numbers," whose significance may not be clear to someone reading the algorithm, we use constant definitions to give each conversion factor a descriptive name:

const *inchesPerFoot* = 12

const *centimetersPerInch* = 2.54

The calculation is best done in two steps. First, express the given length entirely in inches by multiplying the given number of feet by the number of inches in a foot and adding the given number of inches to the result:

lengthInInches ← *inchesPerFoot* ∗ *feet* + *inches*

Multiplying the length in inches by the number of centimeters per inch gives the length in centimeters:

centimeters ← *centimetersPerInch* ∗ *lengthInInches*

As usual, the algorithm must get its data, carry out its calculations, and output the result:

''Prompt for number of feet and inches to be converted''

''Input number of feet and inches''

''Compute length in centimeters''

''Output length in centimeters''

Inches, feet, and *lengthInInches* can be integer variables; *centimeters* must be a real variable, however, since *centimetersPerInch* is a real constant. These considerations give us the algorithm in Figure 7.9. When the algorithm is executed, the dialogue with the user goes like this

```
Length in feet and inches? 6, 4
Length in centimeters is 193.04
```

Making change   An algorithm to make change is a standard example in programming and computer science textbooks. In the past, some authors felt obliged to point out that this example was purely an intellectual exercise, since no one would use an expensive computer—the only kind there was then—for something so trivial as making change. Now, with microprocessors in vending machines, cash registers, and banking terminals, a program for making change is a perfectly reasonable application.

The algorithm we want to write will obtain from the user the amount of change

Figure 7.9   Algorithm for converting feet and inches to centimeters. Note the use of constant definitions for the conversion factors.

```
algorithm Convert

{ Convert feet and inches to centimeters }

declare
        const inchesPerFoot = 12
        const centimetersPerInch = 2.54
        inches, feet, lengthInInches: integer
        centimeters: real
execute
        output 'Length in feet and inches? ', more
        input feet, inches
        lengthInInches ← inchesPerFoot * feet + inches
        centimeters ← centimetersPerInch * lengthInInches
        output 'Length in centimeters is ', centimeters
end Convert
```

(in cents) that is to be returned to the customer. The algorithm will print the number of each denomination coin to be handed back—so many half dollars, so many quarters, and so on. We assume that the amount of change to be handed back is less than one dollar, so the algorithm will need to deal only with coins, not bills. The algorithm will still work for larger amounts of change, but since it can only hand back coins, the customer may receive a large number of half dollars.

For the customer's convenience, we want to use as large coins as possible; we don't want to hand back, say, 90 cents change entirely in pennies, or even in nickels and dimes. Therefore, we start with the largest coin, the half dollar, and see how many half dollars we can hand back without going over the total amount to be returned. After handing out as many half dollars as possible, we consider the amount still to be returned and see how many quarters we can hand back. Out of the amount still to be returned after half dollars and quarters have been handed back, we see how many dimes we can hand back, and so on. After all the larger coins have been handed back, the amount still to be returned is handed back in pennies.

We use quotient-remainder arithmetic to determine how many of a particular coin to hand back and how much change will still remain to be returned after handing back the coin in question. For example, to determine how many half dollars to hand back, we divide the amount to be handed back by 50—the number of cents in a half dollar. The quotient is the number of half dollars to be handed back. The remainder is the amount that remains to be returned after handing back half dollars. For example, if the amount of change to be returned is 70 cents, our work looks like this:

$$\begin{array}{r} 1 \\ 50\overline{)70} \\ \underline{50} \\ 20 \end{array}$$

quotient—number of half dollars to be returned

remainder—amount still to be returned after handing back half dollars

In the algorithmic language, we use **div** to compute the integer quotient and **mod** to compute the integer remainder:

70 **div** 50 = 1   *(number of half dollars to hand back)*
70 **mod** 50 = 20   *(amount still to be returned after handing back half dollars)*

With these considerations, the outline for our algorithm is straightforward:

"Obtain amount of change to be returned"
"Compute and print number of half dollars to hand back and compute amount remaining to be returned after half dollars are handed back"
"Compute and print number of quarters to hand back and compute amount remaining to be returned after quarters are handed back"
"Compute and print number of dimes to hand back and compute amount remaining to be returned after dimes are handed back"
"Compute and print number of nickels to hand back and compute amount remaining to be returned after nickels are handed back"
"Print the amount still remaining as the number of pennies to be handed back"

We define constants to represent the value in cents of each denomination of coin (except the penny):

const

centsPerHalf	=	50
centsPerQuarter	=	25
centsPerDime	=	10
centsPerNickel	=	5

We use the integer variable *numberOfCoins* for the number of coins of a particular denomination to be handed back and *amountRemaining* for the amount that still remains to be handed back. At the beginning of the algorithm, the value of *amountRemaining* is set to the total amount of change to be returned. After each denomination coin is handed back, *amountRemaining* is *updated*—it is assigned a new value—so that its value once again represents the amount of change remaining to be handed back. When all the larger coins have been handed back, the value of *amountRemaining* is the amount that must be handed back in pennies.

Figure 7.10 shows the algorithm *MakeChange*. The first step in our outline is to obtain from the user the amount of change to be returned; this amount is assigned to *amountRemaining*:

output 'Amount of change (in cents)? ', **more**

input *amountRemaining*

The rest of the algorithm is divided into blocks of statements, each of which handles one denomination of coin. Each block of statements computes and prints the value of *numberOfCoins,* the number of coins to be handed back. The same block also updates *amountRemaining* so that its value will once again be the amount that remains to be returned. The first block of statements handles half dollars. We use **div** to compute the number of coins to be returned:

numberOfCoins ← *amountRemaining* **div** *centsPerHalf*

and **mod** to compute the new value of *amountRemaining*—the amount remaining after half dollars have been handed back:

amountRemaining ← *amountRemaining* **mod** *centsPerHalf*

Note that *amountRemaining* appears on both sides of the assignment operator; the old value of *amountRemaining,* the one it had before the statement was executed, is used to evaluate the expression; and the value of the expression becomes the new value of *amountRemaining.*

The statements for each denomination end with an **output** statement that prints the number of coins to be handed back for that denomination:

output 'Halves', **tab**(10), *numberOfcoins*

Figure 7.10   Algorithm for making change. The assertions help us
understand the algorithm by giving the initial and final states
of the computation as well as its state after each
denomination of coin has been dealt with.

---

algorithm *MakeChange*

{ Compute number of half dollars, quarters, dimes, nickels, and pennies to
be returned for amount of change less than one dollar }

declare
    const *centsPerHalf*   = 50
    const *centsPerQuarter* = 25
    const *centsPerDime*   = 10
    const *centsPerNickel* = 5
    amountRemaining, *numberOfCoins*: *integer*
execute

    { No coins have been handed back }

    output ′Amount of change (in cents)? ′, **more**
    input *amountRemaining*

    { No coins have been handed back; *amountRemaining* is amount to be
    handed back in halves, quarters, dimes, nickels, and pennies }

    numberOfCoins ← *amountRemaining* **div** *centsPerHalf*
    amountRemaining ← *amountRemaining* **mod** *centsPerHalf*
    output ′Halves′, **tab**(10), *numberOfCoins*

    { Halves have been handed back; *amountRemaining* is amount to be
    handed back in quarters, dimes, nickels, and pennies }

    numberOfCoins ← *amountRemaining* **div** *centsPerQuarter*
    amountRemaining ← *amountRemaining* **mod** *centsPerQuarter*
    output ′Quarters′, **tab**(10), *numberOfCoins*

    { Halves and quarters have been handed back; *amountRemaining* is
    amount to be handed back in dimes, nickels, and pennies }

    numberOfCoins ← *amountRemaining* **div** *centsPerDime*
    amountRemaining ← *amountRemaining* **mod** *centsPerDime*
    output ′Dimes′, **tab**(10), *numberOfCoins*

{ Halves, quarters, and dimes have been handed back; *amountRemaining* is amount to be handed back in nickels and pennies }

numberOfCoins ← *amountRemaining* **div** *centsPerNickel*
amountRemaining ← *amountRemaining* **mod** *centsPerNickel*
output 'Nickels', **tab**(10), *numberOfCoins*

{ Halves, quarters, dimes, and nickels have been handed back; *amountRemaining* is amount to be handed back in pennies }

output 'Pennies', **tab**(10), *amountRemaining*

{ All coins have been handed back }

end *MakeChange*

A typical exchange between the user and the algorithm goes like this:

```
Amount of change (in cents)? 97
Halves      1
Quarters    1
Dimes       2
Nickels     0
Pennies     2
```

Of the algorithms we have written in the algorithmic language so far, *Make-Change* is the first to include assertions. The algorithms preceding *MakeChange* did straightforward calculations with constants or the values of variables. There was little to assert that was not immediately obvious from the text of the algorithm. With *MakeChange,* on the other hand, the "state of the computation"—the denominations of coins that have been handed back and the significance of the value of *amount-Remaining*—changes as the algorithm is executed in a way that is not immediately obvious. It will help us understand the algorithm to use assertions to give the state of the computation before any statements have been executed, after the input data has been read, and after the statements for each denomination of coin have been executed.

For example, the first assertion states that, to begin with, no coins have been handed back. The second assertion, which follows the statement that reads the amount of change to be returned, states that no coins have been handed back yet and the value of *amountRemaining* is the number of coins to be handed back in halves, quarters, dimes, nickels, and pennies. The third assertion, which follows the statements for half dollars, states that half dollars have been handed back and the value of *amountRemaining* is the amount to be handed back in quarters, dimes, nickels, and pennies. Similar assertions follow the statements for dimes and nickels. The final assertion of the algorithm states that all coins have been handed back.

We can use these assertions to prove the correctness of the algorithm by showing that: (1) the first assertion holds before any statements have been executed; and (2) if the assertion preceding a statement or group of statements is true before the statements are executed, the assertion following the statements will be true after the statements have been executed.

Review questions

1. What is a *variable?* Why is the term ''variable'' used?

2. Describe the correspondence between a variable and its value.

3. What is a *variable-value table?*

4. What do we mean when we say that x is a *real variable* and i is an *integer variable?*

5. When can a value be assigned to a variable of a different type? How is the assignment carried out?

6. In what circumstances are the functions *trunc* and *round* useful in connection with assignment?

7. What is *dereferencing?*

8. In what contexts does a variable represent a value? In what contexts does it represent a memory location?

9. Sometimes we use shorthand phrases such as ''*employeeName* is 'Mary Jones' '' and ''*hoursWorked* equals 40.'' Explain what each of these phrases actually means.

10. Describe the action taken by an assignment statement when there is a single constant to the right of the assignment operator.

11. Describe the action taken by an assignment statement when there is a single variable to the right of the assignment operator.

12. Describe the action taken by an assignment statement when the expression to the right of the assignment operator is a combination of variables, constants, and operators.

13. Describe what happens when the statement

$$i \leftarrow j + k$$

is executed; i, j, and k are integer variables.

14. When a variable appears in the list of items to be printed by an **output** statement, does the variable represent a value or a memory location? Why?

15. Do the variables in the list of items to be read by an **input** statement represent values or memory locations? Why?

16. Distinguish between batch and interactive processing.

17. What is a prompt?

18. Summarize the reasoning process that we use in arriving at an algorithm for solving a given problem.

19. Describe a way of outlining the statement part of an algorithm. What is *stepwise refinement?*

20. Describe how **div** and **mod** are used by the algorithm for making change.

Exercises

1. A *trace* of the execution of an algorithm shows the value that each variable had before and after each statement was executed. The trace shows what statements were executed and how those statements affected the values of the variables. For example, if the integer variables $i, j,$ and k initially have the values 5, 10, and 15, respectively, a trace of the execution of

$$i \leftarrow j$$
$$j \leftarrow k \textbf{ div } i$$
$$k \leftarrow j + k$$

looks like this:

Statement	i	j	k
	5	10	15
$i \leftarrow j$			
	10	10	15
$j \leftarrow k \textbf{ div } i$			
	10	1	15
$k \leftarrow j + k$			
	10	1	16

Let a, b, c, d be integer variables with the initial values 10, 20, 30, and 40, respectively. Construct a trace of the execution of the following statements:

$$a \leftarrow d$$
$$d \leftarrow b$$
$$b \leftarrow c$$
$$c \leftarrow d$$

2. Suppose that the initial values of the integer variables a, b, c, and d are 10, 20, 30, and 40, respectively, and that the input data is

1
2
3

Construct a trace of the execution of the following statements:

$d \leftarrow c$
$c \leftarrow b$
$b \leftarrow a$
input a
$d \leftarrow c$
$c \leftarrow b$
input b
$d \leftarrow c$
input c

3. If a, b, and c are variables of the same type, will

$a \leftarrow b$
$b \leftarrow c$

and

$b \leftarrow c$
$a \leftarrow b$

have the same effect? Under what conditions can we interchange the order of assignment statements without changing their effect?

4. Devise a sequence of assignment statements that will interchange the values of a and b, both of which are of the same type.

Hint: Another variable, say t, will be needed for temporary storage.

5. Write an algorithm to convert centimeters to inches.

6. Write an algorithm to convert temperatures from Fahrenheit to Celsius using the formula

$$C = \frac{5}{9}(F - 32)$$

7. The length of the diagonal of a rectangle is given by the square root of the sum of the squares of the sides. Write an algorithm to input the length and width of a rectangle and output the length of its diagonal.

8. Write an algorithm to input the number purchased of a given item, the cost of the item, and the sales tax rate. The algorithm should output the amount the customer must pay.

9. One can check an automobile speedometer for accuracy by noting the time required to travel a ''measured mile'' while maintaining a certain indicated speed. Write an algorithm that will input the time, in minutes and seconds, required to travel between two milestones and output the speed the car was traveling.

10. Salespeople at a certain company get a 15% commission on their sales. Write an algorithm to input the amount a person sold and to print both the commission the person receives and the amount the company receives after the commission has been deducted.

11. The diameter of a circular pool and the depth to which it is filled are both given. Write an algorithm to calculate how many liters of water are needed to fill the pool to the specified depth. The diameter and depth are given in meters.

    We can calculate the volume of water needed as follows:

    $$\text{volume} = \frac{3.14 \times \text{depth} \times \text{diameter}^2}{4}$$

    This formula gives the volume in cubic meters. Each cubic meter consists of 1000 liters, so

    $$\text{number-of-liters} = 1000 \times \text{volume}$$

12. The *length* of a rectangular object is its longest dimension; the *girth* of the object is the distance around it, measured perpendicular to the length. The combination *length-plus-girth* occurs in postal regulations; for example, a package cannot be sent by first-class mail if its length-plus-girth exceeds 100 inches. Write an algorithm to input the length, width, and height of a package and print its length-plus-girth.

13. A bank account pays interest at the rate of i percent each year, compounded monthly. Let a be the amount currently in the account and suppose that no further deposits are made. After n months, the amount c currently in the amount can be calculated by

    $$c = a(1 + r)^n$$

    where r is the monthly interest rate, expressed as a decimal:

    $$r = \frac{i}{1200}$$

    Write an algorithm to compute the amount currently in the account, given the starting amount, the yearly rate of interest, and the number of months the money was left in the account.

14. Use the assertions in *MakeChange* to prove the correctness of the algorithm.

15. Modify the algorithm *MakeChange* to hand back one, five, ten, and twenty dollar bills as well as coins. The amount of change to be handed back should be entered in the usual dollars and cents notation—12.55, for example, for

twelve dollars and fifty-five cents. The algorithm should convert the amount entered by the user to cents before assigning it to *amountRemaining*.

Pascal Supplement

Variables and declarations

Variables play the same role in Pascal as in the algorithmic language. A variable is a named memory location, the name of which must be a valid Pascal identifier. As in the algorithmic language, variables must be declared in *variable declarations* that give the name of each variable and the type of values that the variable can have.

Variables are declared in a *variable declaration part* similar to the constant definition part with which we are already familiar. The variable declaration part of a Pascal program consists of the keyword **var** followed by any number of variable delcarations:

var

   hoursWorked: *real*;

   hourlyRate: *integer*;

   grossWages: *real*;

Each variable declaration consists of the variable name followed by a colon and the type of the variable. Each declaration ends with a semicolon. Thus the variable declaration part just given declares *hoursWorked* and *grossWages* as real variables and *hourlyRate* as an integer variable.

When several variables are declared with the same type, their declarations can be combined. For example,

var

   x: *real*;

   y: *real*;

   z: *real*;

can be abbreviated to

var

   x, y, z: *real*;

The variable names to the left of the colon are separated by commas; all the variables listed to the left of the colon are declared with the type specified to the right of the colon. The declarations given previously for *hoursWorked, hourlyRate,* and *grossWages* can be written more compactly as

var

   hoursWorked, grossWages: *real*;

   hourlyRate: *integer*;

The definition and declaration parts of a Pascal program always precede the statement part—the compound statement giving the statements to be executed. What's more, the definition and declaration parts must appear in a particular order: constant definitions must always precede variable declarations. Thus, considering only the definition and declaration parts we have taken up so far, we can outline a Pascal program as follows:

program heading

constant definition part

variable declaration part

statement part

terminating period

Any definition or declaration parts not needed by a particular program can be omitted. But the parts that *are* present must appear in the required order.

Assignment and expressions

The assignment operator in Pascal (and many other languages) is $:=$, which approximates the left-pointing arrow of the algorithmic language using symbols available on most computer keyboards. Except for the different symbol for the assignment operator, the assignment statement has the same form in Pascal as in the algorithmic language:

variable $:=$ expression

When an assignment statement is executed, the expression to the right of the assignment operator is evaluated and its value is stored in the memory location corresponding to the variable to the left of the assignment operator. The value of the expression becomes the new value of the variable, and so, as in the algorithmic language, the assignment operator in Pascal can be read as "becomes."

Generally, the value assigned to a variable must belong to the type of the variable: integers are assigned to integer variables, real numbers are assigned to real variables, and so on. Pascal follows the principle of *strong type checking,* according to which the language processor checks to see that each value has the correct type for the variable to which it is to be assigned or the operation that is to be carried out on it. Strong type checking is sometimes frustrating to programmers, since Pascal may refuse to allow an assignment that is logically justified on other grounds. But the frustration is more than made up for by the increased ability of the language processor to detect programmer errors.

To specify precisely what types of values can be assigned to a variable, and to allow some exceptions to the general rule that the type of the value and the variable must be the same, Pascal uses the concept of *assignment compatibility*. A value of type T2 is said to be assignment compatible with a type T1 if the value of type T2 can be assigned to a variable of type T1.

If T1 and T2 are the same type, all values of type T2 are assignment compatible with type T1. For example, all integers are assignment compatible with type *integer,* all real numbers are assignment compatible with type *real,* and so on.* This is just another way of saying that integers can always be assigned to integer variables, real numbers can always be assigned to real variables, and so on.

Like the algorithmic language, Pascal will convert an integer to the corresponding real number, allowing the integer to be assigned to a real variable. For example, if *hourlyRate* is a real variable, the assignment

   hourlyRate := 10

is valid. Pascal converts the integer value 10 to the real value 10.0, which is assigned to *hourlyRate.* Because of this automatic conversion, we can say that values of type *integer* are assignment compatible with type *real.*

As we continue our study of Pascal, we will encounter other situations in which a value of a type T2 can be assignment compatible with another type T1. In each such case, the types T1 and T2 overlap—that is, they have values in common. A value of type T2 that is also a value of type T1 can be assigned to a variable of type T1. A value of type T2 that does not also belong to type T1, however, is not assignment compatible with type T1.

The treatment of variables in expressions is the same in Pascal as in the algorithmic language. As in the latter, the meaning of a variable name depends on the context in which it occurs. If the variable name appears in a context where a value is expected, such as to the right of the assignment operator, the variable name represents the current value of the variable. The same is true when a variable name appears as part of an expression. When a variable name appears where the name of a memory location is expected, as to the left of the assignment operator, the variable name represents a memory location, not a value. Put another way, when a variable appears as part of an expression or where an expression is expected, the variable is automatically *dereferenced*—replaced by its value. When the variable appears where the name of a memory location is expected, no dereferencing takes place.

Input and output

Write and writeln Expressions are expected for the parameters of *write* and *writeln,* so variables in a *write* or *writeln* statement represent values. This is true whether the variables appear as separate items to be printed or as parts of more complex expressions. For example, if *length* and *width* are integer variables, the statements

   length := 7;
   width := 5;
   writeln(length:4, *width*:4, 2 * (*length* + *width*):4)

---

*Pascal *file types,* described in a later chapter, are an exception to this rule. Assignment is not allowed under any circumstances for values of file types. Thus, even if T1 and T2 were the same file type, values of type T2 would not be assignment compatible with type T1.

produce the printout

```
7    5    24
```

Integer variables as well as expressions yielding integer values can be used for field-width parameters. Thus, if *fieldWidth* is an integer variable, the statements

> *fieldWidth* := 4;
> *writeln* ('a', 'b':*fieldWidth*);
> *fieldWidth* := 10;
> *writeln*('a', 'b':*fieldWidth*);
> *writeln*('a', 'b':*fieldWidth* − 3)

produce the output

```
a###b
a#########b
a######b
```

where the #s represent blanks as usual. The actual printout looks like this

```
a    b
a             b
a         b
```

Read and readln   Corresponding to the **input** statement in the algorithmic language are the Pascal procedures *read* and *readln*. For example, if *length* and *width* are integer variables, then

> *read*(*length*, *width*)

reads two values from the standard input file (usually the user's keyboard) and assigns the first value to *length* and the second to *width*. Thus, if the input entered by the user is

```
10 8
```

then 10 is assigned to *length* and 8 is assigned to *width*. The values entered must be assignment compatible with the types of the corresponding variables. Thus, for the *read* statement just given, the input data

```
10.0 8.0
```

would result in an error message, since real values cannot be assigned to integer variables. On the other hand, integer values can be entered for real variables, since integer values are assignment compatible with type *real*.

In general, the parameters for *read* and *readln* are variables whose values are to be read. Only variables, not expressions, can be used in *read* and *readln* statements, since *read* and *readln* need names of memory locations in which values can be stored, and only variables can represent names of memory locations. Just as the expressions in *write* and *writeln* are analogous to the expression to the right of an assignment operator, the variables in *read* and *readln* are analogous to the variable to the left of an assignment operator. Both the parameter positions in *read* and *readln* statements and the position to the left of the assignment operator are contexts in which variables represent memory locations instead of values.

As they are used in this section, *read* and *readln* always read from the standard input file represented by the predefined identifier *input*. Recall that *input* must be listed as a parameter in the program heading of any program that reads from the standard input file.

Read and *readln* can read integer, real, and character values. In typing the input, successive integer and real values are separated by one or more blank spaces (commas may *not* be used). For example, suppose x, y, and z are real variables and i, j, and k are integer variables. If the user responds to the *read* statement

$read(x, y, z, i, j, k)$

with

```
3.5  1.4     3E−4 100     −75    20
```

the variables are assigned values as follows:

Variable	Value
x	3.5
y	1.4
z	0.0003
i	100
j	−75
k	20

For character values, on the other hand, no separators (such as blank spaces) are needed or possible. For example, suppose that c, d, and e are character variables, and the statement

$read(c, d, e)$

is executed. If the input is

```
pqr
```

then the variables receive the following values:

Variable	Value
c	'p'
d	'q'
e	'r'

If the input had been

```
p  r
```

the variables would have received the following values:

Variable	Value
c	'p'
d	' '
e	'r'

The blank between p and r is treated as a character to be read rather than a separator.

Pascal treats successive lines of input as if they were separated by a blank space. Thus the three lines of input

```
3.5
1.4
3E-4
```

are equivalent to the single line

```
3.5  1.4  3E-4
```

and the two lines

```
p
r
```

are equivalent to the single line

```
p  r
```

Thus the input for

read(x, y, z, i, j, k)

could also be typed as

```
3.5
1.4
3E-4
100
-75
20
```

or

```
3.5  1.4
3E-4  100
-75  20
```

or

```
3.5  1.4  3E-4
100  -75  20
```

to mention only a few possibilities.

We can prove that there is an implicit blank space between successive input lines by executing

```
read(c, d, e);
writeln(c, d, e)
```

and entering

```
o
k
```

as input. The *writeln* statement prints

```
o  k
```

showing that variable *d* was assigned the blank space between the two lines of input.

The only difference between *read* and *readln* lies in what is done with the rest of the current input line after values have been read for all the variables in the *read* or *readln* statement. *Read* leaves the rest of the current input line for use by the next *read* or *readln* statement; *readln* discards the rest of the current input line so that the next *read* or *readln* statement must start with the next line of input. For example, suppose that *l* and *m* are also integer variables, and compare the actions of the following two sets of statements:

```
read(i, j);     readln(i, j);
read(k);        readln(k);
read(l, m)      readln(l, m)
```

Suppose that the input is

```
10  20  30  40
1  2  3  4
100  200  300  400
```

Each *read* statement leaves the rest of the current line for use by the next *read* or *readln* statement. Thus the first *read* statement reads the values 10 and 20, the second reads the value 30, and the third reads the values 40 and 1. The next *read* or *readln* statement in the program will begin by reading the value 2. In contrast, each *readln* statement discards the rest of the current line after it finishes reading. Thus, the first *readln* statement reads the values 10 and 20, the second reads the value 1, and the third reads the values 100 and 200. The next *read* or *readln* statement in the program will have to begin with a new line of input. The following table contrasts the values assigned to the variables depending on whether *read* or *readln* was used:

Variable	Value Assigned by read	Value Assigned by readln
i	10	10
j	20	20
k	30	1
l	40	100
m	1	200

Prompts and responses

For many interactive systems, we can use *write* to print a prompt and *readln* to read the user's response. For example,

> *write*('Length and width of rectangle? ');
> *readln*(*length*, *width*)

The *write* statement prints the prompt without going to a new line so that the response will appear on the same line as the prompt. Using *readln* statements for responses requires the user to type a new line in response to each prompt. When the two statements in the example are executed, a dialogue similar to the following takes place:

```
Length and width of rectangle? 7 5
```

The program typed the prompt and the user typed the two numbers. The value 7 was assigned to *length* and the value 5 to *width*.

Using *write* statements for prompts may not produce the desired results for some systems. Systems that process only complete lines of output will not immediately print the partial line produced by the *write* statement but will wait for the line to be completed by a later *writeln* statement. For such systems, *writeln* statements should be used for prompts; the response will appear on the line following the prompt.

Example programs

Figures 7.11 through 7.14 show the Pascal programs corresponding to the four algorithms described in this chapter. As usual, the principles on which the algorithms are based have been discussed in the main text; in the supplement we will confine our comments to the problem of translating the algorithms into Pascal.

Figure 7.11 shows the program *Discounts,* which computes the amount of discount and the discounted price of an item of merchandise from the regular price and the percentage discount. Since the program reads from the standard input file and writes to the standard output file, both *input* and *output* must be listed as parameters in the program heading.

Following the program heading and a comment is the variable declaration part, in which all five variables used by the program are declared as real variables. Note that the combined declaration for the five variables extends over two lines. In general, any Pascal construction can be continued over as many lines as need be, as long as no individual symbol (such as an identifier, literal, or reserved word) is broken between lines.

In the statement part of the program, a *write* statement prompts the user for the regular price and the percentage discount, and a *readln* statement reads the values entered. The calculations are done as in the algorithmic language, and *writeln* statements are used to print the results. Each of the two numbers is printed with two decimal places, as is customary for amounts of money. Each is printed with a field-

Figure 7.11   Pascal program corresponding to the algorithm for
computing discounts, Figure 7.7. Note the file parameters
input and *output* in the program heading and the variable
declaration part introduced by the reserved word **var**.

```
program Discounts(input, output);

{ Compute amount of discount and discounted price from regular price and
percentage discount }

var
    regularPrice, percentDiscount, discountRate,
    amountOfDiscount, discountedPrice: real;
begin
    write('Regular price and percentage discount? ');
    readln(regularPrice, percentDiscount);
    discountRate := percentDiscount / 100.0;
    amountOfDiscount := regularPrice * discountRate;
    discountedPrice := regularPrice − amountOfDiscount;
    writeln('Amount of discount is $', amountOfDiscount:1:2);
    writeln('Discounted price is $', discountedPrice:1:2)
end.
```

width parameter of 1 so that it will take up no more space than required for the
characters making up the number. With standard Pascal, each printed number is
immediately preceded by a dollar sign; with some existing versions of Pascal, a space
may occur between the dollar sign and the number.

Some of the identifiers in our algorithms will present problems with Pascal implementations in which only the first eight characters of an identifier are significant.
For example, such an implementation would consider *discountRate* and
discountedPrice to be the same identifier, since both agree in their first eight characters. If the implementation does not distinguish between lowercase and uppercase
letters, as many do not, then *Discounts* would also be considered identical to the
other two identifiers. One solution to this problem is to abbreviate a frequently occurring long first word. For example, we could use *discntRate* and *discntedPrice* in
place of *discountRate* and *discountedPrice*.

The program for computing batting averages, Figure 7.12, declares both integer
and real variables. The declarations for the three integer variables are combined. The
user is prompted separately for each item of input data. The program uses three
write-readln statement combinations to print the prompts and accept the responses.
If the values entered for *timesAtBat* and *timesWalked* are the same, the program will

Figure 7.12   Pascal program corresponding to the algorithm for
computing batting averages, Figure 7.8. If the values
entered for *timesAtBat* and *timesWalked* are the same, the
program will be terminated with an error message similar to
"division by zero attempted."

```
program ComputeBattingAverage(input, output);

{ Compute baseball player's batting average from number of times at bat,
number of times walked, and number of hits }

var
    hits, timesAtBat, timesWalked: integer;
    battingAverage: real;
begin
    write('Number of times at bat? ');
    readln(timesAtBat);
    write('Number of times walked? ');
    readln(timesWalked);
    write('Number of hits? ');
    readln(hits);
    battingAverage := hits / (timesAtBat − timesWalked);
    writeln('Batting average is ', battingAverage:1:3)
end.
```

attempt to divide by zero when it computes the batting average. Since division by
zero is impossible, execution of the program will be terminated and an error message
will be displayed. The program prints the result of its calculations with three decimal
places, which is the customary format for batting averages.

Convert, Figure 7.13, converts feet and inches to centimeters. This program has
both a constant definition part and a variable declaration part. As required, the constant definition part precedes the variable declaration part. An implementation in
which only the first eight characters of identifiers are significant will not distinguish
between *centimetersPerInch* and *centimeters;* abbreviating the word *centimeters* to
cm in either identifier will avoid the conflict.

In *MakeChange*, Figure 7.14, we want to print the output in two columns, one
column giving the denominations of coins and the other column giving the number
of coins of each denomination to be handed back. In order for the columns to line
up, all values in a given column must be printed with the same field width. For the
denominations, we could achieve this by printing 'Halves', 'Quarters', 'Nickels', and

Figure 7.13   Pascal program corresponding to the algorithm for
converting feet and inches to centimeters, Figure 7.9. Note
the constant definition and variable declaration parts,
introduced by the keywords **const** and **var**, respectively.
The constant definition part must precede the variable
declaration part.

```
program Convert(input, output);

{ Convert feet and inches to centimeters }

const
    inchesPerFoot = 12;
    centimetersPerInch = 2.54;
var
    inches, feet, lengthInInches: integer;
    centimeters: real;
begin
    write('Length in feet and inches? ');
    readln(feet, inches);
    lengthInInches := inchesPerFoot * feet + inches;
    centimeters := centimetersPerInch * lengthInInches;
    writeln('Length in centimeters is ', centimeters:1:2)
end.
```

so on, each with a field-width parameter of 8 (the longest string, 'Quarters', contains
eight characters). This, however, would print the first column as follows

```
  Halves
Quarters
   Dimes
 Nickels
 Pennies
```

Strings, however, look better when justified on the left rather than on the right. We
can achieve left justification by inserting enough spaces to the right of each denomination so that each string is eight characters long. That is, we print the values of

```
'Halves  '
'Quarters'
'Dimes   '
'Nickels '
'Pennies '
```

Figure 7.14   Pascal program corresponding to the algorithm for making change. The strings giving the names of the denominations contain sufficient blanks to the right of the names to make all the strings the same length. This causes the names to be justified (lined up) on the left, which looks better than the right justification produced by Pascal.

```pascal
program MakeChange(input, output);

{ Compute number of half dollars, quarters, dimes, nickels, and pennies to
be returned for amount of change less than one dollar }

const
    centsPerHalf    = 50;
    centsPerQuarter = 25;
    centsPerDime    = 10;
    centsPerNickel  =  5;
var
    amountRemaining, numberOfCoins: integer;
begin

    { No coins have been handed back }

    write('Amount of change (in cents)? ');
    readln(amountRemaining);

    { No coins have been handed back; amountRemaining is amount to be
    handed back in halves, quarters, dimes, nickels, and pennies }

    numberOfCoins := amountRemaining div centsPerHalf;
    amountRemaining := amountRemaining mod centsPerHalf;
    writeln('Halves ', numberOfCoins:3);

    { Halves have been handed back; amountRemaining is amount to be
    handed back in quarters, dimes, nickels, and pennies }

    numberOfCoins := amountRemaining div centsPerQuarter;
    amountRemaining := amountRemaining mod centsPerQuarter;
    writeln('Quarters', numberOfCoins:3);

    { Halves and quarters have been handed back; amountRemaining is
    amount to be handed back in dimes, nickels, and pennies }
```

numberOfCoins := *amountRemaining* **div** *centsPerDime*;
amountRemaining := *amountRemaining* **mod** *centsPerDime*;
writeln('Dimes ', *numberOfCoins*:3);

{ Halves, quarters, and dimes have been handed back;
amountRemaining is amount to be handed back in nickels and
pennies }

numberOfCoins := *amountRemaining* **div** *centsPerNickel*;
amountRemaining := *amountRemaining* **mod** *centsPerNickel*;
writeln('Nickels ', *numberOfCoins*:3);

{ Halves, quarters, dimes, and nickels have been handed back;
amountRemaining is the amount to be handed back in pennies }

writeln('Pennies ', *amountRemaining*:3);

{ All coins have been handed back }

end.

No field-width parameters are required. The entries in the number-of-coins column are printed with a field width of 3, producing two spaces between the two columns. A typical exchange with the program goes like this:

```
Amount of change (in cents)? 81
Halves    1
Quarters  1
Dimes     0
Nickels   1
Pennies   1
```

The four identifiers beginning with *centsPer* will not be distinguished by an implementation in which only the first eight characters of an identifier are significant. A simple remedy is to abbreviate *cents* to *cnts* in each identifier.

Repetition

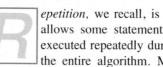

epetition, we recall, is the control structure that allows some statements of an algorithm to be executed repeatedly during a single execution of the entire algorithm. Most notrivial algorithms use repetition. Indeed, if each statement in an algorithm were to be executed only once, we would probably find it easier to execute the statements by hand (perhaps with the aid of a calculator) than to write a computer program and then let the computer execute the statements.

The fact that our instructions must be broken down into extremely small steps before they can be executed by a computer encourages the use of repetition. For example, if we want the computer to search for a particular entry in a table, we cannot (in most programming languages) merely tell the computer to search the table. Instead we must write the statements for examining a single entry into the table, and then arrange for the execution of these statements to be repeated for each table entry that needs to be examined.

As important as repetition is, its use imposes some obligations on the programmer. We must verify that each repetition terminates, lest our programs ''hang up'' the computer by causing it to repeat some statements indefinitely. And we must make sure that we thoroughly understand the effects produced by the repeated execution of a sequence of statements. Usually, the best way to do the latter is to consider an *invariant assertion* that is true before the repeated statements are executed and remains true after each execution of the repeated statements.

In this chapter we will look at three algorithmic-language constructions for specifying and controlling repetition. The three constructions are referred to by the keywords that introduce them: **for, while,** and **repeat.**

8.1

The for construction

The **for** construction is the "safest" of the three since the repetition it produces always terminates. We can never accidentally write a nonterminating repetition—an "infinite loop"—using a **for** construction. On the other hand, the **for** construction requires that the number of repetitions to be carried out be known in advance—that is, before the **for** statement is executed. If we want the repeated statements to be executed until some desired situation occurs, and we do not know in advance how many repetitions will be required to bring about the desired situation, then the **for** construction cannot be used and we must turn to the **while** or **repeat** construction.

The **for** statement is best introduced with an example:

> **for** $i \leftarrow 1$ **to** 5
> > **output** i
>
> **endfor**

The integer variable i is successively assigned the values 1 through 5. For each value of i, the **output** statement is executed, producing the following printout:

> 1
> 2
> 3
> 4
> 5

By using **downto** in place of **to,** we can make the computer count backward:

> **for** $i \leftarrow 5$ **downto** 1
> > **output** i
>
> **endfor**

This **for** construction causes the computer to print:

> 5
> 4
> 3
> 2
> 1

As many statements as needed can appear between **for** and **endfor**. On each repetition, these statements are executed sequentially. For example, the **for** construction

> **for** $i \leftarrow 1$ **to** 3
> > **output** '***', **more**
> > **output** '$$', **more**
>
> **endfor**

prints the pattern

> ***$$***$$***$$

The statements between **for** and **endfor** are usually indented to help us see at a glance which statements are controlled by the **for** construction. Note the use of the **more** command to prevent the output device from going to a new line. One of the most common uses of **more** is to allow repeated executions of **output** statements to produce output on the same line.

The **for** construction has the following two general forms:

> **for** control-variable ← expression-1 **to** expression-2
> > statements
>
> **endfor**

and

> **for** control-variable ← expression-1 **downto** expression-2
> > statements
>
> **endfor**

The *control variable* is the variable whose value is varied from repetition to repetition. Expression-1 gives the initial value of the control variable, and expression-2 gives its final value. The values of expression-1 and expression-2 must be of the same type as the control variable. We will always use control variables of type integer; however, other types with discrete values, such as *char,* can also be used. For example, if c is a character variable, then

> **for** c ← 'a' **to** 'z'
> > **output** c, **more**
>
> **endfor**

prints

> abcdefghijklmnopqrstuvwxyz

and

> **for** c ← 'z' **downto** 'a'
> > **output** c, **more**
>
> **endfor**

prints

> zyxwvutsrqponmlkjihgfedcba

Expression-1 and expression-2 can be any expressions that yield values of the proper type. For example, if i, j, and k are integer variables, the statements

> j ← 3
> k ← 5
> **for** i ← $k - j$ **to** $k + j$
> > **output** i, ' ', **more**
>
> **endfor**

print

2 3 4 5 6 7 8

since the value of $k - j$ is 2 and that of $k + j$ is 8. If the values of j and k are changed, the same **for** construction will step the value of i through a different range of values. For example, the statements

> $j \leftarrow 3$
> $k \leftarrow 4$
> **for** $i \leftarrow k - j$ **to** $k + j$
> > **output** i, ' ', **more**
>
> **endfor**

print

1 2 3 4 5 6 7

The **to** form of the **for** construction will only step through a series of increasing values. Therefore, if the value of expression-1 is greater than that of expression-2, no executions of the repeated statements take place. For example,

> **for** $i \leftarrow 5$ **to** 1
> > **output** i
>
> **endfor**

produces no output. Likewise the **downto** form will only step through decreasing values. Therefore, if the value of expression-1 is less than that of expression-2, the repeated statements are not executed. Thus

> **for** $i \leftarrow 1$ **downto** 5
> > **output** i
>
> **endfor**

also produces no output.

Nested for constructions   The statements controlled by a **for** construction can themselves include **for** constructions. When one construction is contained within another construction of the same kind, we say that the constructions are *nested*. Nested **for** constructions are particularly common. For example, suppose we wish to print the following pattern:

> *
> **
> ***
> ****
> *****

We can print a single line with this pattern with the statements

> **for** $i \leftarrow 1$ **to** n
> 　**output** $'*'$, **more**
> **endfor**
> **output**

where the value of the integer variable n determines how many asterisks will be printed on the line. The final **output** statement with no items to be printed causes the output device to go to a new line, effectively canceling the last **more** command. To print the entire pattern, we need to execute these statements with the value of n equal to 1, 2, 3, 4, and 5. We can do this by enclosing the statements for printing one line within another **for** construction:

> **for** $n \leftarrow 1$ **to** 5
> 　''Print line containing n asterisks''
> **endfor**

Replacing the quoted description with the statements that actually print a line of n asterisks gives the following nested **for** constructions:

> **for** $n \leftarrow 1$ **to** 5
> 　**for** $i \leftarrow 1$ **to** n
> 　　**output** $'*'$, **more**
> 　**endfor**
> 　**output**
> **endfor**

Note that indentation is crucial for clarifying the structure of nested constructions. A nonindented version of the nested **for** statements

> **for** $n \leftarrow 1$ **to** 5
> **for** $i \leftarrow 1$ **to** n
> **output** $'*'$, **more**
> **endfor**
> **output**
> **endfor**

is much more difficult to figure out than the indented version.

8.2

Algorithms using the for construction

Computing a total　For our first example, we will write an algorithm to read a series of integers and compute their total. Simple as this example is, it illustrates several important ideas that are fundamental to many applications of repetition.

In designing an algorithm to do a particular job, it often helps to recall how the job is done manually. To add a series of numbers with a calculator, we clear the calculator display to zero and then enter and add each number. As we work, the display shows a running total of all the numbers added so far.

We will follow the same method in our algorithm. The variable *total* will play the same role as the calculator display; as the algorithm is executed, the value of *total* will be the running total of all the numbers added so far. Before any additions are done, the value of *total* must be cleared to zero:

$total \leftarrow 0$

Each number to be included in the total is accepted from the user and added to the value of *total:*

> **output** 'Enter number: ', **more**
> **input** *number*
> *total* $\leftarrow$ *total* $+$ *number*

Suppose that the user has been asked how many values are to be included in the total, and the user's response has been assigned to *count*. Then the statements for accepting a number and adding it to the running total must be executed "*count* times"—that is, a number of times equal to the value of *count*. A **for** construction repeats the statements the required number of times:

> **for** $i \leftarrow 1$ **to** *count*
> > **output** 'Enter number: ', **more**
> > **input** *number*
> > *total* $\leftarrow$ *total* $+$ *number*
>
> **endfor**

We can outline the algorithm as follows:

"Obtain number of values to be added and assign to *count*"
"Clear value of *total* to zero"
"Repeat *count* times: input a number and add it to the value of *total*"
"Output value of *total* as sum of numbers entered"

Figure 8.1 shows the complete algorithm. A typical exchange between the algorithm and the user looks like this:

```
How many numbers are to be added? 4
Enter number: 348
Enter number: 295
Enter number: 762
Enter number: 590
Total is 1995
```

The key to understanding the repetition is the invariant assertion that precedes the repeated statements in Figure 8.1. The assertion, which states that the value of *total* is the sum of all the numbers entered so far, certainly holds true just before the repeated statements are executed for the first time, since at that point no numbers have been entered and *total* still has its initial value of zero. Each execution of the

Figure 8.1   Algorithm for computing the sum of a series of integers
                  entered by the user. The user must specify in advance how
                  many integers are to be added.

```
algorithm ComputeTotal

{ Compute sum of integers entered by user }

declare
    count, number, total, i: integer
execute
    output 'How many numbers are to be added? ' , more
    input count
    total ← 0
    for i ← 1 to count

        { The value of total is the sum of all the numbers entered so far }

        output 'Enter number: ', more
        input number
        total ← total + number
    endfor
    output 'Total is ', total
end ComputeTotal
```

repeated statements inputs a number and adds it to the value of *total*: thus if the
assertion was true before the repeated statements were executed, it must still be true
afterward.

Since the repetition is controlled by a **for** construction, it is guaranteed to terminate and does so after the repeated statements have been executed *count* times, the
number of times requested by the user. When the repetition terminates, the invariant
assertion is still true, and so the value of *total* is the sum of all the numbers that
were entered. Thus when the repetition terminates, the value of *total* is the desired
total that is to be printed out for the user.

Note that *total* appears on both sides of the repeated assignment statement:

total ← *total* + *number*

Except on the first execution of this statement, the value of *total* used to evaluate the
expression on the right is the value that was computed during the previous execution.
Except on the last execution, the value of the expression, which is stored back in
total, will be used in evaluating the expression on the next execution. Thus *total*
serves to carry a data value forward from one execution of the repeated statements

to the next; the value computed for *total* on one repetition is used on the next repetition. We will often find that a repetition construction involves one or more variables that are used in this way.

Personal investment   Suppose that we have a savings account on which the interest is compounded monthly. If we start with a given amount in the account, and deposit the same amount each month, how much will we have after a given number of months have elapsed?

We will use *amount* for the amount currently in the account. The starting value for *amount* will be obtained from the user. This value will then be updated month by month as interest is earned. The role of *amount* in this algorithm will be analogous to that of *total* in the preceding one.

Additional data needed for the calculation are the monthly deposit (*deposit*), the yearly percentage interest rate (*yearlyRate*), and the number of months over which the calculation is to be done (*months*). After obtaining the necessary data and converting the percentage yearly rate into a decimal monthly rate (*monthlyRate*), the algorithm works through the calculation month by month.

> "Obtain amount initially in account and assign to *amount*"
>
> "Obtain values for *deposit*, *yearlyRate*, and *months*"
>
> "Convert percentage yearly rate *yearlyRate* to decimal monthly rate *monthlyRate*"
>
> **for** $n \leftarrow 1$ **to** *months*
>
>> { The value of *amount* is the amount in the account at the start of the *n*th month }
>>
>> "Update the value of amount to reflect the deposit made and the interest earned during the *n*th month"
>
> **end for**
>
> "Print the value of *amount* as the amount in the account after the given number of months have elapsed"

The invariant assertion is true before the repetitions commence since the value of *amount* was set initially to the starting amount obtained from the user. The repeated statements must update the value of *amount* in such a way as to maintain the truth of the invariant assertion. Specifically, if the invariant assertion is assumed to be true before the repeated statements are executed, the repeated statements must update the value of *amount* in such a way that the invariant assertion will still be true after the execution of the repeated statements.

Consider the situation for the *n*th month—that is, for some arbitrary month during the course of the calculation. Since the invariant assertion can be assumed true before the repeated statements are executed, the value of *amount* is the amount in the account at the beginning of the *n*th month. To update *amount,* we first add the deposit for the month:

$$amount \leftarrow amount + desposit$$

Next we compute the amount of interest earned during the month:

$$interest \leftarrow amount * monthlyRate$$

and add the interest to the amount:

$$amount \leftarrow amount + interest$$

After the deposit and interest for the current month have been added, the value of *amount* is the amount in the account at the beginning of the next month. Since the value of *n* will be increased by 1 for the next repetition, the invariant assertion will be true prior to the next execution of the repeated statements.

When the repetition terminates, the invariant assertion is still true and tells us that the value of *amount* is the amount in the account after the number of repetitions specified by the user. Hence the value of *amount* can be printed as the requested amount. Figure 8.2 shows the complete algorithm. A typical exchange with the program goes like this:

```
Amount in your account now? 1000
Monthly deposit? 100
Yearly interest rate in percent? 6
Number of months? 36
New amount is $5149.96
```

Fibonacci's rabbit problem   The mathematician Leonardo Fibonacci proposed the following problem. Suppose that a pair of rabbits has one pair of offspring each month, and each new pair becomes fertile at the age of one month. If we start with one fertile pair and none of the rabbits die, how many pairs will we have after a year's time?

You will not be surprised to hear that we are going to work through the problem month by month, computing the number of pairs at the beginning of each month. What is slightly different about this problem is that we have two values to keep track of: the number of pairs alive at the beginning of each month and the number of those pairs that are *fertile*.

Let the values of *pairs* and *fertilePairs* be the number of pairs and fertile pairs at the beginning of each month. The initial values of these variables will be accepted from the user. (In the original Fibonacci problem, both initial values are 1.) We will devise a set of statements to calculate the values of *pairs* and *fertilePairs* at the beginning of the following month, given their values at the beginning of the current month, and repeat these statements for the number of months specified by the user (12 in the original problem).

Every fertile pair has one pair of offspring during the month. The number of pairs at the beginning of next month, then, is the number of pairs at the beginning of this month plus one pair of offspring for each fertile pair:

$$pairsNextMonth \leftarrow pairs + fertilePairs$$

Each pair becomes fertile after one month's time. Therefore, all pairs alive at the beginning of the current month will be fertile at the beginning of the following month. Thus, *fertilePairs* is updated as follows:

$$fertilePairs \leftarrow pairs$$

Figure 8.2   Algorithm for computing the amount in a savings account
after a given number of months, assuming that a given
amount is deposited in the account at the beginning of each
month.

```
algorithm Investment

{ Compute amount resulting from monthly deposits in a savings account.
Assume that interest is compounded monthly }

declare
    amount, deposit, yearlyRate,
    monthlyRate, interest: real
    months, n: integer
execute
    output 'Amount in your account now? ', more
    input amount
    output 'Monthly deposit? ', more
    input deposit
    output 'Yearly interest rate in percent? ', more
    input yearlyRate
    output 'Number of months? ', more
    input months
    monthlyRate ← yearlyRate / 1200.0
    for n ← 1 to months

        { The value of amount is the amount in the account at the start of
        the nth month }

        amount ← amount + deposit
        interest ← amount * monthlyRate
        amount ← amount + interest
    endfor
    output 'New amount is $', amount
end Investment
```

Finally, *pairs* is updated by assigning it the number of pairs calculated for the beginning of next month:

   pairs ← *pairsNextMonth*

Note that *pairs* could not have been updated earlier, even though the value it was to receive had been calculated, since the current value of *pairs* was needed to update *fertilePairs*. In calculations such as this one, we must be careful about the order in which calculations are carried out lest we destroy some value that will be needed later.

Figure 8.3 shows the complete algorithm. As usual, the key to the repetition is the invariant assertion, which in this case just states the roles of *pairs* and *fertile-Pairs*. Note that the list of items to be printed in the final **output** statement has been continued onto a second line, something always allowed for lists in the algorithmic

Figure 8.3   Algorithm for solving a slightly generalized version of Fibonacci's rabbit problem. Since the rabbit-raising enterprise must start with at least one pair, the starting number of pairs should be greater than zero. The starting number of fertile pairs can be greater than or equal to zero, however; we can start with no fertile pairs since the remaining pairs will become fertile after one month's time.

```
algorithm Fibonacci

{ Solve Fibonacci's rabbit problem }

declare
    pairs, fertilePairs, months,
    pairsNextMonth, n: integer
execute
    output 'Starting number of pairs? ', more
    input pairs
    output 'Starting number of fertile pairs? ', more
    input fertilePairs
    output 'Number of months? ', more
    input months
    for n ← 1 to months

        { The values of pairs and fertilePairs are, respectively, the
        number of pairs and the number of fertile pairs alive at the
        beginning of the nth month }

        pairsNextMonth ← pairs + fertilePairs
        fertilePairs ← pairs
        pairs ← pairsNextMonth
    endfor
    output 'After ', months, ' months you will have ', pairs, ' pairs'
end Fibonacci
```

language. If we use the algorithm to solve the initial Fibonacci problem, the exchange with the user goes like this:

```
Starting number of pairs? 1
Starting number of fertile pairs? 1
Number of months? 12
After 12 months you will have 377 pairs
```

The inventor's request   According to an old tale, the inventor of chess was called before the king and told to name his own reward. The inventor responded, "All I ask is one grain of wheat for the first square of my chessboard, two grains for the second square, four grains for the third square, and so on for all 64 squares, doubling the number of grains for each square." Should the king grant the request? To find out, we will write an algorithm to determine the number of grains of wheat the inventor has requested.

By now we are old hands at this kind of problem, so we can go right to the heart of the matter. We are going to step through the 64 squares of the chessboard, computing the number of grains on each square, and keeping track of the total number of grains on all the squares considered so far. Assume that the squares are numbered from 1 through 64, and let the value of n be the number of the square currently being considered. We can use *grains* for the number of grains to be placed on the current square, and *total* for the number of grains on all squares considered *prior* to the current one. Our invariant assertion, then, is:

{ *Grains* is the number of grains to be placed on the nth square and *total* is the number of grains placed on squares already considered }

Just prior to the first execution of the repeated statements, the value of n will be 1 and so the value of *grains* must be the number of grains to be placed on the first square, which is 1. The value of *total* is the number of grains placed on squares already considered, of which there are none. Hence, *grains* and *total* are given the following initial values:

grains $\leftarrow 1.0$

total $\leftarrow 0.0$

Suspecting that the number of grains requested is going to be very large, perhaps larger than the largest integer value for most computer systems, we declare *grains* and *total* as real variables and, hence, assign them real intial values.

The repeated statements must maintain the truth of the invariant assertion by updating the values of *grains* and *total* so that they will be appropriate for the next square considered. The new value for *total* must include the number of grains on the current square, so we update *total* as follows:

total $\leftarrow total + grains$

The number of grains is doubled for each square, so the value of *grains* for the next square should be twice its value for the current square:

grains $\leftarrow 2.0 * grains$

Why must *total* be updated before *grains?*

Figure 8.4 shows the complete algorithm. When the algorithm is executed, it prints the following:

```
Inventor requested 1.84467E+19 grains
```

The inventor requested over 18 billion billion grains of wheat, considerably more than is currently produced each year throughout the entire world.

8.3 The while construction

When the computer reaches a **for** construction, it begins by computing the values of expression-1 and expression-2, which determine the values through which the control variable will be stepped and hence the number of repetitions that will be carried out. We can use a **for** construction, then, only when the number of repetitions is known

Figure 8.4   Algorithm for computing the number of grains of wheat supposedly requested by the inventor of chess. *Grains* and *total* are declared as real variables in anticipation of the fact that their values may become very large.

---

algorithm *Wheat*

{ Compute number of grains of wheat requested by inventor of chess }

declare
    grains, total: real { Values may be very large }
    n: integer
execute
    grains ← 1.0
    total ← 0.0
    for *n* ← 1 **to** 64

        { *Grains* is the number of grains to be placed on the *n*th square and *total* is the number of grains placed on squares already considered }

        total ← *total* + *grains*
        grains ← 2.0 * *grains*
    endfor
    output 'Inventor requested ', *grains*, ' grains'
end *Wheat*

before the first repetition is carried out. If the number of repetitions is not known in advance, we must use either the **while** construction (described in this section) or the **repeat** construction (described in the next section).

The **while** construction has the following general form:

while condition

statements

endwhile

The condition is a declarative statement that can be true or false. In the algorithmic language, a condition is represented by a *Boolean expression*—an expression whose value is one of the two Boolean values *true* and *false*. Before each execution of the repeated statements, the condition is tested—that is, the Boolean expression is evaluated. If the value of the Boolean expression is *true,* the repeated statements are executed, after which the condition is tested again, and so on. If the value of the Boolean expression is *false,* the repeated statements are not executed, the repetitions are terminated, and the computer continues execution with the next statement following the **while** construction.

Relational operators   A *relational operator* corresponds to a relation that can exist between two values, such as one number being equal to another or one string preceding another in alphabetical order. The operands for a relational operator are the values to be compared; the relational operator returns *true* if the corresponding relation holds between the operands and *false* otherwise. Since relational operators return Boolean values, we can use them to construct Boolean expressions.

The following relational operators apply to integers and real numbers:

Operator	Relation
=	is equal to
<	is less than
>	is greater than
<=	is less than or equal to
>=	is greater than or equal to
<>	is not equal to

The operands may be integers, real numbers, or a combination of the two. The result returned is always Boolean—*true* if the relation holds and *false* if it does not:

Expression	Value
$3 = 5$	*false*
$2 <= 5$	*true*
$5 >= 5$	*true*
$4 <> 4$	*false*
$7 < 7.5$	*true*
$3.14 > 3.1416$	*false*

The relational operators have a lower priority than any arithmetical operator. This means that, if we place a relational operator between two arithmetical expressions, the arithmetical expressions will be evaluated first, and the relational operator will be applied to the results:

$$9 - 3 * 2 > 5$$

$9 - 6 > 5$	*Multiplications first . . .*
$3 > 5$	*. . . then subtraction . . .*
false	*. . . then "greater than."*

The relational operators are defined for characters and strings as well as for numeric values:

Operator	*Relation*
=	is equal to
<	precedes in alphabetical order
>	follows in alphabetical order
<=	precedes in alphabetical order or is equal to
>=	follows in alphabetical order or is equal to
<>	is not equal to

The term "alphabetical order" needs to be extended to all characters of type *char*. This is done by means of a *collating sequence,* which lists all the characters in alphabetical order. For example, the order in which the characters appear in Figure 4.1 defines the collating sequence for the popular ASCII character set. The collating sequence can vary from one computer system to another. The letters of the alphabet and the numerals will always be in the expected order, but such matters as whether the letters precede the numerals and where the punctuation marks are located vary from one collating sequence to another. Note that uppercase and lowercase letters are not considered equal. The collating sequence determines whether the uppercase letters precede the lowercase ones, or vice versa.

The following are some examples of string comparisons:

Expression	*Value*
'a' > 'z'	*false*
'0' < '9'	*true*
'beak' < 'book'	*true*
'car' = 'auto'	*false*
'zip' <> 'ZIP'	*true*
'o k' <> 'ok'	*true*
'kind' < 'kindly'	*true*

In the last two examples, note that: (1) blank spaces count when doing comparisons; and (2) when one string forms the initial part of another, the shorter string comes first in alphabetical order.

As a simple example of both relational operators and the **while** construction, let's write a **while** construction equivalent to the **for** construction:

> **for** $i \leftarrow 1$ **to** 5
>> **output** i
>
> **endfor**

The **while** construction does not automatically step the value of a control variable, so the value of i must be set to 1 before the first repetition and incremented by 1 at the end of each repetition. The repetitions are to continue as long as the value of i is less than or equal to 5:

> $i \leftarrow 1$
> **while** $i <= 5$
>> **output** i
>> $i \leftarrow i + 1$
>
> **endwhile**

Note that i is given an initial value before the **while** construction is executed. Since **while** tests the condition *before* each execution of the repeated statements, and hence before the first execution, each variable appearing in the condition must be given its initial value before the **while** construction is executed.

To prove that the example repetition terminates—always our responsibility with the **while** construction—we note that each execution of the repeated statements increases the value of i by 1. Therefore, the value of i will eventually exceed 5, at which time the condition $i <= 5$ will become false and no more repetitions will take place.

The **while** construction equivalent to

> **for** $i \leftarrow 5$ **downto** 1
>> **output** i
>
> **endfor**

is

> $i \leftarrow 5$
> **while** $i >= 1$
>> **output** i
>> $i \leftarrow i - 1$
>
> **endwhile**

Now, the value of i is decreased by 1 on each repetition. The repetitions must terminate since repeatedly decreasing the value of i will eventually make it less than 1, causing the condition $i >= 1$ to become false.

8.4 Algorithms using the while construction

Reading data   The algorithm *ComputeTotal* (Figure 8.1) requires the user to begin by entering the number of values to be added. If the number of values is large, counting them is an unreasonable burden on the user. If the values have to be counted, let the computer do it. Instead, we should enter the numbers to be added, then enter a special *sentinel value* indicating that all the data values have been entered. The sentinel value can be any value that cannot be mistaken for a data value; for example, if the data values are all positive numbers, then the sentinel value can be a negative number. When the algorithm recognizes the sentinel value, it prints the number of values previously entered and their sum.

We can outline an algorithm that inputs and processes data in this way as follows:

"Input first value to be processed"
while "value to be processed is not sentinel value"
    "Process current value"
    "Input next value to be processed"
endwhile

The tricky point here is that the first value to be processed must be read before the **while** construction is executed. Thus, the statements for inputting a value occur in two places: before the **while** construction and at the end of the repeated statements. The reason for this arrangement is that, when a value is read, it must be tested to see if it is the sentinel value *before* it is processed, since we don't want to process the sentinel value as if it were a data value. With the arrangement shown, each input value is tested immediately after it has been read and before it has been processed.

People sometimes try to get by with fewer statements by writing the following:

while "value to be processed is not sentinel value"
    "Input next value to be processed"
    "Process value just read"
endwhile

This arrangement has two fatal flaws. First, the variable holding the value to be processed is not given an initial value before the **while** construction is executed; thus, we do not know what value this variable will have the first time its value is tested. Second, an input value is processed before testing to see if it is the sentinel value. Thus, the sentinel value will be processed as if it were an ordinary data value, contrary to our desires.

Figure 8.5 shows the algorithm *ComputeTotal1*, which adds a series of nonnegative numbers. Since the numbers to be added are nonnegative, any negative number will be considered a sentinel value. When the sentinel is read, the algorithm prints both the number of values that were entered and their sum. A typical exchange with the algorithm goes like this:

```
Enter a number: 10
Enter a number: 15
Enter a number: 20
Enter a number: −1
Number of values entered is 3
Total is 45
```

Note that the sentinel value, −1, is not counted as a value entered nor is it included in the sum.

The algorithm uses *count* to keep a running count of the number of values en-

Figure 8.5 Algorithm for counting and computing the sum of a series of nonnegative integers entered by the user. Since the integers being added are nonnegative, a negative integer is used as a sentinel to signal the end of the input data. The sentinel value is not included in either the count or the total.

---

algorithm *ComputeTotal1*

{ Compute sum of integers entered by user }

declare
    count, number, total: *integer*
execute
    count ← 0
    total ← 0
    output 'Enter a number: ', **more**
    input *number*
    while *number* >= 0

        { The values of *count* and *total* are, respectively, the number of and the sum of the values already processed. The value of *number* is the next value to be processed }

        count ← *count* + 1
        total ← *total* + *number*
        output 'Enter a number: ', **more**
        input *number*
    endwhile
    output 'Number of values entered is ', *count*
    output 'Total is ', *total*
end *ComputeTotal1*

tered and *total* to keep a running total of the values. To begin with, both *count* and *total* are cleared to zero:

> *count* ← 0
>
> *total* ← 0

The current value to be processed is assigned to *number*. In accordance with the outline just given, the first value is read and assigned to *number* before the **while** construction is executed:

> **output** 'Enter a number: ', **more**
>
> **input** *number*

The repeated statements are executed as long as the value of *number* is nonnegative—that is, the value of *number* is not the sentinel value:

> **while** *number* >= 0
>
>> ''Add 1 to the value of *count,* add the value of *number* to that of *total,*
>>
>> and read into *number* the next input value to be processed''
>
> **endwhile**

The invariant assertion in Figure 8.5 states that, just before each execution of the repeated statements, the value of *count* is the number of values already processed and the value of *total* is their sum. The value of *number* is the next value to be processed. This assertion holds before the repetitions begin, since at that time no values have been processed, *count* and *total* have been initialized to zero, and the first input value to be processed has been read and assigned to *number*. To maintain the truth of the invariant assertion, the repeated statements must include the current value to be processed in both the count:

> *count* ← *count* + 1

and the total:

> *total* ← *total* + *number*

Also, since the value of *number* has now been processed, the next input value to be processed must be read and assigned to *number*:

> **output** 'Enter a number: ', **more**
>
> **input** *number*

With the **while** construction, we must always convince ourselves that the repetition will eventually terminate. Each execution of the repeated statements must, in some sense, ''make progress'' toward a situation in which the condition tested by the **while** statement will be false. We assume that the input data consists of a finite number of nonnegative data values terminated by a negative sentinel value. Each execution of the repeated statements processes one input value and hence makes progress toward the situation in which the sentinel value is read. When the sentinel value is finally read, the condition *number* >= 0 has the value *false,* and the repetition terminates. The assumption that the data values are followed by a sentinel value is essential for proving termination. If the user forgets to include the sentinel value—a not uncommon error—all bets are off.

The rabbit problem revisited   In the original Fibonacci rabbit problem, we are asked how many pairs there will be after the rabbits have reproduced for a given number of months. Since the number of months is given, we can use a **for** statement to repeat the calculations for one month the required number of times. But suppose the problem is turned around and we are asked for the number of months the rabbits must reproduce in order for the number of pairs to equal or exceed a given value. Now, the number of times the repeated statements are to be executed is not only not known in advance but is the result we are trying to find. Instead of a **for** statement, for which the number of repetitions would have to be specified in advance, we must use a **while** statement so that the repeated statements can be executed until a given condition—the number of pairs equals or exceeds the specified value—holds true.

Figure 8.6 shows an algorithm for solving this version of the rabbit problem. A typical exchange with the algorithm goes like this:

```
Starting number of pairs? 1
Starting number of fertile pairs? 1
Number of pairs desired? 500
After 13 months you will have 610 pairs
```

The end of the 13th month (the beginning of the 14th month) is the first time the number of pairs equals or exceeds 500. The actual number of pairs present at that time is 610.

As usual, *pairs* and *fertilePairs* are the total number of pairs and the number of fertile pairs. *PairsDesired* is the number of pairs that must be reached or exceeded, and the variable *months* is used to count the number of months the rabbits have reproduced. After *pairs* and *fertilePairs* have received their initial values, we initialize *months* to zero and repeat the monthly update of *pairs* and *fertilePairs* until the value of *pairs* equals or exceeds that of *pairsDesired*. Each time the calculation for one month is repeated, the value of *months* is increased by 1:

> *months* ← 0
>
> **while** *pairs* < *pairsDesired*
>
> > "Update *pairs* and *fertilePairs* to reflect the situation one month later"
> >
> > *months* ← *months* + 1
>
> **endwhile**

As usual, the repetition is best summarized by means of an invariant assertion. The invariant assertion in Figure 8.6 states that the values of *pairs* and *fertilePairs* reflect the corresponding populations at the beginning of the current month, and the value of *months* is the number of months the rabbits have already reproduced. The truth of this assertion is established before the repetitions begin by giving *pairs* and *fertilePairs* their starting values and setting the value of *months* to zero. To maintain the truth of the invariant assertion, the repeated statements must update the values of *pairs* and *fertilePairs* to represent the situation at the beginning of the next month and increase the value of *months* by 1 to count the current month.

Figure 8.6   Algorithm for solving a version of the Fibonacci problem in
which we are asked how many months must elapse before
the number of pairs equals or exceeds a given number.
Since we do not know in advance how many times the
calculations for a single month are to be repeated, the
execution of the repeated statements must be controlled by a
while construction rather than a **for** construction.

---

algorithm *Fibonacci1*

{ Determine number of months needed to produce a given number of pairs }

declare
    pairs, fertilePairs, months,
    pairsNextMonth, pairsDesired: integer
execute
    output 'Starting number of pairs? ', **more**
    input *pairs*
    output 'Starting number of fertile pairs? ', **more**
    input *fertilePairs*
    output 'Number of pairs desired? ', **more**
    input *pairsDesired*
    months ← 0
    while *pairs* < *pairsDesired*

        { The values of *pairs* and *fertilePairs* are, respectively, the
        number of pairs and the number of fertile pairs at the beginning of
        the current month. *Months* is the number of months that the
        rabbits have already reproduced }

        pairsNextMonth ← *pairs* + *fertilePairs*
        fertilePairs ← *pairs*
        pairs ← *pairsNextMonth*
        months ← *months* + 1
    endwhile
    output 'After ', *months*, ' months you will have ', *pairs*, ' pairs'
end *Fibonacci1*

The repetition terminates at the beginning of the first month for which the value
of *pairs* equals or exceeds that of *pairsDesired*. According to the invariant assertion,
the value of *months* is the number of months the rabbits reproduced, so we can print
the value of *months* as the number of months required for the number of pairs to
equal or exceed the value entered for *pairsDesired*.

Proving termination is a bit tricky. We must show that the value of *pairs* will eventually equal or exceed the value of *pairsDesired*, regardless of what value was entered for the latter. Let's look again at the statements that update *pairs* and *fertilePairs:*

$$pairsNextMonth \leftarrow pairs + fertilePairs$$
$$fertilePairs \leftarrow pairs$$
$$pairs \leftarrow pairsNextMonth$$

Each month, the value of *pairs* is increased by the value of *fertilePairs*. If the value of *fertilePairs* is always a positive number greater than zero, the value of *pairs* will increase each month and so will eventually exceed the value of *pairsDesired*. We must see, then, under what conditions we can guarantee that the value of *fertilePairs* will remain a positive number greater than zero no matter how many repetitions are carried out.

Let's start by proving the following: if the starting values for *pairs* and *fertilePairs* are positive numbers greater than zero, then this condition will hold no matter how many repetitions are performed. That is, we want to show that the assertion "the values of *pairs* and *fertilePairs* are positive numbers greater than zero" could be included in the invariant assertion for the repetition.

Since we are assuming that the starting values for *pairs* and *fertilePairs* are positive numbers greater than zero, our assertion is true before the first execution of the repeated statements. What's more, we can easily see that the truth of the assertion is left unchanged by the repeated statements. If the values of *pairs* and *fertilePairs* are positive numbers greater than zero, then so must be the value assigned to *pairsNextMonth*. (Why?) But the value assigned to *pairsNextMonth* and the current value of *pairs* become, respectively, the new values for *pairs* and *fertilePairs*. Hence, after the repeated statements have been executed, the values of *pairs* and *fertilePairs* are positive numbers greater than zero, and the assertion is still true.

Thus we can conclude that, if the starting values for *pairs* and *fertilePairs* are positive numbers greater than zero, then the value of *fertilePairs* will remain a positive number greater than zero regardless of how many times the repeated statements are executed. The value of *pairs* will increase each month and so will eventually equal or exceed the value of *pairsDesired*, causing the repetition to terminate.

We can also prove termination when the value of *pairs* is a positive number greater than zero and the value of *fertilePairs* is zero. After the first execution of the repeated statements, the value of *pairs* will be unchanged and the value of *fertilePairs* will be equal to the value of *pairs*. (Why?) Thus after one execution of the repeated statements, the values of both *pairs* and *fertilePairs* are positive numbers greater than zero, and the proof given for that case applies.

We have proved termination for all combinations of input data that make sense in terms of the problem we are trying to solve. Negative values for *pairs* and *fertilePairs* have no meaning for the problem being solved and so can be excluded from the outset. Since we must start our rabbit-raising enterprise with at least one pair, the starting value of *pairs* must be a positive number greater than zero. The starting number of fertile pairs can be zero, however, since any infertile pairs will become fertile after a month's time. Therefore, the starting value for *fertilePairs* can be greater than or equal to zero.

For other combinations of starting values, the repetition may or may not terminate, depending on the particular values entered. For example, if the values entered for *pairs* and *fertilePairs* are both zero, the repetition will not terminate. (Why?) It would be better if the algorithm detected invalid input data and printed an error message for the user, rather than just failing to terminate. We cannot incorporate this improvement now, however, since it requires a selection construction that will not be discussed until Chapter 9.

8.5 The repeat construction

The **repeat** construction has the following form:

repeat
    statements
until condition

The **repeat** construction differs from the **while** construction in two respects:

1. The statements are executed repeatedly until the condition becomes true. The repetition continues as long as the condition is false. We can think of the condition in the **repeat** construction as a *termination* condition: the repetitions terminate when the condition becomes true. In contrast, the condition in a **while** construction is a *continuation condition:* the repetition continues as long as the condition remains true.

2. The condition is checked *after* each execution of the repeated statements, rather than before each execution as is the case with the **while** construction. This means that the repeated statements are always executed at least once, since the termination condition is not checked until after the first execution of the repeated statements. In contrast, the statements controlled by a **while** construction will not be executed at all if the continuation condition is already false when the computer reaches the **while** construction.

The **repeat** construction comes in handy when the condition for terminating a repetition cannot be meaningfully checked until after the repeated statements have been executed. For example, the repeated statements might input or calculate some of the values that must be checked in evaluating the condition.

Figure 8.7 illustrates an application of the **repeat** construction. Usually, when an interactive program has finished processing one set of data entered by the user, the program should give the user the option of entering another set of data for processing. This saves the user the trouble of having to load and execute the program for each set of data to be processed. After processing one set of data, the program asks:

```
Do you wish to enter another set of data (y/n)?
```

Figure 8.7   This version of the algorithm for computing the amount in a
savings account allows the user to repeat the calculation for
as many different sets of data as desired. The **repeat**
construction is appropriate here, since it would be silly to
ask the user if the calculation was to be repeated before it
had been carried out the first time.

```
algorithm Investment1

{ Compute amount resulting from monthly deposits in a savings account.
Assume that interest is compounded monthly. Repeat computation for as
many sets of data as desired by user }

declare
     amount, deposit, yearlyRate,
     monthlyRate, interest: real
     months, n: integer
     answer: char
execute
     repeat
          output 'Amount in your account now? ', more
          input amount
          output 'Monthly deposit? ', more
          input deposit
          output 'Yearly interest rate in percent? ', more
          input yearlyRate
          output 'Number of months? ', more
          input months
          monthlyRate ← yearlyRate / 1200.0
          for n ← 1 to months

               { The value of amount is the amount in the account at the
               start of the nth month }

               amount ← amount + deposit
               interest ← amount * monthlyRate
               amount ← amount + interest
          endfor
          output 'New amount is $', amount
          output
          output 'Do you wish to enter another set of data (y/n)? ', more
          input answer
     until (answer = 'n') or (answer = 'N')
end Investment1
```

If the user enters n or N, the program terminates. Otherwise, the statements for processing a set of data are repeated. Using the character variable *answer* to hold the user's response, we can outline the program as follows:

> **repeat**
>> "Statements for reading and processing one set of data"
>> **output** 'Do you wish to enter another set of data (y/n)? ', **more**
>> **input** *answer*
> **until** (*answer* = 'n') **or** (*answer* = 'N')

Since it is convenient to allow the user to enter a single-character response in either uppercase or lowercase, we have anticipated our work in Chapter 9 by using the compound condition

> (*answer* = 'n') **or** (*answer* = 'N')

which is true if either or both of the conditions joined by **or** are true. Figure 8.7 shows the algorithm for computing interest on a savings account modified so that it can process more than one set of data.

The **repeat** construction is clearly appropriate for this application, since the user's response—the value of *answer*—is not known until *after* the repeated statements have been executed. On the other hand, anything that can be done with a **repeat** construction can also be done with a **while** construction, so some languages provide only a **while** construction but no **repeat** construction. Often, the trick to using **while** in place of **repeat** is to assign suitable initial values to the variables tested by the condition so as to force the repeated statements to be executed at least one time. For example, the following statements behave in exactly the same way as the repeat construction:

> *answer* ← 'y'
> **while** (*answer* <> 'n') **and** (*answer* <> 'N')
>> "Statements for reading and processing one set of data"
>> **output** 'Do you wish to enter another set of data (y/n)? ', **more**
>> **input** *answer*
> **endwhile**

Assigning *answer* the initial value 'y' forces the repeated statements to be executed at least one time. The repetition continues as long as the value of *answer* is not equal to 'n' and not equal to 'N'. (Again, we anticipate our work in Chapter 9 by using a compound condition, which is true only if both the conditions joined by **and** are true.)

Review questions

1. Why do most nontrivial algorithms use repetition?

2. What obligation does the use of repetition impose on the programmer?

3. What are *invariant assertions?* How are they used?

4. Give the names and general forms of the three constructions used for specifying repetition in the algorithmic language.

5. For which repetition construction is the repetition guaranteed to terminate?

6. Which repetition construction requires that the number of repetitions be specified in advance—that is, before the repeated statements are executed?

7. What is a *control variable?*

8. What do we mean when we say that two constructions are *nested?* Give an example of nested **for** constructions.

9. What is a *condition?* What type of expression is used to represent conditions in the algorithmic language?

10. Give the six relational operators and define each for numeric, character, and string operands.

11. Describe the process by which the statements controlled by a **while** construction are executed. When is the condition checked? How does the value of the condition affect the execution of the controlled statements?

12. Suppose that the condition in a **while** construction has the value *false* the first time it is evaluated. How many times are the repeated statements executed?

13. What is a sentinel?

14. Why are two **input** statements needed in the algorithm *Total1?*

15. Describe the process by which the statements controlled by a **repeat** construction are executed.

16. Suppose that the condition in a **repeat** construction has the value *true* the first time it is checked. How many times are the repeated statements executed?

17. Distinguish between a *continuation condition* and a *termination condition*. In which repetition construction is each used?

18. Describe two differences between the **while** construction and the **repeat** construction.

19. In what circumstances is the use of the **repeat** construction rather than the **while** construction indicated?

20. Explain one way in which a **while** construction can be substituted for a **repeat** construction.

Exercises

1. Write an algorithm to compute the sum of all the integers from 1 through 100.

2. The *factorial* of a positive integer greater than zero is defined as the product of all integers from 1 through the number in question. Thus, 3 factorial equals $1 \times 2 \times 3$ or 6; 4 factorial equals $1 \times 2 \times 3 \times 4$ or 24; and so on. Write an algorithm to input an integer greater than zero and output its factorial.

3. You are offered work for one month under the following terms. You will be paid one cent for the first day you work, two cents for the second day, four cents for the third day and so on, doubling the amount for every day of the month. Write an algorithm to determine how much you would earn for the month. The algorithm should accept from the user the number of days in a month, so you can see how much you would lose by working February or June rather than July.

4. Write an algorithm to determine how long it would take you to become a millionaire working under the terms described in Exercise 3.

5. Write an algorithm to input a series of real numbers and compute their average. The algorithm will first prompt the user to enter the number of values to be averaged; it will then prompt the user to enter each value. When all the values have been entered, the algorithm will print their average.

6. Modify the algorithm of Exercise 5 so that the computer, rather than the user, counts the number of values to be averaged. Assume that the values to be included in the average are all positive, and use a negative value as a sentinel. The algorithm will prompt for values to be included in the average until a negative value is entered, after which it will print the average of all values that preceded the negative value.

7. Modify the algorithm *Discounts* (Figure 7.7) so that it will process as many different sets of data as desired by the user. After completing each discount calculation, the algorithm should determine whether the user wishes to terminate the algorithm or process another set of data.

8. When the algorithm *Investment1* (Figure 8.7) asks whether the user wishes to process another set of data, it accepts any answer other than n or N as meaning "yes." Thus if the user accidentally types b or m instead of n, the interest calculation will be repeated. Where the user's response is critical— for example, where important files might be destroyed if the user's desires are misinterpreted—the user should be forced to enter y, Y, n, or N. Modify *Investment1* so that the question as to whether another set of data is to be processed is repeated until the user's response is y, Y, n, or N—that is, until the compound condition

   (*answer* = 'y') **or** (*answer* = 'Y') **or** (*answer* = 'n') **or** (*answer* = 'N')

   is true.

9. Modify the algorithm in Figure 8.2 so that interest is compounded daily rather than monthly. Still assume, however, that deposits are made at the beginning of each month, and that the calculation is to be carried out for the number of months specified by the user. Since we do not know the specific months over which the calculation will be done, we will assume that each month has 30 days.

Hint: Try using two nested **for** constructions. The inner **for** construction will step through the days in a month, while the outer one will step through the number of months requested by the user. Don't forget to change the yearly percentage interest rate to a *daily* decimal interest rate. To be consistent with our assumption of 30 days per month, we will assume 12×30 days in a year; thus the yearly percentage rate is to be divided by $12 \times 30 \times 100$, or 36000.0.

10. In the problem described in Exercise 9, we can get a better approximation to the number of days in a month by alternating 30-day months and 31-day months. Modify the algorithm of Exercise 9 to carry out its calculations in this manner.

Hint: Use two variables, *daysPerMonth* and *alternateDaysPerMonth,* which are given the initial values of 30 and 31. For each month, the value of *days-PerMonth* is used to determine the number of days for which interest is earned, after which the values of *daysPerMonth* and *alternateDaysPerMonth* are exchanged. Since this approximation gives us a 366-day year, we should convert the yearly percentage interest rate to the daily decimal rate by dividing by 366×100, or 36600.0.

11. Some programming languages do not provide the exponentiation operator **. For positive integer exponents, however, we can do exponentiation by repeated multiplication: the value of $x ** n$ is computed by starting with 1.0 and multiplying by the value of x the number of times specified by the value of n. Write an algorithm that uses repeated multiplication to compute the value of $x ** n$ where the value of x is real and that of n is an integer greater than or equal to zero.

12. The sequence of numbers

    0, 1, 1, 2, 3, 5, 8, 13, 21, . . .

is known as *Fibonacci's sequence* and has applications in mathematics and computer science. The first two numbers of the sequence are 0 and 1; each remaining number is the sum of the two preceding ones. Write an algorithm to print any specified number of terms of the Fibonacci sequence. For example, if the user requests six terms, the algorithm will print:

    0   1   1   2   3   5

Hint: How is Fibonacci's sequence related to Fibonacci's rabbit problem? Consider the version of the rabbit problem in which we start with one infertile pair.

13. The king has just been told how many grains of wheat would be required to satisfy the request made by the inventor of chess. Before having the inventor beheaded, the king decides, for amusement, to see how far the kingdom's grain surplus will go in satisfying the inventor's request. Write an algorithm to input the number of grains of wheat available and calculate how many squares of the chessboard the available wheat would take care of if used to satisfy part of the inventor's request.

14. Write algorithms to print each of the following patterns:

```
(a)  *****        (b)      *        (c)      *
     ****             ***              ***
     ***             *****            *****
     **            *******          *******
     *           *********        *********
                                   *******
                                    *****
                                     ***
                                      *
```

The algorithms for (b) and (c) can be written with or without the use of the **tab** command; try both ways. For (c), use a separate repetition construction for the bottom four lines of the pattern.

15. In algebra, the *binomial coefficient*

$$\binom{n}{r}$$

is defined by

$$\frac{(r + 1)(r + 2) \cdots (n - 1)n}{1 \cdot 2 \cdots (n - r - 1)(n - r)}$$

where n and r are nonnegative integers and r is less than or equal to n. When r is equal to n, the value of the binomial coefficient is 1. Write an algorithm to input values for n and r, then print the value of the binomial coefficient.

For further reading

Bently, Jon. "Programming Pearls: Writing Correct Programs." *Communications of the ACM,* December 1983, pp. 1040–1045.

Hearn, Albert D. "Some Words about Program Structure." *Byte,* September 1978, pp. 68–76.

Hughes, Joan K., and Michtom, Jay I. *A Structured Approach to Programming.* Englewood Cliffs, N.J.: Prentice-Hall, 1977.

Knuth, Donald E. "Structured Programming with go to Statements." *Computing Surveys,* December 1974, pp. 261–301.

Ledgard, Henry F., and Marcotty, Michael. "A Genealogy of Control Structures." *Communications of the ACM,* November 1975, pp. 629–639.

Peterson, W. W., Kasami, T., and Tokura, N. "On the Capabilities of While, Repeat, and Exit Statements." *Communications of the ACM,* August 1973, pp. 503–512.

Wirth, Niklaus. "On the Composition of Well Structured Programs." *Computing Surveys,* December 1974, pp. 246–259.

———. *Algorithms + Data Structures = Programs.* Englewood Cliffs, N.J.: Prentice-Hall, 1975.

Yourdan, Edward J. *Techniques of Program Structure and Design.* Englewood Cliffs, N.J.: Prentice-Hall, 1975.

Pascal Supplement

The for statement

As in the algorithmic language, the Pascal **for** statement has a "**to** form" in which the value of the control variable increases with each step:

> **for** control-variable : = expression-1 **to** expression-2 **do**
> > statement

and a "**downto** form" in which the value of the control variable decreases with each step:

> **for** control-variable : = expression-1 **downto** expression-2 **do**
> > statement

Note the keyword **do,** which is not used in the algorithmic language.

Pascal does not have a keyword **endfor** to terminate the block of statements controlled by the **for** statement. Instead, the **for** statement controls the execution of only a single statement, the one that follows the keyword **do.** For example,

> **for** i : = 1 **to** 5 **do** *write*(i:2)

causes the computer to print

> 1 2 3 4 5

and

> **for** i : = 5 **downto** 1 **do** *write*(i:2)

causes the computer to print

> 5 4 3 2 1

For clarity, we will usually write the controlled statement on the line below the

for statement and indent it with respect to the word **for**. Thus the above **for** statements would usually be written:

> **for** $i := 1$ **to** 5 **do**
> > *write*(i:2)

and

> **for** $i := 5$ **downto** 1 **do**
> > *write*(i:2)

The control variable can have any ordinal type. The ordinal types we have discussed so far are *integer, char,* and *Boolean.* An order is defined for the values of every ordinal type, so we can always say whether one value of an ordinal type precedes, equals, or follows another value of the same type. The **to** form of the **for** statement steps through successive values of an ordinal type in ascending order, whereas the **downto** form steps through successive values in descending order.

For type *integer,* the order is ordinary numerical order, and for type *char* it is alphabetical order as defined by the collating sequence for the computer system being used. For type *Boolean, false* is considered to precede *true.* Thus if i is an integer variable, c is a character variable, and b is a Boolean variable, the statements

> **for** $i := -2$ **to** 2 **do**
> > *write*(i:3);
>
> **for** $c :=$ 'z' **downto** 'a' **do**
> > *write*(c);
>
> **for** $b :=$ *false* **to** *true* **do**
> > *write*(b:6)

are all valid and print

```
 -2 -1  0  1  2
zyxwvutsrqponmlkjihgfedcba
 false   true
```

![gray bar] **Compound statements**

The Pascal **for** statement seems limited in that it can control the execution of only a single repeated statement. We can easily get around this limitation, however, by letting the repeated statement be a *compound statement,* which, we recall, is a sequence of statements bracketed by **begin** and **end.** For example, the compound statement

> **begin**
> > *write*('aa');
> > *write*('bb.')
>
> **end**

prints the pattern

```
aabb.
```

To repeat the pattern five times, we use the **for** statement

> **for** $i := 1$ **to** 5 **do**
>   **begin**
>   *write*('aa');
>   *write*('bb.')
>   **end**

On each repetition, the statements making up the compound statement are executed, causing the computer to print:

```
aabb.aabb.aabb.aabb.aabb.
```

We use indentation to make the structure of our statements clear at a glance—to show which statement is controlled by a **for** statement and which statements belong to a compound statement. Styles of indentation vary; some of the other styles you may encounter in your reading are:

> **for** $i := 1$ **to** 5 **do**
> **begin**
>   *write*('aa');
>   *write*('bb.')
> **end**

and

> **for** $i := 1$ **to** 5 **do**
>   **begin**
>   *write*('aa');
>   *write*('bb.')
>   **end**

and even

> **for** $i := 1$ **to** 5 **do begin**
>   *write*('aa');
>   *write*('bb.')
> **end**

Regardless of which style of indentation you prefer, choose one and use it consistently throughout each program.

The repeated statement is considered to be part of the **for** statement. This means that the semicolons separating the **for** statement from surrounding statements come before the **for** statement and after the repeated statement. For example:

$x := 3.5$;
for $i := 1$ **to** 5 **do** *write*(*i*:2);
$y := 7.9$

By writing the repeated statement on the same line as the **for** statement, we emphasize that *write*(*i*:2) is part of the **for** statement. Thus we are not surprised that the semicolon separating the **for** statement from $y := 7.9$ occurs after *write*(*i*:2). Even though we usually write the repeated statement on a line by itself, the punctuation remains the same:

$x := 3.5$;
for $i := 1$ **to** 5 **do**
    write(*i*:2);
$y := 7.9$

The same principle applies when the repeated statement is a compound statement:

$x := 3.5$;
for $i := 1$ **to** 5 **do**
    begin
        write ('aa');
        write ('bb.')
    end;
$y := 7.9$

In this case, the **for** statement includes the compound statement and so consists of everything from the word **for** through the word **end**. Thus, the semicolon separating the **for** statement from the following statement comes after the word **end**.

Programs using the for statement

The programs in Figures 8.8 through 8.11 correspond to the algorithms in Figures 8.1 through 8.4. The programs are straightforward translations of the algorithms and require little further comment. Note the indentation and punctuation associated with the **for** statements. The statements making up the compound statement controlled by a **for** statement are precisely the statements that must leave the truth of the invariant assertion unchanged. We indicate this by placing the invariant assertion immediately before the first statement of the compound statement.

Conditions, Boolean expressions, and relational operators

As in the algorithmic language, a condition is represented in Pascal by a Boolean expression. The condition is true if the Boolean expression evaluates to *true* and the condition is false if the Boolean expression evaluates to *false*.

Figure 8.8   Pascal program corresponding to the algorithm for
computing a total, Figure 8.1. Note that the semicolon
separating the **for** statement from the *writeln* statement
occurs after the word **end** of the compound statement.

```
program ComputeTotal(input, output);

{ Compute sum of integers entered by user }

var
    count, number, total, i: integer;
begin
    write('How many numbers are to be added? ');
    readln(count);
    total := 0;
    for i := 1 to count do
        begin

            { The value of total is the sum of all the numbers entered so
            far }

            write('Enter a number: ');
            readln(number);
            total := total + number
        end;
    writeln('Total is ', total:1)
end.
```

Conditions, or Boolean expressions, can be formed with the six relational operators, which are the same as in the algorithmic language:

Operator	Relation
=	is equal to
<	precedes
>	follows
<=	precedes or is equal to
>=	follows or is equal to
<>	is not equal to

(Pascal has one additional relational operator, **in,** which is used only in connection with set types, which we have not discussed yet.)

Figure 8.9   Pascal program corresponding to the algorithm for computing the amount in a savings account, Figure 8.2.

```pascal
program Investment(input, output);

{ Compute amount resulting from monthly deposits in a savings account.
Assume that interest is compounded monthly }

var
    amount, deposit, yearlyRate,
    monthlyRate, interest: real;
    months, n: integer;
begin
    write('Amount in your account now? ');
    readln(amount);
    write('Monthly deposit? ');
    readln(deposit);
    write('Yearly interest rate in percent? ');
    readln(yearlyRate);
    write('Number of months? ');
    readln(months);
    monthlyRate := yearlyRate / 1200.0;
    for n := 1 to months do
        begin

            { The value of amount is the amount in the account at the
            start of the nth month }

            amount := amount + deposit;
            interest := amount * monthlyRate;
            amount := amount + interest
        end;
    writeln('New amount is $', amount:1:2)
end.
```

A relational operator yields the value *true* if the corresponding relation holds true for its operands and the value *false* if the relation does not hold. The relational operators can be used for comparing values of any of the four Pascal types that we have discussed: *real, integer, char,* and *Boolean*. In general, the two operands of a relational operator must have the same type; we can compare integers with integers and characters with characters but not integers with characters. As a special exception, however, we can compare an integer with a real number; the integer operand is converted to the corresponding real number before carrying out the comparison.

Figure 8.10   Pascal program corresponding to the algorithm for solving
Fibonacci's rabbit problem, Figure 8.3.

```
program Fibonacci(input, output);

{ Solve Fibonacci's rabbit problem }

var
     pairs, fertilePairs, months,
     pairsNextMonth, n: integer;
begin
     write('Starting number of pairs? ');
     readln(pairs);
     write('Starting number of fertile pairs? ');
     readln(fertilePairs);
     write('Number of months? ');
     readln(months);
     for n := 1 to months do
        begin

             { The values of pairs and fertilePairs are, respectively, the
             number of pairs and the number of fertile pairs alive at the
             beginning of the nth month }

             pairsNextMonth := pairs + fertilePairs;
             fertilePairs := pairs;
             pairs := pairsNextMonth
        end;
     writeln('After ', months:1, ' months you will have ', pairs:1, ' pairs')
end.
```

"Precedes" and "follows" must be defined for each type by giving the order
assumed for values of that type. For the ordinal types, this order is the same one
mentioned earlier in connection with the **for** statement. For types *real* and *integer,*
ordinary numerical order is assumed. The order for type *char* is alphabetical order as
defined by the collating sequence for the computer system. And for type *Boolean,*
false is assumed to precede *true.* The following are some examples of Boolean
expressions formed with relational operators:

Expression	Value	Expression	Value
$3 < 5$	*true*	$'a' >= 'z'$	*false*
$3.14 <> 6.28$	*true*	$true < false$	*false*
$2.5 > 3$	*false*		

Figure 8.11   Pascal program corresponding to the algorithm for computing the amount of grain requested by the inventor of chess, Figure 8.4.

```
program Wheat(input, output);

{ Compute number of grains of wheat requested by inventor of chess }

var
    grains, total: real; { Values may be very large }
    n: integer;
begin
    grains := 1.0;
    total := 0.0;
    for n := 1 to 64 do
        begin

            { Grains is the number of grains to be placed on the nth
            square and total is the number of grains placed on squares
            already considered }

            total := total + grains;
            grains := 2.0 * grains
        end;
    writeln('Inventor requested ', grains:1, ' grains')
end.
```

As in the algorithmic language, the relational operators have a lower priority than the arithmetical operators. Thus when the operands of a relational operator are arithmetical expressions, the arithmetical operations are carried out before the relational operator is applied. For example, in

$5 + 3 < 5 * 2$

the arithmetical operators are applied first to give

$8 < 10$

The relational operator is then applied to get the value *true*.

The while statement

The **while** statement in Pascal has the following general form:

while condition **do**
    statement

As with the **for** statement, the general form provides for only a single repeated statement. However, the repeated statement can be a compound statement, thus allowing the execution of any number of statements to be controlled.

The *semantics* of the **while** statement—the way in which it is executed by the computer—is the same as for the **while** construction in the algorithmic language. The condition is evaluated *before* each execution of the repeated statement. If the condition evaluates to *true,* the repeated statement is executed, after which the condition is evaluated again, and so on. If the condition evaluates to *false,* the repetitions are terminated; the computer goes on to the next statement in the program without any further executions of the repeated statement.

Consider the following example:

$i := 0;$
while $i <= 20$ **do**
    $i := i + 5$

The repeated statement is $i := i + 5$. Since each execution of the repeated statement increases the value of i by 5, i takes on the values 0, 5, 10, 15, 20, and 25. Before each repetition, the value of i is checked to see if it is less than or equal to 20. When the value of i is 0, 5, 10, 15, and 20, the test is passed and the repeated statement is executed. When the value of i is 25, however, the value of the Boolean expression $i <= 20$ is *false,* the repetitions are terminated, and the computer goes on to the next statement in the program.

We can get the successive values of i printed out by using a compound statement:

$i := 0;$
while $i <= 20$ **do**
    begin
        write(i:3);
        $i := i + 5$
    end

These statements cause the computer to print:

```
0   5   10   15   20
```

The final value of i, 25, isn't printed. (Why?)

As in the algorithmic language, if the condition is false the first time it is checked, the repeated statements will not be executed at all. For example, the statements

$i := 21;$
while $i <= 20$ **do**
    begin
        write(i:3);
        $i := i + 5$
    end

do not produce any printout. Since the value of $i <= 20$ is *false* the first time the expression is evaluated, the repeated statement is not executed, no printing takes place, and the value of i remains 21.

Programs using the while statement

The programs in Figures 8.12 and 8.13 correspond to the algorithms in Figures 8.5 and 8.6. These programs are straightforward translations of the corresponding algorithms. As with the programs using the **for** statement, note the use of compound

Figure 8.12   Pascal program corresponding to the algorithm for summing a series of nonnegative integers terminated by a sentinel, Figure 8.5. Note that the semicolon separating the **while** statement from the *writeln* statement occurs after the word **end** of the compound statement.

```
program ComputeTotal1(input, output);

{ Compute sum of integers entered by user }

var
     count, number, total: integer;
begin
     count := 0;
     total := 0;
     write('Enter a number: ');
     readln(number);
     while number >= 0 do
        begin

             { The values of count and total are, respectively, the number
               of and the sum of the values already processed. The value of
               number is the next value to be processed }

             count := count + 1;
             total := total + number;
             write('Enter a number: ');
             readln(number)
        end;
     writeln('Number of values entered is ', count:1);
     writeln('Total is ', total:1)
end.
```

Figure 8.13 Pascal program corresponding to the algorithm for solving a modified version of Fibonacci's rabbit problem, Figure 8.6.

```
program Fibonaccil(input, output);

{ Determine number of months needed to produce a given number of pairs }

var
    pairs, fertilePairs, months,
    pairsNextMonth, pairsDesired: integer;
begin
    write('Starting number of pairs? ');
    readln(pairs);
    write('Starting number of fertile pairs? ');
    readln(fertilePairs);
    write('Number of pairs desired? ');
    readln(pairsDesired);
    months := 0;
    while pairs < pairsDesired do
        begin

            { The values of pairs and fertilePairs are, respectively, the
            number of pairs and the number of fertile pairs at the
            beginning of the current month. Months is the number of
            months that the rabbits have already reproduced }

            pairsNextMonth := pairs + fertilePairs;
            fertilePairs := pairs;
            pairs := pairsNextMonth;
            months := months + 1
        end;
    writeln('After ', months:1, ' months you will have ', pairs:1, ' pairs')
end.
```

statements, the use of semicolons, and the positioning of invariant assertions. Detecting the end of a series of input values, as in Figure 8.12, is discussed further in the following section.

Reading data and the eof predicate

We recall that the outline for reading a series of data values terminated by a sentinel is as follows:

"Input first value to be processed"

while "value to be processed is not sentinel value"

"Process current value"

"Input next value to be processed"

endwhile

The outline is easily translated into Pascal:

"Input first value to be processed"

while "value to be processed is not sentinel value" **do**

begin

"Process current value"

"Input next value to be processed"

end

For example, suppose the input values are to be counted and summed, as in Figure 8.12, but without prompting individually for each value. If the data values are all positive and the sentinel is negative, the following Pascal statements do the job:

count := 0;

total := 0;

readln(number);

while *number* >= 0 **do**

begin

count := *count* + 1;

total := *total* + *number;*

readln(number)

end

We can eliminate the need for a sentinel value and simplify the statements for reading and processing the data by using the predefined function *eof* ("end of file"). The argument of *eof* is a file identifier, such as *input;* the function returns *true* if all the data in the file has been read and *false* if more data remains to be read. The argument can be omitted; if it is, *input* is assumed. Thus the expressions *eof* and *eof(input)* are equivalent. *Eof* is a *Boolean function,* since it returns the Boolean values *true* and *false.* A Boolean function is often called a *predicate,* after the corresponding construction in grammar and logic, so we can speak of either the *eof function* or the *eof predicate.*

Using *eof,* we can outline the statements for reading and processing a series of values as follows:

while not *eof(input)* **do**

begin

"Input next value to be processed"

"Process value"

end

In the examples, we will assume that values are read from the file *input*. The operator **not** changes *true* to *false* and vice versa; thus, the value of **not** *eof(input)* is *false* if the end of the file *input* has been reached and *true* otherwise. Following this outline, our statements for counting and summing a series of values become:

count := 0;
total := 0;
while not *eof(input)* **do**
    begin
        readln(number);
        count := *count* + 1;
        total := *total* + *number*
    end

With *eof,* we do not have to check each newly read value to see if it is the sentinel. As long as the value of **not** *eof(input)* is *true,* at least one value remains to be read from file *input;* the repeated statements can read and process that value without further checking. This means that we only need one *readln* statement, and that statement can be followed immediately by the statements for processing the value read. The more awkward arrangement with two *readln* statements is needed only when each input value must be checked to see if it is the sentinel before it can be processed.

Eof is most useful for noninteractive processing—for reading and processing a previously prepared file, such as a disk file or a deck of punched cards, as opposed to prompting the user to type in each value as it is needed. The operating system keeps track of whether the end of a card or disk file has been reached; when *eof* is called, it can check with the operating system to determine whether a value of *true* or *false* should be returned.

For interactive processing, the file *input* is usually the user's keyboard. To allow *eof* to be used with the keyboard, some systems designate a special end-of-file key that the user can press to signal the end of data input. If file *input* is the keyboard, then the value of *eof(input)* is *false* before the end-of-file key is pressed and *true* afterward.

Even with an end-of-file key, *eof* may not be particularly convenient for interactive processing. For example, some Pascal implementations—UCSD Pascal, for example—require that the end-of-file key be pressed immediately after typing the last character of the last data item to be entered. This procedure is likely to be confusing to the user, who is accustomed to pressing the Return or Enter key after responding to a prompt. Typing the end-of-file key at the wrong time causes the program to terminate with an input/output error. For interactive processing, it is probably best to have the user enter a sentinel to indicate the end of the input data or have the program explicitly ask the user whether or not more data is to be entered.

The repeat statement

The **repeat** statement in Pascal is the same as in the algorithmic language:

repeat
> statements

until condition

As in the algorithmic language, any number of statements may be included between **repeat** and **until**. This is in contrast to the **for** and **while** statements, which provide for only a single repeated statement, requiring us to use a compound statement if the execution of more than one statement is to be controlled. Since **repeat** and **until** form a natural pair of brackets for the repeated statements, the **begin** and **end** of a compound statement are not required.

The repeated statements are separated by semicolons, just as if they were part of a compound statement. If the **repeat** statement is followed by another statement, a semicolon following the condition separates the entire **repeat** statement from the statement that follows it. In the following example, note the semicolon separating the two repeated statements and the one separating the entire **repeat** statement from the *writeln* statement that follows it:

$i := 0$;
repeat
> *write(i:3)*;
> $i := i + 5$

until $i > 20$;
writeln;

These statements cause the computer to print

```
 0  5 10 15 20
```

The final value of i is 25, which is not printed. The *writeln* statement just causes the output device to go to a new line after printing the five values.

As in the algorithmic language, the condition is checked *after* each execution of the repeated statements, and the repetitions terminate when the condition becomes true. Since the condition is not checked until after the repeated statements are executed, the repeated statements are always executed at least once, even if the condition is true when the **repeat** statement is executed. For example, consider the following two sets of statements:

$i := 21$;
while $i <= 20$ **do** $i := 21$;
> **begin**   **repeat**
> > *write(i:3)*;   *write(i:3)*;
> > $i := i + 5$ $i := i + 5$

> **end**   **until** $i > 20$

Figure 8.14 Pascal program corresponding to the algorithm in Figure 8.7, the version of the investment algorithm that allows the user to repeat the investment calculation as many times as desired. The **repeat** statement has the same form in Pascal as in the algorithmic language. Since the **repeat** statement is the last statement of this program, it is not followed by a semicolon.

```
program Investment1(input, output);

{ Compute amount resulting from monthly deposits in a savings account.
Assume that interest is compounded monthly. Repeat computation for as
many sets of data as desired by user }

var
      amount, deposit, yearlyRate,
      monthlyRate, interest: real;
      months, n: integer;
      answer: char;
begin
      repeat
            write('Amount in your account now? ');
            readln(amount);
            write('Monthly deposit? ');
            readln(deposit);
            write('Yearly interest rate in percent? ');
            readln(yearlyRate);
            write('Number of months? ');
            readln(months);
            monthlyRate := yearlyRate / 1200.0;
            for n := 1 to months do
                  begin

                        { The value of amount is the amount in the account at the
                        start of the nth month }

                        amount := amount + deposit;
                        interest := amount * monthlyRate;
                        amount := amount + interest
                  end;
            writeln('New amount is $', amount:1:2);
            writeln;
            write('Do you wish to enter another set of data (y/n)? ');
            readln(answer)
      until (answer = 'n') or (answer = 'N')
end.
```

For the statements on the left, we have seen that the repeated statements are not executed. Nothing is printed, and the value of i remains 21. For the statements on the right, however, the repeated statements are executed once before the termination condition is checked. Therefore, the value 21 is printed and the value of i is increased to 26. Since the value of i is 26 when the termination condition is checked, the value of $i > 20$ is *true*, and the repetition terminates after a single execution of the repeated statements.

Figure 8.14 is the Pascal program corresponding to the algorithm *Investment1* in Figure 8.7. This program does personal investment calculations, asking after each calculation whether or not the user wishes to enter another set of data. As in the algorithm, the termination condition is the Boolean expression:

$(answer = 'n')$ **or** $(answer = 'N')$

The operator **or** returns *true* if either or both of its operands have the value *true*, so the termination condition is true if the value of *answer* is 'n' or 'N'. The parentheses around the expressions constructed with relational operators are required. The Boolean operators **not, or,** and **and** are discussed in more detail in the Pascal supplement for Chapter 9.

9

Selection

I n Chapter 2, we saw that an action taken by an algorithm may depend on the problem state at the time the action is taken. For example, a certain step in a sorting algorithm might exchange the positions of two names if they are out of alphabetical order but leave their positions unchanged if they are already in order. At any point in the execution of an algorithm, the possible states can be classified into *cases,* each of which requires that a different action be taken. Algorithmic and programming languages use *selection constructions* to tell the computer how to determine which of the possible cases has actually arisen and to specify the action to be taken in each case.

9.1

One- and two-way selection

In one-way selection, a choice is made between taking a certain action and taking no action at all. In the algorithmic language, we use the following construction for one-way selection:

> **if** condition **then**
>> statements
> **endif**

As in the repetition constructions, the condition is represented by a Boolean expression, which is evaluated when the selection construction is encountered. If the Boolean expression evaluates to *true,* the condition is true and the statements are executed. If the Boolean expression evaluates to *false,* the condition is false and the statements are skipped.

For example, consider the following statements:

seconds ← *seconds* + 1
if *seconds* > 59 **then**
    seconds ← 0
endif
output *seconds*

After increasing the value of *seconds* by 1, the computer checks to see if the new value of *seconds* exceeds 59; if so, the value of *seconds* is reset to zero. If the value of *seconds* does not exceed 59, however, the reset action is not taken. Finally, the value of seconds is printed. If the new value of *seconds* is greater than 59, the actions taken are:

seconds ← *seconds* + 1
seconds ← 0
output *seconds*

If the new value of *seconds* is not greater than 59, the actions taken are:

seconds ← *seconds* + 1
output *seconds*

In two-way selection, a choice is made between two possible actions, one of which is always performed. The algorithmic-language construction for two-way selection is similar to that for one-way selection except that an **else** part is present to handle the second alternative:

if condition **then**
    statements-1
else
    statements-2
endif

If the condition is true, then statements-1 are executed; if the condition is false, statements-2 are executed. Thus, regardless of whether the condition is true or false, one and only one of the two sets of statements is executed.

For example, consider the following statements:

input *answer*
if *answer* = *rightAnswer* **then**
    response ← 'Correct'
else
    response ← 'Incorrect'
endif
output *response*

If the value obtained for *answer* by the **input** statement equals the value of *right-*

Answer, response is set to 'Correct'. If the value obtained for *answer* does not equal the value of *rightAnswer, response* is set to 'Incorrect'. The **output** statement prints the value of *response,* which must be either 'Correct' or 'Incorrect' since one of the two assignments was carried out. In the case in which the answer is correct, the actions taken are:

> **input** *answer*
>
> *response* ← 'Correct'
>
> **output** *response*

In the case in which the answer is incorrect, the actions taken are:

> **input** *answer*
>
> *response* ← 'Incorrect'
>
> **output** *response*

Note that "one way" and "two way" refer to the number of sets of statements from which a selection is made, not to the number of cases involved. Both one-way and two-way selection involve two cases; for one-way selection, however, no statements are executed for the case in which the condition is false. One-way selection is thus a special case of two-way selection, corresponding to a two-way selection in which the **else** part contains no statements. Hence, the following selection constructions are equivalent:

> **if** condition **then**   **if** condition **then**
>
>   statements   statements
>
> **endif**   **else**
>
>   **endif**

Occasionally, a one-way selection will be clearer if written as a two-way selection whose **else** part contains only an assertion or comment detailing the circumstances under which no action is to be taken:

> **if** *seconds* > 59 **then**
>
>   { Seconds counter has overflowed and must be reset to zero }
>
>   *seconds* ← 0
>
> **else**
>
>   { Seconds counter has not overflowed }
>
> **endif**

Both one-way and two-way selection deal with two cases, which are distinguished by the value of a Boolean expression. One-way selection takes a specified action in the case in which the Boolean expression is *true* and takes no action in the case in which the Boolean expression is *false*. Two-way selection takes one action in the case in which the Boolean expression is *true* and takes another action in the case in which the Boolean expression is *false*.

Verifying algorithms containing selections   When proving an algorithm correct, selection constructions are treated just like other statements and constructions: given that the assertion preceding the selection construction (the precondition) is true before the construction is executed, we must show that the assertion following the construction (the postcondition) is true after the construction is executed. Each case must be considered separately. That is, for each case we must show that, if the precondition and the assertion characterizing the case are true before the statements for that case are executed, the postcondition will be true after the statements for that case are executed. For one-way selection, we must not forget to consider the case in which no action is taken.

For example, consider the following statements and assertions:

{ The value of *seconds* lies in the range 0 to 59 }

seconds ← *seconds* + 1

{ The value of *seconds* lies in the range 1 to 60 }

if *seconds* > 59 **then**

{ The value of *seconds* is 60 }

seconds ← 0
else

{ The value of *seconds* lies in the range 1 to 59 }

endif

{ The value of *seconds* lies in the range 0 to 59 }

Originally, the value of *seconds* lies in the range 0 to 59. After the value of *seconds* is increased by 1, it lies in the range 1 to 60. We want to show that, after the selection construction is executed, the value of *seconds* will once again lie in the range 0 to 59.

When the value of the Boolean expression

seconds > 59

is *true,* the value of *seconds* must be greater than 59. Since the precondition for the selection construction tells us that the value of seconds is in the range 1 to 60, the only value that *seconds* can have is 60. This gives us the assertion for the **then** part of the selection construction:

{ The value of *seconds* is 60 }

When the value of the Boolean expression is *false*, the value of *seconds* must be 59 or less. Again, since the precondition assures us that the value of *seconds* lies in the range 1 to 60, we know that the value of *seconds* must lie in the range 1 to 59. This reasoning gives us the assertion for the **else** part of the selection construction:

{ The value of *seconds* lies in the range 1 to 59 }

The **then** part of the selection construction contains one statement

seconds ← 0

which sets the value of *seconds* to 0. After the statements for the first case have been executed, then, the value of *seconds* is zero.

The **else** part of the selection construction contains no statements. Therefore, after the (nonexistent) statements for the second case have been executed, the value of *seconds* remains in the range 1 to 59.

Combining the results for the two cases, we see that after the selection construction has been executed the postcondition

{ The value of *seconds* lies in the range 0 to 59 }

is true. The 0 in the postcondition comes from the first case and the remainder of the range (1 to 59) comes from the second case. Writing a one-way selection as a two-way selection with only an assertion in the **else** part makes explicit the two cases that must be considered in verifying the selection construction.

As with repetition constructions, our study of selection will focus on intuitive understanding rather than on formal proofs of correctness. But assertions and the techniques of reasoning with them provide a basis for that intuitive understanding. Just as formulating an invariant assertion is a good way of understanding how a repetition works and what it accomplishes, so case analysis provides the foundation for understanding the purpose and functioning of selection constructions.

9.2 Algorithms using one- and two-way selection

Balances As our first exercise in selection, we will write an algorithm to read records from a file of customer accounts and print the account number and balance for each customer whose balance is greater than zero. Nothing is printed for customers whose balance is zero (account paid up) or negative (company owes customer money).

In general, a *record* is a collection of data pertaining to a single individual, such as a customer. When a file is divided into lines, such as a file typed with a text editor, usually each record is typed on a separate line, so there is a one-to-one correspondence between lines and records. For simplicity, we assume that each record in the customer file consists only of an account number and a balance, although records in an actual customer file would surely contain additional information, such as the customer's name and address. The last record in the file is a *sentinel record* with an account number of 9999. A short test file might look like this:

```
1295      39.90
2964       0.00
5912       0.00
6412     105.75
7214       2.95
9999       0.00
```

Customer 1295 has a balance of 39.90, customer 2964 has a balance of 0.00, and so on. We can read the record for a single customer with

> **input** *accountNumber, balance*

where *accountNumber* is an integer variable and *balance* is a real variable. If the value read for *accountNumber* is 9999, the end of the file has been reached and processing should terminate. The customer file will be processed noninteractively, as if it were a card or disk file. That is, the customer records will be read and processed one after another without pausing to prompt the user to enter the data for each customer.

Our algorithm follows the already familiar outline for processing data items terminated by a sentinel:

> **input** *accountNumber, balance*
> **while** *accountNumber* <> *sentinel*
>> ''Print account number and balance if balance is greater than zero''
>> **input** *accountNumber, balance*
> **endwhile**

As usual, we read one record before beginning the repetition and one after each execution of the repeated statements so that each record will be tested to see if it is the sentinel record before any attempt is made to process it. *Sentinel* is defined as a constant with the value 9999.

The account number and balance are to be printed for every record whose balance is greater than zero. For each record we have two cases: (1) the balance is greater than zero, and (2) the balance is less than or equal to zero. In the first case, the account number and the balance are to be printed; in the second case, no action is to be taken. The two cases can be distinguished by the value of the Boolean expression

> *balance* > 0.0

which is *true* for the first case and *false* for the second. Since action needs to be taken only in the case in which the Boolean expression is *true*, we can use a one-way selection:

> **if** *balance* > 0.0 **then**
>> **output** *accountNumber*, **tab**(11), *balance*
> **endif**

The **tab** command causes the account numbers and balances to be printed in two columns. The account number column begins at the left margin; the balance column begins at the 11th character position.

Figure 9.1 shows the complete algorithm. The first two statements print headings for the account number and balance columns, and the third statement skips a line between the column headings and the first line of data. (The lines of data are called *detail lines*.) The assertion in the selection construction describes the case in which the **output** statement will be executed. For the sample data given earlier, the algorithm produces the following output:

```
Account     Balance
Number      Due

1295        39.90
6412        105.75
7214        2.95
```

Figure 9.1   This algorithm uses one-way selection to print the account number and balance for only those accounts having balances greater than zero.

```
algorithm Balances

{ Print account number and balance for accounts with balances greater than
  zero }

declare
    const sentinel = 9999
    accountNumber: integer
    balance: real
execute
    output 'Account', tab(11), 'Balance'
    output 'Number', tab(11), 'Due'
    output
    input accountNumber, balance
    while accountNumber <> sentinel
        if balance > 0.0 then

            { Account has balance greater than zero }

            output accountNumber, tab(11), balance
        endif
        input accountNumber, balance
    endwhile
end Balances
```

Payroll We wish to compute the gross wages—wages before taxes or other deductions—of workers who are paid by the hour. If we know the number of hours a person worked (*hoursWorked*) and the number of dollars per hour the person earns (*hourlyRate*), we can easily compute the person's gross wages with the following statement:

grossWages ← *hoursWorked* * *hourlyRate*

There is one catch, though. Persons who are paid by the hour usually earn "time and a half" for overtime, where overtime hours are all hours in excess of 40 hours a week. That is, every hour in excess of 40 must be counted as if it were an hour and a half. We can take this into account by adding an extra half hour to the value of *hoursWorked* for each hour in excess of 40 that was actually worked:

hoursWorked ← *hoursWorked* + 0.5 * (*hoursWorked* − 40.0)

This adjustment must be made, however, only for persons who worked more than 40 hours. If the value of *hoursWorked* were less than 40, the term in parentheses would be negative, and the worker would be penalized time for not having worked 40 hours, which is not what is desired at all. Persons who worked 40 hours or less are to be paid for the hours actually worked without any adjustments being made. The following one-way selection adjusts the value of *hoursWorked* only for persons who worked overtime:

if *hoursWorked* > 40.0 **then**

    hoursWorked ← *hoursWorked* + 0.5 * (*hoursWorked* − 40.0)

endif

Specifically, we have two cases: (1) the employee worked overtime, and (2) the employee did not work overtime. The two cases are distinguished by the values of the Boolean expression

hoursWorked > 40.0

which is *true* in the first case and *false* in the second case. In the first case, the value of *hoursWorked* needs to be adjusted to take overtime into account; in the second case, the value of *hoursWorked* need not (and must not) be adjusted, so no action needs to be taken.

Figure 9.2 shows the complete algorithm. Again, we have a noninteractive algorithm that reads and processes records from a file. Each record consists of an employee number, the hours the employee worked, and the employee's hourly rate. The file is terminated by a sentinel record with an employee number of 9999. The output is to be a four-column listing giving each employee's number, hours worked, hourly rate, and gross wages. The first two statements of the algorithm print column headings and the third statement skips a line between the column headings and the first detail line.

The first statement controlled by the **while** construction prints the number, hours worked, and hourly rate for the current employee. The value of *hoursWorked* must be printed at this point, rather than after the gross wages have been calculated, be-

Figure 9.2 This algorithm for computing gross wages uses one-way selection to adjust the hours worked so that each hour of overtime is counted as an hour and a half.

---

algorithm *Payroll*

{ Compute gross wages for employees who get time and a half for overtime, where all hours in excess of 40 are overtime }

declare
    const *sentinel* = 9999
    employeeNumber: *integer*
    hoursWorked, *hourlyRate*, *grossWages*: *real*
execute
    output 'Employee', **tab**(11), 'Hours', **tab**(21), 'Hourly', **tab**(31),
        'Gross'
    output 'Number', **tab**(11), 'Worked', **tab**(21), 'Rate', **tab**(31),
        'Wages'
    output
    input *employeeNumber*, *hoursWorked*, *hourlyRate*
    while *employeeNumber* <> *sentinel*
        output *employeeNumber*, **tab**(11), *hoursWorked*, **tab**(21),
            hourlyRate, **more**
        if *hoursWorked* > 40.0 **then**

            { Employee worked overtime }

            hoursWorked ← *hoursWorked* + 0.5 ∗ (*hoursWorked* −
                40.0)
        endif
        grossWages ← *hoursWorked* ∗ *hourlyRate*
        output tab(31), *grossWages*
        input *employeeNumber*, *hoursWorked*, *hourlyRate*
    endwhile
end *Payroll*

---

cause the value may be adjusted by the calculations and so must be printed before the calculations are done. The one-way selection adjusts the values of *hoursWorked* for persons who worked overtime, and the following assignment statement calculates the value of *grossWages* using the possibly adjusted value of *hoursWorked*. The **output** statement prints the value of *grossWages* on the same line on which the values of *employeeNumber*, *hoursWorked*, and *hourlyRate* have already been printed.

The following is a typical printout:

Employee Number	Hours Worked	Hourly Rate	Gross Wages
1742	44.0	3.58	164.68
2513	35.0	3.25	113.75
4211	46.0	2.75	134.75
5295	38.0	5.31	201.78
8496	48.0	6.83	355.16

Payroll1   There is another method of computing wages-with-overtime that calls for a two-way rather than a one-way selection. Instead of adjusting the value of *hoursWorked* for persons who worked overtime, a separate calculation for the value of *grossWages* is done for each case.

For a person who did not work overtime, the value of gross wages is calculated as usual by multiplying the hours worked by the hourly rate:

$$grossWages \leftarrow hoursWorked * hourlyRate$$

A person who worked overtime worked 40 regular hours (paid for at the rate *hourlyRate*) and worked *hoursWorked* $-$ 40.0 overtime hours (paid for at the time-and-a-half rate of 1.5 * *hourlyRate*). Thus we can calculate the value of *grossWages* as follows:

$$grossWages \leftarrow 40.0 * hourlyRate +$$
$$1.5 * hourlyRate * (hoursWorked - 40.0)$$

The first term computes the wages earned for regular hours and the second term computes the wages earned for overtime hours.

The value of the Boolean expression

$$hoursWorked <= 40.0$$

is *true* for an employee who worked no overtime and *false* for an employee who worked overtime. Thus we can use the following two-way selection to do the proper calculation for each case:

if *hoursWorked* $<=$ 40.0 **then**
    $grossWages \leftarrow hoursWorked * hourlyRate$
else
    $grossWages \leftarrow 40.0 * hourlyRate +$
        $1.5 * hourlyRate * (hoursWorked - 40.0)$
endif

Note that, in the algorithmic language, we allow an expression, like a list, to be continued onto additional lines if need be.

Figure 9.3 shows the complete algorithm *Payroll1*. Since the value of *hoursWorked* is no longer adjusted during the calculations, there is no reason to print it

Figure 9.3   This version of the algorithm for computing gross wages
uses two-way selection to do different gross-wage
computations for workers who did and did not work
overtime.

---

algorithm *Payroll1*

{ Compute gross wages for employees who get time and a half for
  overtime, where all hours in excess of 40 are overtime }

declare
    const *sentinel* = 9999
    employeeNumber: *integer*
    hoursWorked, *hourlyRate*, grossWages: *real*
execute
    output 'Employee', **tab**(11), 'Hours', **tab**(21), 'Hourly', **tab**(31),
          'Gross'
    output 'Number', **tab**(11), 'Worked', **tab**(21), 'Rate', **tab**(31),
          'Wages'
    output
    input *employeeNumber, hoursWorked, hourlyRate*
    while *employeeNumber* <> *sentinel*
        if *hoursWorked* <= 40.0 **then**

             { Employee did not work overtime }

             grossWages ← *hoursWorked* * *hourlyRate*
        else

             { Employee worked overtime }

             grossWages ← 40.0 * *hourlyRate* +
                    1.5 * *hourlyRate* * (*hoursWorked* − 40.0)
        endif
        output *employeeNumber*, **tab**(11), *hoursWorked*, **tab**(21),
           hourlyRate, **tab**(31), *grossWages*
        input *employeeNumber, hoursWorked, hourlyRate*
    endwhile
end *Payroll1*

before doing the calculations. Hence a single output statement can be used to print each detail line.

PassFail   The algorithm in Figure 9.4 is another illustration of two-way selection. The input data consists of records, each containing a student number and the final grade received by the student. The output consists of three columns: a student number column, a passed column, and a failed column. Passing grades are printed in the passed column and failing grades are printed in the failed column. At the end of the output, the number of persons who passed the course and the number who failed are printed. The following is a typical printout:

```
Number          Passed          Failed

1923            82
2349                            65
3761            72
3995            75
5124                            48

Passed:  3
Failed:  2
```

The variables *passedCount* and *failedCount* are used to keep running counts of the number of students who passed and failed. *StudentNumber* and *grade* hold the number and grade of the next student to be processed. The invariant assertion in Figure 9.4 describes the values of these four variables just before the statements for processing the next student are executed. For each student, there are two cases: (1) the student failed, and (2) the student passed. If the constant *lowestPassingGrade* is defined with the value of the minimum passing grade, the value of the Boolean expression

$grade < lowestPassingGrade$

is *true* in the first case and *false* in the second. In the first case, the student's grade must be printed in the failed column (beginning at character position 21) and the student must be counted as one who failed:

output *studentNumber*, **tab**(21), *grade*
failedCount ← *failedCount* + 1

In the second case, the student's grade must be printed in the passed column and the student must be counted as one who passed:

output *studentNumber*, **tab**(11), *grade*
passedCount ← *passedCount* + 1

The following two-way selection takes the needed action for each case:

Figure 9.4   This algorithm uses two-way selection to print passing grades in one column and failing grades in another. The algorithm also keeps count of the number of students who passed and the number who failed.

```
algorithm PassFail

{ Print student numbers and grades with passing grades in one column and
  failing grades in another. Count number of students who passed and
  failed }

declare
    const sentinel = 9999
    const lowestPassingGrade = 70
    studentNumber, grade, passedCount, failedCount: integer
execute
    output 'Number', tab(11), 'Passed', tab(21), 'Failed'
    output
    passedCount ← 0
    failedCount ← 0
    input studentNumber, grade
    while studentNumber <> sentinel

        { The values of passedCount and failedCount are the numbers of
          previously processed students who passed and failed. The values
          of studentNumber and grade are the data for the next student to
          be processed }

        if grade < lowestPassingGrade then

            { Student failed }

            output studentNumber, tab(21), grade
            failedCount ← failedCount + 1
        else

            { Student passed }

            output studentNumber, tab(11), grade
            passedCount ← passedCount + 1
        endif
        input studentNumber, grade
    endwhile
    output
    output 'Passed: ', passedCount
    output 'Failed: ', failedCount
end PassFail
```

If *grade* < *lowestPassingGrade* **then**
  output *studentNumber*, **tab**(21), *grade*
  failedCount ← *failedCount* + 1
else
  output *studentNumber*, **tab**(11), *grade*
  passedCount ← *passedCount* + 1
endif

9.3 Multiway selection

Two-way selection selects one of two alternative sets of statements for execution. We can generalize two-way selection to *multiway selection* by selecting from among more than two alternative sets of statements. The algorithmic language provides two constructions for multiway selection: the case construction and an extended version of the **if** construction. Also, "do it yourself" multiway selection constructions can be built by nesting **if** constructions: the **then** and **else** parts of an **if** construction can contain other **if** constructions, whose **then** and **else** parts can contain still other **if** constructions, and so on.

Nested if constructions Consider the following nested **if** constructions in which the **then** part of one **if** construction contains another **if** construction:

If condition-1 **then**
  if condition-2 **then**
    statements-1
  else
    statements-2
  endif
else
  statements-3
endif

If condition-1 is true, then the inner **if** construction is executed and the computer must check condition-2 to see what action is to be taken. Thus if condition-1 and condition-2 are both true, statements-1 will be executed, whereas if condition-1 is true but condition-2 is false, statements-2 will be executed. On the other hand, if condition-1 is false, then statements-3 are executed. No other condition has to be checked in this case.

Figure 9.5 uses a *decision tree* to illustrate the order in which the conditions are checked and the way in which their values determine which statements will be executed. Each point or *node* of the tree is labeled with a condition or a set of statements to be executed. The bottommost or *leaf* nodes are labeled with sets of statements; the nonleaf nodes are labeled with conditions. Each *branch* is labeled *true* or *false*. Starting at the top of the diagram (the *root* node of the decision tree), the computer first checks condition-1. If condition-1 is false, the computer follows the false branch to

Figure 9.5   Decision tree for the nested **if** constructions at right. If
condition-1 is true, we must follow the left branch of the
tree and check condition-2. If condition-2 is false,
statements-1 are executed; otherwise, statements-2 are
executed. On the other hand, if condition-1 is false, no
further checking is done and statements-3 are executed.

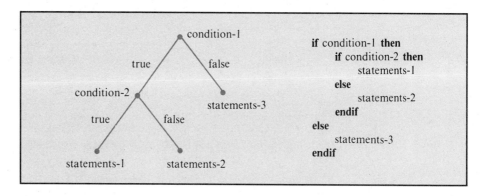

statements-3, which are executed. If condition-1 is true, the computer follows the
true branch to condition-2, which must also be checked. If condition-2 is true, the
computer follows the true branch to statements-1, which are executed. Otherwise, it
follows the false branch and executes statements-2. The following table shows the
conditions under which each set of statements is executed:

Condition-1	Condition-2	Statements Executed
true	true	statements-1
true	false	statements-2
false	true	statements-3
false	false	statements-3

As another example, consider the following **if** construction, which has another
if construction nested in its **else** part:

```
if condition-1 then
    statements-1
else
    if condition-2 then
        statements-2
    else
        statements-3
    endif
endif
```

If condition-1 is true, then statements-1 are executed. If condition-1 is false, then condition-2 must be checked. If condition-1 is true and condition-2 is false, statements-2 are executed; if both condition-1 and condition-2 are false, statements-3 are executed. Figure 9.6 shows the decision tree for this **if** construction; the following table shows the conditions under which each set of statements is executed:

Condition-1	Condition-2	Statements Executed
true	true	statements-1
true	false	statements-1
false	true	statements-2
false	false	statements-3

We see that for each different nesting scheme we get a different decision tree and different conditions under which the various statements are to be executed. If we invent nested **if** constructions on spur of the moment as we need them, then we will have to take the time to study the properties of each nesting scheme we devise. Fortunately, in many cases we can use a standard nesting scheme whose properties we can master once and for all. The following nested **if** constructions illustrate the standard scheme:

```
if condition-1 then
    statements-1
else
    if condition-2 then
        statements-2
    else
        if condition-3 then
            statements-3
        else
            if condition-4 then
                statements-4
            else
                statements-5
            endif
        endif
    endif
endif
```

Figure 9.7 shows the decision tree for this nesting scheme. Note that the conditions are arranged along a line rather than being spread throughout a "bushy" tree. Starting at the root, the computer first checks condition-1. If condition-1 is true, statements-1 are executed. If condition-1 is false, the computer goes on to condition-2, and so on. As long as all the conditions encountered are false, the computer takes only branches marked false and so moves down the right side of the tree, checking

Figure 9.6   Decision tree for the nested **if** constructions at right. If
condition-1 is true, statements-1 are executed. Otherwise,
the result of checking condition-2 determines whether
statements-2 or statements-3 will be executed.

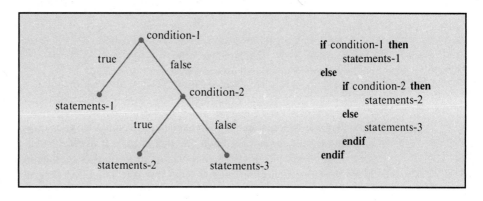

Figure 9.7   Decision tree for the standard nesting scheme at right.
Starting at the root of the tree and moving down the right
side, conditions are checked until the first true condition is
encountered. The statements corresponding to the first true
condition (and only those statements) are executed. If none
of the conditions are true, statements-5 are executed.

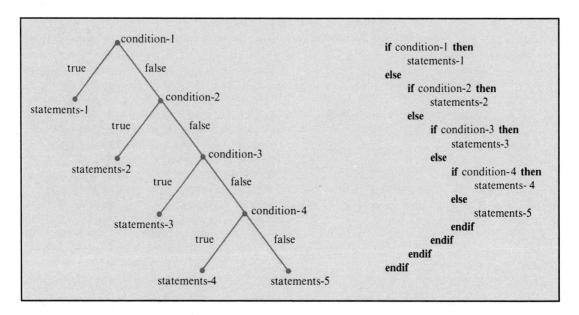

the conditions one after another. As soon as a true condition is encountered, the computer follows the branch marked true and executes the corresponding statements. If all the conditions are false, then statements-5, the statements in the **else** part of the innermost **if** construction, are executed.

We can think of the nested **if** constructions as representing a list of conditions and a list of statements:

condition-1	statements-1
condition-2	statements-2
condition-3	statements-3
condition-4	statements-4
	statements-5

To determine which statements to execute, the computer goes down the condition list checking conditions until it finds one that is true. It then executes the corresponding set of statements in the statements list. At most one set of statements is executed; if more than one condition is true, the *first* true condition determines which set of statements will be executed. If none of the conditions are true, the last set of statements, the one that does not correspond to any condition, is executed.

The rules for finding which statements are executed are much simpler for the standard nesting scheme than for some nesting scheme we might invent on the spur of the moment. For this reason, we would like to use the standard nesting scheme whenever possible. Unfortunately, the nested **if** constructions are somewhat cumbersome to write in the algorithmic language; the large number of **endif**s at the end of the construction are particularly annoying. We get around this problem by defining an extended **if** construction that provides the same correspondence between conditions and sets of statements as the standard nesting scheme but is somewhat easier to write.

The extended if construction   The extended **if** construction has the following form:

> **if** condition-1 **then**
> >   statements-1
> **elseif** condition-2 **then**
> >   statements-2
> **elseif** condition-3 **then**
> >   statements-3
> **elseif** condition-4 **then**
> >   statements-4
> **else**
> >   statements-5
> **endif**

The rules for determining which set of statements will be executed are the same as for the standard nesting scheme. The conditions are checked in the order in which they appear in the extended **if** construction. The statements corresponding to the first condition found to be true are executed. If none of the conditions are true, the statements in the **else** part are executed.

The extended **if** construction differs from the corresponding nested **if** statements in three ways: (1) **else** followed by **if** has been contracted into a single word, **elseif**; (2) only a single **endif** is required to terminate the entire extended **if** construction; and (3) the indentation has been revised so that the keywords **if, elseif, else,** and **endif** are aligned. The revised indentation scheme serves better than the original one to suggest a list of corresponding conditions and sets of statements.

The extended **if** construction can have any number of **elseif** parts, depending on how many conditions need to be tested. The **else** part may be omitted. If the **else** part is omitted, then no action is taken when none of the conditions are true. If we think of the extended **if** construction with the **else** part as a generalization of two-way selection, then the extended **if** construction without the **else** part is a generalization of one-way selection.

An algorithm using the extended if construction Figure 9.8 shows an algorithm for simulating a calculator. Numbers and operators are entered in the order number-operator-number. For example, to have the calculator compute the sum 2 + 3 we would enter the number 2 followed by the operator + followed by the number 3. Each time the calculator carries out an operation it prints an updated value for the calculator display—the number that would appear in the display register of an actual calculator. The algorithm prompts for each number and operator. In calculating the sum 2 + 3, for example, the dialogue with the user would go like this:

```
Number: 2
Operator: +
Number: 3
Display: 5
```

The user enters 2, +, and 3 in response to the algorithm's prompts. The algorithm prints the value of the display after doing the addition.

The algorithm permits *chained calculations,* in which the current result is used as one of the operands for the next operation. For example, to compute the sum

7 + 5 + 4 + 3

we just enter the numbers and operators 7, +, 5, +, 4, +, and 3 in that order:

```
Number: 7
Operator: +
Number: 5
Display: 12
Operator: +
Number: 4
Display: 16
Operator: +
Number: 3
Display: 19
```

Figure 9.8   Algorithm for simulating a calculator. An extended **if**
construction is used for multiway selection.

```
algorithm Calculator

{ Simulate calculator }

declare
    display, entry: real
    operator: char
execute
    operator ← 'E'
    while operator <> 'Q'
        if operator = ' + ' then
            output 'Number: ', more
            input entry
            display ← display + entry
        elseif operator = ' − ' then
            output 'Number: ', more
            input entry
            display ← display − entry
        elseif operator = '*' then
            output 'Number: ', more
            input entry
            display ← display * entry
        elseif operator = '/' then
            output 'Number: ', more
            input entry
            display ← display / entry
        elseif operator = 'C' then
            display ← 0.0
        elseif operator = 'E' then
            output 'Number: ', more
            input display
        elseif operator = 'S' then
            display ← − display
        endif
        output 'Display: ', display
        output 'Operator: ', more
        input operator
    endwhile
end Calculator
```

The operator E ("enter") allows us to terminate a chained calculation by discarding the current display value and entering a new one. E plays somewhat the same role as the = sign does on many actual calculators. For example, in the following dialogue, we first compute 7 + 5 and then compute 4 + 3. The E operator allows 4 to be entered into the display instead of being added to the current contents of the display:

```
Number: 7
Operator: +
Number: 5
Display: 12
Operator: E
Number: 4
Display: 4
Operator: +
Number: 3
Display: 7
```

The calculator simulation algorithm accepts the following operators:

Operator	Description
+	Accept number and add to contents of display
−	Accept number and subtract from contents of display
*	Accept number and multiply by contents of display
/	Accept number and divide into contents of display
C	Clear—set display to zero
E	Accept number and enter into display
S	Change sign of contents of display
Q	Quit—terminate algorithm

We can think of the operators as commands from the user that are to be carried out by the algorithm. An algorithm, or a part of one, that carries out commands from the user is called a *command interpreter*. Command interpreters are quite common; for example, many programs display a *menu* of acceptable commands and ask the user to press the key corresponding to the desired command. A command interpreter then carries out the operation requested by the user. All command interpreters use some form of multiway selection to execute the set of statements that carry out the command selected by the user.

The algorithm in Figure 9.8 uses an extended **if** construction to carry out the +, −, *, /, C, E, and S commands:

> **if** *operator* = ' + ' **then**
>   "add number to display"
> **elseif** *operator* = ' − ' **then**
>   "subtract number from display"

elseif *operator* = '*' **then**

"multiply number by display"

elseif *operator* = '/' **then**

"divide number into display"

elseif *operator* = 'C' **then**

"clear display"

elseif *operator* = 'E' **then**

"enter number into display"

elseif *operator* = 'S' **then**

"change sign of display"

endif

The value of *operator* is the operator entered by the user. The extended **if** construction executes the statements corresponding to the value of *operator*. Since the extended **if** construction has no **else** part, no action is taken if *operator* has some value other than ' + ', ' − ', '*', '/', 'C', 'E', or 'S' (The Q operator is handled by the **while** construction.) Thus no operation is carried out if the user enters an invalid operator.

The algorithm initially sets the value of *operator* to 'E' so as to begin by allowing the user to enter a value into the display. The **while** construction carries out operations and accepts new operators until the user enters the operator Q, which terminates the **while** construction and the algorithm. After each operation is carried out, the contents of the display are printed:

operator ← 'E'

while *operator* <> 'Q'

"Carry out the requested operation"

output 'Display: ', *display*

output 'Operator: ', **more**

input *operator*

endwhile

The case construction A Boolean expression can have only two values. With a single Boolean expression, therefore, we can select from at most two alternatives, which limits us to one-way and two-way selection. The extended **if** construction arrives at the statements to be executed via a series of two-way decisions, each of which is governed by the value of a Boolean expression. Sometimes, however, we can construct a non-Boolean expression whose value determines directly which set of statements is to be executed. In the calculator simulation algorithm, for example, the variable *operator* constitutes such an expression: if the value of *operator* is ' + ', the statements for performing an addition should be carried out; if the value of *operator* is ' − ', the statements for performing a subtraction should be carried out, and so on. The case construction allows the value of a non-Boolean expression to determine directly which set of statements should be executed.

The case construction in the algorithmic language has the following form:

select case expression
    case list-1
        statements-1
    case list-2
        statements-2
            .
            .
            .
    case list-n
        statements-n
endselect

Note that this construction is usually referred to as a case construction even when it begins with another keyword such as **select.**

The value of the expression determines which set of statements will be executed. Each set of statements is preceded by a *case list*—a list of constants specifying the values of the expression for which the statements are to be executed. The constants in the case lists must have the same type as the value returned by the expression. For example, consider the following case construction:

select case *command*
    case 'e', 'E'
        ''edit file''
    case 'l', 'L'
        ''load file''
    case 's', 'S'
        ''save file''
    case others
        output 'Invalid command—please try again'
endselect

The expression is the character variable *command*. If the value of *command* is 'e' or 'E', the statements for editing a file will be executed. If the value of *command* is 'l' or 'L', the statements for loading a file will be executed. A case list consisting of the keyword **others** represents all values not specified in other case lists. Thus, if the user enters a command other than e, E, l, L, s, or S, the statement corresponding to **others** is executed and the user is warned of an invalid command.

It is an error if the value of the selecting expression is not found on any of the case lists. Therefore, when the expression can have values other than those explicitly listed, we should always include **case others** to handle the additional values. If **case others** contains no statements, then no action will be taken for values not listed in other case lists.

We can use the keyword **to** in case lists to specify a range of values. For example, the following construction classifies a nonnegative number as having one, two, three, or more than three digits:

    select case *number*
        case 0 **to** 9
            output 'One digit number'
        case 10 **to** 99
            output 'Two digit number'
        case 100 **to** 199
            output 'Three digit number'
        case others
            output 'Number has more than three digits'
    endselect

Ranges and individual values can be intermixed in a single case list; for example, the statements corresponding to

    case 'a' **to** 'z', 'A' **to** 'Z', '$', '&'

are selected if the value of the expression is a lowercase letter, an uppercase letter, a dollar sign, or an ampersand.

    The case lists of a given case construction must be disjoint; no constant may occur on more than one case list. If the same value appeared on more than one case list, the computer would not know which set of statements to execute for that value.

    An algorithm using the case construction   The calculator simulation algorithm in Figure 9.9 is similar to that in Figure 9.8 except that a case construction is used to execute the statements corresponding to the operator entered by the user:

    select case *operator*
        case ' + '
            "add number to display"
        case ' − '
            "subtract number from display"
        case '*'
            "multiply number by display"
        case '/'
            "divide number into display"
        case 'C'
            "clear display"
        case 'E'
            "enter number into display"
        case 'S'
            "change sign of display"

Figure 9.9   This version of the algorithm for simulating a calculator,
uses a case construction for multiway selection.

```
algorithm Calculator1

{ Simulate calculator }

declare
    display, entry: real
    operator: char
execute
    operator ← 'E'
    while operator <> 'Q'
        select case operator
            case '+'
                output 'Number: ', more
                input entry
                display ← display + entry
            case '−'
                output 'Number: ', more
                input entry
                display ← display − entry
            case '*'
                output 'Number: ', more
                input entry
                display ← display * entry
            case '/'
                output 'Number: ', more
                input entry
                display ← display / entry
            case 'C'
                display ← 0.0
            case 'E'
                output 'Number: ', more
                input display
            case 'S'
                display ← − display
            case others

                { Ignore invalid operator }

        endselect
        output 'Display: ', display
        output 'Operator: ', more
        input operator
    endwhile
end Calculator1
```

case others

{ Ignore invalid operator }

endselect

The selecting expression is the value of *operator*. Since a separate set of statements is executed for each operator, each case list except the last specifies only a single value. The case list **others** specifies all values of *operator* other than $'+'$, $'-'$, $'*'$, $'/'$, $'C'$, $'E'$, and $'S'$. Since we wish this program to just ignore invalid operators, there are no statements corresponding to the **others** case list.

9.4 Compound conditions and Boolean operators

Conditions such as $x < y$ are often called *simple conditions* because each corresponds to a simple sentence in English. For example, the simple sentence corresponding to $x < y$ is "the value of x is less than the value of y." We also sometimes need *compound conditions* that correspond to compound sentences, such as "the value of x is less than the value of y and the value of y is less than the value of z." The *Boolean operators* (or *logical operators*) **and, or,** and **not** allow us to construct Boolean expressions representing compound conditions. Each Boolean operator takes Boolean values as operands and returns a Boolean value as a result.

And   The operator **and** returns *true* only if both of its operands are *true*. Thus, the value of

p **and** q

is *true* only if both the value of p is *true* and the value of q is *true*. We can also describe the behavior of **and** with the following *truth table:*

p	q	p **and** q
true	true	true
true	false	false
false	true	false
false	false	false

Or   The operator **or** returns *true* if either or both of its operands are *true*. Thus, the value of

p **or** q

is *true* if the value of p is *true* or the value of q is *true* or both. We can also describe the behavior of **or** with the following truth table:

p	q	p **or** q
true	true	true
true	false	true
false	true	true
false	false	false

Not   The operator **not** returns *true* if its operand is *false* and returns *false* if its operand is *true*. Thus, the value of

not p

is *true* if the value of p is *false* and vice versa. We can also describe the behavior of **not** with the following truth table:

p	**not** p
true	false
false	true

Priorities of Boolean operators   Unfortunately, the priorities of the Boolean operators vary from one language to another. Some languages use the following reasonable priority scheme:

**	*highest priority*
/, *	
+, −	
=, <>, <, <=, >, >=	
not	
and	
or	*lowest priority*

In an expression involving arithmetical, relational, and Boolean operators, the arithmetical operators are applied first, then the relational operators, and finally the Boolean operators. For example, no parentheses are required in the following expression:

$x + 3 < y - 5$ **and** $y + 5 > z - 3$

Since arithmetical operators have a higher priority than relational operators, the arithmetical expressions $x + 5$, $y - 5$, $y + 5$, and $z - 3$ are evaluated first. The relational operators are applied next, after which the Boolean operator **and** is applied to the Boolean values returned by the relational expressions. If the values of x, y, and z are 1, 6, and 9, the evaluation goes like this:

$x + 3 < y - 5$ **and** $y + 5 > z - 3$
$1 + 3 < 6 - 5$ **and** $6 + 5 > 9 - 3$
$4 < 1$ **and** $11 > 6$ *Arithmetical operators first . . .*
false **and** *true*   *. . . relational operators next . . .*
false   *. . . and Boolean operators last.*

The priorities of **not, and,** and **or** relative to one another are those used in *Boolean algebra,* the algebra of logic invented by George Boole.

Unfortunately, some languages do not use the reasonable priority scheme given above. In Pascal, for example, **and** has the same priority as $*$ and $/$, **or** has the same priority as $+$ and $-$, and **not** has a higher priority than any arithmetical operator. As a result, the expression

$x + 3 < y - 5$ **and** $y + 5 > z - 3$

is invalid in Pascal. Since **and,** with the same priority as $*$ and $/$, has a higher priority than $-$ and $+$, the computer would start by attempting to apply **and** to 5 and y, rather than first evaluating the two relational expressions and applying **and** to the results. The attempt to apply **and** to 5 and y would fail, since **and** can be applied only to Boolean values and the values of 5 and y are integers. Hence, the expression is invalid.

In the algorithmic language, we will always enclose the operands of Boolean operators in parentheses when the operands are expressions involving other operators. The parenthesized expressions are probably easier to read than nonparenthesized ones and are valid regardless of the priorities assigned to the Boolean operators by a particular programming language. Thus our example expression will be written:

$(x + 3 < y - 5)$ **and** $(y + 5 > z - 3)$

indicating that the relational expressions are to be evaluated before the Boolean operator is applied. Note that we are still assuming that the relational operators have a lower priority than the arithmetical operators, so the operands of relational operators do not have to be enclosed in parentheses. We also assume that repeated occurrences of the same operator are applied in left-to-right order, so we can write

p **and** q **and** r **and** s

instead of

$((p$ **and** $q)$ **and** $r)$ **and** s

9.5

Algorithms using Boolean operators

Classifying triangles   A triangle is *equilateral* if the lengths of all three of its sides are equal, *isosceles* if the lengths of only two sides are equal, and *scalene* if none of its sides have the same length. The algorithm in Figure 9.10 inputs the lengths of the sides of triangles and classifies each as *equilateral, isosceles,* or *scalene*. The task performed by this algorithm is a simple example of *pattern recognition*—classifying geometrical figures or other objects according to a given criterion.

Let the values of a, b, and c be the lengths of the sides of the triangle to be classified. The triangle is equilateral if all three sides have the same length, that is, if the value of

$(a = b)$ **and** $(b = c)$ **and** $(a = c)$

Figure 9.10   This algorithm uses Boolean operators and multiway selection to classify triangles as equilateral, isosceles, or scalene.

---

algorithm *Triangles*

{ Classify triangles as equilateral, isosceles, and scalene }

declare
    a, b, c: *real*   { sides of triangle }
    response: *char*   { Does user wish to continue? }
execute
    repeat
        output 'Enter three sides of triangle: ', **more**
        input *a, b, c*
        If $(a = b)$ **and** $(b = c)$ **then**
            output 'Equilateral'
        elseif $(a = b)$ **or** $(b = c)$ **or** $(a = c)$ **then**
            output 'Isosceles'
        else
            output 'Scalene'
        endif
        output
        repeat
            output 'Classify another triangle (y/n)? ', **more**
            input *response*
        unit $(response = \text{'y'})$ **or** $(response = \text{'Y'})$ **or**
            $(response = \text{'n'})$ **or** $(response = \text{'N'})$
    until $(response = \text{'n'})$ **or** $(response = \text{'N'})$
end *Triangles*

---

is *true*. We can simplify this expression by noting that, if $a = b$ and $b = c$ are *true*, then so is $a = c$, since the values of a and c are both equal to the value of b. We need to check only the first two equalities, therefore, and so can use the following simplified expression:

    $(a = b)$ **and** $(b = c)$

If the triangle is not equilateral, it may still be isosceles: two of its sides may have the same length. We can use the following Boolean expression to check for an isosceles triangle:

    $(a = b)$ **or** $(b = c)$ **or** $(a = c)$

This expression, unlike the corresponding one for equilateral triangles, cannot be further simplified.

Every equilateral triangle is also isosceles. Therefore, we must check for equilateral triangles before checking for isosceles triangles; we must apply the test for isosceles triangles only to those triangles that have failed the test for equilateral triangles. If we were to check for isosceles triangles first, then all equilateral triangles would be classified as isosceles. Triangles that fail both the test for equilateral triangles and the test for isosceles triangles are classified as scalene. We use an extended **if** construction to carry out the tests in the desired order:

if $(a = b)$ **and** $(b = c)$ **then**
    output 'Equilateral'
elseif $(a = b)$ **or** $(b = c)$ **or** $(a = c)$ **then**
    output 'Isosceles'
else
    output 'Scalene'
endif

Dealing blackjack   Figure 9.11 shows an algorithm for simulating the actions of a blackjack dealer. On each turn, a blackjack player has the option to ''hit''— take another card—or to ''stay''—elect to take no more cards. The player's hand consists of all cards the player has taken, and the value, or *count,* of the hand is the sum of the values of all the cards in the hand. The player with the highest count not exceeding 21 wins; any player whose count goes over 21 ''busts,'' or loses. A player hits to increase the count of his or her hand and stays out of fear of busting.

The cards 2 through 10 are counted at their face values, regardless of suit. The face cards (jack, queen, and king) are counted as 10. The ace can be counted as either 1 or 11; it is counted as 11 unless doing so would put the count over 21, in which case it is counted as 1. A count that includes an ace counted as 11 is said to be *soft*. Note that two aces counted as 11 would always put the count over 21. Therefore, a count can be soft only by virtue of a single ace being counted as 11.

The dealer plays a hand just like the other players, but the dealer has no options. If the dealer's count is 16 or less, the dealer must hit—take another card. If the dealer's count is greater than 16, the dealer must stay. And, like the players, the dealer will bust if his or her count goes over 21.

The algorithm in Figure 9.11 hits by prompting the user to enter the value of a card. The ace is represented by the value 1; it is up to the algorithm to determine when an ace should be counted as 11. Other cards are represented by integers in the range 2 through 10. The algorithm inputs card values until the dealer stays or busts, at which time the algorithm prints the action taken by the dealer and the dealer's final count:

```
Card? 4
Card? 10
Card? 3
Dealer stays
Dealer's count is 17
```

Figure 9.11   Algorithm for simulating a blackjack dealer.

```
algorithm Dealer

{ Simulate blackjack dealer }

declare
    count,                    { current count of dealer's hand }
    card: integer             { card just drawn }
    softCount: Boolean    { true if count includes ace counted as 11 }
execute
    count ← 0
    softCount ← false
    repeat
        output 'Card? ', more
        input card
        count ← count + card
        if (card = 1) and (not softCount) then

            { Ace was drawn and current count is not soft }

            count ← count + 10
            softCount ← true
        endif
        if (count > 21) and softCount then

            { Count exceeds 21 and is soft }

            count ← count − 10
            softCount ← false
        endif
    until count > 16
    if count <= 21 then
        output 'Dealer stays'
    else
        output 'Dealer busts'
    endif
    output 'Dealer''s count is ', count
end Dealer
```

The following exchange illustrates an ace counted as 11:

```
Card? 1
Card? 9
Dealer stays
Dealer's count is 20
```

In this example, the dealer busts:

```
Card? 9
Card? 6
Card? 10
Dealer busts
Dealer's count is 25
```

Let's use the integer variable *count* for the dealer's count. The algorithm will read the values of cards and update the value of *count* until the value of *count* exceeds 16. If, at this point, the value of *count* does not exceed 21, then the dealer stays. If the value of *count* has gone over 21, however, the dealer busts. We can outline the algorithm as follows:

"Initialize variables"

repeat

"Obtain value of card and update *count*. If the card was an ace and the count is not already soft, make the count soft and count the ace as 11. If the current card makes the count go over 21, check if the count is soft. If so, try to avoid busting by counting the ace as 1 instead of 11"

until *count* > 16

if *count* <= 21 **then**

output 'Dealer stays'

else

output 'Dealer busts'

endif

output 'Dealer''s count is ', *count*

We will use the Boolean variable *softCount* to keep track of whether the count is soft; the value of *softCount* will be *true* when the count is soft and *false* otherwise. A Boolean variable used to keep track of whether some event has occurred or some situation exists is often called a *flag;* we can think of the flag *softCount* as being raised (*true*) when the count is soft and lowered (*false*) when the count is not soft.

The algorithm begins by initializing *count* to 0 and *softCount* to *false*:

count ← 0

softCount ← *false*

The value of the current card is read into *card*

output 'Card? ', **more**

input *card*

and used to update the value of *count*:

    card ← *count* + *card*

An ace is entered and counted as a 1. If the count is not currently soft, however, it should be made soft and the ace should be counted as 11. Since the ace has already been counted as 1, we count it as 11 by adding 10 to the value of *count*:

if (*card* = 1) **and** (**not** *softCount*) **then**
    count ← *count* + 10
    softCount ← *true*
endif

If the current card made the count go over 21, and if the count is soft, then we may be able to avoid busting by counting the ace as 1 instead of 11:

if (*count* > 21) **and** *softCount* **then**
    count ← *count* − 10
    softCount ← *false*
endif

Decreasing the value of *count* by 10 reverses the change that was made when the ace was counted as 11. Note that the ace in question need not be the current card, but may have been taken on some previous turn.

Review questions

1. Give two functions performed by a selection construction in an algorithmic or programming language.

2. Give the general form of the one-way selection construction in the algorithmic language.

3. Give the general form of the two-way selection construction in the algorithmic language.

4. How many cases are involved in a one-way selection? In a two-way selection?

5. In "one-way selection" and "two-way selection," to what do the terms "one way" and "two way" refer?

6. Why is it sometimes convenient to use the two-way selection construction for writing a one-way selection?

7. Describe the procedure that must be followed when a selection construction is encountered while proving the correctness of an algorithm.

8. Why are assertions and their use in proving algorithms correct important to us even though we won't usually take the time to construct a detailed correctness proof for each algorithm we study?

9. What are *nested* **if** constructions?

10. What is a *decision tree?* How can we use a decision tree to illustrate how the computer will process a set of nested **if** constructions?

11. How can we use a table to illustrate how the computer will process a set of nested **if** constructions?

12. Describe the standard nesting scheme and illustrate it with a set of nested **if** constructions and the corresponding decision tree.

13. Give the rules for determining which set of statements will be executed in the standard nesting scheme.

14. Describe the extended **if** construction. How it is related to nested **if** constructions?

15. What is a *command interpreter?* For what purpose do command interpreters use multiway selection?

16. Describe the case construction.

17. The extended **if** construction uses the values of two or more Boolean expressions to determine which set of statements should be executed. How does the case construction achieve the same result more directly?

18. What is a *case list?* How is a range of values indicated in a case list?

19. Define each of the Boolean operators **and, or,** and **not.** Give each definition first in words and then by constructing a *truth table.*

20. Describe the convention we will follow in the algorithmic language for using parentheses in expressions involving Boolean operators. Why do we follow this convention even though it requires more parentheses than would be needed if an appropriate set of operator priorities were assumed? What is an advantage of using the parentheses?

21. What is a *flag?* For what purpose is it used?

Exercises

1. Evaluate each of the following expressions. Assume that the integer variables a, b, and c and the Boolean variables p, q, and r have the following values:

Variable	Value	Variable	Value
a	3	p	*true*
b	4	q	*false*
c	12	r	*true*

(a) **not** p

(b) p **or** q

(c) p **and** q

(d) p **and** $(q$ **or** $r)$

(e) $(b > a)$ **and** $(b > c)$

(f) $(b > a)$ **or** $(b > c)$

(g) **not** $((a = b)$ **or** $(a = c))$

(h) $(a < b)$ **and** $(a < c)$ **and** $(c < b)$

(i) $(a > b)$ **or** $(b > c)$ **or** $(c > a)$

(j) $(a > c - b)$ **or** $(c > a + b)$

2. State the conditions under which each of the Boolean expressions in Exercise 1 has the value *true*. Consider all possible values for the variables, not just the values given in Exercise 1. *Example:* the value of the expression in part (a) is *true* whenever the value of p is false.

3. A salesperson gets a 5% commission on sales of $1,000 or less and a 10% commission on sales over $1,000. (Someone who sold $1,500 worth would get a 5% commission on $1,000 and a 10% commission on $500.) Write an algorithm to input amounts sold and output each salesperson's commission and the amount received by the company after the commission is deducted from the amount sold.

4. We recall that a package cannot be sent by first-class mail if its length-plus-girth (its length plus the distance around it in the width-height direction) exceeds 100 inches. Write an algorithm to read the length, width, and height for rectangular packages and print whether or not each package can be sent by first-class mail.

5. Suppose that temperatures are recorded every hour. Write an algorithm to input the 24 temperatures recorded during a day and output the high and low for the day.

Hint: Use the variables *high* and *low* for the high and low temperatures. The repetition that reads and processes temperatures should maintain the truth of the following invariant assertion:

{ The value of *low* is the lowest temperature processed so far and the value of *high* is the highest temperature processed so far }

This assertion will hold before the repetition begins if *low* and *high* are both set initially to the first temperature to be processed. The repetition will then begin with the second temperature to be processed.

6. A machine part in the shape of a cylindrical rod will only fit properly if the diameter of the rod is in the range 9.95 cm through 10.07 cm. Write an algorithm to input the diameters of rods and print "accept" for each rod whose diameter is in the required range and "reject" for each that is too large or too small.

7. A machine part has the shape of a rectangular block whose length, width, and height must lie in the following ranges:

 length: 7.49–7.51 cm
 width: 0.95–1.05 cm
 height: 0.42–0.43 cm

 Write an algorithm to read sets of data each consisting of the length, width, and diameter of a part and print whether or not each part is to be accepted or rejected.

8. Write an algorithm that inputs sets of data each consisting of the length, width, and height of a box and the diameter and height of a cylindrical jar. For each set of data, the algorithm should print whether or not the jar will fit inside the box. The jar can sit upright in the box or it can lie on its side with its top parallel to one of the sides of the box.

9. Write an algorithm to input two integers and output them in ascending numerical order regardless of the order in which they were entered.

10. Write an algorithm to input three integers and output them in ascending numerical order. One approach is to assign the integers to three variables, say i, j, and k. Following the sorting algorithm in Chapter 1, exchange the values of i and j, j and k, and i and k as needed until i contains the smallest integer, j the next largest, and k the largest. Remember that, to exchange the values of two variables, an additional variable, say *temp*, is needed for temporary storage:

 $temp \leftarrow i$
 $i \leftarrow j$
 $j \leftarrow temp$

11. Here is another approach to solving the problem of printing three integers in ascending order (Exercise 10). Again let the three integers be assigned to variables i, j, and k. Instead of exchanging the values of the variables and then printing the result with a single **output** statement, we will use a separate **output** statement for each of the six possible orders of the values of i, j, and k. For example, if the value of i precedes or equals the value of j, which in turn precedes or equals the value k, the output will be printed with

 output $i, ' ', j, ' ', k$

 On the other hand, if the value of i precedes the value of k, which in turn precedes the value of j, then the statement

 output $i, ' ', k, ' ', j$

 will be used. Our algorithm will use nested **if** constructions to cause the proper statement to be used for each possible order of the input values.

 Hint: Figure 9.12 shows a decision tree for the problem of sorting three numbers.

Figure 9.12   Decision tree for sorting the values of i, j, and k. The nonleaf nodes are labeled with conditions comparing the values of i, j, and k. Each leaf node is labeled with a possible order for the values of i, j, and k. The results of checking the conditions lead us to a particular leaf node giving the order in which the three values should be printed. For example, if $i <= j$ and $j <= k$ are both true, the values should be printed in the order ijk.

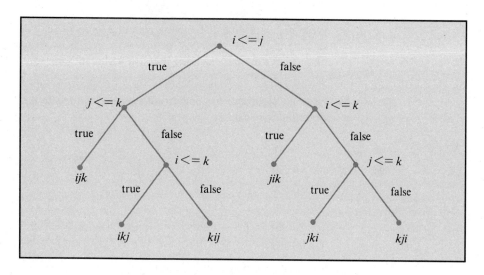

Each leaf node is labeled with the order in which the values of i, j, and k should be printed: ijk, for example, indicates that the value of i should be followed by the value of j, which should be followed by the value of k. The nonleaf nodes are labeled with conditions comparing the values of i, j, and k. For example, following the leftmost branch, if $i <= j$ and $j <= k$ are both true, then the values should be printed in the order ijk. On the other hand, following the next-to-leftmost branch, if $i <= j$ is true, $j <= k$ is false, and $i <= k$ is true, the value of k lies between those of i and j and the values should be printed in the order ikj. Note that the condition at the root node determines the order in which the values of i and j should be printed. Each *subtree* (tree contained within a larger tree) hanging from the root node determines the position of the value of k relative to the values of i and j. Using the decision tree in Figure 9.12 as a guide, write the nested **if** constructions needed to print the three integers in ascending order.

12. Using the method of Exercise 11, write an algorithm that inputs three integers and prints the smallest of the three. Draw a decision tree for the problem and write an algorithm based on the decision tree.

13. The cost of a certain item depends on the quantity ordered, as given by the following table:

Quantity Ordered	Cost per Item
0–99	$5.95
100–199	$5.75
200–299	$5.40
300 or more	$5.15

Write an algorithm that inputs quantities ordered and outputs the cost of each item and the total cost of the order. Write two versions of the algorithm, one using an extended **if** construction and one using a case construction.

14. Write an algorithm to convert numeric scores to letter grades according to the following scale:

Score	Letter Grade
0–59	F
60–69	D
70–79	C
80–89	B
90–100	A

15. Write an algorithm that will, at the user's request, print one of the following figures:

```
*****            *              *
*****           ***            ***
*****          *****          *****
*****         *******          ***
*****        *********          *
```

When the algorithm starts, it presents the user with the following menu and prompt:

```
R. Rectangle
T. Triangle
D. Diamond
Enter letter for figure desired:
```

The algorithm will print the rectangle, triangle, or diamond depending on whether the user enters R, T, or D. The letters can be entered in uppercase or lowercase. After printing one figure, the algorithm will determine if the user desires another figure to be printed; if so, the algorithm will again print the menu and prompt the user to enter the letter corresponding to the figure desired.

Pascal Supplement

One- and two-way selection

The **if** statement in Pascal has two possible forms:

if condition **then** statement-1

if condition **then** statement-1 **else** statement-2

The form without the **else** part is used for one-way selection; the form with the **else** part is used for two-way selection.

Usually, the controlled statements and the word **else** are written on separate lines, with the controlled statements indented relative to **if** and **else**:

if condition **then**
    statement-1

and

if condition **then**
    statement-1
else
    statement-2

As with the repetition constructions, styles of indentation vary from one programmer to another. Feel free to experiment with styles of indentation, but use one style consistently through each program.

As in the algorithmic language, the condition is represented by a Boolean expression that is evaluated when the **if** statement is executed. For one-way selection, statement-1 is executed if the value of the Boolean expression is *true,* and no action is taken if the value of the Boolean expression is *false*. For two-way selection, statement-1 is executed if the value of the Boolean expression is *true,* and statement-2 is executed if the value of the Boolean expression is *false*.

In the general forms, statement-1 and statement-2 each represents a single statement. However, as in the **while** and **for** statements, the single statement can be a compound statement, thus allowing the execution of any number of statements to be controlled. For example in

if $i > j$ **then**
    begin
        temp := *i*;
        i := *j*;
        j := *temp*
    end

the three statements making up the compound statement are all executed if the value of $i > j$ is *true* and none of them are executed if the value is *false*.

The semicolon that separates an **if** statement from the next statement in the program comes after statement-1 if there is no **else** part and after statement-2 if an **else** part is present:

```
if i > 9 then          if i > 9 then
    i := 0;                i := 0
writeln(i)             else
                           i := i + 1;
                       writeln(i)
```

Note carefully that when an **else** part is present there is no semicolon after statement-1. Thus in the example on the right, there is no semicolon after $i := 0$. When the statements in question are compound statements, the semicolon comes after the **end** of the compound statement:

```
if i > 9 then              if i > 9 then
    begin                      begin
        i := 0;                    i := 0;
        j := j + 1                 write('*')
    end;                       end
writeln(i)                 else
                               begin
                                   i := i + 1;
                                   write('-')
                               end;
                           writeln(i)
```

Again note that there is no semicolon following the statement in the **then** part of an **if** statement that also has an **else** part.

Figures 9.13 through 9.16 give the Pascal programs corresponding to the algorithms in Figures 9.1 through 9.4. The translations into Pascal are straightforward and require little comment.

In Figure 9.13, the **if** statement

```
if balance > 0.0 then
    writeln(accountNumber:10, balance:10:2)
```

is used to print the account number and balance for those accounts that have a balance greater than zero.

In Figure 9.14, the **if** statement

```
if hoursWorked > 40.0 then
    hoursWorked := hoursWorked + 0.5 * (hoursWorked - 40.0)
```

adjusts the value of *hoursWorked* for those persons, and only those persons, who worked overtime.

Figure 9.13 Pascal program *Balances* corresponding to the algorithm in
Figure 9.1

```
program Balances(input, output);

{ Print account number and balance for accounts with balances greater than
  zero }

const
    sentinel = 9999;
var
    accountNumber: integer;
    balance: real;
begin
    writeln('Account ':10, 'Balance ':10);
    writeln('Number ':10, 'Due     ':10);
    writeln;
    readln(accountNumber, balance);
    while accountNumber <> sentinel do
        begin
            if balance < 0.0 then

                { Account has balance greater than zero }

                writeln(accountNumber:10, balance:10:2);
            readln(accountNumber, balance)
        end
end.
```

The program in Figure 9.15 achieves the same result by doing different calculations for gross wages depending on whether or not the person worked overtime:

if *hoursWorked* $\leq$ 40.0 **then**
    grossWages := *hoursWorked* * *hourlyRate*
else
    grossWages := 40.0 * *hourlyRate* +
                    1.5 * *hourlyRate* * (*hoursWorked* − 40.0)

In Figure 9.16, an **if** statement with compound statements in its **then** and **else**
parts is used to count a grade as a pass or a fail and print it in the passed or failed
column:

Figure 9.14   Pascal program *Payroll* corresponding to the algorithm in
Figure 9.2

```
program Payroll(input, output);

{ Compute gross wages for employees who get time and a half for
  overtime, where all hours in excess of 40 are overtime }

const
    sentinel = 9999;
var
    employeeNumber: integer;
    hoursWorked, hourlyRate, grossWages: real;
begin
    writeln('Employee':10, 'Hours  ':10, 'Hourly':10, 'Gross ':10);
    writeln('Number  ':10, 'Worked':10, 'Rate   ':10, 'Wages':10);
    writeln;
    readln(employeeNumber, hoursWorked, hourlyRate);
    while employeeNumber <> sentinel do
        begin
            write(employeeNumber:10, hoursWorked:10:1,
                hourlyRate:10:2);
            if hoursWorked > 40.0 then

                { Employee worked overtime }

                hoursWorked := hoursWorked + 0.5 * (hoursWorked -
                                40.0);
            grossWages := hoursWorked * hourlyRate;
            writeln(grossWages:10:2);
            readln(employeeNumber, hoursWorked, hourlyRate)
        end
end.
```

Figure 9.15   Pascal program *Payroll1* corresponding to the algorithm in
Figure 9.3

---

program *Payroll1*(*input*, *output*);

{ Compute gross wages for employees who get time and a half for
overtime, where all hours in excess of 40 are overtime }

const
    sentinel = 9999;
var
    employeeNumber: *integer*;
    hoursWorked, *hourlyRate*, *grossWages*: *real*;
begin
    writeln('Employee ':10, 'Hours ':10, 'Hourly':10, 'Gross':10);
    writeln('Number   ':10, 'Worked':10, 'Rate ':10, 'Wages':10);
    writeln;
    readln(*employeeNumber*, *hoursWorked*, *hourlyRate*);
    while *employeeNumber* <> *sentinel* **do**
        begin
            if *hoursWorked* <= 40.0 **then**

                { Employee did not work overtime }

                grossWages := *hoursWorked* * *hourlyRate*
        else

                { Employee worked overtime }

                grossWages := 40.0 * *hourlyRate* +
                        1.5 * *hourlyRate* * (*hoursWorked* −
                        40.0);
            writeln(*employeeNumber*:10, *hoursWorked*:10:1,
                hourlyRate:10:2, *grossWages*:10:2);
            readln(*employeeNumber*, *hoursWorked*, *hourlyRate*)
        end
end.

```
program PassFail(input, output);

{ Print student numbers and grades with passing grades in one column and
  failing grades in another. Count number of students who passed and
  failed }

const
    sentinel = 9999;
    lowestPassingGrade = 70;
var
    studentNumber, grade, passedCount, failedCount: integer;
begin
    writeln('Number':10, 'Passed':10, 'Failed':10);
    writeln;
    passedCount := 0;
    failedCount := 0;
    readln(studentNumber, grade);
    while studentNumber <> sentinel do
        begin

            { The values of passedCount and failedCount are the numbers
              of previously processed students who passed and failed. The
              values of studentNumber and grade are the data for the next
              student to be processed }

            if grade < lowestPassingGrade then
                begin

                    { Student failed }

                    writeln(studentNumber:10, grade:20);
                    failedCount := failedCount + 1
                end
            else
                begin

                    { Student passed }

                    writeln(studentNumber:10, grade:10);
                    passedCount := passedCount + 1
                end;
            readln(studentNumber, grade)
        end;
    writeln;
    writeln('Passed: ', passedCount:2);
    writeln('Failed: ', failedCount:2)
end.
```

```
if grade < lowestPassingGrade then
    begin
        writeln(studentNumber:10, grade:20);
        failedCount := failedCount + 1
    end
else
    begin
        writeln(studentNumber:10, grade:10);
        passedCount := passedCount + 1
    end
```

Note that in

```
writeln(studentNumber:10, grade:20)
```

the field-width parameter of 20 skips over the 10-character-wide passed column and prints the grade in the 10-character-wide failed column.

In translating these programs, we have followed the algorithms in assuming that each file is terminated by a sentinel record. However, the *eof* predicate can be used to good effect for these noninteractive programs. For example, if *eof* is used instead of a sentinel to indicate the end of the input file, the statement part of *Balances* (Figure 9.13) can be rewritten as follows:

```
writeln('Account':10, 'Balance':10);
writeln('Number':10, 'Due     ':10);
writeln;
while not eof(input) do
    begin
        readln(accountNumber, balance);
        if balance > 0.0 then
            writeln(accountNumber:10, balance:10:2)
    end
```

Only one *readln* statement is needed, and this statement precedes the other repeated statements instead of following them as in Figure 9.13. As a rule, we will translate the algorithms as literally as possible and so will use a sentinel to signal the end of a file. But note that using *eof* instead of a sentinel is more idiomatic Pascal.

Multiway selection

Nested if statements　　The statement occurring in the **then** or **else** part of an **if** statement can itself be an **if** statement, thus allowing **if** statements to be nested. For example, if we let the statement in the **then** part be another **if** statement, we get the following:

if condition-1 **then**
    if condition-2 **then**
        statement-1
    else
        statement-2
else
    statement-3

These nested **if** statements correspond to the nested **if** constructions illustrated in Figure 9.5. The decision trees for the two are the same (except for the substitution of "statement" for "statements"). Thus the computer begins by checking condition-1; if it is false, statement-3 is executed. If condition-1 is true, then condition-2 must be checked. If condition-2 is true, then statement-1 is executed; if condition-2 is false, then statement-2 is executed. The following table, which is essentially the same as the one for the corresponding nested **if** constructions, shows the conditions under which each statement is executed:

condition-1	*condition-2*	*statement executed*
true	true	statement-1
true	false	statement-2
false	true	statement-3
false	false	statement-3

Likewise, if we replace the statement in the **else** part of an **if** statement with another **if** statement, we get the following:

if condition-1 **then**
    statement-1
else
    if condition-2 **then**
        statement-2
    else
        statement-3

These nested **if** statements correspond to the nested **if** constructions in Figure 9.6. Again, the decision tree and the table showing the conditions under which each statement is executed are essentially the same for the nested **if** statements and the nested **if** constructions.

Because Pascal does not terminate an **if** statement with **endif,** ambiguity can arise as to which **if** statement a particular **else** part goes with. Consider the following example, where c1 and c2 stand for conditions and s1 and s2 stand for statements:

    if c1 **then if** c2 **then** s1 **else** s2

Does the **else** part go with the first or the second **if** statement? That is, if the nested **if** statements are written in indented form, which of the following is correct:

```
if c1 then          if c1 then
    if c2 then          if c2 then
        s1                  s1
    else                else
        s2                  s2
```

Note that the two indented forms differ in the conditions under which s2 is executed. For the form on the left, s2 is executed when c1 is true and c2 is false; for the form on the right, s2 is executed when c1 is false.

Pascal provides the following special rule to remove this ambiguity: *each else part goes with the nearest if statement that does not already have an else part*. Thus in our example, the **else** part goes with the second **if** statement, not the first. The indented form on the left is correct; the one on the right is incorrect. Note that Pascal language processors pay no attention to indentation, so if we used the indented form on the right, we would just be misleading ourselves as to how Pascal would process the statement.

Note that the **endif**s prevent this ambiguity from arising in the algorithmic language, even if we allow an entire **if** construction to be written on a single line. In the algorithmic language, we would write

> **if** c1 **then if** c2 **then** s1 **endif else** s2 **endif**

if we wanted the **else** part to go with the first **if** construction, and

> **if** c1 **then if** c2 **then** s1 **else** s2 **endif endif**

if we wanted the **else** part to go with the second **if** construction. The corresponding indented forms are:

```
if c1 then          if c1 then
    if c2 then          if c2 then
        s1                  s1
    endif               else
else                        s2
    s2                  endif
endif               endif
```

The standard nesting scheme   The following nested **if** statements illustrate the standard nesting scheme in Pascal:

```
if condition-1 then
    statement-1
else
    if condition-2 then
        statement-2
    else
        if condition-3 then
            statement-3
```

   else

     if condition-4 **then**

      statement-4

     else

      statement-5

As in the algorithmic language, the computer checks the conditions in the order in which they appear in the nested **if** statements. The statement corresponding to the first condition found to be true is executed. If none of the conditions are found to be true, statement-5, the statement in the **else** part of the last **if** statement, is executed.

Since Pascal does not use **endif,** the problem of **endif**s piling up at the end of a set of nested **if** constructions does not occur. We can thus use the nested **if** statements directly, rather than devising an equivalent extended **if** construction as was done in the algorithmic language. Nevertheless, we will find it convenient to revise the indentation so as to emphasize the list of condition-statement pairs rather than emphasizing the nesting scheme:

  if condition-1 **then**

    statement-1

  else if condition-2 **then**

    statement-2

  else if condition-3 **then**

    statement-3

  else if condition-4 **then**

    statement-4

  else

    statement-5

This is not a new statement type, but just the same nested **if** statements written in a different format. Note that the words **else if** are not (and cannot be) combined into a single word **elseif,** as was done in the algorithmic language.

Figure 9.17 shows the program for simulating a calculator, corresponding to the algorithm in Figure 9.8. The multiway selection is implemented with nested **if** statements following the standard nesting scheme and written in the ''**else if** format'' just described. Note that many of the controlled statements are compound statements; this does not affect the overall format. Also note that the last **if** statement does not have an **else** part. Therefore, if none of the conditions tested are true—if the operator is not $+$, $-$, $*$, $/$, C, E, or S—then no action is taken by the nested **if** statements. (As in the algorithm, the operator Q is handled by the **while** statement rather than the nested **if** statements.)

Figure 9.17 Pascal program *Calculator* corresponding to the algorithm in Figure 9.8

```
program Calculator(input, output);

{ Simulate calculator }

var
    display, entry: real;
    operator: char;
begin
    operator := 'E';
    while operator <> 'Q' do
        begin
            if operator = '+' then
                begin
                    write('Number: ');
                    readln(entry);
                    display := display + entry
                end
            else if operator = '-' then
                begin
                    write('Number: ');
                    readln(entry);
                    display := display - entry
                end
            else if operator = '*' then
                begin
                    write('Number: ');
                    readln(entry);
                    display := display * entry
                end
            else if operator = '/' then
                begin
                    write('Number: ');
                    readln(entry);
                    display := display / entry
                end
            else if operator = 'C' then
                display := 0.0
            else if operator = 'E' then
                begin
                    write('Number: ');
                    readln(display)
                end
            else if operator = 'S' then
                display := -display;
            writeln('Display: ', display:1:2);
            write('Operator: ');
            readln(operator)
        end
end.
```

The case statement   The Pascal **case** statement, which corresponds to the case construction in the algorithmic language, has the following form:

case expression **of**

    case-list-1: statement-1;

    case-list-2: statement-2;

    case-list-3: statement-3;

       .

       .

       .

    case-list-n: statement-n

end

As in the algorithmic language, each case list consists of a list of constants giving possible values of the expression. The constants must be of the same type as the value returned by the expression, and the case lists must be disjoint—the same constant cannot occur on more than one case list. A colon separates each case list from the statement to be executed for that case. Each statement except the last is followed by a semicolon; the semicolon is optional for the last statement. When the **case** statement is executed, the expression is evaluated, the case list containing the value of the expression is located, and the corresponding statement is executed. It is an error if none of the case lists contain the value of the expression.

Standard Pascal does not allow ranges such as $'a'$ **to** $'z'$ in case lists; each value must be listed separately. Also there is no default case list, such as **others**, that includes all possible values of the expression not appearing on other case lists. Because of these restrictions, the Pascal **case** statement is somewhat more cumbersome to use than the algorithmic language case construction. Often we must list a large number of constants, such as all the letters of the alphabet, or else use an **if** statement to "filter out" expression values that the **case** statement is not prepared to handle.

For example, suppose we try to translate the following case construction into Pascal:

    select case *command*

        case $'e'$, $'E'$

            "edit file"

        case $'1'$, $'L'$

            "load file"

        case $'s'$, $'S'$

            "save file"

        case others

            output $'$Invalid command—please try again$'$

    endselect

Our first attempt is:

```
case command of
      'e', 'E': "edit file";
      'l', 'L': "load file";
      's', 'S': "save file"
end
```

This, however, is wrong because it has no case corresponding to **case others** in the algorithmic language. If, for example, the user accidentally type a or d instead of s, the program would terminate with an error message, and the user's file would probably be lost.

The simplest fix is to use an **if** statement to execute the **case** statement if the command is e, E, l, L, s, or S and to print an error message otherwise:

```
if "command is e, E, l, L, s, or S" then
      "execute case statement"
else
      writeln('Invalid command--please try again')
```

The **if** statement protects the **case** statement from values it is not prepared to handle. Often the simplest way to write the condition for such a protective **if** statement is to use Pascal *sets*. Sets will be discussed in detail later in the book. For now, note that a set is a collection of values that can be represented by listing the values in the set between square brackets. Thus the set

```
['e', 'E', 'l', 'L', 's', 'S']
```

contains the character values 'e', 'E', 'l', 'L', 's', and 'S'. The condition

```
command in ['e', 'E', 'l', 'L', 's', 'S']
```

is true if the value of *command* is one of the listed characters and false otherwise. With the **if** statement and sets, we can translate the algorithmic language case construction into Pascal as follows:

```
if command in ['e', 'E', 'l', 'L', 's', 'S'] then
      case command of
            'e', 'E': "edit file";
            'l', 'L': "load file";
            's', 'S': "save file"
      end
else
      writeln('Invalid command—please try again')
```

Figure 9.18 shows the program corresponding to the algorithm in Figure 9.9, the calculator simulation using a case construction. The translation is straightforward except that an **if** statement must be used to protect the **case** statement from operators it cannot handle:

```
if operator in ['+', '-', '*', '/', 'C', 'E', 'S'] then
      "execute case statement"
```

Since the calculator simulation just ignores invalid operators, the **if** statement has no **else** part; no action is taken if the operator is invalid.

Figure 9.18   Pascal program *Calculator1* corresponding to the algorithm
in Figure 9.9

```pascal
program Calculator1(input, output);

{ Simulate calculator }

var
    display, entry: real;
    operator: char;
begin
    operator := 'E';
    while operator <> 'Q' do
        begin
            if operator in ['+', '-', '*', '/', 'C', 'E', 'S'] then
                case operator of
                    '+':
                        begin
                            write('Number: ');
                            readln(entry);
                            display := display + entry
                        end;
                    '-':
                        begin
                            write('Number: ');
                            readln(entry);
                            display := display - entry
                        end;
                    '*':
                        begin
                            write('Number: ');
                            readln(entry);
                            display := display * entry
                        end;
                    '/':
                        begin
                            write('Number: ');
                            readln(entry);
                            display := display / entry
                        end;
                    'C': display := 0.0;
                    'E':
                        begin
                            write('Number: ');
                            readln(display)
                        end;
                    'S': display := -display
                end; { case }
            writeln('Display: ', display:1:2);
            write('Operator: ');
            readln(operator)
        end
end.
```

Boolean operators

The Boolean operators **and, or,** and **not** are defined in Pascal precisely as in the algorithmic language. The priorities of the Boolean, relational, and arithmetical operators are as follows:

not	*highest priority*
*, /, **and**	
+, −, **or**	
=, <>, <, >, <=, >=, **in**	*lowest priority*

Since the Boolean operators have higher priorities than the relational operators, we must use parentheses to force relational expressions to be evaluated before Boolean operators are applied. For example, if i, j, and k are integer variables, the expression

$i < j$ **and** $j < k$

is invalid. Since **and** has a higher priority than $<$, the computer would begin by trying to evaluate

j **and** j

which it cannot do since the **and** operator applies only to Boolean values, not integers. We must use parentheses around the relational expressions to force them to be evaluated first:

$(i < j)$ **and** $(j < k)$

The revised expression is probably clearer than the original one, however, so it may be just as well that Pascal forces us to use parentheses that other languages might allow us to omit. In fact, it is a good idea to follow the rule given for the algorithmic language and use parentheses around any operand of a Boolean operator that is itself an expression involving operators. Thus, for clarity,

(**not** p) **and** q

is preferable to

not p **and** q

even though the two expressions are equivalent in Pascal since **not** has a higher priority than **and**. We will, however, use the fact that operators with the same priority are evaluated in left-to-right order to write expressions such as

p **and** q **and** r **and** s

p **or** q **or** r **or** s

instead of

$((p$ **and** $q)$ **and** $r)$ **and** s

$((p$ **or** $q)$ **or** $r)$ **or** s

Figures 9.19 and 9.20 give the Pascal programs corresponding to the algorithms in Figures 9.10 and 9.11. The translations are straightforward and require little comment. In Boolean expressions, only those parentheses required by Pascal have been used. For example, in

> (*card* = 1) **and not** *softCount*

parentheses are not required around **not** *softCount* since **not** has a higher priority than **and**. On the other hand, it might possibly be clearer to write

> (*card* = 1) **and** (**not** *softCount*)

Using optional parentheses is something of an art; either too few or too many or poorly placed parentheses can adversely affect the clarity of an expression.

Figure 9.19   Pascal program *Triangles* corresponding to the algorithm in Figure 9.10

```
program Triangles(input, output);

{ Classify triangles as equilateral, isosceles, and scalene }

var
      a, b, c: real;      { sides of triangle }
      response: char;     { Does user wish to continue? }
begin
   repeat
      write('Enter three sides of triangle: ');
      readln(a, b, c);
      if (a = b) and (b = c) then
         writeln('Equilateral')
      else if (a = b) or (b = c) or (a = c) then
         writeln('Isosceles')
      else
         writeln('Scalene');
      writeln;
      repeat
         write('Classify another triangle (y/n)? ');
         readln(response)
      until (response = 'y') or (response = 'Y') or
            (response = 'n') or (response = 'N')
   until (response = 'n') or (response = 'N')
end.
```

Figure 9.20 Pascal program *Dealer* corresponding to the algorithm in Figure 9.11

```
program Dealer(input, output);

{ Simulate blackjack dealer }

var
    count,                  { current count of dealer's hand }
    card: integer;          { card just drawn }
    softCount: Boolean;     { count includes ace counted as 11 }
begin
    count := 0;
    softCount := false;
    repeat
        write('Card? ');
        readln(card);
        count := count + card;
        if (card = 1) and not softCount then
            begin

                { Ace was drawn and current count is not soft }

                count := count + 10;
                softCount := true
            end;
        if (count > 21) and softCount then
            begin

                { Count exceeds 21 and is soft }

                count := count - 10;
                softCount := false
            end
    until count > 16;
    if count <= 21 then
        writeln('Dealer stays')
    else
        writeln('Dealer busts');
    writeln('Dealer''s count is ', count:1)
end.
```

In Figure 9.19, the terminating conditions for the **repeat** statements can be simplified by using sets. In place of

(response = 'y') **or** *(response* = 'Y')

we can use

response **in** ['y', 'Y']

and in place of

(response = 'y') **or** *(response* = 'Y') **or**
(response = 'n') **or** *(response* = 'N')

we can use

response **in** ['y', 'Y', 'n', 'N']

10

Subalgorithms

A *subalgorithm* is an algorithm that is invoked by an algorithm or another subalgorithm rather than directly by the user. We will consider two kinds of subalgorithms, *functions* and *procedures,* which differ in the ways they return the results of their calculations. We are already familiar with *predefined functions,* such as *round* and *sqrt;* in this chapter we will see how to define our own functions when no predefined function meets our needs.

Algorithms, functions, and procedures are all algorithms in the most general sense of the word: all are sets of instructions for solving particular problems. The three differ only in such technical details as how they are invoked, how they receive their input data, and how they return their results.

We can think of subalgorithms as building blocks for constructing algorithms. We can assemble an algorithm from functions and procedures rather than directly from statements in the algorithmic language, just as an automobile is assembled from previously manufactured parts such as tires, spark plugs, and headlights, rather than directly from rubber, glass, and metal.

Such building blocks offer a number of advantages. Just as the person who designs the tires of a car does not have to worry about the design of the spark plugs, we can focus our attention on one building block at a time, allowing us to break our work down into manageable parts. Different persons can work on different building blocks at the same time, provided they agree in advance as to how the different building blocks are to communicate with one another. Because the difficulty of proving an algorithm correct increases rapidly with the size and complexity of the algorithm, it may be much easier to verify many small building blocks individually than to verify one large algorithm. If an algorithm malfunctions, we can often isolate the problem to a single building block on which we can concentrate our efforts at finding and correcting the error. And if a building block is needed at more than one place in an algorithm, we can write it once and invoke it in as many places as needed.

10.1 Functions

We recall that functions are invoked by using them in expressions. A function is supplied with one or more *arguments* or *actual parameters*. The function returns a value that is used in evaluating the expression. For example, in the expression

3 * *round*(4.9) + 2

the actual parameter for the predefined function *round* is 4.9. *Round* returns the value 5, the result of rounding 4.9 up to the nearest integer. The value returned by the function is used in evaluating the expression:

$$3 * 5 + 2$$
$$15 + 2$$
$$17$$

A function definition looks very much like an algorithm, which is to be expected since algorithms, functions, and procedures are just variations on the same underlying concept. A function definition, however, must declare *formal parameters,* which will be used to refer to the values of the actual parameters supplied when the function is invoked. The function definition must also state the type of values returned by the function and the particular value returned when the function is invoked.

For example, let's define a function *Maximum* that takes two integers as actual parameters and returns the larger of the two:

Expression	*Value*
Maximum(5, 10)	10
Maximum(9, 2)	9
Maximum(7, 7)	7

The function *Maximum* is defined as follows:

```
function Maximum(m, n): integer
declare
    m, n: in integer
execute
    if m > n then
        Maximum ← m
    else
        Maximum ← n
    endif
end Maximum
```

The first line of the function definition is the *function heading,* which has the following form:

    function function-name(formal-parameter-list): return-type

The function name is an identifier, which should be chosen by the programmer to reflect the nature of the function. Thus, we choose *Maximum* as the name of the function that returns the larger of two numbers. We will follow the convention of capitalizing function names.

A function must have some way to refer to the values of the actual parameters that will be supplied when the function is invoked. This is done with identifiers called *formal parameters.* The list of formal parameters, enclosed in parentheses, comes immediately after the function name. There is a one-to-one correspondence between the formal and actual parameters: the first formal parameter refers to the first actual parameter, the second formal parameter refers to the second actual parameter, and so on. When possible, formal parameters should be given names that suggest their significance. For example, because of well-chosen function and parameter names, we can see at a glance that the function with the heading

    function *Perimeter*(*length*, *width*): *real*

computes the perimeter of a geometrical figure from its length and width. When, as in the case of the function *Maximum,* the parameters have no special significance, we can use noncommittal names like *m* and *n*.

A function heading ends with a colon followed by the type of the values returned by the function. Thus, without analyzing or even seeing the entire function definitions, we can see that *Maximum* returns integer values and *Perimeter* returns real values.

Like an algorithm, a function definition has a **declare** part containing definitions and declarations and an **execute** part containing statements to be executed. The formal parameters, which are introduced in the formal parameter list, are declared in the **declare** part. (Some programming languages declare the formal parameters in the formal parameter list; this, however, clutters the formal parameter list, making it difficult to see at a glance just what the formal parameters are.)

The formal parameters for the function *Maximum* are declared as follows:

    declare

        m, n: **in** *integer*

Formal parameters, like variables, are given types; *m* and *n* are declared as integer parameters. The types of the values supplied as actual parameters must be the same as the types declared for the corresponding formal parameters.

There are three kinds of formal parameters: *input parameters, output parameters,* and *input/output parameters.* Input parameters, the only kind we will consider for the moment, are used to transmit input data to a subalgorithm. Input parameters are declared with the keyword **in** preceding the parameter type. Thus, both *m* and *n* are declared as input parameters.

When a function is invoked, input parameters are replaced with the values of the corresponding actual parameters. The statements in the **execute** part of the function definition are executed just as if every occurrence of a formal parameter had been replaced by the corresponding actual parameter. Thus, if *Maximum* is invoked with the expression

$2 * Maximum(5, 7) + 3$

then the statements in the **execute** part are carried out as if every occurrence of *m* had been replaced with 5 and every occurrence of *n* had been replaced with 7.

If the actual parameters are expressions, the expressions are evaluated and their values replace the formal parameters. Thus, if *Maximum* is invoked by

$Maximum(7 * 2, 5 * 3)$

the expressions are evaluated to give 14 and 15 as the values of the actual parameters. Each occurrence of *m* in the **execute** part of the algorithm is replaced by 14, and each occurrence of *n* is replaced by 15.

Another way of looking at the correspondence between actual parameters and formal input parameters is that the latter behave as if they had been defined as constants with values equal to the corresponding actual parameters. Thus, when *Maximum* is invoked by

$2 * Maximum(5, 7) + 3$

the statements in the **execute** part of the function definition are executed as if *m* and *n* had been defined by

const $m = 5$
const $n = 7$

Likewise, if the function is invoked by

$Maximum(7 * 2, 5 * 3)$

the statements are executed as if *m* and *n* were defined by

const $m = 14$
const $n = 15$

Since input parameters behave like constants, their values remain the same throughout the execution of the function. The values of the input parameters are determined when the function is invoked and cannot be changed by any statement in the function definition.

The value the function is to return is assigned to the function name. When a function is invoked, a memory location is reserved for holding the value the function is to return. Every time a statement of the form

function-name $\leftarrow$ expression

is executed, the expression is evaluated and its value is stored in the reserved memory location. When the execution of the function terminates, the contents of the reserved memory location are returned as the value of the function. Thus if more than one value is assigned to the function name, only the last assignment is effective.

At least one assignment to the function name must be made; otherwise, the value returned by the function will be undefined.

The **execute** part of *Maximum* consists of a single statement:

if *m* > *n* **then**

    Maximum ← *m*

else

    Maximum ← *n*

endif

The **if** statement compares the values of *m* and *n*, which are, of course, the same as the values of the actual parameters. If the value of *m* is greater than that of *n*, the value of *m* is assigned to *Maximum* and is the value returned by the function. On the other hand, if the value of *n* is greater than or equal to the value of *m*, the value of *n* is assigned to *Maximum* and is the value returned by the function.

For example, suppose the function is invoked by the following expression:

2 ∗ *Maximum*(5, 7) + 3

The statements defining the function are executed with *m* replaced by 5 and *n* replaced by 7:

if 5 > 7 **then**

    Maximum ← 5

else

    Maximum ← 7

endif

Since the condition 5 > 7 is false, the statement in the **else** part is executed, and 7 is assigned to the function name as the value to be returned. Thus, the expression that invoked the function is evaluated as follows:

$$2 * Maximum(5, 7) + 3$$
$$2 * 7 + 3$$
$$14 + 3$$
$$17$$

The factorial function Let's look at a slightly more complicated function definition. The *factorial* of a positive integer is defined as the product of all the integers from 1 through the integer in question. For example, 3 factorial is equal to $1 \times 2 \times 3$, or 6; 4 factorial is equal to $1 \times 2 \times 3 \times 4$, or 24; and so on. The function *Factorial* returns the factorial of a positive integer (the function returns 1 if the argument is 0 or a negative integer):

function *Factorial*(*n*): *integer*

declare

    n: **in** *integer*

    product, *i*: *integer*

execute

$product \leftarrow 1$

for $i \leftarrow 1$ **to** n

$product \leftarrow product * i$

endfor

$Factorial \leftarrow product$

end *Factorial*

The **for** statement steps the value of i from 1 to the value of n. Thus, if the function is invoked with the expression *Factorial*(5), the value of i will be stepped from 1 to 5; if the function is invoked with *Factorial*(10), the value of i will be stepped from 1 to 10; and so on. The value of *product* is set initially to 1 and then multiplied in turn by each value of i. The invariant assertion for the repetition is as follows:

{ The value of *product* is the product of all integers in the range 1 to $i - 1$.

(When the value of i is 1 the value of *product* is 1) }

When the **for** statement terminates, therefore, the value of *product* is the product of all positive integers in the range 1 to n. Since this is, by definition, equal to the factorial of n, the value of *product* is assigned to *Factorial* as the value to be returned.

Although values can be assigned to the function name as possible values to be returned, the current value to be returned *cannot* be referenced by using the function name in an expression. Thus, we cannot eliminate the variable *product* by writing the statement part of *Factorial* like this:

$Factorial \leftarrow 1$

for $i \leftarrow 1$ **to** n

$Factorial \leftarrow Factorial * i$

endfor

The right-hand side of

$Factorial \leftarrow Factorial * i$

is invalid since a value assigned to the function name cannot be referenced by using the function name in an expression. When used to transmit a return value, the function name is a special case of an *output parameter*—a parameter to which values can be assigned but whose current value cannot be accessed.

Figure 10.1 shows the function *Factorial* along with an algorithm that uses the function to print a table of integers and their factorials. The computer begins by executing the algorithm *PrintFactorials*; the function *Factorial* is executed only when the expression

$Factorial(i)$

is encountered in

output i, **tab**(16), *Factorial*(i)

The function is invoked with the value of *i* as its actual parameter. The value returned by the function is printed as the value of *Factorial(i)*.

Unless explicitly declared otherwise, identifiers are *local* to the algorithm or subalgorithm in which they are declared. This means that identifiers in different algorithms or subalgorithms have nothing to do with one another, even if they are spelled the same. In Figure 10.1, for example, the *i* declared in *PrintFactorials* and the *i* declared in *Factorial* are distinct identifiers that have nothing to do with one another, even though both are represented by the letter *i*.

Figure 10.1   The algorithm *PrintFactorials* tests the function *Factorial* by using it to print a table of factorials.

```
algorithm PrintFactorials

{ Test Factorial function by printing a short table of factorials }

declare
    i: integer
execute
    output 'Number', tab(16), 'Factorial'
    output
    for i ← 1 to 7
        output i, tab(16), Factorial(i)
    endfor
end PrintFactorials


function Factorial(n): integer

{ Compute factorial of positive integer }

declare
    n: in integer
    product, i: integer
execute
    product ← 1
    for i ← 1 to n
        product ← product * i
    endfor
    Factorial ← product
end Factorial
```

For convenience, we will use the term *unit* for an algorithm or subalgorithm. A unit, then, is an algorithm, a function, or a procedure. We will also find it convenient to use the term ''algorithm'' for all the units required to do a particular job, rather than just for the unit introduced with the keyword **algorithm.** To distinguish the unit introduced with **algorithm,** we will refer to it as the *main algorithm.* Using this terminology, we can say that Figure 10.1 shows an algorithm for printing a table of factorials. The algorithm consists of two units, a main algorithm *PrintFactorials* and one subalgorithm, the function *Factorial.*

The computer always begins execution with the first statement of the main algorithm and stops after executing the last statement of the main algorithm. The other units of the algorithm—the procedures and functions—are executed only when invoked, either directly by the main algorithm or indirectly by another procedure or function.

10.2 Procedures

A function returns a single value, which is to be used in evaluating an expression. Sometimes, however, we may wish a subalgorithm to return no value or several values, and we may want to use the value or values returned for some purpose other than evaluating an expression. In these situations we use a *procedure* rather than a *function.* A procedure begins with a *procedure heading,* which has the following form:

procedure procedure-name(formal-parameter-list)

No return type is specified since there is no return value associated with a procedure. The remainder of a procedure definition is made up of **declare** and **execute** parts, just like an algorithm or a function definition. The **execute** part *does not* contain an assignment to the procedure name since the name of a procedure is not used to return a value.

For example, the following procedure rounds a value to two decimal places and prints it preceded by a dollar sign:

procedure *PrintCurrency(amount)*
declare
    amount: **in** *real*
    cents: *integer*
    roundedAmount: *real*
execute
    cents ← *round*(100.0 ∗ *amount*)
    roundedAmount ← *cents* / 100.0
    output '$', *roundedAmount*, **more**
end *PrintCurrency*

A procedure is invoked by a *procedure statement,* which consists of the procedure name followed by a list of actual parameters. The list of actual parameters is enclosed in parentheses:

procedure-name(actual-parameter-list)

For example, the procedure statement

PrintCurrency(3.1416)

causes the computer to print

`$3.14`

PrintCurrency does not return any value to the algorithm or subalgorithm that invokes it. Nevertheless, it is still useful because it prints the value of its actual parameter in the desired format—rounded to two decimal places and preceded by a dollar sign.

If procedures are to be generally useful, they must have ways of returning results to the algorithms and subalgorithms that invoke them. Since formal parameters are used to transmit input data to a procedure, it is only reasonable to also use formal parameters for returning results.

10.3

Input, output, and input/output parameters

As mentioned earlier, the algorithmic language allows three kinds of parameters: input, output, and input/output. The following table summarizes the properties of each kind of parameter:

Parameter	Keyword	Use	Actual Parameter	Formal Parameter
input	**in**	transmits input data	expression	constant
output	**out**	returns result	variable	variable (assignment only)
input/ output	**in out**	transmits input data and returns result	variable	variable

The first line of the table summarizes what we already know about input parameters: they are declared with the keyword **in** and are used to transmit input data to a subalgorithm. The actual parameter can be an expression including, of course, constants and variables as well as expressions constructed with operators. In the **execute** part of the subalgorithm, the formal parameter functions as a constant whose value is the value of the expression that was supplied as an actual parameter.

Output parameters are declared with the keyword **out**, and input/output parameters are declared with the keywords **in out**. An output parameter can be used only to return a result; an input/output parameter can be used both to transmit input data to the subalgorithm and to return a result.

Since both output and input/output parameters are used to return results, the corresponding actual parameters must be able to receive the returned results. Only a variable can be used to store a result; a constant or an expression constructed with operators cannot. Therefore, the actual parameter corresponding to an output or input/output formal parameter must always be a variable.

Formal output and input/output parameters function as variables in the **execute** part of the subalgorithm. Input/output parameters can be used just like any other variables: they can be assigned new values, and they can be used in contexts, such as expressions, in which their values will be accessed. Output parameters, however, can only be assigned new values; the current value of an output parameter cannot be accessed. Thus an output parameter can appear to the left of an assignment operator, in an **input** statement, or as an actual parameter corresponding to an output parameter of a procedure. It cannot, however, appear in any context in which its value will be used, such as in an expression, to the right of an assignment operator, in an **output** statement, or as an actual parameter corresponding to an input or input/output parameter of a procedure.

For all three kinds of parameters, the type of the actual parameter must be the same as the type of the corresponding formal parameter.

When the execution of a subalgorithm begins, each formal input/output parameter has the same value as the corresponding actual parameter. (Remember that both the actual parameter and the formal parameter are variables.) After the execution of the subalgorithm terminates, each actual parameter corresponding to an output or input/output formal parameter has the last value that was assigned to the formal parameter. Thus, results are returned by assigning values to output and input/output parameters; the last value assigned to the formal parameter is the result that is returned.

For example, consider the following procedure, which computes the area and the perimeter of a rectangle:

> **procedure** *Rectangle*(*length*, *width*, *area*, *perimeter*)
> **declare**
> > *length*, *width*: **in** *real*
> > *area*, *perimeter*: **out** *real*
>
> **execute**
> > *area* ← *length* * *width*
> > *perimeter* ← 2.0 * (*length* + *width*)
>
> **end** *Rectangle*

Suppose that *Rectangle* is invoked with the procedure statement

> *Rectangle*(5.0, 3.0, *a*, *p*)

where *a* and *p* are real variables. Since *length* and *width* are input parameters, they function as constants whose values are those of the corresponding actual parameters. Thus the statements in the **execute** part of *Rectangle* are equivalent to

$area \leftarrow 5.0 * 3.0$

$perimeter \leftarrow 2.0 * (5.0 + 3.0)$

When these statements are executed, the value 15.0 is assigned to *area* and the value 16.0 is assigned to *perimeter*. After the procedure returns, the values of *a* and *p* will be the same as the last values assigned to the corresponding formal parameters. Thus, after the procedure returns, the value of *a* is 15.0 and the value of *p* is 16.0. The statements

$a \leftarrow 1.0$

$p \leftarrow 4.0$

Rectangle(5.0, 3.0, *a*, *p*)

output 'Area is ', *a*

output 'Perimeter is ', *p*

cause the computer to print

```
Area is 15.0
Perimeter is 16.0
```

Note that the procedure statement replaces the current values of *a* and *p* (1.0 and 4.0) with the values returned by the procedure.

For an example of an input/output parameter, let's write a procedure to increment the seconds or minutes display of a digital clock. Each time the procedure is called, the displayed value should be increased by 1. When the value reaches 60, however, it should be reset to zero:

procedure *Increment*(*display*)

declare

   display: **in out** *integer*

execute

   $display \leftarrow display + 1$

   if $display = 60$ **then**

      $display \leftarrow 0$

   endif

end *Increment*

Suppose that this procedure is invoked with the statements

$d \leftarrow 30$

Increment(*d*)

output *d*

where *d* is an integer variable. When execution of the procedure begins, the value of *display* is 30, the value of the corresponding actual parameter. After

$display \leftarrow display + 1$

is executed, the value of *display* is 31. The **if** construction compares the value of *display* with 60; since the two are not equal, the controlled statement is not executed, and the procedure returns. After the procedure returns, the value of *d* is the last value that was assigned to *display*. The **output** statement, therefore, prints 31.

Now consider the following statements:

$d \leftarrow 59$

Increment(*d*)

output *d*

When execution of the procedure begins, the value of *display* is 59. The statement

$display \leftarrow display + 1$

assigns *display* the value 60. The **if** construction compares the value of *display* with 60; since the two are equal, the controlled statement

$display \leftarrow 0$

is executed and *display* is assigned the value 0. When the procedure returns, *d* has the last value assigned to *display*, which was 0. Hence the **output** statement prints 0.

10.4
Parameter-passing methods

A computer system can use two methods, *copy* and *reference,* to pass input data to a procedure and return results from a procedure. In most cases, we do not have to worry about which method is used. In certain tricky situations, however, the two will give different results. These situations should be avoided, thus assuring that an algorithm will work as desired regardless of the parameter-passing method used by a particular language implementation.

Parameter passing by copy works like this. When a procedure is invoked, a private memory area is set up for use by that particular invocation. For each of the formal parameters, a corresponding memory location is reserved in the private memory area. Before execution of the procedure begins, the values of all actual parameters corresponding to **in** and **in out** formal parameters are copied into the memory locations corresponding to the formal parameters.

During execution of the procedure, all references to formal parameters refer to the corresponding memory locations in the private memory area. Referring to the value of an input or input/output parameter refers to the value in the corresponding memory location; assigning a value to an output or input/output parameter stores a new value in the corresponding memory location. When the procedure returns, the contents of the memory locations corresponding to all output and input/output parameters are copied into the memory locations associated with the actual parameters (remember that the actual parameters must be variables). Figure 10.2 illustrates parameter passing by copy.

The problem with parameter passing by copy is that in some situations enormous amounts of data may have to be needlessly copied. For example, suppose a procedure is used to change one entry in a large table having thousands of entries. If the table

Figure 10.2   Parameter passing by copy. The procedure P has f as a
formal input/output parameter and is invoked with a as the
corresponding actual parameter. Before the execution of P
begins, the value of the actual parameter a is copied into the
formal parameter f. During the execution of P, the value of f
can change but that of a cannot, so the values of a and f
may differ. After the execution of P, the value of the formal
parameter f is copied into the actual parameter a, so the
values of a and f are once again the same.

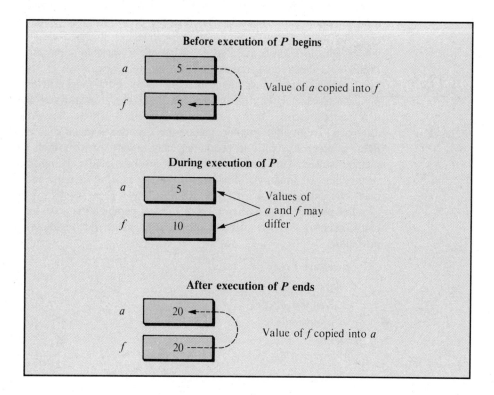

is accessed via an input/output parameter, the entire table must be copied into the
procedure's private memory area before execution of the procedure begins. Then,
after the procedure changes the single entry of interest, the entire table must be
copied from the procedure's private memory area to the memory area corresponding
to the actual parameter. Since only one table entry was changed, many thousands of
values were copied back and forth needlessly.

 We can avoid needless copying by passing parameters by *reference*. Again, a
memory location corresponding to each formal parameter is set up in the procedure's
private memory area. Now, however, this location holds not the value of the actual
parameter but a reference to that value—specifically, the machine address of the

memory location containing the value of the actual parameter. Only the address, which usually occupies only a single memory location, need be passed to the procedure. The value of the actual parameter need not be copied. When the formal parameter is encountered in a statement in the **execute** part of the procedure, the corresponding address is used to refer to the memory location containing the value of the actual parameter.

Specifically, if the actual parameter corresponding to an input parameter is a constant or a variable, the address of the memory location containing the value of the constant or variable is passed to the procedure. If the actual parameter is an expression, the expression must be evaluated and its value stored in a memory location, the address of which is passed to the procedure. The actual parameter corresponding to an output or input/output parameter is always a variable; the address of the memory location containing the value of the variable is passed to the procedure. Figure 10.3 illustrates parameter passing by reference.

Lanaguage implementations sometimes choose the most efficient method of passing each parameter. If a parameter value occupies at most a few memory locations, it is passed by copy. If the value is a large block of data, however, it is passed by reference. To give the implementation the freedom to make such choices, we would like for procedure calls to work the same regardless of which parameter-passing method is used. This is the case for most procedure calls encountered in practice. In certain unusual situations, however, parameter passing by copy and by reference can give different results.

The problem arises when the same actual parameter is accessed by two different paths, such as via two different formal parameters. For example, suppose that the procedure

> **procedure** *Foo*(*i*, *j*)
> **declare**
> > *i*: **in out** *integer*
> > *j*: **out** *integer*
> **execute**
> > $i \leftarrow 3$
> > **output** *i*
> > $j \leftarrow 5$
> > **output** *i*
> **end** *Foo*

is invoked with the procedure statement

> *Foo*(*k*, *k*)

As a result of this invocation, the two formal parameters *i* and *j* both correspond to the same actual parameter *k*.

Suppose that parameter passing is by copy; *i* and *j* correspond to memory locations in the procedure's private memory area. When the procedure is invoked, *i* is given the value of *k* (whatever that might be). The first two statements of the proce-

Figure 10.3   Parameter passing by reference. The procedure P has f as a
formal input/output parameter and is invoked with a as the
corresponding actual parameter. Before the execution of P
begins, the formal parameter f is set to refer to the actual
parameter a; thus any reference to f in the **execute** part of P
will be interpreted as a reference to a. When the procedure
uses the value of f in evaluating an expression, the value of
a will actually be used. When the procedure assigns a new
value to f, the new value will actually be assigned to a.
After the the execution of P ends, the value of a will be the
last value that was assigned to f. If no assignment to f was
made, a will retain the value that it had when P was
invoked.

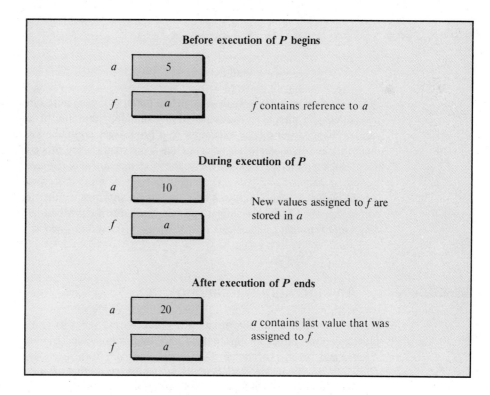

dure assign i the value 3 and print the value of i; the value printed is, of course, 3.
The second two statements assign j the value 5 and again print the value of i. Since
i and j correspond to different memory locations, the assignment to j has no effect
on the value of i, and the value 3 is again printed. When the procedure terminates,
it is an open question as to what value k will receive since this depends on the order
in which the values of i and j are copied into the memory location corresponding to

k. If they are copied in the order in which they appear in the procedure heading, then *k* will receive the value of *j*, which is 5.

Now suppose that parameter passing is by reference. In this case *i* and *j* both refer to the memory location corresponding to *k*. An assignment to *i* or *j* immediately changes the values of *i*, *j*, and *k* since all three refer to the same memory location. The first assignment statement in the procedure assigns 3 as the value of *i*, *j*, and *k*; the first **output** statement prints 3. The second assignment changes the value of *i*, *j*, and *k* to 5; the second **output** statement therefore prints 5. When the procedure returns, the value of *k* is 5.

The following table contrasts the behavior of the procedure call when parameters are passsed by copy and by reference:

	By Copy	*By Reference*
Output	3	3
	3	5
Final value of k	3 or 5	5

More than one access path to an actual parameter can cause other problems when parameters are passed by reference. For example, the value of an input parameter can be changed during the execution of a procedure, contradicting our earlier statement that an input parameter behaves like a constant during procedure execution. To avoid such problems, we will make the rule that *an actual parameter may be accessed by at most one path*. The actual parameter must correspond to at most one formal parameter, and it cannot be accessed by any means other than via the formal parameter, such as by the global variable mechanism described later in this chapter. Any algorithm that violates this rule will be considered erroneous.

10.5
An algorithm for playing craps

As an example of an algorithm using procedures, we will use the algorithm for playing craps shown in Figure 10.4. The algorithm consists of a main algorithm, *Craps,* and seven procedures: *GetStartingBankroll, GetPlayersBet, PlayOneRound, UpdatePlayersBankroll, RollDice, PlayRemainingRolls,* and *Random.*

We begin by considering the rules of craps. The player rolls a pair of dice, each of which is marked with numbers in the range 1 to 6. The sum of the numbers showing on the dice, which ranges from 2 to 12, determines the outcome of the roll as follows:

Case 1   7 or 11 rolled. The player wins.

Case 2   2, 3, or 12 rolled. The player loses.

Figure 10.4   Algorithm for playing craps with the user. The algorithm
consists of the main algorithm *Craps* and seven procedures:
*GetStartingBankroll, GetPlayersBet, PlayOneRound,
UpdatePlayersBankroll, RollDice, PlayRemainingRolls,* and
Random.

```
algorithm Craps

{ Play craps with user }

declare
    bankroll,          { Amount available to player for betting }
    bet,               { Amount bet on this round }
    seed: real         { Value used for generating random numbers }
    won,               { True if player has won current round }
    playing: Boolean   { True if game is to continue }
execute
    output 'Enter number between 0 and 1: ', more
    input seed
    GetStartingBankroll(bankroll)
    repeat
        output
        GetPlayersBet(bankroll, bet)
        PlayOneRound(seed, won)
        UpdatePlayersBankroll(bankroll, bet, won, playing)
    until not playing
end Craps




procedure GetStartingBankroll(bankroll)

{ Find out how much money player has }

declare
    bankroll: in out real
execute
    output 'How much money do you have to play with? ', more
    input bankroll
    while bankroll <= 0.0
        output 'Please enter an amount greater than zero: ', more
        input bankroll
    endwhile
end GetStartingBankroll
```

procedure *GetPlayersBet*(*bankroll*, *bet*)

{ Get amount player wishes to bet on current round }

declare
    bankroll: **in** *real*
    bet: **in out** *real*
execute
    output ′How much do you want to bet? ′, **more**
    input *bet*
    while (*bet* < 0.0) **or** (*bet* > *bankroll*)
        output ′Invalid bet--please try again: ′, **more**
        input *bet*
    endwhile
end *GetPlayersBet*

procedure *PlayOneRound*(*seed*, *won*)

{ Play one round; determine whether player wins or loses }

declare
    seed: **in out** *real*
    won: **out** *Boolean*
    dice: *integer*
execute
    RollDice(*dice*, *seed*)
    select case *dice*
        case 7, 11   { Player wins }
            won ← *true*
        case 2, 3, 12   { Player loses }
            won ← *false*
        case 4 **to** 6, 8 **to** 10 { More rolls needed to determine outcome }
            PlayRemainingRolls(*dice*, *seed*, *won*)
    endselect
end *PlayOneRound*

procedure *UpdatePlayersBankroll*(*bankroll*, *bet*, *won*, *playing*)

{ Update *bankroll* and report results of round. If player is broke, set
playing to *false*. Otherwise, determine if user wishes to play another
round and set value of *playing* to *true* or *false* accordingly }

```
declare
    bankroll: in out real
    bet: in real
    won: in Boolean
    playing: out Boolean
    response: char
execute
    if won then
        output 'You win'
        bankroll ← bankroll + bet
    else
        output 'You lose'
        bankroll ← bankroll − bet
    endif
    if bankroll < 0.005 then
        output 'You''re broke'
        playing ← false
    else
        output 'You have ', bankroll, ' dollars'
        repeat
            output 'Do you want to play again (y/n)? ', more
            input response
        until (response = 'y') or (response = 'n') or
              (response = 'Y') or (response = 'N')
        playing ← (response = 'y') or (response = 'Y')
    endif
end UpdatePlayersBankroll



procedure RollDice(dice, seed)

{ Simulate roll of dice; print value rolled on each die and return their sum
  as value of dice }

declare
    dice: out integer
    seed: in out real
    die1, die2: integer
execute
    Random(6, die1, seed)
    Random(6, die2, seed)
    output 'You rolled a ', die1, ' and a ', die2
    dice ← die1 + die2
end RollDice
```

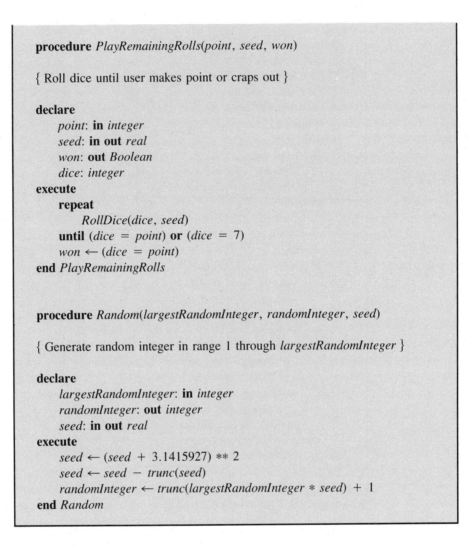

```
procedure PlayRemainingRolls(point, seed, won)

{ Roll dice until user makes point or craps out }

declare
    point: in integer
    seed: in out real
    won: out Boolean
    dice: integer
execute
    repeat
        RollDice(dice, seed)
    until (dice = point) or (dice = 7)
    won ← (dice = point)
end PlayRemainingRolls



procedure Random(largestRandomInteger, randomInteger, seed)

{ Generate random integer in range 1 through largestRandomInteger }

declare
    largestRandomInteger: in integer
    randomInteger: out integer
    seed: in out real
execute
    seed ← (seed + 3.1415927) ** 2
    seed ← seed − trunc(seed)
    randomInteger ← trunc(largestRandomInteger * seed) + 1
end Random
```

Case 3   4, 5, 6, 8, 9, or 10 rolled. The number showing on the first roll becomes the player's *point*. The player now continues to roll the dice until he wins by "making his point"—rolling the same number as on the first roll—or loses by "crapping out"—rolling a 7.

To simulate rolling the dice, the algorithm uses *pseudorandom numbers* (often just called *random numbers*). These are numbers that seem to have been generated by some process involving chance, such as rolling dice or spinning a roulette wheel, but are actually computed by a procedure called a *pseudorandom number generator*. The operation of the pseudorandom number generator is governed by a variable *seed,* whose current value determines the sequence of random numbers that will be produced by future calls to the pseudorandom number generator. The algorithm begins by obtaining the starting value of *seed* from the user. Each time the pseudorandom number generator is called, it uses the current value of *seed* and assigns *seed* a new value. To give the pseudorandom number generator access to *seed*, which is declared in the main algorithm, *seed* must be passed as an input/output parameter to the pseudorandom number generator and to any procedure that directly or indirectly invokes the pseudorandom number generator.

Not only must the algorithm simulate the rolling of the dice and determine the results of each roll, it must also obtain the amount the player wishes to bet on each round and keep track of the player's winnings or losses. The following dialogue illustrates a typical execution of the algorithm (the number between 0 and 1 requested from the player is used as the initial value of *seed*):

```
Enter number between 0 and 1: .678
How much money do you have to play with? 1000

How much do you want to bet? 100
You rolled a 4 and a 6
You rolled a 3 and a 2
You rolled a 2 and a 1
You rolled a 4 and a 3
You lose
You have 900 dollars
Do you want to play again (y/n)? n
```

In constructing the algorithm, we will follow the method of *top-down design*. We write the main algorithm first, invoking as-yet-unwritten procedures for each major operation the main algorithm must carry out. We can think of the main algorithm as an executive that coordinates the activities of the algorithm but calls on one of its subordinates—a procedure—to accomplish each major task. When we have completed the main algorithm, we go on to write each of the procedures it invokes. Here the top-down design method can be used again: in writing each procedure, we can invoke still other not-yet-written procedures.

We can outline the main algorithm, *Craps,* as follows:

"Have user enter initial value of seed for pseudorandom number generator"

"Get player's starting bankroll—amount that player has for betting"

repeat

"Skip a line on display"

"Get player's bet for this round"

"Play one round"

"Update player's bankroll. Inform player of outcome of round. If player is broke, set *playing* to *false.* Otherwise, see if player wishes to continue and set *playing* to *true* or *false* accordingly."

until not *playing*

As to variables, we need real variables *bankroll* for the player's bankroll, *bet* for the player's bet on the current round, and *seed* to hold the seed for the pseudorandom number generator. We also need two Boolean variables: *won* to indicate whether the player won or lost the current round, and *playing* to indicate whether or not another round is to be played. Using these variables as parameters, we can write *Craps* using a procedure call for each major operation in the outline, as shown in Figure 10.4.

The call

GetStartingBankroll(bankroll)

obtains from the player the starting value for *bankroll*. The procedure requires the user to enter a valid value for *bankroll*; zero and negative values are rejected. Likewise, the call

GetPlayersBet(bankroll, bet)

gets the amount the player wishes to bet on the current round. The value of *bankroll* is passed to the procedure so it can check that the player is not betting more than he has. Negative bets are also rejected.

The procedure call

PlayOneRound(seed, won)

plays one round, printing out for the player the numbers that come up on each roll of the dice, and sets *won* to *true* or *false* depending on whether the player won or lost the round. Since *PlayOneRound* uses the pseudorandom number generator, it must be passed *seed* as an input/output parameter.

Finally, the call

UpdatePlayersBankroll(bankroll, bet, won, playing)

increases the value of *bankroll* by that of *bet* if *won* is *true* and decreases the value of *bankroll* by that of *bet* if *won* is *false*. The outcome of the round and the new value of *bankroll* are printed for the player. If the player is now broke, *playing* is set to *false*. Otherwise, the procedure determines whether the user wishes to continue playing and sets the value of *playing* accordingly.

GetStartingBankroll prompts the player to enter the amount of money he has to bet with. If a negative or zero amount is entered, the player is prompted to enter a value greater than zero. The latter prompt is repeated as long as the player continues to enter negative or zero values. Note that as far as the use of the procedure is concerned, *bankroll* could be an output parameter since it is used only to return a result to the invoking algorithm. However, making *bankroll* an input/output parameter allows its value to be accessed by the procedure and thus to be tested to see if the user has entered a zero or negative value.

The parameter *bankroll* is local to the procedure *GetStartingBankroll* and has nothing to do with the variable *bankroll* declared in the main algorithm or with the parameter *bankroll* declared in any other procedure. An algorithm is sometimes easier to understand if the same name is given to variables and parameters that, although declared in different units and distinct from one another, are nevertheless used to represent the same quantity, such as a player's bankroll. We must take care, however, not to confuse different variables and parameters having the same name.

GetPlayersBet obtains the amount that the user wishes to bet on the current round. If the amount entered is less than zero or greater than the value of *bankroll*, the user is asked to enter another value. *Bet* is another example of a parameter that could have been an output parameter since it is used only to return a result to the invoking unit. Making it an input/output parameter, however, allows its value to be accessed within the procedure.

PlayOneRound plays one round of craps. Again, we use the top-down design principle by calling as-yet-unwritten procedures to perform major operations. The call

    RollDice(dice, seed)

rolls the simulated dice, prints the numbers rolled for the user, and sets *dice* to the sum of the numbers rolled. Since *RollDice* uses the pseudorandom number generator, it must be given access to *seed*. Note that *seed* is a formal input/output parameter for *PlayOneRound* and is passed to *RollDice* as an actual parameter corresponding to a formal input/output parameter. This is permissible since a formal input/output parameter behaves like a variable and so can serve as an actual parameter corresponding to another formal input/output parameter.

A case construction is used to execute the proper statement corresponding to the value of *dice,* the value rolled by the player. If a 7 or 11 was rolled, the player wins, so *won* is set to *true*. If a 2, 3, or 12 was rolled, the player loses, so *won* is set to *false*. If the number rolled is in the range 4 to 6 or 8 to 10, the procedure *PlayRemainingRolls* is called to roll the dice until the player makes his point or craps out. The current value of *dice* is passed to *PlayRemainingRolls* as the player's point—the value the player must match to win. Since *PlayRemainingRolls* uses the pseudorandom number generator, *seed* must also be passed. *PlayRemainingRolls* sets *won* to *true* or *false* depending on the final outcome of the remaining rolls.

Note that the formal output parameter *won* is used as an actual parameter corresponding to another formal output parameter, which is permissible since a formal output parameter behaves like a variable. A formal output parameter *cannot,* however, be used as an actual parameter corresponding to a formal input or input/output parameter since the value of a formal output parameter cannot be accessed.

UpdatePlayersBankroll begins by checking the value of *won*, which indicates whether the player won or lost the last round. If the value of *won* is *true*, the player is informed of the win and the value of *bet* is added to that of *bankroll*; otherwise, the player is informed of the loss and the value of *bet* is subtracted from that of *bankroll*.

Because of the inaccuracies possible in floating-point arithmetic, one should avoid testing two floating-point values for equality. This is particularly true if one or both values have been subjected to arithmetical operations, since the test might fail because one or both values are slightly inaccurate. Therefore, instead of using the Boolean expression

    bankroll = 0.0

to test if the player is broke, we use

    bankroll < 0.005

If the player is broke, a message to that effect is printed and *playing* is set to *false,* terminating the game. Otherwise, the player is informed of the size of his bankroll and is asked whether or not he wishes to play again. The question is repeated until the player's response is one of the following four acceptable values: y, n, Y, or N. The assignment

$$playing \leftarrow (response = \text{'}y\text{'}) \textbf{ or } (response = \text{'}Y\text{'})$$

sets *playing* to *true* if the user responded with y or Y and to *false* otherwise. Note that the expression to the right of the assignment operator is a Boolean expression whose value, *true* or *false,* is assigned to the Boolean variable *playing.*

Having looked at the procedures called by the main algorithm, let's move down a level and look at the procedures called by the procedures called by the main algorithm. Specifically, we turn our attention to *RollDice* and *PlayRemainingRolls,* both of which are called by *PlayOneRound.* (*PlayRemainingRolls* also calls *RollDice.*)

RollDice simulates the rolling of a pair of dice. The sum of the numbers on the two dice is returned via the output parameter *dice.* Since *RollDice* uses the pseudorandom number generator, it must have access to the seed via the input/output parameter *seed.*

The procedure *Random* is the pseudorandom number generator. The call

$$Random(6, die1, seed)$$

assigns a pseudorandomly chosen integer in the range 1 to 6 to *die1,* therefore simulating the rolling of one die. The value of *seed* is used to generate the pseudorandom integer, and the pseudorandom number generator assigns a new value to *seed.* A similar call

$$Random(6, die2, seed)$$

assigns another pseudorandomly chosen integer to *die2,* thereby simulating the rolling of the second die. The **output** statement prints the values of *die1* and *die2* for the user, and the sum of the values of *die1* and *die2* is returned via the output parameter *dice.*

PlayRemainingRolls is called with the input parameter *point* equal to the player's point—the value that came up on the first roll. The procedure repeatedly calls *RollDice* to roll the simulated dice until the value rolled is equal to the value of *point* or to 7. If the rolls were stopped because the value rolled—the value of *dice*—was equal to *point,* the player wins; otherwise, the player craps out and loses. The assignment

$$won \leftarrow (dice = point)$$

returns *true* via the output parameter *won* if the values of *dice* and *point* are equal, and returns the value *false* if they are unequal.

Finally, we come to *Random,* the pseudorandom number generator called by *RollDice.* The value of *seed* is a pseudorandom real number in the range 0 to 1 (including 0 but not 1). Each time *Random* is called, it should compute a new value of *seed* in such a way that: (1) there is no obvious relationship between the new value and the old, and (2) the values of *seed* produced by repeated calls to *Random* are evenly distributed throughout the interval 0 to 1. The new value of *seed* is used to compute a pseudorandom integer in the range 1 through *largestRandomInteger*.

There are many methods of generating random numbers, none of which is suitable for every purpose for which random numbers are used. We will use a "quick and dirty" method which is suitable for uncritical applications such as game playing but may not yield random numbers with the statistical properties required by advanced applications such as simulation and cryptography. A constant is added to the value of *seed* (the mathematical constant *pi* is chosen here), the sum is squared, and the fractional part of the result—the part to the right of the decimal point—becomes the new value of *seed:*

$$seed \leftarrow (seed + 3.1415927) ** 2$$
$$seed \leftarrow seed - trunc(seed)$$

The value of *trunc(seed)* is the integer part of *seed*—the part to the left of the decimal point. Subtracting the integer part of a number from the number leaves the fractional part.

We recall that the main algorithm asks the user to enter a number between 0 and 1 as the initial value of *seed*. Regardless of the value entered by the user, however, the procedure for updating *seed* yields a value in the range 0 to 1 (including 0 but not 1). Since *seed* is updated before being used to calculate a pseudorandom integer, the calculation for a pseudorandom integer will work properly even if the user failed to follow instructions and entered a value outside the range 0 to 1.

We use the value of *seed* to compute a random integer as follows. Since the value of *seed* lies in the interval 0 to 1 (not including 1), the value of

$$largestRandomInteger * seed$$

lies in the interval 0 to *largestRandomInteger* (not including *largestRandomInteger*). The integer part of the product

$$trunc(largestRandomInteger * seed)$$

is an integer ranging from 0 to *largestRandomInteger* − 1. Adding 1

$$trunc(largestRandomInteger * seed) + 1$$

gives us a random integer in the range 1 to *largestRandomInteger*. This random integer is returned via the output parameter *randomInteger*.

Figure 10.5 is a *structure chart* showing the calling relationships between the units making up the algorithm for playing craps. Each unit is represented by a box; lines connect the box representing a unit to the boxes representing the units it calls. The main algorithm, which is on the *top level* of the chart, calls procedures *GetStartingBankroll*, *GetPlayersBet*, *PlayOneRound*, and *UpdatePlayersBankroll*. *PlayOneRound*, in turn, calls procedures *RollDice* and *PlayRemainingRolls*. *RollDice* calls the pseudorandom number generator *Random* and *PlayRemainingRolls* calls *RollDice*. The shaded corner of the box for *RollDice* warns that it is called by more than one unit and hence appears more than once in the structure chart. The procedures called by a unit that appears more than once in the structure chart are shown only for the unit's first (topmost, leftmost) appearance.

Figure 10.5   Structure chart for the algorithm *Craps*. Since *RollDice* is called by two different procedures, it appears twice in the structure chart; the shaded corner on the box for *RollDice* warns of the multiple appearance. When a procedure appears more than once in a structure chart, the procedures that it calls are, for brevity, shown only for one appearance. Thus *Random* is shown only for the uppermost, leftmost occurrence of *RollDice*.

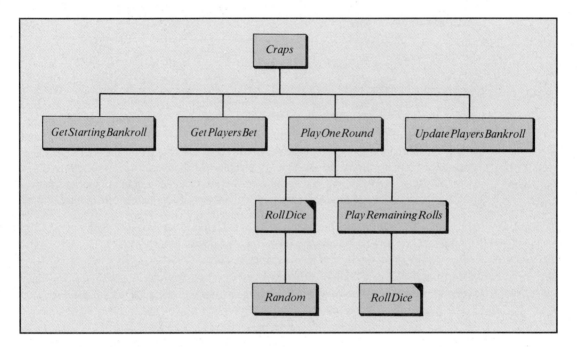

10.6

Scope and lifetime

The objects with which an algorithm works, such as constants, variables, procedures, and functions, each has a scope and a lifetime.

The *scope* of an object is the part of the algorithm from which the object can be accessed. For example, the formal parameters and variables declared in the **declare** part of a subalgorithm can be referred to only from within the subalgorithm containing the declarations. Thus the scope of such a formal parameter or variable is the unit in which it is declared.

The *lifetime* of an object is the time that it remains in existence. For example, when a subalgorithm is invoked, a private memory area is created for the formal parameters and variables declared in the subalgorithm. When the subalgorithm returns, this private memory area is discarded, and the values of all the parameters and variables are lost. The lifetime of the formal parameters and variables, then, is the duration of the invocation. If a subalgorithm is invoked more than once, the same parameter and variable *names* will be used for each invocation. However, the objects to which the names refer—the memory locations holding the values of variables, for example—will be different for each invocation.

We use the term *local* for objects whose scope is a single unit and whose lifetime is limited to a single invocation of that unit. For example, that variables and formal parameters declared in a function or procedure definition are said to be local to the unit in which they are declared.

On the other hand, we use the term *global* for objects whose scope includes more than one unit and whose lifetime may exceed a single invocation of a particular unit. For example, according to the conventions we have used so far, function and procedure definitions (not to be confused with invocations of the functions or procedures) are global. The scope of a function or procedure definition is the entire algorithm, since any unit of an algorithm can refer to a function or procedure definition by name for the purpose of invoking the function or procedure. Function and procedure definitions remain in existence throughout the execution of an algorithm, so their lifetimes coincide with the execution time of the algorithm.

Local and global variables   The variables declared in a unit, which can be accessed only from within the unit and whose lifetime is limited to a single invocation of the unit, are called the *local variables* of the unit. A *global variable*, in contrast, can be accessed from more than one unit. The lifetime of a global variable may exceed some of the function or procedure invocations that assign values to the variable or make use of its values.

Global variables have two uses. First, they can be used to pass data from one unit to another; one of the units with access to a global variable can assign a value to the variable and another of the units can make use of that value. Thus global variables provide an alternative to formal parameters and the function value return mechanism for passing input data to a subalgorithm and passing results back to the invoking unit. Second, global variables can be used to pass data from one invocation to the next of the same function or procedure; a value assigned to a global variable during one invocation can be used during another invocation. The local variables of a function or procedure cannot be used for this purpose; since local variables are created anew for each invocation, their values are not retained between invocations.

Unfortunately, subalgorithms that use global variables may be much more difficult to understand than those using formal parameters to receive input data and return results. The names of the formal parameters, their declarations, and any accompanying comments describe the input data the subalgorithm will use and the results it will return. The actual parameters supplied for each invocation of the subalgorithm give the expressions used to supply input data and the variables used to receive the results returned. On the other hand, we may have to examine every statement of a subalgorithm to see if any global variables are accessed. And since it is not obvious what other subalgorithms access the same global variables, we may have trouble determining from where a subalgorithm receives its input data and to where it sends its results. We can think of the formal parameters as the front door of a subalgorithm through which data and results pass in plain view. Global variables are the back door through which data and results can slip unnoticed.

Because ease of understanding is one of the primary goals of the algorithmic language, it might seem that we have sufficient reason for forbidding the use of global variables. Their use, however, is often demanded by another important principle, that of *information hiding*. According to this principle, the person who uses a subalgorithm—who writes units that invoke it—should not have to be concerned with the details of the internal operation of the subalgorithm, but only with the input data it requires and the results that it produces.

It often happens, however, that some of the data structures used during the internal operation of a subalgorithm must be accessed by more than one subalgorithm and must be preserved between invocations of the subalgorithms. We could leave it up to the user to declare variables to hold these data structures and to pass the structures to the various subalgorithms as parameters, but then the principle of information hiding is violated since the user must be concerned with data structures used only by the internal manipulations of the subalgorithms. A better approach is to let the subalgorithms use global variables for accessing these internal data structures. The formal parameters and function value return mechanism can be reserved for the input data and results with which the user is concerned.

For example, suppose we want to maintain a table with two columns, *key* and *value*. The *key* column contains values to be looked up, such as people's names, and the corresponding entries in the *value* column contain the information we are seeking, such as people's telephone numbers. The table must be accessible to all of the various procedures that maintain it, and it must be preserved between procedure invocations. One approach, which violates information hiding, is to require the user to declare a variable to hold the table and to pass this variable as a parameter to each procedure that manipulates the table. Using this approach, the procedures that maintain the table can be called by procedure statements with the following forms:

Initialize(*table*)

Lookup(*key*, *value*, *table*)

Insert(*key*, *value*, *table*)

Delete(*key*, *table*)

Initialize creates an empty table; *Lookup* looks up a particular key (say a person's name) and returns the corresponding value (say the person's telephone number) via the output parameter *value*. *Insert* inserts a particular key-value pair in the table, and *Delete* deletes the entry corresponding to a particular key.

An alternative that satisfies the principle of information hiding is to store the table as the value of a global variable that can be accessed by all four procedures. Now the user need not be concerned with the table or its structure, but only with the data to be stored and looked up. The procedures can now be invoked with the following procedure statements:

Initialize

Lookup(*key*, *value*)

Insert(key, value)

Delete(key)

The variable *seed* in the algorithm for playing craps illustrates another violation of information hiding. The value of *seed* must be preserved between procedure invocations, and it must be accessible to two units: the main algorithm *Craps*, which assigns *seed* its initial value, and the pseudorandom number generator *Random*, which uses *seed* for generating random numbers. To achieve these results with parameter passing, access to *seed* must be passed from *Craps* to *PlayOneRound*, from *PlayOneRound* to *RollDice* and *PlayRemainingRolls*, from *PlayRemainingRolls* to *RollDice*, and, finally, from *RollDice* to *Random*. Three procedures, *PlayOneRound*, *PlayRemainingRolls*, and *RollDice*, must pass along access to *seed* even though they do not access the variable. How much better it would be if the authors of those three procedures could remain blissfully ignorant of the very existence of *seed*.

In the following subsections, we will look at three commonly used methods for declaring and accessing global variables. We will use the craps-playing algorithm as an example, showing in each case how *Craps* and *Random* can be given access to *seed*, and how the value of *seed* can be preserved between invocations of *Random* without having to pass access to *seed* through *PlayOneRound*, *PlayRemainingRolls*, and *RollDice*.

The common declaration. A common declaration specifies that certain variables are to be stored in a common memory area accessible to all units, rather than in the private memory area of any one unit. Variables in common memory areas remain in existence and retain their values throughout the execution of the algorithm. They can be accessed by any unit containing an appropriate common declaration. The common declaration originated in FORTRAN but is sometimes found in other languages as well.

A common declaration declares a common memory area and states which variables will be stored in it. For example, the **declare** part

declare

    common /*Area1*/ *x*, *y*, *j*

    x, *y*, *z*: *real*

    i, *j*, *k*: *integer*

declares a common memory area, *Area1*, containing the real variables *x* and *y* and the integer variable *j*. The other declared variables, *z*, *i*, and *k*, are local variables of the unit and are stored in the unit's private memory area. The variables in *Area1* can be referenced by any other unit containing the common declaration

    common /*Area1*/ *x*, *y*, *j*

The variables in *Area1* remain in existence as long as any unit containing a common declaration for *Area1* is being executed. If a common declaration for *Area1* is placed in the main algorithm, the variables in *Area1* will remain in existence throughout the execution of the entire algorithm.

Figure 10.6 shows how common declarations can be used to allow both *Craps* and *Random* to access *seed* directly without passing access to *seed* as a parameter through a series of intervening procedures. Both *Craps* and *Random* contain the declarations:

common */RandomNumberSeed/ seed*

seed: *real*

Seed remains in existence throughout the execution of the algorithm. Statements in both *Craps* and *Random* can refer directly to *seed*; *seed* is not passed to *Random* as a formal parameter. The other procedures of the algorithm are the same as in Figure 10.4 except that the formal parameter *seed* is omitted from *PlayOneRound*, *RollDice*, and *PlayRemainingRolls*.

Common declarations achieve the desired effect but do little to make the algorithm more understandable. There is no grouping together of the logically related units that refer to a given common area; a person reading an algorithm may have to examine all the common declarations in all the units of an algorithm to see what common areas exist and which units reference them.

One problem with common declarations lies not so much in their concept as in the way are often implemented. Correspondence between the variables in different common declarations for the same common area is by position rather than by variable name, so one unit might contain the common declaration

common */Area1/ x, y, j*

and another might contain

common */Area1/ a, b, n*

In this case, *a*, in the second unit will refer to the same memory location as *x* in the first unit, *b* will refer to the same location as *y*, and *n* will refer to the same location as *j*.

Suppose, however, that we wished to place identical common declarations in two units, but due to a typing error one contains

common */Area1/ x, y, j*

and the other contains

common */Area1/ y, x, j*

The error will not be detected by the language processor, so *x* in one unit will erroneously correspond to *y* in the other, and vice versa. Even worse, corresponding variables may not be checked to determine if they are of the same data type. Thus, if one unit contains

common */Area/ x, y, j*

and the other contains

common */Area1/ x, j, y*

a real variable in one unit will correspond to an integer variable in the other, and

Figure 10.6   This version of *Craps* uses a common area to make the
variable *seed* accessible to both the main algorithm and the
procedure *Random*. Only the main algorithm and the
procedure *Random* are shown; the other procedures differ
from the corresponding ones in Figure 10.4 only in that *seed*
is not passed as a parameter.

```
algorithm Craps

{ Play craps with user }

declare
    common /RandomNumberSeed/ seed
    bankroll,            { Amount available to player for betting }
    bet,                 { Amount bet on this round }
    seed: real           { Value used for generating random numbers }
    won,                 { True if player has won current round }
    playing: Boolean     { True if game is to continue }
execute
    output 'Enter number between 0 and 1: ', more
    input seed
    GetStartingBankroll(bankroll)
    repeat
        output
        GetPlayersBet(bankroll, bet)
        PlayOneRound(won)
        UpdatePlayersBankroll(bankroll, bet, won, playing)
    until not playing
end Craps



procedure Random(largestRandomInteger, randomInteger)

{ Generate random integer in range 1 through largestRandomInteger }

declare
    common /RandomNumberSeed/ seed
    largestRandomInteger: in integer
    randomInteger: out integer
    seed: real
execute
    seed ← (seed + 3.1415927) ** 2
    seed ← seed − trunc(seed)
    randomInteger ← trunc(largestRandomInteger * seed) + 1
end Random
```

vice versa. Chaos will result because of the completely incompatible coding schemes normally used for real and integer values.

Nested scopes   The local variables of a unit are accessible throughout the unit definition. If one unit definition is nested inside another, the local variables of the outer unit should also be accessible from the inner unit definition which, after all, is enclosed in and is part of the definition of the outer unit. Thus, the local variables of the outer unit serve as global variables for the inner unit. If there are several inner units, all can access the local variables of the outer unit. And if several invocations of the inner units take place during one invocation of the outer unit, the local variables of the outer unit remain in existence throughout all the invocations of the inner units.

The scope of an identifier is the unit definition in which it is declared. If unit definitions are nested, so are the scopes of the identifiers. Languages that permit this kind of nesting are said to have *identifiers with nested scopes*. Nested scopes were introduced in the programming language Algol-60 which, along with FORTRAN, was among the first higher-level languages to achieve widespread use. Identifiers with nested scopes have since been incorporated in many languages derived from Algol-60, including Pascal, now the most widely used language for teaching computer science.

The unit definitions are nested as follows. The **declare** part of a unit can contain function and procedure definitions as well as constant definitions and variable and parameter declarations. The **declare** parts of those function and procedure definitions can, in turn, contain still other function and procedure definitions, and so on, so that function and procedure definitions can be nested as deeply as desired.

Figure 10.7 illustrates nested unit definitions with the algorithm *Guess*, which plays a guessing game with the user. The **declare** part of *Guess* contains the definition of the procedure *Random*, which is the same as the random number generator used in the algorithm for playing craps except that *seed* is accessed as a global variable rather than passed as a parameter.

Note that the definition of *Random*, like the other declarations in the **declare** part of *Guess*, provides information that will be used during the execution of *Guess*. Execution still begins with the first statement in the **execute** part of *Guess*; the statements in the **execute** part of *Random* are executed only when *Random* is invoked by a procedure statement in the **execute** part of *Guess*.

The local variables of *Guess* are *playersGuess*, *secretNumber*, *playAgain*, and *seed*. These are accessible throughout the definition of *Guess* and hence are accessible throughout the definition of *Random*, which is included in the definition of *Guess*. On the other hand, the formal parameters declared in *Random*—*largestRandom-Integer* and *randomInteger*—are local to *Random* and cannot be accessed from those part of *Guess* outside of the definition of *Random*.

Specifically, *Random* can access the variable *seed*, which is local to *Guess* but global to *Random*. Because *seed* remains in existence throughout the execution of *Guess*, its value is preserved between invocations of *Random*.

We can see here a major problem of nested unit definitions: *Random* gets access not only to *seed* but to *playersGuess*, *secretNumber*, and *playAgain* as well. Someone reading the algorithm would have to study the statements of *Random* to see which of these four global variables, if any, it actually accesses. And access to unneeded global variables increases the danger that an erroneous statement in *Random* will unintentionally access or modify the value of a global variable.

Nested unit definitions are often diagrammed as in Figure 10.8. Each box corresponds to a unit definition and shows the scope of the identifiers declared within the unit. Identifiers declared within a box are accessible throughout the box and so are accessible from within any other boxes nested within the box in question. We can think of the boxes as being made of one-way glass that let us look out but not in. From within a box, we can look out and see identifiers declared in surrounding boxes. On the other hand, we cannot look into a box from the outside and see the local identifiers declared within the box.

Figure 10.7   The algorithm *Guess* illustrates nested unit definitions: the definition of the procedure *Random* is nested in the **declare** part of *Guess*. All the variables declared in *Guess* can be referred to by *Random;* these variables are local to *Guess* but global to *Random*. The only global variable actually referred to by *Random* is *seed*.

---

algorithm *Guess*

{ Play guessing game with user }

declare { *Guess* }
    playersGuess, secretNumber: *integer*
    playAgain: *char*
    seed: *real*   { Global variable accessed by *Guess* and *Random* }

    procedure *Random(largestRandomInteger, randomInteger)*

    { Generate random integer in range 1 through *largestRandomInteger.*
     Accesses global variable *seed* }

    declare { *Random* }
    largestRandomInteger: **in** *integer*
    randomInteger: **out** *integer*
    execute { *Random* }
        seed ← (*seed* + 3.1415927) ** 2
        seed ← *seed* − *trunc*(*seed*)
        randomInteger ← *trunc*(*largestRandomInteger* * *seed*) + 1
    end *Random*

```
execute { Guess }
    output 'Enter number between 0 and 1: ', more
    input seed
    output 'I am thinking of a number from 1 to 100'
    output 'You are to try to guess the number. I will tell'
    output 'you whether your guess is right or whether it is'
    output 'too large or too small.'
    repeat
        output
        Random(100, secretNumber)
        output 'I have my number. What is your guess? ', more
        repeat
            input playersGuess
            if playersGuess > secretNumber then
                output 'Too large. Guess again: ', more
            elseif playersGuess < secretNumber then
                output 'Too small. Guess again: ', more
            endif
        until playersGuess = secretNumber
        output 'You are right!'
        output 'Would you like to play again (y/n)? ', more
        input playAgain
    until (playAgain = 'n') or (playAgain = 'N')
end Guess
```

For example, from within the *Random* box we can look out and see the variables *playersGuess*, *secretNumber*, *playAgain*, and *seed* declared in the *Guess* box. On the other hand, from a point inside the *Guess* box but outside the *Random* box, we cannot look in and see the formal parameters *largestRandomInteger* and *randomInteger* declared in *Random*. Note that the name of a function or procedure appears outside its box and hence is accessible throughout the unit containing the function or procedure definition. Thus, the identifier *Random* is accessible throughout *Guess*; if this were not so, it would be impossible to invoke *Random* with a procedure statement in the **execute** part of *Guess*.

Figure 10.9 illustrates a slightly more complicated situation. Two subalgorithms, *Q1* and *Q2*, are defined in the main algorithm *P*. Still another subalgorithm, *R*, is defined within *Q1*. *Q1* and *Q2* can by invoked from the **execute** parts of *P*, *Q1*, *Q2*, and *R*. From inside *R* we can look out through the walls of *R* and see the definitions of *Q1* and *Q2*. On the other hand, *R* cannot be invoked from the **execute** parts of *Q2* or *P*. From outside *Q1* we cannot look into *Q1* and see the definition of *R*.

Variables *a* and *b* are declared in *P* and are accessible from *P*, *Q1*, *Q2*, and *R*. Variables *c* and *d* are declared in *Q1* and are accessible from *Q1* and *R*. They cannot

Figure 10.8   Diagram for nested unit definitions. Each box corresponds to
a unit definition and shows the scope of the identifiers
declared within the unit. Identifiers declared within a box
are accessible throughout the box and so are accessible from
other boxes nested within the box in question.

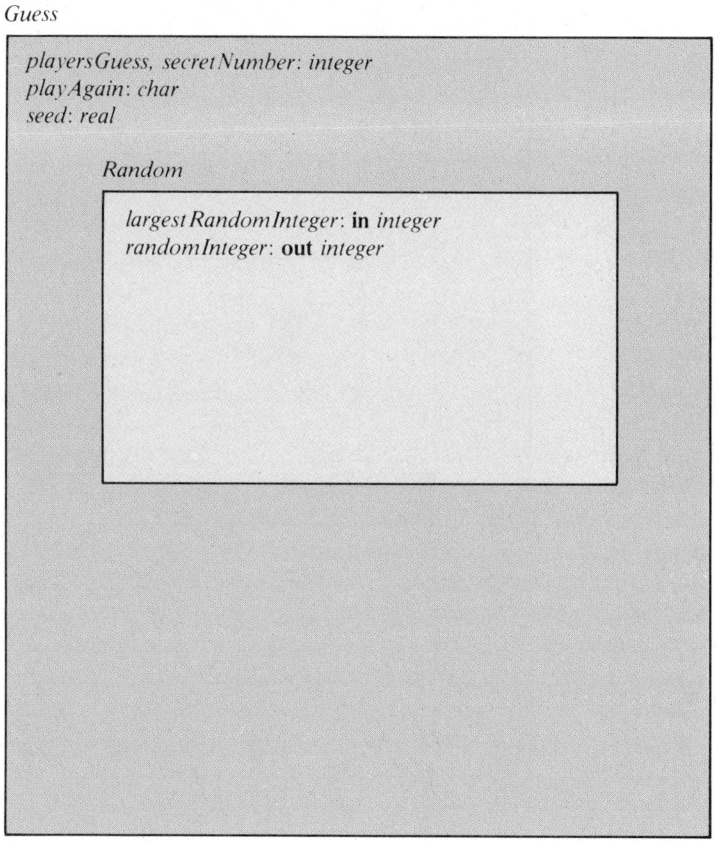

Guess

> *playersGuess, secretNumber*: *integer*
> *playAgain*: *char*
> *seed*: *real*
>
> *Random*
>
>> *largestRandomInteger*: **in** *integer*
>> *randomInteger*: **out** *integer*

be accessed from *P* and *Q2*. Variables *e* and *f* are declared in *R* and are accessible
only from *R*; they cannot be accessed from *P*, *Q1*, or *Q2*. Variables *h* and *i* are
declared in *Q2* and are accessible only from *Q2*. They cannot be accessed from *P*,
Q1, or *R*.

Figure 10.10 illustrates another important feature of nested scopes. What is different about Figure 10.10 is that identifiers declared in different units have the same
spelling. There is an *a* in *P* and an *a* in *Q1*, a *b* in *P* and a *b* in *Q2*, and an *f* in *Q1*
and an *f* in *Q2*.

Figure 10.9   Diagram for nested unit definitions. Units *Q1* and *Q2* are
defined within *P*, and unit *R* is defined within *Q1*. Variables
a and *b* are accessible from *P*, *Q1*, *Q2*, and *R*; *c* and *d* are
accessible from *Q1* and *R*; *e* and *f* are accessible from *R*
only; and *h* and *i* are accessible from *Q2* only.

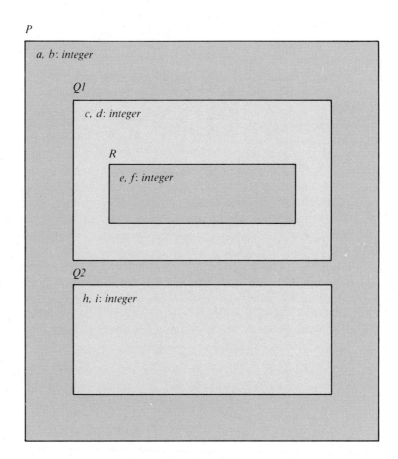

We recall that identifiers declared in different units have nothing to do with one
another, even if their names are spelled in the same way. Thus, the variable *a* declared in *P* corresponds to a different memory location than the variable *a* declared
in *Q1*; the variable *b* declared in *P* corresponds to a different memory location than
the variable *b* declared in *Q2*; and the variable *f* declared in *Q1* corresponds to a
different memory location than the variable *f* declared in *Q2*.

As a result, the same statement can refer to different memory locations depending on where it occurs in the algorithm. For example, if

$$f \leftarrow 25$$

Figure 10.10   Diagram for nested unit definitions. The declaration of *a* in
Q1 "hides" the declaration of *a* in *P*. Therefore, a reference
to *a* in *Q1* refers to the *a* declared in *Q1*, whereas a
reference to *a* in *P* or *Q2* refers to the *a* declared in *P*.
Likewise, the declaration of *b* in *Q2* hides the declaration of
b in *P*, so a reference to *b* in *Q2* refers to the *b* declared in
Q2, whereas a reference to *b* in *P* or *Q1* refers to the *b*
declared in *P*.

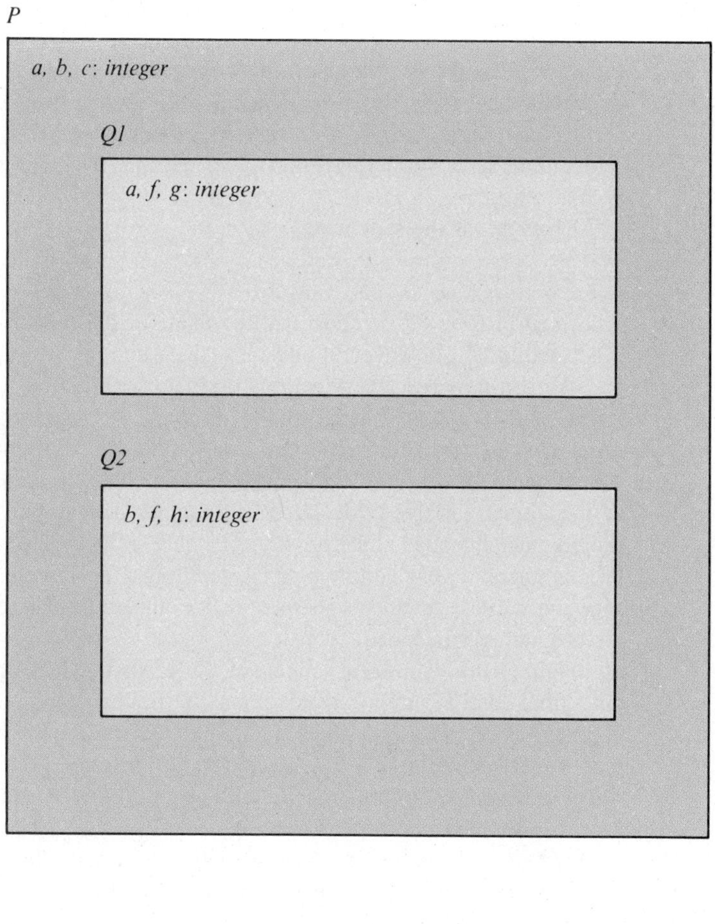

P

a, b, c: integer

Q1

a, f, g: integer

Q2

b, f, h: integer

occurs in the **execute** part of *Q1*, it stores 25 in the memory location corresponding
to the *f* declared in *Q1*. If the same statement occurs in the **execute** part of *Q2*,
however, it stores 25 in an entirely different memory location, the memory location
corresponding to the *f* declared in *Q2*.

Now consider the following statement:

$a \leftarrow 100$

If this statement is located in *P* or *Q2*, it assigns 100 to the variable *a* declared in *P*. But what if the statement is located in *Q1*? There seem to be two variables named *a* that are visible in *Q1*: the variable *a* declared in *P* and the variable *a* declared in *Q1*. To which *a* should the value 100 be assigned?

This question is resolved by the following rule: *when several objects with the same name are visible at a particular point in an algorithm, the name applies to the object having the smallest scope.* The variable *a* declared in *Q1* has a smaller scope than the variable *a* declared in *P*; therefore, when *a* is used within *Q1*, it refers to the *a* declared in *Q1*. If

$$a \leftarrow 100$$

is located in *Q1*, it assigns 100 to the *a* declared in *Q1*. We can think of the declaration of *a* in *Q1* as "hiding" the declaration of *a* in *P*, so that only the former declaration is visible from within *Q1*. Still another way of stating the rule is that *local indentifiers take precedence over global ones*. Thus, a reference to *a* in *Q1* refers to the local variable *a*—the *a* declared in *Q1*—rather than to the global variable *a*—the *a* declared in *P*.

Likewise, if the statement

$$b \leftarrow b + 1$$

is located in *P* or *Q1*, it adds 1 to the value of the *b* declared in *P*. If the statement is located in *Q2*, however, it adds 1 to the value of the *b* declared in *Q2*.

We can now see a very serious problem with nested scopes. Suppose the declaration of *a* in *Q1* were accidentally omitted. A language processor would give no error message since the algorithm is still syntactically correct—no rule of the algorithmic language has been violated. However, every reference to *a* in *Q1* now refers to the global variable *a* declared in *P* rather than to the local variable *a* that the programmer intended, but forgot, to declare in *Q1*. What a fiendish trap to lay for programmers: a very common error, omitting a declaration, produces no error message but causes statements to refer to a completely different memory location than the programmer intended.

Figure 10.11 shows a version of the craps-playing algorithm using nested unit definitions, and Figure 10.12 diagrams the nested scopes. Each procedure definition is nested as deeply as possible. Looking at the structure chart in Figure 10.5, we see that *RollDice* and *PlayRemainingRolls* are invoked, directly or indirectly, from *PlayOneRound*; therefore, the definitions of *RollDice* and *PlayRemainingRolls* are nested in the definition of *PlayOneRound*. Likewise, since *Random* is invoked only by *RollDice*, its definition is nested within that of *RollDice*. For simplicity, Figure 10.12 shows only one variable, *seed*, which is declared in *Craps* and accessed from both *Craps* and *Random*.

Looking at Figure 10.12, we see that nested scopes provide good control over access to procedure and function names. *RollDice* and *PlayRemainingRolls* can be invoked from *PlayOneRound* but not from *GetStartingBankroll*, *GetPlayersBet*, or *UpdatePlayersBankroll*. Likewise, the procedure name *Random* is accessible only from *RollDice*, the only procedure that invokes *Random*. On the other hand, control of access to variable names is poor. Although *seed* is referred to only by *Craps* and

Figure 10.11 Version of *Craps* using nested unit definitions. Note how
much more difficult this version is to read than the version
in Figure 10.4.

---

algorithm *Craps*

{ Play craps with user }

declare
  bankroll,   { Amount available to player for betting }
  bet,   { Amount bet on this round }
  seed: *real*   { Value used for generating random numbers }
  won,   { True if player has won current round }
  playing: *Boolean*   { True if game is to continue }

  procedure *GetStartingBankroll*(*bankroll*)

  { Find out how much money player has }

  declare { *GetStartingBankroll* }
    bankroll: **in out** *real*
  execute { *GetStartingBankroll* }
    output 'How much money do you have to play with? ', **more**
    input *bankroll*
    while *bankroll* <= 0.0
      output 'Please enter an amount greater than zero: ', **more**
      input *bankroll*
    endwhile
  end *GetStartingBankroll*

  procedure *GetPlayersBet*(*bankroll*, *bet*)

  { Get amount player wishes to bet on current round }

  declare { *GetPlayersBet* }
    bankroll: **in** *real*
    bet: **in out** *real*
  execute { *GetPlayersBet* }
    output 'How much do you want to bet? ', **more**
    input *bet*
    while (*bet* < 0.0) **or** (*bet* > *bankroll*)
      output 'Invalid bet--please try again: ', **more**
      input *bet*
    endwhile
  end *GetPlayersBet*

procedure *PlayOneRound(won)*

{ Play one round; determine whether player wins or loses }

declare { *PlayOneRound* }
  won: **out** *Boolean*
  dice: *integer*

  procedure *RollDice(dice)*

  { Simulate roll of dice; print value rolled on each die and return
    their sum as value of *dice* }

  declare { *RollDice* }
    dice: **out** *integer*
    die1, *die2*: *integer*

    procedure *Random(largestRandomInteger, randomInteger)*

    { Generate random integer in range 1 through
      largestRandomInteger }

    declare { *Random* }
      largestRandomInteger: **in** *integer*
      randomInteger: **out** *integer*
    execute { *Random* }
      seed ← (*seed* + 3.1415927) ∗∗ 2
      seed ← *seed* − *trunc(seed)*
      randomInteger ← *trunc(largestRandomInteger* ∗ *seed)* + 1
    end *Random*

  execute { *RollDice* }
    Random(6, *die1*)
    Random(6, *die2*)
    output 'You rolled a ', *die1*, ' and a ', *die2*
    dice ← *die1* + *die2*
  end *RollDice*

  procedure *PlayRemainingRolls(point, won)*

  { Roll dice until user makes point or craps out }

```
            declare { PlayRemainingRolls }
                point: in integer
                won: out Boolean
                dice: integer
            execute { PlayRemainingRolls }
                repeat
                    RollDice(dice)
                until (dice = point) or (dice = 7)
                won ← (dice = point)
            end PlayRemainingRolls



execute { PlayOneRound }
    RollDice(dice)
    select case dice
        case 7, 11              { Player wins }
            won ← true
        case 2, 3, 12           { Player loses }
            won ← false
        case 4 to 6, 8 to 10   { More rolls needed to determine
                                    outcome }
            PlayRemaining Rolls(dice, won)
    endselect
end PlayOneRound



procedure UpdatePlayersBankroll(bankroll, bet, won, playing)

{ Update bankroll and report results of round. If player is broke, set
  playing to false. Otherwise, determine if user wishes to play another
  round and set value of playing to true or false accordingly }

declare { UpdatePlayersBankroll }
    bankroll: in out real
    bet: in real
    won: in Boolean
    playing: out Boolean
    response: char
execute { UpdatePlayersBankroll }
    if won then
        output 'You win'
        bankroll ← bankroll + bet
```

```
        else
            output 'You lose'
            bankroll ← bankroll − bet
        endif
        if bankroll < 0.005 then
            output 'You''re broke'
            playing ← false
        else
            output 'You have ', bankroll, ' dollars'
            repeat
                output 'Do you want to play again (y/n)? ', more
                input response
            until (response = 'y') or (response = 'n') or
                (response = 'Y') or (response = 'N')
            playing ← (response = 'y') or (response = 'Y')
        endif
    end UpdatePlayersBankroll


execute { Craps }
    output 'Enter number between 0 and 1: ', more
    input seed
    GetStartingBankroll(bankroll)
    repeat
        output
        GetPlayersBet(bankroll, bet)
        PlayOneRound(won)
        UpdatePlayersBankroll(bankroll, bet, won, playing)
    until not playing
end Craps
```

Random, it is accessible to every unit of the algorithm. In fact, all the variables declared in *Craps* are accessible from every unit, except where declarations of local identifiers take precedence over declarations of global variables having the same names.

We can summarize the properties of nested scopes as follows:

1. Nested scopes provide good control of access to function and procedure names.

2. Nested scopes provide poor control of access to variables. Usually, each function or procedure has access to far more global variables than it needs; even a subalgorithm that does not make use of global variables still has access

Figure 10.12 Diagram illustrating the nested unit definitions of Figure 10.11.

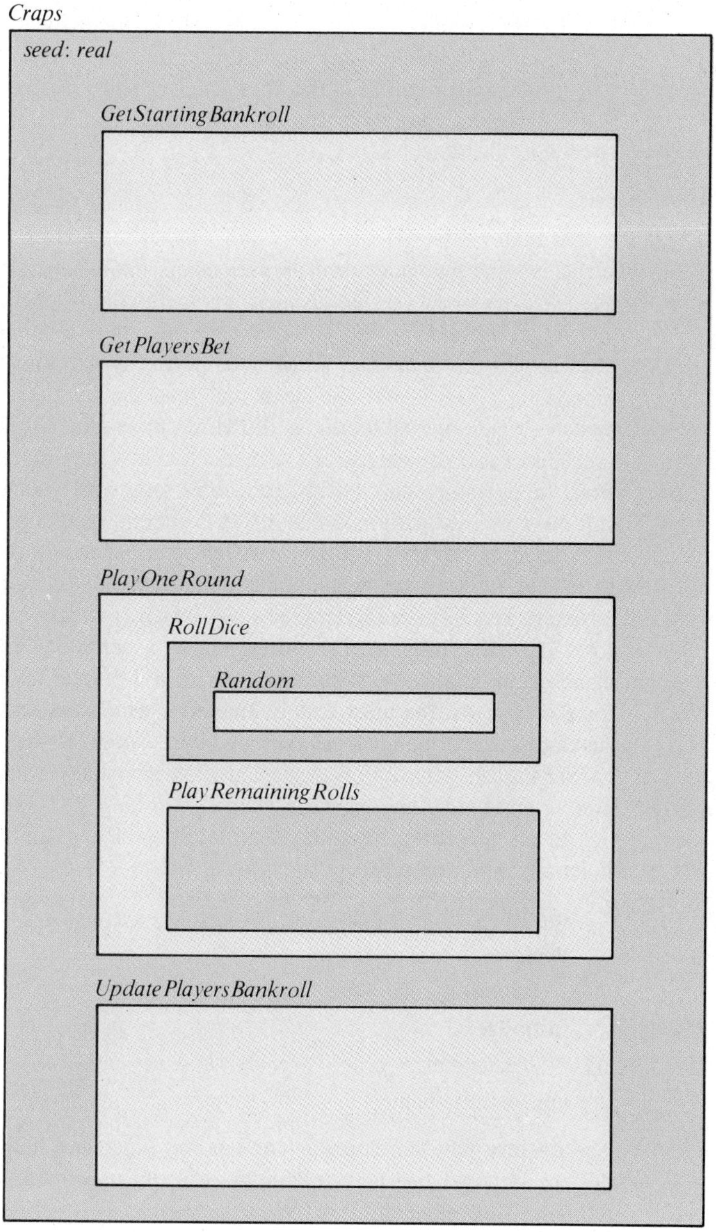

to all variables declared in enclosing scopes and not overriden by declarations of local identifiers. Someone studying a subalgorithm must examine each statement to determine which of the accessible global variables, if any, are actually referred to.

3. Accidentally omitting the declaration for a local variable may cause references to that variable to refer instead to a global variable with the same name. This error can be difficult to uncover since no error message is given by the language processor and since the missing declaration does not call attention to itself.

Modules   Now let's look at still another method of controlling access to global variables, one that is less widely used but far more satisfactory than either of the two already discussed. The idea behind this method is to package one or more functions and procedures along with the data structures they manipulate. The package constitutes as *abstract machine*, which we operate by invoking the various functions and procedures, just as we operate a real machine by pressing buttons and throwing switches. The internal workings of the machine—the definitions of the functions and procedures and the details of the data structures they manipulate—can all be hidden from the operator, who need be concerned only with *what* each function or procedure call does and not with *how* that effect is acomplished.

Just about every term that can signify an enclosure or a set of related parts has been used for such packages; typical names are *module*, *capsule*, *envelope*, *unit*, and *package*. We will use the term *module*, which is widely understood as a general term for a part of a program that accomplishes a definite purpose. Modules (under one name or another) have been incorporated in a number of recently devised programming languages, the most widely known of which are *Ada* and *Modula-2*. Although standard Pascal does not provide modules, certain Pascal implementations, such as UCSD Pascal, Microsoft Pascal, and IBM Personal Computer Pascal, provide modules as nonstandard extension.

In the algorithmic language, a module is a unit similiar in form to algorithms, functions, and procedures:

module module-name
declare
    declarations
initialize
    statements
end module-name

The **declare** part can contain function and procedure definitions as well as variable declarations and constant definitions. Identifiers defined in the **declare** part can be referenced by other units if they are *exported* as described below. Otherwise, they can be referenced only by the functions and procedures defined in the module and the statements in the **initialize** part. Like a main algorithm, a module as a whole is not invoked by another unit, although functions and procedures exported from the module can be invoked by other units. The objects declared in a module remain in existence throughout the execution of the algorithm.

The **initialize** part of a module is similar to the **execute** part of an algorithm, function, or procedure; however, the **initialize** parts of all the modules in an algorithm are executed before the first statement of the main algorithm. Thus, the **initialize** parts can be used to assign initial values to variables declared in the module, and we can be sure that such initializations will always be performed before execution of the main algorithm begins. The **initialize** parts of different modules may be executed in any order; an algorithm cannot rely on the order in which the **initialize** parts of different modules will be executed.

A module uses an **export** declaration to specify which identifiers can be accessed by other units. Thus,

> **export** *Clear, Increment, Reading*

specifies that the identifiers *Clear, Increment,* and *Reading* are to be exported; all other identifiers declared in the module can be accessed only from within the module. To gain access to the exported identifiers, another unit must use an **import** declaration specifying the identifiers to be accessed and the module from which they are to be imported. Suppose, for example, the above **export** declaration occurs in the module *Counter*. A main algorithm, function, or procedure containing the **import** declaration

> **import** *Clear, Increment* **from** *Counter*

can refer to *Clear* and *Increment*; it cannot refer to *Reading*, which it does not import.

Let's look in detail at a module that embodies a counting device. The operations that can be performed on a counter are clearing it to zero, incrementing its reading by one (counting one item), and noting its current reading. Our module will export a function or procedure for each operation:

> **module** *Counter*
> **declare**
>> **export** *Clear, Increment, Reading*
>> *count*: *integer*
>>
>> **procedure** *Clear*
>> **execute**
>>> *count* ← 0
>>
>> **end** *Clear*
>>
>> **procedure** *Increment*
>> **execute**
>>> *count* ← *count* + 1
>>
>> **end** *Increment*

> **function** *Reading*: *integer*
> **execute**
> > *Reading* ← *count*
>
> **end** *Reading*
>
> **initialize**
> > *Clear*
>
> **end** *Counter*

Other units of an algorithm containing this module can refer to *Clear*, *Increment*, and *Reading*, which are exported, but not to *count*, which is not exported. We can think of the *Counter* module as a black box having three buttons. Pressing the *Clear* button (invoking the *Clear* procedure) clears the counter; pressing the *Increment* button increases the count by one; and pressing the *Reading* button displays the current count. A new mechanical counter usually reads zero when it is first taken out of its box. We can arrange the equivalent for *Counter* by having the **initialize** part of the module call *Clear* to clear the counter to zero; the counter is cleared to zero before any statements of the main algorithm are executed.

We could have exported *count*, thereby allowing the counter to be read directly rather than via the function *Reading*. But exporting *count* would allow its value to be changed in arbitrary ways by other units. The function *Reading*, on the other hand, can only be used to obtain the current reading of the counter; it cannot be used to change that reading.

Figure 10.13 shows the module *RandomNumberGenerator*, which can be used to provide random numbers for the craps-playing algorithm or any other algorithm that needs random integers. (A well-designed module can often be used in many different algorithms.) Also shown are the two units, *Craps* and *RollDice*, that make use of the module. The other units of the craps-playing algorithm are the same as before except that all references to the parameter *seed* are omitted.

The module *RandomNumberGenerator* defines and exports two procedures, *Reseed* and *Random*. The variable *seed* is declared but not exported; other units can affect the value of *seed* only by invoking *Reseed* or *Random*. *Reseed* is used to set the starting value of *seed* before generating a series of random numbers; the value of *seed* is set to that of the input parameter *newSeed*. *Random* uses the method described previously to generate and return a random integer in the range 1 to *largestRandomInteger*; *Random* also assigns a new value to *seed*. Since it is the user's responsibility to initialize the random number generator by invoking *Reseed*, no **initialize** part is provided. Thus, no statements of *RandomNumberGenerator* are automatically executed before execution of the main algorithm begins.

The main algorithm, *Craps*, needs only to invoke *Reseed* to initialize the random number generator; thus, only *Reseed* needs to be imported:

> **import** *Reseed* **from** *RandomNumberGenerator*

A value entered by the user is used to reseed the random number generator:

> **output** '*Enter number between 0 and 1: *', **more**
> **input** *seed*
> *Reseed*(*seed*)

Figure 10.13 This version of *Craps* imports the procedures *Reseed* and *Random* from the module *RandomNumberGenerator*. Only the main algorithm and the procedure *RollDice* of *Craps* are shown. The remaining procedures of *Craps* are the same as in Figure 10.4 except that: (a) *Random* is not present (it is imported from the module), and (b) *seed* is not passed as a parameter. In the module *RandomNumberGenerator,* the variable *seed* is accessible to both *Reseed* and *Random* but not the units that use the module.

```
algorithm Craps

{ Play craps with user }

declare
    import Reseed from RandomNumberGenerator
    bankroll,           { Amount available to player for betting }
    bet,                { Amount bet on this round }
    seed: real          { Value used for generating random numbers }
    won,                { True if player has won current round }
    playing: Boolean    { True if game is to continue }
execute
    output 'Enter number between 0 and 1: ', more
    input seed
    Reseed(seed)
    GetStartingBankroll(bankroll)
    repeat
        output
        GetPlayersBet(bankroll, bet)
        PlayOneRound(won)
        UpdatePlayersBankroll(bankroll, bet, won, playing)
    until not playing
end Craps



procedure RollDice(dice)

{ Simulate roll of dice; print value rolled on each die and return their sum
  as value of dice }

declare
    import Random from RandomNumberGenerator
    dice: out integer
    die1, die2: integer
```

```
execute
    Random(6, die1)
    Random(6, die2)
    output 'You rolled a ', die1, ' and a ', die2
    dice ← die1 + die2
end RollDice


module RandomNumberGenerator
declare
    export Reseed, Random
    seed: real


    procedure Reseed(newSeed)

    { Set initial value of seed }

    declare
        newSeed: in real
    execute
        seed ← newSeed
    end Reseed


    procedure Random(largestRandomInteger, randomInteger)

    { Generate random integer in range 1 through largestRandomInteger }

    declare
        largestRandomInteger: in integer
        randomInteger: out integer
    execute
        seed ← (seed + 3.1415927) ** 2
        seed ← seed − trunc(seed)
        randomInteger ← trunc(largestRandomInteger * seed) + 1
    end Random
end RandomNumberGenerator
```

RollDice needs only to import *Random*:

> **import** *Random* **from** *RandomNumberGenerator*

Calls to random are used to generate random integers in the range 1 to 6:

> *Random*(6, *die1*)
> *Random*(6, *die2*)

Figure 10.14 shows a version of *RandomNumberGenerator* that automatically assigns an initial value to *seed* so that the procedure *Reseed* is not needed. *Seed* should be given a different initial value each time an algorithm using *RandomNumberGenerator* is executed; otherwise, *Random* would always produce the same sequence of random numbers. One way to achieve this is to let the initial value of

Figure 10.14   This version of the module *RandomNumberGenerator* uses
the function *TimeInSeconds,* imported from the module
System, to compute the initial value for *seed*.

```
module RandomNumberGenerator
declare
    export Random
    import TimeInSeconds from System
    const secondsPerDay = 86400
    seed: real


    procedure Random(largestRandomInteger, randomInteger)

    { Generate random integer in range 1 through largestRandomInteger }

    declare
        largestRandomInteger: in integer
        randomInteger: out integer
    execute
        seed ← (seed + 3.1415927) ** 2
        seed ← seed − trunc(seed)
        randomInteger ← trunc(largestRandomInteger * seed) + 1
    end Random


initialize
    seed ← TimeInSeconds / secondsPerDay
end RandomNumberGenerator
```

seed depend on the exact time of day at which the **initialize** part is executed. Since different executions of the algorithm are unlikely to commence at exactly the same time of day, it is likely that a different sequence of random numbers will be produced each time the algorithm is executed.

Operating systems usually provide a variety of useful functions and procedures that can be called by user programs; we can think of these functions and procedures as being exported by a module named *System*. One such function returns the time of day. The format in which the time is returned, and the units in which it is expressed, vary from system to system. We will assume that the module *System* exports a parameterless function *TimeInSeconds* whose value is an integer giving the number of seconds that have elapsed since midnight. Since there are 86400 seconds in a 24-hour day, the value returned by *TimeInSeconds* ranges from 0 (at midnight) to 86399 (at one second before midnight).

The version of *RandomNumberGenerator* shown in Figure 10.14 uses the time of day to assign an initial value to *seed*. Since the algorithm using the module no longer needs to initialize *seed*, the procedure *Reseed* is no longer needed and is eliminated. (*Reseed* could have been retained, however, to give the algorithm using the module the option of assigning a different initial value to *seed*.) The only identifier to be exported, therefore, is *Random*, the procedure that generates the next random number. The time-of-day function *TimeInSeconds* is imported from the module *System*:

> **export** *Random*
>
> **import** *TimeInSeconds* **from** *System*

A constant, *secondsPerDay*, is defined, and the variable *seed* is declared:

> **const** *secondsPerDay* = 86400
>
> *seed*: *real*

Since neither *secondsPerDay* nor *TimeInSeconds* is exported, both are accessible only from within the module in which they are declared.

The **initialize** section of the algorithm contains a single statement:

> *seed* ← *TimeInSeconds* / *secondsPerDay*

This statement is executed before any of the statements of the algorithm using the module. Note that, when a function or procedure has no parameters, as is the case with *TimeInSeconds*, the parentheses around the parameter list are also omitted. Since the value returned by *TimeInSeconds* ranges from 0 through 86399, and since the value of *secondsPerDay* is 86400, *seed* is assigned a value in the range 0 to 1 (not including 1) as desired.

Up to this point in our discussion, algorithms (in the most general sense of the word) have been presented as main algorithms, which received their input data via **input** statements and returned their results via **output** statements. Often we were forced to concern ourselves with details of input and output formatting and user interaction that were irrelevant to the algorithmic ideas in which we were interested. To avoid having to concern ourselves with such details, we will henceforth frequently present algorithms as functions or procedures, which receive input and return results via formal parameters and the function return mechanism, rather than with **input** and **output** statements. When several functions and procedures access a common set of data structures, the functions, procedures, and data structures will usually be packaged as a module.

10.7 Recursion revisited

Recursive algorithms were introduced in Section 2.4, which you may wish to review at this point. A recursive algorithm calls itself to solve a simplified version of the problem that it was called to solve. Execution of a recursive algorithm consists of a series of such *recursive calls*, which terminate when the original problem to be solved has been simplified to one or more *trivial cases* or *base cases* that can be solved without further recursive calls. In this section we will see how to express recursive algorithms as functions or procedures containing calls to themselves.

When a function or procedure is invoked, a private data area is created for its local variables and formal parameters. For recursive functions or procedures, it is crucial that a separate private data area be set up for each invocation. When a function or procedure calls itself, a second invocation is begun before the first one is completed. If the function or procedure calls itself again, a third invocation will commence before either of the first two have been completed, and so on. The values of local variables and formal parameters will generally be different for each invocation. Consequently, each invocation requires its own private data area. The private data area for an invocation must be retained until that invocation is completed, even though other invocations of the same function or procedure are carried out in the interim.

Towers of Hanoi   Let's begin by writing a recursive procedure for solving the Towers of Hanoi problem discussed in Chapter 2. We recall that, as shown in Figure 2.5, the problem involves three pegs labeled A, B, and C. Peg A contains n disks stacked in order of decreasing size, the largest on the bottom and the smallest on top. The disks are numbered in order of increasing size, with disk 1 being the smallest and disk n being the largest. The disks are to be moved from peg A to peg C, using peg B as needed. Only one disk can be moved at a time, and a larger disk may never be placed on top of a smaller one.

In Chapter 2, we devised the following plan for solving the Towers of Hanoi problem, which is illustrated in Figure 2.6:

"Move disks 1 through $n - 1$ from peg A to peg B"

"Move disk n from peg A to peg C"

"Move disks 1 through $n - 1$ from peg B to peg A"

The middle step consists of moving only a single disk, and so can be carried out directly. The first and last steps, however, generally involve moving more than one disk, and so must be handled by recursive calls to the disk-moving procedure.

Figure 10.15 shows the procedure *MoveDisks*, which prints the moves needed to move a given number of disks from a given source peg to a given destination peg. A call to *MoveDisks* has the form

MoveDisks(n, source, dest, aux)

where *n* is an integer parameter giving the number of disks to be moved, and *source*, *dest*, and *aux* are character parameters giving, respectively, the source peg from which the disks are to be moved, the destination peg to which they are to be moved, and the auxiliary peg that will be used as needed during the move.

A recursive function or procedure always involves at least two cases: the trivial case, which can be solved without further recursive calls, and the nontrivial case, which requires that the function or procedure be called recursively. For *MoveDisks*, the trivial case occurs when only one disk is to be moved, whereas the nontrivial case involves moving more than one disk. The following two-way selection executes the proper statements for each case:

if *n* = 1 **then**
  ''trivial case''
else
  ''nontrivial case''
endif

For the trivial case, there is only one disk to be moved, which is always disk number 1. Therefore, the procedure needs only to print the instructions for moving disk 1:

output 'Move disk 1 from peg ', *source*, ' to peg ', *dest*

For the nontrivial case, we begin by calling *MoveDisks* recursively to move the *n* − 1 disks on top of disk *n* to the auxiliary peg, using the destination peg as needed:

MoveDisks(n − 1, *source, aux, dest)*

Since all the disks on top of disk *n* have been removed, disk *n* can be moved to the destination peg in a single step:

output 'Move disk ', *n*, ' from peg ', *source*, ' to peg', *dest*

Finally, the *n* − 1 disks that have been moved to the auxiliary peg must now be moved to the destination peg, where they will be placed on top of disk *n*. Again, a recursive call is used to move the *n* − 1 disks:

MoveDisks(n − 1, *aux, dest, source)*

In Chapter 2 we saw how to use the principle of mathematical induction to prove correct the algorithm for solving the Towers of Hanoi problem. According to this principle, a recursive function or procedure with a parameter *n* works for all positive integer values of *n* greater than zero provided that:

Figure 10.15   Algorithm for solving the Towers of Hanoi problem using the recursive procedure *MoveDisks*.

```
algorithm Towers

{ Solve the Towers of Hanoi problem }

declare
    NumberOfDisks: integer
execute
    output 'How many disks? ', more
    input NumberOfDisks
    while NumberOfDisks > 0
        MoveDisks(NumberOfDisks, 'A', 'C', 'B')
        output
        output 'How many disks? ', more
        input NumberOfDisks
    endwhile
end Towers



procedure MoveDisks(n, source, dest, aux)

{ Move n disks from peg source to peg dest using peg aux as the auxiliary
  peg }

declare
    n: in integer
    source, dest, aux: in char
execute
    if n = 1 then
        output 'Move disk 1 from peg ', source, ' to peg ', dest
    else
        MoveDisks(n − 1, source, aux, dest)
        output 'Move disk ', n, ' from peg ', source, ' to peg ', dest
        MoveDisks(n − 1, aux, dest, source)
    endif
end MoveDisks
```

1. (*base case*) the function or procedure works when the value of the parameter is 1; and

2. (*inductive step*) for any value of *n* greater than 1, if we assume the function of procedure works for the parameter value $n - 1$, we can prove that it works for the parameter value *n*.

For *MoveDisks*, the induction is on *n*, the number of disks to be moved. When the value of *n* is 1, we have the trivial case, which is handled by a single **output** statement; the procedure obviously works for this case. For the value of *n* greater than 1, we have the nontrivial case, which we can easily prove since in doing so we are allowed to assume that *MoveDisks* works for parameter value $n - 1$.

Figure 10.15 also shows a main algorithm that invokes *MoveDisks* to print the moves required for a given number of disks. The disks are always moved from peg A to peg C using peg B as an auxiliary. The procedure is invoked by the following statement:

MoveDisks(NumberOfDisks, 'A', 'C', 'B')

The following is a typical exchange with the user:

```
How many disks? 3
Move disk 1 from peg A to peg C
Move disk 2 from peg A to peg B
Move disk 1 from peg C to peg B
Move disk 3 from peg A to peg C
Move disk 1 from peg B to peg A
Move disk 2 from peg B to peg C
Move disk 1 from peg A to peg C
```

The factorial function Let's write a recursive function to compute the factorial of a number, a task for which we have already written a nonrecursive function. We recall that the factorial of a positive integer greater than zero is the product of all positive integers in the range 1 through the number in question. Thus,

$$Factorial(1) = 1$$

and

$$Factorial(n) = n * (n - 1) * (n - 2) * \ldots * 3 * 2 * 1$$

For *n* greater than 1, however, the latter can be written as follows:

$$Factorial(n) = n * [(n - 1) * (n - 2) * \ldots * 3 * 2 * 1]$$

The expression in brackets, however, is the product of all positive integers from 1 through $n - 1$, and so is equal to $Factorial(n - 1)$:

$$Factorial(n) = n * Factorial(n - 1)$$

These considerations suggest the following *recursive definition* for the factorial function:

$Factorial(1) = 1$

$Factorial(n) = n * Factorial(n - 1)$ for $n > 1$

The definition is called recursive since, in the second equation, the function *Factorial* is defined in terms of itself.

Working in the other direction, we can use mathematical induction to show that the recursive definition is equivalent to the original one, that the recursively defined *Factorial(n)* is equal to the product of all positive integers from 1 through n. For n equal to 1, the first equation of the recursive definition states that the value of *Factorial(n)* is 1, as it should be. For n greater than 1, assume that the equivalence holds for parameter value $n - 1$, that is, that the value of *Factorial(n − 1)* is the product of the positive integers 1 through $n - 1$. By the second equation of the recursive definition, the value of *Factorial(n)*

$= n * Factorial(n - 1)$

$= n * $ "product of positive integers from 1 through $n - 1$"

$= $ "product of positive integers from 1 through n"

As shown in Figure 10.16, a recursive version of the *Factorial* function can be written directly from the recursive definition. For n equal to 1, the first equation of the recursive definition tells us that *Factorial* should return the value 1; for n greater than 1, the second equation of the recursive definition tells us the *Factorial* should return the product of n and *Factorial(n − 1)*. The following selection executes the proper statement depending on the value of n:

if $n = 1$ **then**

    $Factorial \leftarrow 1$

else

    $Factorial \leftarrow n * Factorial(n - 1)$

endif

When n is equal to 1, the computer executes the statement

$Factorial \leftarrow 1$

which assigns 1 to the function name as the value to be returned by the function. For n greater than 1, the computer executes the statement

$Factorial \leftarrow n * Factorial(n - 1)$

which may require further explanation. The identifier *Factorial* is used in two different ways in this statement. To the left of the assignment operator, it represents the memory location in which the value to be returned is stored. To the right of the assignment operator, it represents the *Factorial* function and calls for a recursive invocation of that function. Thus, the value to be returned by *Factorial* is computed by calling the function recursively with parameter $n - 1$ and multiplying the result returned by n.

It was mentioned earlier that only when the function name appears to the left of an assignment operator does it represent the memory location that holds the value to

Figure 10.16   Algorithm for testing the recursive function *Factorial*.

```
algorithm PrintFactorials

{ Test Factorial by printing a short table of factorials }

declare
    i: integer
execute
    output 'Number', tab(16), 'Factorial'
    output
    for i ← 1 to 7
        output i, tab(16), Factorial(i)
    endfor
end PrintFactorials


function Factorial(n): integer

{ Compute factorial of positive integer }

declare
    n: in integer
execute
    if n = 1 then
        Factorial ← 1
    else
        Factorial ← n * Factorial(n − 1)
    endif
end Factorial
```

be returned. When the function name appears to the right of the assignment operator, or indeed in any expression, it signals a recursive invocation of the function.

If *Factorial* is called with an actual parameter less than 1, the recursion will fail to terminate. *Factorial* will invoke itself repeatedly until the system runs out of memory for private memory areas for the not-yet-completed invocations, at which time the algorithm that invoked *Factorial* will be terminated with a (probably obscure) error message. Systems with inadequate memory management may crash (stop working until the operating system is reloaded) when a nonterminating recursion occurs. This can be avoided by having the function print its own error message when it is called with an invalid parameter value. In the following, we assume that *Error* is a system procedure that prints the specified error message and terminates execution of the algorithm from which it was invoked:

function *Factorial*(*n*): *integer*
declare
    import *Error* **from** *System*
    n: **in** *integer*
execute
    if *n* = 1 **then**
        Factorial ← 1
    elseif *n* > 1 **then**
        Factorial ← *n* ∗ *Factorial*(*n* − 1)
    else
        Error('Factorial called with invalid argument')
    endif
end *Factorial*

Pitfalls of recursion   Recursion is essentially a form of repetition since execution of an algorithm using recursion results in repeated calls to the recursive function or procedure. Any problem that can be solved with a recursive algorithm can be solved with a nonrecursive algorithm using repetition, and vice versa. Although by no means always the case, often the recursive algorithm is easier to understand while the nonrecursive one is more efficient—executes faster and requires less memory.

One reason an iterative algorithm is often more efficient than the corresponding recursive algorithm is that the computer must do far less work in jumping back to the beginning of a series of repeated statements than in invoking a subalgorithm, setting up its private memory area, and passing parameters. Also, a recursive function or procedure is typically invoked many times before any of the invocations is completed. Thus, many uncompleted invocations, each with its private memory area, are in existence at the same time, taking up far more memory than is required for the corresponding iterative algorithm.

Our two versions of the function *Factorial* illustrate this problem. Both the iterative and the recursive version do the same number of multiplications, and so do the same amount of *useful* work. But the time required for the function invocations in the recursive version is much greater than that required for manipulating the control variable of the **for** construction in the iterative version.

What's more, if the recursive version of *Factorial* is invoked with the parameter 5, then the function will be invoked again with parameter 4, then again with parameter 3, then with parameter 2, and finally with parameter 1. Only when the invocation with parameter 1 returns the value of *Factorial*(1) can the invocation with parameter 2 be completed. Only when the invocation with parameter 2 returns the value of *Factorial*(2) can the invocation with parameter 3 be completed, and so on. Thus all five invocations, together with their private memory areas, are in existence at the same time. The iterative version of *Factorial* needs only one private memory area, regardless of the number whose factorial is to be computed, and so uses less memory than the recursive version.

Sometimes, however, the inefficiency of a recursive algorithm lies not only in the overhead of function and procedure invocations but in that the recursive algorithm demands far more computation than the corresponding iterative one. A recursive function for computing members of *Fibonacci's sequence* illustrates this problem: the recursive definition of the function is very simple and intuitive but calls for much unneccesary computation.

The *Fibonacci sequence*

0, 1, 1, 2, 3, 5, 8, 13, 21, . . .

arises out of Fibonacci's rabbit problem. The first two members of the sequence are 0 and 1; each remaining member is the sum of the two preceding ones. We can define a function *Fibonacci(n)* such that the value of *Fibonacci(0)* is the first member of the sequence, the value of *Fibonacci(1)* is the second member of the sequence, and so on:

n	*Fibonacci(n)*
0	0
1	1
2	1
3	2
4	3
5	5
6	8
7	13
8	21

The relation between the Fibonacci sequence and the rabbit problem is as follows. If we start with one fertile pair of rabbits, the number of pairs we will have after m months is the value of *Fibonacci(m + 2)*.

From the definition of the Fibonacci sequence, it is easy to write a recursive definition of *Fibonacci*:

Fibonacci(0) = 0
Fibonacci(1) = 1
Fibonacci(n) = *Fibonacci*(n − 1) + *Fibonacci*(n − 2) for $n > 1$

The first two equations give the first two members of the sequence; the third equation states that each member after the second one is the sum of the two preceding members.

As shown in Figure 10.17, we can readily translate the recursive definition into a recursive function. The function definition is unusual only in that there are two trivial, or base, cases requiring no recursive call, rather than the more usual one base

Figure 10.17   This algorithm for Fibonacci's rabbit problem uses the recursive function *Fibonacci* to compute Fibonacci numbers. Unfortunately, the function *Fibonacci* is extremely inefficient, since during the recursive calls *Fibonacci* is often evaluated many times with the same argument value, even though one such evaluation is sufficient to yield the corresponding Fibonacci number.

```
algorithm RabbitProblem

{ Solve Fibonacci's rabbit problem }

declare
     months: integer
execute
     output 'Number of months? ', more
     input months
     output 'After ', months, ' months you will have ',
              Fibonacci(months + 2), ' pairs'
end RabbitProblem


function Fibonacci(n): integer

{ Compute nth term of Fibonacci sequence }

declare
     n: in integer
execute
     if n = 0 then
          Fibonacci ← 0
     elseif n = 1 then
          Fibonacci ← 1
     else
          Fibonacci ← Fibonacci(n − 1) + Fibonacci(n − 2)
     endif
end Fibonacci
```

case. If the value of the parameter *n* is 0, *Fibonacci* returns 0; if the value of *n* is 1, *Fibonacci* returns 1; otherwise, *Fibonacci*(*n* − 1) and *Fibonacci*(*n* − 2) are evaluated, and their sum is returned:

> **if** *n* = 0 **then**
>> *Fibonacci* ← 0
>
> **elseif** *n* = 1 **then**
>> *Fibonacci* ← 1
>
> **else**
>> *Fibonacci* ← *Fibonacci*(*n* − 1) + *Fibonacci*(*n* − 2)
>
> **endif**

Figure 10.17 also shows a main algorithm, *RabbitProblem*, that uses *Fibonacci* to solve Fibonacci's rabbit problem of computing the number of rabbit pairs present after a given number of months if we start with one fertile pair. If we execute this algorithm on a not-too-fast computer system, such as a language implemented by an interpreter running on a microcomputer, we will notice a definite delay while the computer calculates the number of pairs after 12 months, and a much longer delay while it calculates the number of pairs after 18 months. Yet the latter calculation involves evaluating *Fibonacci*(20), which should require only 19 additions, one for each member of the sequence after the first two. Even the most modest computer system should not require a noticeable amount of time to do 19 additions.

To find out what is going wrong, let's use the module *Counter*, described earlier in the chapter, to find out how many times *Fibonacci* is being invoked during a calculation. Figure 10.18 shows the algorithm of Figure 10.17 modified for counting the invocations of *Fibonacci*. The main algorithm imports *Clear* and *Reading* from *Counter*. Before *Fibonacci* is invoked, *Clear* is called to clear the counter. (The call to *Clear* is optional since the counter is cleared automatically when the module *Counter* is initialized.) After *Fibonacci* has been invoked, the function *Reading* is used to obtain the number of invocations of *Fibonacci* that took place. *Fibonacci* imports the procedure *Increment* and calls it at the beginning of each invocation, thus counting the invocation. The following two interactions with the modified algorithm show that we have problems:

```
Number of months? 12
After 12 months you will have 377 pairs
Number of calls to Fibonacci: 1219

Number of months? 18
After 18 months you will have 6765 pairs
Number of calls to Fibonacci: 21891
```

More than one thousand calls to *Fibonacci* are needed to evaluate *Fibonacci*(14), and more than 21 thousand calls are needed to evaluate *Fibonacci*(20)! No wonder the computer is taking its time about calculating the result. What's going on?

To evaluate *Fibonacci*(20), *Fibonacci* is called recursively to evaluate *Fibonacci*(19) and to evaluate *Fibonacci*(18). To evaluate *Fibonacci*(19), *Fibonacci*(18)

Figure 10.18   To try to find out why the function *Fibonacci* is so
inefficient, we use the module *Counter* to count the number
of times *Fibonacci* is invoked during a calculation. The
procedures *Clear* and *Increment*, and the function *Reading*,
are imported from *Counter*. *Clear* is invoked before any
calls to *Fibonacci* are made; the call to *Clear* is optional
since the counter is cleared in the **initialize** section of the
module. *Increment* is called each time *Fibonacci* is invoked,
thus counting the invocation. After all calls to *Fibonacci*
have returned, the value returned by *Reading* is the number
of times *Fibonacci* was invoked.

```
algorithm RabbitProblem

{ Solve Fibonacci's rabbit problem }

declare
    inport Clear, Reading from Counter
    months: integer
execute
    Clear { optional }
    output 'Number of months? ', more
    input months
    output 'After ', months, ' months you will have ',
            Fibonacci(months + 2), ' pairs'
    output 'Number of calls to Fibonacci: ', Reading
end RabbitProblem



function Fibonacci(n): integer

{ Compute nth term of Fibonacci sequence }

declare
    import Increment from Counter
    n: in integer
execute
    Increment
    if n = 0 then
        Fibonacci ← 0
    elseif n = 1 then
        Fibonacci ← 1
    else
        Fibonacci ← Fibonacci(n − 1) + Fibonacci(n − 2)
    endif
end Fibonacci
```

and *Fibonacci*(17) must be evaluated. And here we see the problem. *Fibonacci*(18) is evaluated twice: once to compute *Fibonacci*(20), and once to compute *Fibonacci*(19). All the invocations of *Fibonacci* required to compute *Fibonacci*(18) are carried out twice. The further we go back toward the beginning of the *Fibonacci* sequence, the worse things become. For example, to compute *Fibonacci*(18), *Fibonacci*(17) and *Fibonacci*(16) must be evaluated. Thus *Fibonacci*(17) is evaluated three times: once in evaluating *Fibonacci*(19), and twice in the two redundant evaluations of *Fibonacci*(18). By the time the computation reaches the trivial cases *Fibonacci*(0) and *Fibonacci*(1), an enormous number of calls to *Fibonacci* have taken place.

The purpose of this discussion is not to scare you away from recursion, which is an important programming technique. For example, the Towers of Hanoi problem is one for which recursion is quite appropriate; although nonrecursive algorithms for this problem exist, they are more difficult to understand than the recursive algorithm and are probably not much more efficient. On the other hand, when a recursive algorithm and a simple, straightforward iterative algorithm exist for the same problem, as is the case for *Factorial* and *Fibonacci*, then the iterative algorithm is probably preferable to the recursive one. And we must watch out for recursive definitions that, like the definition of *Fibonacci*, are simple and intuitive but lead to large amounts of redundant computation when translated into algorithms.

10.8 Verifying algorithms that use functions and procedures

A function or procedure is characterized by a *precondition* the condition that must hold before the function or procedure is called, and a *postcondition* which states the condition that is guaranteed to hold after the function or procedure returns. For example, for the function *Factorial*(n), the two assertions are as follows:

Precondition: The value of *n* is an integer greater than or equal to 1.

Postcondition: The value returned by *Factorial*(n) is the product of all the integers in the range 1 to *n*.

The precondition *must* be satisfied before the function or procedure is invoked; if it isn't, all bets are off. For example, one of our recursive definitions of *Factorial* will cause an error message or even a system crash if the function is invoked with a zero or negative value for *n*. *If* the precondition holds before the function or procedure is invoked, *then* we can rest assured that the postcondition will hold after the function or procedure returns.

For example, let's prove that the following statements will print the factorial of a positive integer of 1 or greater entered by the user. If the integer is less than 1, an error message will be printed. Assume that *n* has been declared as an integer variable:

output 'Enter integer of 1 or greater: ', **more**
input *n*

> **if** $n >= 1$ **then**
>> **output** 'The factorial of ', n, ' is ', $Factorial(n)$
>
> **else**
>> **output** 'Error: Number entered was less than 1'
>
> **endif**

The user can enter any integer value for n. The **if** construction distinguishes two cases: n greater than or equal to 1, and n less than 1. In the first case, the precondition for *Factorial* is satisfied, so we can rest assured that the value returned by *Factorial* is the factorial of n. Thus when n is greater than or equal to 1, the **output** statement in the **then** part of the **if** construction prints the facotrial of n. When n is less than 1, the **output** statement in the **else** part of the **if** construction prints an appropriate error message.

As another example, consider the procedure

> $GetPlayersBet(bankroll, bet)$

which is part of the algorithm for playing craps. The precondition and postcondition are as follows:

> *Precondition*: The value of *bankroll* is greater than zero.

> *Postcondition*: The value of *bankroll* remains unchanged and the value of *bet* (which was accepted from the user) lies in the range 0.0 through *bankroll*.

Note that, if the value of *bankroll* is less than zero, no value of *bet* satisfies the postcondition. (If the value of *bankroll* equals zero, only a zero value for *bet* satisfies the postcondition.) Checking the statements for *GetPlayersBet*, we see that if *bankroll* is less than zero then no value for *bet* (except zero when *bankroll* is zero) can be accepted from the user, and so the procedure will not function as desired. *GetPlayersBet* is called in the following context:

> $GetStartingBankroll(bankroll)$
> **repeat**
>> $GetPlayersBet(bankroll, bet)$
>> $PlayOneRound(seed, won)$
>> $UpdatePlayersBankroll(bankroll, bet, won, playing)$
>
> **until not** $playing$

To see that the precondition for *GetPlayersBet* always holds just before the procedure is invoked, let's look at the preconditions and postconditions for the procedures affecting *bankroll* and *bet*. *GetStartingBankroll* has no precondition—there is no restriction on the state of the computation when it is invoked. The postcondition for *GetStartingBankroll* states that *bankroll* is greater than zero; hence the first time through the repeated statements the precondition for *GetPlayersBet* is satisfied. The postcondition for *GetPlayersBet* assures us that the value of *bankroll* is still greater than zero, the value of *bet* is greater than zero, and the value of *bet* is less than or equal to that of *bankroll*.

PlayOneRound does not affect *bankroll* or *bet* and so can be ignored for our present purposes. The precondition for *UpdatePlayersBankroll* is the same as the postcondition for *GetPlayersBet*: *bankroll* is greater than zero, *bet* is greater than or equal to zero, and *bet* is less than or equal to *bankroll*. The postcondition for *UpdatePlayersBankroll* states, in part,* that if *playing* is *true* then *bankroll* is greater than zero. (If *playing* is *false*, *bankroll* can be greater than or equal to zero.) The controlled statements are repeated only if the value of *playing* is *true*. Hence, if the controlled statements are repeated, the value of *bankroll* is greater than zero.

Thus, when execution of the repeated statements begins, the value of *bankroll* is greater than zero, either because *GetPlayersBankroll* has just been executed or because *UpdatePlayersBankroll* has been executed and has returned the value *true* for *playing*. Hence the statement that *bankroll* is greater than zero is an invariant assertion of the repetition; it always holds just before the first repeated statement is executed. We can conclude, therefore, that the precondition for *GetPlayersBet* always holds just before that procedure is invoked.

When proving the correctness of a function or procedure, our task is always to prove that *if* the precondition holds before the statements of the procedure have been executed, *then* the postcondition will hold afterward. If the function or procedure we are trying to verify calls other functions or procedures, we use the preconditions and postconditions for those other functions and procedures to prove that each invocation receives valid input data and produces the desired results.

Recursive functions and procedures are verified in basically the same way as nonrecursive ones; that is, again, we must prove that if the precondition holds before the function or procedure is invoked, then the postcondition will hold after the function or procedure returns. But when proving this for a function or procedure invoked with parameter value n, we encounter calls to the same function or procedure with parameter value $n - 1$. To complete our proof, we need some justification for assuming that the invocations with parameter value $n - 1$ work properly—that is, if the precondition holds before the function or procedure is invoked with parameter value $n - 1$, then the postcondition will hold after the function or procedure returns. Mathematical induction allows us to make this crucial assumption. It imposes the additional requirement, however, that we verify the base case by showing that if the precondition holds before the function or procedure is called for the base case, then the postcondition will hold after the function or procedure returns.

Review questions

1. What two kinds of *subalgorithms* are discussed in this chapter?

2. What are some of the advantages of using subalgorithms as building blocks, rather than trying to construct algorithms directly from the raw material of algorithmic-language statements?

---

*The complete postcondition also states how the value of *bankroll* after the procedure has returned depends on the values of *bankroll*, *bet*, and *won* before the procedure was invoked.

3. Give the general form of a function definition; include both the function heading as well as the **declare** and **execute** parts of the function definition.

4. What is the purpose of *formal parameters?* What is the purpose of *actual parameters?* Which kind of parameters are the *arguments* of a function?

5. How does the function definition specify the value that the function is to return?

6. Contrast procedures and functions.

7. Contrast *input, output,* and *input/output* parameters. For which kind of parameter can the corresponding actual parameter be an expression? For which kinds must it be a variable?

8. Which kind of parameter functions as a constant in the **execute** part of the function or procedure? Which kinds of parameters function as variables?

9. For each of the three kinds of parameters, describe how values are passed and results returned *by copy.*

10. For each of the three kinds of parameters, describe how values are passed and results returned *by reference.*

11. Distinguish between *local* and *global* variables.

12. What are some problems with the use of global variables? Why are global variables sometimes needed, nevertheless?

13. Describe the use of *common areas* to provide and control access to global variables.

14. Describe the use of *nested scopes* to provide and control access to global variables.

15. Describe the use of *modules* to provide and control access to global variables. What advantage do modules have that are not possessed by common areas and (especially) by nested scopes?

16. Using the module *Counter* as an example, explain why we can think of a module as defining an abstract machine that we "operate" by means of function and procedure calls. What features of the abstract machine correspond to the controls and instruments of a real machine?

17. Why is it essential that each invocation of a recursive function or procedure have its own private data area?

18. Give an example of a recursive definition of a function and show how the recursive definition can be converted straightforwardly into a function definition in the algorithmic language.

19. Give three reasons why recursive algorithms can be less efficient than iterative ones.

20. How do we go about verifying algorithms containing function and procedure calls?

Exercises

In the following exercises, we will usually illustrate a function or procedure by giving the function or procedure name followed by the list of formal parameters, as in *Min(m, n)* and *Smallest(i, j, k)*. The names of the formal parameters will sometimes be used to refer to the corresponding actual parameters; for example, we might say that *Min(m, n)* returns the smaller of *m* and *n*.

1. Write a function *Min(m, n)* whose value is the minimum of its two integer arguments.

2. Write a function *Smallest(i, j, k)* whose value is the smallest of the values of its three integer arguments.

3. Write a function *FractionalPart(x)* that returns the part of the value of *x* that lies to the right of the decimal point.

4. To round a real number to *n* decimal places, we multiply it by 10 ** *n*, round the result to the nearest integer, and divide the rounded result by 10 ** *n*. For example, to round 21.6472 to two decimal places, we multiply by 10 ** 2, or 100, to get 2164.72, round to the nearest integer to get 2165, and divide by 10 ** 2 to get 21.65. Write a function *RoundOff(x, n)* that returns the value of *x* rounded to *n* decimal places.

5. Write a function

   AdjustedHours(hoursWorked, overtimeLimit)

   that returns the value of *hoursWorked* adjusted so that each hour in excess of *overtimeLimit* is counted as an hour and a half.

6. Write a procedure

   Discount(Price, PercentDiscount, AmountOfDiscount, DiscountedPrice)

   that computes the amount of discount and discounted price of an item, given the price of the item and the percent discount.

7. Write a procedure

   AdjustHours(hoursWorked, overtimeLimit)

   to adjust the value of *hoursWorked* so that each hour in excess of *overtimeLimit* is counted as an hour and a half. For example, the statements

   $h \leftarrow 50.0$
   AdjustHours(h, 40.0)
   output *h*

cause the computer to print 55.0. On the other hand, the statements

$h \leftarrow 30.0$

AdjustHours(h, 40.0)

output *h*

cause the computer to print 30.0

8. If a subalgorithm accesses the same variable both as a global variable and via a formal parameter, the variable is being accessed by two different paths, and the results of executing the subalgorithm may depend on whether parameters are passed by copy or by reference. Write a procedure and give procedure invocations illustrating this statement.

9. Modify the module *RandomNumberGenerator* (Figure 10.13 or Figure 10.14) so that *Random* is a function,

Random(largestRandomInteger)

that returns a random integer in the range 1 to *largestRandomInteger*.

10. Write a module to simulate a calculator. The module exports procedures *Enter, Add, Subtract, Multiply,* and *Divide* and the function *Display*:

Enter(number)

Add(number)

Subtract(number)

Multiply(number)

Divide(number)

Display

Enter enters the value of *number* into the calculator's display. *Add, Subtract, Multiply,* and *Divide* each carries out the specified operation with the value in the display as the first operand and *number* as the second operand; the result is stored in the display. The function *Display* returns the current contents of the display.

11. Write a module *BlackjackDealer* to simulate a blackjack dealer. (The rules by which a blackjack dealer operates are given in Chapter 8.) The module exports two procedures:

NewGame

NextCard(card)

and three functions:

StayP

BustP

Count

NewGame initializes the module for a new game. *NextCard* causes the module to accept the value of *card* as its next card; if the dealer has stayed or busted, however, invoking *NextCard* has no effect. *StayP* and *BustP* are predicates—*Boolean functions. StayP* returns *true* if the dealer has stayed and *false* otherwise; *BustP* returns *true* if the dealer has busted and false otherwise. *Count* returns the current count of the dealer's hand. After *NewGame* has been executed, *StayP* and *BustP* both return *false,* and *Count* returns 0. Each call to *NextCard* updates the values returned by *StayP, BustP,* and *Count* to reflect the effect of the new card. After either *StayP* or *BustP* has returned *true,* additional calls to *NextCard* do not change the values returned by *StayP, BustP,* and *Count.*

12. It is customary to extend the definition of *Factorial* to zero argument values by defining *Factorial*(0) to be equal to 1. Modify the recursive function *Factorial* so that it is in accord with the extended definition.

Hint: Use $n = 0$ rather than $n = 1$ as the base case.

13. Write a function

    Power(*x, n*)

    that uses repeated multiplication to compute the value of the real number x raised to the power of the nonnegative integer n. The value of *Power*(*x, n*) should be equal to $x \ast\ast n$.

14. The function *Power* described in Exercise 13 can be defined recursively as follows:

    Power(*x*, 0) = 1
    Power(*x, n*) = $x \ast$ *Power*(*x, n* − 1) for $n > 0$

    Using mathematical induction, show that this definition is equivalent to the one using repeated multiplication. Use this definition to write a recursive version of the function *Power.*

15. The greatest common divisor of two nonnegative integers m and n is the largest integer that can be divided evenly into both m and n. For example, the greatest common divisor of 12 and 8 is 4, and the greatest common divisor of 40 and 30 is 10. The following two statements (which math students may wish to prove but we will not bother to) provide the basis for computing greatest common divisors:

    1. The greatest common divisor of any number m and 0 is m. For example, the greatest common divisor of 9 and 0 is 9, since 9 is the largest integer that divides evenly into both 9 and 0.

    2. The greatest common divisor of m and n is the same as the greatest common divisor of n and m **mod** n. For example, the greatest common divisor of 24 and 10 is the same as the greatest common divisor of 10

and 4 ($=$ 24 **mod** 10). The greatest common divisor of each pair of numbers is 2.

We can use these statements to construct a recursive definition of the function $Gcd(m, n)$, which returns the greatest common divisor of the non-negative integers m and n:

From statement 1:
  $Gcd(\text{m}, 0) = m$
From statement 2:
  $Gcd(m, n) = Gcd(n, m \textbf{ mod } n)$ for $n > 0$

Use this recursive definition to write a function definition for Gcd in the algorithmic language. How can we be sure that the recursion terminates, that is, that repeated recursive calls to Gcd will lead to the trivial case that can be handled without any further recursive calls?

For further reading

The following papers point out some of the difficulties that arise in using nested scopes to control access to global variables:

Cailliau, R. "How to Avoid Getting *Schlonked* by Pascal." *SIGPLAN Notices,* December 1982, pp. 31–40.

Clarke, Lori A., Wileden, Jack C., and Wolf, Alexander L. "Nesting in Ada Programs is for the Birds." *SIGPLAN Notices,* November 1980, pp. 139–145.

Levy, Eric B. "The Case against Pascal as a Teaching Tool." *SIGPLAN Notices,* November 1982, pp. 39–41.

Pascal Supplement

Functions and procedures

Just as a function in the algorithmic language is similar to a main algorithm, but with a function heading instead of an algorithm heading, so a function in Pascal is similar to a Pascal program, but with a function heading substituted for the program heading. A Pascal function heading has the following form:

function function-name(formal-parameter-declarations): return-type;

Pascal declares the formal parameters in the function heading, in contrast to the algorithmic language which *lists* the formal parameters in the function heading but *declares* them in the **declare** part of the function definition. For example, the function heading

function *Volume(length: real; width: real; height: real): real;*

declares the three formal parameters *length*, *width*, and *height* all to be of type *real*. The parameter declarations have the same form as variable declarations: each consists of the formal parameter name, a colon, and the declared type. Formal parameter declarations are *separated* by semicolons; there is no semicolon between the right-most declaration and the closing parenthesis. As in the algorithmic language, the return type gives the type of the values the function is to return. The entire function heading is terminated by a semicolon.

As with variable declarations, we can combine the declarations of formal parameters having the same type. Thus, our example could be written more simply as follows:

> **function** *Volume(length, width, height: real): real*;

Like the algorithmic language, Pascal designates the value the function is to return by assigning it to the name of the function. For example, the following is the Pascal function declaration for *Volume:*

> **function** *Volume(length, width, height: real): real*;
> **begin**
> > *Volume := length * width * height*
>
> **end**;

The statement part of the function contains a single statement, which computes the product of the actual parameters and assigns the result to *Volume,* thereby designating this result as the value to be returned by the function. Thus, the value of

> *Volume*(10, 5, 4)

is 200, the product of 10, 5, and 4.

A function or procedure declaration can contain any of the definition or declaration sections that can appear in a program, so the declaration for *Volume* could have contained a constant definition section and a variable declaration section if these had been needed. Note the semicolon following the statement part; a function or procedure declaration is terminated with a semicolon, just as a program is terminated by a period.

Here is the Pascal version of the function *Maximum,* which was discussed in the main text:

> **function** *Maximum(m, n: integer): integer*;
> **begin**
> > **if** *m > n* **then**
> > > *Maximum := m*
> >
> > **else**
> > > *Maximum := n*
>
> **end**;

Maximum takes two integers as arguments and returns an integer result. The **if** statement in the statement part of the function determines which parameter value will be assigned to *Maximum* and so determines which value the function will return.

The function declaration for *Factorial* has a variable declaration part as well as a statement part:

function *Factorial*(*n*: *integer*): *integer*;
var
    product, *i*: *integer*;
begin
    product := 1;
    for *i* := 1 **to** *n* **do**
        product := *product* * *i*;
    Factorial := *product*
end;

Factorial takes an integer argument and returns an integer result. Variables *product* and *i* are local to the function declaration, cannot be accessed from outside it, and have nothing to do with any variables named *product* and *i* that might occur elsewhere in the program in which *Factorial* is used. As in the algorithmic language version of the function, the factorial of *n* is computed as the value of *product*, then assigned to *Factorial* as the value the function should return.

Figure 10.19 shows the program corresponding to the algorithm *PrintFactorials* (Figure 10.1) described in the main text. Comparing Figures 10.1 and 10.19, we see at once a difference between the algorithmic language and Pascal. In the algorithmic language, function and procedure definitions are listed separately rather than being included in the text of the main algorithm. In Pascal, however, function and procedure declarations, like constant definitions and variable declarations, are included in the text of the program that uses them.

The following shows the general form of a program, function declaration, or procedure declaration (the list of declaration and definition parts is not complete):

program, function, or procedure heading

constant definition part

variable declaration part

function and procedure declarations

statement part

Thus the variable declaration part can be followed by any number of "function or procedure declaration parts," each of which declares a single function or procedure. The order given for the definition and declaration parts must be observed: constant definitions must precede variable declarations; variable declarations must precede function and procedure declarations; and all definitions and declarations must precede the statement part of a program, function, or procedure.

In Figure 10.19, *PrintFactorials* has a variable declaration part, in which the integer variable *i* is declared, and a function declaration for the function *Factorial*. The *i* declared in variable declaration part of *PrintFactorials* has nothing to do with the *i* declared in the variable declaration part of *Factorial*. References to *i* in the

Figure 10.19   Pascal program *PrintFactorials* corresponding to the
algorithm in Figure 10.1.

```
program PrintFactorials(input, output);

{ Test Factorial function by printing a short table of factorials }

var
    i: integer;


function Factorial(n: integer): integer;

{ Compute factorial of positive integer }

var
    product, i: integer;
begin
    product := 1;
    for i := 1 to n do
        product := product * i;
    Factorial := product
end; { Factorial }


begin { PrintFactorials }
    writeln ('Number':15, 'Factorial':15);
    writeln;
    for i := 1 to 7 do
        writeln (i:15, Factorial(i):15)
end.
```

statement part of *PrintFactorials* refer to the *i* declared in *PrintFactorials;* references
to *i* in the statement part of *Factorial* refer to the *i* declared in *Factorial*.

Execution of the program begins with the statement part of *PrintFactorials;* the
statement part of *Factorial* is executed only when the function is invoked by means
of the expression *Factorial(i)* in the statement part of *PrintFactorials*.

A procedure declaration is similar to a function declaration except that the procedure heading is introduced by the keyword **procedure**:

procedure procedure-name(formal-parameter-declarations);

No return type is specified since the procedure name is not used to return a value.
Note, however, that the procedure heading also ends with a semicolon. The statement

part of a procedure *does not* contain an assignment to the procedure name, again because the name of a procedure is not used to return a value.

For example, the following is the Pascal version of the procedure *PrintCurrency* discussed in the main text:

> **procedure** *PrintCurrency(amount: real)*;
> **begin**
> > *write('$', amount:*1:2)
> **end**;

This is not a literal translation of the corresponding procedure in the algorithmic language. The availability of field-width parameters in Pascal allows the procedure to be considerably simpler in Pascal than in the algorithmic language.

Parameters and parameter passing

Pascal provides two kinds of parameters for passing and returning data values: *value parameters* and *variable parameters*. Except for one difference to be mentioned later, value parameters in Pascal are the same as input parameters in the algorithmic language. Parameter passing for value parameters is always by copy. Variable parameters are the same as input/output parameters in the algorithmic language. Parameter passing for variable parameters is always by reference.

Pascal does not provide any analog of output parameters in the algorithmic language. Pascal programs use variable parameters (which permit both input and output) where the algorithmic language uses output parameters. This is, in fact, the course followed by most programming languages; as mentioned in the main text, output-only parameters are rare.

As is the case for the corresponding kinds of parameters in the algorithmic language, value parameters can be used only to pass data to a function or procedure, whereas variable parameters can be used both to pass data to a function or procedure and to return results. The actual parameter corresponding to a value parameter can be any expression: a constant, a variable, or an expression constructed with operators. The actual parameter corresponding to a variable parameter must be a variable (from whence comes the name "variable parameter"). For value parameters, the value of the actual parameter must be assignment compatible with the type of the formal parameter. For variable parameters, the type of the actual parameter must be the same as that of the formal parameter.

Variable parameters are specified by the keyword **var** at the beginning of a parameter declaration; if **var** is not present, the parameters are declared as value parameters. Thus, in

> **procedure** *Rectangle(length, width: real*;
> > **var** *area, perimeter: real)*;

length and *width* are value parameters, since the keyword **var** is not present in their declaration. On the other hand, *area* and *perimeter* are variable parameters, since their combined declaration begins with the keyword **var.** Here is the complete procedure declaration for *Rectangle:*

proceaure *Rectangle*(*length*, *width*: *real*;

                    var *area*, *perimeter*: *real*);

begin

    area := *length* ∗ *width*;

    perimeter := 2.0 ∗ (*length* + *width*)

end;

In the algorithmic language, *area* and *perimeter* are declared as output parameters; in Pascal, we must use variable parameters, which permit both input and output, even though in reality *area* and *perimeter* are used only for output.

Since parameter passing for variable parameters is by reference, assignments to formal variable parameters cause the values in question to be assigned to the corresponding actual parameters. Thus, the procedure statement

    Rectangle(5.0, 3.0, *a*, *p*);

causes the procedure to be executed as if the formal parameter *area* was replaced by the actual parameter *a* and the formal parameter *perimeter* was replaced by the actual parameter *p*. Thus, the assignment

    area := *length* ∗ *width*

is executed as if it had been written

    a := *length* ∗ *width*

and

    perimeter := 2.0 ∗ (*length* + *width*)

is executed as if it had been written

    p := 2.0 ∗ (*length* + *width*)

Input/output parameters in the algorithmic language also become variable parameters in Pascal, as illustrated by the procedure *Increment*:

procedure *Increment*(**var** *display*: *integer*);

begin

    display := *display* + 1;

    if *display* = 60 **then**

        display := 0

end;

When *Increment* is invoked with the procedure statement

    Increment(*d*)

the statement part is executed as if each occurrence of the formal parameter *display* were replaced with the actual parameter *d*. For example, *display* := *display* + 1

is executed as if it had been written

d := *d* + 1

When the statement is executed, the value of the actual parameter *d* is increased by 1.

As mentioned earlier, there is one respect in which value parameters in Pascal differ from input parameters in the algorithmic language. A formal input parameter behaves like a constant whose value is that of the corresponding actual parameter. A value parameter, on the other hand, behaves like a local variable whose initial value is that of the corresponding actual parameter.

In the algorithmic language, for example, if the function *Volume* with input parameters *length, width,* and *height* is invoked by

v ← *Volume*(10.0, 5.0, 20.0)

the statement part of the procedure is executed as if the formal parameters were defined by

const *length* = 10.0
const *width* = 5.0
const *height* = 20.0

In Pascal, on the other hand, *length, width,* and *height* are treated like local variables declared by

var

    length, width, height: real;

and assigned initial values as follows

length := 10.0;
width := 5.0;
height := 20.0

before execution of the statement part of the function begins.

Since Pascal value parameters behave like local variables rather than constants, their values can be changed during the execution of a function or procedure. If a new value is assigned to a value parameter, its original value—the value of the corresponding actual parameter—is, of course, lost. Assigning a new value to a value parameter has no effect whatever on the corresponding actual parameter. The actual parameter is used only to give the formal parameter its initial value; thereafter, the formal parameter behaves just like any other local variable.

For example, the following rather tricky version of the *Factorial* function uses the value parameter *n* as a local variable:

function *Factorial*(*n*: *integer*): *integer*;
var

    product: *integer*;

```
begin
    product := 1;
    for n := n downto 1 do
        product := product * n;
    Factorial := product
end;
```

Since the formal parameter *n* behaves like a local variable, it can be used as the control variable in a **for** statement. The **for** statement

```
for n := n downto 1 do
    product := product * n
```

steps *n* from its initial value—the value of *n* before the **for** statement is executed—down to 1. Since the initial value of *n* is the value of the actual parameter, the value of *n* is stepped from the value of the actual parameter down to 1. The values through which *n* is stepped are multiplied together, their product being formed as the value of *product*. When the **for** statement terminates, therefore, the value of *product* is the product of all integers from 1 through the value of the actual parameter.

Pascal allows us to use a value parameter for two purposes: as a formal parameter whose value is equal to the corresponding actual parameter, and as a local variable whose value can be changed at will. However, using the same object for two different purposes can make things more difficult for anyone trying to understand the program. For the sake of clarity, therefore, it is worthwhile to treat formal value parameters as if they were constants and to declare additional local variables to hold values that are to be changed during the course of a computation.

The program *craps*

Figure 10.20 shows a version of the algorithm for playing craps (Figure 10.4). The procedure declarations are included in the program *Craps* following the variable declarations but preceding the statement part of the program. In general, the program heading and the definitions and declarations at the beginning of a Pascal program are separated from the statement part of the program by the declarations of all the functions and procedures that the program uses. Given a long Pascal program, we will find part of the main program at the beginning of the listing and the rest (the statement part) at the end of the listing.

The procedures declared in the Pascal program correspond directly to the ones used in the algorithmic language. Note that, where the algorithmic language uses an input parameter, Pascal uses a value parameter; and where the algorithmic language uses an input/output or output parameter, Pascal uses a variable parameter. As an aid to the reader, a comment at the end of each procedure gives the name of the procedure. Also, when the statement part of a program, function, or procedure is separated from the rest of the program, function, or procedure, as is the case for *Craps,* it's helpful to include the program, function, or procedure name in a comment near the **begin** of the statement part.

Figure 10.20 Pascal program *Craps* corresponding to the algorithm in Figure 10.4. In this version of *Craps,* procedure declarations are part of the main program, as is required in Pascal, but procedure declarations are not nested inside other procedure declarations.

```
program Craps(input, output);

{ Play craps with user }

var
    bankroll,          { Amount available to player for betting }
    bet,               { Amount bet on this round }
    seed: real;        { Value used for generating random numbers }
    won,               { True if player has won current round }
    playing: Boolean;  { True if game is to continue }


procedure GetStartingBankroll (var bankroll: real);

{ Find out how much money player has }

begin
    write('How much money do you have to play with? ');
    readln(bankroll);
    while bankroll <= 0.0 do
        begin
            write('Please enter an amount greater than zero: ');
            readln(bankroll)
        end
end; { GetStartingBankroll }


procedure GetPlayersBet(bankroll: real; var bet: real);

{ Get amount player wishes to bet on current round }

begin
    write('How much do you want to bet? ');
    readln(bet);
    while (bet < 0.0) or (bet > bankroll) do
        begin
            write('Invalid bet--please try again: ');
            readln(bet)
        end
end; { GetPlayersBet }
```

```
procedure Random(largestRandomInteger: integer;
                 var randomInteger: integer;
                 var seed: real);

{ Generate random integer in range 1 through largestRandomInteger }

begin
    seed := sqr(seed + 3.1415927);
    seed := seed - trunc(seed);
    randomInteger := trunc(largestRandomInteger * seed) + 1
end; {Random }



procedure RollDice(var dice: integer; var seed: real);

{ Simulate roll of dice; print value rolled on each die and return their sum
  as value of dice }

var
    die1, die2: integer;
begin
    Random(6, die1, seed);
    Random(6, die2, seed);
    writeln('You rolled a ', die1:1, ' and a ', die2:1);
    dice := die1 + die2
end; { RollDice }



procedure PlayRemaningRolls(point: integer;
                           var seed: real;
                           var won: Boolean);

{ Roll dice until user makes point or craps out }

var
    dice: integer;
begin
    repeat
        RollDice(dice, seed)
    until (dice = point) or (dice = 7);
    won := (dice = point)
end; { PlayRemainingRolls }
```

```pascal
procedure PlayOneRound(var seed: real; var won: Boolean);

{ Play one round; determine whether player wins or loses }

var
    dice: integer;
begin
    RollDice(dice, seed);
    case dice of
        7, 11:                  won := true;
        2, 3, 12:               won := false;
        4, 5, 6, 8, 9, 10:      PlayRemainingRolls(dice, seed, won)
    end
end; { PlayOneRound }


procedure UpdatePlayersBankroll(var bankroll: real;
                                bet: real;
                                won: Boolean;
                                var playing: Boolean);

{ Update bankroll and report results of play. If player is broke, set playing
  to false. Otherwise, determine if user wishes to play another round and
  set value of playing to true or false accordingly }

var
    response: char;
begin
    if won then
        begin
            writeln('You win');
            bankroll := bankroll + bet
        end
    else
        begin
            writeln('You lose');
            bankroll := bankroll - bet
        end;
    if bankroll < 0.005 then
        begin
            writeln('You''re broke');
            playing :=false
        end
```

```
        else
            begin
                writeln('You have ', bankroll:1:2, ' dollars');
                repeat
                    write('Do you want to play again (y/n)? ');
                    readln(response)
                until (response = 'y') or (response = 'n') or
                    (response = 'Y') or (response = 'N');
                playing := (response = 'y') or (response = 'Y')
            end
end; { UpdatePlayersBankroll }


begin {Craps }
    write('Enter number between 0 and 1: ');
    readln(seed);
    GetStartingBankroll(bankroll);
    repeat
        writeln;
        GetPlayersBet(bankroll, bet);
        PlayOneRound(seed, won);
        UpdatePlayersBankroll(bankroll, bet, won, playing)
    until not playing
end.
```

In Pascal, a function or procedure declaration must precede all references to the function or procedure name. This means that a function or procedure declaration must precede the declarations of functions and procedures from which the function or procedure in question is invoked. Thus, the declaration of *RollDice* must precede those of *PlayOneRound* and *PlayRemainingRolls,* the declaration of *Play-RemainingRolls* must precede that of *PlayOneRound,* and the declaration of *Random* must precede that of *RollDice*. This order is just the opposite of the one that is most natural for top-down design and construction, in which we write a program, function, or procedure *before* writing the functions and procedures it calls. Of course, modern text editors make it easy to insert a function or procedure declaration at any point in a program, so the order in which the functions and procedures are written need not be the same as the order in which they appear in the program.

Access to variables

Standard Pascal uses only the method of nested scopes for controlling access to global variables. Because of the limitations of nested scopes, some versions of Pascal also provide *units,* a construction similar to the modules discussed in the main text.

Nested scopes A Pascal program, function, or procedure can itself contain declarations for functions and procedures, and these can contain still other function and procedure declarations, and so on, allowing function and procedure declarations to be nested. The scope of a Pascal identifier is the program, function, or procedure in which the identifier is declared. (More precisely, the scope extends from the declaration of the identifier to the end of the statement part of the program, function, or procedure.) When function and procedure declarations are nested, the scopes of the identifiers declared in them are nested accordingly.

Figure 10.21 shows the Pascal program corresponding to the algorithm for playing a guessing game (Figure 10.7). The diagram in Figure 10.8 applies to the Pascal program as well as to the algorithm.* Variables *playersGuess, secretNumber, playAgain,* and *seed* are local to the main program *Guess.* The scope of each extends from its point of definition to the end of the statement part of the program. Since the declaration for *Random* is within the scopes of these variables, each is accessible from within *Random;* these variables are local to *Guess* but global to *Random.* Specifically, *Random* can access the global variable *seed.* The procedure name *Random* is considered declared in *Guess,* so that its scope extends from the beginning of the procedure declaration to the end of *Guess.* Specifically, *Random* can be invoked from the statement part of *Guess.* The formal parameters, however, are local to *Random;* the scope of each extends from its declaration to the end of the statement part of *Random.*

The version of *Craps* given in Figure 10.20 uses as little nesting as possible; all the program's procedures are nested within the main program but not within one another. Thus, only the main program suffers from having its statement part separated from the rest of the program by a mass of procedure declarations. In contrast, the program in Figure 10.22, which is a literal translation of the algorithm in Figure 10.11, uses as much nesting as possible. Since *Random* is invoked only by *RollDice,* for example, the declaration of *Random* is nested within that of *RollDice.* And since *RollDice* and *PlayRemainingRolls* are invoked only by *PlayRemainingRolls* and *PlayOneRound,* the declarations of *RollDice* and *PlayRemainingRolls* are nested within the declaration of *PlayOneRound.* The diagram in Figure 10.12 applies to both Figure 10.11 and Figure 10.22. In each case, the global variable *seed* is accessed from both *Craps* and *Random.* Although the nesting scheme of Figure 10.22 may seem theoretically neat, the program listing in Figure 10.20 is surely the easier to read.

Forward declarations The scope of an identifier begins at the point at which the identifier is declared; therefore, declarations of identifiers must always precede their uses. In particular, the declaration of a function or procedure must precede the first point in the program where the function or procedure is invoked.

---

*Except that the formal parameter declarations for *Random* are given in the algorithmic language rather than in Pascal. In Pascal, *largestRandomInteger* is a value parameter and *randomInteger* is a variable parameter.

Figure 10.21   Pascal program *Guess* corresponding to the algorithm in Figure 10.7.

```
program Guess(input, output);

{ Play guessing game with user }

var
    playersGuess, secretNumber: integer;
    playAgain: char;
    seed: real; { Global variable accessed by Guess and Random }


procedure Random(largestRandomInteger: integer;
                      var randomInteger: integer);

{ Generate random integer in range 1 through largestRandomInteger.
  Accesses global variable seed }

begin
    seed := sqr(seed + 3.1415927);
    seed := seed − trunc(seed);
    randomInteger := trunc(largestRandomInteger * seed) + 1
end; { Random }


begin { Guess }
    write('Enter number between 0 and 1: ');
    readln(seed);
    writeln('I am thinking of a number from 1 to 100');
    writeln('You are to try to guess the number. I will tell');
    writeln('you whether your guess is right or whether it is');
    writeln('too large or too small.');
    repeat
        writeln;
        Random(100, secretNumber);
        write('I have my number. What is your guess? ');
        repeat
            readln(playersGuess);
            if playersGuess > secretNumber then
                write('Too large. Guess again: ')
            else if playersGuess < secretNumber then
                write('Too small. Guess again: ')
        until playersGuess = secretNumber;
        writeln('You are right!');
        write('Would you like to play again (y/n)? ');
        readln(playAgain)
    until (playAgain = 'n') or (playAgain = 'N')
end.
```

Figure 10.22 This version of the Pascal program *Craps* corresponds to the algorithm in Figure 10.11, in which procedures are nested to the greatest possible degree. Note that Figure 10.22 is more difficult to read than Figure 10.20, in which procedure declarations are not nested inside other procedure declarations.

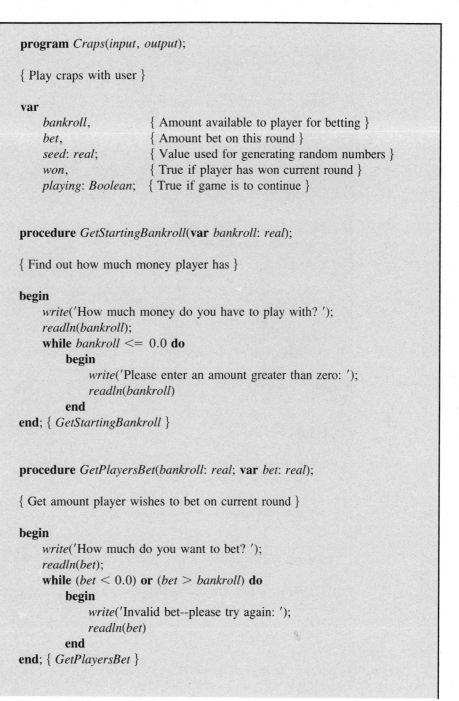

```pascal
program Craps(input, output);

{ Play craps with user }

var
    bankroll,           { Amount available to player for betting }
    bet,                { Amount bet on this round }
    seed: real;         { Value used for generating random numbers }
    won,                { True if player has won current round }
    playing: Boolean;   { True if game is to continue }


procedure GetStartingBankroll(var bankroll: real);

{ Find out how much money player has }

begin
    write('How much money do you have to play with? ');
    readln(bankroll);
    while bankroll <= 0.0 do
        begin
            write('Please enter an amount greater than zero: ');
            readln(bankroll)
        end
end; { GetStartingBankroll }


procedure GetPlayersBet(bankroll: real; var bet: real);

{ Get amount player wishes to bet on current round }

begin
    write('How much do you want to bet? ');
    readln(bet);
    while (bet < 0.0) or (bet > bankroll) do
        begin
            write('Invalid bet--please try again: ');
            readln(bet)
        end
end; { GetPlayersBet }
```

procedure *PlayOneRound*(**var** *won*: *Boolean*);

{ Play one round; determine whether player wins or loses }

var
    dice: *integer*;

procedure *RollDice*(**var** *dice*: *integer*);

{ Simulate roll of dice; print value rolled on each die and return their sum
  as value of *dice* }

var
    die1, *die2*: *integer*;

procedure *Random*(*largestRandomInteger*: *integer*;
                    var *randomInteger*: *integer*);

{ Generate random integer in range 1 through *largestRandomInteger* }

begin
    seed := *sqr*(*seed* + 3.1415927);
    seed := *seed* − *trunc*(*seed*);
    randomInteger := *trunc*(*largestRandomInteger* * *seed*) + 1
end; { *Random* }

begin { *RollDice* }
    Random(6, *die1*);
    Random(6, *die2*);
    writeln('You rolled a ', *die1*:1, ' and a ', *die2*:1);
    dice := *die1* + *die2*
end; { *RollDice* }

procedure *PlayRemaingRolls*(*point*: *integer*; **var** *won*: *Boolean*);

{ Roll dice until user makes point or craps out }

var
    dice: *integer*;

```pascal
begin
    repeat
        RollDice(dice)
    until (dice = point) or (dice = 7);
    won := (dice = point)
end; { PlayRemainingRolls }


begin { PlayOneRound }
    RollDice(dice);
    case dice of
        7, 11:              won := true;
        2, 3, 12:           won := false;
        4, 5, 6, 8, 9, 10:  PlayRemainingRolls(dice, won)
    end
end; { PlayOneRound }


procedure UpdatePlayersBankroll(var bankroll: real;
                                bet: real;
                                won: Boolean;
                                var playing: Boolean);

{ Update bankroll and report results of round. If player is broke, set
  playing to false. Otherwise, determine if user wishes to play another
  round and set value of playing to true or false accordingly }

var
    response: char;
begin
    if won then
        begin
            writeln('You win');
            bankroll := bankroll + bet
        end
    else
        begin
            writeln('You lose');
            bankroll := bankroll - bet
        end;
    if bankroll < 0.005 then
        begin
            writeln('You''re broke');
            playing := false
        end
```

```
        else
            begin
                writeln('You have ', bankroll:1:2, ' dollars');
                repeat
                    write ('Do you want to play again (y/n)? ');
                    readln(response)
                until (response = 'y') or (response = 'n') or
                      (response = 'Y') or (response = 'N');
                playing := (response = 'y') or (response = 'Y')
            end
    end; { UpdatePlayersBankroll }


begin { Craps }
    write('Enter number between 0 and 1: ');
    readln(seed);
    GetStartingBankroll(bankroll);
    repeat
        writeln;
        GetPlayersBet(bankroll, bet);
        PlayOneRound(won);
        UpdatePlayersBankroll(bankroll, bet, won, playing)
    until not playing
end.
```

There are situations, however, in which this requirement cannot be met. For example, two procedures, say P and Q, may be *mutually recursive*—P invokes Q and Q invokes P:

procedure P(**var** x, y: *integer*);
var
    a, b: *integer*;
begin

    . . .

    $Q(a, b)$;   { invocation of Q }

    . . .

end; { P }

procedure Q(**var** u, v: *integer*);
var
    c, d: *integer*;

begin

. . .

$P(c, d)$;   { invocation of P }

. . .

end; { Q }

Regardless of the order in which the two procedure declarations appear, one of the two procedure names is referred to before it is declared.

To avoid this problem, Pascal allows a function or procedure to be declared by means of its heading only. Such a *forward declaration* consists of the function or procedure heading followed by the keyword **forward:**

procedure Q(**var** u, v: *integer*); **forward**;

Note the semicolons after the procedure heading and after **forward.** The body of the function or procedure—the part that follows the heading—is declared later in the program at a point where all the identifiers to which it refers have been declared:

procedure Q;
var

c, d: *integer*;

begin

. . .

$P(c, d)$;   { invocation of P }

. . .

end; { Q }

The body is preceded by an abbreviated procedure heading that gives *only* the name of the procedure. The abbreviated heading does not declare formal parameters or a return type for functions since these have already been declared in the forward declaration.

Now consider the following sequence of declarations:

procedure Q(**var** u, v: *integer*); **forward**;

procedure P(**var** x, y: *integer*);
var

a, b: *integer*;

begin

. . .

$Q(a, b)$;   { invocation of Q }

. . .

end; { P }

procedure Q;
var

c, d: *integer*;

begin

. . .

$P(c, d)$;   { invocation of P }

. . .

end; { Q }

Procedure Q is declared in the forward declaration, which precedes the reference to Q in the body of procedure P. Since the body of Q is placed after the declaration of P, the reference to P in the body of Q follows the declaration of P, and all is well.

Units Standard Pascal does not provide any construction corresponding to the modules in the algorithmic language. However, some versions of Pascal, including UCSD Pascal, IBM Personal Computer Pascal, and Microsoft Pascal, provide module-like constructions called *units* as a nonstandard extension. In translating from the algorithmic language to Pascal, we will translate algorithmic-language modules into UCSD-Pascal units. Persons using versions of Pascal that do not provide units should consider a unit as merely a convenient means of presenting a series of declarations and statements that can be incorporated in Pascal programs.

A unit has the following form:

unit unit-name;

interface

declarations of exported identifiers

implementation

declarations of identifiers not to be exported

bodies of procedures declared in interface

begin

initialization statements

end

The interface and implementation sections of a unit accomplish the same purpose as **export** declarations in the algorithmic language. Identifiers declared in the interface are exported for use by programs and other units; identifiers declared in the implementation are local to the unit and are not exported.

Functions and procedures that are to be exported are declared in the interface by means of their headings only, exactly as in forward declarations, although the keyword **forward** is not used. The bodies of functions and procedures declared in the interface are given in the implementation with abbreviated headings, exactly as for forward declarations.

If initialization statements are present, they are executed before commencing the execution of the program that uses the unit. If no initialization statements are present, the keyword **begin** can be omitted.

For example, Figure 10.23 shows the unit *RandomNumberGenerator*, corresponding to the module of the same name discussed in the main text. *RandomNumberGenerator* exports two procedures, *Reseed* and *Random*, which are therefore declared in the interface:

Figure 10.23 Pascal unit *RandomNumberGenerator* corresponding to the module in Figure 10.13

```
unit RandomNumberGenerator;

interface
    procedure Reseed(newSeed: real);
    procedure Random(largestRandomInteger: integer;
                       var randomInteger: integer);

implementation
    var
        seed: real;

    procedure Reseed;
    begin
        seed := newSeed
    end; { Reseed }

    procedure Random;
    begin
        seed := sqr(seed + 3.1415927);
        seed := seed − trunc(seed);
        randomInteger := trunc(largestRandomInteger * seed) + 1
    end; { Random }
end. { RandomNumberGenerator }
```

```
unit RandomNumberGenerator;
interface
    procedure Reseed(newSeed: real);
    procedure Random(largestRandomInteger: integer;
                       randomInteger: integer);
```

The declarations are identical to **forward** declarations, except that the keyword **forward** does not actually appear.

The variable *seed* is *not* exported by the unit and is therefore declared in the implementation rather than in the interface. The bodies of the procedures *Reseed* and *Random* are also given in the implementation; each procedure body is preceded by an abbreviated procedure heading, exactly as for procedures that have been declared by forward declarations. Since no automatic initialization is to take place, no initialization statements are present and the keyword **begin** that would normally precede them is omitted.

Figure 10.28 shows the unit *Counter,* corresponding to the module of the same name discussed in the main text. The procedures *Clear* and *Increment,* and the function *Reading,* are exported, but the variable *count* is local to the unit. *Counter* contains one initialization statement, an invocation of *Clear,* which sets the counter to zero before the execution of the program using the unit.

A program that uses a unit names the unit in a **uses** declaration, which precedes all other declarations and definitions in the program. For example, in Figure 10.20 the declaration

    uses *RandomNumberGenerator*;

specifies that the program *Craps* uses the unit *RandomNumberGenerator.* In Figure 10.29, the **uses** declaration

    uses *Counter*;

specifies that the program *RabbitProblem* uses the unit *Counter.* More than one unit can be specified in a **uses** declaration; for example, a program that uses both *RandomNumberGenerator* and *Counter* would have the **uses** declaration

    uses *RandomNumberGenerator, Counter*;

When a program uses a unit, all the identifiers declared in the interface part of the unit are imported for use by the program. The scope of the imported identifiers is the entire program, so they are accessible to all functions and procedures declared in the program. In contrast to the corresponding situation in the algorithmic language, functions and procedures cannot specify units in **uses** declarations; they can only refer to identifiers imported by **uses** declarations in the main program.

A unit can also use another unit. A **uses** declaration can appear in the interface or in the implementation part of a unit (in each case the uses declaration immediately follows the keyword **interface** or **implementation**). In the most common case, the **uses** declaration appears in the implementation part, allowing the functions and procedures in the implementation to invoke functions and procedures imported from the used units. When one unit uses a second unit, the initialization statements for the second unit are carried out before those for the first.

When using a version of Pascal that does not support units, we may regard a unit as a convenient way of presenting a series of declarations and statements that can be included in Pascal programs. All the variable, function, procedure, and other declarations in the unit must be incorporated in the appropriate parts of any program that would otherwise use the unit. Any initialization statements for the unit must be placed at the beginning of the statement part of the program. The disadvantage of this approach is that the distinction between the interface and implementation sections of the unit is lost, so all identifiers declared in the unit—and not just those declared in the interface—are accessible throughout the program in which the declarations and statements were incorporated.

Figure 10.24 shows a version of the program *Craps* that uses the unit *RandomNumberGenerator*; to shorten the program listing, some procedure declarations are indicated by comments rather than being given in full. *Reseed* and *Random,* which are imported from *RandomNumberGenerator,* are accessible from throughout

Figure 10.24   A version of the Pascal program *Craps* using the unit
RandomNumberGenerator. For brevity, some procedure
declarations are indicated by comments rather than being
written out in full.

```
program Craps (input, output);

{ Play craps with user }

uses RandomNumberGenerator;

var
    bankroll,          { Amount available to player for betting }
    bet,               { Amount bet on this round }
    seed: real;        { Value used for generating random numbers }
    won,               { True if player has won current round }
    playing: Boolean;  { True if game is to continue }


{ Declaration for GetStartingBankroll goes here }


{ Declaration for GetPlayersBet goes here }


procedure RollDice(var dice: integer);

{ Simulate roll of dice; print value rolled on each die and return their sum
  as value of dice }

var
    die1, die2: integer;
begin
    Random(6, die1);
    Random(6, die2);
    writeln('You rolled a ', die1:1, ' and a ', die2:1);
    dice := die1 + die2
end; { RollDice }


procedure PlayRemainingRolls (point: integer;
                                    var won: Boolean);

{ Roll dice until user makes point or craps out }
```

```
var
    dice: integer;
begin
    repeat
        RollDice(dice)
    until (dice = point) or (dice = 7);
    won := (dice = point)
end; { PlayRemainingRolls }


procedure PlayOneRound(var won: Boolean);

{ Play one round; determine whether player wins or loses }

var
    dice: integer;
begin
    RollDice (dice);
    case dice of
        7, 11:                  won := true;
        2, 3, 12:               won := false;
        4, 5, 6, 8, 9, 10:      PlayRemainingRolls (dice, won)
    end
end; { PlayOneRound }


{ Declaration for UpdatePlayersBankroll goes here }


begin { Craps }
    write('Enter number between 0 and 1: ');
    readln(seed);
    Reseed(seed);
    GetStartingBankroll(bankroll);
    repeat
        writeln;
        GetPlayersBet(bankroll, bet);
        PlayOneRound(won);
        UpdatePlayersBankroll(bankroll, bet, won, playing)
    until not playing
end.
```

Figure 10.25   Pascal program *Towers* corresponding to the algorithm in
Figure 10.15.

```
program Towers(input, output);

{ Solve the Towers of Hanoi problem }

var
    NumberOfDisks: integer;


procedure MoveDisks(n: integer; source, dest, aux: char);

{ Move n disks from peg source to peg dest using peg aux as the auxiliary
  peg }

begin
    if n = 1 then
        writeln('Move disk 1 from peg ', source,
                ' to peg ', dest)
    else
        begin
            MoveDisks(n − 1, source, aux, dest);
            writeln('Move disk ', n:1, ' from peg ', source,
                    ' to peg ', dest);
            MoveDisks(n − 1, aux, dest, source)
        end
end; { MoveDisks }


begin { Towers }
    write('How many disks? ');
    readln(NumberOfDisks);
    while NumberOfDisks > 0 do
        begin
            MoveDisks(NumberOfDisks, 'A', 'C', 'B');
            writeln;
            write('How many disks? ');
            readln(NumberOfDisks)
        end
end.
```

Figure 10.26 Pascal program *PrintFactorials* corresponding to the algorithm in Figure 10.16.

```pascal
program PrintFactorials(input, output);

{ Test Factorial by printing a short table of factorials }

var
    i: integer;


function Factorial(n: integer): integer;

{ Compute factorial of positive integer }

begin
    if n = 1 then
        Factorial := 1
    else
        Factorial := n * Factorial(n − 1)
end; { Factorial }


begin { PrintFactorials }
    writeln('Number':15, 'Factorial':15);
    writeln;
    for i := 1 to 7 do
        writeln(i:15, Factorial(i):15)
end.
```

Craps. Reseed is invoked from the statement part of *Craps,* and *Random* is invoked from the procedure *RollDice.*

Recursion

Like most modern programming languages, Pascal provides a separate private data area for each invocation of a function or procedure, thus allowing recursive invocations. (FORTRAN, in constrast, does not necessarily provide a separate data area for each invocation of a function or procedure, so recursion is not allowed in FORTRAN.) Since Pascal supports recursion, recursive functions and procedures can be translated from the algorithmic language into Pascal with little change.

Figure 10.27 Pascal program *RabbitProblem* corresponding to the algorithm in Figure 10.17.

```
program RabbitProblem(input, output);

{ Solve Fibonacci's rabbit problem }

var
    months: integer;


function Fibonacci(n: integer): integer;

{ Compute nth term of Fibonacci sequence }

begin
    if n = 0 then
        Fibonacci := 0
    else if n = 1 then
        Fibonacci := 1
    else
        Fibonacci := Fibonacci(n − 1) + Fibonacci(n − 2)
end; { Fibonacci }


begin { RabbitProblem }
    write('Number of months? ');
    readln(months);
    writeln('After ', months:1, ' months you will have ',
            Fibonacci(months + 2):1, ' pairs')
end.
```

Figures 10.25, 10.26, and 10.27 show programs incorporating recursive functions and procedures. The program in Figure 10.25 solves the Towers of Hanoi problem; the program in Figure 10.26 prints a table of factorials; and the program in Figure 10.27 uses a grossly inefficient recursive implementation of the function *Fibonacci* to solve Fibonacci's rabbit problem.

Figure 10.29 shows a version of the rabbit-problem program that uses the unit *Counter* to count the number of calls to the function *Fibonacci* and thus reveal the computational inefficiency of the recursive definition of *Fibonacci*. The unit *Counter* itself is given in Figure 10.28.

Figure 10.28   Pascal unit *Counter* corresponding to the module *Counter*
discussed in the main text.

```pascal
unit Counter;

interface
    procedure Clear;
    procedure Increment;
    function Reading: integer;

implementation
    var
        count: integer;

    procedure Clear;
    begin
        count := 0
    end; { Clear }

    procedure Increment;
    begin
        count := count + 1
    end; { Increment }

    function Reading;
    begin
        Reading := count
    end; { Reading }

begin
    Clear
end. { Counter }
```

Figure 10.29   This version of the Pascal program *RabbitProblem*
corresponds to the algorithm in Figure 10.18. The program
uses the unit *Counter* to count the number of times the
function *Fibonacci* is invoked.

```pascal
program RabbitProblem(input, output);

{ Solve Fibonacci's rabbit problem }

uses Counter;

var
    months: integer;


function Fibonacci(n: integer): integer;

{ Compute nth term of Fibonacci sequence }

begin
    Increment;   { Count current call to Fibonacci }
    if n = 0 then
        Fibonacci := 0
    else if n = 1 then
        Fibonacci := 1
    else
        Fibonacci := Fibonacci(n − 1) + Fibonacci(n − 2)
end; { Fibonacci }


begin { RabbitProblem }
    Clear; { Clear counter (optional) }
    write('Number of months? ');
    readln(months);
    writeln('After ', months:1, ' months you will have ',
            Fibonacci(months + 2):1, ' pairs');
    writeln('Number of calls to Fibonacci: ',
            Reading:1)   { Display counter reading }
end.
```

11

Software design, coding, and testing

omputer hardware technology has continually advanced since the earliest days of electronic computers. The cost of computers has steadily declined while their memory capacity and speed of operation has steadily increased. The microprocessor revolution has brought low-cost computing to millions of people. Recent advances in microprocessor and memory-chip technology should allow owners of personal computers to run many programs that would have once required minicomputers or mainframes.

Unfortunately, there has been no such dramatic advance in software technology. As computers have become capable of executing larger and more complex programs, the difficulty of writing those programs has increased enormously. Software development projects are often completed far behind schedule, and the programs they produce still contain many errors or *bugs*. For example, one mainframe operating system developed in the 1960s consumed 5,000 worker-years of effort, was completed years after the scheduled release date, and when released contained about 1,000 bugs. What's more, the number of bugs remained about the same through successive revisions of the system because changes intended to correct one bug usually introduced others.

The difficulty of developing reliable software at predictable cost and on a predictable schedule is often referred to as the *software crisis*. Since computers require software for every useful function they perform, the software crisis prevents us from taking full advantage of the dramatic advances in computer hardware technology.

11.1

Software engineering

The software crisis has given rise to the discipline of *software engineering*. Engineers apply scientific and technical knowledge to create useful products. The engineer must be concerned not only with the scientific and technical details of a product, but with the practical problems of developing a usable product on an acceptable schedule at an acceptable cost. Characteristics such as performance, reliability, ease of use, and cost of the finished product often must be traded off to meet customer needs or to stay within the time schedule and budget for product development. Software engineering seeks to apply such technical, economic, and managerial considerations to the development of computer programs.

Software engineering emphasizes a systematic approach to designing, implementing, and testing programs. In the past, programmers often plunged immediately into *coding*—writing statements in a programming language—without first gaining sufficient information about the problem to be solved and the best program design for solving it. Software engineering, in contrast, advocates the following *software development life cycle:*

Requirements analysis

Specification

Design

Implementation (coding)

Testing

Maintenance

Requirements analysis determines what requirements a program must satisfy to solve the problem at hand and to meet the user's needs for acceptable performance, reliability, cost, and development time. The *specification* phase determines the detailed operation of the program, such as what output must be produced for each possible set of input data. The *design* phase determines the overall structure of the program, such as how it will be divided into modules.* In the *implementation* phase, modules are coded in a programming language, then compiled and linked into an executable program. *Testing* seeks to determine if the resulting program meets its specifications. Testing often overlaps other phases, particularly implementation. For example, modules are often tested individually before being combined into a single program. *Maintenance* refers to changes that must be made after a program has been released and is in use. Such changes are needed to correct bugs that were not discovered during testing and to modify the program to meet changes in the user's needs.

---

*In this chapter we will use the term *module* for any program that performs a well-defined function. The term thus applies to algorithms, functions, and procedures as well as to the algorithmic-language modules introduced in Chapter 10. To designate the algorithmic-language modules we will use the term ''module construction.''

Software engineering is oriented toward large software projects in which the problems of specification, design, testing, and project management are at their worst. But the principles of software engineering can be applied to much smaller projects, such as programs that individuals write for personal use or as classroom assignments. Individuals will not, of course, need to produce all the formal documents required for a large project. The specifications and design, for example, may be scribbled on the back of an envelope or even kept in the programmer's head. Yet taking time to think through the requirements, specification, design, and testing strategy will result in a much better program than if the programmer had plunged immediately and thoughtlessly into coding.

11.2 Characteristics of high-quality software

Low-quality software is easily recognized. A poor-quality program may produce erroneous output, or it may "crash." This term refers to two kinds of malfunction: (1) the program is terminated prematurely by the operating system for attempting an erroneous operation, such as trying to divide by zero; and (2) the program causes the computer to hang up in a nonterminating repetition.

Recognizing high-quality software is more difficult. It is generally accepted, however, that a high-quality program will be *reliable, testable, usable, efficient, portable,* and *maintainable.*

Reliability A program is reliable if it is *correct* and *robust.* A correct program is one that meets its specifications. For any valid input data, the program produces the output called for by the specifications. A robust program is one that continues to execute despite such problems as invalid input data, hardware malfunctions, and even errors within the program itself.

A robust program never crashes or produces erroneous output because of problems in its operating environment. If the user enters invalid input data, the program responds with an informative error message detailing precisely why the input was unacceptable. If a hardware device, such as a printer, malfunctions, the program informs the user of the problem. It then gives the user the opportunity to correct the problem and continue execution of the program. If the program finds that it cannot continue execution, it should terminate only after informing the user of the problem and making sure that none of the data entrusted to it will be lost.

Testability Testability refers to the ease with which the program can be tested for proper operation. The specifications should state precisely the behavior that the program is to exhibit; testing is meaningless if we are not sure what the program is to do in the first place. Sets of test data that exercise every function of the program should be prepared. The program should be constructed from well-defined modules, which can be tested individually. To help monitor the internal workings of a program, we can provide it with a *test mode.* When the test mode is activated, the program prints many data values that it uses in its internal calculations but that are not normally produced as output.

Usability   Regardless of its technical characteristics, a program must be a practical and convenient tool for accomplishing the task for which it was designed. For example, the proper use of the program should be reasonably obvious to someone who understands the task to be accomplished but has little or no experience with computers. It should not be necessary to study lengthy and complex user's manuals before being able to use the program. Programs with these characteristics are called user-friendly. Most mainframe and minicomputer software is not user-friendly. Microcomputer software is steadily becoming more user-friendly as software publishers strive to sell their wares to managers, doctors, teachers, shopkeepers, and others who wish to use computers as tools without having to become computer experts.

Efficiency   An efficient program executes as rapidly as possible and uses as little memory as possible. Users of large computers are often charged according to the central-processor time and the amount of memory that a program uses, so an inefficient program may be too expensive to run. An interactive program may be inconvenient to use if it is so inefficient that there is a long delay between the user's request and the computer's response. A program can be so inefficient as to be completely unusable, such as if it must run for days or weeks to produce an answer needed in minutes or hours.

Important as efficiency is, programmers are often prematurely concerned with it. They tend to write obscure, hard-to-understand programs because the obscure code is marginally more efficient than a more straightforward and understandable version. Experience shows, however, that only a small part of a program's code has a significant effect on the program's running time. Thus, the modern approach is to design and code a program for clarity and simplicity. One can then later modify any small sections that are shown through testing to be bottlenecks for program efficiency.

Portability   A program is portable if it can be readily adapted for use on computer systems other than the one for which it was originally written. Portability is important whenever programs are to be distributed to persons or organizations who may not all use the same computer system. Portability is clearly important to software publishers, who would like to sell their wares to users of many different kinds of computer systems.

One method of making a program portable is to write it in a standardized, widely used higher-level language. Unfortunately, the best standardized and most widely used programming languages are the older ones, such as FORTRAN and COBOL, which do not provide many of the language features demanded by modern structured programming. Thus, there may be a tradeoff between portability and program structure and clarity.

What's more, there may be a tradeoff between portability and user-friendliness. The latter is often enhanced by making full use of the hardware features of a particular computer system: color and graphics displays, pointing devices such as light pens and mice, and special-purpose function keys that can be used as pushbuttons for controlling a program. But a program written to use such features would be difficult to adapt to a computer system that lacks some or all of them.

Maintainability Maintainability refers to the ease with which a program can be modified to correct bugs or to improve its performance. The programmers who maintain a program usually are not the same ones who wrote it originally. Since a programmer cannot modify a program without first understanding how it works, simplicity and clarity are keys to maintainability. Also important are modularity, which allows part of the program to be modified without affecting other parts, and testability, which allows the program to be tested for correct operation after changes have been made.

11.3 Requirements analysis

In the remainder of this chapter, one section is devoted to each of the six stages of the software development life cycle. To provide a concrete example of the development process, we will specify, design, and implement a simple simulation program.

Requirements analysis seeks to understand the problem at hand and produce a *requirements definition* describing an appropriate solution. The considerations of requirements analysis may go far beyond merely specifying a piece of computer software. First it must be determined whether a general-purpose computer is the best tool for solving the problem. Perhaps the job in question should be done manually, or perhaps a special-purpose machine, such as a dedicated word processor, should be used. If a computer solution is decided upon, will a microcomputer, minicomputer, mainframe, or supercomputer be needed? Can an existing computer system be used, can the needed computer time be purchased from a service bureau, or should one or more new computers be acquired for this application?

Once a computer system is selected, the next step is to determine the requirements for the software that will enable the system to solve the problem at hand. The requirements definition for the software focuses on the task to be accomplished. Details of program operation are specified only to the degree needed to assure that the task will be accomplished as desired. The remaining operational details will be determined in the specification phase. For example, the requirements definition might specify that a program will print certain reports containing certain information. It will probably be left to the specification phase, however, to determine the exact format in which each report is to be printed.

The requirements definition must also detail the level of performance required for the program. How much memory will the program require? How rapidly should the program respond to user input? Will the program be used by experienced computer operators or by computer novices who will require a high degree of user-friendliness? What degree of reliability is required? To what extent can erroneous output and program failures be tolerated? What features are needed to prevent unauthorized persons from gaining access to sensitive data manipulated by the program?

Our first thought might be to specify that the program be perfectly reliable, or at least come as close to that goal as possible. We must not forget, however, the impact of such a high reliability requirement on the cost and time for program development and perhaps on other factors, such as program efficiency. In certain critical applications, such as a program for controlling a nuclear reactor, no effort can be spared to assure the highest possible reliability. In less critical applications, however, an occasional program failure may be a reasonable price to pay for developing the program on an acceptable schedule and at an acceptable cost.

One problem with developing a requirements definition is that the prospective users may be unsure about what they really want. They may be unfamiliar with the capabilities of computer systems and unsure about the best ways to apply computers to their problems. They may have difficulty in visualizing exactly how the use of a computer system will affect their day-to-day work. Possible solutions are to study the computer systems used by other organizations in the same or related areas and to use a consultant experienced in applying computers in the desired area. It is not unusual for the requirements definition and specification to be changed after the implementation phase when users realize that the system that was implemented is not what they "really wanted."

Simulation of a waiting line   Simulation programs mimic the behavior of real-world systems such as factories, airports, and automobile traffic. The simulation programs serve as tools for investigating the behavior of the actual systems. As an example of program development, we will specify, design, and implement a program for simulating a waiting line. Waiting-line simulations are the basis for many more complex simulations, which often involve many interacting waiting lines.

Our task for now is to define the requirements for a program to simulate the waiting line. We begin, as requirements analysis always should, with the problem to be solved or, in this case, the system to be simulated.

We imagine a store having a single checkout counter. As customers complete their purchases, they line up at the counter to be checked out. It is the waiting line at the checkout counter that we wish to simulate. We can think of the waiting line as being interposed between the shopping area and the checkout counter. The shopping area serves as a source of customers arriving at the end of the line. The checkout counter serves as a destination for customers leaving the front of the line.

We have no way of knowing the times at which customers will arrive at the end of the line or the time required to check out each customer. What we can do, however, is collect statistics on checkout times and times between arrivals. Observation might show, for example, that 15% of the customers are checked out in one minute, 30% in two minutes, 40% in three minutes, 10% in four minutes, and 5% in five minutes. In the simulation, the checkout times and times between arrivals will be determined by a random number generator, so these will not coincide with the corresponding times for any actual line. We will make sure, however, that the statistics for arrivals and checkouts are the same for both the simulation and the actual line. That is, for both the simulation and the actual line, 15% of the customers will get checked out in one minute, 30% in two minutes, and so on.

We would normally run a waiting-line simulation to determine if the line will be long enough to seriously inconvenience customers, perhaps causing them to do their shopping elsewhere in the future. Therefore, we are interested in the average length of the line and the greatest length to which it is likely to grow. We are also interested in the general behavior of the line. Does it steadily become longer, or does it maintain a fixed length? Or is it, perhaps, usually empty, growing longer only occasionally when a number of customers happen to arrive within a short time interval?

Our program, then, will print for each simulation run the average length of the line and the greatest length that was reached during the run. To help us judge the overall behavior of the line, the program will print the length of the line minute by minute during the run. The minute-by-minute behavior of the line would best be displayed graphically, perhaps with a line on the display screen that would become longer and shorter as people entered and left the simulated checkout line. To avoid complex and hardware-dependent graphics programming, however, we will simply have our program print the number of customers in the line after each minute of simulated time.

These considerations allow us to write the requirements definition shown in Figure 11.1. Without going too deeply into details, the requirements definition states what the program will do, what type of input it will receive, and what type of output it will produce. Note that the statistics for checkout times and times between arrivals are to be written into the program; the alternatives would be to have them entered by the user or read from a data file.

The program must be able to handle simulation runs of up to 20 days of simulated time, which is much longer than is actually likely to be needed. If a longer run is requested, the program is allowed to fail. For example, the program might be terminated by the operating system with the error message "integer overflow," indicating that the program attempted to exceed the largest available value for type *integer*.

Figure 11.1   Requirements definition for the waiting-line simulation.

Requirements Definition for Waiting-Line Simulation

The program will simulate a waiting line at a checkout counter. Statistics for checkout times and times between arrivals at the end of the line will be incorporated in the program. The program is to be run interactively on a microcomputer. At the start of each program run, the program will ask the user to enter a seed for the random number generator and to enter the number of minutes of simulated time that the simulation is to be run. The program will print the length of the line for each minute of simulated time. After the simulation has run for the requested number of minutes, the program will print the average and maximum lengths of the simulated line.

The program must be able to handle simulation runs of up to 20 days (28,800 minutes) of simulated time. If a longer time is requested, a program failure may occur.

Allowing the program to fail for unreasonable input data simplifies the program, making it easier to develop and understand, at the expense of its robustness and user-friendliness. This part of the requirements definition is included not to demonstrate the best possible programming practice but to illustrate a situation in which some reliability and robustness are traded for a compensating advantage.

11.4 Specification

The *functional specification* describes as precisely as possible the operations that a program must carry out. The specification states *what* the program must do but not *how* the program is to do it. The functional specification is an elaboration of the requirements definition, and the two are sometimes combined into a single document. The requirements definition, however, focuses on what is needed to solve the problem at hand in a manner satisfactory to the user. The functional specification, in contrast, describes one particular program (one of many, perhaps) that meets the needs set forth in the requirements definition.

The functional specification describes in detail the inputs and outputs for the program. Where will the input data be obtained? From the operator's keyboard? From remote terminals? From punched cards? From tape or disk files? What outputs are to be produced? Reports? Bills? Checks? Graphics displays? What is the format of the records in the input files? Of data entered at the keyboard? Of the operator's display screen? Of the reports and other documents that the program is to produce? What permanent data files, such as a file of customer accounts, are to be accessed? Which are to be updated? What are the formats of the records in the permanent files?

The functional specification must also state how the program's output is related to its input. Sometimes this is easy to do. In business applications, for example, many data items, such as people's names, are passed unchanged from input to output. Other output data items, such as a worker's gross wages, are obtained by means of simple calculations done on the input data. It's easy for the functional specification to describe exactly how each output data item is to be obtained or computed from the input data.

For more sophisticated programs, however, stating the relation between the input and output data precisely may be extremely difficult, and we may have to be satisfied with an intuitive description. Consider a compiler. In general, we know that the input to the compiler is a program written in a given higher-level language and that the compiler's output is an equivalent program in the machine language of a particular computer. But no one has yet discovered any concise, precise method of stating the relation between the input and output of a compiler, one that would let us easily see what machine codes the compiler would produce as output for each higher-level language program presented as input.

The functional specification can be used to produce test data for determining whether the finished program meets the specification. Each set of test data consists of a set of input data and the corresponding output data that, according to the specification, the program should produce. Such sets of test data are most easily generated when there is a simple, easily described relationship between the program's input and output.

The functional specification may elaborate on the requirements definition by setting additional performance goals in such areas as response time, memory usage, reliability, and portability. Because the specification clearly indicates the size and complexity of the software to be produced, it can be used for estimating the time, funds, and personnel that will be required for development.

Figure 11.2 shows the functional specification for the program for simulating a waiting line. The input, output, and the relation between the two are described in much more detail than in the requirements definition. Note that this program is one of those in which there is no simple, easily described relation between input and output. The only way to actually predict the program's output would be to simulate the program's operation either by hand or by another computer program. The simulation would have to duplicate the operation of the program's pseudorandom number generator, which is used to determine arrival and checkout times.

11.5 Design

The design phase determines how the program will carry out the operations called for by the functional specification. The program is divided into small, manageable parts, each of which serves a clearly defined purpose. The programmer chooses data structures—that is, decides how the data processed by the program is to be represented inside the computer. Algorithms are chosen for major operations such as sorting. When the design is completed, all the difficult decisions will have been made, and coding the program in a particular programming language should be a straightforward process.

Modularity and information hiding   The functional specification describes the overall operation of the entire program. The entire program, however, is likely to be far too complex for the programmer to keep all the details in mind at the same time. The first task of the program designer is to divide the program into smaller, more manageable parts in such a way that the operations of the individual parts as well as the relationships among different parts will be as clear as possible. These parts are called *modules* and are usually implemented as functions, procedures, or special module constructions such as those introduced in Chapter 10.

One of the most important principles for dividing a program into modules is *information hiding*. The variables that the program is to manipulate are divided into groups, each of which plays some well-defined role in the program. Each group of variables is hidden inside a module construction. The module construction provides functions and procedures for accessing and manipulating the variables in ways that are meaningful according to the roles they play in the program. All access to the variables from outside the module construction is via these functions and procedures.

Hiding variables in module constructions is often referred to as *data abstraction,* since we can think of the data manipulations not in terms of assignments to the hidden variables but rather in terms of the abstract operations defined by the functions

Figure 11.2   Functional specification for the waiting-line simulation.

Functional Specification for Waiting-Line Simulation

The program is to simulate the behavior of a waiting line. Simulated time is measured in minutes. Checkout times and times between customer arrivals at the end of the line are determined by a pseudorandom number generator. Checkout times and times between customer arrivals are governed by the following tables, each of which gives the percentage of cases in which the time interval in question is one, two, three, four, or five minutes:

Time Between Arrivals		*Checkout Time*	
Time (min)	*Percentage*	*Time (min)*	*Percentage*
1	10	1	15
2	25	2	30
3	50	3	40
4	10	4	10
5	5	5	5

The simulation begins with the waiting line empty. At one minute into the simulation, a customer arrives at the end of the line and, because the line is empty, immediately begins to check out. (Thus the waiting line remains empty.) Thereafter, arrivals and checkout completions occur at random times governed by the statistics given in the previous paragraph.

Input to the program is entered on the keyboard by the user. The program requires two items of input: a seed for the pseudorandom number generator and the number of minutes of simulated time that the simulation is to run. The dialogue with the user is as follows, with underlined items showing typical user responses:

```
Enter seed for random number generator: .7321945
Number of minutes simulation is to run: 500
```

The random number generator seed should be in the range 0 to 1 (not including 1). The number of minutes the simulation is to run should be in the range 1 through 28,800. Input values outside these ranges may cause program failure or meaningless output. Improperly formatted input data, such as a real number with two decimal points, may also cause program failure.

Output is sent to the computer's standard output device, usually a video display. As the simulation runs, the program outputs a table giving the length of the line at one-minute intervals. The table has the following form:

Time	Length
1	0
2	1
3	1
4	2
5	1
etc	

When the simulation is completed (the maximum simulated time specified by the user is reached), the program prints the average length of the simulated line and the maximum length reached in the following form:

```
Average length: 1.1
Maximum length: 5
```

and procedures. The software designer can specify a module construction by describing the abstract operations. It is then left to the person coding the module construction to determine how the data is to be represented as values of variables and how those variables are to be manipulated by the functions and procedures that implement the abstract operations.

Function, procedure, and data packages such as the module constructions in the algorithmic language are introduced into programming languages specifically for the purpose of information hiding. When information hiding is not an issue, modules can be implemented equally well as functions or procedures.

Top-down design   Top-down design derives from the problem-solving technique whereby a problem is broken down into subproblems, these subproblems are broken down into still simpler subproblems, and so on until subproblems that can be readily solved are obtained. In program design, we start with a top-level module whose job is to solve the problem described in the program specifications. We break this problem down into subproblems, and allow the top-level module to call on a subordinate module to handle each subproblem. The problem to be solved by each subordinate module can be broken down into still further subproblems, which are handled by other subordinate modules, and so on.

One successful application of top-down design is *stepwise refinement,* which is usually used to design a single algorithm, function, or procedure that does not call on other modules. We first write an English-language description of the job that the entire algorithm, function, or procedure is to accomplish. We then *refine* this description by replacing it with a series of descriptions giving the steps by which the original task can be accomplished. Each of these steps can, in turn, be replaced by a series of smaller steps until we arrive at steps that can be expressed as statements in a programming language rather than by English-language descriptions.

Top-down design is also effective when all modules are functions and procedures. At the top level, we decide what steps are needed to carry out the task specified for the main algorithm and call a function or procedure for each step. When writing each of these functions or procedures, we can break its assigned task down into still smaller steps, which additional functions and procedures are called to carry out, and so on.

This approach to top-down design is well illustrated by the craps-playing algorithm in Figure 10.4. The structure chart in Figure 10.5 illustrates the procedure hierarchy, with the main algorithm at the top and the procedures that perform the simplest tasks at the bottom. The program design can be presented as a structure chart together with a description of the task to be carried out by each function and procedure.

Top-down design with functions and procedures is popular in programming languages that do not provide module constructions. Two languages with which this technique is often used are standard Pascal and COBOL. Neither language supports information hiding. In standard Pascal, variables accessed by functions and procedures must either be global variables or passed as parameters. COBOL provides two procedurelike constructions: *paragraphs* and *subroutines.* Paragraphs can only access global variables, whereas subroutines can only access variables passed as parameters.

When a program is organized around module constructions rather than procedures and functions, the principle of information hiding may play as great a role as that of top-down design for structuring the program into modules. Rather than starting with the problem to be solved and asking how it can be divided into subproblems, we may look instead at the data structures needed to solve the problem and specify a module to manage each.

Top-down design and information hiding can sometimes complement one another. For example, we may have to break a problem down into subproblems in order to see what data structures will be needed for the program's calculations. Once the data structures have been decided upon, information hiding can be applied to determine the modular structure of the program.

In direct contrast to top-down design is *bottom-up design,* in which the bottom-level modules are designed first, then the modules on the next higher level, and so on until the top-level module is reached. While bottom-up design would probably not be applied systematically to a large programming project, there are sometimes good reasons for designing, and perhaps even implementing, some low-level modules before designing the rest of the program. The low-level modules are usually responsible for such basic tasks as updating the display screen and storing data on disk. The speed with which these tasks can be accomplished may strongly influence the design of the rest of the program. For example, the design of a word processor is likely to be influenced by whether the display can be updated fast enough to keep up with the user's typing, and the data structures selected for storing a data base may depend on how rapidly data can be transferred to and from disk.

Top-down design assumes that we know enough about solving the problem at hand with a computer that we can readily determine the best way to divide the problem into subproblems. Such is most likely to be true when the program to be written is a routine one, such as a business data-processing program, or when it is based on well-understood principles, as is the case for most compilers. If, however, we start with no idea of how to solve the given problem with a computer, considerable thought and experimentation with a computer may be needed to arrive at a suitable design. Such thought and experimentation is unlikely to follow a strict top-down pattern. While we may have an inspiration as to how a certain needed operation can be broken down into simpler steps, our next inspiration may tell us how some of the low-level operations with which we have experimented can be combined to achieve a higher-level result.

In short, dividing a problem into subproblems is an important problem-solving technique, and likewise the top-down approach is an important program-design technique. But other principles, such as information hiding, the need to evaluate the performance of low-level modules, and the need to understand the solution before beginning the design may also play important roles. We should not follow one design principle rigidly to the exclusion of all others, but should try to bring all our knowledge of the programming process to bear on the problem at hand. In programming, we need all the help we can get and can ill afford to ignore any principles that experience has shown to be fruitful.

The waiting-line simulation: modular structure   We will now return to our example for this chapter, the program for simulating a waiting line, and determine how to structure it into modules. Our design approach will be basically top-down; however, the principle of information hiding will also play an important role.

A fundamental design decision for any simulation program is how time is to be handled. In the real world, time flows continuously, so that between any two instants of time there is an infinite number of intermediate instants. Computers can only deal with finite, discrete quantities, however, so a simulation program must compute the state of the simulated system only at certain discrete instants of time, such as every second, every minute, or every hour.

The specifications for the waiting-line simulation require that the length of the waiting line be printed every minute of simulated time. The statistics for checkout times and times between arrivals are also given in terms of minutes. Thus, we will choose the minute as our basic unit of simulated time and compute the state of the waiting line every minute. A fundamental operation of the program will be to advance the simulation by one minute. Given the current state of the simulated system, the program must calculate the state the system will be in after one minute has elapsed.

We begin in proper top-down fashion with the top-level module, which is the main algorithm *SimulationOfWaitingLine*. The main algorithm will handle such routine chores as accepting the input data, stepping the simulation through the number of minutes requested by the user, printing the time and length of the line each minute, and computing and printing the average and maximum line lengths. After printing each time and length, the main algorithm will call the procedure *AdvanceToNextState* to advance the simulation by one minute. So far, then, our simulation consists of a main algorithm and one procedure, as shown in Figure 11.3.

To advance the state of the simulation, *AdvanceToNextState* must invoke operations provided by the modules that actually represent the simulated system. How are these modules to be chosen? One suggestion comes from the physical structure of the system being simulated: customers come from the shopping area, pass through the waiting line, and end up at the checkout counter. Therefore, we might use one module for the shopping area, which serves as a source of customers; one for the waiting line, through which customers pass; and one for the checkout counter, which is the customers' final destination.

This modularization also makes sense in terms of information hiding. With the shopping area we associate one value, the time at which a customer will next be ready to get in line. With the waiting line we associate one value, the length of the line. And with the checkout counter we associate one value, the time at which the counter will next be free. If each value is hidden inside the corresponding module and manipulated only by the operations of that module, the principle of information hiding will be observed.

Figure 11.4 shows the structure chart with the addition of the modules *ShoppingArea, WaitingLine,* and *CheckoutCounter. AdvanceToNextState* uses operations provided by these modules to move customers from the shopping area to the waiting line and from the waiting line to the checkout counter.

Two additional modules are needed to complete the design. Several modules need to know the current simulated time; this is provided by a module *Clock*. And the modules *ShoppingArea* and *CheckoutCounter* each needs a source of pseudorandom numbers for determining times between arrivals and checkout times; these are

Figure 11.3   Modularization of the the waiting-line simulation after the first- and second-level modules have been chosen. The top-level module, the main algorithm *SimulationOfWaitingLine*, calls one second-level module, the procedure *AdvanceToNextState*. The unterminated lines labeled *Time, Length,* and *Reseed* indicate that the top-level module needs access to these two functions and a procedure; at this point in the design, however, it is not clear which modules will provide *Time, Length,* and *Reseed.*

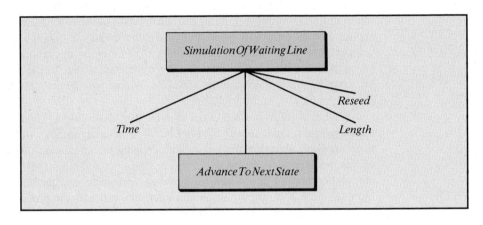

provided by the module *RandomNumberGenerator*. In terms of information hiding, the *Clock* module hides the current time and the *RandomNumberGenerator* module hides the current random number seed.

Figure 11.5 shows the complete modularization of the waiting-line simulation. Note that modules may make use not only of the modules on the next level down but of those on any lower level. For example, the top-level module must read the clock and get the length of the waiting line to print times and lengths, and it must provide a new seed to the random number generator. The second-level module, *AdvanceToNextState,* must advance the time shown on the clock.

The waiting-line simulation: specifying the modules   To complete the design, we must describe precisely the operations carried out by each module. It is usually much easier to provide a concise, precise specification for a module than it is to do the same for the entire program, which is one reason for dividing the program into modules in the first place. Figure 11.6 shows the module specifications.

One popular method for specifying algorithms, functions, and procedures is *pseudocode*—a high-level, Englishlike description of what the module is to accomplish. We will use this technique for the main algorithm *SimulationOfWaitingLine* and the procedure *AdvanceToNextState.*

The pseudocode for the main algorithm tells us that the algorithm must take the following steps:

Figure 11.4   Modularization of the waiting-line simulation after the third-level modules *ShoppingArea, WaitingLine,* and *Checkout-Counter* have been chosen. Unterminated lines indicate that various modules need access to the functions and procedures *Time, AdvanceClock, Rnd,* and *Reseed.*

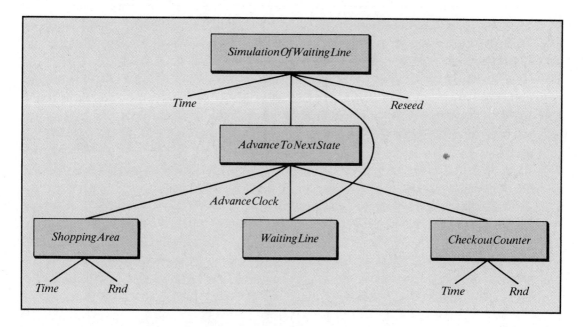

1. Obtain a random number seed from the user and pass the seed to the module *RandomNumberGenerator.*

2. Obtain from the user the number of minutes the simulation is to run.

3. For each minute of the simulation, call *AdvanceToNextState* to advance the state of the simulation by one minute. After each call to *AdvanceToNextState,* print the simulated time (obtained from the module *Clock*) and the length of the simulated line (obtained from the module *WaitingLine*). Keep a running total of the waiting line lengths and keep track of the longest length reached.

4. Compute the average length of the waiting line by dividing the total of the waiting line lengths (computed in step 3) by the number of minutes the simulation ran. Print the average length and the maximum length of the waiting line.

The procedure *AdvanceToNextStep* must advance the clock reading by one minute and, when possible, move a person from the shopping area to the waiting line and a person from the waiting line to the checkout counter:

1. Advance the clock reading by one minute.

Figure 11.5   The complete modularization of the waiting-line simulation.
The fourth-level modules *Clock* and *RandomNumber-*
Generator provide the remaining functions and procedures
required by the higher-level modules.

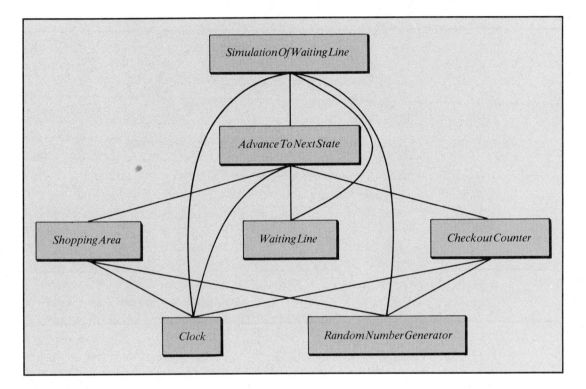

2. If a person in the shopping area is waiting to get in line, remove the person
   from the shopping area and place him or her in the waiting line.

3. If the waiting line is not empty and the checkout counter is free, remove a
   person from the waiting line and start that person getting checked out.

For specifying module constructions, another method is often used. A module
construction typically provides *functions,* which return values to the calling module,
and *procedures,* which change the internal state of the module. We can specify the
module by describing the values returned by the functions and specifying how these
values are changed by the execution of the procedures. An advantage of this method
is that it tells us *what* the module does—what values it provides and how those values
can be changed—but it tells us nothing about *how* the module stores and manipulates
its data internally. Thus the implementor is left with maximum freedom to choose
the data structures and algorithms that the module is to use internally.

Figure 11.6   Module specifications for the waiting-line simulation.

Module Specifications for Waiting-Line Simulation

algorithm *SimulationOfWaitingLine*

PSEUDOCODE

1. Obtain a random number seed from the user and pass the seed to the module *RandomNumberGenerator*.

2. Obtain from the user the number of minutes the simulation is to run.

3. For each minute of the simulation, call *AdvanceToNextState* to advance the state of the simulation by one minute. After each call to *AdvanceToNextState*, print the simulated time (obtained from the module *Clock*) and the length of the simulated line (obtained from the module *WaitingLine*). Keep a running total of the waiting line lengths and keep track of the longest length reached.

4. Compute the average length of the waiting line by dividing the total of the waiting line lengths (computed in step 3) by the number of minutes the simulation ran. Print the average length and the maximum length of the waiting line.

procedure *AdvanceToNextState*

PSEUDOCODE

1. Advance the clock reading by one minute.

2. If a person in the shopping area is waiting to get in line, remove the person from the shopping area and place him or her in the waiting line.

3. If the waiting line is not empty and the checkout counter is free, remove a person from the waiting line and start that person getting checked out.

module *ShoppingArea*

FUNCTIONS

NewArrivalP: Returns *true* if a person in the shopping area is waiting to get in line and *false* otherwise.

PROCEDURES

AcceptNewArrival: Accepts (removes from the shopping area) a person who is ready to get in line. *AcceptNewArrival* can be called only when the value returned by *NewArrivalP* is *true*. After *AcceptNewArrival* is executed, *NewArrivalP* returns the value *false* and continues to do so until the simulated time has advanced to the point where another person is ready to get in line.

INITIAL VALUES

Before any calls to *AcceptNewArrival* have been executed, *NewArrivalP* returns the value *true*.

ERROR CONDITIONS

It is an error to call *AcceptNewArrival* when the value returned by *NewArrivalP* is *false*.

module *WaitingLine*

FUNCTIONS

Length: Returns an integer value giving the number of people currently in line.

PROCEDURES

PutPersonInLine: Puts one person in the waiting line. The value returned by *Length* is one greater after a call to *PutPersonInLine* than before.

RemovePersonFromLine: Removes one person from the waiting line. The value returned by *Length* is one less after a call to *RemovePersonFromLine* than before.

INITIAL VALUES

Before any calls to *PutPersonInLine* or *RemovePersonFromLine* have been executed, *Length* returns the value zero.

ERROR CONDITIONS

It is an error to call *RemovePersonFromLine* when the value returned by *Length* is zero.

module *CheckoutCounter*

FUNCTIONS

CounterFreeP: Returns *true* if the checkout counter is free to check out another customer and *false* otherwise.

PROCEDURES

StartCheckout: Initiates checkout of a customer. *StartCheckout* can be called only when the value returned by *CounterFreeP* is *true*. After *StartCheckout* has been called, the value returned by *CounterFreeP* is *false* and remains so until the simulated time has advanced to the point where the counter is once again free.

INITIAL VALUES

Before any calls to *StartCheckout* have been executed, *CounterFreeP* returns the value *true*.

ERROR CONDITIONS

It is an error to call *StartCheckout* when the value returned by *CounterFreeP* is *false*.

module *Clock*

FUNCTIONS

Time: Returns an integer value equal to the current time.

PROCEDURES

AdvanceClock: Advances the clock reading by one minute. The value returned by *Time* is one greater after a call to *AdvanceClock* than before.

INITIAL VALUES

Before any calls to *AdvanceClock* have been made, *Time* returns the value zero.

module *RandomNumberGenerator*

FUNCTIONS

Rnd: Returns a pseudorandomly generated real number in the range 0 to 1 (not including 1).

PROCEDURES

Reseed(*newSeed*): Provides the value *newSeed* as a seed value to the random number generator. The value of *newSeed* should be in the range 0 to 1 (not including 1), although most values outside that range will not cause an error. After a call to *Reseed,* the next value returned by *Rnd* is computed as if the previous value returned by *Rnd* was the value of *newSeed*.

ALGORITHMS
   The following algorithm is used for random number generation. Let r' be the value returned by a call to *Rnd* and r the value returned by the immediately preceding call to *Rnd*. The value of r' is related to that of r by

$$r' = FractionalPartOf((r + 3.1415927) ** 2)$$

where the function *FractionalPartOf* returns the part of its argument that lies to the right of the decimal point. After a call to *Reseed*, the value r' returned by the next call to *Rnd* is computed by the above formula with r replaced by the value of *newSeed*.

The simplest module construction in our design is the module *Clock,* which we can specify as follows:

FUNCTIONS
   Time: Returns an integer value equal to the current time.

PROCEDURES
   AdvanceClock: Advances the clock reading by one minute. The value returned by *Time* is one greater after a call to *AdvanceClock* than before.

INITIAL VALUES
   Before any calls to *AdvanceClock* have been made, *Time* returns the value zero.

The module *ShoppingArea* can be specified in like manner. This module serves as a source of customers; it must tell us when a new customer has arrived to get in line and must allow us to remove that customer from the shopping area to be placed in line. We will follow the convention of ending the name of a predicate—a Boolean function—with *P*. We can think of the *P* as a question mark; we invoke the predicate *NewArrivalP* to ask whether there is a new arrival at the end of the checkout line.

FUNCTIONS
   NewArrivalP: Returns *true* if a person in the shopping area is waiting to get in line and *false* otherwise.

PROCEDURES
   AcceptNewArrival: Accepts (removes from the shopping area) a person who is ready to get in line. *AcceptNewArrival* can be called only when the value returned by *NewArrivalP* is *true*. After *AcceptNewArrival* is executed, *NewArrivalP* returns the value *false* and continues to do so until the simulated time has advanced to the point where another person is ready to get in line.

INITIAL VALUES

Before any calls to *AcceptNewArrival* have been executed, *NewArrivalP* returns the value *true*.

ERROR CONDITIONS

It is an error to call *AcceptNewArrival* when the value returned by *NewArrivalP* is *false*.

The same technique is used to specify the other module constructions. The module *RandomNumberGenerator* is unique in that it provides a function, *Rnd,* that both returns a value and changes the internal state of the module. Although such state-changing functions are sometimes convenient, the specifications will usually be clearer if we restrict functions to returning values and use only procedures to change the internal state of the module.

Choosing algorithms   Algorithms for simple tasks such as printing tables and computing averages are best left to the implementor rather than being specified by the designer. However for some tasks, such as sorting, a number of algorithms have been studied and analyzed in the computer science literature. Thus such performance factors as running time and memory usage are known for each algorithm. Some algorithms are known to be better suited than others for use with particular hardware configurations. In this situation, the designer may choose an algorithm known to be able to provide the desired performance on the hardware to be used.

The only algorithm specified in the design for the waiting-line simulation is the algorithm for generating pseudorandom numbers. Many such algorithms are known and have been analyzed. Unfortunately, the details of many of these depend on the largest available value of type *integer*. It is difficult to use these algorithms effec-, tively with a computer that provides only 16-bit integers (maximum value 32,767), as do many minicomputers and microcomputers. To allow the simulation to be run on as many types of computers as possible, a simple "quick and dirty" algorithm is specified, even though the resulting numbers might not simulate truly random numbers as closely as those obtained with a hardware-dependent algorithm.

11.6   Implementation

In the implementation phase, the program is coded into the statements of a programming language. If the design has been done well, the implementation can be carried through by programmers of modest skills. On the other hand, if unanticipated difficulties are encountered during implementation—perhaps the program performs a certain operation too slowly—then it may be necessary to modify the design.

Usually the implementation and testing phases overlap, with substantial testing being done during implementation. The plan for testing may dictate the order in which modules are implemented. Nevertheless, this section focuses on implementation only, and all considerations of testing are deferred to the next section.

The techniques of *structured programming* should be followed in coding the program. That is, the code should be based on the three fundamental control constructions: *sequencing, selection,* and *repetition.* Selection and repetition should be implemented by means of high-level program constructions such as the **while, repeat, if,** and **select** constructions in the algorithmic language.

Occasionally, for reasons such as portability or compability with existing programs, one may have to use an older language that does not provide these high-level control constructions. In this case it may be possible to use a *preprocessor,* a translator that accepts a program containing the desired control constructions and translates it into a program in the standard version of the language.

The rest of this section describes the implementation of the waiting-line simulation. Although our implementation will be written in the algorithmic language, in practice one would use an actual programming language, such as Pascal, rather than a pseudolanguage. Figure 11.7 shows the implementation of the waiting-line simulation.

We assume that the maximum possible value of type *integer* is at least 32,767, which is likely to be true even for implementations on microcomputers. Since the specification only requires the program to handle simulated times up to 28,800 minutes, we can use integers for the various times with which the program must deal. We can also use an integer for the length of the waiting line, since this length can increase by at most one for each minute of the simulation. Since the specification allows the program to fail if a running time greater than 28,800 minutes is requested, the program does not have to check for the possibility of integer overflow—exceeding the maximum possible value of type *integer.*

SimulationOfWaitingLine   Given the pseudocode in the design, the implementation of the main algorithm is straightforward. The main algorithm uses the procedure *AdvanceToNextState* and the module constructions *WaitingLine, Clock,* and *RandomNumberGenerator.* From *WaitingLine* it imports the function *Length,* the current length of the waiting line. From *Clock* it imports the function *Time,* which returns the current simulated time. And from *RandomNumberGenerator* it imports the procedure *Reseed,* which provides a new seed for the random number generator.

To run the simulation, *AdvanceToNextState* is called repeatedly to advance the simulation by one minute. After each call to *AdvanceToNextState,* the values returned by *Time* and *Length* are printed. During the run, *totalLength* is used to hold a running total of all the lengths, and *maxLength* is used to hold the largest length reached. We declare *totalLength* as a real variable because the sum of a large number of line lengths could exceed the largest possible integer even though each of the lengths being added is less than this value.

After the simulation has run for the number of minutes requested by the user, the value of *totalLength* is used to calculate the average line length, and the average and maximum lengths are displayed for the user.

AdvanceToNextState   Like the main algorithm, the procedure *AdvanceToNextState* is straightforward to implement from the pseudocode given in the design. The procedure first calls *AdvanceClock* to advance the clock by one minute. Next it

Figure 11.7 Algorithmic-language implementation of the waiting-line simulation.

```
algorithm SimulationOfWaitingLine

{ Simulate waiting line at checkout counter }

declare
    import Length from WaitingLine
    import Time from Clock
    import Reseed from RandomNumberGenerator

    totalLength, averageLength, seed: real
    numberOfSteps, maxLength, i: integer
execute
    output 'Enter seed for random number generator: ', more
    input seed
    Reseed(seed)
    output 'Number of minutes simulation is to run: ', more
    input numberOfSteps
    totalLength ← 0.0
    maxLength ← 0
    output
    output 'Time', tab(11), 'Length'
    for i ← 1 to numberOfSteps
        AdvanceToNextState
        output Time, tab(11), Length
        totalLength ← totalLength + Length
        if Length > maxLength then
            maxLength ← Length
        endif
    endfor
    if numberOfSteps > 0 then
        averageLength ← totalLength / numberOfSteps
    else
        averageLength ← 0.0
    endif
    output
    output 'Average length: ', averageLength
    output 'Maximum length: ', maxLength
end SimulationOfWaitingLine


procedure AdvanceToNextState

{ Advances simulated system by one time unit }
```

```
declare
    import NewArrivalP, AcceptNewArrival from ShoppingArea
    import Length, PutPersonInLine, RemovePersonFromLine
            from WaitingLine
    import CounterFreeP, StartCheckout from CheckoutCounter
    import AdvanceClock from Clock
execute
    AdvanceClock
    if NewArrivalP then
        AcceptNewArrival
        PutPersonInLine
    endif
    if CounterFreeP and (Length > 0) then
        RemovePersonFromLine
        StartCheckout
    endif
end AdvanceToNextState
```

module *ShoppingArea*

{ Represents source of customers who are to get in line }

```
declare
    import Time from Clock
    import Rnd from RandomNumberGenerator
    export NewArrivalP, AcceptNewArrival

    timeOfNextArrival: integer
```

function *NewArrivalP*: *Boolean*

{ Check if customer is ready to get in line }

```
execute
    NewArrivalP ← (Time >= timeOfNextArrival)
end NewArrivalP
```

procedure *AcceptNewArrival*

{ Remove customer from shopping area. Set time at which another
  customer will be ready to get in line }

```
        declare
            random: real
        execute
            if NewArrivalP then
                random ← Rnd
                if random <= 0.10 then
                    timeOfNextArrival ← Time + 1
                elseif random <= 0.35 then
                    timeOfNextArrival ← Time + 2
                elseif random <= 0.85 then
                    timeOfNextArrival ← Time + 3
                elseif random <= 0.95 then
                    timeOfNextArrival ← Time + 4
                else
                    timeOfNextArrival ← Time + 5
                endif
            else
                output 'Internal Error: Bad call to AcceptNewArrival'
            endif
        end AcceptNewArrival



initialize
    timeOfNextArrival ← 0
end ShoppingArea



module WaitingLine

{ Simulates waiting line }

declare
    export Length, PutPersonInLine, RemovePersonFromLine

    lineSize: integer


function Length: integer

{ Return the current length of the line }

execute
    Length ← lineSize
end Length
```

procedure *PutPersonInLine*

{ Increase the length of the line by one }

execute
    lineSize ← *lineSize* + 1
end *PutPersonInLine*

procedure *RemovePersonFromLine*

{ Decrease the length of the line by one }

execute
    if *lineSize* > 0 **then**
        lineSize ← *lineSize* − 1
    else
        output 'Internal Error: Bad call to RemovePersonFromLine'
    endif
end *RemovePersonFromLine*

initialize
    lineSize ← 0
end *WaitingLine*

module *CheckoutCounter*

{ Simulates checkout counter }

declare
    import *Time* **from** *Clock*
    import *Rnd* **from** *RandomNumberGenerator*
    export *CounterFreeP*, *StartCheckout*

    timeWhenFree: *integer*

    function *CounterFreeP*: *Boolean*

    { Determine if checkout counter is ready for new customer }

    execute
        CounterFreeP ← (*Time* >= *timeWhenFree*)
    end *CounterFreeP*

```
        procedure StartCheckout

        { Start checking out customer. Set time at which checkout counter will
          next be free }

        declare
            random: real
        execute
            if CounterFreeP then
                random ← Rnd
                if random <= 0.15 then
                    timeWhenFree ← Time + 1
                elseif random <= 0.45 then
                    timeWhenFree ← Time + 2
                elseif random <= 0.85 then
                    timeWhenFree ← Time + 3
                elseif random <= 0.95 then
                    timeWhenFree ← Time + 4
                else
                    timeWhenFree ← Time + 5
                endif
            else
                output 'Internal Error: Bad call to StartCheckout'
            endif
        end StartCheckout


initialize
    timeWhenFree ← 0
end CheckoutCounter


module Clock

{ Maintains simulated time }

declare
    export Time, AdvanceClock

    currentTime: integer


function Time: integer

{ Return current time }
```

```
    execute
        Time ← currentTime
    end Time


procedure AdvanceClock

{ Advance clock reading by one time unit }

    execute
        currentTime ← currentTime + 1
    end AdvanceClock


initialize
    currentTime ← 0
end Clock


module RandomNumberGenerator

{ Provides source of pseudorandom real numbers }

declare
    export Rnd, Reseed

    seed: real


function Rnd: real

{ Return pseudorandom real number in range 0 to 1 (not including 1) }

    execute
        seed ← (seed + 3.1415927) ** 2
        seed ← seed − trunc(seed)
        Rnd ← seed
    end Rnd


procedure Reseed

{ Provide seed for random number generator }
```

```
        declare
            newSeed: in real
        execute
            seed ← newSeed
        end Reseed
    end RandomNumberGenerator
```

uses *NewArrivalP* to determine if a new arrival is ready to get in line. If so, *AcceptNewArrival* is called to remove the new arrival from the shopping area and *PutPersonInLine* is called to put the person in line. Finally, *CounterFreeP* and *Length* are used to determine if the checkout counter is free and if anyone is waiting in line. If both are true, *RemovePersonFromLine* is called to remove a person from the line and *StartCheckout* is called to start that person checking out.

ShoppingArea   The *ShoppingArea* module determines when persons arrive at the end of the checkout line. *NewArrivalP* returns *true* if a new person is ready to get in line and *false* otherwise. *AcceptNewArrival* removes the new arrival from the shopping area; that is, it resets the value returned by *NewArrivalP* to *false*.

The program specification gives statistics for the times between successive arrivals. Since the method for determining arrivals is based on time, the easiest way to implement the *ShoppingArea* module is to have it maintain the time at which the next person will be ready to get in line. This value, which constitutes the information hidden by the module, is stored as the value of *timeOfNextArrival*.

The implementation of *NewArrivalP* now becomes straightforward. The value of *Time*, the current simulated time, is compared with the value of *timeOfNextArrival*, the next time at which a person will be ready to get in line. If the value returned by *Time* is greater than or equal to the value of *timeOfNextArrival, NewArrivalP* returns *true;* otherwise, it returns *false*.

The external effect defined for *AcceptNewArrival* is to reset the value returned by *NewArrivalP* to *false*. *AcceptNewArrival* does this by setting *timeOfNextArrival* to the time at which the next person will be ready to get in line. The new value of *timeOfNextArrival* will always be greater than the current simulated time, so the value returned by *NewArrivalP* becomes *false* and remains *false* until the time of the next arrival is reached. Thus, the burden of determining the times at which people are ready to get in line falls on *AcceptNewArrival*. *NewArrivalP* merely checks whether the time of the next arrival, as set by *AcceptNewArrival*, has been reached.

A call to *AcceptNewArrival* is valid only if the value returned by *NewArrivalP* is *true*. Thus *AcceptNewArrival* begins by checking the value returned by *NewArrivalP;* if the value is *false,* the procedure prints an error message and takes no action. This error is classed as an internal error since only a bug in the procedure *AdvanceToNextState* could produce an invalid call to *AcceptNewArrival*. No input data entered by the user could produce this error.

If the call to *AcceptNewArrival* is valid, the procedure must set *timeOfNext-Arrival* to the time at which the next person is to arrive. The time of the next arrival is to be chosen at random but in accordance with the statistics given in the specification. That is, the time between successive arrivals is to be one minute in 10% of the cases, two minutes in 25% of the cases, and so on.

We can proceed as follows. We divide the interval 0 to 1 into subintervals such that the length of the first subinterval is 0.10, the length of the second subinterval is 0.25, and so on, as shown in Figure 11.8. If a number in the interval 0 to 1 is now chosen at random, it will have a 10% chance of lying in the first subinterval, a 25% chance of lying in the second subinterval, and so on. Thus if the random number is less than or equal to 0.10, the time to the next arrival should be one minute. If the random number is greater than 0.10 but less than or equal to 0.35, the largest value in the second interval, the time to the next arrival is 2 minutes, and so on.

AcceptNewArrival calls the function *Rnd* to obtain a random number in the range 0 to 1 and assigns this number to the variable *random*. An extended **if** construction compares the value *random* with the upper limits of the first four intervals. If the value falls in the first interval, *timeOfNextArrival* is set to *Time* + 1; if the value falls in the second interval, *timeOfNextArrival* is set to *Time* + 2; and so on. If the value does not fall in any of the first four intervals, then it must fall in the fifth interval, and so *timeOfNextArrival* is set to *Time* + 5.

The variable *timeOfNextArrival* is given the initial value zero. Since the value returned by *Time* is always greater than or equal to zero, *NewArrivalP* will initially return the value *false,* as required by the module specification.

Figure 11.8   Division of the interval 0 to 1 into subintervals whose lengths are proportional to the probabilities that various events will occur. If an event has 10% chance of occurring, the length of the corresponding subinterval is 0.10; if an event has a 25% chance of occurring, the length of the corresponding subinterval is 0.25, and so on. To determine which event occurs, we generate a pseudorandom number in the interval 0 to 1 and note the subinterval into which it falls.

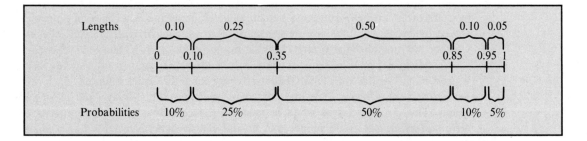

WaitingLine The module *WaitingLine* represents the line being simulated. Since this simulation is only concerned with the length of the line, the line can be represented entirely by its length; *WaitingLine* does not have to keep track of the position of each customer within the line.

The length of the waiting line is maintained as the value of the variable *lineSize*. The function *Length* returns the current value of *lineSize;* the procedure *PutPerson-InLine* increases the value of *lineSize* by one; and the procedure *RemovePerson-FromLine* decreases the value of *lineSize* by one. If *RemovePersonFromLine* is called with the value of *lineSize* equal to zero, an error message is printed and the value of *lineSize* remains unchanged. *LineSize* is given the initial value zero so that *Length* will initially return zero, as called for by the specifications.

CheckoutCounter *CheckoutCounter* works exactly the same as *ShoppingArea,* with *CounterFreeP* playing the same role as *NewArrivalP, StartCheckout* playing the same role as *AcceptNewArrival,* and *timeWhenFree* playing the same role as *time-OfNextArrival.* Aside from different names for functions, procedures, and variables, the only difference between the two modules is that the statistics for checkout times are different than those for times between arrivals.

Clock The module *Clock* maintains the current simulated time as the value of the variable *currentTime*. The function *Time* returns the value of *currentTime,* and the procedure *AdvanceClock* increases the value of *currentTime* by one. The value of *currentTime* is initially set to zero.

RandomNumberGenerator The Module *RandomNumberGenerator* produces random numbers in the range 0 to 1 (not including 1). The variable *seed* holds the current seed value for the random number generator. The function *Rnd* computes the next value of *seed* according to the algorithm for random number generation given in the module specification and returns the new value of seed as the next random number. The procedure *Reseed* assigns the value of its parameter to *seed*.

11.7

Validation, verification, and testing

Validation is the process of assuring that software meets the users' needs. *Verification* is the process of assuring that a program meets its functional specification. Verification is an essential part of validation; but if the requirements definition and specification are incorrect or inadequate, a program may be verified successfully but still fail to meet the needs of its users. *Testing* is one method of verification, in which the program is supplied with input data and the output that it produces is compared with the output that it should produce. The output may be the normal output of the program, or it may be special output intended for use only during testing.

Although testing follows implementation in the software development life cycle, the modern trend is to conduct validation, verification, and testing activities throughout software development. In the requirements analysis and specification phases, requirements and specifications can be analyzed for correctness, completeness, and consistency. The specifications can be used to generate test data that will later be used to test the program. During implementation, the code produced by one programmer can be reviewed by others. When the first attempts are made to compile the code, the compiler will discover a variety of oversights such as misspelled words, improper punctuation, invalid format for program statements, and invalid use of data types. Individual modules are usually compiled and tested separately before being combined into a complete program.

Testing is the phase of software development that is least likely to be successful; bugs are frequently found in programs that have been extensively tested. To completely verify a program by means of testing, we would have to test it for every possible combination of input values. This is almost always impractical because of the large number of possible sets of input data. For example, consider our simulation program, which uses only a very small amount of input data—one real number and one integer, the latter in the range 1 to 28,800. If a real number can have up to seven digits, then there are 10 million possible real values and $28,800 \times 10,000,000$ or 288 billion possible sets of input data—far too many to test the program for every set. And because most programs use far more input data than does the simulation program, their number of possible sets of input data is enormously larger.

Because of the difficulty of adequately testing programs, software engineers have devised a number of other validation and verification techniques. We will look briefly at these before returning to the problem of testing.

Document analysis   During its development, a program is described by a number of *documents* such as the requirements definition, the functional specification, and the program code itself. Many problems can be uncovered by having persons other than the ones who wrote the documents analyze them for correctness, consistency, and completeness. Document analysis is standard procedure in many areas; for example, a paper submitted to a scientific journal is usually sent to a number of other scientists for analysis before being accepted for publication. The most important methods of document analysis are desk checking, document inspection, and walkthrough.

Desk checking refers to an author checking his or her own specification, design, or program. Desk checking can locate many errors, particularly those that resulted from carelessness or inattention but that are immediately recognized as errors when seen in print. The main limitation of desk checking is that authors tend to overlook their own errors. When reading a document with which we are very familiar, we tend to perceive what we know it should say rather than what it actually does say; someone less familiar with the document may be better able to spot errors. Also, the more subtle errors often result from the author's failure to understand some aspect of the problem or from some oversight in the author's reasoning. Another person who looks at the problem from a different perspective and solves it by a different reasoning process is more likely to catch these kinds of errors.

In *document inspection,* a document is examined line by line using a checklist. The following is a general checklist that can be applied to programming documents:

Correctness: Are facts included in the document, such as mathematical formulas and data tables, correct?

Completeness: Does the document describe the software in sufficient detail? Are any important program properties, such as performance requirements and details of input and output, missing, or incomplete?

Necessity: Is each item in the document actually necessary?

Consistency: Do any of the items in the document contradict one another?

Clarity: Does each item in the document have only one possible interpretation?

Feasibility: Can the software described in the document actually be developed with the time, funds, computer hardware, and programming personnel available?

Testability: Can tests be constructed for every program property called for by the document?

In a *walkthrough,* the person who wrote the document explains it to others. Usually this is done by assuming sample input data and explaining how the data will be manipulated by each part of the program; the data is "walked through" the program. The other persons participating in the walkthrough ask questions whenever the explanation seems unclear or incomplete. Errors are often discovered by the author of the document while attempting to respond to such questions.

Like other creative people, programmers and designers are often reluctant to expose their work to their colleagues' criticisms, particularly when the work is in preliminary form. To avoid a defensive attitude, every effort must be made to emphasize that the purpose of the walkthrough is to help rather than to judge the document's author. The other persons participating in the walkthrough should be the author's peers; management personnel should be excluded. The author should conduct the walkthrough session. The other participants should not try to rewrite the document, but should confine themselves to locating errors and other problems. Supplying corrections should be left to the author. Records kept during the walkthrough should be used only for improving the document, not for evaluating its author.

Persons examining program code should be particularly alert for commonly made errors. For example, nonterminating repetitions are the bane of poorly designed and poorly tested software. Every repetition construction needs to be scrutinized for the conditions under which it will and will not terminate.

Selection constructions, we recall, correspond to the problem-solving technique of case analysis: each possible set of statements to be executed corresponds to one of the cases that must be considered in solving the problem. Sometimes, each case corresponds to a particular class of input data. Frequently, the programmer or designer overlooks one or more possible cases, with the result that input data corresponding to the overlooked cases causes incorrect output or a program failure. Each selection construction needs to be checked to make sure that the programmer has provided for all possible cases.

A very common programming error is the *off-by-one* or *fencepost* error. The latter name comes from the following typical example. Suppose you are building a fence 30 meters long and posts are to be placed every three meters. The ends of the fence are to be supported by posts, rather than attached to existing structures. How many posts do you need? If you answer 10, you have committed a fencepost error. Eleven posts are needed, one at the beginning of each three-meter section and one more at the end of the last section.

Here is another fencepost error often made by computer science students. The character positions on a typed line or a punched card are usually numbered—1 for the leftmost position, 2 for the next position to the right, and so on. Suppose you need to process a data item that occupies positions 20 through 30. How many characters must be processed? If you answered 10, you have committed another fencepost error. Characters 21 through 30 constitute 10 characters; including character 20 makes 11 characters. In general, if you must process item m through item n in a list of sequentially numbered items, the number of items to be processed is not $n - m$, but $n - m + 1$.

Fencepost errors are often revealed by considering extreme cases. If we consider a fence consisting of only one three-meter segment, it is obvious that two posts, rather than one, are required. If we consider a data item occupying positions 20 through 20, it is obvious that one character, rather than zero characters, must be processed. Therefore, extreme values of input data, such as the smallest and largest values allowed, are useful for walkthroughs and for program testing.

Checking done by compilers When a program or module is compiled, the compiler checks for *syntax errors* such as errors in spelling, punctuation, and grammar. For many modern languages such as Pascal, the compiler checks for errors in the use of data types, such as attempting to assign a real value to an integer variable. Invalid use of types usually reflects some confusion in the programmer's mind as to the kind of data the program is dealing with at a particular point. Future compilers may use *data flow analysis* to detect such problems as variables to which no values are assigned, variables whose values are never used, and variables whose values are used before any values are assigned to them. *Control flow analysis* can detect segments of code that will never be executed. Such data and control flow anomalies usually reflect confusion or oversights on the part of the programmer.

Proving programs correct The object of this approach is to prove programs correct by mathematical reasoning. Initial and final assertions (preconditions and postconditions) are used to characterize the effect of each program, function, procedure, and statement. Invariant assertions are used to characterize repetitions. We begin a proof by assuming that the initial assertion is true, then work through the program proving the intermediate assertions until we are finally able to establish that the final assertion follows from the intial assertion.

Proofs can be formal or informal. In a formal proof, assertions are expressed as formulas in mathematical logic, and an assertion is proved by deriving the corresponding formula from the formulas corresponding to assertions that are assumed true or have previously been proven. In an informal proof, the assertions are stated in English, perhaps augmented by elementary mathematical notation. The programmer's intuitive knowledge of the effect of a statement, rather than a formal mathematical derivation, is used to derive the assertion following the statement from the one preceding it. Several informal proofs of correctness are given in Chapters 1 and 2.

With current techniques, it is not possible to prove large programs correct. Because formal proofs are extremely complex and tedious, they are just as subject as programs to careless mistakes. Informal proofs, on the other hand, are likely to suffer from oversights in the programmer's reasoning and from the failure of the programmer to fully understand the implications of assertions and the effects of statements. In practice, proofs do not guarantee correctness. A number of algorithms that were published with proofs of correctness have later been found to be incorrect. For that matter, many of the proofs published in mathematics journals have later been found to be incorrect.

To avoid human errors, we can automate the process of proving programs correct. The programmer supplies the initial and final assertions and probably at least some of the intermediate assertions as well. The assertions must be stated formally so that they can be processed by the computer. Under the control of a theorem-proving program, the computer either proves that the final assertion follows from the initial assertion, thus verifying the program, or it calls the programmer's attention to the errors that prevented the proof from being carried through. Unfortunately, current theorem-proving programs are unable to handle proofs of the complexity needed for verifying programs.

Formulating the assertions can itself present problems. The specifications for the program must be translated into initial and final assertions; often this is extremely difficult to do, and the resulting assertions are extremely complex and tedious. Even when the proof is to be derived automatically, the programmer must usually supply at least some of the intermediate assertions, particularly the invariant assertions associated with repetitions, which are often particularly difficult to derive.

Despite these difficulties, correctness proofs will probably play an increasing role in the program development process in the future. Informal proofs can increase a programmer's understanding of a program by forcing him or her to consider it from a different perspective. Advances in automated theorem-proving techniques are likely to make automated correctness proofs practical for small modules if not for entire programs. Some of the machinery of correctness proofs, such as assertions, can aid our understanding of programs and play a role in program testing.

Simulation   Simulation allows us to observe the behavior of a program at the specification or design stage rather than waiting until the implementation is complete. The specification or design must be stated in a formal specification or design language that can be processed by a computer. The formal specification or design is processed by a simulation program, which then simulates the program described by the specification or design. The simulation is actually an implementation of the desired program; however, this implementation may be inefficient, may be able to process only small volumes of data, and may run on a different computer system than the one on which the finished program is to be executed.

A simulation based on the specification allows users to determine whether the specified program actually meets their needs; if not, it is much easier to make changes at the specification stage than to wait until after the program has been implemented. Simulation can be used to determine the proposed program's response to various sets of input data, thereby allowing test data to be derived from the program's specifications. At the design stage, simulation allows us to test the design before proceeding with the implementation.

Simulation is widely used in hardware design. A new computer chip is invariably simulated at several different levels of detail before actually being constructed. Currently, however, simulation is much less widely used in software development.

Program synthesis If a program can be simulated from its specifications, why not go a step further and automatically derive the final program from its specifications, thus avoiding the design and implementation stages altogether. This technique, known as *program synthesis,* has enjoyed success in some areas, but currently is not practical for many kinds of programs.

Program synthesis is not a validation technique but allows much verification and validation activity to be avoided by synthesizing a program directly from its specifications, bypassing the design and implementation stages. In particular, program synthesis can be considered an alternative to proving programs correct. It may turn out to be easier to synthesize correct programs from their specifications than to prove that manually written programs meet their specifications.

An area in which program synthesis is proving practical is in business data processing. Most data-processing programs involve the same elements. Input data is read from designated files or accepted from computer terminals. The program carries out simple mathematical computations, such as those for wages, tax deductions, or cost of merchandise, after which the data is sent to output files or used to print reports, checks, bills, or other documents. Existing files, such as a file of customer accounts, may have to be accessed and updated.

The specification for such a program identifies the files to be accessed, generated, and updated, the output documents to be produced, the formats for the file records and the output documents, the mathematical calculations to be carried out, and the overall flow of information through the system. With these details at hand, it is in principle straightforward to produce the desired program. In practice, however, if the program is written in a standard programming language, such as COBOL, human errors will result in the usual problems of software development: bugs, delays, and cost overruns.

The solution is to produce the program directly from its specifications. The specifications are stated in what is sometimes called a *very-high-level language* or a *fourth-generation language.* The specifications are then compiled directly into the final program. With some training, users can write the specifications for the programs they need, allowing them to develop their own programs without the need of programmers or other computer specialists. This is particularly important in many companies in which development of requested programs by computer-center personnel is running years behind schedule.

Unfortunately, program synthesis can currently be applied only to relatively routine programs. More complex programs still require skills of designers and programmers. Frequently, the difficulty lies not so much in compiling the program from its specifications but in stating the specifications in the first place.

A case in point is *compiler generators.* The input to the compiler generator program is a description of a high-level language and of the machine language into which it is to be translated; the output from the compiler generator is a compiler program that will do the desired translation. The obstacle to compiler generation is providing precise descriptions of the source and object languages and of the relation between them. It is straightforward to describe the *syntax,* or grammar, of a programming language. To describe the *semantics,* or the meaning, of the statements in the language is much more difficult, as is describing the correspondence between statements in a higher-level language and the corresponding machine code for a particular computer. Thus, although a number of compiler generators have been written, they are not widely used because of the complexity of specifying the compiler to be generated. (Another reason, to be sure, is that compilers produced by compiler generators are usually much less efficient than hand-coded compilers.)

Program testing   Having surveyed various other approachs to validation and verification, let's return to the most widely used verification technique of all—testing programs by observing their responses to sample input data. Testing is one of the least certain of the verification techniques, since testing can never guarantee that a program is correct but can only show that it works for the particular input data for which it was tested. On the other hand, testing is one of the most widely applicable methods since it can be used for programs of any size and complexity. This cannot be said for some theoretically superior methods such as correctness proofs.

Specifications and designs can be tested only if they have been simulated. If they have not been simulated, then testing proper begins with the implementation phase, although test data may have been chosen during earlier phases. *Module testing* refers to testing modules individually as they are completed. *Integration testing* refers to testing groups of modules. When all the modules have been included in integration testing, the entire program will have been tested. *Integration testing* may be followed by *beta testing,* in which copies of the program are provided to individuals and organizations who agree to use the program and report any errors they discover. Prospective purchasers or users of the program may insist on *acceptance tests* to determine if the program meets their needs. *Benchmark tests* are used to compare the performance of different programs—to see which can carry out a particular kind of calculation most rapidly, for example.

Top-down and bottom-up implementation and testing   We have already considered the arguments for top-down and bottom-up order for specifying and designing modules. Once the design is complete, however, these arguments no longer apply, and we are free to implement the modules in any order that we choose. By making an appropriate choice, however, we can test larger and larger portions of the system as additional modules are completed, and each newly completed module can be tested within the framework of the partially completed system. Again, the question of top-down versus bottom-up order arises.

In top-down implementation and testing, the top-level module is implemented and tested first. During testing, the lower-level modules used by the top-level module are replaced by *stubs*—dummy modules that accept data from the top-level module and return dummy results, but do not actually perform the functions specified for the modules they represent. As each second-level module is completed, it replaces the corresponding stub, allowing a larger portion of the final system to be tested. The second-level modules will make use of still other stubs, which will be replaced as lower-level modules are completed, and so on.

In bottom-up implementation and testing, the lowest-level modules are implemented and tested first. No stubs are needed since the modules under test do not use any other modules. On the other hand, for each module tested we must write a special *test driver,* a program that uses the module, passes it test data, and reports the results that it produces. As each module on the next highest level is completed, it too can be tested without the need for stubs since the lower-level modules it uses have already been completed and tested. On the other hand, a test driver is again needed to supply data to the module under test and to report the results that it returns.

The question of top-down versus bottom-up implementation and testing, then, often hangs on which are easier to produce, stubs or test drivers. In many cases the answer is stubs, and in those cases top-down implementation and testing is recommended.

In some cases, however, stubs seem inadequate for program testing. For example, much of the output produced by a graphics program may pass through a low-level screen-handling module. Observing the displays produced by this module can reveal many errors in the higher-level modules. On the other hand, if this module is replaced by a stub that does not actually produce a display, the main output channel for the higher-level modules has been cut off, and it is difficult to see how they can be adequately tested. Likewise, a low-level memory manager may be responsible for allocating regions of main memory for use by higher-level modules. It is difficult to see how the higher-level modules could be tested with the memory manager replaced by a stub that does not actually allocate memory areas.

Because of examples like these, some people recommend "top-down design and bottom-up implementation." But this, like all other simplistic prescriptions, is probably too rigid for practical use. The design, implementation, and testing strategies must be chosen to meet the needs of the project at hand. Sometimes these will indicate top-down implementation and testing, sometimes bottom-up implementation and testing, and sometimes a combination of the two.

Choosing test data   The most difficult problem of testing is selecting the input data for which a program is to be tested. Since we can test a program for only a small fraction of possible input data items, each test item must be chosen to reveal as many errors as possible. Another problem is determining how much test data to use. That is, at what point can we conclude that the program has been adequately tested and terminate the testing phase? Finally, for each test input we must determine the correct output that the program should produce, which may not be easy for complex programs such as language processors.

Each test data set consists of input data for the program and the corresponding output called for by the specifications. For some programs the correct output is easy to determine. In business data-processing programs, for example, output data items are often either the same as some of the input data items or are derived from them by simple arithmetical computations. For such programs the correct output for each input is readily derived by hand, using the specifications as a guide.

For more complex programs, however, the correct outputs may be more difficult to determine. The specifications may describe the complex process that the program is to carry out, such as translating from one language to another, but may not give any simple rules for determining the output corresponding to a particular input. If the specifications are sufficiently detailed and formal to serve as the basis of a computer simulation of the program, the simulation can be used to determine the outputs produced by various inputs. An existing program that solves the same problem can be used in the same way. Hand or computer simulation of the algorithms employed by the program can also be used. Experts in the application area can often provide data for problems whose solutions are known.

It may be almost impossible to predict the output for some programs, either because of the complexity of the calculations they carry out or because random number generators are used to deliberately produce unpredictable output. To evaluate such programs, we can first determine that the overall behavior of the program is reasonable—the program doesn't crash or hang up in a nonterminating repetition, and its output is in the desired format. An expert in the application area can then determine if the program's output is reasonable. For example, if the program is to play chess, is it doing a reasonably good job of it? Or is it making moves so absurd that they are probably due to bugs rather than to weaknesses in the underlying chess-playing algorithm? Finally, we can monitor the internal operation of the program to make sure that the calculations called for by the specifications and design are actually being carried out.

There are two basic approaches to choosing input data for testing. In "black box,"* or functional testing, the selection of test data is based entirely on the program specifications. The internal operation and construction of the program are ignored. In "glass box," or structural testing, on the other hand, the structure and operation of the program serve as a guide to test data selection. For example, test data items may be chosen to cause a specific sequence of statements to be executed or to cause a repetition to be executed a specific number of times.

In functional testing, the input data is normally divided into *input classes*—classes of data items that, according to the specifications, are to be processed differently by the program. For example, depending on the amount of the unpaid balance for a customer's account, the program may send the customer a normal bill, a reminder, a threatening letter, or a notice that the account is being turned over to a collection agency. Accounts for which different actions were to be taken would belong to different input classes.

---

*"Black box" is the engineer's traditional term for a device that can accept input and produce output but whose internal workings are hidden. The opposite of a black box is a "glass box," a device whose internal workings are subject to observation.

We will certainly want to test the program for values in each input class. If an input class were overlooked, then the part of the program that handles the corresponding situation would go untested. Experience shows that many errors are found by testing *boundary values*—the largest and smallest value in each class. Testing based on boundary values is called *boundary value analysis* or *stress testing*.

For example, suppose that customers with less than $1.00 due are not billed, those with up to $500.00 due are sent normal bills, and those with $500.00 or more due are sent sterner demands for payment. The boundary values for the input class corresponding to normal bills are $1.00 and $499.99. We would normally test these boundary values as well as other values, such as $275.95, that do not lie on the boundaries of the input class.

Input values can be classified as *extreme, nonextreme,* and *special*. Extreme values lie at the boundaries of input classes; nonextreme values lie within the classes. Special values do not belong to any input class but require individual treatment by the program. Programs should always be tested for all extreme and special values and for some nonextreme values within each input class.

Extreme values for which the program should take no action are particularly likely to produce errors. These include input files containing no records as well as requests that the program process zero input values, produce zero output values, or set up a table containing zero entries.

Sometimes the output values produced by a program also fall into distinct classes. It is then helpful to test the program with input values that produce extreme, nonextreme, and special output values.

Functional testing can be applied to individual modules as well as to the entire program. The specifications for each module are used to determine input and output classes, to choose extreme, nonextreme, and special input values, and to choose input values that produce extreme, nonextreme, and special output values. This approach is sometimes referred to as design-based functional testing since it works from the design, which specifies the individual modules, rather than from the specification, which describes the behavior of the overall program.

In contrast to functional testing, which considers only classes of input and output data, structural testing uses knowledge of the internal structure of a program to choose input data that adequately tests each part of the program. The paths that the computer can take in going from one program instruction to another can be represented by a diagram called a *flowchart* or *flowgraph*. Test data is chosen to test the program for as many as possible of the paths that the computer can take through the flowchart.

For example, Figure 11.9 shows the flowchart corresponding to the following segment of code:

```
while m <> n
    if m > n then
        m ← m − n
    else
        n ← n − m
    endif
endwhile
```

Figure 11.9 A code segment and its flowchart.

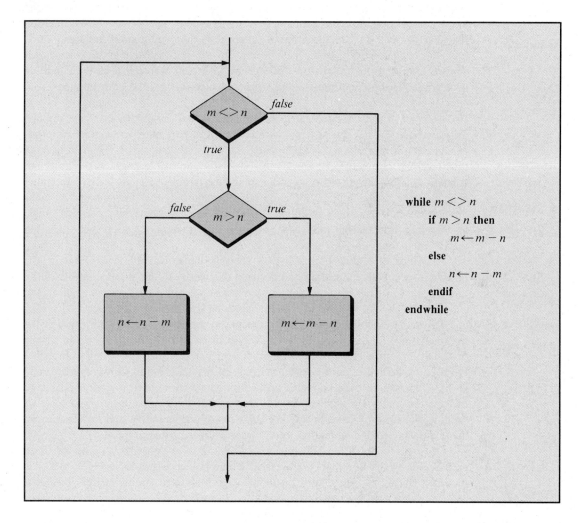

while $m <> n$
  if $m > n$ then
    $m \leftarrow m - n$
  else
    $n \leftarrow n - m$
  endif
endwhile

Each rectangular box in the flowchart contains a statement to be executed and each diamond-shaped box contains a condition to be tested. The computer follows the lines connecting the boxes, executing statements and testing conditions as it encounters the corresponding boxes. Leaving each diamond-shaped box are two lines, one to be followed if the condition tested by the box is true, and the other to be followed if the condition is false.

In Figure 11.9, the **if** construction corresponds to the diamond-shaped box containing the condition $m > n$, the rectangular boxes containing the statements $m \leftarrow m - n$ and $n \leftarrow n - m$, and the connecting lines that leave the decision diamond and rejoin after passing through the statement boxes. If the condition $m > n$ is true, the computer takes the path leading to the statement $m \leftarrow m - n$; if the condition is false, the computer takes the path leading to the statement $n \leftarrow n - m$.

The **while** construction is the circular structure, or *loop,* consisting of the decision diamond that tests the condition $m <> n,$ the part of the flowchart representing the **if** construction, and the path that returns to a point just preceding the decision diamond. On entering the loop, the computer tests the condition. If the condition is true, the computer follows the path leading to the **if** construction, executes the **if** construction, and then returns to the decision diamond, where it tests the condition once again. If the condition is false, the computer follows the path marked false, which exits from the loop.

Each set of test data will cause the computer to follow a particular path through the flowchart. To test the program as thoroughly as possible, we would like to use enough sets of test data to force the computer to follow every possible path through the flowchart. In practice, however, this is usually impossible to do. If the flowchart contains a large number of decision diamonds, the number of paths through the flowchart may be astronomical. If the flowchart contains loops, the number of paths through the flowchart may be infinite. One path may traverse the loop zero times, another may traverse the loop once, another may traverse the loop twice, another may traverse the loop three times, and so on.

A *branch* of a flowchart is a path entering the flowchart, a path leaving the flowchart, or a path connecting two decision diamonds. In the absence of our ability to test every possible path through the flowchart, we can do the next best thing and choose test data that will cause each branch to be traversed at least once.

Traversing every branch is not the same as traversing every path through the flowchart since the branches are not traversed in every possible combination. In the flowchart of Figure 11.10, for example, let ac denote the path consisting of branch a followed by branch c, ad the path consisting of branch a followed by branch d, and so on. To traverse every possible path through the flowchart, we would have to traverse the four paths denoted ac, ad, bc, and bd. To traverse every branch, however, we would only have to traverse the two paths denoted ac and bd. Traversing the two paths denoted ad and bc would accomplish the same purpose.

One way to judge the effectiveness of testing is to count the number of times each branch of the flowchart is traversed. If one branch is not traversed at all, or is traversed much less frequently than the other branches, additional test data that causes the branch in question to be traversed is needed. We can monitor the number of times each branch is traversed during testing by inserting a statement in each branch that counts each time the branch is traversed. Figure 11.11 shows the flowchart of Figure 11.9 with statements inserted for counting the number of traversals of each branch. The variables *counter1* through *counter5* are used as counters. The counting statements would be inserted in the corresponding program code as follows:

$$counter1 \leftarrow counter1 + 1$$
while $m <> n$
$$\quad counter2 \leftarrow counter2 + 1$$
$\quad$ **if** $m > n$ **then**
$$\quad\quad counter3 \leftarrow counter3 + 1$$
$$\quad\quad m \leftarrow m - n$$

Figure 11.10   Flowchart illustrating that it is possible traverse all the branches of a flowchart without traversing all paths through the flowchart. To traverse all paths, one must traverse the four paths ac, ad, bc, and bd (ac represents branch a followed by branch c, ad represents branch a followed by branch d, and so on). To traverse all branches, however, we can traverse either the two paths ac and bd or the two paths ad and bc.

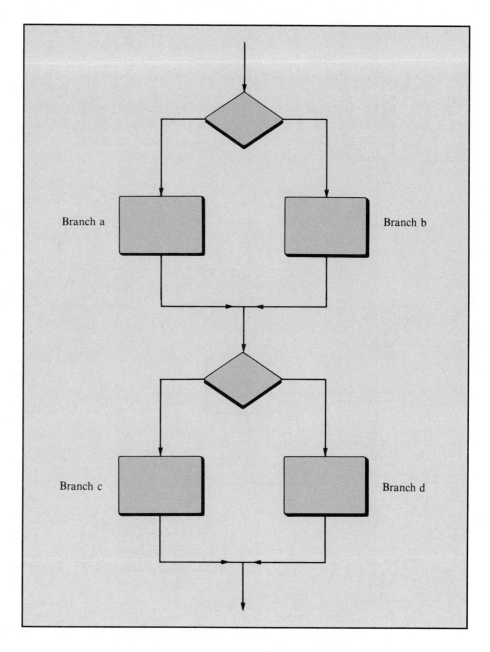

Figure 11.11 Flowchart of Figure 11.9 with statements inserted to count the number of times each branch is traversed during testing.

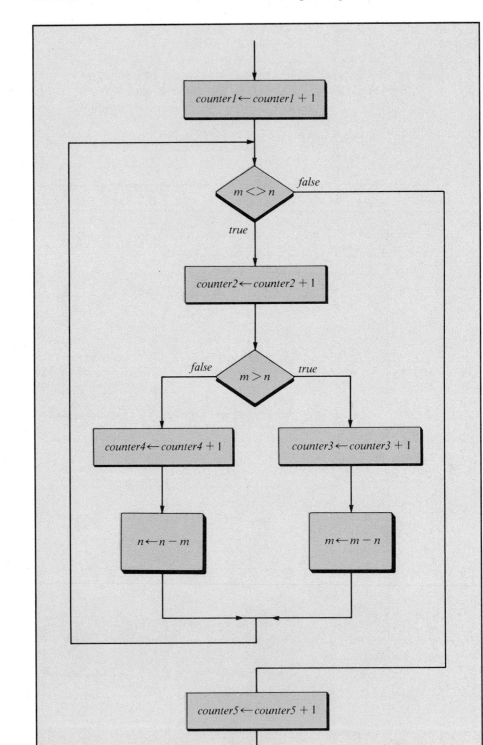

else

$\qquad$ *counter4* $\leftarrow$ *counter4* $+$ 1

$\qquad$ $n \leftarrow n - m$

endif

endwhile

counter5 $\leftarrow$ *counter5* $+$ 1

The values of some of the counts will be related. For example, after each set of tests, the values of *counter1* and *counter5* will be the same, and the value of *counter2* will be the sum of the values of *counter3* and *counter4*. Such relationships could be used to allow some of the counter variables and counting statements to be eliminated.

Debugging Testing attempts only to determine whether a program is correct; it makes no effort to locate the errors in incorrect programs. Debugging, in contrast, attempts to pinpoint the erroneous statements so that they can be corrected.

For testing it is often sufficient to consider only a program's input and output. For debugging we must usually monitor the internal operation of the program as well. The situation is similar to that faced by a service technician. From external observation it may be obvious that a piece of equipment isn't working right: the car doesn't start, the refrigerator doesn't get cold, or the picture on the television set is distorted. But to locate the trouble, the technician will usually have to use special test instruments to monitor the internal operation of the equipment.

The programmer's test instruments are *tracing* and *variable monitoring*. A *trace* of a program's execution is a printout showing each statement that the computer executes. A trace allows the programmer to determine the path that the computer is taking through the program for a particular set of input data. Tracing can locate such errors as the wrong part of an **if** construction being executed, or repeated statements being executed the wrong number of times.

Variable monitoring allows the programmer to monitor selected variables as program execution proceeds. In the early days of programming, this was often done by getting a *memory dump*—a printout of the contents of the computer's memory—one or more times during program execution. Memory dumps, however, are very difficult to interpret because of the difficulty of establishing a relation between the codes stored in memory and the variables and values with which the programmer is concerned. Some programming systems will print out on request a program's variable-value list (often called the *symbol table*); this printout is a higher-level language version of the memory dump. Even better, some programming systems provide means by which the values of particular variables can be monitored as the program executes. Variable monitoring allows programmers to detect such errors as incorrect assignments and erroneous computations.

Some recent programming language implementations have excellent provisions for monitoring program execution. During execution several windows appear on the screen. One window shows the user's input and the output produced by the program. Another window shows the part of the program currently being executed; the statement being executed is highlighted. The remaining window shows the values of the variables the program is manipulating. Execution of the program can be slowed to the point that the programmer can follow the order in which the statements are executed and examine the changes that are made in the values of the variables.

11.8 Maintenance

Hardware requires maintenance because parts wear out and have to be replaced. Software doesn't wear out but still requires maintenance for two reasons: (1) errors may be found that escaped discovery during testing; and (2) the task that the program is to carry out changes. The latter reason occurs frequently in business applications. Changes in the way a business conducts its operations, or in the laws that regulate it, may require changes in the computer programs it uses.

The programmers who perform maintenance usually are not the same ones who originally developed the program. A program is easy to maintain, then, if persons not familiar with it can with reasonable effort understand it well enough to make corrections or changes. This means that the program's structure must be as clear and logical as possible. It must be accompanied by documentation that clearly and thoroughly describes its internal operation. And it must be modular, so that changes made to one part of a program will not accidentally affect conceptually unrelated parts.

Review questions

1. What is the *software crisis?*

2. What is *software engineering?* What are some matters with which engineers must be concerned that go beyond the technical details of the product?

3. List the six phases of the software development life cycle.

4. List and briefly describe six characteristics of high-quality software.

5. Describe the process of *requirements analysis.* What document does it produce? What difficulties can arise if prospective users are unaware of the capabilities and limitations of computer technology in their area of application?

6. Give the considerations that go into producing the *functional specification* for a program.

7. How is the principle of *information hiding* used to determine how a program should be divided into modules?

8. What is *top-down design?* From what powerful problem-solving technique does it derive? Give some reasons why it may occasionally be necessary to deviate from strict top-down design.

9. Give two program design situations to which strict top-down design is particularly applicable.

10. What activity other than coding is usually begun during the implementation phase?

11. Contrast *validation, verification,* and *testing.*

12. Describe how document analysis is used for program validation. Define *desk checking, document inspection,* and *walkthrough.*

13. Give an example of a *fencepost* error.

14. Why are correctness proofs in principle superior to program testing? Why are they usually less useful in practice?

15. How can simulation of specifications and designs aid program validation and verification?

16. Why can *program synthesis,* although not strictly a validation technique, enormously simplify the task of validating programs?

17. Define *module testing, integration testing, beta testing, acceptance testing,* and *benchmark testing.*

18. Contrast *top-down* and *bottom-up* implementation and testing. What are *stubs* and *test drivers?* How can the relative difficulty of writing stubs and test drivers influence the order in which modules will be implemented and tested?

19. Contrast *functional* and *structural* testing.

20. Describe how test data is chosen for functional testing. What are *input classes* and *output classes?* Define *extreme, nonextreme,* and *special* data values.

21. What is a *flowgraph* or *flowchart?* In terms of flowcharts, describe first the ideal and then the realistic objectives of structural testing.

22. How can *counters* be used to determine the extent to which each branch of a flowchart has been tested?

23. Contrast *testing* and *debugging.*

24. What is *tracing?* What kinds of errors can it reveal?

25. What is *variable monitoring?* What kinds of errors can it reveal? What is a *memory dump?* A *symbol table?*

Exercises

The following exercises are based on carrying a project of moderate complexity through all six stages of the software development life cycle. The exercises will be more realistic if a number of students work on the same project. One team of students, representing the prospective users of the software, will define the requirements for the project. Other teams will be responsible for specification, design, implementation, testing, and maintenance. The teams should avoid looking over one another's shoulders throughout the project but should communicate through formal meetings and documents.

No specific project is described here, since defining the requirements of the program to be written is the responsibility of the user team. If the user team needs an idea, it should note that programs to play casino games such as roulette and blackjack are at the desired level of complexity. If the project is postponed until elementary data structures such as records, files, arrays, and strings have been discussed, then a simple information retrieval system, text editor, or text formatter would also provide a suitable project.

1. The user team should decide on the task to be accomplished, set reasonable levels for performance, convenience, reliability and development time, and write the requirements definition. It will help if the user team investigates and, if possible, experiments with existing programs carrying out the same or similar tasks before defining the requirements for the program it wants written. Software reviews in computer magazines are a good source of critical descriptions of existing programs.

2. Working mainly from the requirements definition, but consulting with the user team when questions arise, the specification team should write the functional specification for the program. The completed specification should be submitted to the user team for approval.

3. Working from the functional specification, the design team should divide the program into modules, write the specifications for the individual modules, and specify any nontrivial algorithms that are needed. Difficulties encountered during design may require changes in the requirements or specifications, in which case the project must backtrack to the appropriate earlier phase.

4. The implementation team should code the various modules from the design and do enough testing to catch gross errors. When each module seems to be working properly, it can be passed to the testing team for more rigorous testing. Walkthroughs should be used to attempt to discover coding errors. The implementation and testing teams should agree on the order in which modules are to be implemented and tested. As in the design phase, problems arising in the implementation phase may force a return to earlier phases. Since users often request changes when they actually see the implementation, it may be well to demonstrate a working implementation to the user team as soon as possible, even if the program has not yet been fully debugged.

5. The testing team is responsible for thoroughly testing the individual modules and the complete program. The team should devise a testing strategy, select test data, and carry out the tests. When errors are discovered, the module or program should be returned to the implementation team for debugging.

6. The user team should request and the maintenance team should implement an enhancement to the completed program. The maintenance team should have no knowledge of the program other than that provided by the documents created during the development process (including, of course, the program listing).

For further reading

Adrion, W. Richards, et al. "Validation, Verification, and Testing of Computer Software." *Computing Surveys,* June 1982, pp. 159–192.

Brooks, Jr., Frederick P. *The Mythical Man-Month.* Reading, Mass.: Addison-Wesley Publishing Co., 1975.

Brown, P. J. "Programming and Documenting Software Projects." *Computing Surveys,* December 1974, pp. 213–220.

Howden, William E. "Validation of Scientific Programs." *Computing Surveys,* June 1982, pp. 193–227.

Huang, J. C. "An Approach to Program Testing." *Computing Surveys,* September 1975, pp. 113–128.

Hughes, Joan K., and Michtom, Jay I. *A Structured Approach to Programming.* Englewood Cliffs, N. J.: Prentice-Hall, 1977.

Myers, Ware. "Software Engineering." *McGraw-Hill Encyclopedia of Electronics and Computers.* New York: McGraw-Hill Book Company, 1982, pp. 756–762.

Parnas, D. L. "A Technique for Software Module Specification with Examples." *Communications of the ACM,* May 1972, pp. 330–336

––––––. "On the Criteria To Be Used in Decomposing Systems into Modules." *Communications of the ACM,* December 1972, pp. 1053–1058.

Wirth, Nilaus. "On the Composition of Well-Structured Programs." *Computing Surveys,* December 1974, pp. 247–259.

Yohe, J. M. "An Overview of Programming Practices." *Computing Surveys,* December 1974, pp. 221–245.

Yourdon, Edward J. *Techniques of Program Structure and Design.* Englewood Cliffs, N. J.: Prentice-Hall, 1975.

Zelkowitz, Marvin V. "Perspectives on Software Engineering." *Computing Surveys,* June 1978, pp. 197–216.

Pascal Supplement

Figure 11.12 shows an implementation of the waiting-line simulation in UCSD Pascal. Units are the only nonstandard feature of UCSD Pascal that is used; each module construction in the algorithmic language is implemented as a UCSD-Pascal unit. In standard Pascal, the hidden variables such as *timeOfNextArrival* and *lineSize* would

Figure 11.12   Pascal implementation of the waiting-line simulation.

```pascal
program SimulationOfWaitingLine(input, output);

{ Simulate waiting line at checkout counter }

uses Clock, RandomNumberGenerator, ShoppingArea, WaitingLine,
    CheckoutCounter;
var
    totalLength, averageLength, seed: real;
    numberOfSteps, maxLength, i: integer;


procedure AdvanceToNextState;

{ Advances simulated system by one time unit }

begin
    AdvanceClock;
    if NewArrivalP then
        begin
            AcceptNewArrival;
            PutPersonInLine
        end;
    if CounterFreeP and (Length > 0) then
        begin
            RemovePersonFromLine;
            StartCheckout
        end
end;


begin
    write('Enter seed for random number generator: ');
    readln(seed);
    Reseed(seed);
    write('Number of minutes simulation is to run: ');
    readln(numberOfSteps)
    totalLength := 0.0;
    maxLength := 0;
    writeln;
    writeln('Time':10, 'Length':10);
```

```pascal
      for i := 1 to numberOfSteps do
          begin
              AdvanceToNextState;
              writeln(Time:10, Length:10);
              totalLength := totalLength + Length;
              if Length > maxLength then
                  maxLength := Length
          end;
      if numberOfSteps > 0 then
          averageLength := totalLength / numberOfSteps
      else
          averageLength := 0.0;
      writeln;
      writeln('Average length: ', averageLength:1:1);
      writeln('Maximum length: ', maxLength:1)
  end.


  unit ShoppingArea;

  { Represents source of customers who are to get in line }

  interface
      function NewArrivalP: Boolean;
      { Check if customer is ready to get in line }

      procedure AcceptNewArrival;
      { Remove customer from shopping area. Set time at which another
        customer will be ready to get in line }

  implementation
      uses Clock, RandomNumberGenerator;

      var
          timeOfNextArrival: integer;

      function NewArrivalP;
      begin
          NewArrivalP := (Time >= timeOfNextArrival)
      end;

      procedure AcceptNewArrival;
      var
          random: real;
```

```
    begin
        if NewArrivalP then
            begin
                random := Rnd;
                if random <= 0.10 then
                    timeOfNextArrival := Time + 1
                else if random <= 0.35 then
                    timeOfNextArrival := Time + 2
                else if random <= 0.85 then
                    timeOfNextArrival := Time + 3
                else if random <= 0.95 then
                    timeOfNextArrival := Time + 4
                else
                    timeOfNextArrival := Time + 5
            end
        else
            writeln('Internal Error: Bad call to AcceptNewArrival')
    end;

begin
    timeOfNextArrival := 0
end.


unit WaitingLine;

{ Simulates waiting line }

interface
    function Length: integer;
    { Return the current length of the line }

    procedure PutPersonInLine;
    { Increase the length of the line by one }

    procedure RemovePersonFromLine;
    { Decrease the length of the line by one }

implementation
    var
        lineSize: integer;

    function Length;
```

```
        begin
            Length := lineSize
        end;

        procedure PutPersonInLine;
        begin
            lineSize := lineSize + 1
        end;

        procedure RemovePersonFromLine;
        begin
            if lineSize > 0 then
                lineSize := lineSize − 1
            else
                writeln('Internal Error: Bad call to RemovePersonFromLine')
        end;

begin
    lineSize := 0
end.


unit CheckoutCounter;

{ Simulates checkout counter }

interface
    function CounterFreeP: Boolean;
    { Determine if checkout counter is ready for new customer }

    procedure StartCheckout;
    { Start checking out customer. Set time at which checkout counter will
      next be free }

implementation
    uses Clock, RandomNumberGenerator;

    var
        timeWhenFree: integer;

    function CounterFreeP;
    begin
        CounterFreeP := (Time >= timeWhenFree)
    end;
```

```
        procedure StartCheckout;
        var
            random: real;
        begin
            if CounterFreeP then
                begin
                    random := Rnd;
                    if random <= 0.15 then
                        timeWhenFree := Time + 1
                    else if random <= 0.45 then
                        timeWhenFree := Time + 2
                    else if random <= 0.85 then
                        timeWhenFree := Time + 3
                    else if random <= 0.95 then
                        timeWhenFree := Time + 4
                    else
                        timeWhenFree := Time + 5
                end
            else
                writeln('Internal Error: Bad call to StartCheckout')
        end;

begin
    timeWhenFree := 0
end.


unit Clock;

{ Maintains simulated time }

interface
    function Time: integer;
    { Return current time }

    procedure AdvanceClock;
    { Advance clock reading by one time unit }

implementation
    var
        currentTime: integer;

    function Time;
```

```
     begin
          Time := currentTime
     end;

     procedure AdvanceClock;
     begin
          currentTime := currentTime + 1
     end;

begin
     currentTime := 0
end.


unit RandomNumberGenerator;

{ Provides source of pseudorandom real numbers }

interface
     function Rnd: real;
     { Return pseudorandom real number in range 0 to 1 (not including 1; }

     procedure Reseed(newSeed: real);
     { Provide seed for random number generator }

implementation
     var
          seed: real;

     function Rnd;
     begin
          seed := sqr(seed + 3.1415927);
          seed := seed − trunc(seed);
          Rnd := seed
     end;

     procedure Reseed;
     begin
          seed := newSeed
     end;
end.
```

have to be declared in the main program and either be passed as parameters to the functions and procedures that access them or be accessed as global variables. In either case, information hiding would be impossible.

UCSD Pascal requires that a **uses** declaration list not only the units that are used directly but also those that are used indirectly, that is, those that are used by other units appearing in the **uses** declaration. The units must be listed in bottom-up order. Thus, if unit *A* uses unit *B*, unit *B* uses unit *C*, and unit *C* uses unit *D*, the **uses** declaration appearing in unit *B* is

   uses *D, C*

and that appearing in unit *A* is

   uses *D, C, B*

Thus the **uses** clause for the main program in Figure 11.12 lists in bottom-up order all the units used directly or indirectly by the main program and the procedure *AdvanceToNextState*:

   uses *Clock, RandomNumberGenerator, ShoppingArea, WaitingLine,*
      CheckoutCounter

Part IV
Data structures

12

Types, records, and files

I n Part III we concentrated on control structures such as sequencing, selection, and repetition as well as on larger units of program organization such as functions, procedures, and modules. In Part IV we turn our attention to *data structures*, methods for organizing the data processed by an algorithm.

We implement data structures be defining appropriate data types. Data types can be classified as *simple types*, *structured types*, and *pointer types*. Values of simple types cannot be broken down into simpler components; they are the raw material out of which more complex structures are built. The simple types in the algorithmic language are the predefined types *integer*, *real*, *Boolean*, and *char*.

Values of structured types *are* built from simpler components. The predefined type *string* is a structured type since strings are built from values of type *char*. Values of pointer types serve as cross references for linking together values of structured types. Data structures are realized by values of structured types, possibly linked to one another by values of pointer types.

The definition of a data structure often involves not just the layout of the data in memory, which is described by a type definition, but also the operations that are to be carried out on the data. For example, the array data types provide a general-purpose facility for constructing lists and tables. They can serve as a basis for a number of quite different structures depending on what operations are carried out on the entries in the lists and tables. Modules provide a powerful means of defining data structures by packaging type definitions along with functions and procedures for manipulating values of the defined types. Data structures defined by modules are sometimes said to be realizations of *abstract data types*.

This chapter introduces the facilities for defining new types in the algorithmic language and considers two important and related structured types: *record types* and *file types*.

477

12.1 Type definitions

Type definitions, which are similar in structure to constant definitions, can appear in the **declare** sections of algorithms, functions, procedures, and modules. A type definition consists of the keyword **type** followed by the identifier that is to designate the new type, an equal sign, and a description of the type being defined:

type type-identifier = type-description

The type description can be the name of a predefined type or a type that is defined elsewhere, or it can be a description giving the structure of the values belonging to the type being defined.

For example, consider the following **declare** section:

declare
    type *floatingPoint* = *real*
    type *logical* = *Boolean*
    x, *y*, *z*: *floatingPoint*
    p, *q*, *r*: *logical*

In the two type definitions, the type descriptions to the right of the equal signs are the names of predefined types. Thus, type *floatingPoint* is defined to be equivalent to type *real* and type *logical* is defined to be equivalent to type *Boolean*. The newly defined types are used to declare x, y, and z as variables of type *floatingPoint* and p, q, and r as variable of type *logical*. Because of the type definitions, x, y, and z act like real variables and p, q, and r act like Boolean variables; therefore, statements such as the following are valid:

$x \leftarrow y \,/\, x$
$r \leftarrow p$ **and** q
$p \leftarrow (x > 3.1416)$

Normally we do not use type definitions to give new names to the predefined types (particularly in pseudolanguages, in which we can call the predefined types whatever we want to anyway). Instead, the equal sign in the type definition is usually followed by a description giving the structure of the values of the type being defined.

12.2 Record types

A *record* is a collection of data values, each of which occupies a designated position called a *field*. The fields of a record can be referred to individually by means of *field identifiers*. The meaning of the term *record* in computer science is similar to its everyday meaning, as exemplified by school records, medical records, and tax records.

Record types and values   A *record type* is a type whose values are records having a given structure. We define a record type by giving the structure of the corresponding records. We give the structure of a record by defining its fields. The type description for a record type has the following general form:

record

    list of field definitions

endrecord

A field definition has the same form as a variable declaration:

field-identifier: type-description

The field identifier is used to designate the field; the type description gives the type of values that can be stored in the field. For example, the type description

record

    name: *string*

    major: *string*

    gradePointAverage: *real*

endrecord

describes records having three fields designated by the field identifiers *name*, *major*, and *gradePointAverage*. Fields *name* and *major* store string values; field *gradePointAverage* stores a real value. As in variable declarations, we can combine the definitions of field identifiers having the same type. Thus, the type description above can also be written as follows:

record

    name, *major*: *string*

    gradePointAverage: *real*

endrecord

or

record

    name,

    major: *string*

    gradePointAverage: *real*

endrecord

We can define a record type by using this type description to the right of the equal sign in a type definition:

type *student* = **record**

        name: *string*

        major: *string*

        gradePointAverage: *real*

      endrecord

Values of type *student* are records having two string fields *name* and *major* and a real field *gradePointAverage*.

We can represent a value of a record type by giving the name of the type followed by a list of the values of its fields. The list of field values is enclosed in parentheses, and the field values must appear in the same order that the corresponding field definitions appear in the record type description. For example,

student('Jane Doe', 'English', 3.7)

represents a value of type student in which the *name* field has the value 'Jane Doe', the *major* field has the value 'English', and the *gradePointAverage* field has the value 3.7.

Figure 12.1 shows how the student record for Jane Doe can be stored in three memory locations, one for each field. Only the field values are stored in memory. The field identifiers are not needed since programs manipulating the record will refer to the fields by their positions in the record rather than by their names.

A value of a structured type is called an *entire value*. The values from which an entire value is constructed are called *component values*. The component values of a record are its field values. Thus,

student('John Jones', 'Physics', 2.9)

is an entire value whose component values are 'John Jones', 'Physics', and 2.9.

Record variables and field designators The declaration

s1, *s2*: *student*

declares *s1* and *s2* as variables of type *student*. Thus, the following assignments are valid:

s1 ← *student*('Jane Doe', 'English', 3.7)
s2 ← *student*('John Jones', 'Physics', 2.9)
s1 ← *s2*
s2 ← *s1*

Variables such as *s1* and *s2* are called *entire variables* since they hold entire values. Just as an entire value is composed of component values, so is an entire

Figure 12.1 Layout in memory of a value of type *student*. The field identifiers at left are not stored in memory; compiled programs designate fields by their positions in the record rather than by their names.

name	'Jane Doe'
major	'English'
gradePointAverage	3.7

variable composed of *component variables*, each of which holds one of the components of the value of the entire variable. For record variables, the component variables are denoted by *field designators*, each of which consists of a record variable followed by a period and a field identifier. For example, the component variables of *s1* are denoted by the following field designators:

> *s1.name*
> *s1.major*
> *s1.gradePointAverage*

After the assignment

> *s1* ← *student*('Jane Doe', 'English', 3.7)

the component variables of *s1* have the following values:

Variable	Value
s1.name	'Jane Doe'
s1.major	'English'
s1.gradePointAverage	3.7

We can also make assignments to component variables. For example, after the assignments

> *s1.name* ← 'J. Random Nerd'
> *s1.major* ← 'Phys. Ed.'
> *s1.gradePointAverage* ← 1.5

the value of *s1* is

> *student*('J. Random Nerd', 'Phys. Ed.', 1.5)

Instead of defining a record type and using the type identifier to declare variables, we can declare variables directly using the record description. For example, we might declare the variable *book* as follows:

> *book*: **record**
> > *author*: *string*
> > *title*: *string*
> > *publisher*: *string*
> > *year*: *integer*
>
> **endrecord**

The type of *book* is that given by the type description—the type of all records with string fields *author*, *title*, and *publisher* and with integer field *year*. This type is said to be *anonymous* since no name has been given to it in a type definition.

We have no way of representing a value of an anonymous type since a value representation must begin with the name of the type whose value is being represented. Thus, the only way to assign a constant value to *book* is to assign the corresponding field values to the component variables:

> *book.author* ← 'Neill Graham'
> *book.title* ← 'Introduction to Computer Science'
> *book.publisher* ← 'West Publishing Company'
> *book.year* ← 1985

For this and other reasons, defining type identifiers and using them to declare variables is usually preferable to using anonymous types.

Scopes of field indentifiers   With one exception, the scope of a field identifier is the record description in which it is defined; the field identifiers of a record type are not ''visible'' from outside the record description. The one exception is that field identifiers can be used in field designators. We can think of the period that precedes a field identifier in a field designator as an operator that ''opens up'' the record description and allows the field identifiers to become visible.

Because of the limited scope of field identifiers, no confusion results if records of different types have the same field identifiers or if variables and field identifiers have the same name.

For example, consider the following definitions and declarations:

type *s* = **record**
  a: *real*
  b: *integer*
endrecord
type *t* = **record**
  a: *Boolean*
  b: *char*
endrecord
a, b: *string*
u: *s*
v: *t*

No confusion can arise between the field identifiers of type *s* and the field identifiers of type *t* nor between the field identifiers and the variables *a* and *b*. For example, *u* is a variable of type *s* and *v* is a variable of type *t*. Hence *u.a* refers to field *a* of a record of type *s*, and *v.a* refers to field *a* of a record of type *t*. Just plain *a* refers to the string variable *a*. Thus, the following assignments are valid:

> *u.a* ← 3.5
> *v.a* ← *true*
> *a* ← 'This is a string'

When an identifier designating a record type is exported or imported by a module, the field identifiers are also automatically exported or imported. For example, if the following appear in the declaration section of module *Alpha*:

export *s*

> **type** s = **record**
>> a: *real*
>> b: *integer*
>
> **endrecord**

and module *Beta* contains the following declarations:

> **import** s **from** *Alpha*
>
> w: s

then a and b can be used in module *Beta* as field designators for records of type s. Thus, the following statements are valid in module *Beta*:

> $w.a \leftarrow 6.28$
>
> $w.b \leftarrow 100$

Nested records   One or more fields of a record may themselves contain records; some fields of those records may contain still other records; and so on. When a field of a record itself contains a record, we say that the records are *nested*. For example, consider the following **declare** section:

> **declare**
>> **type** *fullName* = **record**
>>> *first*, *middle*, *last*: *string*
>>
>> **endrecord**
>>
>> **type** *student* = **record**
>>> *name*: *fullName*
>>>
>>> *major*: *string*
>>>
>>> *gradePointAverage*: *real*
>>
>> **endrecord**
>>
>> *stdnt*: *student*

In this version of type *student*, the name field of a student record holds not a string but a record of type *fullName*. Thus, nested within every student record is a record of type *fullName*.

A value of type *fullName* has three string fields: *first*, *middle*, and *last*. We can represent a value of type *fullName* by

> *fullName*('John', 'Random', 'Nerd')

and a value of type student by

> *student*(*fullName*('John', 'Random', 'Nerd'), 'Physics', 2.9)

Now consider the variable *stdnt*, whose values are of type *student*. After the assignment

> *stdnt* $\leftarrow$ *student*(*fullName*('John', 'Random', 'Nerd'), 'Physics', 2.9)

the component variables of *stdnt* have the following values:

Variable	*Value*
stdnt.name	*fullName*('John', 'Random', 'Nerd')
stdnt.major	'Physics'
stdnt.gradePointAverage	2.9

Stdnt.name is itself a record variable of type *fullName* and so has three component variables. We designate the component variables of *stdnt.name* by adjoining an additional period and field identifier:

Variable	*Value*
stdnt.name.first	'John'
stdnt.name.middle	'Random'
stdnt.name.last	'Nerd'

Figure 12.2 shows how *stdnt* and its component variables are laid out in memory.

Record descriptions can also be nested. For example, type *student* could be defined as follows:

type *student* = **record**

        name: **record**

                first, *middle*, *last*: *string*

          endrecord

        major: *string*

        gradePointAverage: *real*

      endrecord

Figure 12.2   The entire variable *stdnt* has three component variables: *stdnt.name, stdnt.major,* and *stdnt.gradePointAverage. Stdnt.name,* in turn, has three component variables of its own: *stdnt.name.first, stdnt.name.middle,* and *stdnt.name.last.* The value of *stdnt* is represented in memory by the values of the three components of *stdnt.name,* the value of *stdnt.major,* and the value of *stdnt.gradePointAverage.*

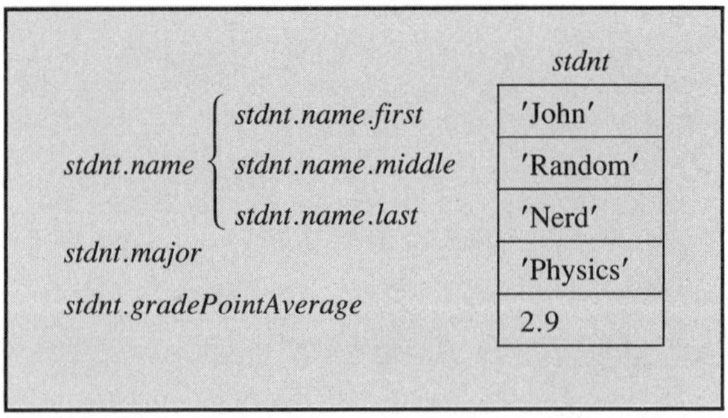

This definition clearly illustrates the nesting of records in values of type *student*. On the other hand, the type of the name field is now anonymous and, as mentioned earlier, anonymous types present certain difficulties. For example, there is now no way to represent a constant value of the name field and hence no way to represent a constant value of type *student*.

Type equivalence   We have seen that a type can be defined as equivalent to another type. For example,

type *logical* = *Boolean*

defines type *logical* as equivalent to type *Boolean*. Both types have the two values *true* and *false*. Values of Boolean variables can be assigned to logical variables and vice versa. The question that now arises is under what circumstances, if any, are types defined by different type descriptions equivalent.

For example, consider the following definitions:

type *s* = **record**
        x: *real*
        i: *integer*
    endrecord

type *t* = **record**
        x: *real*
        i: *integer*
    endrecord

Since values of *s* and *t* clearly have the same structure, we might wish to consider types *s* and *t* equivalent. Equivalence of two types because their values have the same structure is called *structural equivalence*.

Unfortunately, structural equivalence raises many hard-to-answer questions. For example, suppose type *u* is defined as follows:

type *u* = **record**
        y: *real*
        j: *integer*
    endrecord

Is type *u* equivalent to types *s* and *t*? Values of the three types have the same structure since each value consists of a real field followed by an integer field. On the other hand, the different field identifiers suggest that values of type *u* have a different meaning and are intended for different uses than values of types *s* and *t*.

On the other hand, suppose type *v* is defined as follows:

type *v* = **record**
        i: *integer*
        x: *real*
    endrecord

Conceptually, values of types s and v have the same structure since the field identifiers and the types of the fields are the same for each. On the other hand, the order in which the field values are stored in memory is different for types s and v, so that in practice it would be extremely difficult to treat values of the two types as equivalent.

To avoid these kinds of problems, most modern programming languages abandon structural equivalence and allow only *name* equivalence. We will also follow this course in the algorithmic language. Two types are name equivalent only if

1. they are designated by the same type identifier;

2. the type identifier of one type is defined as equivalent to the type identifier of the other in a type definition; or

3. the two types are defined by the same occurrence of a type description.

By these criteria, s, t, u, and v are all distinct, inequivalent, types. If we declare variables a and b by

a: s

b: s

then the types of a and b are equivalent by rule 1, since they are represented by the same type identifier. Rule 2 tells us that if we define type w by

type $w = s$

then types w and s are equivalent. If we declare a and b by

a: s

b: w

then values of a can be assigned to b and vice versa. On the other hand, if we declare a and b by

a: s

b: t

then a and b have different types, so values of a cannot be assigned to b nor vice versa. Rule 3 *does not* apply, since s and t are defined by *different occurrences* of the same type description.

Rule 3 usually comes up in connection with anonymous types. If we declare a and b by

a: **record**

    x: *real*

    i: *integer*

  endrecord

b: **record**

    x: *real*

    i: *integer*

  endrecord

then the types of *a* and *b* are not equivalent. In fact, the types of *a* and *b* cannot be equivalent to the types of any other variables in the algorithm, so there is no way whatever to assign an entire value to *a* or *b*. On the other hand, if we combine the declarations of *a* and *b*

> *a*, *b*: **record**
>> *x*: *real*
>> *i*: *integer*
> **endrecord**

then rule 3 applies since the types of *a* and *b* are defined by the *same occurrence* of a type description. The types of *a* and *b* are equivalent, and the following assignment statements are valid:

> $a \leftarrow b$
> $b \leftarrow a$

12.3 Files and streams

Physically, a file is any source from which data can be obtained or any destination to which data can be sent. Examples of files are input devices such as keyboards, output devices such as displays and printers, and blocks of data stored on disk or tape.

Conceptually, a file is a sequence of values, all of the same type. The number of values in the file is not fixed but can vary during processing and may even be indefinite. At any time only one of the values in the file is accessible for processing. The keyboard, which can be considered to be a file of characters, illustrates the last two statements. The number of characters in the keyboard file is indefinite since it depends on the number of characters that the user happens to type while a particular program is running. And since the keyboard does not remember all the characters that are typed on it, the only character that can actually be obtained from the keyboard file is the one most recently typed.

We can model a file by means of a data abstraction called a *stream*. The operations defined for streams include all those that can be carried out on any kind of file. For a particular kind of a file, such the keyboard or a disk file, only a subset of the operations defined on streams will be available.

We can picture a stream as a sequence of values, all of the same type. The number of values in the stream is not fixed, but can vary during processing. Associated with every stream is a *current position* that indicates the point in the stream at which values can be stored or retrieved; in illustrations we will designate the current position by an upward arrow. The following example illustrates a stream of integers:

> 25   30   45   10   12 78
>   ↑

The current position is at the third value in the stream.

The current position may be at any of the values in the stream or it may be beyond the end of the stream. We will refer to the position beyond the end of the stream as the *end position*. The following example illustrates a stream in which the current position is the end position:

25 30 45 10 12 78

                  ↑

To designate the current position numerically, we assume that the positions in a stream are numbered sequentially. The first value is in position 1, the second value is in position 2, and so on. Let n represent the number of values currently in the stream (remember that this number can change as the stream is processed). Then position 1 is the position of the first value, position n is the position of the last value, and position $n + 1$ is the end position. The value of the current position can vary from 1 through $n + 1$.

The stream of integers we have been using as an example contains six values, so the value of n is 6. The first value is in position 1, the last value is in position 6, and the end position is position 7. The value of the current position can range from 1 through 7. The following illustrates the positions for this stream:

Values: 25 30 45 10 12 78
Positions: 1   2   3   4   5   6 7

We define a data abstraction by describing the operations that can be carried out on the data. In principle, a data abstraction should be defined entirely by giving the effects of various sequences of operations. In practice, such a definition is somewhat complex and technical, so we will define the operations on streams in terms of the intuitive picture of a stream that we have just finished developing. The operations can be classified as functions, which just return values, and procedures, which affect the state of the stream:

FUNCTIONS

AtEndP	Returns *true* if the current position is the end position and *false* otherwise.
Position	Returns the current position as an integer in the range 1 through $n + 1$, where n is the number of values currently in the stream.
Size	Returns n, the number of values currently in the stream.

PROCEDURES

Read(x)	Assigns the value at the current position to the output parameter x and increases the value of the current position by 1. A call to *Read* is valid only when the value returned by *AtEndP* is *false*.
Write(x)	Stores the value of the input parameter x at the current position and increases the value of the current position by 1. If the current position is not the end position, the value of x replaces the value at the current position. If the current po-

sition *is* the end position, the value of *x* is added to the end of the stream.

Reset	Sets the value of the current position to 1.
SetToEnd	Sets the current position to the end position.
SetPosition(p)	Sets the value of the current position to that of the input parameter *p*. After *SetPosition* has been executed, *Position* returns the value of *p*.
Delete	Deletes all the values in a stream, yielding the *empty stream*, which contains no values. After *Delete* has been executed, the current position and the end position are both at position 1. *AtEndP* returns *true* and *Position* returns 1.

To illustrate these operations, let's return to our example stream:

$$25 \quad 30 \quad 45 \quad 10 \quad 12 \quad 78$$
$$\uparrow$$

For this state of the stream, *AtEndP* returns *false* and *Position* returns 3. On the other hand, for the state

$$25 \quad 30 \quad 45 \quad 10 \quad 12 \quad 78$$
$$\uparrow$$

AtEndP returns *true* and *Position* returns 7. In either state, *Size* returns 6.

Read can be called only when the current position is not the end position, thus assuring that there is a value to be read at the current position. *Read(x)* reads the value at the current position into *x* and advances the current position by 1. If the state of the stream is given by

$$25 \quad 30 \quad 45 \quad 10 \quad 12 \quad 78$$
$$\uparrow$$

Read(x) assigns 12 to *x* and changes the state of the stream to

$$25 \quad 30 \quad 45 \quad 10 \quad 12 \quad 78$$
$$\uparrow$$

A second call to *Read(x)* assigns 78 to *x* and changes the state of the stream to

$$25 \quad 30 \quad 45 \quad 10 \quad 12 \quad 78$$
$$\uparrow$$

A third call to *Read* is not allowed, since the current position is now at the end position and there are no more values to be read.

Write(x) stores the value of *x* at the current position and advances the current position. If the state of the stream is

$$25 \quad 30 \quad 45 \quad 10 \quad 12 \quad 78$$
$$\uparrow$$

executing *Write*(99) changes the state of the stream to

25   30   45   99   12   78
                    ↑

If the state of the stream is

25   30   45   10   12   78
                         ↑

executing *Write*(55) changes the state of the stream to

25   30   45   10   12   78   55
                              ↑

Thus, executing *Write* when the current position is at the end position adds a new value to the end of the stream. The current position is then advanced to the new end position.

Reset sets the current position to the beginning of the stream:

25   30   45   10   12   78
↑

SetToEnd sets the current position to the end position:

25   30   45   10   12   78
                         ↑

Executing *SetPosition*(4) produces the following state:

25   30   45   10   12   78
               ↑

Delete removes all the values from a stream, producing the empty stream, which we represent as follows:

↑

Note that *Read* cannot be executed for the empty stream but *Write* can. Thus, the sequence

Delete
Write(10)
Write(20)

produces the following stream:

10   20
     ↑

12.4

File types

We can think of files as streams constrained by the properties of actual input, output, and storage devices. Because of these constraints, there are different *modes* of file access. In each access mode, only certain of the stream operations are allowed, and circumstances under which some of the allowed operations can be carried out may be restricted.

File types and variables   Like a stream, a file can be pictured as a sequence of values, all of the same type. The type of the values is called the *component type* of the file type. The type description for a file type has the following form:

file of component-type

For example, the type definition

type *intFile* = **file of** *integer*

defines *intFile* as a type whose values are files of integers, and the definitions

type *student* = **record**

> *name*: *string*
> *major*: *string*
> *gradePointAverage*: *real*

>> **endrecord**

type *studentFile* = **file of** *student*

define *studentFile* as a type whose values are files of student records.

A file is represented in an algorithm as the value of a file variable. File variables are declared as variables of file types in the usual way:

workFile: *intFile*

oldFile, *newFile*: *studentFile*

The value of *workFile* can be a file of type *intFile*, and the values of *oldFile* and *newFile* can be values of type *studentFile*.

Assignment is not allowed for file variables. Assignment implies copying a value from one area of main memory to another. Since files are stored on external devices and not all the values of the file may be in existence at the same time, such copying is impossible. For similar reasons there is no method of representing constant values of file types. In the absence of assignment and constant values, there is often little reason to use named types for file variables; therefore, file variables are frequently declared with anonymous types:

workFile: **file of** *integer*

oldFile, *newFile*: **file of** *student*

On the other hand, the component type of a file type is usually named, since variables for holding values read from a file and values to be written to a file must be declared with the same type as the component type.

Access modes and the open and close statements   A file is *opened* when it is associated with a file variable and *closed* when that association is terminated. A file must be opened before processing begins and closed after processing is finished.

Because not all stream operations can be carried out on every file, a file is opened with a particular *access mode* that determines the available operations and the manner in which they can be carried out. Basically, there are two methods of accessing a file: *sequential access* and *direct access*. For direct access, also called random access, the values in a file can be accessed in any order. All stream operations are allowed for direct access. For sequential access, values must be accessed in the order in which they are stored in the file. Jumping from one arbitrary file position to another is not allowed. Thus, *SetPosition* is not allowed for sequential access.

What's more, sequential access must be confined to either input or output; the two operations cannot be mixed. For input, *Read* is allowed but *Write* is not; for output, the reverse is true. During sequential output, *Write* is allowed only when the current position is the end position. That is, *Write* can only be used to add new values to the end of the file: it cannot be used to change values already in the file.

These restrictions give rise to four access modes, **input**, **output**, **extend**, and **direct**, which are described in the following table:

Mode	Allowed Functions and Procedures	Comments
input	*AtEndP, Read, Reset*	Sequential input. *Reset* is executed automatically when the file is opened.
output	*Delete, Write*	Sequential output: creating a new file. *Delete* is executed automatically when the file is opened.
extend	*SetAtEnd, Write*	Sequential output: extending an existing file. *SetAtEnd* is executed automatically when the file is opened.
direct	All stream operations	Direct or random access. Values can be read or written at any position within the file, and *Write* can be used to add new values to the end of the file.

Note that, for **output** and **extend** modes, the current position is set to the end position when the file is opened and remains there throughout processing. *AtEndP* is not needed since it would always return the value *true*.

As a rule, no data conversion is done during file processing. Values read from a file are represented in memory by the same binary codes that were received from the external device, and the binary codes for values written to a file are transmitted unchanged to the external device.

Files with component type *char* are an exception, however. Character files *can* be processed without conversion, in which case at most one character can be read by a single call to *Read* or written by a single call to *Write*. Frequently, however, we wish certain sequences of characters in the file to be interpreted as representing other data values, such as integers and real numbers. On input, for example, we want the character sequence "525" to be converted to the binary code for the corresponding integer, and the character sequence "3.14" to be converted to the binary code for the corresponding real number. On output, we want the reverse conversions from binary codes to character sequences to be performed.

Character files for which data conversion is to be performed are called *text files*. Text files contain not only the codes for printable characters but also control codes such as CR (carriage return), LF (line feed), and FF (form feed) for dividing the file into lines and pages. The noncontrol characters occur in sequences representing such data values as integers, real numbers, Boolean values, characters, and strings. Input from the file and output to it are handled as has been previously described for the **input** and **output** statements. **Output** statements can contain formatting commands such as **tab** and **more**.

In the algorithmic language, we will use the keyword **text** in an access mode to indicate that a file of characters is to be processed as a text file. Since text files can only be processed sequentially, they give rise to three more access modes:

text input

text output

text extend

These modes are the same as the corresponding ones without the keyword **text**, except that data conversion is carried out when **text** is present and is not carried out when **text** is absent. Thus, integers, real numbers, Boolean values, characters, and strings can be read from a character file in mode **text input**; in mode **input** only characters can be read, one at a time. Likewise, integers, real numbers, Boolean values, characters, and strings can be written to a character file in modes **text output** and **text extend**; in modes **output** and **extend**, only characters can be written, one at a time.

A file is opened with an **open** statement, which has the following from:

open file-variable **as** external-name **mode** access-mode

The file variable is the *internal name* for the file—the name by which the file is known to the algorithm processing it. The **external name** is the name by which the file is known to the computer system. The external name typically designates a particular input, output, or storage device and perhaps a particular file stored on that device. The external name is not an identifier but is represented by a string constant, variable, or expression. This allows the external name to be included in the program as a constant, obtained from the user, or even computed by the program. The access mode states which of the previously discussed modes governs access to the file.

Files are closed with a **close** statement. The keyword **close** is followed by a list of file-variables representing files to be closed:

close file-variable1, file-variable2, ...

Closing files that have had data written to them is extremely important. Data to be written to a file is often stored temporarily in main memory and transferred to the external device in blocks. The last block is transferred when the file is closed. Failing to close the file may cause part of the data written to it to be lost; this is particularly likely if the program terminates abnormally due to a hardware or software failure.

Consider the following definitions and declarations:

type *student* = **record**

      name: *string*

      major: *string*

      gradePointAverage: *real*

   endrecord

type *studentFile* = **file of** *student*

stdnt: *student*

oldFile, *newFile*: *studentFile*

The file variables *oldFile* and *newFile* serve as internal names for files of student records. Suppose we wish to read the records of *oldFile*, update them as needed, and create a file *newFile* containing the updated records. We might open *oldFile* with the statement

  open *oldFile* **as** 'c:gpa-sem1.dat' **mode input**

and open *newFile* with the statement

  open *newFile* **as** 'c:gpa-sem2.dat' **mode output**

The internal name *oldFile* is to refer to the disk file with the external name c:gpa-sem1.dat, and the internal name *newFile* is to refer to the disk file with the external name c:gpa-sem2.dat. *OldFile* is opened for sequential input, and *newFile* will be created using sequential input. Any existing file with the external name c:gpa-sem2.dat will be deleted since *Delete* is automatically excuted when a file is opened in **output** mode. If no file with that external name exists, a new, empty file with that name will be created.

External file names are completely system dependent. Our examples follow the conventions of the MS-DOS operating system, which is widely used on microcomputers. In c:gpa-sem1.dat, for example, the *device name* c: indicates disk drive c, the disk drive on which the file is stored. The file name gpa-sem1 (Grade Point Averages, First Semester) and the extension .dat (data) designate a particular file on disk drive c. Extensions are used to designate such general classifications as data files (.dat), text files (.txt), BASIC programs (.bas), Pascal programs (.pas), and executable machine-language programs (.exe).

Instead of writing the external file names in our algorithm as string constants, we could obtain them from the user when the algorithm is executed. If *oldFileName* and *newFileName* are string variables, the following statements open the two files with user-supplied external names:

> **output** 'Enter name of input file: ', **more**
> **input** *oldFileName*
> **open** *oldFile* **as** *oldFileName* **mode input**
> **output** 'Enter name of output file: ', **more**
> **input** *newFileName*
> **open** *newFile* **as** *newFileName* **mode output**

Input and output statements   We are already familiar with the **input** statement for reading from the standard input device and the **output** statement for writing to the standard output device. With slight extensions, these statements will serve for all file input and output. We will use these statements rather than the underlying stream procedures *Read* and *Write*.

The following is the most general form of the input statement:

> **input** v1, v2, ..., vn **from** file-variable **at** position

V1, v2, ..., vn are the variables that are to receive values read from the file. Except for text files, the type of the variables must be the same as the component type of the file. For text files, the types of the variables can be any of the types *integer, real, Boolean, char,* and *string* whose values can be read from text files.

The **from** phrase gives the internal name of the file from which data is to be read. If the **from** phrase is omitted, data is read from the standard input file, which is automatically opened with mode **text input** before execution of the program begins. The standard input file normally corresponds to the user's keyboard; however, many operating systems allow it to be reassigned to other files, such as a disk file or the standard output file of another program.

The **at** phrase gives the file position at which reading will begin. The **at** phrase is allowed only in direct access mode. When it is omitted, as it must be in sequential modes, reading begins at the current position.

For example, the statement

> **input** *x, y, z* **from** *realFile* **at** 500

reads the values of *x, y,* and *z* from *realFile*. The value of *x* is read from position 500; the value of *y* is read from position 501; and the value of *z* is read from position 502. This statement is equivalent to the following stream operations on *realFile*:

> *SetPosition*(500)
> *Read*(*x*)
> *Read*(*y*)
> *Read*(*z*)

The statement

> **input** *x, y, z* **from** *realFile*

also reads three values from *realFile*, but with the value of *x* read from the current position and the values of y and z from the two positions following the current position. This statement is equivalent to the following stream operations on *realFile*:

Read(x)

Read(y)

Read(z)

The following is the most general form of the **output** statement:

output e1, e2, ..., en **to** file-variable **at** position

E1, e2, ..., en are expressions whose values are to be written to the file. Except for text files, the type of e1, e2, ..., en must be the same as the component type of the file. For text files, the values of e1, e2, ..., en can have any of the five types that can be stored in text files. Also for text files, the output list can contain formatting commands such as **tab** and **more**.

The **to** phrase gives the internal name of the file to which data is to be written. If the **to** phrase is omitted, the standard output file is assumed. Before execution of a program begins, the standard output file is automatically opened with mode **text output**.

The **at** phrase gives the file postition at which writing will begin. The **at** phrase is allowed only in direct access mode. If it is omitted, as it must be in sequential access modes, writing begins at the current position.

For example,

output 3.5, 2.98, 51.7 **to** *realFile* **at** 250

writes 3.5 to *realFile* at position 250, writes 2.98 at position 251, and writes 51.7 at position 252. This statement is equivalent to the following stream operations for *realFile*:

SetPosition(250)

Write(3.5)

Write(2.98)

Write(51.7)

The statement

output 3.5, 2.98, 51.7 **to** *realFile*

writes the same three values to *realFile*, but writing begins at the current position rather than at position 250. This statement is equivalent to the following stream operations for *realFile*:

Write(3.5)

Write(2.98)

Write(51.7)

Stream functions   The stream procedures such as *Read* and *Write* are not invoked directly by the user but are executed only in response to **open**, **close**, **input**, and **output** statements. The stream functions *AtEndP, Position,* and *Size* can be invoked directly. Each must be supplied with the internal name of the file as an argument. Thus, the value of

    AtEndP(oldFile)

returns *true* if the current position of *oldFile* is at the end position and *false* otherwise. In modes **input** and **text input**, only *AtEndP* is available; no functions are available in modes **output**, **extend**, **text output**, and **text extend**; and all three functions are available in mode **direct**.

12.5   Sequential file processing

In the remainder of this chapter, we will look at some of the details of sequential file processing. Although some techniques applicable to direct access files will be discussed later in the book, a thorough study of direct access file processing is beyond the scope of an introductory computer science course.

In sequential file processing, values (usually records) are read from one or more input files and written to one or more output files. The records are read from the input files in the order in which they are stored in the files and written to the output files in the order in which they are to be stored. Input files are opened with mode **input** or **text input**. If a new output file is being created, it is opened with mode **output** or **text output**. If new records are being added to the end of an existing file, it is opened with mode **extend** or **text extend**.

We must determine when the end of the input file is reached so as to know when to stop reading and processing records. We can use the predicate *AtEndP* for this purpose, or we can terminate the input file with a special sentinel record.

To illustrate the use of *AtEndP*, assume that *stdnt* is a variable of type *student*, and *oldFile* and *newFile* are variables of type *studentFile*. The following statements read the records from *oldFile*, modify them as needed, and write the modified records to *newFile*:

    open *oldFile* **as** 'c:testin.dat' **mode input**
    open *newFile* **as** 'c:testout.dat' **mode output**
    while not *AtEndP(oldFile)*
        input *stdnt* **from** *oldFile*
        ''Modify the value of *stdnt* as needed''
        output *stdnt* **to** *newFile*
    endwhile
    close *oldFile, newFile*

As long as the value of *AtEndP(oldFile)* is *false*, the end of *oldFile* has not yet been reached, and hence the repeated statements can be safely executed. Note that a *false* value for *AtEndP* guarantees only that at least one record remains to be processed. Therefore, reading more than one record with the same **input** statement can be dangerous because in reading the second and succeeding records the **input** statement may attempt to read beyond the last record in the file.

The following statements illustrate the use of a sentinel record to terminate processing of the input file. The sentinel record is assumed to be a record whose *name* field has the value *'zzzzzz'*:

> **open** *oldFile* **as** *'c:testin.dat'* **mode input**
> **open** *newFile* **as** *'c:testout.dat'* **mode output**
> **input** *stdnt* **from** *oldFile*
> **while** *stdnt.name* $<>$ *'zzzzzz'*
>> ''Modify the value of *stdnt* as needed''
>> **output** *stdnt* **to** *newFile*
>> **input** *stdnt* **from** *oldFile*
> **endwhile**
> **output** *stdnt* **to** *newFile* { write sentinel record }
> **close** *oldFile, newFile*

We now use two **input** statements: one preceding the **while** construction and one as the last repeated statement. The latter **input** statement reads the record that will be processed and written on the next execution of the repeated statements. The use of two **input** statements serves two purposes: (1) a record is read before the **while** construction is executed, assuring that a value is assigned to *stdnt* before *stdnt.name* is tested by the **while** statement; and (2) because each record is tested to see if it is the sentinel record after it is read but before it is processed, the sentinel record is never processed as if it were a valid data record.

Since the repeated **output** statement is not executed for the sentinel record, an additional **output** statement following the **while** construction is needed to write the sentinel record to the output file. When the output file is later read, the sentinel record will again be used to terminate processing.

12.6   Three examples of sequential file processing

Classifying accounts   Figure 12.3 shows an algorithm for classifying account records according to the outstanding balance for each account. Account records are read from the file *accounts*. Those with a balance of $500 or less are written to the file *goodAccounts*; those with a balance of more than $500 are written to the file *badAccounts*. The file *goodAccounts* can then be used to generate normal bills, and *badAccounts* can be used to generate notices warning of an excessively large unpaid balance.

The constant *balanceLimit* is defined as 500.00, the largest balance allowed for a good account. Values of type *accountRecord* are defined as records with two fields: an integer field *accountNumber* and a real field *balance*. Variables *accounts*,

Figure 12.3 Algorithm for classifying account records as good or bad according to the balance shown on each record.

```
algorithm ClassifyAccounts

{ Classify account records as good or bad according to outstanding balance }

declare
    const balanceLimit = 500.00
    type accountRecord = record
                            accountNumber: integer
                            balance: real
                         endrecord
    accounts, goodAccounts, badAccounts: file of accountRecord
    inRec: accountRecord
execute
    open accounts as 'c:accts.dat' mode input
    open goodAccounts as 'c:gdaccts.dat' mode output
    open badAccounts as 'c:badaccts.dat' mode output
    while not AtEndP(accounts)
        input inRec from accounts
        if inRec.balance > balanceLimit then
            output inRec to badAccounts
        else
            output inRec to goodAccounts
        endif
    endwhile
    close accounts, goodAccounts, badAccounts
end ClassifyAccounts
```

goodAccounts, and *badAccounts* are declared to represent files of account records; *inRec* is declared as a record variable of type *accountRecord.*

File *accounts* is opened for sequential input, and files *goodAccounts* and *badAccounts* are opened for sequential output. For simplicity, the external file names are written into the **open** statements as string constants; in practice, these names would more likely be obtained from the user as the values of string variables. That method of obtaining external file names is illustrated in the file update algorithm in Figure 12.7.

Processing is to continue until all input records have been processed—that is, until *AtEndP(accounts)* returns the value *true.* An **input** statement reads each account record into the record variable *inRec.* The *balance* field of the record, the value of *inRec.balance,* is compared with *balanceLimit.* If the value of *inRec.balance* exceeds that of *balanceLimit,* the value of *inRec* is written to *badAccounts;* otherwise, the value of *inRec* is written to *goodAccounts.*

When all the records in *accounts* have been processed, the three files are closed and the algorithm terminates.

Merging files Merging was introduced in Chapter 1. We are given a number files, each of whose records are in ascending order according to the values of a *key field,* such as a name or account number. We wish to combine the files in such a way that the records in the combined file will also be ascending order according to values of the key field.

We recall the algorithm for merging from Chapter 1. At any time only one record from each of the input files will be in main memory and available for processing. At each step of the merging procedure, we compare the keys of the available records and write the record with the smallest key to the output file. A new record is then read from the input file that supplied the record just written to the output file.

When the end of an input file is reached, that file should be ignored thereafter and processing should continue with the remaining files whose ends have not been reached. The easiest way to arrange for this to happen is to provide each input file with a sentinel record whose key is larger than the largest key allowed for a valid data record. When the end of a file is reached, its sentinel record will be read into main memory. Since the available record with the smallest key is always selected to be written to the output file, valid data records from files whose ends have not been reached will always be selected in preference to sentinel records from files whose ends have been reached. Processing terminates when all the records in main memory are sentinel records.

Figure 12.4 show an algorithm for merging two input files, *inFile1* and *inFile2,* into a single output file *outFile.* The records in the files are account records of the same type as processed by the record-classifying algorithm in Figure 12.3. The account number field is the key field, and a sentinel record has an account number of 9999. All valid data records must have account numbers less than 9999.

InFile1 and *inFile2* are opened for sequential input, and *outFile* is opened for sequential output. As is usual when sentinels are employed, we read the first record from each file before executing the repetition construction that processes the remaining records.

At the beginning of each repetition, *inRec1* and *inRec2* hold the available records from *inFile1* and *inFile2.* Processing continues until both *inRec1* and *inRec2* hold sentinel records. On each repetition, the values of *inRec1.accountNumber* and *inRec2.accountNumber* are compared. If *inRec1* holds the record with the smaller account number, then the value of *inRec1* is written to *outFile* and another record is read from *inFile1.* Otherwise, the value of *inRec2* is written to *outFile* and another record is read from *inFile2.*

When the repetition terminates, both *inRec1* and *inRec2* hold sentinel records. The value of *inRec1* is written to *outFile* so that *outFile* will also end with a sentinel record. The three files are then closed, and the algorithm terminates.

Figure 12.4 Algorithm for merging two files.

```
algorithm Merge

{ Merge inFile1, inFile2 to form outFile }

declare
    const sentinel = 9999
    type accountRecord = record
                            accountNumber: integer
                            balance: real
                        endrecord
    inFile1, inFile2, outFile: file of accountRecord
    inRec1, inRec2: accountRecord
execute
    open inFile1 as 'c:infile1' mode input
    open inFile2 as 'c:infile2' mode input
    open outFile as 'c:outfile' mode output
    input inRec1 from inFile1
    input inRec2 from inFile2
    while (inRec1.accountNumber <> sentinel) or
          (inRec2.accountNumber <> sentinel)
        if inRec1.accountNumber <= inRec2.accountNumber then
            output inRec1 to outFile
            input inRec1 from inFile1
        else
            output inRec2 to outFile
            input inRec2 from inFile2
        endif
    endwhile
    output inRec1 to outFile
    close inFile1, inFile2, outFile
end Merge
```

Updating a master file   We conclude our discussion of sequential file processing with one of the classic problems of business data processing—updating a master file from a transaction file. The master file is a permanent file such as a file of customer accounts. Records in the transaction file represent changes that need to be made in the master file, such as increasing a customer's balance when new purchases are made and decreasing it when payments are made. Transaction records can also add new records to the master file and delete existing records from it.

Figure 12.5 shows a *system flowchart* for the file update problem. A system flowchart shows the sources from which data is obtained, the processing steps to

Figure 12.5   System flowchart for the file update problem. A system
flowchart shows the flow of information from one processing
step to another. The cylinders represent disk files; the box
represents the processing carried out by the computer. The
broken line indicates that this month's new master file will
become next month's old master file.

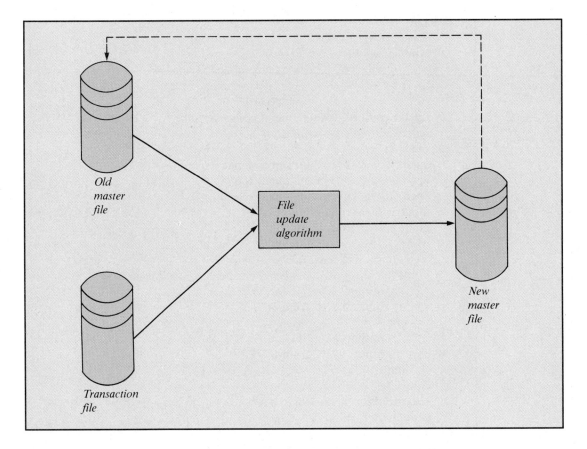

which it is subjected, and the destinations to which it is sent. The cylinders in Figure
12.5 represent disk files, and the box represents computer processing. The master
file to be updated is called the *old master file*. Records from the old master file and
the transaction file are combined by the file update algorithm to produce the updated
new master file. The broken line in the diagram indicates that the new master file
produced by this run of the processing algorithm will be the old master file the next
time a file update run is done.

The main problem of updating a master file is matching transaction records with
the master records that they are supposed to update. Both master and transaction
records have a key field; each transaction record applies to the master record having

the same key value as the transaction record. The solution is to merge the old master and transaction files into a common stream. The merged stream consists of groups of records, with all the records in a group having the same key value. The first record of a group is either a master record or a transaction record that adds a master record. The remaining records of the group make changes in the master record; the last transaction record of the group may delete the master record. Once the master and transaction records have been grouped in this way, it is easy to change the master records as called for by the transaction records and write the updated master records to the new master file.

In order for the old master file and the transaction files to be merged, the records in both files must be in ascending order according to the values of their key fields. The records written to the new master file will also be in ascending order. To simplify the merging process, the old master file and the transaction file each ends with a sentinel record whose key value is greater than the key value of any valid data record. A sentinel record is also written at the end of the new master file.

Figure 12.6 shows the modules for the file update algorithm. *Merge* inputs rec-

Figure 12.6   Modules for the file update problem. Module *Merge* merges
the old master file and transaction file into a common
stream. *Update* processes this stream to produce the new
master file. The main algorithm *FileUpdate* moves records
from the input stream represented by *Merge* to the output
stream represented by *Update*. *CommonDefinitions* provides
constant and type definitions used by the main algorithm and
the other two modules.

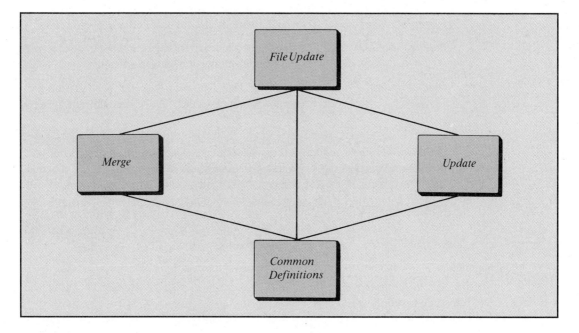

ords from the old master file and the transaction file and merges them into a single stream. *Update* processes this stream by applying the transactions to the master records and writing the updated master records to the new master file. The main algorithm calls the initialization procedures of *Merge* and *Update* before processing begins, transfers each record of the merged stream from *Merge* to *Update,* then calls finalization procedures to terminate processing. *CommonDefinitions* provides constant and type definitions used by the main algorithm and the two modules. *Common-Definitions* is a *passive* module: it contains no executable code.

Module *Merge* provides a function *EndFilesP* and three procedures:

EndFilesP	Returns *true* if the ends of both the old master file and transaction file have been reached and *false* otherwise.
InputInitialize	Opens old master file and transaction file and inputs the first record from each file.
GetRecord(outRec)	Assigns to *outRec* the next record in the merged stream.
InputFinalize	Closes the old master file and transaction file.

Merge provides a module implementation of the data abstraction *sequential input stream. EndFilesP, InputInitialize*, and *GetRecord* correspond respectively to the stream operations *AtEndP, Reset*, and *Read*.

Likewise, module *Update* provides a module implementation of the data abstraction *sequential output stream*, with *PutRecord* corresponding to the stream operation *Write*:

OutputInitialize	Opens the new master file and initializes variables.
PutRecord(inRec)	Processes the value of *inRec*, which is the next record in the merged master-transaction stream.
OutputFinalize	Outputs the last data record to the new master file, outputs a sentinel record, and closes the new master file.

CommonDefinitions exports three identifiers: *sentinel, accountRecord,* and *transRecord. Sentinel* is the key value for the sentinel record; it is defined as equal to 9999. The records in the old and new master files are of type *accountRecord*:

type *accountRecord* = **record**

   accountNumber: *integer*

   balance: *real*

endrecord

Records in the transaction file as well as those in the merged stream of master and transaction records are of type *transRecord*:

```
type transRecord = record
                    accountNumber: integer;
                    recordType: char
                    amount: real
              endrecord
```

The field *recordType* contains one of the four values 'M', 'A', 'C', 'D', which have the following significance:

'M'   Master record. *AccountNumber* contains the account number of the master record and *amount* contains the balance of the master record. Type M records occur only in the merged stream, not in the transaction file.

'A'   Add transaction. The *accountNumber* and *amount* fields contain the account number and balance of the master record to be added.

'C'   Change transaction. *AccountNumber* contains the account number of the master record to be changed. The value of *amount* is added to the *balance* field of the master record. Since the value of *amount* can be positive or negative, a Change transaction can increase or decrease the balance of a master record.

'D'   Delete transaction. The *accountNumber* field gives the account number of the master record to be deleted. The *amount* field is not used.

Figure 12.7 shows the file update algorithm. The main algorithm *FileUpdate* begins by calling *InputInitialize* and *OutputInitialize* to open files and otherwise initialize the *Merge* and *Update* modules. It then transfers records from the input stream to the output stream as long as *EndFilesP* returns *false*. After all records have been transferred, the main algorithm calls *InputFinalize* and *OutputFinalize* to terminate file processing and close the files.

In the module *Merge*, *acctFile* is the old master file and *transFile* is the transaction file. *AcctRec* holds the next record to be processed from *acctFile*, and *transRec* holds the next record to be processed from *transFile*.

The function EndFilesP returns *true* only when the ends of both the old master and the transaction file have been reached. This will have occurred when both *acctRec* and *transRec* contain sentinel records. Thus *EndFilesP* returns *true* only when both *acctRec.accountNumber* and *transRec.accountNumber* have the value *sentinel*.

InputInitialize obtains from the user the external names of the old master and transaction files, which it assigns to the string variables *acctName* and *transName*. *AcctFile* and *transFile* are opened as sequential input files with external names equal to the values of *acctName* and *transName*. Finally, the first record in *acctFile* is read into *acctRec*, and the first record in *transFile* is read into *transRec*.

GetRecord(outRec) returns the next record in the merged stream as the value of *outRec*. This is the crucial procedure for module *Merge* because it is responsible for merging records from the old master file and the transaction file. If the

Figure 12.7   Algorithm for the file update problem.

```
algorithm FileUpdate

{ Update old master file from transaction file producing new master file }

declare
    import transRecord from CommonDefinitions
    import EndFilesP, InputInitialize, GetRecord, InputFinalize
            from Merge
    import OutputInitialize, PutRecord, OutputFinalize
            from Update
    currentRec: transRecord
execute
    InputInitialize
    OutputInitialize
    while not EndFilesP
        GetRecord(currentRec)
        PutRecord(currentRec)
    endwhile
    InputFinalize
    OutputFinalize
end FileUpdate


module Merge

{ Merge old master and transaction files into common stream }

declare
    import sentinel, accountRecord, transRecord
            from CommonDefinitions
    export EndFilesP, InputInitialize, GetRecord,
            InputFinalize
    acctFile: file of accountRecord
    transFile: file of transRecord
    acctRec: accountRecord
    transRec: transRecord


    function EndFilesP: Boolean

    { Return true when there are no more old master or transaction records
      to be processed }
```

```
execute
    EndFilesP ← (acctRec.accountNumber = sentinel) and
                (transRec.accountNumber = sentinel)
end EndFilesP


procedure InputInitialize

{ Get input file names, open files, and read initial records }

declare
    acctName, transName: string
execute
    output 'Name of input account file? ', more
    input acctName
    output 'Name of transaction file? ', more
    input transName
    open acctFile as acctName mode input
    open transFile as transName mode input
    input acctRec from acctFile
    input transRec from transFile
end InputInitialize


procedure GetRecord(outRec)

{ Get next record from merged stream }

declare
    outRec: out transRecord
execute
    if acctRec.accountNumber <= transRec.accountNumber then
        outRec.accountNumber ← acctRec.accountNumber
        outRec.recordType ← 'M'
        outRec.amount ← acctRec.balance
        input acctRec from acctFile
    else
        outRec ← transRec
        input transRec from transFile
    endif
end GetRecord
```

```
        procedure InputFinalize

        { Close files }

        execute
            close acctFile, transFile
        end InputFinalize
end Merge



module Update

{ Process merged stream of old master and transaction records to produce
  new master file }

declare
        import sentinel, accountRecord, transRecord
                from CommonDefinitions
        export OutputInitialize, PutRecord, OutputFinalize
        acctFile: file of accountRecord
        buffer: accountRecord
        currentAcctNo: integer
        bufferFull: Boolean


        procedure OutputInitialize

        { Open output file and initialize variables }

        declare
            acctName: string
        execute
            input 'Name of output account file? ', more
            input acctName
            open acctFile as acctName mode output
            currentAcctNo ← −1
            bufferFull ← false
        end OutputInitialize


        procedure PutRecord(inRec)

        { Process one master or transaction record }
```

```
declare
    inRec: in transRecord
execute

    if inRec.accountNumber <> currentAcctNo then
        currentAcctNo ← inRec.accountNumber
        NewAccount
    endif
    select case inRec.recordType
        case 'M'
            Master(inRec)
        case 'A'
            Add(inRec)
        case 'C'
            Change(inRec)
        case 'D'
            Delete(inRec)
        case others
            output 'Transaction code error for key ',
                        inRec.accountNumber
    endselect
end PutRecord


procedure OutputFinalize

{ Empty buffer, write sentinel record, and close output file }

execute
    if bufferFull then
        output buffer to acctFile
    endif
    buffer.accountNumber ← sentinel
    buffer.balance ← 0.0
    output buffer to acctFile
    close acctFile
end OutputFinalize


procedure NewAccount

{ Empty buffer in preparation for processing records for new account }
```

```
execute
    if bufferFull then
        output buffer to acctFile
    endif
    bufferFull ← false
end NewAccount


procedure Master(inRec)

{ Process master record }

declare
    inRec: in transRecord
execute
    if bufferFull then
        output 'Duplicate master record for key ',
                inRec.accountNumber
    else
        buffer.accountNumber ← inRec.accountNumber
        buffer.balance ← inRec.amount
        bufferFull ← true
    endif
end Master


procedure Add(inRec)

{ Process Add transaction }

declare
    inRec: in transRecord
execute
    if bufferFull then
        output 'Attempt to add existing record for key ',
                inRec.accountNumber
    else
        buffer.accountNumber ← inRec.accountNumber
        buffer.balance ← inRec.amount
        bufferFull ← true
    endif
end Add
```

```
    procedure Change(inRec)

    { Process Change transaction }

    declare
        inRec: in transRecord
    execute
        if bufferFull then
            buffer.balance ← buffer.balance + inRec.amount
        else
            output 'Attempt to change nonexistent record for key ',
                    inRec.accountNumber
        endif
    end Change



    procedure Delete(inRec)

    { Process Delete transaction }

    declare
        inRec: in transRecord
    execute
        if bufferFull then
            bufferFull ← false
        else
            output 'Attempt to delete nonexistent record for key ',
                    inRec.accountNumber
        endif
    end Delete
end Update



module CommonDefinitions

{ Constant and type definitions used by main program and other units }

declare
    export sentinel, accountRecord, transRecord
    const sentinel = 9999
    type accountRecord = record
                            accountNumber: integer
                            balance: real
                        endrecord
```

```
        type transRecord = record
                           accountNumber: integer
                           recordType: char
                           amount: real
                     endrecord
     end CommonDefinitions
```

accountNumber field of *acctRec* is less than or equal to that of *transRec*, the master record in *acctRec* is sent to the merged stream; otherwise, the transaction record in *transRec* is sent. If the value of *acctRec* is sent to the merged stream, a new record from *acctFile* is read into *acctRec*; if the value of *transRec* is sent, a new record from *transFile* is read into *transRec*.

In comparing the two account numbers, the "equal" in "less than or equal to" is crucial. If the current master and transaction records have the same key, the master record and not the transaction record must be sent to the merged stream. This assures that in the merged stream a master record always precedes the transaction records that apply to it.

OutRec is declared with type *transRecord*, the type of the records in the merged stream. Thus a transaction record can be transmitted unchanged to the merged stream by assigning the value of *transRec* to *outRec*. Master records, however, must be converted to type *transRecord* before being transmitted to the merged stream. This is done by assigning the account number of the master record to *outRec.accountNumber*, setting *outRec.recordType* to 'M', and assigning the value of the balance field of the master record to *outRec.amount*.

OutputFinalize closes the old master file and the transaction file.

Module *Update* accepts the stream of merged master and transaction records, applies the transactions to the master records, and writes the updated master records to the new master file.

Three variables, *buffer*, *bufferFull*, and *currentAccountNo*, are crucial to the processing carried out by *Merge*. *Buffer* holds one master record; *bufferFull* is a flag whose value is *true* when *buffer* contains a valid record and *false* otherwise. When a master record (or a transaction that adds a new master record) is received from the merged stream, the master record is stored in *buffer* and *bufferFull* is set to *true*. Change transactions modify the *balance* field of *buffer*. A Delete transaction sets *bufferFull* to *false*, effectively deleting the master record strored in *buffer*.

CurrentAccountNo contains the account number of the master record currently being updated; when a record with a different account number is received from the merged stream, all transactions that apply to the current master record have been processed. If *bufferFull* is *true*, indicating that the current master record has not been deleted, the value of *buffer* is written to the new master file.

OutputInitialize obtains the external name for the new master file; *acctFile* is opened as a sequential output file with this name. *CurrentAccountNo* is set to the invalid account number -1 so that the first record received from the merged stream will be processed as the first record of a new account. *BufferFull* is set to false, indicating that *buffer* does not currently hold a valid master record.

PutRecord(inRec) accepts a record from the merged stream. The account number of the new record is compared with the value of *currentAccountNo*; if the two are not the same, *currentAccountNo* is set to the account number of the new record, and the procedure *NewAccount* is called to begin processing for a new account. Finally, the value of the record type field for the new record is used in a case construction to call the proper procedure for processing the record. *Master* is called to process a master record, *Add* to process an Add transaction, *Change* to process a Change transaction, and *Delete* to process a Delete transaction. If *inRec.recordType* has some value other than 'M', 'A', 'C', or 'D', an error message warns the user of a "transaction code error" and the record is ignored.

OutputFinalize begins by checking the value of *bufferFull*; if the value is *true*, *buffer* contains a master record, which *OutputFinalize* writes to the new master file. *OutputFinalize* then writes a sentinel record to the new master file and closes the file.

Note that only *InputInitialize*, *PutRecord*, and *OutputInitialize* are exported by *Update*. The five procedures *NewAccount*, *Master*, *Add*, *Change*, and *Delete* are not exported and are only for internal use within the module; all are called by *PutRecord*.

NewAccount terminates processing for the current account—a sequence of master and transaction records with the same account number. If *bufferFull* is *true*, indicating that *buffer* contains a valid master record, the contents of *buffer* are written to the new master file. *BufferFull* is then set to *false*, indicating that *buffer* no longer contains a record to be written to the new master file.

Master stores a master record in *buffer*. If *bufferFull* is *true*, *buffer* already contains a master record with the same key as the record being processed. In this case the user is warned of a "duplicate master record" error and the current input record is not processed.

Like *Master*, *Add* stores a master record in *buffer*. If *bufferFull* is *true*, *buffer* already contains a master record with the same key as the master record to be added. In this case, the user is warned of an "attempt to add an existing record" and the Add transaction is not processed.

Change adds the value of the *amount* field of the transaction record to that of the *balance* field of the current master record. If the value of *bufferFull* is *false*, there is no current master record to be updated; *Change* complains of an "attempt to change a nonexistent record" and the Change transaction is not processed.

Delete deletes the current master record. If *bufferFull* is *true*, it is set to *false*; if *bufferFull* is *false*, *Change* complains of an "attempt to delete a nonexistent record."

Review questions

1. What is a *data structure*?

2. Contrast *simple*, *structured*, and *pointer* types.

3. What is a *record*? What are *fields*? *Field identifiers*? *Field designators*?

4. Contrast *entire values* and *component values*.

5. Contrast *entire variables* and *component variables*.

6. Give an example of *nested records*.

7. Contrast *structural equivalence* of types with *name equivalence*. Which kind of equivalence is used in the algorithmic language? What are some of the difficulties of determining structural equivalence?

8. What is a *file*?

9. What is a *data abstraction*?

10. Describe one way of visualizing a *stream*.

11. What is the *current position* of a stream?

12. Describe the three functions defined for streams.

13. Describe the six procedures defined for streams.

14. What is the *component type* of a file type?

15. Why is assignment not allowed for file variables?

16. Contrast sequential and direct access files.

17. Describe the access modes **input**, **output**, **extend**, and **direct access**. Which stream operations are allowed in each mode?

18. Contrast text and nontext files.

19. What are the *internal* and *external* names for a file?

20. Describe the **open** and **close** statements and give the function performed by each. Why may data be lost if an output file is not closed?

21. Describe the statements for reading records from and writing records to a file.

Exercises

1. Modify the algorithm *Classify Accounts* so that it obtains the names of external files from the user rather than the file names being written into the program. What is the advantage of the modified algorithm over the original one?

2. Only the text files can be sent to display devices such as the screen and the printer. Frequently, we need to *list* a nontext file—print its contents in a form people can read. Using the definition for type *accountRecord* given in the text, write an algorithm to read a file of account records and print its contents in two columns: one column for the *accountNumber* fields of the records and one column for the *balance* fields.

3. Suppose that the formatting command **page** in an **output** statement causes a form-feed code to be placed in a text file; the form-feed code will cause a printer to advance to the top of a new page. Thus, if the standard output file is a printer, the statement

   output page

   causes the printer to advance to the top of a new page. Modify the algorithm of Exercise 1 so that it prints at most 60 lines on each page.

4. Each record of a time-card file contains an employee number, the hours the employee worked, and the employee's hourly pay rate. Each record of a payroll file contains an employee number and the gross wages that the employee earned. Write an algorithm to read a time-card file, calculate the gross wages for each employee, and write the results to a payroll file. Employees are paid time and a half for overtime, which is all hours in excess of 40.

5. Data-base management and information retrieval systems must often merge files according to logical operations specified by the user. For example, an **and**-merge sends a record to the output file only if it occurs in each of the input files; an **or**-merge sends a record to the output file if it occurs in any or all of the input files. Note that only one copy of each record is sent to the output file, even though the record may occur in more than one input file. Write algorithms for **and**-merge and **or**-merge.

For further reading

Programs for updating master files are often poorly structured and may not allow some reasonable sequences of transaction records. Recently a structured algorithm for updating files, known as the "balanced line" algorithm, has become popular. The following references describe the balanced line algorithm. The version used in this book follows most closely the one given by Levy.

Dijkstra, E. W. *A Discipline of Programming*. Englewood Cliffs, N.J.: Prentice-Hall, 1976, pp. 117–122.

Dwyer, B. "One More Time—How to Update a Master File." *Communications of the ACM*, January 1981, pp. 3–8.

Levy, Michael R. "Modularity and the Sequential File Update Problem." *Communications of the ACM*, June 1982, pp. 362–367.

Pascal Supplement

This supplement describes the Pascal versions of the record and file types discussed in the main text of this chapter. In addition, it briefly introduces three kinds of types that occur in Pascal but not in the algorithmic language: *enumerated types*, *subrange types*, and *set types*. Enumerated types are included for reference only; they are not used in any of the Pascal programs in this book. Subrange types are important for defining *array types*, which are discussed in Chapter 13. In this book, set types will be used only for translating certain case constructions; the use of sets helps to make up for the lack of an **others** case in Pascal.

Type definitions

Type definitions in a Pascal program, function, or procedure appear in a *type definition section*, which is similar in construction to a constant definition section. Type definitions must follow constant definitions but precede variable declarations. The following list shows the required order for the definitions and declarations that precede the executable part of a program, function, or procedure:

constant definitions

type definitions

variable declarations

function and procedure declarations

Any declaration or definition sections that are not needed may be omitted, but those that are present must be in the order shown.

A type definition section has the following form:

type
     type definitions

Each type definition has the following form:

type-identifier = type-denoter;

A "type denoter" is either a type identifier or a construction defining a new type. A type definition, like a constant definition, is terminated by a semicolon.

For example, the type declaration section

type
    floatingPoint = real;
    logical = Boolean;

defines type *floatingPoint* as equivalent to type *real*, and type *logical* as equivalent to type *Boolean*.

Enumerated types

Pascal allows programmers to define new ordinal types by listing, or enumerating, the values of each new type. The values of enumerated types are represented by identifiers. The following are some definitions of enumerated types:

type

    day = (*sun, mon, tue, wed, thurs, fri, sat*);

    chessman = (*pawn, knight, bishop, rook, queen, king*);

    grade = (*f, d, c, b, a*);

Type *day*, for example, consists of seven values denoted by the identifiers *sun, mon, tue, wed, thurs, fri,* and *sat*. The order in which the identifiers are listed is important because it allows us to define the relations "precedes" and "follows" for the type. Thus, *sun* precedes *mon*, and *tue* precedes *fri*. Similarly, *sat* follows *fri*, and *fri* follows *mon*.

    The same identifier cannot be used for values of more than one enumerated type. If we define

    rank = (*private, corporal, sergeant, lieutenant, captain, major, colonel,*

            general);

then we cannot also define

    officer = (*lieutenant, captain, major, colonel, general*);

since doing so would define *lieutenant, captain, major, colonel,* and *general* as values of more than one type. In the next section we will see how *officer* can be defined as a subrange type.

    We can think of the predefined type *Boolean* as if it were defined as follows:

    Boolean = (*false, true*);

We can use enumerated types whenever we need a type with a relatively small number of named values. One such application occurs in the file update program, discussed in the main text and later in this supplement. That program uses one of the characters 'M', 'A', 'C', 'D' to specify whether a record in the merged stream represents a master record, an Add transaction, a Change transaction, or a Delete transaction. Instead of using four values of type *char* for this purpose, we could define an enumerated type

    recType = (*master, add, change, delete*);

and use a value of type *recType* to classify each record. The *recordType* field for transaction records and records in the merged stream would be defined by

    recordType: *recType*;

Subrange types

For every ordinal type we can define a new type whose values are some subrange of the original type. For example,

    digit = 0 . . 9;

defines a subrange of type *integer* whose values are 0 through 9. (The two dots in the definition can be read as "to" or "through.") Likewise, the type definition *workday* = *mon* . . *fri*;

defines a subrange of type *day* whose values are *mon* through *fri*, and

officer = *lieutenant* . . *general*;

defines a subrange of type *rank* whose values are *lieutenant* through *general*.

The type whose values are used to define a subrange type is called the *host* type. All operations that can be performed on values of the host type can also be performed on values of the subrange type. The only difference between the subrange type and the host type is that values of the subrange type are required to lie in the specified subrange.

For example, suppose that *i* and *n* are declared as follows:

var
    i: *integer*;
    n: *digit*;

The assignment

    $i := n$

is always valid since a value of type *digit* is also a value of type *integer*. On the other hand,

    $n := i$

is valid only if the value of *i* lies in the range of 0 through 9. A value of type *integer* is also a value of type *digit* only if it lies in the range 0 through 9.

All the operations that can be carried out on integers are allowed for digits as well. For example, the statements

    $n := 5$;
    $n := n - 3$;
    $n := 2 * n$

are valid (when executed in the order shown). In each statement the value assigned to *n* lies in the range 0 through 9. On the other hand, consider the following statements:

    $n := 7$;
    $n := n + 3$

After 7 is assigned to *n*, the value of $n + 3$ is 10. When an attempt is made to assign 10 to *n*, the computer reports an error.

Use of a subrange type rather than its host type serves two purposes. First, it notifies someone reading the program that only a small range of values is meaningful for a certain variable, parameter, or record field. Second, it allows the computer to check that the values assigned to the variable, parameter, or record field lie in the designated subrange and to warn of an error if they do not.

Operations on values of ordinal types

The ordinal types in Pascal are *integer*, *Boolean*, *char*, enumerated types, and sub-range types. As the name implies, an order is defined for the values of each of these types. For integers, this order is the usual numerical order. For Boolean values, *false* precedes *true*. For characters, the order is given by the collating sequence for a particular computer system. For enumerated types, the order of the values is the order in which they are listed in the type definition. Values have the same order in a subrange type as they do in the host type.

As a consequence of this ordering, the relational operators

$$= \quad < \quad > \quad <= \quad >= \quad <>$$

can be applied to values of any ordinal type. The following examples illustrate relational operators applied to values of enumerated types:

Expression	Value
sun < *thurs*	*true*
queen >= *rook*	*true*
f = *a*	*false*
private > *general*	*false*

The functions *pred* and *succ* apply to values of all ordinal types. *Pred* returns the value (if any) immediately preceding the value of its argument; *succ* returns the value (if any) immediately following the value of its argument. If no such value exists, the value of the function is undefined and the function call results in an error. The following table illustrates *pred* and *succ*:

Expression	Value
pred(5)	4
succ(5)	6
succ(*sun*)	*mon*
pred(*true*)	*false*
succ('a')	'b'
pred(*queen*)	*rook*
pred(*sun*)	undefined
succ(*king*)	undefined

The values of enumerated types are numbered, starting with 0 for the first value. For example, the values of type *day* are numbered as follows:

$$day = \begin{matrix} (sun, & mon, & tue, & wed, & thurs, & fri, & sat); \\ 0 & 1 & 2 & 3 & 4 & 5 & 6 \end{matrix}$$

The numbers are called the *ordinal numbers* of the corresponding values. Pascal provides a predefined function, *ord*, which returns the ordinal number of its argument:

Expression	Value
ord (*sun*)	0
ord (*sat*)	6
ord(*true*)	1
ord(*false*)	0
ord(*bishop*)	2

The *ord* function can be applied to values of ordinal types other than *Boolean* and the enumerated types. For integer values, *ord* returns the value of its argument; for character values, the ordinal numbers depend on the collating sequence. In the following examples, the ASCII character set is assumed:

Expression	Value
ord(100)	100
ord(−100)	−100
ord('a')	97
ord('z')	122
ord('0')	48
ord('9')	57

For type *char* only, there is a function, *chr*, that converts ordinal numbers back into the corresponding characters:

Expression	Value
chr(97)	'a'
chr(122)	'z'
chr(48)	'0'
chr(57)	'9'

Set types

A *set* is a collection of values. For example, the set that contains the values 1, 3, 5, and 9 is denoted in Pascal as

[1, 3, 5, 9]

The set that contains the characters 'a', 'e', 'i', 'o', and 'u' is denoted as

['a', 'e', 'i', 'o', 'u']

The values that belong to a set are called its *elements*. The elements of [1, 3, 5, 9] are 1, 3, 5, and 9.

The type denoter for a set type has the following form:

set of base-type

The base type is the type of the elements of the sets and must be an ordinal type. Each Pascal implementation imposes additional restrictions on possible base types; for example, some implementations allow *char* as a base type while others do not. These restrictions destroy much of the usefulness of set types because they prevent a program that uses set types from being portable between different Pascal implementations.

For example, the type definition

letterset = **set of** 'a' . . 'z'

defines *letterset* as a type whose values are all possible sets of lowercase letters. The following are some possible values of type *letterset*:

['a'], ['a', 'c'], ['a', 'e', 'i', 'o', 'u'], []

Note that [] denotes the empty set, the set that has no elements. Every set type includes the empty set as a value, regardless of the base type.

Now consider the following type definitions:

primary = (*red, yellow, blue*);

primarySet = **set of** *primary*;

Type *primarySet* contains the following values:

[]   [*red*]   [*yellow*]   [*blue*]   [*red, yellow*]
[*red, blue*]   [*yellow, blue*]   [*red, yellow, blue*]

A variable of type *primarySet* must have one of these eight values.

Set values are created by means of *set constructors*. We have been using set constructors all along to display set values:

[1, 3, 5, 9]   ['a', 'b', 'c', 'd']   [*red, yellow*]

A set constructor is an expression that is evaluated as the program executes. This means that it can contain variables and expressions as well as constants. For example, suppose the variables i and j have the values 5 and 3. The set constructor

[$i, j, i + j, i - j, i * j, i$ **div** j]

has the value

[5, 3, 8, 2, 15, 1]

(The order in which the elements are listed is immaterial.) On the other hand, if the values of i and j were 7 and 2, the same set constructor would have the following value:

[7, 2, 9, 5, 14, 3]

The list of elements in a set constructor can contain subranges as well as the values of individual elements. Thus, the set constructor

[1 . . 5]

is equivalent to

[1, 2, 3, 4, 5]

and

[1 . . 3, 7, 12 . . 15]

is equivalent to

[1, 2, 3, 7, 12, 13, 14, 15]

There are three operations that can be carried out on sets to yield other sets. These are *union, intersection,* and *difference,* which in Pascal are denoted by + , *, and − . They are defined as follows, where s and t represent values of the same set type:

$s + t$ The union of s and t, which contains those elements that belong to s, to t, or to both s and t.

$s * t$ The intersection of s and t, which contains those elements belonging to both s and t.

$s - t$ The difference of s and t, which contains those elements that belong to s but do not belong to t.

The following examples illustrate union, intersection, and difference:

Expression	*Value*
[1, 2, 3, 4] + [3, 4, 5, 6]	[1, 2, 3, 4, 5, 6]
[1, 2, 3, 4] * [3, 4, 5, 6]	[3, 4]
[1, 2, 3, 4] − [3, 4, 5, 6]	[1, 2]

The following relational operators apply to sets of the same base type and yield Boolean Values:

  =   <>   <=   >=   **in**

These operators can be defined as follows, where s and t represent sets of the same base type, and e represents a value belonging to the base type of s and t:

$s = t$ yields *true* if s *equals* t, that is, if s and t contain the same elements.

$s <> t$ yields *true* if s is *not equal* to t, that is, if s and t do not contain the same elements.

$s <= t$ yields *true* if s is a *subset* of t, that is, if every element of s is also an element of t.

$s >= t$ yields *true* if s is a *superset* of t, that is, if every element of t is also an element of s.

e **in** t yields *true* if e is an element of s.

The following examples illustrate the relational operators for sets:

Expression	*Value*
[1, 2, 3] = [1, 2, 4]	*false*
[1, 2, 3] <> [1, 2, 4]	*true*
[2, 3] <= [1, 2, 3]	*true*
[1, 2, 3] >= [1, 2, 3, 4]	*false*
2 **in** [1, 2, 3]	*true*
4 **in** [1, 2, 3]	*false*

Sets are useful for avoiding complex Boolean expressions. For example, consider the following **if** statement, in which c is a character variable:

if $(c = \text{'a'})$ **or** $(c = \text{'e'})$ **or** $(c = \text{'i'})$ **or**
  $(c = \text{'o'})$ **or** $(c = \text{'u'})$ **then**
    ProcessVowel

This statement will be easier to read and will execute more rapidly if written as follows:

if c **in** ['a', 'e', 'i', 'o', 'u'] **then**
    ProcessVowel

Record types

Definitions of record types have much the same form in Pascal as in the algorithmic language. The type denoter for a record type has the following form:

record
    list of field definitions
end

Field definitions have the same form as variable declarations. Note two differences between Pascal and the algorithmic language. First, in Pascal, field definitions are separated by semicolons, which are not used in the algorithmic language. Second, a record description in Pascal is terminated by **end** instead of **endrecord**, which is used for the same purpose in the algorithmic language.

For example, consider the following type definition section:

type
    skyCondition = (*cloudy, partlyCloudy, clear*);
    precipitation = (*rain, snow, sleet, hail, none*);

> *weather* = **record**
> > *sky*: *skyCondition*;
> > *precip*: *precipitation*;
> > *low*,
> > *high*: *integer*
>
> **end**;

SkyCondition and *precipitation* are both enumerated types. A record of type *weather* contains four fields: *sky*, which holds a value of type *skyCondition*; *precip*, which holds a value of type *precipitation*; and *low* and *high*, which hold values of type *integer*. In the record description, note that each field definition except the last ends with a semicolon. What's more, the last definition is a combined one that defines both *low* and *high* as integer fields.

Fields are referred to by field designators, exactly as in the algorithmic language. For example, suppose *v* and *w* are declared as entire variables of type *weather*:

> **var**
> > *v, w*: *weather*;

The four component variables of *w* are designated as follows:

> *w.sky*
> *w.precip*
> *w.low*
> *w.high*

The following assignment of an entire value

> *w* := *v*

is equivalent to the following four assignments of component values:

> *w.sky* := *v.sky*;
> *w.precip* := *v.precip*;
> *w.low* := *v.low*;
> *w.high* := *v.high*

Pascal does not provide any means for representing structured constants; this is a major deficiency of the language. To assign to *w* the value that would be denoted in the algorithmic language by

> *weather*(*cloudy, rain*, 50, 75)

we must assign the appropriate component value to each of the component variables of *w*:

> *w.sky* := *cloudy*;
> *w.precip* := *rain*;
> *w.low* := 50;
> *w.high* := 75

Records can be nested in Pascal. Consider, for example, the following type definitions:

date = **record**
 month: 1 . . 12;
 day: 1 . . 31;
 year: *integer*
 end;
report = **record**
 dt: *date*;
 wx: *weather*
 end;

Each report record contains a date record and a weather record. If *r* is declared by

var
 r: *report*;

the component variables of *r* are *r.dt* and *r.wx*. Each of these, however, is a record variable with component variables of its own. The component variables of *r.dt* are

r.dt.month
r.dt.day
r.dt.year

and the component variables of *r.wx* are

r.wx.sky
r.wx.precip
r.wx.low
r.wx.high

As in the algorithmic language, the scope of a field identifier is the record description in which it is defined. The period that precedes a field identifier in a field designator can be regarded as an operator that opens up a record description and allows the field identifiers inside to become visible. Because of the limited scopes of field identifiers, no confusion arises if the same field identifiers are used for fields of different records or if field identifiers are the same as variable names.

The with statement The **with** statement allows field designators to be abbreviated. For example, instead of

w.sky := *cloudy*;
w.precip := *rain*;
w.low := 50;
w.high := 75

we can write

```
with w do
    begin
        sky := cloudy;
        precip := rain;
        low := 50;
        high := 75
end
```

The assignments to the field identifiers are interpreted as assignments to component variables of *w*. Put another way, the **with** statement causes *w*. to be prefixed to each of the field identifiers *sky, precip, low,* and *high*.

Any number of record variables can be listed between **with** and **do**. The record variables should have different types; otherwise, there is no way for the system to determine which record variable to prefix to which field identifier. The following **with** statement assigns a value to the record variable *r*:

```
with r, dt, wx do
    begin
        month := 5;
        day := 24;
        year := 1984;
        sky := cloudy;
        precip := rain;
        low := 55;
        high := 75
end;
```

Once the system encounters *r* in the **with** list, it will prefix *r*. to *dt* and *wx*. In the remainder of the **with** list, therefore, we can write *dt* and *wx* instead of *r.dt* and *r.wx*. The type of a record variable determines which field identifiers it will be prefixed to. Since *r* is of type *report*, *r*. will be prefixed to *dt* and *wx*; since *r.dt* is of type *date*, *r.dt*. will be prefixed to *month, day,* and *year*; since *r.wx* is of type *weather*, *r.wx*. will be prefixed to *sky, precip, low,* and *high*.

Record variants   It is sometimes convenient to allow records belonging to the same type to have different structures. To accommodate this situation, Pascal allows a record to have a *fixed part* followed by a *variant part*. The fixed part is the same for all records of a given type. The variant part, however, can differ for records belonging to the same type.

For example, suppose that student records can refer to both undergraduate and graduate students. An undergraduate has a class (freshman, sophomore, junior, or senior) and a grade-point average. A graduate student does not have a class and has a standing rather than a grade-point average. Consider the following definitions:

```
statusType = (undergrad, grad);
classType = (freshman, sophomore, junior, senior);
standingType = (satisfactory, unsatisfactory);
student = record
                id: integer;
                case status: statusType of
                    undergrad:
                        (class: classType;
                         gpa: real);
                    grad:
                        (standing: standingType)
        end;
```

The fields *id* and *status* belong to the fixed part; they are present in every record of type *student*. The status field is the *tag field* for the record; its value determines the structure of the variant part. If the value of the status field is *undergrad,* the variant part contains the fields *class* and *gpa*. If the value of the status field is *grad,* the variant part contains the single field *standing*. Note that each possible variant part is enclosed in parentheses and labeled with the corresponding value of the tag field.

For example, a value of type *student* having the value *undergrad* for its status field has the same structure as if it were described as follows:

```
record
    id: integer;
    status: statusType;
    class: classType;
    gpa: real
end
```

Likewise, a value of type *student* having the value *grad* for its status field has the same structure as if it were described as follows:

```
record
    id: integer;
    status: statusType;
    standing: standingType
end
```

If *s* is a variable of type *student,* the assignments

```
s.id := 3794;
s.status := undergrad;
s.class := junior;
s.gpa := 2.9
```

are valid, as are the statements

$s.id := 7196;$

$s.status := grad;$

$s.standing := satisfactory$

The fields of a given record must be designated by distinct field identifiers even if the fields belong to different variants. For example, the following declaration is invalid:

t: **record**

    case b: *Boolean* **of**

        true:

            (c: *real*);

        false:

            (c: *integer*)

   end;

We must use different field identifiers for the real and integer fields, even though they belong to different variants:

t: **record**

    case b: *Boolean* **of**

        true:

            (r: *real*);

        false:

            (i: *integer*)

   end;

With the correct declaration, the Pascal compiler knows that $t.r$ is a real variable and that $t.i$ is an integer variable. If the incorrect definition were allowed, the compiler would not be able to determine whether $t.c$ were a real variable or an integer variable. The compiler would thus be unable to do the strong type checking required in Pascal.

Variant parts can be nested. Each possible variant part can contain both a fixed part and another variant part. Those variant parts can contain still other variant parts, and so on.

File types

Type definitions   File types are described in Pascal in the same way as in the algorithmic langauge. The type denoter for a file type has the following form:

file of component-type

The component type is the type of the values stored in the file. The only restriction on the component type is that the components of a file may not themselves be files or contain files as components. Thus the component type may not be a file type nor a structured type whose values contain files at any level of nesting.

Pascal handles text files (spelled "textfiles" in books on Pascal) differently than does the algorithmic language. Pascal textfiles have the predefined file type *text*. Files of type *text* are similar to files of type **file of** *char*. The contents of a textfile, however, are divided into lines and perhaps also into pages. On input from a textfile, sequences of characters representing integers, real numbers, and Boolean values are automatically converted into the binary representations for those values. On output to a textfile, the binary representations of integer, real, and Boolean values are automatically converted to the corresponding sequences of characters. The standard files *input* and *output* are of type *text*.

File variables   As in the algorithmic language, file variables serve as the internal names of files. The following definition and declarations illustrate how file variables are declared in Pascal:

type

    studentFile = **file of** *student*

var

    roll: *studentFile*;

    data: **file of** *real*;

    report: *text*;

Roll is declared as a file of student records, *data* as a file of real numbers, and *report* as a textfile.

Input and *output* are predeclared as file variables of type *text*. These file variables must not be redeclared by the programmer.

Standard Pascal does not provide any statement for associating internal and external file names. Instead, file variables that represent external files must be listed as parameters in the program heading. It is left up to the operating system to obtain from the user the external names of the files listed in the program heading. The correspondence between internal and external file names is set up before program execution begins and cannot be changed while the program is being executed.

For example, if the program *FileProcessing* uses files *roll*, *data*, and *report* as well as the standard files *input* and *output*, it must have the following program heading:

program *FileProcessing*(*input, output, roll, data, report*);

Unless the user requests otherwise, files *input* and *output* will probably be associated with standard input and output devices such as the user's keyboard and display. The user must supply the names of the remaining files when requesting the operating system to execute the program. This is usually done in a cryptic command line such as the following:

fileproc classlst stat3.dat lpt1

In this command line, "fileproc" is the name of the disk file containing the program *FileProcessing*, the program to be executed; "classlst" is the name of the external file corresponding to *roll*; "stat3.dat" is the name of the external file corresponding to *data*; and "lpt1" is the name of the external file corresponding to *report*. Classlst and stat3.dat are the names of disk files; lpt1 is the name of an output device, "line printer 1."

This method of associating internal and external file names is unsatisfactory for many purposes. For example, user-friendly programs usually prompt the user to enter the names of the files to be processed, instead of requiring the file names to be included in a cryptic command line. Some programs even allow the user to select the files to be processed from a menu of relevant file names by means of a pointing device such as a mouse.

To allow user-friendly programs to be written, many versions of Pascal provide, as a nonstandard extension, means by which internal and external file names can be associated within a Pascal program. The program in Figure 12.10 illustrates the method by which this is done in UCSD Pascal.

Reset and rewrite Standard Pascal provides two modes for file access: *inspection* and *generation*. These correspond respectively to modes **input** and **output** in the algorithmic language. (For a file of type *text*, inspection and generation correspond to the algorithmic-language modes **text input** and **text output**.) Standard Pascal does not provide access modes corresponding to **extend** and **direct**, although some Pascal implementations provide such modes as nonstandard extensions.

Standard Pascal does not provide **open** and **close** statements. One job done by the **open** statement—establishing a correspondence between internal and external file names—is accomplished automatically in standard Pascal. The remaining jobs done by the **open** statement, such as establishing an access mode, are handled by the predefined procedures *reset* and *rewrite*. Files are closed automatically when execution of a program terminates. Since data can be lost if a program failure occurs before files are closed, some implementations of Pascal provide a *close* procedure as a nonstandard extension.

If *f* is a file variable, the procedure call

reset(*f*)

accomplishes three things: (1) the current position of *f* is set to the beginning of the file; (2) inspection mode is established; and (3) the first value in the file is transferred to main memory. The procedure call

rewrite(*f*)

accomplishes two things: (1) the current contents of file *f* are deleted, so the value of *f* becomes the empty file; and (2) generation mode is established. We invoke *reset* before beginning to read from a file and *rewrite* before beginning to write to a file.

Buffer variables, get, put, and eof A *buffer* is an area of main memory for holding values read from a file or values to be written to a file. Normally, the operating system maintains at least one buffer for each file that a program accesses. To read a value from a file, the program requests the operating system to transfer the value from the file to the buffer area. To write a value to a file, the program places the value in the buffer area and requests the operating system to transfer the contents of the buffer area to the file.

The algorithmic language automatically transfers values between the buffer area and variables declared by the programmer. The programmer cannot refer to the buffer area directly. For example, when the statement

input x **from** f

is executed, the operating system is requested to transfer the next value in file f to the buffer area. The contents of the buffer area are then assigned to the variable x. Likewise, when

output x **to** f

is executed, the value of x is first moved to the buffer area for file f. The operating system is then requested to write the contents of the buffer area to the file.

In contrast, Pascal allows programmers to access the buffer area directly. Associated with each file variable is a *buffer variable* that refers to the buffer area. The buffer variable is denoted by the file variable followed by an upward arrow. Thus, $f\uparrow$ denotes the buffer variable corresponding to the file variable f. A buffer variable can be used just like any other variable: the program can refer to the value of the buffer variable, and the buffer variable can be assigned new values.

For example, suppose that the file variable f is declared by

f: **file of** *integer*;

and the current contents of the file are as follows:

    10   30   15   99   75

Executing

   reset(f)

resets the current position to the beginning of the file, establishes inspection mode, and assigns the first value in the file to the buffer variable. After executing *reset*, we can represent the state of the file and the buffer variable as follows:

    10   30   15   99   75   f↑ = 10
    ↑

The value of $f\uparrow$ can be accessed just like the value of any other variable. For example, the statement

   $x := f\uparrow$

assigns the value 10 to x.

To access the next value in the file, we use the procedure *get*, which can be called only in inspection mode. The procedure call

   get(f)

moves the current position to the next value and assigns that value to the buffer variable. The new state of the file and buffer variable is as follows:

10 30 15 99 75 $\qquad$ $f\uparrow = 30$
$\quad\;\;\uparrow$

Each time *get* is called, the current position is moved to the next file position and the value at that position is assigned to the buffer variable. Thus after *get* has been called three more times, the state of the file and buffer variable is as follows:

10 30 15 99 75 $\qquad$ $f\uparrow = 75$
$\qquad\qquad\;\;\uparrow$

Now suppose that *get* is called yet another time. The current position is advanced to the end position. Since no value is stored at the end position, none can be transferred to the buffer variable, and the value of the buffer variable is undefined. This situation can be represented as follows:

10 30 15 99 75 $\qquad$ $f\uparrow = ?$
$\qquad\qquad\qquad\uparrow$

The program must be alerted to this situation so that it will not attempt to refer to the value of the buffer variable when the buffer variable has no valid value. This is done with the predefined predicate *eof*, which corresponds to *AtEndP* in the algorithmic language. The function call *eof(f)* returns *true* if the current position of the file is at the end position and *false* otherwise. The value of the buffer variable is defined when *eof* returns *false* and undefined when *eof* returns *true*. If we include the value returned by *eof* in the state of the file, we can represent the state just before the end position is reached as follows:

10 30 15 99 75 $\qquad$ $f\uparrow = 75$
$\qquad\qquad\;\;\uparrow$ $\qquad\qquad\quad$ *eof(f) = false*

The state after the end position has been reached is represented as follows:

10 30 15 99 75 $\qquad$ $f\uparrow = ?$
$\qquad\qquad\qquad\uparrow$ $\qquad\qquad\;$ *eof(f) = true*

The procedure call

rewrite(f)

deletes the current contents of file *f* and establishes generation mode. After the call, the value of file *f* is the empty file and the value of *f* $\uparrow$ is undefined. We can represent the state of file *f* as follows:

$\qquad\qquad\qquad\qquad\qquad f\uparrow = ?$

$\uparrow$

To store a value in the file, we first assign the value to the buffer variable:

$f\uparrow := 64$

The state of the file and the buffer variable is now as follows:

$$f\uparrow \ = \ 64$$

$$\uparrow$$

The predefined procedure *put,* which can only be called in generation mode, transfers the value of the buffer variable to the file and moves the current position forward to the new end position. After the procedure call

> *put(f)*

the state of the file and buffer variable is as follows:

64 $f\uparrow \ = \ ?$

   $\uparrow$

Note that, after the call to *put,* the value of the buffer variable is once again undefined.

Succeeding values are stored in the file in the same way. For example, the statements

> $f\uparrow \ := \ 50;$
> *put(f)*

store 50 in the file; the statements

> $f\uparrow \ := \ 13;$
> *put(f)*

store 13 in the file; and the statements

> $f\uparrow \ := \ 88;$
> *put(f)*

store 88 in the file. After these three sets of statements have been executed, the state of the file and the buffer variable is as follows:

64   50   13   88 $f\uparrow \ = \ ?$

            $\uparrow$

In generation mode, the current position of a file is always at the end position, and so *eof* always returns the value *true.*

Sequential file processing with get and put Let us define an account record by

> **type**
>   *accountRecord* =**record**
>   *accountNumber: integer;*
>   *balance: real*
>   **end**;

and delcare *oldFile* and *newFile* as account records:

>**var**
>
>>*oldFile*, *newFile*: **file of** *accountRecord*;

Suppose that we want to read account records from *oldFile*, increase the balance of each record by $10 to reflect a service charge, and write the updated records to *newFile*. The following statements accomplish this task:

>*reset(oldFile)*;
>
>*rewrite(newFile)*;
>
>**while not** *eof(oldFile)***do**
>
>>**begin**
>>
>>>*newFile↑.accountNumber* := *oldFile↑.accountNumber*;
>>>
>>>*newFile↑.balance* := *oldFile↑.balance* + 10.00;
>>>
>>>*put(newFile)*;
>>>
>>>*get(oldFile)*
>>
>>**end**

Reset assigns the first value in *oldFile* to the buffer variable *oldFile↑*. Since *oldFile↑* and *newFile↑* are record variables, we can use them to construct field designators. The value of *oldFile↑.accountNumber* is assigned to *newFile↑.accountNumber*; $10 is added to the value of *oldFile↑.balance*; and the sum is assigned to *newFile↑* *.balance*. *Put* is called to write the value of *newFile↑* to *newFile*, and *get* is called to read the next value in *oldFile* into *oldFile↑*. Processing continues until *eof(oldFile)* returns the value *false*, indicating that all the records in *oldFile* have been processed.

Sequential file processing with read and write   *Read* and *write* in Pascal correspond respectively to **input** and **output** in the algorithmic language. Specifically, the procedure call

>*read(f, x)*

corresponds to the **input** statement

>**input** x **from** *f*

and the procedure call

>*write(f, x)*

corresponds to **output** statement

>**output** x **to** *f*

If the file parameter *f* is omitted, *read* is assumed to read from the standard file *input*, and *write* is assumed to write to the standard file *output*.

The procedure call *read(f, x)* is defined as equivalent to the following statements:

>$x := f↑$;
>
>*get(f)*

The value of the buffer variable is assigned to *x*, and *get* is called to obtain a new value from the file.

Likewise, the procedure call *write(f, x)* is defined as equivalent to

$$f\uparrow := x;$$
$$put(f)$$

The value of *x* is assigned to the buffer variable, and *put* is called to write the value to the file.

The definitions of *read* and *write* can be extended so that more than one value can be read or written during a single invocation. The procedure statement

$$read(f, x1, x2, \ldots, xn)$$

is defined as equivalent to the following sequence of statements:

$$read(f, x1); read(f, x2); \ldots; read(f, xn)$$

Likewise, the procedure statement

$$write(f, x1, x2, \ldots, xn)$$

is defined as equivalent to the following sequence of statements:

$$write(f\ x1); write(f, x2); \ldots; write(f, xn)$$

Taken literally, the definition of *read* presents problems for interactive programming. Suppose file *f* is the user's keyboard. The call *read(f, x)* assigns the character just typed by the user to *x* and then calls *get* to obtain the next character that the user types. *The user must type another character before the previously typed character will be returned to the program for processing.* This rules out the common situation in which the user gives commands to a program by striking a key for each command. The user would have to strike the key for the next command before the previous command could be obeyed.

One solution to this problem uses *lazy evaluation*, which puts off operations as long as possible rather than carrying them out as soon as they are requested by the program. With lazy evaluation, a new value is not obtained from the file when *get* is called; the system merely notes that a new value has been requested. When the program actually refers to the value of *f*↑, the system gets busy and obtains the new value that was previously requested by *get*.

Now suppose *read(f, x)* is used to read a character from the user's keyboard. The following statements are executed:

$$x := f\uparrow;$$
$$get(f)$$

Because of lazy evaluation, the reference to the value of *f*↑ causes the system to obtain a new character from the user's keyboard, a character that was requested by an earlier call to *get*. The call to *get* requests another character from the keyboard, but this request will be put off until the value of *f*↑ is referred to again. Thus *read* does not have to wait for another character to be typed before returning for character that was assigned to *x*.

Let's rewrite our example of sequential file processing to use *read* and *write* instead of *get* and *put*. Since we will not refer to the buffer variables, we will need a variable *accnt* to hold the account record currently being updated. *Accnt* is declared as follows:

> *accnt*: *accountRecord*;

The following statements read records from *oldFile* and write updated records to *newFile*:

> *reset*(*oldFile*);
> *rewrite*(*newFile*);
> **while not** *eof*(*oldFile*) **do**
>> **begin**
>>> *read*(*oldFile*, *accnt*);
>>> *accnt.balance* := *accnt.balance* + 10.00;
>>> *write*(*newFile*, *accnt*)
>> **end**

Note that *reset*, *rewrite*, and *eof* are used in the same way in both versions of the example.

Textfiles Textfiles, files of type *text*, have two properties. First, the characters in a textfile are divided into lines and possibly into pages. (Usually, only files that are to be sent to a printer are divided into pages.) Second, values of types *integer*, *real*, *char*, and *Boolean* can be read from and written to textfiles. The procedures *read* and *write* perform data conversion for integer, real, and Boolean values. *Read* converts from the sequences of characters (such as ''3.14'') that represent values in a textfile to the binary codes that represent values in main memory. *Write* performs the reverse conversion from binary codes to sequence of characters. Field-width parameters can be used to control the exact format in which values are written to textfiles.

The *read* and *write* statements that we have been using all along read from the textfile *input* and write to the textfile *output*. Thus we are already familiar with many details of input from and output to textfiles, details that do not need to be discussed again here. For example, we know the formats in which values must be stored in a textfile so that they can be read by a *read* statement, and we know how to use field-width parameters to control the formats in which values will be stored in a textfile by a *write* statement.

Different computer systems may use different methods for dividing a textfile into lines. Some use a special end-of-line character to terminate each line; the code for the end-of-line character can vary from system to system. Some systems use two special characters to terminate each line. This method is a concession to printers, most of which require two control characters, carriage-return and line-feed, to move the printing mechanism to the beginning of a new line. Still another method is to extend each line with enough blank spaces so that all lines contain the same number of characters. Since the number of characters in a line is known, no special character is required to signal the end of a line.

The Pascal procedures for processing textfiles are designed to be independent of the method actually used to divide the file into lines. Pascal processes a textfile as if each line is terminated by a single end-of-line character. The end-of-line character is read as a blank space; this allows the Pascal program to be independent of whatever code or codes are used to represent the end of a line in the textfile. To distinguish the end-of-line character from an ordinary blank space, Pascal provides the predicate *eoln* ("end of line"). The value of *eoln(f)* is *true* when the current position of *f* is at an end-of-line character and *false* otherwise.

For example, consider the textfile that would be printed as follows:

```
Line one
Line two
Line three
```

If we use a / to represent the end-of-line character, we can represent this textfile as follows:

Line one/Line two/Line three/

Suppose that the file is being read and the current file position is at some character other than the end-of-line character. We can represent the state of the file, the buffer variable, and *eoln* as follows:

Line one/Line two/Line three/ $\qquad f\uparrow = $ 'n'
$\uparrow \qquad\qquad\qquad\qquad\qquad eoln(f) = $ *false*

Now suppose, that the current file position is at an end-of-line character. The value of $f\uparrow$ is a blank space (since the end-of-file character is read as a blank space) and *eoln* returns *true*:

Line one/Line two/Line three/ $\qquad f\uparrow = $ ' '
$\uparrow \qquad\qquad\qquad\qquad\qquad eoln(f) = $ *true*

The procedure *readln* moves the current file position to the beginning of the next line. The procedure call *readln(f)* has the same effect as the following statements:

while not *eoln(f)* **do**

    get(f);

get(f)

Readln can be extended to read values from the file before moving to the beginning of a new line. The procedure statement

readln(f, x1, x2, . . ., xn)

is defined as equivalent to the following two-statement sequence:

read(f, x1, x2, . . ., xn); *readln(f)*

The procedure call *writeln(f)* terminates the line currently being written to file *f*. *Writeln* can be extended to write a series of values before terminating the line. The procedure statement

writeln(f, x1, x2, . . ., xn)

is defined to be equivalent to the following two-statement sequence:

write(f, x1, x2, . . ., xn); *writeln(f)*

The procedure *page(f)* terminates the page currently being written to file *f*. If the last line on the page to be terminated does not end with an end-of-line character, the system executes *writeln(f)* before terminating the page. The method of dividing a textfile into pages varies from system to system. One method is to end each page with a form-feed control character. When a printer receives a form-feed character, it advances to the top of a new page.

If the file parameter *f* is omitted for *read*, *readln*, *eof*, or *eoln*, the standard file *input* is assumed. If the file parameter is omitted for *write*, *writeln*, or *page*, the standard file *output* is assumed. Thus we can write *eof* instead of *eof(input)*, *eoln* instead of *eoln(input)*, and *page* instead of *page(output)*. We are already familiar with using *read*, *readln*, *write*, and *writeln* with the file parameter omitted. Note that the file parameter cannot be omitted for *reset*, *rewrite*, *get*, and *put*.

Examples of sequential file processing   Figure 12.8 shows the Pascal program *ClassifyAccounts*, which is the Pascal translation of the algorithm in Figure 12.3. The file variables *accounts*, *goodAccounts*, and *badAccounts* are listed as parameters in the program heading. *Reset* is executed for the input file *accounts*, and *rewrite* is executed for the output files *goodAccounts* and *badAccounts*. *Get* is used to obtain records from the input file, and *put* is used to store records in the two output files.

Figure 12.9 shows the Pascal program *Merge*, which is the Pascal translation of the algorithm in Figure 12.4. This program uses *read* and *write*, rather than *get* and *put*, to transfer values to and from the files. Since *read* and *write* are used, it is not necessary to access the buffer variables, as it would be if *get* and *put* were used. A good exercise is to rewrite this program to use *get* and *put* instead of *read* and *write*.

Figure 12.10 shows the Pascal program *Fileupdate*, which is the Pascal translation of the algorithm in Figure 12.7. The program was written in UCSD Pascal so that the modules in the algorithm could be translated into UCSD-Pascal units. A few nonstandard features of UCSD Pascal need to be explained before the program can be understood.

UCSD Pascal provides a standard data type *string*, which is equivalent to the *string* data type in the algorithmic langauge. Strings can be read from textfiles by *read* and *readln* statements and written to textfiles by *write* and *writeln* statements.

UCSD Pascal uses a completely different method than standard Pascal for establishing a correspondence between internal and external file names. The internal file names do not need to be listed in the program heading (listing them there is allowed but has no effect). Instead, extended versions of the procedures *reset* and *rewrite* are used to set up the correspondence between internal and external file names. The standard internal file names *input* and *output*, which do not appear in *reset* and *rewrite* statements, are automatically set to correspond to the user's keyboard and display.

A call to *reset* in UCSD Pascal has the following form:

reset(internal-name, external-name)

Figure 12.8 Pascal program for classifying account records as good or bad according to the balance shown on each record.

```
program ClassifyAccounts(accounts, goodAccounts, badAccounts);

{ Classify account records as good or bad according to outstanding balance }


const
    balanceLimit = 500.00;
type
    accountRecord = record
                            accountNumber: integer;
                            balance: real
                    end;
var
    accounts, goodAccounts, badAccounts: file of accountRecord;
begin
    reset(accounts);
    rewrite(goodAccounts);
    rewrite(badAccounts);
    while not eof(accounts) do
        begin
            if accounts↑.balance > balanceLimit then
                begin
                    badAccounts↑:= accounts↑;
                    put(badAccounts)
                end
            else
                begin
                    goodAccounts↑:= accounts↑;
                    put(goodAccounts)
                end
            get(accounts)
        end
end.
```

The external name is represented by a string constant or the value of a string variable. In addition to performing the functions of *reset* in standard Pascal, the UCSD-Pascal *reset* procedure also causes the internal file name to represent the file designated by the external file name.

Figure 12.9   Pascal program for merging two files.

```pascal
program Merge(inFile1, inFile2, outFile);

{ Merge inFile1, inFile2 to form outFile }

const
    sentinel = 9999;
type
    accountRecord = record
                        accountNumber: integer;
                        balance: real
                    end;
var
    inFile1, inFile2, outFile: file of accountRecord;
    inRec1, inRec2: accountRecord;
begin
    reset(inFile1);
    reset(inFile2);
    rewrite(outFile);
    read(inFile1, inRec1);
    read(inFile2, inRec2);
    while (inRec1.accountNumber <> sentinel) or
          (inRec2.accountNumber <> sentinel)       do
        begin
            if inRec1.accountNumber <= inRec2.accountNumber then
                begin
                    write(outFile, inRec1);
                    read(inFile1, inRec1)
                end
            else
                begin
                    write(outFile, inRec2);
                    read(inFile2, inRec2);
                end
        end;
        write(outFile, inRec1)
end.
```

Figure 12.10   Pascal program for the file update problem.

```
program FileUpdate;

{ Update old master file from transaction file producing new master file }

uses CommonDefinitions, Merge, Update;
var
    currentRec: transRecord;
begin
    InputInitialize;
    OutputInitialize;
    while not EndFilesP do
        begin
            GetRecord(currentRec);
            PutRecord(currentRec)
        end;
    OutputFinalize
end.


unit Merge;

{ Merge old master file and transaction file into common stream }

interface
    uses CommonDefinitions;

    function EndFilesP: Boolean;
    { Return true when there are no more old master or transaction records
      to be processed }

    procedure InputInitialize;
    { Get input file names and open files }

    procedure GetRecord(var outRec: transRecord);
    { Get next record from merged stream }

implemenetation
    var
        acctFile: file of accountRecord;
        transFile: file of transRecord;

    function EndFilesP;
```

```
begin
    EndFilesP := (acctFile↑.accountNumber = sentinel) and
                 (transFile↑.accountNumber = sentinel)
end


procedure InputInitialize;
var
        acctName, transName: string;
    begin
        write('Name of input account file? ');
        readln(acctName);
        write('Name of transaction file? ');
        readln(transName);
        reset(acctFile, acctName);
        reset(transFile, transName)
    end;


    procedure GetRecord;
    begin
        if acctFile↑.accountNumber <= transFile↑.accountNumber then
            begin
                outRec.accountNumber := acctFile↑.accountNumber;
                outRec.recordType := 'M';
                outRec.amount := acctFile↑.balance;
                get(acctFile)
            end
        else
            begin
                outRec := transFile↑;
                get(transFile)
            end
    end;
end. { Merge }


unit Update;

{ Process merged stream of master and transaction records to produce new
  master file }

interface
    uses CommonDefinitions;
```

```
    procedure OutputInitialize;
    { Open output file and initialize variables }

    procedure PutRecord(var inRec: transRecord);
    { Process one master or transaction record }

    procedure OutputFinalize;
    { Empty buffer, write sentinel record, and close output file }

implementation
    var
        acctFile: file of accountRecord;
        currentAcctNo: integer;
        bufferFull: Boolean;

    procedure OutputInitialize;
    var
        acctName: string;
    begin
        write('Name of output account file? ');
        readln(acctName);
        rewrite(acctFile, acctName);
        currentAcctNo := -1;
        bufferFull := false
    end;

    procedure NewAccount;

    { Empty buffer in preparation for processing records for new account }

    begin
        if bufferFull then
            put(acctFile);
        bufferFull := false
    end;

    procedure Master(var inRec: transRecord);

    { Process master record }

    begin
        if bufferFull then
            writeln('Duplicate master record for key ',
                inRec.accountNumber:1)
```

```
        else
            begin
                acctFile↑.accountNumber := inRec.accountNumber;
                acctFile↑.balance := inRec.amount;
                bufferFull := true
            end
end;

procedure Add(var inRec: transRecord);

{ Process Add transaction }

begin
    if bufferFull then
        writeln('Attempt to add existing record for key ',
                inRec.accountNumber:1)
    else
        begin
            acctFile↑.accountNumber := inRec.accountNumber;
            acctFile↑.balance := inRec.amount;
            bufferFull := true
        end
end;

procedure Change(var inRec: transRecord);

{ Process Change transaction }

begin
    if bufferFull then
        acctFile↑.balance := acctFile↑.balance + inRec.amount
    else
        writeln('Attempt to change nonexistent record for key ',
                inRec.accountNumber:1)
end;

procedure Delete(var inRec: transRecord);

{ Process Delete transaction }

begin
    if bufferFull then
        bufferFull := false
```

```
        else
            writeln('Attempt to delete nonexistent record for key ',
                    inRec.accountNumber:1)
end;

procedure PutRecord;
begin
    if inRec.accountNumber <> currentAcctNo then
        begin
            currentAcctNo := inRec.accountNumber;
            NewAccount
        end;
    if not (inRec.recordType in ['M', 'A', 'C', 'D']) then
        writeln('Transaction code error for key ',
                in Rec.accountNumber:1)
    else
        case inRec.recordType of
            'M': Master(inRec);
            'A': Add(inRec);
            'C': Change(inRec);
            'D': Delete(inRec)
        end
end;

    procedure OutputFinalize;
    begin
        if bufferFull then
            put(acctFile);
        acctFile↑.accountNumber := sentinel;
        acctFile↑.balance := 0.0;
        put(acctFile);
        close(acctFile, lock)
    end;
end. { Update }


unit CommonDefinitions;

{ Constant and type definitions used by main program and other units }

interface
    const
        sentinel = 9999;
```

```
    type
        accountRecord = record
                            accountNumber: integer;
                            balance: real
                        end;
        transRecord = record
                            accountNumber: integer;
                            recordType: char;
                            amount: real
                        end;
    implementation

        { No implementation part }

    end. { CommonDefinitions }
```

A call to *rewrite* in UCSD Pascal has the following form:

rewrite(internal-name, external-name)

In addition to performing functions of *rewrite* in standard Pascal, the UCSD-Pascal *rewrite* procedure also causes the internal file name to represent the file designated by the external file name.

In Figure 12.10, the procedure *InputInitialize* in unit *Merge* and the procedure *OutputInitialize* in unit *Update* illustrate how UCSD Pascal allows external file names to be obtained from the user after execution of the program begins. The procedure calls

reset(acctFile, acctName);
reset(transFile, transName)

cause the internal file names *acctFile* and *transFile* to represent the files whose external names are the values of the string variables *acctName* and *transName*. The procedure call

rewrite(accFile, acctName)

causes the internal file name *acctFile* to represent the file whose external name is the value of the string variable *acctName*.

In UCSD Pascal, an output file must be closed if it is to be retained after the program terminates. An output file that is not closed is discarded when the program terminates. The procedure call

close(acctFile, lock)

closes the file *acctFile* and specifies that it is to be retained after the program terminates.

13

Arrays

Arrays serve to represent lists and tables in main memory. We use arrays to organize large amounts of data in main memory, just as we use files to organize large amounts of data in auxiliary memory. Records, in contrast, are used to organize small blocks of data, such as the data pertaining to a particular person or inventory item. Both arrays and files often have records as components.

13.1

One-dimensional arrays

Array types and values We can think of a one-dimensional array as a list of values such as the following:

1. 3.5

2. 6.9

3. 7.2

4. 9.5

5. 4.2

The values on the list are the components of the array. All the components have the same type, which is the component type of the array. In the example, the component type is type *real,* and the components of the array are 3.5, 6.9, 7.2, 9.5, and 4.2

Each component of an array is labeled with a unique *index value*. Values of types *integer, char,* and *Boolean* can be used as index values. The range of allowable index values determines the number of components in the array. Since the array in the example is indexed by integers in the range 1 to 5, it has five components, one for each of the integers from 1 to 5.

All arrays belonging to a particular array type have the same component type and the same range of index values. Since the range of index values is the same, all arrays belonging to the same type have the same number of components. We describe an array type by giving the range of index values and the component type:

array[range-of-index-values] **of** component-type

The range of index values is given in the following form:

lower-limit **to** upper-limit

For example,

array[1 **to** 5] **of** *real*

describes the type of all five-component arrays with real components indexed by integers in the range 1 to 5. The example array belongs to this type.

Let's define the array type *list* as follows:

type *list* = **array**[1 **to** 5] **of** *real*

We can represent values of array types in the same form that we used for values of record types. Each value is represented by the name of the array type followed by a parenthesized list of component values. The following are some representations of values of type *list:*

list(3.5, 6.9, 7.2, 9.5, 4.2)
list(−100.5, −25.4, 0.0, 33.3, 48.9)
list(−0.25, −0.03, 0.69, 0.82, 0.99)

The first of these represents the example array given at the beginning of this section.

Array variables   The variable *a* declared by

a: *list*

is an *array variable* whose values are arrays of type *list*. Each of the following assignment statements is valid:

a ← *list*(3.5, 6.9, 7.2, 9.5, 4.2)
a ← *list*(−100.5, −25.4, 0.0, 33.3, 48.9)
a ← *list*(−0.25, −0.03, 0.69, 0.82, 0.99)

Figure 13.1 shows the layout in memory of the value of *a* after each of the above assignments. Note that only the components of an array are stored in memory. The index values need not be stored because the computer can calculate which component corresponds to each index value.

Figure 13.1   Memory layout of the value of *a* after each of the
assignments shown. Only the component values, and not the
index values, are stored in memory.

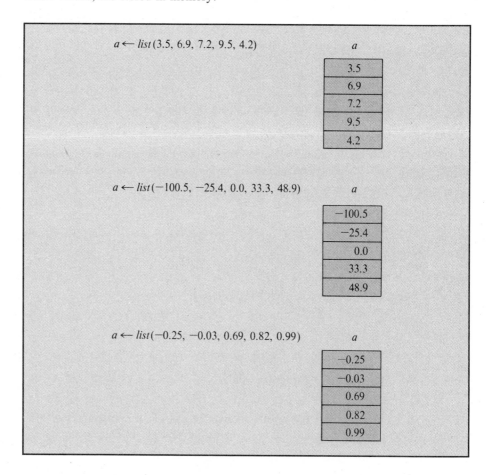

The value of one array variable can be assigned to another as long as the array
variables are of the same type. As with records, type equivalance is based on name,
not structure. Thus if *a* and *b* are declared by

　　a, b: *list*

or

　　a: *list*
　　b: *list*

then *a* and *b* have the same type and the assignments

　　a ← *b*

and

　　b ← *a*

are permissible. On the other hand, if a and b are declared by

a: **array**[1 **to** 5] **of** *real*

b: **array**[1 **to** 5] **of** *real*

then a and b have different types and the above assignments are not allowed.

The array variable a of type *list* is an entire variable to which we assign entire values such as *list*(3.5, 6.9, 7.2, 9.5, 4.2). As with record variables, we can think of an array variable such as a as being composed of *component variables,* each of which holds one component of the value of a. Each component variable is designated by a unique index value, which is written in brackets following the name of the array variable. Thus the component variables of a are written $a[1]$, $a[2]$, $a[3]$, $a[4]$, and $a[5]$. Figure 13.2 shows the values of the component variables of a after each of the three assignment statements given at the beginning of this section.

Component variables can be assigned values and used in expressions just like any other variables. For example, after the assignments

$a[1] \leftarrow 0.5$

$a[2] \leftarrow 0.7$

$a[3] \leftarrow 0.2$

$a[4] \leftarrow 0.9$

$a[5] \leftarrow 0.3$

the value of a is

list(0.5, 0.7, 0.2, 0.9, 0.3)

and the value of the expression

$3.0 * a[1] + 4.0 * a[2]$

is 4.3.

One of the most important properties of components of array variables is that the index value can be given as the value of an expression. Thus if we write

$a[i + 2 * j]$

in an algorithm, the values of i and j determine which component of a is referred to. These values do not need to be known when the algorithm is written. They might be read from an input file, for example, or arrived at as the result of a calculation. If $a[i + 2 * j]$ appears within a repetition construction, i and j may have different values on each repetition, so that $a[i + 2 * j]$ refers to a different component of a on each execution of the repeated statements.

13.2

Elements of array processing

Arrays and for constructions   A **for** construction is frequently used to step through the components of an array so that similar or identical operations can be carried out on each component. For example, let a be an array variable of type *list*

Figure 13.2   The component variables of the array variable a. The values of the component variables are shown after each of three assignments to a. After the first assignment, for example, the value of $a[1]$ is 3.5, the value of $a[2]$ is 6.9, and so on.

	a
$a \leftarrow list(3.5, 6.9, 7.2, 9.5, 4.2)$	
$a[1]$	3.5
$a[2]$	6.9
$a[3]$	7.2
$a[4]$	9.5
$a[5]$	4.2
$a \leftarrow list(-100.5, -25.4, 0.0, 33.3, 48.9)$	
$a[1]$	-100.5
$a[2]$	-25.4
$a[3]$	0.0
$a[4]$	33.3
$a[5]$	48.9
$a \leftarrow list(-0.25, -0.03, 0.69, 0.82, 0.99)$	
$a[1]$	-0.25
$a[2]$	-0.03
$a[3]$	0.69
$a[4]$	0.82
$a[5]$	0.99

and assume that we want to set all the component variables of a to zero. Since a has only five component variables, we could do the job with the following assignment:

$a \leftarrow list(0.0, 0.0, 0.0, 0.0, 0.0)$

or with the following five assignments:

$a[1] \leftarrow 0.0$
$a[2] \leftarrow 0.0$
$a[3] \leftarrow 0.0$
$a[4] \leftarrow 0.0$
$a[5] \leftarrow 0.0$

The method that is most effective for larger arrays, however, is to use a **for** construction to step through the components of *a*, setting each component to zero:

> **for** $i \leftarrow 1$ **to** 5
> $\quad a[i] \leftarrow 0.0$
> **endfor**

The integer variable *i* is stepped from 1 to 5, and the repeated statement

> $a[i] \leftarrow 0.0$

is executed for each value of *i*. When the value of *i* is 1, the repeated statement is equivalent to

> $a[1] \leftarrow 0.0$

When the value of *i* is 2, the repeated statement is equivalent to

> $a[2] \leftarrow 0.0$

and so on. When the repetition terminates, each of the component variables of *a* will have been assigned the value 0.0.

Averaging the components of an array   Let's compute the average of the components of the array *a* of type *list*. The first step is to compute the sum of the component values. We will use the real variable *total* to hold a running total of all the values added so far. We begin by clearing the value of *total* to zero:

> $total \leftarrow 0.0$

We then step through the components of *a*, adding the value of each component in turn to the value of *total:*

> **for** $i \leftarrow 1$ **to** 5
> $\quad total \leftarrow total + a[i]$
> **endfor**

Finally, the value of *total* is divided by 5, the number of components of *a*, to get the average. The complete set of statements for computing the average is as follows:

> $total \leftarrow 0.0$
> **for** $i \leftarrow 1$ **to** 5
> $\quad total \leftarrow total + a[i]$
> **endfor**
> $average \leftarrow total \ / \ 5$

Finding the largest and smallest components of an array   Suppose that the temperature is recorded each hour and the 24 temperatures recorded on a given day are stored as the components of a 24-component array. We wish to find the high and low temperature for the day. We define the type *tempArray* and declare the array variable *temp* as follows:

type *tempArray* = **array**[1 **to** 24] **of** *real*
temp: *tempArray*

As we step through the components of *temp*, we will use the real variable *low* to record the lowest temperature encountered so far. Likewise, we will use the real variable *high* to record the highest temperature encountered so far. When a temperature lower than the value of *low* is encountered, that temperature becomes the new value of *low*. When a temperature higher than the value of *high* is encountered, that temperature becomes the new value of *high*. *High* and *low* are set initially to the value of *temp*[1], the first temperature in the array. After the entire array *temp* has been scanned, the values of *high* and *low* are the largest and smallest components of the value of *temp*:

```
low ← temp[1]
high ← temp[1]
for i ← 2 to 24
    if temp[i] < low then
        low ← temp[i]
    elseif temp[i] > high then
        high ← temp[i]
    endif
endfor
```

Now suppose that the value of *temp*[1] is the temperature recorded at 1:00 a.m., *temp*[2] is the temperature recorded at 2:00 a.m., and so on. We want to know not only the high and low temperatures but the times at which the high and low first occurred. That is, we want to know the index of the first occurrence of the largest component value of *temp* and the index of the first occurrence of the smallest component of *temp*.

We proceed as follows. As we step through the array, we will use the integer variables *lowIndex* and *highIndex* to keep track of the index values of the first occurrences in *temp* of the values of *low* and *high*. Each time the value of a component of *temp* is assigned to *low*, the index of that component must be assigned to *lowIndex*. Likewise, each time the value of a component of *temp* is assigned to *high*, the index of that component must be assigned to *highIndex:*

```
low ← temp[1]
lowIndex ← 1
high ← temp[1]
highIndex ← 1
for i ← 2 to 24
    if temp[i] < low then
        low ← temp[i]
        lowIndex ← i
```

> **elseif** *temp*[*i*] > *high* **then**
>> *high* ← *temp*[*i*]
>> *highIndex* ← *i*
> **endif**
endfor

When the repetition terminates, the value of *low* is the smallest component of the value of *temp,* and the value of *lowIndex* is the smallest index value for which the condition

$$low = temp[lowIndex]$$

is true. Likewise, the value of *high* is the largest component of the value of *temp,* and the value of *highIndex* is the smallest index value for which the condition

$$high = temp[highIndex]$$

is true.

Input and output of arrays   To input the value of an array variable from a text file, we use a **for** construction to step through the components of the array variable and input the value of each. For example, the following statements input the value of the array variable *temp* from the standard input file:

> **for** *i* ← 1 **to** 24
>> **input** *temp*[*i*]
> **endfor**

We recall that each execution of an **input** statement begins by reading data from a new line of the input file. Thus, the above statements require that each component of the array appear on a separate line in the input data. As with the **output** statement, however, we can use the command **more** to require that the **input** statement remain on the same line after reading its data. If we use the statements

> **for** *i* ← 1 **to** 24
>> **input** *temp*[*i*], **more**
> **endfor**

the values being read can be arranged in lines in any way that we please. The **input** statement will automatically go to a new line when all the values on the current line have been exhausted.

Likewise, we can write the components of the value of *temp* to the standard output file with the following statements:

> **for** *i* ← 1 **to** 24
>> **output** *temp*[*i*]
> **endfor**

Each component, however, is printed on a separate line. To print all 24 components on the same line, we can use the following:

```
for i ← 1 to 24
    output temp[i], ' ', more
endfor
```

With the aid of the **tab** command, we can produce more elaborate formatting. For example, suppose that we want to print the 24 components of the array in six lines with four values to a line. The four values on each line are arranged in columns 10 characters wide. The following statements produce this printout.

```
column ← 1
for i ← 1 to 24
    output tab(10 * column), temp[i], more
    column ← column + 1
    if column > 4 then
        column ← 1
        output
    endif
endfor
```

The integer variable *column* has the value 1, 2, 3, or 4, depending on which of the four columns the value of *temp*[i] is to be printed on. The statement

output tab(10 * *column*), *temp*[i], **more**

moves the printer to character position 10 * *column* before printing the value of *temp*[i]. Thus, the first column begins at character position 10, the second column at character position 20, and so on. The **more** command keeps the printer on the same line after the value of *temp*[i] is printed.

After printing the value of *temp*[i], the value of *column* is increased by 1 so that the next value printed will be in the next column to the right. If the new value of *column* is greater than 4, however, all four values have been printed on the current line. In that case the value of *column* is reset to 1, and the statement

output

is executed to cause the printer to go to a new line.

13.3 Searching arrays

We frequently need to search a list for a particular entry. Typical examples from everyday life are looking up a telephone number and looking up a word in a dictionary. Each entry on the list being searched has a *key field*, which identifies the entry, and one or more *value fields*, which contain the information we are trying to retrieve. In the case of a telephone book, for example, the key field is the person's name and the value fields are the person's address and telephone number. In a dictionary, each key field contains a word, and the corresponding value fields contain the word's pronunciation, definition, and derivation.

Now let's see how such a list might be searched by a computer. Depending on the size of the list, it will be stored in either main or auxiliary memory; searching will be faster if the list is small enough to be stored in main memory. The list will be stored as a file if it is stored in auxiliary memory and as an array if it is stored in main memory. Since arrays are the subject of this chapter, it is the second possibility that we will consider here.

We begin by looking at the definitions and declarations needed to describe the list to be searched. For simplicity, we will assume that the key field of each entry holds an integer and the value field holds a real number. For example, the key field might hold a customer's account number and the value field might hold the balance in the account. The following are the definitions and declarations we need:

> **type** *dataRecord* = **record**
>> *key*: *integer*
>>
>> *value*: *real*
>
> **endrecord**
>
> **const** *size* = 500
>
> *data*: **array**[1 **to** *size*] **of** *dataRecord*
>
> *free*: *integer*

Each data record is of type *dataRecord* and contains an integer field *key* and a real field *value*. *Size* is the number of records that can be stored in the data array; the value chosen for *size* depends on the amount of data to be stored. The array variable *data* holds the data array, which is an array of data records indexed by an integer in the range 1 to *size*.

Normally, not all the components of the data array will actually be used. The unused components remain available if any additional records need to be stored. Also, one of our searching algorithms requires at least one unused component for storing a sentinel value. The integer variable *free* is used to hold the index of the first unused component of the data array. Thus the components

> *data*[1] through *data*[*free* − 1]

are in use and hold valid data records. The components

> *data*[*free*] through *data*[*size*]

are unused and hold garbage (meaningless values). Figure 13.3 illustrates this situation.

Sequential search   The most obvious way to search a list is to begin with the first entry and work through the list entry by entry until we find the entry we are searching for or until we reach the end of the list. This method of search is called *linear search* or *sequential search*.

Let the value of *searchKey* be the value we are searching for, and let the value of *i* be the index of the record that is currently being examined. The value of *i* is stepped through the values 1, 2, 3, and so on. For each value of *i*, we compare the value of *data*[*i*].*key,* the key of the "*i*th" data record, with the value of *searchKey,*

Figure 13.3   The array *data* used by the sequential and binary search
algorithms. For convenience, *data* is shown with only 12
components instead of the 500 declared in the text. The
value of *free* is the index of the first unused component of
data. When the value of a variable designates an array
component, we say that the variable *points to* the component
and draw an arrow from the variable to the component that
it points to.

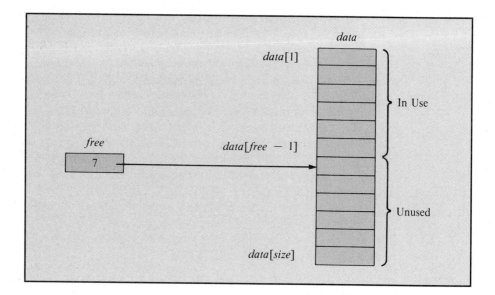

the key value we are searching for. If the two key values are equal, the search stops.
Otherwise, the value of *i* is increased by 1 and the search continues:

$i \leftarrow 1$
while *searchKey* <> *data*[*i*].*key*
    $i \leftarrow i + 1$
endwhile

The repetition terminates when a record is found whose key is equal to the value
of *searchKey*. The value of *i* when the repetition terminates is the index of the record
that was found, and the value of *data*[*i*] is the record itself. The value of *data*[*i*].*key*
is equal to the value of *searchKey*, and the value of *data*[*i*].*value* is the value that
was looked up.

Unfortunately, this method has a fatal flaw. If the part of the array that is in use
does not contain a record whose key is equal to *searchKey*, the search will continue
into the unused part of the array. If, by accident, one of the garbage records in the
unused part of the array has a key equal to *searchKey*, then the search will find a

garbage record. Otherwise, the search will "run off the end" of the data array, and the search algorithm will be terminated with an error message when it attempts to access the nonexistent array component with index *size* + 1.

We need some method to terminate the search when it reaches the end of the part of the array that is in use. The easiest way to terminate the search is to store a sentinel record immediately following the last valid data record. That is, the sentinel record is stored in *data[free]*, the first unused component of the data array. This method requires that the data array always have at least one unused component for storing the sentinel record.

What sentinel value should we use? We are already searching for a record whose key is equal to *searchKey*, and the search will terminate when such a record is found. If we use the value of *searchKey* for the key of the sentinel record, only one test must be made for each record examined. If we use some other sentinel value, however, we will have to make two tests for each record: one test to see if the value of *data[i].key* is equal to that of *searchKey*, and another to see if the value of *data[i].key* is equal to the sentinel value. Two tests will also be needed if we use some other means to control the search, such as continuing the search only as long as the condition *i* < *free* is true.

The only modification that must be made to the statements for sequential search is to set *data[free].key*, the key of the sentinel record, to the value of *searchKey* before the search begins:

> *data[free].key* ← *searchKey*
> *i* ← 1
> **while** *searchKey* <> *data[i].key*
>   *i* ← *i* + 1
> **endwhile**

Since a record whose key is equal to the value of *searchKey* will always be found, the repetition will always terminate with the value of *i* equal to the index of the record that was found. If the condition *i* < *free* is true when the repetition terminates, a valid data record was found. Otherwise, the sentinel record was found, indicating that there is no valid data record whose key is equal to the value of *searchKey*.

Figure 13.4 illustrates a procedure for sequential search. The declarations for *data* and *free* are assumed to be global to the procedure; for example, the declarations and the procedure definition may be part of the same module. In the procedure call

> *SequentialSearch(searchKey, found. index)*

the input parameter *searchKey* is the key value to be looked up. If a data record with this key is found, the value of the output parameter *found* is set to *true* and the value of *index* is set to the index of the record that was found. If no such record is found, the value of *found* is set to *false* and the value assigned to *index* is meaningless.

The procedure uses the statements given above to search the array. When the repetition terminates, the value of the Boolean expression *i* < *free* is *true* if a valid data record with the desired key was found and *false* if the search was stopped by

Figure 13.4   Procedure for sequential search.

```
procedure SequentialSearch(searchKey, found, index)

{ Locate record with given key }

declare
    searchKey: in integer
    found: out Boolean
    index: out integer
    i: integer
execute
    data[free].key ← searchKey
    i ← 1
    while searchKey <> data[i].key
        i ← i + 1
    endwhile
    found ← (i < free)
    index ← i
end SequentialSearch
```

the sentinel. Thus, the value of $i < free$ is returned as the value of the output parameter *found:*

$found \leftarrow (i < free)$

The final value of i is returned as the value of the output parameter *index:*

$index \leftarrow i$

If a data record with the desired key was found, then the index of that record is returned as the value of *index*. If no valid data record was found, the value returned via *index* is meaningless. (Actually, the index value returned in this case is the value of *free* [why?], which, however, is of no use to the algorithm that invoked the procedure.)

Efficiency of sequential search   There are two types of efficiency for algorithms: space efficiency (concerning how much memory the algorithm uses), and time efficiency (concerning how much time the algorithm takes to do its job). The space efficiency is about the same for all the searching and sorting algorithms described in this chapter. Most of the required memory space is taken up by the array being searched or sorted. A small amount of additional memory is needed for the variables used to control the searching or sorting process. On the other hand, the running time of searching and sorting algorithms can vary enormously from one algorithm to another. We will thus be interested in only the time efficiency of the algorithms developed in this chapter.

How efficient is the sequential search algorithm? The running time of the algorithm is clearly proportional to the number of records that must be examined before finding the desired record. In the best case, the record we are searching for is the first one in the array, so only one record needs to be examined. In the worst case, the record we are looking for is the last one in the array, so all the records need to be examined. In the worst case, then, the running time is proportional to n, the number of data records in the array being searched. (Note that the value of n is equal to that of *free* -1.) If all the records are equally likely to be searched for, then on the average about $n / 2$ records will need to be examined before finding the desired one. The average running time, then, is also proportional to n.

We often express this result by saying that sequential search has a worst case and an average running time of $O(n)$, where O can be read as "the order of" or "on the order of." This *O-notation* implies the following:

1. A running time of $O(n)$, for example, means that the running time is proporational to n. The factor of proportionality depends on the particular programming language and computer system for which the algorithm is implemented. For example, one implementation of sequential search may give a running time in microseconds of, say, $10n$. For other, less efficient systems, the running time might be $100n$, $1000n$, or worse. In each case, however, the running time is still $O(n)$.

2. The proportionality is accurate only for large values of n. For small values of n, statements for initializing variables and returning results may take almost as much time as the search itself. Also, when deriving the running time, we will often simplify expressions by making approximations that are valid only for large values of n.

Intuitively, we might expect a searching or sorting algorithm to have a running time of $O(n)$ since we would expect that the amount of time the algorithm takes should be proportional to the number of array components with which it must contend. But algorithms often defy intuition in this respect. The running times of some algorithms considered in this chapter are much better than $O(n)$, and the running times of others are much worse than $O(n)$.

Binary search   Sequential search is satisfactory for small lists but is too inefficient for use with large ones. Imagine how long it would take to look up a name in a telephone directory by starting on the first page and scanning the directory column by column, page by page, until the desired name was found.

How is it that we are able to look up names in a telephone directory much more rapidly than would be possible with a sequential search? The answer is that the names in a telephone directory are in alphabetical order, and we use this order to guide us quickly to the part of the directory containing the name we are looking for. Likewise, if the records in an array are in ascending order according to their key fields, much more efficient search algorithms than sequential search are possible. *Binary search* is a simple and highly efficient algorithm for searching an ordered array.

Binary search works by dividing the list to be searched in half and determining which half contains the entry being sought. The half that does not contain the entry being sought is discarded; the division and discarding step is repeated for the half that does contain the entry being sought. After one division-and-discard step, the search has been narrowed down to one half of the original list; after two steps, it is narrowed down to one quarter of the original list; after three steps, to one eighth of the original list; and so on. After a relatively small number of steps, the search will have narrowed down to a single entry.

We can illustrate a binary search by using it to locate the page of a telephone directory that contains a given name. We start by opening the directory in the middle and examining the right-hand page. Using the guide words at the top of the page, we determine whether the name we are looking for lies on that page; if it does, we have found the page we are looking for and the search terminates. Otherwise, we compare the name we are looking for with the first name on the right-hand page. If the name we are looking for comes first in alphabetical order, the name is in the first half of the directory. If the name we are looking for follows in alphabetical order the first name on the right-hand page, the name we are looking for is in the second half of the directory. Depending on the outcome of the comparison, the search is narrowed down to either the first or second half of the directory. The selected half can itself be divided into halves and the narrowing down process repeated. After surprisingly few repetitions—no more than 10 for a 1,024-page directory—the search will have narrowed down to a single page.

Figure 13.5 shows a procedure for binary search of the array *data*. The parameters of the procedure have the same significance as for the sequential search procedure. The value of *searchKey* is the key to be searched for. If a record with this key is found, *found* is set to *true* and *index* is set to the index of the record that was found. Otherwise, *found* is set to *false* and the value of *index* is meaningless.

As the search proceeds, the part of *data* that remains to be searched becomes smaller and smaller. The integer variables *low* and *high* are used to hold the indexes of the first and last components of the part of *data* that remains to be searched. Thus, at any time during the search, the part of *data* that remains to be searched consists of the components *data*[*low*] through *data*[*high*]. Before the search begins, the entire part of the array that is in use needs to be searched. Therefore, *low* and *high* are intially set to the indexes of the first and last components of the part of the array that is in use:

$$low \leftarrow 1$$
$$high \leftarrow free - 1$$

Note that if the value of *free* is 1—none of the array is in use—the binary search routine will fail by attempting to access the nonexistent array component *data*[0]. One way to avoid this problem is simply to provide the array with a dummy component *data*[0], as is done in the table-handling module discussed later.

At the beginning of each execution of the repeated statements, the value of *mid* is set to the index of the component at the approximate midpoint of the part of the array still to be searched:

$$mid \leftarrow (low + high) \textbf{ div } 2$$

Figure 13.5.   Procedure for binary search.

```
procedure BinarySearch(searckKey, found, index)

{ Locate record with given key }

declare
    searchKey: in integer
    found: out Boolean
    index: out integer
    low, mid, high: integer
execute
    low ← 1
    high ← free − 1
    repeat
        mid ← (low + high) div 2
        if searchKey < data[mid].key then
            high ← mid − 1
        elseif searchKey > data[mid].key then
            low ← mid + 1
        endif
    until (searchKey = data[mid].key) or (low > high)
    found ← (searchKey = data[mid].key)
    index ← mid
end BinarySearch
```

The component *data*[*mid*] divides the other components of the part of the array to be searched into two parts of approximately equal size. The first part consists of the components preceding *data*[*mid*]:

data[*low*] through *data*[*mid* − 1]

The second part consists of the components following *data*[*mid*]:

data[*mid* + 1] through *data*[*high*]

The value of *searchKey* is compared with the key of the value of *data*[*mid*]. If the condition

searchKey < *data*[*mid*].*key*

is true, the record being sought, if present at all, lies in the first of the two parts. The value of *high* is set to *mid* − 1, narrowing down the search to the first part. One the other hand, if the condition

searchKey > *data*[*mid*].*key*

is true, the record being sought, if present at all, lies in the second of the two parts. The value of *low* is set to *mid* + 1, narrowing down the search to the second part. Figure 13.6 illustrates the narrowing down process.

There are two conditions under which the search should terminate. If

searchKey = *data*[*mid*].*key*

is true, the value of *mid* is the index of the record being sought. The desired record has been found, and the search terminates successfully. If

low > *high*

is true, then the values of *low* and *high* have passed one another. The part of the array remaining to be searched has been narrowed down to "less than nothing," indicating that the record being sought is not present in the array, and the search terminates unsuccessfully.

How do we know that the repetition will eventually terminate? On each execution of the repeated statements, either the value of *low* is increased or the value of *high* is decreased. Eventually, therefore, the values of *low* and *high* will pass each other, the condition

low > *high*

will become true, and the repetition will terminate.

After the search terminates, *found* must be set to reflect whether the search was successful; if it was, the index of the record found must be returned as the value *index*. If the search terminated successfully, the condition

searchKey = *data*[*mid*].*key*

is true and the value of *mid* is the index of the record that was found. Therefore, the values of *found* and *index* are set as follows:

found ← (*searchKey* = *data*[*mid*].*key*)
index ← *mid*

If the search was unsuccessful, the value assigned to *found* is *false,* and the value assigned to *index* is just the index of the last record examined by the search, which is of no significance to the algorithm that called the procedure.

Efficiency of binary search In the worst case, the running of time of a binary search is proportional to the number of times the list being searched must be divided in half to narrow down the search to a single record. If the list being searched contains two records (2^1 in exponential notation), then one division is required to narrow down the search down to a single record. If the list contains four records (2^2 in exponential notation), then two divisions are required to narrow down the search to a single record. If the list contains eight records (2^3 in exponential notation), then three divisions are required, and so on. In general, if the number of records n is equal to 2^m, then m divisions are required to narrow down the search to a single record, and the running time of the binary search is proportional to m.

Figure 13.6   The step in a binary search in which the search is narrowed
down to the first or second half of the list. The variables
low, *mid*, and *high* point to the first, middle, and last
components of the part of the list that remains to be
searched. If the value of *searchKey* is less than the key of
data[*mid*], the record being sought lies in the first half of the
list, and *high* is set to the value of *mid* − 1. If the value of
searchKey is greater than they key of *data*[*mid*], the record
being sought lies in the second half of the list, and *low* is
set to the value of *mid* + 1.

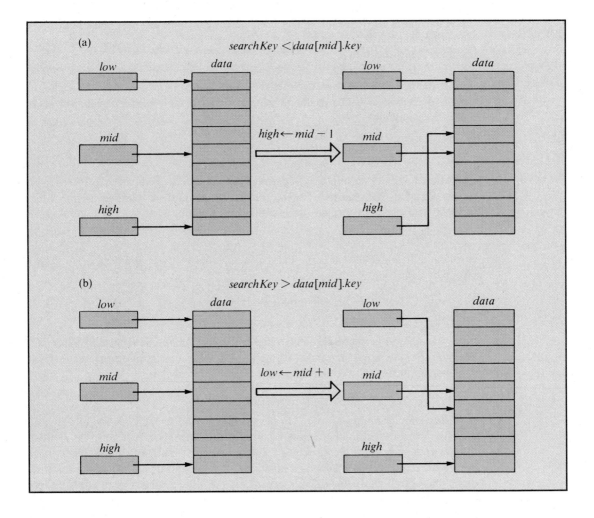

If $n = 2^m$, we say that m is the *logarithm of n to base 2* and write

$m = \log(n)$

The definition of the logarithm function can be extended to arguments that are not powers of 2; the logarithms of such arguments are not integers, but have fractional parts. Most scientific calculators provide a logarithm function, but usually not to base 2. We can compute logarithms to base 2 with a calculator by dividing the logarithm of n by the logarithm of 2, that is, by evaluating the expression

$\log(n) / \log(2)$

This will yield the logarithm of n to base 2 regardless of the base of the logarithms provided by the calculator.

We can thus write the running time for a binary search as $O(\log(n))$. The following table compares some values of n and $\log(n)$. We see that, especially for large n, a running time of $O(\log(n))$ is *much* better than a running time of $O(n)$:

n	$\log(n)$
2	1
4	2
8	3
16	4
32	5
1,024	10
1,048,576	20
1,073,741,824	30

Hashing It would be nice if we could do away with searching altogether by devising some calculation that would compute the index at which a record is stored from the value of its key. While such calculations are possible, they usually impose restrictions that make their use impractical. For example, once the calculation has been devised, no additional records may be stored in the array nor can any existing ones be deleted.

Fortunately, we can do almost as well without imposing burdensome restrictions. We can devise a calculation that computes from the key of a record the index at which we should begin searching the array for that record. Although a few searches beginning at the computed index may be lengthy, most will be quite short, and will need to examine only a few records before finding the desired one. This technique is called *hashing*, since the key-to-index calculation scrambles, or "makes a hash of," the record key. It is also called *scatter storage*, since the array has valid data records and unused components scattered throughout, instead of being divided into used and unused parts.

For hashing we must modify slightly the definitions and declarations that we used in our discussions of sequential and binary search. The following are the modified definitions and declarations:

type *dataRecord* = **record**

        inUse: *Boolean*

        key: *integer*

        value: *real*

endrecord

const *size* = 503

const *limit* = *size* − 1

data: **array**[0 **to** *limit*] **of** *dataRecord*

Since hashing intermixes valid data records with unused array components, we need some way of distinguishing used and unused components. We can do this by giving each component a Boolean field *inUse* which has the value *true* if the component holds a valid data record and the value *false* if the component is unused.

The hashing method that we will discuss here requires that the number of components of the array, the value of the constant *size*, be a *prime number*. A prime number is an integer that cannot be evenly divided by any other integer except 1 and itself. The following are examples of prime numbers:

    2   3   5   7   11   13   17   19   23

Tables of prime numbers can be found in mathematical handbooks or calculated by computer programs. We generally have to modify the desired size of the data array slightly in order to make the size a prime number. Thus instead of defining *size* as 500, which is not a prime number, we define it as 503, which is. If a slightly smaller array were permissible, we could define *size* as 499, which is also a prime number.

The hashing calculation is slightly simpler if array indexes begin with 0 instead of 1. Therefore, we define *limit* as *size* − 1 and let the index values for the array *data* range from 0 to *limit* instead of from 1 to *size*.

The variable *free* is not needed since there are no used and unused parts of the array.

Before storing any data records in the array, we mark each component of the array as unused by setting its *inUse* field to *false*:

for *i* ← 0 **to** *limit*

    data[*i*] ← *dataRecord*(*false*, 0, 0.0)

endfor

The heart of any hashing method is the *hashing function*, *Hash*(*key*), which computes an index value for each possible record key. The hashing function is used for two purposes: (1) when storing a new record in the array, the search for an unused component in which to store the new record begins at the index given by the hashing function; and (2) when attempting to find the record having a given key, the search for that record begins at the index given by the hashing function.

The index values computed by the hashing function should be scattered throughout the array so that valid data records and unused array components will be thoroughly intermixed. When a new record is stored in the array, there is a good chance that the index computed by the hashing function will be that of an unused array component, and no search for an unused component will be needed. If the component designated by the hashing function is already in use—a situation known as a *collision*—it is likely that an unused component will be near and will be found after a short search.

If no collision occurred when a record was stored in the array, then the hashing function will yield the index of that record and no search for the record is needed. If a collision did occur when the record was stored, then the record can be found by a (usually) short search beginning at the component designated by the hashing function.

Many different hashing functions have been proposed. The one used here, although simple, is often highly effective. The key, assumed to be a positive integer, is divided by the size of the data array and the remainder is returned as the value of the hashing function:

> **function** *Hash*(*key*): *integer*
> **declare**
> > *key*: **in** *integer*
> **execute**
> > *Hash* ← *key* **mod** *size*
> **end** *Hash*

When a positive integer is divided by *size,* the remainder lies in the range 0 to *size* − 1 or 0 to *limit*, which is exactly the range of index values allowed for the data array. Thus the value returned by *Hash* is always a valid index value. In order for the computed index values to be scattered as widely as possible throughout the array, the value of *size* must be a prime number.

The following table gives some values of *Hash*:

key	Hash(key)
9653	96
7421	379
8397	349
6123	87
2145	133

If we are lucky, the value of *Hash* will be the index of an unused record when we are storing a new record and the index of the desired record when we are trying to retrieve a record. If we are not quite so lucky, we must conduct a search for the unused record or the record to be retrieved. The question then arises as to the order in which the array components should searched. This order is defined by a function *Next*(*index*). If *index* is the index of the component currently being examined by the search, the value of *Next*(*index*) is the index of the next component to be examined.

The most obvious search method is to step through the array component by component as in sequential search. In that case, *Next* might be defined by the following statement:

> *Next* ← *index* + 1

However, since the search begins somewhere within the array (at the index value computed by *Hash*), it will not be finished when the end of the array is reached. Instead, when the end of the array is reached, we need to step back to the beginning of the array and continue the search. For this purpose, we define *Next* by the following statement:

$$Next \leftarrow (index + 1) \bmod size$$

If the value of *index* is in the range 0 to *size* − 1, then the value of *Next* is *index* + 1. If the value of *index* is *size*, however, then the value of *Next* is 0 (why?). Thus the search steps from the last component of the array (with index *size* − 1 or *limit*) back to the first component (with index 0). The complete function definition for *Next* is as follows:

function *Next*(*index*): *integer*
declare
    index: **in** *integer*
execute
    Next ← (*index* + 1) **mod** *size*
end *Next*

This definition of *Next* has the disadvantage that it tends to produce *clusters*—large blocks of data records containing no unused components. If the hashing function yields an index within a cluster when a new record is stored, a collision will occur. With the definition given for *Next*, the new record will be stored at the end of the cluster, making the cluster even larger. For this reason, more complex definitions of *Next* are sometimes used; however, we will stick with the simpler definition.

Figure 13.7 shows the procedure

FindUnusedRecord(*searchKey*, *found*, *index*)

which finds an unused array component for storing a given record. The input parameter *searchKey* is the key of the record to be stored. The output parameter *found* is set to *true* if an unused record was found and to *false* otherwise. If an unused record was found, *index* is set to the index of the unused record.

Three variables, *start*, *c*, and *n*, are used during the search. The value of *start* is the index at which the search starts, the index returned by the hashing function. The value of *c* is the index of the current record, the one that is currently being examined. The value of *n* is the index of the next record, the one that will be examined after the current record. Initially, both *start* and *n* are set to the index returned by the hashing function:

start ← *Hash*(*searchKey*)
n ← *start*

The repeated statements move the search forward to the next record to be examined. The value of *c*, the index of the current record, is set to the value of *n*, the index of the next record to be examined. The function *Next* is then used to compute a new value for *n*:

Figure 13.7   Procedure for finding an unused record in a hash table.

```
procedure FindUnusedRecord(searchKey, found, index)

{ Locate unused record }

declare
    searchKey: in integer
    found: out Boolean
    index: out integer
    start, c, n: integer
execute
    start ← Hash(searchKey)
    n ← start
    repeat
        c ← n
        n ← Next(c)
    until (not data[c].inUse) or (n = start)
    found ← not data[c].inUse
    index ← c
end FindUnusedRecord
```

$$c \leftarrow n$$
$$n \leftarrow Next(c)$$

There are two conditions under which the search should terminate. We will have found the unused component we are looking for if the *inUse* field of *data[c]* has the value *false*, that is, if the condition

not *data[c].inUse*

is false.

But what if the array contains no unused components? After examining all components of the array, the search will return to the point at which it started, the component whose index is the value of *start*. Therefore, the search should also terminate if the next record to be examined is the record with which the search started, that is, if the condition

$n = start$

is true.

When the search terminates after finding an unused record, the value of c is the index of the unused record that was found, and the value of **not** *data[c].inUse* is *true*. Hence the values of *found* and *index* are set as follows:

$found \leftarrow \textbf{not } data[c].inUse$

$index \leftarrow c$

If no unused record was found, then the value of c is just the index of the last record that was examined, and the value of **not** $data[c].inUse$ is *false*. Hence *found* is set to *false* and *index* is set to a value that has no significance for the algorithm that invoked the procedure.

Figure 13.8 shows the procedure

$FindRecord(searchKey, found, index)$

which finds the record having a given key. The search for finding a record duplicates the search that was used to find an unused record when the record in question was stored in the file. Therefore, the procedures *FindUnusedRecord* and *FindRecord* are quite similar. The only differences between them are the conditions under which the search is terminated and the value returned by *found*.

There are three conditions under which the search for a given record can be terminated. Two of these are obvious. If the desired record has been found, then the condition

$searchKey = data[c].key$

Figure 13.8   Procedure for finding the record with a given key in a hash table.

```
procedure FindRecord(searchKey, found, index)

{ Locate record with given key }

declare
    searchKey: in integer
    found: out Boolean
    index: out integer
    start, c, n: integer
execute
    start ← Hash(searchKey)
    n ← start
    repeat
        c ← n
        n ← Next(c)
    until searchKey = data[c].key) or
        (not data[c].inUse) or (n = start)
    found ← (searchKey = data[c].key)
    index ← c
end FindRecord
```

is true. If the entire array has been searched without finding the desired record, we will eventually return to the point at which the search started, and the condition

$n = start$

will be true.

The third condition under which the search can be terminated is less obvious, yet it is very important because it allows most searches for records that are not present to be terminated quickly. When a new record is stored, it is placed in the first unused component that is encountered during the search. When searching for the record then, we should not encounter any unused component during the search. If we do encounter an unused component, we know that the record we are searching for is not present. Therefore, we also terminate the search if an unused component is encountered, that is, if the condition

not $data[c].inUse$

is true.

If the search terminates successfully, the key of the current record will be equal to the key that was being searched for. Thus, the value of *found* is set as follows:

$found \leftarrow (searchKey = data[c].key)$

We can delete a record merely by setting its *inUse* field to *false*. Unfortunately, deletions can cause problems for *FindRecord*, which relies on the assertion that no unused component will be encountered while searching for a record that is present in the array. Deleting a record can introduce an unused component that violates this assertion. After a record is deleted, therefore, some of the remaining records may have to be rearranged to restore the truth of the assertion. Consequently, the procedure for deleting a record, which we will not discuss here, is somewhat more complicated than the two procedures that we did discuss.

For hashing to be efficient, we need a good supply of unused components so that collisions will be infrequent and, when one does occur, the search for an unused record will be short. Therefore, no more than 75% to 80% of the array components should be in use. When this *loading factor* is exceeded, collisions become frequent and searches become lengthy.

The worse-case running time of the hashing algorithm described here is $O(n)$, the same as for sequential search. The *average* running time, however, can be much better, with an average of only a few records being examined per search. In spite of this excellent average performance, however, some records may still require lengthy searches. For this reason, hashing may be ruled out for *real-time* systems, such as air-traffic control systems and robot control systems, which must respond rapidly to external events. For such systems, worst-case performance is important because an unexpected delay in retrieving a single data item might result in a disaster.

13.4 A table-handling module

In this section we will construct a module that maintains a table of data records. Each record consists of a positive integer key and a real value. New records can be inserted into the table, existing records can be deleted, and the value corresponding to a given key can be retrieved. The array in which the data records are stored is hidden inside the module and can be manipulated only by the procedures provided by the module. The user of the module does not have to know anything about how the data records are stored. Indeed, we will later construct another version of the module that is externally indistinguishable from the current version but that stores the data records in a completely different way.

The module exports a Boolean function *Error* and four procedures: *New*, *Lookup*, *Insert*, and *Delete*. We specify the function and the four procedures as follows:

Error	Returns *true* if an error occurred during the immediately preceding operation and *false* otherwise.
New	Creates an empty table. Any data currently stored in the table is lost.
Lookup(searchKey, valueFound)	Sets *valueFound* to the data value associated with the key *searchKey*. An error occurs if the table does not have an entry with key *searchKey*.
Insert(insertKey, insertValue)	Inserts a table entry with key *insertKey* and value *insertValue*. An error occurs if the table is full or if an entry with key *insertKey* is already present.
Delete(deleteKey)	Deletes entry with key *deleteKey*. An error occurs if the table does not have an entry with key *deleteKey*.

Our fundamental design decisions are to store the data as an array of records and to use binary search to locate the data record having a given key. Binary search requires that the records in the array be in ascending order according to their keys. Maintaining this order will be the responsibility of *Insert*.

Figure 13.9 shows the module *TableHandler*. The module exports the function *Error* and the procedures *New*, *Lookup*, *Insert*, and *Delete*. With one exception, the definitions of *dataRecord* and *size* and the declarations of *data* and *free* are the same as used in the sections on sequential and binary search. The exception is that index values for *data* run from 0 to *size* instead of from 1 to *size*. The component *data*[0] holds a dummy record whose key is less than the key of any valid data record. This dummy record serves as a sentinel when new records are inserted into the table. It also prevents erroneous operation of the binary search procedure, which will not work properly if applied to a table containing no data records.

The array *data* is divided into used and unused parts as shown in Figure 13.3. The integer variable *free* is the index of the first component in the unused part of the array. The Boolean variable *errorFlag* is set to *true* if an error occurs during an operation and to *false* otherwise.

Figure 13.9   A table-handling module. The module provides a function
for reporting errors and procedures for initializing a new
table, inserting a record, looking up the value associated
with a given key, and deleting a record.

module *TableHandler*

{ Maintain a table of data records }

declare
    export *Error, New, Lookup, Insert, Delete*
    type *dataRecord* = **record**
                        key: *integer*
                        value: *real*
                endrecord
    const *size* = 500
    data: **array**[0 **to** *size*] **of** *dataRecord*
    free: *integer*
    errorFlag: *Boolean*

function *Error*: *Boolean*

{ Return value of and clear error indicator }

execute
    Error ← *errorFlag*
    errorFlag ← *false*
end *Error*

procedure *New*

{ Initialize empty table }

execute
    data[0] ← *dataRecord*(−1, 0.0)
    free ← 1
    errorFlag ← *false*
end *New*

```
procedure Lookup(searchKey, valueFound)

{ Find value corresponding to given key }

declare
    searchKey: in integer
    valueFound: out real
    found: Boolean
    index: integer
execute
    BinarySearch(searchKey, found, index)
    errorFlag ← not found
    if found then
        valueFound ← data[index].value
    endif
end Lookup



procedure Insert(insertKey, insertValue)

{ Insert new record in table }

declare
    insertKey: in integer
    insertValue: in real
    found: Boolean
    i, index: integer
execute
    BinarySearch(insertKey, found, index)
    if found or (free > size) or (insertKey < 0) then
        errorFlag ← true
    else
        errorFlag ← false
        i ← free
        free ← free + 1
        while insertKey < data[i − 1].key
            data[i] ← data[i − 1]
            i ← i − 1
        endwhile
        data[i].key ← insertKey
        data[i].value ← insertValue
    endif
end Insert
```

```
procedure Delete(deleteKey)

{ Delete record with given key }

declare
    deleteKey: in integer
    found: Boolean
    i, index: integer
execute
    BinarySearch(deleteKey, found, index)
    if (not found) or (deleteKey < 0) then
        errorFlag ← true
    else
        errorFlag ← false
        for i ← index to free − 2
            data[i] ← data[i + 1]
        endfor
        free ← free − 1
    endif
end Delete
```

```
procedure BinarySearch(searchKey, found, index)

{ Locate record with given key }

declare
    searchKey: in integer
    found: out Boolean
    index: out integer
    low, mid, high: integer
execute
    low ← 0
    high ← free − 1
    repeat
        mid ← (low + high) div 2
        if searchKey < data[mid].key then
            high ← mid − 1
        elseif searchKey > data[mid].key then
            low ← mid + 1
        endif
    until (searchKey = data[mid].key) or (low > high)
    found ← (searchKey = data[mid].key)
    index ← mid
end BinarySearch
```

> **initialize**
> *New*
> **end** *TableHandler*

Error   The Boolean function *Error* returns the value of the *errorFlag*. Since no error can occur during a call to *Error*, *errorFlag* is cleared to *false*.

New   The procedure *New* builds an empty table containing the dummy record *data*[0] but no valid data records. The component *data*[0] is assigned a record with key −1 and value 0.0. *Free* is set to 1, indicating that *data*[1] is the first unused component of the array. Since no error can occur during a call to *New*, *errorFlag*, is cleared to *false*.

Lookup   The procedure *Lookup* finds the data value corresponding to a given key. *BinarySearch*, which is the same as the binary search procedure we have already discussed, is called to locate the record with index *searchKey*. If the search procedure sets *found* to *true*, the desired record was found and *errorFlag* should be set to *false*. If *found* is set to *false*, however, the desired record was not found, and *errorFlag* should be set to *true*. Hence *errorFlag* is set to **not** *found*. If *found* is set to *true*, *index* is the index of the desired record and *value*[*index*].*value* is the data value corresponding to the given key. This value is returned as the value of *valueFound*.

Insert   The procedure *Insert* stores a record having a given key and value. The new record must be inserted in such a way that the records remain in ascending order according to their keys.

It is an error to insert a record with the same key as an existing record (the existing record must be deleted first). Therefore, *Insert* begins by calling *BinarySearch* to search for a record with key *insertKey*. An error condition exists if *BinarySearch* sets the value of *found* to *true*.

It is also an error if

   $free > size$

or

   $insertKey < 0$

is true. If the first condition is true, the array has no unused components, and hence there is no room for another record. If the second condition is true, the key of the record being inserted is negative. Data records with negative keys are forbidden to assure that the key of the dummy record *data*[0] precedes the keys of all valid data records.

If one or more of the three error conditions is true, *errorFlag* is set to *true* and the procedure returns. Otherwise, *errorFlag* is set to *false* and the new data record is inserted into the array.

The variable i is set to the value of *free*, the first unused component of the array. The value of *free* is increased by 1, effectively transferring this component from the unused to the used part of the array. Thus, the value of *data*[i] is an unused record that can be replaced with the new record we wish to store.

The problem is that the unused record is probably in the wrong place. It is at the end of the used part of the array, whereas the new record must be positioned so that the records will remain in ascending order according to their keys. Hence, the unused record must be "moved up" in the array until it is at the position at which the new record must be inserted.

Throughout the process of moving the unused record, the value of i will always be the index of the unused record. We move the unused record up one position in the array by moving the record preceding it down one position. More precisely, we assign *data*[i] the value of the record that precedes it in the array:

$$data[i] \leftarrow data[i - 1]$$

Now both *data*[i] and *data*[$i - 1$] have the same value. Since only one copy of this value is needed, either *data*[i] or *data*[$i - 1$] can be considered an unused record. Since we wish to move the unused record up one position in the array, we make *data*[$i - 1$] the unused record, which we do by decreasing the value of i by 1:

$$i \leftarrow i - 1$$

The unused record is moved upwards as long as the record to be inserted should be positioned still further up in the list. This will be true if the condition

$$insertKey < data[i - 1].key$$

is true, that is, if the record to be inserted should come before the record immediately preceding the unused record. The following repetition moves the unused record to the proper position:

while *insertKey* < *data*[$i - 1$].*key*
    data[i] ← *data*[$i - 1$]
    i ← $i - 1$
endwhile

How can we be sure that the repetition will terminate, that the unused record will not "run off the beginning" of the array? If the unused record is moved to *data*[1], the value of i is 1 and the continuation condition becomes

$$insertKey < data[0].key$$

However, *data*[0] contains the dummy record whose key precedes the key of every valid data record. Hence the continuation condition is false and the repetition terminates. The dummy record serves as a sentinel to prevent the insertion process from running off the beginning of the array.

When the repetition terminates, the value of i is still the index of the unused record, which has been moved to the proper position for inserting the new data record. The components of the new data record are assigned to the component variables of *data*[i]:

$$data[i].key \leftarrow insertKey$$
$$data[i].value \leftarrow insertValue$$

Delete The procedure *Delete* deletes the record with key *deleteKey*. *Delete* begins by calling *BinarySearch* to locate the record to be deleted. If the record cannot be found, or if the key of the record to be deleted is negative, *errorFlag* is set to *false*. Deletion of records with negative keys is forbidden to assure that the dummy record stored in *data*[0] cannot be deleted.

If neither of the error conditions is true, *errorFlag* is set to *false* and the record found by *BinarySearch* is deleted. Deletion is essentially the opposite of insertion. The record to be deleted is an unused record that must be moved down to the end of the used part of the array where it can join the other unused records in the unused part of the array.

As in *Insert*, the value of *i* is the index of the unused record. We move the unused record down one position by moving the record below it up one position. More precisely, we set the value of *data*[*i*] to that of *data*[*i* + 1]

$$data[i] \leftarrow data[i + 1]$$

Since *data*[*i*] and *data*[*i* + 1] both have the same value, either one can be considered unused. We designate *data*[*i* + 1] as the unused record by increasing the value of *i* by 1. The index of the unused record is initially the value of *index*, which was set by *BinarySearch*. The following repetition moves the unused record to the end of the array:

for *i* ← *index* **to** *free* − 2
    data[*i*] ← *data*[*i* + 1]
endfor

When the repetition terminates, the index of the last record that is in use is the value of *free* − 2, and the index of the unused record that was moved down is the value of *free* − 1. The statement

free ← *free* − 1

transfers the unused record from the used to the unused part of the array.

BinarySearch With one difference, the binary search procedure is the same as the one discussed in the section on binary search. The difference is that *low* is initialized to 0 instead of 1, since our data array begins with *data*[0]. Since the part of the data array that is in use always contains one record—the dummy record at *data*[0]—the binary search routine cannot fail as a result of being applied to an empty array.

13.5

Sorting

Binary search is just one of many procedures that require the records in an array to be in ascending order according to the value of a key field. The process of placing records in order according to a given key is known as *sorting*; the records are said to be "sorted on" the given key. Often records must be sorted on different keys for different applications. One application may require customer records to be sorted on account numbers, another application may require that they be sorted on names, and still another application may require that they be sorted on zip codes. Computers used for business data processing may spend as much as half their time sorting.

There are two classes of sorting procedures: *internal sorting* procedures, which are applied to records stored in main memory as arrays, and *external sorting* procedures, which are applied to records stored in auxiliary memory as files. Since this chapter is about arrays, we will confine our discussion to internal sorting. Before leaving external sorting, however, we note that it is based on sequential access, which is the most efficient type of access for files. Specifically, external sorting procedures are based on merging, which combines two files sorted on a given key to produce a combined file sorted on the same key. The file to be sorted is broken down into short segments called *runs* that are already in order. The runs are then merged to form larger runs, which are merged to form still larger runs, and so on until we are left with a single run consisting of the entire file. External sorting procedures differ from one another mainly in the manner in which the merging process is managed.

In this section we will look at two internal sorting procedures: a straightforward but relatively inefficient procedure *InsertionSort*, and a more complex but much more efficent procedure *Quicksort*. We assume the same definitions and declarations as for the table-handling module:

type *dataRecord* = **record**

           key: *integer*

           value: *real*

     endrecord

const *size* = 500
data: **array**[0 **to** *size*] **of** *dataRecord*
free: *integer*

The part of the data array that is to be sorted extends from *data*[1] through *data*[*free* − 1]. *InsertionSort* stores a sentinel value in *data*[0]; *Quicksort* does not use *data*[0].

InsertionSort The procedure *InsertionSort* is based on the same technique that was used to insert records into the array maintained by the table-handling module. At each step of the sorting, the array being sorted consists of a sorted part followed by an unsorted part. The value of *j* is the index of the first record in the unsorted part. Thus, the values of

    data[1] through *data*[*j* − 1]

are sorted, and the values of

    data[*j*] through *data*[*free* − 1]

are unsorted. The insertion procedure employed by the table-handling module is used to insert the value of *data*[*j*] into its proper position in the sorted part of the array, and the value of *j* is increased by one. This process is repeated until all the records in the unsorted part have been inserted into the sorted part.

Figure 13.10 shows the procedure *InsertionSort*. We can outline the procedure as follows:

for $j \leftarrow 2$ **to** *free* $- 1$

''Insert the value of *data*[*j*] at its proper position among the values *data*[1] through *data*[*j* $- 1$]''

endfor

To make the insertion, we begin by setting *i* to the index of the record to be inserted:

$i \leftarrow j$

The record to be inserted is saved by assigning it to the record variable *temp*:

temp $\leftarrow$ *data*[*i*]

Since the value of *data*[*i*] has been saved, *data*[*i*] becomes an ''unused record'' that can be moved up in the array, exactly as in the *Insert* procedure of the table-handling module.

The key of the record being inserted is the value of *temp.key*. Therefore, the unused record is moved up as long as the condition

temp.key $<$ *data*[*i* $- 1$]

remains true. To assure that the repetition terminates when the value of *i* is 0, we must give *data*[0] a value such that the condition

temp.key $<$ *data*[0]

is false. We could give *data*[0].a special dummy value, as was done in the table-handling module. Another approach, which we will follow here, is to set *data*[0]. *key* to *temp.key*, the key of the record to be inserted:

data[0].*key* $\leftarrow$ *temp.key*

This is similar to the method we used for sequential search, in which we set the key of the sentinel record to the key being searched for.

The process of moving the unused record to the proper position is the same as for the *Insert* procedure of the table-handling module:

while *temp.key* $<$ *data*[*i* $- 1$].*key*

data[*i*] $\leftarrow$ *data*[*i* $- 1$]

$i \leftarrow i - 1$

endwhile

When the repetition terminates, *i* is the index of the unused record, which has been moved to the desired position. The record to be inserted is stored in *data*[*i*]:

Figure 13.10 The procedure *InsertionSort*.

```
procedure InsertionSort

{ Sort records into ascending order on field key }

declare
    i, j: integer
    temp: dataRecord
execute
    for j ← 2 to free − 1
        i ← j
        temp ← data[i]
        data[0].key ← temp.key
        while temp.key < data[i − 1].key
            data[i] ← data[i − 1]
            i ← i − 1
        endwhile
        data[i] ← temp
    endfor
end InsertionSort
```

$data[i] \leftarrow temp$

Efficiency of insertionSort   We can gauge the efficiency of a sorting procedure based on either the number of key-comparisons made or the number of records moved. Let's consider the number of comparisons made by *InsertionSort*. In the worst case, the key of the record being inserted must be compared with the key of each record preceding it in the array, the sentinel record included. Thus, the key of *data*[2] must be compared with the keys of two records: *data*[0] and *data*[1]. The key of *data*[3] must be compared with the keys of three records: *data*[0], *data*[1], and *data*[2]. The key of *data*[4] must be compared with the keys of four records: *data*[0], *data*[1], *data*[2], and *data*[3]. In general, the key of *data*[j] must be compared with the keys of *j* records. Since *j* varies from 2 to *n*, the total number of key-comparisons is given by the following sum:

$$2 + 3 + 4 + \ldots + n$$

In mathematics handbooks, we find the following formula for the sum of the first *n* integers:

$$1 + 2 + 3 + 4 + \ldots + n = \tfrac{1}{2}n^2 + \tfrac{1}{2}n$$

Subtracting 1 from both sides of the equation gives the following:

$$2 + 3 + 4 + \ldots + n = \tfrac{1}{2}n^2 + \tfrac{1}{2}n - 1$$

When n is large, the values of n and 1 are negligible in comparison with that of n^2. For large n, then, the number of comparisons made by an insertion sort in the worst case is proportional to n^2. In a similar fashion, we can show that, in the worst case, the number of moves—the number of record assignments—is also proportional to n^2 for large n. We can thus conclude that the worst-case running time for an insertion sort is $O(n^2)$.

A running time of $O(n^2)$ is *much* worse than a running time of $O(n)$. An algorithm with a running time of $O(n^2)$ will work well enough for small values of n but is likely to prove too slow for even moderately large values of n. Specifically, *InsertionSort* will serve well enough for sorting 10 records, may be usable (although slow) for 100 or so records, and will almost surely be too slow to be practical for 1,000 records.

Quicksort   *Quicksort* is one of the fastest methods known for internal sorting. It divides the list to be sorted into two partitions such that all records in the first partition come before all records in the second partition. The *Quicksort* procedure then calls itself recursively to sort each of the two partitions.

For example, let's see how *Quicksort* might be used to sort the following list of numbers:

    3 9 6 5 7 4 1 2 8

We want to divide this list into two sublists in such a way that all the values on the first sublist are less than or equal to all the values on the second sublist. To do this, we choose one of the numbers to serve as a dividing line between the two sublists. All numbers less than the dividing-line value go on the first sublist; all values greater than the dividing-line value go on the second sublist. The dividing-line value itself may end up on either sublist.

For example, let's choose the dividing-line value as 7, the value at the midpoint of the original list. We can then divide the list into sublists as follows:

    3 2 6 5 1 4   7 9 8

All values less than 7 are on the first sublist, and all those greater than 7 (together with 7 itself) are on the second sublist.

Now if each of the two sublists is sorted separately

    1 2 3 4 5 6   7 8 9

the entire list will be in order and the sorting will be complete. Our plan for *Quicksort* then is as follows. Divide the list to be sorted into two sublists as just illustrated. Then call the *Quicksort* procedure recursively to sort each of the sublists. When the recursive calls return, both the sublists and the original list will be sorted, and the *Quicksort* procedure can terminate.

Let's go back to the division of the original list into two sublists:

    3 2 6 5 1 4   7 9 8

Each of the sublists will itself be sorted by the *Quicksort* procedure. Therefore, each of the sublists will be divided into smaller sublists, which will be divided into still smaller sublists, and so on. Let's follow this process through and see exactly how the original list gets sorted.

Consider the second sublist:

   7   9   8

We take the middle value, 9, as the dividing line. The list can be divided as follows:

   7 8   9

Since the "list" 9 contains only one value, it cannot be divided any further. The list

   7 8

can be divided in only one way:

   7   8

This is as far as we can go with the second sublist of the original division. Now let's apply the same process to the first sublist of the original division:

   3 2 6 5 1 4

If we take 6 as the dividing-line value, we get the following division:

   3 2 4 5 1   6

The second list contains only a single value and so cannot be divided any further. The first list can be divided as follows, using 4 as the dividing-line value:

   3 2 1   5 4

Of these two sublists, the second can be divided into

   4   5

and the first can be divided into

   1   2   3

(*Quicksort* occasionally divides a list into three sublists instead of two. The middle sublist always consists of only a single value. Since the middle sublist cannot be further subdivided and needs no further sorting, it can be ignored.)

Now let's see how these repeated divisions into sublists have put the original list in order:

```
                                3 9 6 5 7 4 1 2 8
                    3 2 6 5 1 4                      7 9 8
              3 2 4 5 1                  6          7 8        9
        3 2 1              5 4                      7      8
    1   2   3          4   5
```

In this illustration, the first line shows the original list, the second line the two sublists of the original list, the third line the sublists of the sublists of the original list, and so on. The end results of the repeated subdivision into sublists are the one-component lists, which cannot be divided any further. The values on the one-component lists, read from left to right (even though they appear on different levels in the diagram) are in the desired numerical order.

Let's summarize the steps in dividing the original list into successively smaller sublists:

1. Choose the dividing-line value.

2. Rearrange the values on the original list so that all those less than the dividing-line value are to the left of a certain point and all those greater than the dividing-line value are to the right of the same point, thus dividing the list into two sublists.

3. Repeat the same process for each sublist containing more than one item. (A one-item sublist cannot be further sorted.) This is done by calling the *Quicksort* procedure recursively for each sublist to be sorted.

Our first job is to find the dividing-line value. *Quicksort* works most efficiently when the two sublists are nearly the same size. They will be most nearly the same size if the dividing-line value is the *median* of the values on the original list—the value that has as many values less than or equal to it as values greater than or equal to it. For example, the median of the original list that we used to illustrate *Quicksort* is 5.

Unfortunately, because finding the median of a list of values is almost as difficult as sorting the values, using the median is not practical. We must choose one of the values and hope that it is close to the median. If the values are in arbitrary order, than one choice is just as good as another, since any value is as likely as any other to be close to the median.

However, there is an argument for taking a value near the middle of the list. Often we are asked to sort a list that is almost in order—only a few values are out of order. In fact, a list that is supposed to be sorted may be sorted again just to make sure. In these cases, a value near the middle of the list has a good chance of being close to the median. Therefore, we will choose the middle value for the dividing-line value.

Thus, for the list

3 9 6 5 7 4 1 2 8

we chose the middle value 7 for the dividing-line value. This choice wasn't too bad, since 7 is not too far from the median, 5. On the other hand, for the sublist

3 2 6 5 1 4

we chose 6, a terrible choice. Since 6 is the largest value on the list, using it as a dividing-line value produces the following very unequal subdivision:

3 2 4 5 1   6

Fortunately, it usually turns out that the terrible choices are few enough so that they do not seriously affect the efficiency of *Quicksort*.

Having chosen the dividing-line value, the next step is to rearrange the values on the list so as to produce the two sublists. We start with two arrows, one at each end of the list:

```
3  9  6  5  7  4  1  2  8
↑                    ↑
i                    j
```

The two arrows are labeled i and j, since i and j are the variables whose values will represent the arrows in the procedure *Quicksort*.

The arrow i is moved forward through the list as long as it points to a value less than the dividing-line value. When it reaches a value greater than or equal to the dividing-line value, it stops. The arrow j is moved backward through the list as long as it points to a value greater than the dividing-line value. When it reaches a value less than or equal to the dividing-line value, it stops. Since the dividing-line value for the example is 7, moving arrow i gives

```
3  9  6  5  7  4  1  2  8
   ↑                 ↑
   i                 j
```

and moving arrow j gives

```
3  9  6  5  7  4  1  2  8
   ↑              ↑
   i              j
```

The values pointed to by i and j are exchanged

```
3  2  6  5  7  4  1  9  8
   ↑              ↑
   i              j
```

after which i is moved forward one position and j is moved backward one position:

```
3  2  6  5  7  4  1  9  8
      ↑        ↑
      i        j
```

This process is repeated: i is moved forward until it encounters a value too large for the first sublist, and j is moved backward until it encounters a value too small for the second sublist:

```
3  2  6  5  7  4  1  9  8
            ↑  ↑
            i  j
```

(Note that j does not move since it is already pointing to a value too small for the second sublist.) Again, we exchange the values

```
3  2  6  5  1  4  7  9  8
            ↑  ↑
            i  j
```

and move i forward one place and j backward one place:

```
3   2   6   5   1   4   7   9   8
                    ↑
                    i

                    j
```

Once more, we move i forward and j backward in search of out-of-place values. Again, the position of j doesn't change since it is already pointing to a value too small for the second sublist:

```
3   2   6   5   1   4   7   9   8
                    ↑   ↑
                    j   i
```

At this point, however, the two arrows have passed one another, which signals that our job is done. Everything from the beginning of the list through the value pointed to by j constitutes the first sublist, and everything from the value pointed to by i through the end of the list constitutes the second sublist. Thus, the list is divided as follows:

```
3   2   6   5   1   4       7   9   8
                    ↑           ↑
                    j           i
```

Once the division into sublists is completed, the *Quicksort* procedure is called recursively for each of the two sublists.

Figure 13.11 shows the procedure

Quicksort(first, last)

The input parameters *first* and *last* are the indexes of the first and last components of the list to be sorted. The parameters are necessary since *Quicksort* is called recursively to sort various sublists; the values of *first* and *last* specify the sublist to be sorted. The top-level call, which requests the sorting of the part of *data* that is in use, is

Quicksort(1, *free* − 1)

The values of i and j are indexes corresponding to the arrows in our previous illustrations. Like the arrows, i and j are initially set to designate the first and last components of the list or sublist to be sorted:

$i \leftarrow first$

$j \leftarrow last$

The dividing-line value, *dividingLine,* is set to the key of the middle component of the list or sublist to be sorted:

dividingLine ← *data*[(*first* + *last*) **div** 2].*key*

Like the corresponding arrows, i is moved forward in the list as long as the key of the record indexed by i is less than the dividing-line value:

Figure 13.11 The procedure *Quicksort*.

```
procedure Quicksort(first, last)

{ Sort records into ascending order on field key }

declare
    first, last: in integer
    i, j, dividingLine: integer
    temp: dataRecord
execute
    i ← first
    j ← last
    dividingLine ← data[(first + last) div 2].key
    repeat
        while data[i].key < dividingLine
            i ← i + 1
        endwhile
        while data[j].key > dividingLine
            j ← j - 1
        endwhile
        if i <= j then
            temp ← data[i]
            data[i] ← data[j]
            data[j] ← temp
            i ← i + 1
            j ← j - 1
        endif
    until i > j
    if first < j then
        Quicksort(first, j)
    endif
    if i < last then
        Quicksort(i, last)
    endif
end Quicksort
```

```
while data[i].key < dividingLine
    i ← i + 1
endwhile
```

Likewise, *j* is moved backward in the list as long as the key of the record indexed by *j* is greater than the dividing-line value:

> **while** *data*[*j*].*key* > *dividingLine*
>
> $j \leftarrow j - 1$
>
> **endwhile**

If *i* and *j* have not passed each other, the values of *data*[*i*] and *data*[*j*] are exchanged. Then *i* is moved forward one component and *j* is moved backward one component:

> **if** *i* <= *j* **then**
>
> $temp \leftarrow data[i]$
>
> $data[i] \leftarrow data[j]$
>
> $data[j] \leftarrow temp$
>
> $i \leftarrow i + 1$
>
> $j \leftarrow j - 1$
>
> **endif**

The process of moving *i* and *j* and exchanging the values of *data*[*i*] and *data*[*j*] is repeated until *i* and *j* pass each other, that is, until the condition

> $i > j$

is true.

When the **repeat** construction terminates, the list

> *data*[*first*] through *data*[*last*]

has been divided into two sublists:

> *data*[*first*] through *data*[*j*]

and

> *data*[*i*] through *data*[*last*]

Quicksort is called recursively to sort each sublist that contains more than one component:

> **if** *first* < *j* **then**
>
> *Quicksort*(*first*, *j*)
>
> **endif**
>
> **if** *i* < *last* **then**
>
> *Quicksort*(*i*, *last*)
>
> **endif**

One-component and zero-component sublists are the "trivial cases" that require no further recursive calls and so allow the recursion to terminate.

Efficiency of quicksort   Suppose that, whenever a list is divided into two sublists, we are lucky enough to choose a dividing-line value that divides the list into two sublists of equal size. In this case *Quicksort,* like a binary search, repeatedly divides the list it is working with in half. As in binary search, $\log(n)$ divisions are required to narrow a list down to a sublist containing only a single value. We can organize the list to be sorted and the sublists into which it is divided into a series of levels. On the top level we have the original list. On the second level we have the two sublists obtained by dividing the original list in half. On the third level we have the four sublists obtained by dividing the the sublists on the second level in half, and so on. On level $\log(n) + 1$ each sublist contains at most a single value. Since a sublist containing only a single value cannot be divided further, no work need be done dividing the sublists on level $\log(n) + 1$. Thus there are $\log(n)$ levels on which work must be done dividing the sublists.

In dividing a sublist arrows i and j are started at opposite ends of the sublist and moved toward each other until they meet. In this process each value on the sublist is compared with the dividing-line value. In dividing the sublists on a given level, a total of n comparisons must be made.

The running time of *Quicksort* is proportional to n, the number of comparisons made on each level, multiplied by $\log(n)$, the number of levels on which comparisons are made. Thus *Quicksort* has a running time of $O(n*\log(n))$. Just as a running time of $O(\log(n))$ is much better than a running time of $O(n)$, so a running time of $O(n*\log(n))$ is much better than a running time of $O(n^2)$.

In deriving the running time, we assumed that we were always lucky enough to choose a dividing-line value that would cause each list or sublist to be divided precisely in half. But what if we were always unlucky enough to choose a dividing-line value that produced the worst possible division, in which one sublist contained only a single value? In that case, each call to *Quicksort* would reduce the size of the original list by only a single value. We would need n subdivision levels, rather than $\log(n)$, to sort the original list. In this case the running time for *Quicksort* becomes $O(n*n)$ or $O(n^2)$, the same as for *InsertionSort*. Thus the worst-case performance is very poor. Fortunately, the worst case is very unlikely to occur, so the average running time can be shown to be $O(n*log(n))$. Quicksort is like hashing in that the average performance is excellent but one always takes the chance of getting very poor performance in a particular case.

A question of space efficiency also arises in connection with *Quicksort*. A private data area must be set up for each invocation of *Quicksort*. Since *Quicksort* is recursive, a number of invocations of *Quicksort* may exist at the same time; a private data area must be set up for each invocation. In the best case and on the average, there are about $\log(n)$ calls to *Quicksort,* and the space required for private data areas is not large. But in the worst case, there can be up to n invocations of *Quicksort* in existence at the same time. For large n, the space for n private data areas could easily exhaust the memory capacity of the computer.

13.6 Multidimensional arrays

Suppose we wish to represent the table in Figure 13.12 as an array. Each row of the table can be represented as a one-dimensional array having three components. For example, we might define the array type *row* as follows:

    type *row* = **array**[1 **to** 3] **of** *integer*

Figure 13.12 A table that can be stored as a two-dimensional array. The first index of the array designates the row of the table and ranges from 1 to 4. The second index designates the column and ranges from 1 to 3.

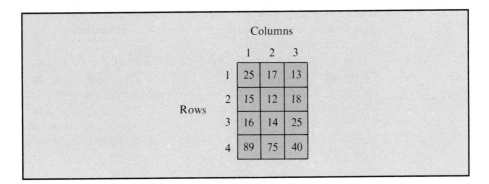

We can now write the value of the first row as

$row(25, 17, 13)$

the value of the second row as

$row(15, 12, 18)$

the value of the third row as

$row(16, 14, 25)$

and the value of the fourth row as

$row(89, 75, 40)$

To represent the entire table as a single array, we need an array of four components, each of which holds one of the four rows of the table. Let's define the array type

type *table* = **array**[1 **to** 4] **of** *row*

and declare the variable *t* by

t: *table*

After the assignments

$t[1] \leftarrow row(25, 17, 13)$
$t[2] \leftarrow row(15, 12, 18)$
$t[3] \leftarrow row(16, 14, 25)$
$t[4] \leftarrow row(89, 75, 40)$

the value of *t*[1] is the first row of the table, the value of *t*[2] is the second row of the table, and so on.

We can represent an entire value of type *table* as follows:

table(*row*(25, 17, 13), *row*(15, 12, 18),

$\quad$ *row*(16, 14, 25), *row*(89, 75, 40))

Each component of type table is a value of type *row*. The assignment

$t \leftarrow$ *table*(*row*(25, 17, 13), *row*(15, 12, 18),

$\quad$ *row*(16, 14, 25), *row*(89, 75, 40))

is valid and equivalent to the four assignments given above.

Since $t[1]$ is itself an array variable of type *row,* it is made up of three component variables: $t[1][1]$, $t[1][2]$, and $t[1][3]$. The value of $t[1][1]$ is 25, the value at the intersection of row 1 and column 1 of the table. The value of $t[1][2]$ is 17, the value at the intersection of row 1 and column 2. The value of $t[1][3]$ is 13, the value at the intersection of row 1 and column 3. In general, the value of $t[i][j]$ is the value at the intersection of row i and column j.

Arrays of type *table* are *two-dimensional arrays,* since each represents a structure that extends in two dimensions or directions: up-down and left-right. However, our method of defining *table* is somewhat cumbersome, as is our method of designating the component variables that hold individual table entries. In common with most programming languages, the algorithmic language provides more concise means of defining the types and designating the components of two-dimensional arrays.

The two-dimensional-array type *table* can be defined in a single type definition as follows:

type *table* = **array**[1 **to** 4, 1 **to** 3] **of** *integer*

This definition states that a value of type *table* is composed of integers, each of which is labeled with two index values. One index ranges from 1 to 4, and the other ranges from 1 to 3. For some purposes it is helpful to think of the components of a value of type *table* as arranged in rows and columns, with the first index designating a particular row and the second index designating a particular column. For other purposes, it may be best to forget the table picture and just note that each component of a value of type table is labeled with two index values.

As before, we declare the variable t to be of type *table:*

t: *table*

The notation

$t[i][j]$

for the component of t corresponding to an individual table entry is also somewhat cumbersome. Like most programming languages, the algorithmic language allows the following alternate notation:

$t[i, j]$

Thus the value of $t[i, j]$ is the value at the intersection of row i and column j of the table. If the value of t is the table shown in Figure 13.12, then the value of $t[1, 2]$ is 17, the value of $t[2, 3]$ is 18, and the value of $t[4, 3]$ is 40.

We can represent an entire value of type *table* as follows:

table((25, 17, 13), (15, 12, 18),

(16, 14, 25), (89, 75, 40))

Since our concise notation does not define a type for the rows of the table, the components of each row are listed in parentheses without any preceding type identifier. The assignment

$t \leftarrow$ *table*((25, 17, 13), (15, 12, 18),

(16, 14, 25), (89, 75, 40))

is valid and assigns to t the table shown in Figure 13.12.

The concept of a multidimensional array can be generalized to more than two dimensions. For example, consider the three-dimensional-array type defined as follows:

type *book* = **array**[1 **to** 10, 1 **to** 4, 1 **to** 3] **of** *integer*

We could think of a value of type *book* as a book with 10 pages, each of which contains a table of integers having four rows and three columns. Or, perhaps better, we can abandon such pictures and just think of a value of type *book* as a collection of integers, each of which is labeled with three index values. The first index value ranges from 1 to 10, the second index value ranges from 1 to 4, and the third index value ranges from 1 to 3.

Suppose b is declared as a variable of type *book:*

b: *book*

Then the value of $b[3, 4, 1]$ is the value on page 3 at the intersection of row 4 and column 1. The value of $b[6, 2, 3]$ is the value on page 6 at the intersection of row 2 and column 3, and so on.

We can define array types of any number of dimensions. For example:

type *hyperbook* = **array**[1 **to** 5, 1 **to** 10, 1 **to** 4, 1 **to** 3] **of** *integer*

Values of type *hyperbook* are four-dimensional structures that are not easily visualized by three-dimensional creatures such as ourselves. But the inability to visualize four-dimensional arrays does not make them any less useful when we wish to organize component values in such a way that each is labeled by four index values.

Magic squares   A *magic square* is a square array of numbers in which the numbers in each row, column, and diagonal have the same sum. The number of rows, which is the same as the number of columns, is the *order* of the square. For example, the following is a magic square of order 3:

4 9 2
3 5 7
8 1 6

The numbers in each row, column, and diagonal add up to 15.

We will use an algorithm for generating magic squares as an example of processing two-dimensional arrays. The algorithm we will use generates squares of odd order—of order 3, 5, 7, 9, and so on. Each square will contain all the integers from 1 through *order* ∗∗ 2, where the value of *order* is the order of the square. Thus, a square of order 3 contains the integers 1 through 9, a square of order 5 contains the integers 1 through 25, and so on. The algorithm must state how the integers are to be placed in the square to make it magic.

The rules for placing the integers tell us how to move from the position in which the previous integer was placed to the position in which the next integer will be placed. In making such moves, we must use the idea of *wraparound*. We treat the square as if it had been bent into a cylinder and its top and bottom edges pasted together. Moving up from the top row puts us on the bottom row, and moving down from the bottom row puts us on the top row. Likewise, we treat the square as if the left and right edges were pasted together. Moving left from the leftmost column puts us in the rightmost column, and moving right from the rightmost column puts us in the leftmost column.

Given the idea of wraparound, we use the following rules to place the integers 1 through *order* ∗∗ 2 in the magic square:

1. The integer 1 goes in the middle of the bottom row.

2. Let the *current position* be the one in which we have just placed an integer. To determine the position of the next integer, we move diagonally down and to the right by one position. (This move may require wraparound.) If the new position does not already contain an integer, the next integer is placed in this position.

3. If the position diagonally down and to the right from the current position is already occupied, we move up one position from the current position and place the next integer there. This move will never require wraparound.

Figure 13.13 shows the algorithm *MagicSquare*. The constant *maxOrder* is the largest order square that the algorithm can generate; *maxOrder* is set to 19, the largest order square that can be conveniently shown on most computer displays. As the magic square is constructed, it is stored in the array variable *square*, whose value is a two-dimensional array with *maxOrder* rows and *maxOrder* columns:

   square: **array**[1 **to** *maxOrder*, 1 **to** *maxOrder*] **of** *integer*

The values of *i* and *j* are the indexes of the current position, the component of *square* in which the last integer was stored. The values of *iNext* and *jNext* are the indexes of the next position, the position diagonally down and to the right from the current position. The value of *number* is the integer placed in the current square, and the value of *order* is the order of the square being generated.

The algorithm begins by asking the user to enter the order of the magic square to be printed. The user is asked to enter an odd number in the range 1 through *maxOrder*, but the user's response is not checked for validity. The algorithm will not work properly if an even number or a number outside the specified range is entered.

We will use a zero value to indicate an empty component of *square*—a component in which no number has yet been placed. Before beginning to place num-

Figure 13.13   Algorithm for printing a magic square of odd order. Note
the use of nested **for** constructions for processing a two-
dimensional array.

```
algorithm MagicSquare

{ Generate a magic square of odd order }

declare
    const maxOrder = 19
    square: array[1 to maxOrder, 1 to maxOrder] of integer
    i, j, iNext, jNext, number, order: integer
execute
    output 'Order of square (odd integer in range 1 − ', maxOrder, ')?',
            more
    input order
    for i ← 1 to order
        for j ← 1 to order
            square[i, j] ← 0
        endfor
    endfor
    i ← order
    j ← (1 + order) div 2
    for number ← 1 to order ** 2
        square[i, j] ← number
        iNext ← i mod order + 1
        jNext ← j mod order + 1
        if square[iNext, jNext] = 0 then
            i ← iNext
            j ← jNext
        else
            i ← i − 1
        endif
    endfor
    for i ← 1 to order
        for j ← 1 to order
            output tab(4 * j), square[i, j], more
        endfor
        output
    endfor
end MagicSquare
```

bers, therefore, we must set the components of *square* to zero.* The statement

   square[*i, j*] ← 0

assigns zero to the component at the intersection of row *i* and column *j*. To assign zero to the components of row *i*, we execute this statement for all values of *j* from 1 to *order*:

   for *j* ← 1 **to** *order*
      square[*i, j*] ← 0
   endfor

To assign zero to the components of the rows of *square,* the above **for** construction must be executed for all values of *i* from 1 through *order*:

   for *i* ← 1 **to** *order*
      for *j* ← 1 **to** *order*
         square[*i, j*] ← 0
      endfor
   endfor

Nested **for** constructions are typical of multidimensional array processing. Two nested **for** constructions are needed to carry out an operation on each component of a two-dimensional array; three nested **for** constructions are needed for a three-dimensional array; four nested **for** constructions are needed for a four-dimensional array; and so on.

Throughout the process of placing the numbers in the square, *i* and *j* are the indexes of the component in which the next number is to be placed. We begin by setting *i* and *j* to the indexes of the component in the middle of the bottom row, the component in which the first number is to be placed:

   i ← *order*

   j ← (1 + *order*) **div** 2

The statements for placing the numbers can be outlined as follows:

   for *number* ← 1 **to** *order* ** 2
      square[*i, j*] ← *number*
      ''Compute indexes *i* and *j* of the component in which next number is to be placed''
   endfor

To determine the component in which the next *number* is to be placed, we must compute the indexes *iNext* and *jNext* of the component that is one position diagonally down and to the right from the current position. If it were not for wraparound, we could use the following statements:

   iNext ← *i* + 1
   jNext ← *j* + 1

_____

*Only those components of *square* whose row and column indexes lie in the range 1 to *order* will be set to zero.

Because of wraparound, however, we must use the following statements:

> *iNext* ← *i* **mod** *order* + 1
>
> *jNext* ← *j* **mod** *order* + 1

If the value of *i* is in the range 1 to *order* − 1, the value of *i* **mod** *order* is the same as the value of *i,* and *iNext* will be set to the value of *i* + 1, the index of the next row down. If the value of *i* is equal to the value of *order,* the index of the bottom row, the value of *i* **mod** *order* is 0, and *iNext* will be set to 1, the index of the top row. Likewise, *jNext* will be set to the index of the next row to the right unless the value of *j* is the index of the rightmost row, in which case *jNext* will be set to the index of the leftmost row.

If the value of *square[iNext, jNext]* is zero, no number has been placed in this component, and hence this is the component in which the next number should be placed. Thus *i* and *j* are set to *iNext* and *jNext.* If a number has already been placed in *square[iNext, jNext]*, the next number is to be placed one position up from the current position. In this case, therefore, the value of *i* is decreased by 1. The following **if** construction sets *i* and *j* to the indexes of the component in which the next number is to be placed:

> **if** *square[iNext, jNext]* = 0 **then**
>> *i* ← *iNext*
>>
>> *j* ← *jNext*
>
> **else**
>> *i* ← *i* − 1
>
> **endif**

To print the magic square that has been generated, we again use nested **for** constructions. The statements

> **for** *j* ← 1 **to** *order*
>> **output tab**(4 ∗ *j*), *square[i, j]*, **more**
>
> **endfor**
>
> **output**

print one row of the magic square. The values on each row are printed beginning at character positions 4, 8, 12, 16, and so on, thus assuring that values on different rows will line up in columns. The **output** statement following the **for** construction causes the output device to go to a new line. To print the entire magic square, the above statements must be executed for all values of *i* in the range 1 to *order:*

> **for** *i* ← 1 **to** *order*
>> **for** *j* ← 1 **to** *order*
>>> **output tab**(4 ∗ *j*), *square[i, j]*, **more**
>>
>> **endfor**
>>
>> **output**
>
> **endfor**

Again. note the use of nested **for** constructions.

Review questions

1. Contrast arrays with records and files.

2. How is an array type described? What is the *component type*? How is the permissible range of index values specified? How is the number of components in an array related to the range of index values?

3. How is an entire value of an array type denoted?

4. If a and b are two array variables, under what circumstances is the assignment $a \leftarrow b$ allowed?

5. How are the component variables of an array variable designated? Do the index values have to be known when the program is written? Explain why or why not.

6. Which construction in the algorithmic language is most frequently used for stepping through the components of an array?

7. What is a *key field*?

8. Explain the principle of *sequential search*.

9. How is a sentinel value used in sequential search?

10. When a sequential search terminates, how can the algorithm determine whether the value being searched for was found?

11. Define *space efficiency* and *time efficiency*.

12. Explain the *O-notation* used to express running times.

13. Give an expression for the running time of a sequential search.

14. Explain the principle of binary search. What characteristic of the list being searched is used by binary search but not by sequential search?

15. Give an expression for the running time of a binary search. Compare the running times of sequential and binary searches.

16. Explain hashing. What is the worst-case running time for insertion or retrieval of a record? What average performance can be expected from hashing? What is the significance of the *loading factor*? For what kind of application is hashing unacceptable?

17. Describe the technique of record insertion used by the table-handling module and the insertion sort procedure.

18. Contrast internal and external sorting.

19. Explain the principle of *InsertionSort*.

20. Give an expression for the running time of *InsertionSort*.

21. Explain the principle of *Quicksort*.

22. Assuming that a reasonable choice is made for most dividing-line values, given an expression for the running time of *Quicksort*. What is the running time of *Quicksort* if the worst possible choice is made for each dividing-line value? Compare the running times for *InsertionSort* and *Quicksort*.

23. What are multidimensional arrays? How are multidimensional array types defined? How are components of multidimensional array variables designated?

24. Define *wraparound*. Contrast the uses of wraparound in the algorithm for printing magic squares and in the function *Next* used in hashing.

25. Describe the use of nested **for** constructions in processing multidimensional arrays.

Exercises

1. Write an algorithm to read in a list of real numbers and store them in a one-dimensional array. The algorithm should then find and print the smallest, the largest, and the average of the numbers stored in the array. The algorithm should make only one pass over the array.

2. Write an algorithm to read in a list of real numbers and find their average. The algorithm will then print each number accompanied by one of the words "below," "average," or "above," depending on whether the value in question is less than, equal to, or greater than the average.

3. Write an algorithm to shuffle a deck of cards. Represent each card by its value and suit in some convenient abbreviated form, such as "5h" for "five of hearts" and "as" for ace of spades. Read in the strings representing the 52 cards and store them as the components of an array variable *card,* which is indexed by integers in the range 1 to 52. To shuffle the cards, generate a pseudorandom integer in the range 1 to 52 and assign it to the integer variable *i*; then exchange the values of *card*[*i*] and *card*[52]. Next, assign *i* a pseudorandom integer in the range 1 to 51 and exchange the values of *card*[*i*] and *card*[51], and so on. On the last step, assign *i* a pseudorandom number in the range 1 to 2 and exchange the values of *card*[*i*] and *card*[2]. When finished, the algorithm should print the shuffled array. Give an expression in the *O*-notation for the running time of the shuffling algorithm.

4. A *histogram* is a bar graph that displays the number of data values falling within each range of a set of given ranges. For example, suppose our data consists of real numbers ranging from 0 up to (but not including) 1. The ranges of interest are 0 to 0.25, 0.25 to 0.5, 0.5 to 0.75, and 0.75 to 1. (Each range includes the lower limit but does not include the upper limit.) Write an algorithm to read a list of data values and print a histogram in the following form:

```
0.00–0.25  * * * * * * *
0.25–0.50  * * * * * * * * * *
0.50–0.75  * * * * * *
0.75–1.00  * * * * * * * * * * * * * *
```

According to this histogram, there were seven data values in the range 0 to 0.25, 10 data values in the range 0.25 to 0.50, and so on. Use one array to store the lower limit of each range (The upper limit need not be stored. Why?) and another to hold a running count of the number of values in each range.

5. Many tests exist for the apparent randomness of pseudorandom number generators; no single pseudorandom number generator will pass all tests. Here is one such test. Generate a large number (say about 500) of pseudorandom integers in the range 1 to 10. Keep count of the number of 1s, 2s, 3s, and so on, that occur. Display those counts in a histogram. For a good pseudorandom number generator, the number of 1s, the number of 2s, the number of 3s, and so on should be roughly the same. The histogram shouldn't have any high peaks or deep valleys. Write an algorithm to test the pseudorandom number generator described in Chapter 10 in this way.

6. Write a change-making algorithm that stores the name and value of each coin or bill in an array. Each component of the array should be of type *denomination*, defined as follows:

> **type** *denomination* = **record**
>
> > *name*: *string*
> >
> > *value*: *integer*
>
> **endrecord**

The *name* field contains the name of the coin or bill in plural form: 'pennies', 'nickels', 'dimes', and so on. The *value* field contains the value of each coin or bill in cents. The algorithm should use a single **for** construction to step through the components of the array and print the number of each coin or bill to be handed back. The algorithm should be able to hand back 1, 10, and 20 dollar bills as well as pennies, nickels, dimes, quarters, and half dollars.

7. Write an algorithm to read in the names and grades of the students in a class and print this information in such a way that the students' names are in alphabetical order.

8. One way to compute the *median* of a list of numbers is to first arrange the numbers in numerical order. If the number of values is odd, the middle value on the sorted list is the median. If the number of values is even, the median is the average of the two middle values. Write an algorithm to read in a list of numbers and print its median.

9. The *percentile rank* of a student in a class is the percent of students in the

class who received a lower grade than the student in question. Note that students who receive the same grade must have the same percentile rank. Write an algorithm to read in the names and grades of the students in a class and print their names, grades, and percentile ranks.

Hint: Use an array of records with each record having fields for a student's name, grade, and percentile rank. Store the names and grades in the array, sort the records into ascending order on grades, and compute the percentile ranks. Then sort the records into ascending order on names and print the names, grades, and percentile ranks.

10. Show that, in the worst case, the number of moves, or record assignments, needed to sort n records with an insertion sort is given by

$$\tfrac{1}{2}n^2 + \tfrac{3}{2}n - 2$$

To insert the jth record in the sorted part of the list, we assign the value of *data[j]* to *temp*, move the empty record up into the sorted part of the list, and then assign the value of *temp* to the empty record. Moving the empty record up involves $j - 1$ record assignments in the worst case. Inserting the jth record, then, involves at most $(j - 1) + 2$ or $j + 1$ record assignments.

11. Write an algorithm to read in a two-dimensional array of integers and print the sum of the numbers in each row and the sum of the numbers in each column. The input data should consist of the numbers in the first row, followed by the numbers in the second row, followed by the numbers in the third row, and so on.

12. Write an algorithm to read in an alleged magic square and determine whether it is really magic by checking whether all the rows, columns, and diagonals have the same sum.

13. A company has four salespeople and five products. Let the salespeople be denoted by numbers from one to four and the products by numbers from one to five. Suppose we are given as data the yearly sales of each product by each salesperson. For example, the data item

    3, 5, 750.00

means that salesperson number 3 sold $750 worth of product number 5. Write an algorithm to read data items of this type and print the following: (1) the total amount sold by each person; (2) the total amount sold of each product; (3) the people who sold the largest and smallest amount of each product; and (4) the products for which each person sold the largest and smallest amount. If a particular combination of salesperson and product does not occur in the data, assume that the person in question did not sell any of the product.

Hint: Store the sales amounts in a two-dimensional array indexed by salesperson number and product number.

14. We wish to compute the average grades of college students having particular classifications and major fields. The classifications, the major fields, and the codes we will use to represent them in the data are as follows:

Classification	Code	Classification	Code
freshman	1	English	1
sophomore	2	history	2
junior	3	mathematics	3
senior	4		

In the data, we will give the classification code, major field code, and grade for each student. Thus, 3, 1, 85 represents a grade of 85 earned by a junior English major. Your algorithm should read the grades of all the students, then print a table showing the average grade for each classification and major field.

Hint: You will need two arrays, one for the number of students with each combination of classification and major field and the other for the total of the grades for each combination. Your program must take into account the possibility that there will be no students in some combinations; there may be no junior history majors, for example. In that case, the program should leave a blank space in the appropriate position in the table it prints.

15. Four candidates are running for a certain office. A political analyst wants to use data collected in a poll to determine the preferences of Democrats, Republicans, and Independents for each of the four candidates. Each data item consists of two numbers: the political affiliation of the person questioned (coded 1 for Democrat, 2 for Republican, and 3 for Independent) and the candidate the person preferred (coded 1 to 4). Write an algorithm to read this data and print a table showing what percent of people of a given political affiliation prefer each candidate. For example, 50% of the Democrats questioned might have been for candidate 1, 20% for candidate 2, 0% for candidate 3, and 30% for candidate 4. Your algorithm should give this kind of result for Democrats, Republicans, and Independents. Your algorithm should also print the percent of people for each candidate, regardless of party, and the percent of the people questioned who were affiliated with each party.

Pascal Supplement

One-dimensional arrays

Array types and values   An array type is described in Pascal as follows:

array[index-type] **of** component-type

Each value of the array type is composed of components drawn from the component type. Each component is labeled with an index value drawn from the index type.

Pascal differs from the algorithmic language in that the permissible index values are specified by an index type rather than by a range of values. The index type can be any ordinal type. This index type is frequently a subrange type, which is, of course, defined as a range of values. However, other ordinal types, such as enumerated types, can also serve as index types. An index type can be designated by either a type denoter (such as 1 . . 5) or by a type identifier (such as *range*).

For example, the array type *list* can be defined in Pascal as follows:

type
$\quad$ *list* = **array**[1 . . 5] **of** *real*;

If we prefer an identifier for the index type instead of a type denoter, we can use the following definitions:

type
$\quad$ *range* = 1 . . 5;
$\quad$ *list* = **array**[*range*] **of** *real*;

The following definitions illustrate an array type whose index type is an enumerated type:

type
$\quad$ *weekday* = (*mon, tue, wed, thur, fri*);
$\quad$ *timeCard* = **array**[*weekday*] **of** *real*;

A value of type *timeCard* has five components, which are labeled by the identifiers *mon, tue, wed, thur,* and *fri*.

Array variables$\quad$Array variables are declared and used as in the algorithmic language. If *a* and *b* are declared by

$\quad$ *a, b*: *list*;

or

$\quad$ *a*: *list*;
$\quad$ *b*: *list*:

or

$\quad$ *a, b*: **array**[1 . . 5] **of** *real*;

then *a* and *b* have the same type, and the assignments

$\quad$ $a := b$

and

$\quad$ $b := a$

are allowed. On the other hand, if *a* and *b* are declared by *a*: **array**[1 . . 5] **of** *real*;

b: **array**[1 . . 5] **of** *real*;

then *a* and *b* do not have the same type and neither of the above assignments is allowed.

Component variables are denoted exactly as in the algorithmic language. If *a* is an array variable of type *list*, then the five component variables of *a* are denoted as follows:

a[1]   *a*[2]   *a*[3]   *a*[4]   *a*[5]

If *tc* is an array variable of type *timeCard*, the component variables of *tc* are denoted as follows:

tc[*mon*]   *tc*[*tue*]   *tc*[*wed*]   *tc*[*thur*]   *tc*[*fri*]

Pascal does not provide any means of representing constant array values. To assign a constant entire value to an array variable, we must assign the appropriate component value to each component variable. For example, the following statements assign a value to the array *a*:

a[1] := 3.5;

a[2] := 6.9;

a[3] := 7.2;

a[4] := 9.5;

a[5] := 4.2

and the following statements assign a value to the array *tc*:

tc[*mon*] := 8.0;

tc[*tue*] := 7.5;

tc[*wed*] := 9.25;

tc[*thur*] := 7.25;

tc[*fri*] := 6.75

Multidimensional arrays

A multidimensional array type is denoted in Pascal as follows:

array[index-type, index-type, . . . , index-type] **of** component-type

For example, the type definition

table = **array**[1 . . 4, 1 . . 3] **of** *integer*;

defines a two-dimensional-array type whose values can be thought of as tables having four rows and three columns.

A component variable of a multidimensional array variable is denoted as in the algorithmic language:

variable[expression, expression, . . . , expression]

The value of each expression must belong to the corresponding index type listed in the definition of the array type. For example, let *t* be an array variable of type *table*:

t: *table*;

The twelve component variables of *t* are denoted as follows:

$t[1, 1]$ $t[1, 2]$ $t[1, 3]$
$t[2, 1]$ $t[2, 2]$ $t[2, 3]$
$t[3, 1]$ $t[3, 2]$ $t[3, 3]$
$t[4, 1]$ $t[4, 2]$ $t[4, 3]$

Since Pascal does not provide any way to represent constant array values, the only way to assign a constant entire value to *t* is to assign the appropriate component value to each of the component variables of *t*. The following twelve statements assign to *t* the table in Figure 13.12:

$t[1, 1] := 25; t[1, 2] := 17; t[1, 3] := 13;$
$t[2, 1] := 15; t[2, 2] := 12; t[2, 3] := 18;$
$t[3, 1] := 16; t[3, 2] := 14; t[3, 3] := 25;$
$t[4, 1] := 89; t[4, 2] := 75; t[4, 3] := 40$

The three-dimensional-array type *book* and the four-dimensional-array type *hyperbook*, used as examples in the main text, are defined in Pascal as follows:

type
    book = **array**[1 . . 10, 1 . . 4, 1 . . 3] **of** *integer*;
    hyperbook = **array**[1 . . 5, 1 . . 10, 1 . . 4, 1 . . 3] **of** *integer*;

Examples

Figure 13.14 shows the Pascal version of the procedure *SequentialSearch* and Figure 13.15 shows the Pascal version of the procedure *BinarySearch*. The global definitions and declarations referred to by these procedures are given in Pascal as follows:

const
    size = 500;
type
    dataRecord = **record**
                    key: *integer*;
                    value: *real*
                end;
var
    data: **array**[1 . . *size*] **of** *dataRecord*;
    free: *integer*;

Figure 13.14   Pascal procedure for sequential search.

```pascal
procedure SequentialSearch(searchKey: integer;
                           var found: Boolean;
                           var index: integer);

{ Locate record with given key }

var
    i: integer;
begin
    data[free].key := searchKey;
    i := 1;
    while searchKey <> data[i].key do
        i := i + 1;
    found := (i < free);
    index := i
end;
```

Figure 13.15   Pascal procedure for binary search.

```pascal
procedure BinarySearch(searchKey: integer;
                       var found: Boolean;
                       var index: integer);

{ Locate record with given key }

var
    low, mid, high: integer;
begin
    low := 1;
    high := free − 1;
    repeat
        mid := (low + high) div 2;
        if searchKey < data[mid].key then
            high := mid − 1
        else if searchKey > data[mid].key then
            low := mid + 1
    until (searchKey = data[mid].key) or (low > high);
    found := (searchKey = data[mid].key);
    index := mid
end;
```

Note that the order of the definitions has been changed because in Pascal constant definitions must preced type definitions.

Figure 13.16 shows the procedure *FindUnusedRecord* for finding an unused record in a hash table; Figure 13.17 shows the procedure *FindRecord* for finding a record with a given key in a hash table. The global definitions and declarations referred to by these procedures are as follows:

const
    size = 503;
    limit = 502;
type
    dataRecord = **record**
                inUse: *Boolean*;
                key: *integer*;
                value: *real*
        end;
var
    data: **array**[0 . . *limit*] **of** *dataRecord*;

Figure 13.16 Pascal procedure for finding an unused record in a hash table.

```
procedure FindUnusedRecord(searchKey: integer;
                           var found: Boolean;
                           var index: integer);

{ Locate unused record }

var
    start, c, n: integer;
begin
    start := Hash(searchKey);
    n := start;
    repeat
        c := n;
        n := Next(c)
    until (not data[c].inUse) or (n = start);
    found := not data[c].inUse;
    index := c
end;
```

Figure 13.17   Pascal procedure for finding the record with a given key in a
hash table.

```
procedure FindRecord(searchKey: integer;
                        var found: Boolean;
                        var index: integer);

{ Locate record with given key }

var
     start, c, n: integer;
begin
     start := Hash(searchKey);
     n := start;
     repeat
         c := n;
         n := Next(c)
     until (searchKey = data[c].key) or
         (not data[c].inUse) or (n = start);
     found := (searchKey = data[c].key);
     index := c
end;
```

Note that the constant definition

$limit = size - 1$

is invalid in standard Pascal, which does not allow a constant to be defined in terms
of an arithmetical expression, even an expression that involves only other constants.
The hashing function *Hash* is expressed in Pascal as follows:

function *Hash(key: integer): integer;*
begin
    Hash := *key* **mod** *size*
end;

The function *Next* is expressed in Pascal as follows:

function *Next(index: integer): integer;*
begin
    Next := (*index* + 1) **mod** *size*
end;

The table-handling module described in the text is translated into UCSD-Pascal
unit. The unit *TableHandler* is shown in Figure 13.18.

Figure 13.18 Table-handling module implemented as a UCSD-Pascal unit. The procedure *BinarySearch* is placed before the other procedures rather than after them because in Pascal a procedure declaration must precede any procedure statements that call the procedure.

```
unit TableHandler;

{ Maintain a table of data records }

interface
    function Error: Boolean;
    { Return value of and clear error indicator }

    procedure New;
    { Initialize empty table }

    procedure Lookup(searchKey: integer;
                         var valueFound: real);
    { Find value corresponding to given key }

    procedure Insert(insertKey: integer;
                         insertValue: real);
    { Insert new record in table }

    procedure Delete(deleteKey: integer);
    { Delete record with given key }

implementation
    const
        size = 500;
    type
        dataRecord = record
                            key: integer;
                            value: real
                        end;
    var
        data: array[0 . . size] of dataRecord;
        free: integer;
        errorFlag: Boolean;
```

```
procedure BinarySearch(searchKey: integer;
                            var found: Boolean;
                            var index: integer);

{ Locate record with given key }

var
    low, mid, high: integer;
begin
    low := 0;
    high := free - 1;
    repeat
        mid := (low + high) div 2;
        if searchKey < data[mid].key then
            high := mid - 1
        else if searchKey > data[mid].key then
            low := mid + 1
    until (searchKey = data[mid].key) or (low > high);
    found := (searchKey = data[mid].key);
    index := mid
end; { BinarySearch }


function Error;
begin
    Error := errorFlag;
    errorFlag := false
end; { Error }

procedure New;
begin
    data[0].key := -1;
    data[0].value := 0.0;
    free := 1;
    errorFlag := false
end; { New }

procedure Lookup;
var
    found: Boolean;
    index: integer;
```

```
begin
    BinarySearch(searchKey, found, index);
    errorFlag := not found;
    if found then
        valueFound := data[index].value
end; { Lookup }


procedure Insert;
var
    found: Boolean;
    i, index: integer;
begin
    BinarySearch(insertKey, found, index);
    if found or (free > size) or (insertKey < 0) then
        errorFlag := true
    else
        begin
            errorFlag := false;
            i := free;
            free := free + 1;
            while insertKey < data[i − 1].key do
                begin
                    data[i] := data[i − 1];
                    i := i − 1
                end;
            data[i].key := insertKey;
            data[i].value := insertValue
        end
end; { Insert }

procedure Delete;
var
    found: Boolean;
    i, index: integer;
begin
    BinarySearch(deleteKey, found, index);
    if (not found) or (deleteKey < 0) then
        errorFlag := true
```

```
        else
            begin
                errorFlag := false;
                for i := index to free − 2 do
                    data[i] := data[i + 1];
                free := free − 1
            end
    end; { Delete }

begin
    New
end. { TableHandler }
```

Figure 13.19 shows the Pascal version of the procedure *InsertionSort*, and Figure 13.20 shows the Pascal version of the procedure *Quicksort*. The global definitions and declarations referred to by these procedures are given in Pascal as follows:

const
    size = 500;

type
    dataRecord = **record**
                    key: *integer*:
                    value: *real*
             end;

var
    data: **array**[0 . . *size*] **of** *dataRecord*;
    free: *integer*;

Figure 13.21 shows the Pascal program for printing a magic square. Pascal does not feature a **tab** command, but field-width parameters can be used for the same purpose when printing an array in table form. The program *MagicSquare* uses the following statements to print a magic square:

for $i := 1$ **to** *order* **do**
    begin
        for $j := 1$ **to** *order* **do**
            write(square[i, j]:4);
        writeln
    end

The *write* procedure remains on the same line of the printout after printing a value; the call to *writeln* causes the printer to go to a new line.

Figure 13.19   Pascal procedure *InsertionSort*.

```
procedure InsertionSort;

{ Sort records into ascending order on field key }

var
    i, j: integer;
    temp: dataRecord;
begin
    for j := 2 to free − 1 do
        begin
            i := j;
            temp := data[i];
            data[0].key := temp.key;
            while temp.key < data[i − 1].key do
                begin
                    data[i] := data[i − 1];
                    i := i − 1
                end;
            data[i] := temp
        end
end;
```

Figure 13.20   Pascal procedure *Quicksort*.

```
procedure Quicksort(first, last: integer);

{ Sort records into ascending order on field key }

var
    i, j, dividingLine: integer;
    temp: dataRecord;
begin
    i := first;
    j := last;
    dividingLine := data[(first + last) div 2].key;
    repeat
        while data[i].key < dividingLine do
            i := i + 1;
        while data[j].key > dividingLine do
            j := j - 1;
        if i <= j then
            begin
                temp := data[i];
                data[i] := data[j];
                data[j] := temp;
                i := i + 1;
                j := j - 1
            end
    until i > j;
    if first < j then
        Quicksort(first, j);
    if i < last then
        Quicksort(i, last)
end;
```

Figure 13.21   Pascal program for printing a magic square. Note the use of
a field-width parameter to arrange the printout in columns.

```pascal
program MagicSquare(input, output);

{ Generate a magic square of odd order }

const
    maxOrder = 19;
var
    square: array[1 . . maxOrder, 1 . . maxOrder] of integer;
    i, j, iNext, jNext, number, order: integer;
begin
    write('Order of square (odd integer in range 1 − ', maxOrder:1, ')? ');
    readln(order);
    for i := 1 to order do
        for j := 1 to order do
            square[i, j] := 0;
    i := order;
    j := (1 + order) div 2;
    for number := 1 to sqr(order) do
        begin
            square[i, j] := number;
            iNext := i mod order + 1;
            jNext := j mod order + 1;
            if square[iNext, jNext] = 0 then
                begin
                    i := iNext;
                    j := jNext
                end
            else
                i := i − 1
        end;
    for i := 1 to order do
        begin
            for j := 1 to order do
            write(square[i, j]:4);
            writeln
        end
end.
```

14

Stacks and queues

n this chapter we return to the concept referred to by the terms *abstract machine, data abstraction*, and *abstract data type*. We define an *abstract machine* by describing its external behavior but not the details of its internal operation. The external behavior is usually described by giving the effects of function and procedure calls. The procedures are analogous to the controls of an actual machine, and the functions are analogous to its readouts.

The term *data abstraction* emphasizes that the purpose of an abstract machine often is to store and retrieve data. The abstract machine usually corresponds to a particular concept of data storage, such as the streams discussed in Chapter 12. The term *abstract data type* draws an analogy between abstract machines and the data types with which we are already familiar, such as integers, real numbers, file types, and array types. We have already seen how the operations associated with data storage and retrieval for files can be formulated abstractly. The same could be done with the operations of retrieving a component value of an array and changing the value of an array component.

In this chapter we will consider two data abstractions: *stacks* and *queues*. For each abstraction we can form a simple mental picture. A stack corresponds to a stack of objects such as cards, papers, or books. A queue corresponds to a waiting line (''queue'' is the British term for a waiting line). Stacks are used in almost all branches of computer science. Queues are frequently found in operating systems and simulation programs.

14.1 Stacks

We picture a stack as a stack of physical objects such as books or cards. New objects can be placed on top of the stack, and the topmost item can be removed or examined. Objects below the top one are inaccessible, however. To get to a particular object, we must remove all the objects that are on top of it.

Some of the terminology for stacks is based on a slightly different analogy—the spring-operated mechanism sometimes used to hold a stack of plates in a cafeteria. The topmost plate on the stack is always at the level of the counter. If the topmost plate is removed, the next plate pops up to the counter level. If a new plate is placed on top of the stack, the plates below are pushed down so that the new plate is at counter level. With this analogy in mind, we say that an item is "pushed onto a stack" when it is placed on top of the stack, and we say that the topmost item is "popped off" when it is removed from the stack.

The first item to be popped off a stack is the last item that was pushed on. For this reason, we say that a stack obeys a *last-in-first-out (LIFO)* discipline.

Each implementation of a stack must provide the following functions and procedures:

FUNCTIONS

Error Returns *true* if the previous function or procedure call caused an error and *false* otherwise.

Top Returns the value of the topmost item on the stack. Calling *Top* when the stack is empty causes a *stack underflow* error.

PROCEDURES

New Creates an empty stack.

Push(x) Places the value of the input parameter x on top of the stack. If the memory space set aside for the stack has been exhausted, calling *Push* causes a *stack overflow* error.

Pop Removes the topmost item from the stack. Calling *Pop* when the stack is empty causes a *stack underflow* error.

The function *Top* and the procedure *Pop* are often combined into a single function (usually called *Pop*) that removes the top item from the stack and returns its value. The formal specifications are clearer if removing the top item and examining its value are separate operations. In practice, however, the combined operation is often more convenient.

Axiomatic definition In referring to such concepts as the top item on a stack and the empty stack, the above specifications draw on our mental picture of a stack of physical objects. But how can we describe a stack to a computer program that has no such mental picture? One way is to give a series of statements, called *axioms*, from which the behavior of the stack can be deduced. The axioms describe the inter-

actions of the functions and procedures defined for a stack. The axioms do not refer
to any external mental picture, such as a stack of physical objects.

The following is one possible set of axioms for a stack. When the axioms state
that two sequences of operations are equivalent, every occurrence of one sequence
as part of a larger sequence can be replaced by the other without changing the effect
of the larger sequence. If, however, such a replacement changes the last operation of
the larger sequence, the value returned by *Error* after execution of the larger sequence may be changed.

1. After the operation

   New

   Error returns *false* and a call to *Top* is invalid. An invalid call to *Top* returns
   an undefined value and causes *Error* to return *true*.

2. After the sequence of operations

   New

   Pop

   Error returns *true*. Except for the value returned by *Error*, this sequence is
   equivalent to the one consisting of the single operation

   New

3. After the operation

   Push(x)

   Error returns *false* and *Top* returns the value of *x*.

4. After the sequence of operations

   Push(x)

   Pop

   Error returns *false*. This sequence is equivalent to the null sequence that
   contains no operations. Put another way, for every sequence containing a
   push followed by a pop as a subsequence, an equivalent sequence can be
   obtained by deleting the push-pop subsequence.

Axiom 1 tells us that *New* cannot cause an error but that it is an error to attempt
to examine the top value of the empty stack created by *New*. Axiom 2 tells us that it
is an error to attempt to pop a value off the empty stack, and the erroneous pop
operation is ignored. Axiom 3 tells us that pushing a value on the stack cannot cause
an error. After a push operation, a call to *Top* is valid and returns the value that was
pushed. Axiom 4 tells us that pushing a value on the stack and then popping it off
again cannot cause an error and leaves the stack unchanged.

The axioms consider only underflow errors, the possibility of which are inherent
in the definition of a stack. Overflow errors, which result from limits imposed by a
particular implementation, are ignored. Taking overflow errors into account would

make the axioms much more complex; axioms 3 and 4 do not hold true if the push operation causes an overflow.

Thus, the axioms describe an ideal stack onto which an arbitrarily large number of items can be pushed. Such ideal data structures are the computer-science analog of the frictionless machines and resistance-free electrical circuits sometimes studied by engineers. In each case, ignoring certain practical complications leads to a better understanding of the fundamental principles involved.

Now let's see how we can use the axioms to deduce the effects of various sequences of operations. For our example we will use a stack of integers: a stack onto which only integer values can be pushed. After the operation

New

we cannot examine the top value of the stack (axiom 1) or pop a value off the stack (axiom 2). It is thus reasonable to call the resulting stack the empty stack.

Now let's create an empty stack and push the value 9 onto it. We execute the following sequence of operations:

New

Push(9)

The last operation in the sequence is a push. Axiom 3 tells us that, after a push operation, *Error* returns *false* and *Top* returns the value that was pushed on. Thus after the given sequence of operations has been carried out, *Error* returns *false* and *Top* returns 9.

Now let's push 7 onto the stack. The complete sequence of operations for creating the empty stack and pushing on 9 and 7 is

New

Push(9)

Push(7)

Again, because the last operation of the sequence is a push, we can apply axiom 3. After the operations of the sequence have been executed, *Error* returns *true* and *Top* returns 7.

Let's pop a value from the stack on which 9 and 7 have been pushed. Now the complete sequence of operations is as follows:

New

Push(9)

Push(7)

Pop

Since this sequence does not end with a push, we cannot apply axiom 3 immediately. We can, however, apply axiom 4, which tells us that a push followed by a pop causes *Error* to return *false,* and that the sequence is equivalent to the one obtained by deleting the push and pop:

New

Push(9)

But axiom 3 tells us that after this sequence *Top* returns 9. Thus after the sequence

   New

   Push(9)

   Push(7)

   Pop

Error returns *false* and *Top* returns 9. Intuitively, Popping 7 allows 9 to become the new top item.

   Suppose we pop still another item from the stack. The overall sequence of operations is now

   New

   Push(9)

   Push(7)

   Pop

   Pop

By axiom 4, the subsequence

   Push(7)

   Pop

can be deleted, leaving us with

   New

   Push(9)

   Pop

We use axiom 4 again to eliminate the subsequence

   Push(9)

   Pop

leaving

   New

Thus after the original sequence has been executed, *Error* returns *false* (because of axiom 4) and the state of the stack is the same as after *New* has been executed. Intuitively, after both of the values that were pushed on have been popped off, the stack is once again empty. Note that the order in which values are popped off a stack is the reverse of the order in which they were pushed on.

   Suppose that yet another pop operation is executed. The overall sequence is now

   New

   Push(9)

   Push(7)

   Pop

   Pop

   Pop

As before, we use axiom 4 to eliminate first the subsequence

Push(7)
Pop

and then the subsequence

Push(9)
Pop

The original sequence is thus equivalent to

New
Pop

By axiom 2, this sequence causes *Error* to return *true* and leaves the stack in the same state as produced by executing *New* alone. (The invalid *Pop* is ignored.) Thus after the original sequence has been executed, *Error* returns *true* and the stack is empty.

14.2 Array implementations of stacks

Figure 14.1 shows how to implement a stack as an array *stackArray*. The index values for *stackArray* range from 1 through *size;* in the diagrams a value of 8 is used for *size*. The variable *topIndex* contains the index of the top value on the stack; we say that *topIndex* points to the top value. The stack is contained in array components

stackArray[1] through *stackArray*[*topIndex*]

Array components

stackArray[*topIndex* + 1] through *stackArray*[*size*]

are unused. *StackArray*[1] contains the bottom value on the stack, and *stackArray*[*topIndex*] contains the top value. Note that when *stackArray* is diagrammed in the usual way, the stack is shown upside down, with its bottom toward the top of the page and its top toward the bottom of the page.

When the value of *topIndex* is the invalid index value 0, the stack is empty; all the components of *stackArray* are unused. When the value of *topIndex* is *size* (8 in the diagrams), the stack is full. All the components of *stackArray* are in use, and no additional values can be pushed onto the stack.

Figure 14.2 illustrates the operation of pushing a value onto a stack. To push the value 4 onto a stack of integers, we first increase the value of *topIndex* by 1 so that *topIndex* points to the unused array component following the component containing the current top value:

topIndex ← *topIndex* + 1

The value to be pushed on is stored in the unused component pointed to by *topIndex*:

stackArray[*topIndex*] ← 4

Figure 14.1   Array implementation of a stack. *TopIndex* points to the top
of the stack. A value of zero for *topIndex* indicates an
empty stack.

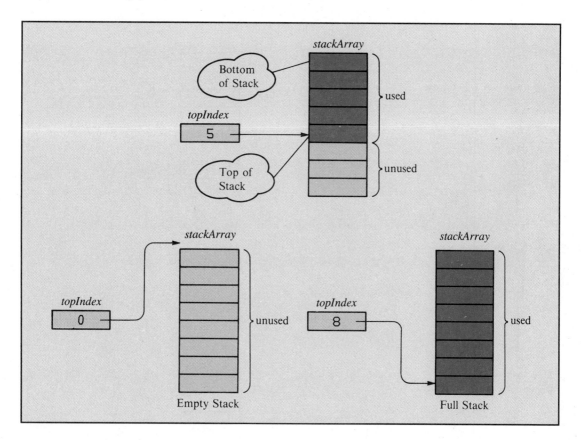

Remembering that the stack is diagrammed upside down, we see that the new top
value is stored immediately "above" the previous top value. *TopIndex* now points
to the new top value so at any time we can access the top value on the stack by
referring to the value of *stackArray[topIndex]*.

Figure 14.3 illustrates the operation of popping a value off a stack. The value of
topIndex is decreased by 1, causing it to point to the value immediately "below" the
current top value:

$$topIndex \leftarrow topIndex - 1$$

The value now pointed to by *topIndex* becomes the new top value. The component
that previously contained the top value becomes unused. If we wanted *Pop* to return
the value that was popped off, we would have it return the value of *stack-
Array[topIndex]* before decreasing the value of *topIndex*.

Figure 14.2   Pushing a value onto a stack.

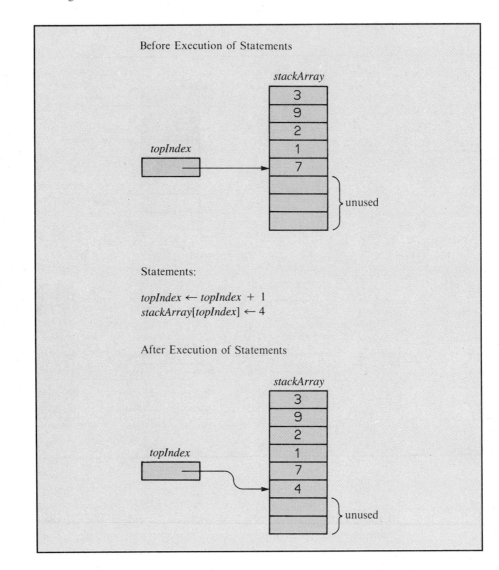

There are two ways to implement a stack as a module. We can write a module that implements a single stack and provides functions and procedures for manipulating that stack. Alternatively, the module can export a type *stack* that can be used to declare as many stacks as needed. In this case the module provides functions and procedures for manipulating values of type *stack*.

The module IntegerStack   Figure 14.4 shows the module *IntegerStack*, which implements a stack of integers. The module exports the functions *Error* and *Top* and

Figure 14.3   Popping a value off a stack.

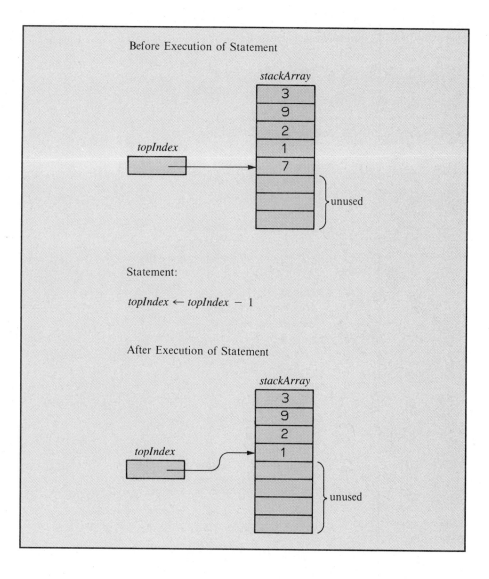

the procedures *Push* and *Pop* for manipulating the stack. The maximum number of values that can be pushed onto the stack is given by *size,* which is defined to have the (arbitrary) value 100. The module declares three variables:

stackArray: **array**[1 **to** *size*] **of** *integer*

topIndex: *integer*

errorFlag: *Boolean*

Figure 14.4   Module *IntegerStack* implements a single stack of integers.

```
module IntegerStack

{ Implements a stack of integers }

declare
    export Error, Top, New, Push, Pop
    const size = 100
    stackArray: array[1 to size] of integer
    topIndex: integer
    errorFlag: Boolean


    function Error: Boolean

    { Return value of and clear error flag }

    execute
        Error ← errorFlag
        errorFlag ← false
    end Error


    function Top: integer

    { Return top value on stack }

    execute
        if topIndex = 0 then
            errorFlag ← true
            Top ← 0
        else
            errorFlag ← false
            Top ← stackArray[topIndex]
        endif
    end Top


    procedure New

    { Create empty stack }
```

```
    execute
        topIndex ← 0
        errorFlag ← false
    end New


    procedure Push(x)

    { Push value onto stack }

    declare
        x: in integer
    execute
        if topIndex = size then
            errorFlag ← true
        else
            errorFlag ← false
            topIndex ← topIndex + 1
            stackArray[topIndex] ← x
        endif
    end Push


    procedure Pop

    { Pop value off stack }

    execute
        if topIndex = 0 then
            errorFlag ← true
        else
            errorFlag ← false
            topIndex ← topIndex - 1
        endif
    end Pop


initialize
    New
end IntegerStack
```

As in our previous examples, *stackArray* holds the stack and *topIndex* points to the top value on the stack. Each function and procedure sets *errorFlag* to *true* if the function or procedure causes an error and to *false* if no error occurs.

The function *Error* returns the value of *errorFlag*. Since the function *Error* cannot itself cause an error, it always clears *errorFlag* to *false*:

$Error \leftarrow errorFlag$
$errorFlag \leftarrow false$

The function *Top* returns the current top value on the stack. If the stack is empty, however, there is no top value to return, and a call to *Top* is invalid. In that case, *errorFlag* is set to *true*, and *Top* returns the arbitrary value 0. Otherwise, *errorFlag* is set to *false* and *Top* returns the value of *stackArray[topIndex]*:

if *topIndex* $= 0$ **then**
 $errorFlag \leftarrow true$
 $Top \leftarrow 0$
else
 $errorFlag \leftarrow false$
 $Top \leftarrow stackArray[topIndex]$
endif

The procedure *New* initializes a stack to the empty state. *TopIndex* is set to 0 and *errorFlag* is cleared to *false*:

$topIndex \leftarrow 0$
$errorFlag \leftarrow false$

The procedure *Push* pushes the value of its parameter, *x*, onto the stack. If the stack is full, *errorFlag* is set to *true*. Otherwise, *errorFlag* is set to *false* and the value of *x* is pushed onto the stack:

if *topIndex* $= size$ **then**
 $errorFlag \leftarrow true$
else
 $errorFlag \leftarrow false$
 $topIndex \leftarrow topIndex + 1$
 $stackArray[topIndex] \leftarrow x$
endif

The procedure *Pop* removes the top value from the stack. If the stack is empty, *errorFlag* is set to *true*. Otherwise, *errorFlag* is set to *false* and the value of *topIndex* is decreased by 1:

if *topIndex* $= 0$ **then**
 $errorFlag \leftarrow true$
else
 $errorFlag \leftarrow false$
 $topIndex \leftarrow topIndex - 1$
endif

As mentioned earlier, *Top* and *Pop* are often combined into a single function that removes and returns the top value on the stack. This version of *Pop* can be written as follows:

function *Pop*: *integer*
execute
    if *topIndex* = 0 **then**
        errorFlag ← *true*
        Pop ← 0
    else
        errorFlag ← *false*
        Pop ← *stackArray*[*topIndex*]
        topIndex ← *topIndex* − 1
    endif
end *Pop*

Note that the value *stackArray*[*topIndex*] is assigned to *Pop before* the value of *topIndex* is decreased by 1.

The module *IntegerStack* is initialized by calling *New* to create an empty stack.

The module IntegerStackType The module *IntegerStackType* (Figure 14.5) exports type *stack* along with functions and procedures for manipulating values of type *stack*. We can declare as many variables as we wish to be of type *stack*, so we are not limited to a single stack as we were with the module *IntegerStack*.

To use *IntegerStackType*, we begin by declaring one or more variables to be of type *stack*:

s, *t*: *stack*

The values of *s* and *t* are stacks. We can push and pop integers on and off these stacks just as we did with the stack implemented by the module *IntegerStack*.

The functions and procedures provided by *IntegerStackType* are the same as those provided by *IntegerStack* except that the former require a stack variable as a parameter. The functions and procedures provided by *IntegerStack* did not need this stack parameter, since they all referred to the single stack embedded within the module *IntegerStack*.

For example, we can call *New* to set the value of the stack variable *s* to the empty stack:

New(*s*)

To set the value of *t* to the empty stack, we use

New(*t*)

and so on.

Figure 14.5   Module *IntegerStackType* implements type *stack,* which can
be used to declare any number of integer stacks.

```
module IntegerStackType

{ Defines type stack and provides functions and procedures for
  manipulating stacks }

declare
    export stack, Error, Top, New, Push, Pop
    const size = 100
    type stack = record
                        errorFlag: Boolean
                        topIndex: integer
                        stackArray: array[1 to size] of integer
                 endrecord


function Error(s): Boolean

{ Return value of and clear error flag }

declare
    s: in out stack
execute
    Error ← s.errorFlag
    s.errorFlag ← false
end Error


function Top(s): integer

{ Return top value on stack }

declare
    s: in out stack
```

```
      execute
          if s.topIndex = 0 then
              s.errorFlag ← true
              Top ← 0
          else
              s.errorFlag ← false
              Top ← s.stackArray[s.topIndex]
          endif
      end Top


procedure New(s)

{ Create empty stack }

declare
      s: out stack
execute
      s.topIndex ← 0
      s.errorFlag ← false
end New


procedure Push(s, x)

{ Push value onto stack }

declare
      s: in out stack
      x: in integer
execute
      if s.topIndex = size then
          s.errorFlag ← true
      else
          s.errorFlag ← false
          s.topIndex ← s.topIndex + 1
          s.stackArray[s.topIndex] ← x
      endif
end Push


procedure Pop(s)

{ Pop value off stack }

declare
      s: in out stack
```

```
        execute
            if s.topIndex = 0 then
                s.errorFlag ← true
            else
                s.errorFlag ← false
                s.topIndex ← s.topIndex − 1
            endif
        end Pop

    end IntegerStackType
```

To push the values 3, 4, and 5 onto *s*, we use:

Push(*s*, 3)

Push(*s*, 4)

Push(*s*, 5)

To pop the top value off *s*, we use:

Pop(*s*)

The function call

Top(*s*)

returns the top value on *s*. After the procedure calls given above, *Top*(*s*) returns the value 4. The value returned by

Error(*s*)

is *true* or *false* depending on whether or not the immediately preceding function or procedure call was invalid.

The module *IntegerStackType* does not store any data; all data is stored in the stack variables declared by the user. *IntegerStackType* merely provides the type *stack* for declaring stack variables and the functions and procedures for manipulating the values of stack variables. Thus, all the variable declarations in *IntegerStack* are wrapped up in a record description, which is used to define the type *stack*:

type *stack* = **record**

        errorFlag: *Boolean*

        topIndex: *integer*

        stackArray: **array**[1 **to** *size*] **of** *integer*

     endrecord

A value or variable of type *stack* has three fields: a Boolean field *errorFlag*, an integer field *topIndex*, and an integer-array field *stackArray*.

The functions and procedures are the same as for *IntegerStack* except that each takes a stack variable as a parameter. If *s* is the formal parameter corresponding to the stack variable, then all references to fields of *s* must be preceded by "*s.*". For example, the procedure *Push* is written as follows:

procedure *Push(s, x)*
declare
    s: **in out** *stack*
    x: **in** *integer*
execute
    if *s.topIndex = size* **then**
        s.errorFlag ← true
    else
        s.errorFlag ← false
        s.topIndex ← s.topIndex + 1
        s.stackArray[s.topIndex] ← x
    endif
end *Push*

Instead of referring to *topIndex*, we refer to *s.topIndex*; instead of referring to *errorFlag*, we refer to *s.errorFlag*, and so on.

IntegerStackType has no **initialize** part since it contains no variables to be initialized. It is up to the user to initialize each stack variable by means of a call to *New*.

14.3 Applications of stacks

Generally, a stack is useful when an ongoing process must be interrupted for some other process to be carried out. Information about the state of the ongoing process is pushed onto a stack, after which the interrupting process is started. When the interrupting process is complete, the state information is popped off the stack and used to resume the original process at the point at which it was interrupted.

Use of a stack allows interruptions to be nested; the interrupting process can be interrupted by another process, which itself can be interrupted in turn. Every time a process is interrupted, another set of state information is pushed onto the stack. Whenever a process is completed, a set of state information is popped off the stack and used to resume an interrupted process.

The three most common applications of stacks are evaluating expressions, translating expressions into a form more suitable for evaluation, and managing subprogram calls and returns.

Evaluating expressions   Consider an operator such as + that takes two operands. In writing an expression involving the operator and its operands, we have three options for positioning the operator relative to its operands.

1. We can place the operator before the operands:

   $+ \ 3 \ 5$

   This is called *prefix notation*. Because it was invented by the Polish logician Lukasiewicz, it is also often called *Polish notation*.

2. We can place the operator between the operands:

   $3 + 5$

   This is called *infix notation* and seems to be the notation that people find most natural. Ordinary arithmetical and algebraic notation is infix notation.

3. We can place the operator after the operands:

   $3 \ 5 \ +$

   This is called *postfix notation*. Since postfix notation is just the reverse of prefix, or Polish, notation, it is often called *reverse Polish notation*, abbreviated "RPN."

Prefix and postfix notation each has an enormous advantage not possessed by infix notation. From our studies of expressions in the algorithmic language, we know that infix notation requires a scheme of operator priorities and the use of parentheses to determine the order in which the operators will be applied. Prefix and postfix notations require neither operator priorities nor parentheses; the order in which the operators appear in the expression determine the order in which they will be applied. For this reason, prefix and postfix notations are referred to as *parenthesis-free* notations.

Because priorities and parentheses are cumbersome for computers to work with, infix expressions are often translated into parenthesis-free notation before being evaluated. The two parenthesis-free notations differ in the direction in which an expression is scanned during evaluation: prefix notation requires a right-to-left scan; postfix notation requires a left-to-right scan. Because persons whose native languages are read from left to right have a strong left-to-right bias, postfix notation usually proves to be the most convenient to use.

To get a better idea of how postfix notation works, let's translate some infix expressions into postfix notation. Consider the following infix expression:

$3 * 4 + 9 * 5$

The operands of $+$ are the values of $3 * 4$ and $9 * 5$. In postfix notation, each operator follows the expressions for its operands. Therefore we can partially translate the infix expression as follows:

$(3 * 4) \ (9 * 5) \ +$

The parts enclosed in parentheses are still in infix notation. To complete the translation, the parenthesized parts must be translated into postfix notation. The postfix translation of $3 * 4$ is $3 \ 4 \ *$; the postfix translation of $9 * 5$ is $9 \ 5 \ *$; and the translation of the entire expression is

3 4 ∗ 9 5 ∗ +

Suppose that in our original infix expression we wanted the addition to be done before the two multiplications. We can force the addition to be done first by enclosing the subexpression 4 + 9 in parentheses:

3 ∗ (4 + 9) ∗ 5

To translate this expression into postfix notation, we note that the operands of the first ∗ are 3 and 4 + 9. Placing the operator after its operands gives

3 (4 + 9) ∗

and replacing (4 + 9) by its translation 4 9 + gives

3 4 9 + ∗

The operands of the second ∗ are 3 ∗ (4 + 9), which we have just translated, and 5. Placing the operator after the translations of its operands gives the postfix translation of the entire expression:

3 4 9 + ∗ 5 ∗

Let's compare the postfix translations of the two versions of the infix expression:

Infix	*Postfix*
3 ∗ 4 + 9 ∗ 5	3 4 ∗ 9 5 ∗ +
3 ∗ (4 + 9) ∗ 5	3 4 9 + ∗ 5 ∗

The different order of operator application, which is expressed by the presence or absence of parentheses in infix notation, is expressed in postfix notation by the order of the operators and operands. In postfix notation the operators always occur in the order in which they are to be applied; as the examples show, this is not always true for infix expressions. In postfix notation, the order of operators and operands replaces the priorities and parentheses of infix notation.

We can use the following extremely simple rule to evaluate expressions in postfix notation. *Scan the expression from left to right. When an operator is encountered, apply it to the two immediately preceding operands. Replace the operator and its operands by the results of the operation and continue scanning.*

Let's apply this rule to the following postfix expression:

3 4 ∗ 9 5 ∗ +

Scanning from left to right, the first operator we encounter is ∗. Following the rule, we apply ∗ to the two immediately preceding operands, 3 and 4, to get 12. We then replace the operator and operands by the result of the operation:

12 9 5 ∗ +

The next operator encountered is ∗, which is applied to the two immediately preceding operands, 9 and 5. Again the operator and operands are replaced by the result of the operation:

12 45 +

At this point the expressions representing the operands of + have both been evaluated. Applying + to the two preceding operands gives 57, the value of the expression.

Now let's try the following postfix expression:

3 4 9 + * 5 *

The first operator we encounter is +, which we apply to the two preceding operands, 4 and 9:

3 13 * 5 *

The next operator encountered is *, which is applied to its two operands. Note that the second operand of * was obtained by evaluating the subexpression 4 9 +. Replacing operator and operands by the result of the operation gives

39 5 *

The remaining * operator can now be applied to its operands, giving 195, the value of the entire expression. Note that in this case the first operand of * is the result of evaluating the subexpression

3 4 9 + *

Where do stacks come into all of this? It isn't practical to actually go through a postfix expression and replace each combination of operator and operands by the result of the operation. But we can achieve the same result with a stack and the following modified rule for evaluating a postfix expression. *Scan the expression from left to right. When an operand is encountered, push it onto the stack. When an operator is encountered, pop the top two values from the stack, apply the operator to them, and push the result onto the stack. When the scan is completed, the value on the stack is the value of the expression.* Let's apply this rule to the following postfix expression:

3 4 * 9 5 * +

For convenience we will depict the stack horizontally, with its top to the right. In the postfix expression we will use an arrow to indicate the operator or operand to be scanned next; in the stack we will use an arrow to indicate the top value. The evaluation proceeds as follows:

Postfix Expression	Stack
3 4 * 9 5 * +	
↑	↑
3 4 * 9 5 * +	3
↑	↑
3 4 * 9 5 * +	3 4
↑	↑

```
3 4 * 9 5 * +            12
      ↑                   ↑
3 4 * 9 5 * +            12 9
        ↑                 ↑
3 4 * 9 5 * +            12 9 5
          ↑                 ↑
3 4 * 9 5 * +            12 45
            ↑               ↑
3 4 * 9 5 * +            57
              ↑             ↑
```

Note that just before an operator is applied, the stack contains the operands that would have preceded the operator if our previous rule for evaluation had been used. To apply the operator to the immediately preceding operands and replace operator and operands with the result of the operation, we pop the top two values from the stack, apply the operator to them, and push the result back onto the stack.

Let's again use a stack to evaluate the following expression:

3 4 9 + * 5 *

The evaluation proceeds as follows:

Postfix Expression   *Stack*

```
3 4 9 + * 5 *
↑                       ↑
3 4 9 + * 5 *           3
↑                       ↑
3 4 9 + * 5 *           3 4
  ↑                       ↑
3 4 9 + * 5 *           3 4 9
    ↑                       ↑
3 4 9 + * 5 *           3 13
      ↑                     ↑
3 4 9 + * 5 *           39
        ↑                 ↑
3 4 9 + * 5 *           39 5
          ↑                 ↑
3 4 9 + * 5 *           195
            ↑               ↑
```

In the introduction to this section, it was stated that stacks are usually used when a process must be resumed after being interrupted by another process. Can we apply this interpretation to using a stack to evaluate postfix expressions? Consider once again the expression

$$3 \; 4 \; * \; 9 \; 5 \; * \; +$$

We can think of the addition operation as being interrupted twice, once to evaluate each of the operands of the addition operator. After the first operand is evaluated, its value, 12, remains on the stack where it will eventually be used to continue the addition operation. After the second operand is evaluated, both of the operands of + are on the stack. At this point the addition operation can be completed using the information on the stack, which consists of the two values to be added.

Translating from infix to postfix notation We have seen how easy it is to evaluate expressions written in postfix notation. Unfortunately, most programming languages use infix notation, which most people find more natural than postfix notation. To realize the advantages of postfix notation, we need some method of translating expressions from infix to postfix notation. Fortunately, this translation is easily accomplished with the aid of a stack.

Let's begin by comparing some corresponding infix and postfix expressions:

Infix	*Postfix*
$3 * 4 + 9 * 5$	$3 \; 4 \; * \; 9 \; 5 \; * \; +$
$3 * (4 + 9) * 5$	$3 \; 4 \; 9 \; + \; * \; 5 \; *$
$3 - 4 + 5$	$3 \; 4 \; - \; 5 \; +$
$3 - (4 + 5)$	$3 \; 4 \; 5 \; + \; -$

Notice two things. First, the operands appear in the same order in the infix and postfix expressions; there is no need to change the order of the operands. Second, each operator occurs further to the right in the postfix expression than in the infix expression, and the order of the operators may be changed. To translate an infix expression into postfix notation, then, we can scan the infix expression from left to right and copy each operand to the postfix expression as it is encountered. Operators, however, cannot be copied directly to the postfix expression but need to be "delayed"—stored temporarily—before being copied. What's more, the operators may be copied to the postfix expression in a different order than they appeared in the infix expression. We will see that the required delay and reordering can be accomplished with a stack.

The following three rules suffice to translate an infix expression that does not contain parentheses into postfix notation. Operands are copied directly from the infix to the postfix expression, but operators are stored temporarily on a stack:

1. Scan the infix expression from left to right. When an operand is encountered, copy it immediately to the postfix expression.

2. When an operator is encountered in the infix expression, remove operators from the stack and place them in the postfix expression until (1) the stack is empty or (2) the operator on top of the stack has a lower priority than the operator encountered in the infix expression. Then push the operator encountered in the infix expression onto the stack.

3. When the entire infix expression has been scanned, pop operators from the stack and place them in the postfix expression until the stack is empty.

To illustrate these rules, we will translate the infix expression

$3 * 4 + 9 * 5$

into postfix notation:

Infix	*Stack*	*Postfix*
3 * 4 + 9 * 5		
↑	↑	↑
3 * 4 + 9 * 5		3
↑	↑	↑
3 * 4 + 9 * 5	*	3
↑	↑	↑
3 * 4 + 9 * 5	*	3 4
↑	↑	↑
3 * 4 + 9 * 5		3 4 *
↑	↑	↑
3 * 4 + 9 * 5	+	3 4 *
↑	↑	↑
3 * 4 + 9 * 5	+	3 4 * 9
↑	↑	↑
3 * 4 + 9 * 5	+ *	3 4 * 9
↑	↑	↑
3 * 4 + 9 * 5	+ *	3 4 * 9 5
↑	↑	↑
3 * 4 + 9 * 5	+	3 4 * 9 5 *
↑	↑	↑
3 * 4 + 9 * 5		3 4 * 9 5 * +
↑	↑	↑

When the + operator is encountered in the infix expression, the higher-priority operator * is removed from the stack and placed in the postfix expression. Thus the higher-priority operator precedes the lower-priority one in the postfix expression. On the other hand, when the second * operator is encountered in the infix expression, it is stacked on top of the lower-priority + operator. When the two operators are unstacked, the higher-priority operator comes off before the lower-priority one. Again, the higher-priority operator precedes the lower-priority one in the postfix expression.

A parenthesized subexpression is treated as a single operand by the operators on either side of it in the infix expression. Just as an operand is moved directly to the postfix expression without removing any operators from the stack, so the operators on the stack when a parenthesized subexpression is encountered cannot be removed until the entire subexpression has been translated. The left parenthesis that precedes the subexpression is pushed onto the stack and serves as a temporary bottom to the stack. The subexpression is translated using the part of the stack above the left parenthesis. When the right parenthesis following the subexpression is encountered, the left parenthesis is popped from the stack, exposing the operators beneath it.

Specifically, we can extend our translation rules to handle infix expressions containing parentheses by adding the following three rules.

4. When a left parenthesis is encountered in the infix expression, push it onto the stack.

5. If a left parenthesis is encountered while unstacking operators according to rule 2, stop the unstacking and push the operator encountered in the infix expression onto the stack. Thus rule 2 treats a left parenthesis as if it were the bottom of the stack.

6. When a right parenthesis is encountered in the infix expression, unstack the operators and place them in the postfix expression until a left parenthesis is encountered on the stack. Discard both left and right parentheses.

To illustrate the translation of infix expressions containing parentheses, we will translate the expression

$$2 * (3 + 4 * 5) * 6$$

into postfix notation:

Infix	*Stack*	*Postfix*
2 * (3 + 4 * 5) * 6		
↑	↑	↑
2 * (3 + 4 * 5) * 6		2
↑	↑	↑
2 * (3 + 4 * 5) * 6	*	2
↑	↑	↑
2 * (3 + 4 * 5) * 6	* (	2
↑	↑	↑
2 * (3 + 4 * 5) * 6	* (	2 3
↑	↑	↑
2 * (3 + 4 * 5) * 6	* (+	2 3
↑	↑	↑
2 * (3 + 4 * 5) * 6	* (+	2 3 4
↑	↑	↑
2 * (3 + 4 * 5) * 6	* (+ *	2 3 4
↑	↑	↑

2 * (3 + 4 * 5) * 6   * (+ *   2 3 4 5
    ↑   ↑   ↑

2 * (3 + 4 * 5) * 6   * (+   2 3 4 5 *
    ↑   ↑   ↑

2 * (3 + 4 * 5) * 6   * (2 3 4 5 * +
    ↑   ↑   ↑

2 * (3 + 4 * 5) * 6   *   2 3 4 5 * +
     ↑   ↑   ↑

2 * (3 + 4 * 5) * 6   2 3 4 5 * + *
     ↑   ↑   ↑

2 * (3 + 4 * 5) * 6   *   2 3 4 5 * + *
      ↑   ↑   ↑

2 * (3 + 4 * 5) * 6   *   2 3 4 5 * + * 6
       ↑   ↑   ↑

2 * (3 + 4 * 5) * 6   2 3 4 5 * + * 6 *
       ↑   ↑   ↑

When the + is encountered in the infix expression, the * below the left parenthesis is *not* unstacked. The left parenthesis "protects" the * from being unstacked by any operator in the subexpression. Only when the entire subexpression has been translated and the left parenthesis has been removed can the * be unstacked.

When a parenthesized subexpression is encountered, translation of the main expression is interrupted while the subexpression is translated, after which translation of the main expression resumes. During translation of the subexpression, the stack retains the information needed to resume translation of the main expression. (That information consists of those operators of the main expression that have been pushed onto the stack but have not yet been unstacked and moved to the translated expression.) Operator priorities have the same effect as parentheses. For example,

3 * 4 + 9 * 5

is translated as if it had been written

(3 * 4) + (9 * 5)

The translation of the addition is interrupted twice, once for the translation of each of the operands of the addition operator. Thus in expression translation, too, we can think of a stack as storing information that allows a process to be resumed after it has been interrupted by another process.

Managing subprogram calls and returns   This application provides the most obvious example of a stack that stores the information needed to resume a process after it has been interrupted. We recall that a private data area is set up for each execution of a program and each invocation of a procedure or function. When a call is made to a procedure or function, the private data area of the caller must be preserved so that the caller can continue executing after the called procedure or function has returned. We can accomplish this by creating private data areas on a stack; the private data areas so created are called *stack frames* or *activation records*.

Figure 14.6 shows how a stack can be used for managing private data areas. As in our previous diagrams, the top of the stack faces the bottom of the page, and vice versa. Suppose that program *P* calls procedure *Q* and procedure *Q* calls procedure *R*. A stack frame for *P* is created before *P* begins executing. When *P* calls *Q*, the stack frame for *Q* is stacked on top of the stack frame for *P*. When *Q* calls *R*, the stack frame for *R* is stacked on top of the stack frame for *Q*.

The usefulness of a stack for managing private data areas depends on two facts: (1) subprograms return in the reverse of the order in which they were called, and (2) items are popped off a stack in the reverse of the order in which they were pushed on. Thus *R* returns first, at which time its stack frame is popped from the stack to

Figure 14.6   Use of a stack for the private data areas of algorithms, functions, and procedures.

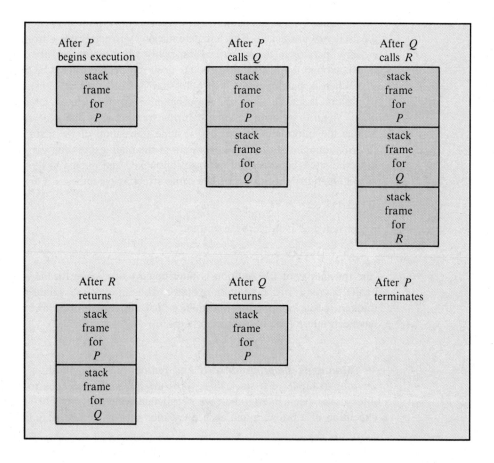

reveal the stack frame for Q, which is used to resume the execution of Q. Q returns next, at which time its stack frame is popped from the stack to reveal the stack frame for P, which is used to resume the execution of P. When the execution of P terminates, its stack frame is popped and the stack is empty.

Figure 14.7 shows the details of a typical stack frame for a subprogram. (These details vary from one language implementation to another.) The actual parameter area holds the parameters that were passed to the subprogram. If parameters are passed by copy, the values of the parameters are stored in this area. If the parameters are passed by reference, the addresses of the locations that actually contain the parameters are stored in the actual parameter area.

The return address and the control link are used to resume execution of the calling program, function, or procedure. The return address is the address of the next instruction to be executed in the caller's code. The control link points to the caller's stack frame. The control link will be discussed in more detail later.

A stack frame contains only the parameters and *local* variables for a procedure or function. *Global* variables are in other stack frames. In the algorithmic language, for example, global variables are always declared in modules. When a module is initialized, a stack frame containing the variables declared in the module is created. The access link area contains pointers to those stack frames that contain variables accessible to the subprogram. The details of the access link area—how many access links are present and which stack frames they point to—depend strongly on how global variables are handled in a particular language.

The access link area is followed by the area containing the local variables of the

Figure 14.7   Organization of a *stack frame*, the private data area of an algorithm, function, or procedure.

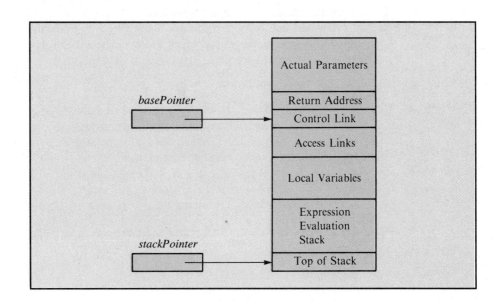

subprogram. Following the local variable area is an expression evaluation stack, which is used to evaluate expressions in postfix notation. The size of the expression evaluation stack is not fixed but varies with the number of values that are pushed onto it during expression evaluation. When the currently executing subprogram calls another subprogram, the stack frame for the new subprogram is constructed on top of the expression evaluation stack.

It is convenient to think of the computer's memory as an array of integers, which we will call *memory*. Pointers into the memory array are stored in two variables, *basePointer* and *stackPointer*, which are usually central processor registers. Thus, *memory*[*basePointer*] is the memory location that contains the control link, and *memory*[*stackPointer*] is the top location on the expression stack. Note that *stackPointer*, which always points to the top of the expression stack, plays the same role as *topIndex* played in our stack modules.

Variables and parameters in the stack frame are always addressed relative to the value of *basePointer*. That is, every reference to a variable or parameter has the form

> *memory*[*basePointer* + *offset*]

where *offset* is the value that must be added to the address of the control link to get the address of the variable or parameter. The value of *offset* is positive for local variables and negative for parameters.

Values of *basePointer* are always used for pointing to stack frames. The control link is the *basePointer* value for the caller's stack frame. The access links are *basePointer* values for stack frames containing global variables.

Let's look in detail at how a subprogram is called. The stack frame is created partly by the caller and partly by the called subprogram. The caller pushes the actual parameters onto its expression stack. It then executes a **call** instruction, which pushes the address of the next instruction in the caller's code onto the expression stack and transfers control to the first instruction of the called subprogram.

When the called subprogram begins executing, the stack frame contains only the actual parameters and the return address. *BasePointer* still contains the caller's base pointer; *stackPointer* points to the return address. The called subprogram's first step is to save the caller's base pointer by pushing it onto the stack:

> *stackPointer* ← *stackPointer* + 1
>
> *memory*[*stackPointer*] ← *basePointer*

The top of the stack, which is pointed to by *stackPointer*, contains the control link (the caller's base pointer), which should be pointed to by *basePointer*. Thus *basePointer* is set to point to the current top of the stack:

> *basePointer* ← *stackPointer*

Next the memory block containing the access links and local variables must be allocated. This is done by moving the stack pointer to the end of the block in question. If *blockSize* is the number of locations in this block, the value of *stackPointer* is modified as follows:

> *stackPointer* ← *stackPointer* + *blockSize*

StackPointer now points to the last location of the local variable area; it will move beyond the local variable area as values are pushed onto the expression stack.

Finally, pointers to frames containing global variables must be stored in the access link area. The method of determining the access links varies from one language to another and even varies among implementations of the same language.

When the subprogram is ready to return, it discards everything beyond the control link by setting the stack pointer to point to the control link (the control link becomes the new top of the stack):

$$stackPointer \leftarrow basePointer$$

The caller's base pointer—the control link—is popped and stored in *basePointer*:

$$basePointer \leftarrow memory[stackPointer]$$
$$stackPointer \leftarrow stackPointer - 1$$

The return address is now on top of the stack. The subprogram executes a **return** instruction, which pops the return address and resumes execution of the caller's code at that address.

After the subprogram returns, the caller must copy to their appropriate destinations the values of any **in out** or **out** parameters that were passed by copy. The parameters are then popped from the caller's expression evaluation stack:

$$stackPointer \leftarrow stackPointer - parameterAreaSize$$

The values of both *basePointer* and *stackPointer* are now the same as they were before the subprogram call was begun by pushing parameters onto the expression evaluation stack.

A function call differs from a procedure call only in that the value of the function must be returned to the caller. A location in the local variable area is reserved for holding the value to be returned. Every time an assignment to the function name is made, the assigned value is stored in this reserved memory location. Before discarding the local variable area, the function saves the value to be returned in a temporary location, usually a central processor register. After the parameters have been popped from the caller's expression stack, the return value is pushed on. Thus the parameters, or operands, of the function are replaced by the value of the function, in accordance with the rules for evaluating expressions in postfix notation.

14.4 Queues

We picture a queue as a waiting line. Items are inserted at the rear of the queue and removed from the front of the queue. The first item to be inserted in the queue is the first item to be removed; for this reason we say that a queue obeys a *first-in-first-out (FIFO)* discipline. An implementation of a queue must provide the following functions:

FUNCTIONS

Error   Returns *true* if the previous function or procedure call caused an error and *false* otherwise.

Front   Returns the value of the item at the front of the queue. Calling *Front* when the queue is empty causes a *queue underflow* error.

PROCEDURES

New   Creates an empty queue.

Insert(x)   Places the value of the input parameter x at the rear of the queue. If the memory space set aside for the queue has been exhausted, calling *Insert* causes a *queue overflow* error.

Remove   Removes the front item from the queue. Calling *Remove* when the queue is empty causes a *queue underflow* error.

We can give an axiomatic definition for a queue just as we did for a stack. As for a stack, the axioms deal only with underflow errors, which are inherent in the definition of a queue, and not with overflow errors, which are caused by limits imposed on a particular implementation. Axioms 3 and 4 are somewhat more complicated than the corresponding ones for stacks because they must deal with arbitrarily long sequences of operations:

1. After the operation

    New

    Error returns *false* and a call to *Front* is invalid. An invalid call to *Front* returns an undefined value and causes *Error* to return *true*.

2. After the sequence of operations

    New

    Remove

    Error returns *true*. Except for the value returned by *Error*, this sequence is equivalent to the one consisting of the single operation

    New

3. Consider the sequence of operations consisting of *New* followed by one or more *Insert* operations:

    New

    Insert(x)

       .

       .

       .

    Insert(z)

    After this sequence has been executed, *Error* returns *false* and *Front* returns the value of x, the first value to be inserted.

4. Consider the sequence of operations consisting of *New*, one or more *Insert* operations, and *Remove*:

New

Insert(x)

Insert(y)

.

.

.

Insert(z)

Remove

After this sequence has been executed, *Error* returns *false*. This sequence is equivalent to the sequence obtained from it by deleting the first *Insert* and the *Remove*:

New

Insert(y)

.

.

.

Insert(z)

We can use these axioms to prove that the effects of various sequences of operations correspond to our intuitive idea of a waiting line. For example, consider the following sequence:

New

Insert(5)

Insert(7)

Insert(9)

Intuitively, this sequence creates a queue of three integers, with 5 first, 7 next, and 9 last. Axiom 3 tells us that, after this sequence has been executed, *Front* returns the value 5, as we would expect.

Now suppose that *Remove* is executed. Axiom 4 tells us that the sequence

New

Insert(5)

Insert(7)

Insert(9)

Remove

is equivalent to the sequence

New

Insert(7)

Insert(9)

Thus after *Remove* has been executed, *Front* returns the value 7, the second value on the original *queue*.

Suppose that *Remove* is executed again. By two applications of axiom 4, we show that

New
Insert(5)
Insert(7)
Insert(9)
Remove
Remove

is equivalent to

New
Insert(7)
Insert(9)
Remove

and that this sequence, in turn, is equivalent to

New
Insert(9)

Thus after *Remove* has been executed twice, *Front* returns the value 9, the third value on the original queue. Likewise, we can show that executing *Remove* a third time yields the empty queue and that a fourth call to *Remove* is invalid.

14.5

Array implementations of queues

The diagram at the top left of Figure 14.8 shows a possible implementation of a queue using an array *queueArray*. The queue is stored with its front toward the beginning of the array and its rear toward the end of the array. *FrontIndex* points to the array component containing the front value; *RearIndex* points to the first unused component following the rear value. (The latter is slightly more convenient than letting *rearIndex* point to the component containing the rearmost value.) To insert the value of x at the rear of the queue, we execute

queueArray[*rearIndex*] $\leftarrow x$
rearIndex $\leftarrow$ *rearIndex* + 1

To remove the front value from the queue, we execute

frontIndex $\leftarrow$ *frontIndex* + 1

To examine the current front value, we access the value of

queueArray[*frontIndex*]

The problem with this implementation is that, as values are inserted in and removed from the queue, the area occupied by the queue moves forward in the array.

Figure 14.8 Array implementation of a queue. *FrontIndex* points to the value at the front of the queue; *rearIndex* points to the unused location following the value at the rear of the queue. Because of wraparound, the array behaves as if its components were arranged in a circle with the last component adjacent to the first. If *frontIndex* and *rearIndex* point to the same component, the queue is empty. When the component pointed to by *rearIndex* is immediately followed by the component pointed to by *frontIndex,* the array is full. One component of the array must remain unused; if this were not so, it would be impossible to distinguish between the full and the empty configurations.

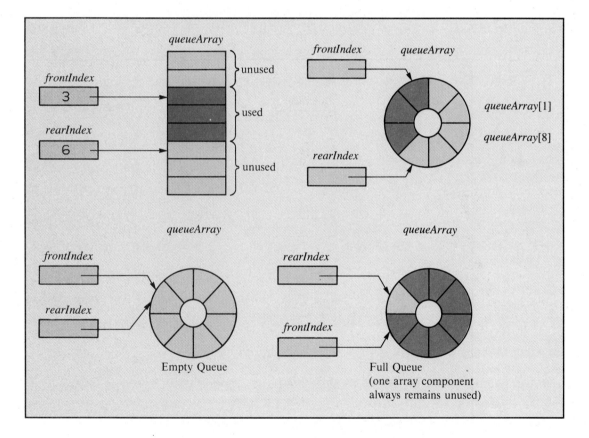

The unused components preceding the queue cannot be reused; the unused components following the queue will be quickly exhausted. The solution is to use wraparound to join the last component of *queueArray* to the first, thereby joining the unused components preceding the queue to the unused components following the queue and so allowing all unused components to be reused. The diagram at the top right of Figure 14.8 illustrates the array implementation with wraparound.

Statements that increase an index by 1 must be modified to allow for wrap-around. Suppose that the index values for *queueArray* range from 1 through *size*. The statements for inserting the value of *x* at the rear of a queue become

queueArray[*rearIndex*] ← *x*
rearIndex ← *rearIndex* **mod** *size* + 1

The statement for removing a value from the front of the queue becomes

frontIndex ← *frontIndex* **mod** *size* + 1

Figure 14.9 illustrates inserting a value at the rear of a queue; Figure 14.10 illustrates removing a value from the front of a queue.

Figure 14.9   Inserting a value at the front of a queue.

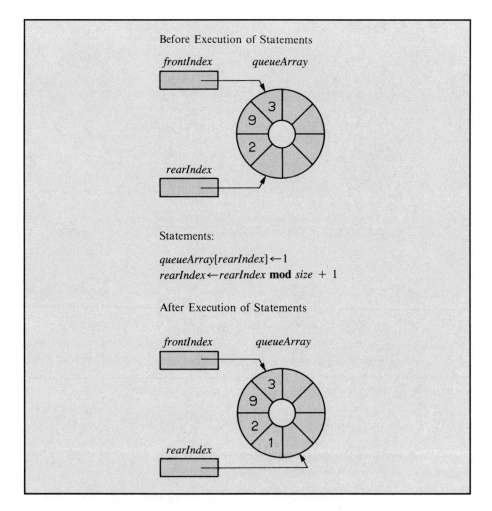

Figure 14.10   Removing a value from the rear of a queue.

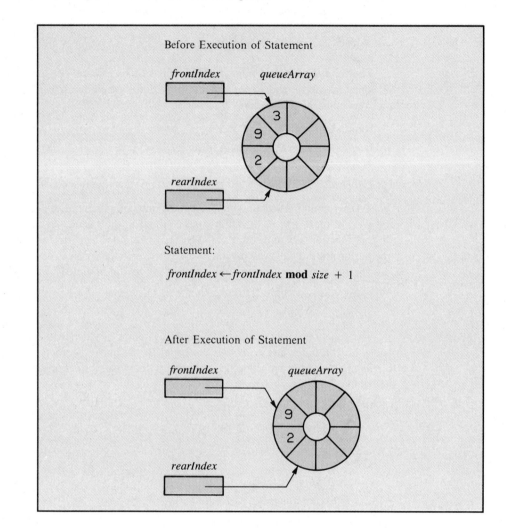

After all the values have been removed from a queue, *frontIndex* will point to the same array component as *rearIndex*. This configuration, illustrated at bottom left in Figure 14.8, represents an empty queue, a queue that contains no values.

The diagram at bottom right in Figure 14.8 illustrates a full queue, one that holds as many values as possible. In a full queue, *rearIndex* points to the array component immediately preceding the one pointed to by *frontIndex*. One array component remains unused in a full queue. If we allowed all array components to be used, we would have the value of *frontIndex* equal to that of *rearIndex* for both the empty queue and the full queue, and it would be impossible to distinguish between the two situations.

As with stacks, we will look at two ways of implementing a queue as a module. Module *IntegerQueue* implements a single queue of integers. Module *IntegerQueueType* provides a type *queue* that can be used to declare as many integer queues as needed.

The module IntegerQueue The module *IntegerQueue* (Figure 14.11) exports the functions *Error* and *Front* and the procedures *Insert* and *Remove*. The module fines one constant and declares four variables:

const *size* = 100

queueArray: **array**[1 **to** *size*] **of** *integer*

frontIndex, rearIndex: *integer*

errorFlag: *Boolean*

QueueArray contains *size* components; since one component always remains unused, however, at most *size* − 1 values can be stored in the queue. As in the stack modules, a function or procedure call sets *errorFlag* to *true* or *false* depending on whether or not the call was invalid.

The function *Error* returns the value of *errorFlag* and clears *errorFlag* to *false*:

Error ← *errorFlag*

errorFlag ← *false*

The function *Front* checks if the queue is empty, which will be the case if the values of *frontIndex* and *rearIndex* are equal. If the queue is empty, *errorFlag* is set to *true* and the arbitrary value 0 is returned. Otherwise, *errorFlag* is set to *false* and the value of *queueArray[frontIndex]* is returned:

if *frontIndex* = *rearIndex* **then**

    errorFlag ← *true*

    Front ← 0

else

    errorFlag ← *false*

    Front ← *queueArray[frontIndex]*

endif

The procedure *New* creates an empty queue. The values of *frontIndex* and *rearIndex* could be set to any value in the range 1 to *size*, as long as both are set to the *same* value:

frontIndex ← 1

rearIndex ← 1

errorFlag ← *false*

The procedure *Insert* checks to see if the queue is full. This will be the case if the component pointed to by *rearIndex* is immediately followed by the component pointed to by *frontIndex,* that is, if the condition

(*rearIndex* **mod** *size* + 1) = *frontIndex*

Figure 14.11   Module *IntegerQueue* implements a single queue of integers.

---

module *IntegerQueue*

{ Implements a queue of integers }

declare
    export *Error, Front, New, Insert, Remove*
    const *size* = 100
    queueArray: **array**[1 **to** *size*] **of** *integer*
    frontIndex, rearIndex: *integer*
    errorFlag: *Boolean*

function *Error*: *Boolean*

{ Return value of and clear error flag }

execute
    Error ← *errorFlag*
    errorFlag ← *false*
end *Error*

function *Front*: *integer*

{ Return value at front of queue }

execute
    if *frontIndex* = *rearIndex* **then**
        errorFlag ← *true*
        Front ← 0
    else
        errorFlag ← *false*
        Front ← *queueArray*[*frontIndex*]
    endif
end *Front*

procedure *New*

{ Create empty queue }

```
    execute
        frontIndex ← 1
        rearIndex ← 1
        errorFlag ← false
    end New


    procedure Insert(x)

    { Insert value at end of queue }

    declare
        x: in integer
    execute
        if (rearIndex mod size + 1) = frontIndex then
            errorFlag ← true
        else
            errorFlag ← false
            queueArray[rearIndex] ← x
            rearIndex ← rearIndex mod size + 1
        endif
    end Insert


    procedure Remove

    { Remove value from front of queue }

    execute
        if frontIndex = rearIndex then
            errorFlag ← true
        else
            errorFlag ← false
            frontIndex ← frontIndex mod size + 1
        endif
    end Remove


initialize
    New
end IntegerQueue
```

is true. If the queue is full, *errorFlag* is set to *true*. Otherwise, *errorFlag* is set to *false* and the value of *x* is inserted at the rear of the queue:

if (*rearIndex* **mod** *size* + 1) = *frontIndex* **then**
    errorFlag ← *true*
else
    errorFlag ← *false*
    queueArray[*rearIndex*] ← *x*
    rearIndex ← *rearIndex* **mod** *size* + 1
endif

The procedure *Remove* checks if the queue is empty. If it is, *errorFlag* is set to *true*; otherwise, the front value is removed from the queue:

if *frontIndex* = *rearIndex* **then**
    errorFlag ← *true*
else
    errorFlag ← *false*
    frontIndex ← *frontIndex* **mod** *size* + 1
endif

The module *IntegerQueue* is initialized by calling *New* to create an empty queue.

The module IntegerQueueType In the module *IntegerQueueType* (Figure 14.12), all the variable declarations of *IntegerQueue* are wrapped up in a record description, which is used to define a type *queue*:

type *queue* = **record**
                errorFlag: *Boolean*
                frontIndex, *rearIndex*: *integer*
                queueArray: **array**[1 **to** *size*] **of** *integer*
          endrecord

The type *queue*, which is exported, can be employed by the user of the module to declare as many queues as needed. For example, the declaration

    q1, *q2*: *queue*

declares *q1* and *q2* as variables, each capable of holding a queue of up to *size* − 1 integers.

The functions and procedures of *IntegerQueueType* are the same as for *IntegerQueue* except that each takes as an additional parameter the queue variable holding the queue to be manipulated. If *q* is the formal parameter corresponding to the queue variable, then all references to fields of *q* must be preceded by "*q*.". For example, the procedure *Insert* is written as follows:

Figure 14.12 Module *IntegerQueueType* implements type *queue*, which can be used to declare any number of integer queues.

```
module IntegerQueueType

{ Defines type queue and provides functions and procedures for
  manipulating queues }

declare
    export queue, Error, Front, New, Insert, Remove
    const size = 100
    type queue = record
                    errorFlag: Boolean
                    frontIndex, rearIndex: integer
                    queueArray: array[1 to size] of integer
                 endrecord


function Error(q): Boolean

{ Return value of and clear error flag }

declare
    q: in out queue
execute
    Error ← q.errorFlag
    q.errorFlag ← false
end Error


function Front(q): integer

{ Return value at front of queue }

declare
    q: in out queue
execute
    if q.frontIndex = q.rearIndex then
        q.errorFlag ← true
        Front ← 0
    else
        q.errorFlag ← false
        Front ← q.queueArray[q.frontIndex]
    endif
end Front
```

```
procedure New(q)

{ Create empty queue }

declare
    q: out queue
execute
    q.frontIndex ← 1
    q.rearIndex ← 1
    q.errorFlag ← false
end New


procedure Insert(q, x)

{ Insert value at end of queue }

declare
    q: in out queue
    x: in integer
execute
    if (q.rearIndex mod size + 1) = q.frontIndex then
        q.errorFlag ← true
    else
        q.errorFlag ← false
        q.queueArray[q.rearIndex] ← x
        q.rearIndex ← q.rearIndex mod size + 1
    endif
end Insert


procedure Remove(q)

{ Remove value from front of queue }

declare
    q: in out queue
execute
    if q.frontIndex = q.rearIndex then
        q.errorFlag ← true
    else
        q.errorFlag ← false
        q.frontIndex ← q.frontIndex mod size + 1
    endif
end Remove

end IntegerQueueType
```

```
procedure Insert(q, x)
declare
    q: in out queue
    x: in integer
execute
    if (q.rearIndex mod size + 1) = q.frontIndex then
        q.errorFlag ← true
    else
        q.errorFlag ← false
        q.queueArray[q.rearIndex] ← x
        q.rearIndex ← q.rearIndex mod size + 1
    endif
end Insert
```

Instead of referring to *rearIndex*, we refer to *q.rearIndex*; instead of referring to *frontIndex*, we refer to *q.frontIndex*; and so on.

IntegerQueueType contains no **initialize** part since it contains no variables to be initialized. It is up to the user to initialize queue variables with calls to *New*. Thus, the variables *q1* and *q2*, declared above, would be initialized to the empty queue with the following calls:

> *New(q1)*
> *New(q2)*

Applications of queues

Computer simulation Computer simulation uses computer programs to model the behavior of such real-world systems as factories, telephone exchanges, and airports. With the aid of computer simulation, we can predict the performance of proposed systems and explore the effects of proposed changes to existing systems.

Frequently systems contain bottlenecks at which persons or things must wait in line for service. Examples are persons waiting to be checked out at a supermarket, parts waiting to be processed by a certain machine in a factory, persons waiting for dial tones from a telephone exchange, and airplanes waiting to land at an airport. Concern about the effects of these bottlenecks is often the very reason why it was considered advisable to do a computer simulation of the system. The simulation program uses queues to represent the waiting lines that occur at the various bottlenecks.

For example, consider the checkout counter simulation that we designed and implemented in Chapter 11. Since all we were interested in there was the length of the waiting line, we did not have to represent the line by a queue. It was sufficient for the simulation program to keep track of the number of people who were in line.

In practice, however, we would probably also be interested in the average time a customer is kept waiting, which is likely to be more important than the length of the line in determining customer satisfaction or dissatisfaction. To determine the average waiting time, we must follow each customer through the waiting line and so must represent the waiting line by a queue.

The queue holds the times at which the customers got in line. When a customer gets in line, an integer equal to the current time is placed at the rear of the queue. When the checkout counter is free, the integer at the front of the queue is removed and sent to the checkout counter module. When a person has finished checking out, the time at which the person got in line is subtracted from the current time, and the difference is added to a running total of waiting times. At the end of the simulation run, the sum of the waiting times is divided by the number of customers checked out to get the average waiting time.

As another example, consider a factory containing a number of machines that break down at unpredictable times. The machines are scheduled for repair in the order in which they break down. Thus there is a waiting line for machines to be repaired. We wish to compute the utilization of each machine, that is, the percentage of the time that the machine is up and running as opposed to waiting to be repaired.

In the simulation, we represent each machine by a record having fields for the time at which a machine broke down and the total down time to date. Using the method described in Chapter 11, a random number generator and a table of statistics for intervals between breakdowns are used to compute when the machine will next break down based on the time it was returned to last service. This computation is made when the machine is returned to service, and the breakdown time is entered in the record for that machine.

When the breakdown time arrives, the record for the machine is placed in a repair queue. After each repair is completed, the record for the next machine to be repaired is removed from the front of the queue. A random number generator and a table of statistics determine the duration of the repair. When the machine is repaired, the time at which the machine broke down is subtracted from the current time, and the difference is added to the total down time for the machine. The time at which the machine will next break down is computed, and the machine is returned to service. (The records for all the machines can be conveniently stored in an array. Each record can have a Boolean field whose value indicates whether the machine is in service or awaiting repair. Only indexes into this array, rather than the records themselves, need be placed in the repair queue.)

When the simulation run is complete, the utilization for each machine can be computed by subtracting the total down time for the machine from the duration of the simulation run and dividing the difference by the duration of the simulation run. The utilizations for all the machines in the factory can be averaged to get the average machine utilization.

Computer systems We recall from Chapter 5 that a multiprogramming or multiprocessing computer system can be visualized as a set of concurrently executing processes, each consisting of a program and the data the program is currently manipulating. Processes can communicate with input and output devices, transmit messages to one another, and manipulate various data areas in the computer's memory, but are otherwise independent of one another.

Frequently, processes must wait in line for the use of some computer resource, such as a printer, a tape drive, or the central processor. Messages sent from one process to another may have to wait in line to be accepted by the receiving process. Processes or data items that must wait in line are placed in queues. We will look at three kinds of queues frequently managed by operating systems: *the dispatch queue, semaphores,* and *buffers.*

Each process is described by a record called a *process control block.* The process control block contains pointers to the process's program, to its data area, and to the next instruction to be executed in the program. When a process must wait for a resource, its process control block is inserted at the rear of a queue. When the resource becomes available, it is granted to the process whose process control block is at the front of the queue.

Dispatch queue   As described in Chapter 5, a process can be *running, ready,* or *blocked.* A running process is currently being executed by the central processor. A ready process is waiting its turn at the central processor. A blocked process is waiting for some other resource, such as an input or output device.

The process control blocks for the ready processes are kept in a queue called the *dispatch queue.* When the central processor becomes available, the process control block at the front of the dispatch queue is removed and that process is given control of the central processor. (The process is said to have been *dispatched.*) When that process's time slice expires, its process control block is placed at the rear of the dispatch queue, and the process whose control block is at the front of the queue is dispatched.

Processes frequently have different priorities for execution. For example, a process that must service a fast input or output device, such as a disk drive, must have a high priority, since data can be lost if the process is too slow in responding to a request from the device to transfer data. Likewise, interactive processes, which must respond to their users in a timely fashion, are given higher priorities than batch processes, which do not interact with their users. The priority of a process is represented by an integer that is stored in the process control block.

When processes can have priorities, the dispatch queue becomes a *priority queue,* in which a process with the highest priority must be run if one is available. If all the highest priority processes are blocked, then a process with the next lowest priority is run, and so on. One way to implement a priority queue is to maintain a separate queue for each priority level. To remove a record, the queue corresponding to the highest priority is checked. If that queue is not empty, the record at the front of the queue is removed and returned. Otherwise, the queue corresponding to the next lowest priority is checked. If this queue is not empty, the record at the front of the queue is removed and returned. Otherwise, the queue corresponding to the next lowest priority is checked, and so on. When a process control block is inserted in a priority queue, it is inserted at the rear of the queue corresponding to the priority of the process.

Semaphores   The process control blocks for ready processes reside on the dispatch queue, where the processes await their turns at the central processor. The process control blocks for blocked processes reside on queues associated with data structures called *semaphores*.

We can visualize a semaphore by considering the plight of a restaurant owner who wishes patrons to wait outside the dining room until a table becomes available. Too cheap to hire a maitre d', the owner devises the following scheme. A bowl containing one marble for each table in the dining room is placed outside the dining room door. A sign instructs each party to take a marble from the bowl before entering the dining room and to replace it upon leaving. If the bowl is empty, patrons must wait in line until a departing party places a marble in the bowl. At that time, the party at the front of the line will take the marble and enter the dining room.

A semaphore is a data structure consisting of an integer variable, which corresponds to the bowl of marbles, and a queue, which corresponds to the waiting line. The value of the integer variable indicates how many units of a resource (such as how many printers) are available. A process can perform two operations on a semaphore: *Wait* and *Signal*.

Before attempting to use the resource guarded by the semaphore, a process executes *Wait*. If the value of the integer variable is greater than zero, the value of the variable is decreased by one and the process is allowed to continue executing. If the value of the integer variable is zero, however, the execution of the process is suspended and its process control block is placed at the end of the queue associated with the semaphore. The process is now blocked.

When a process finishes using the resource guarded by the semaphore, it executes *Signal*. The integer variable is increased by one, indicating that another unit of the resource is now available. If the semaphore queue is not empty, the process that called *Signal* is inserted at the rear of the dispatch queue and the process at the front of the semaphore queue is dispatched. This procedure assures that a process waiting for a resource will gain access to it as soon as the resource becomes available.

If only one unit of a resource is available, the integer variable can be replaced by a Boolean variable whose value is *true* when the resource is available and *false* when the resource is in use. A semaphore that uses a Boolean variable is called a *binary semaphore*. A binary semaphore assures *mutually exclusive* use of a resource; only one process can use the resource at a time. Semaphores were named after the railroad signals used to insure mutually exclusive use of a segment of track by trains going in opposite directions. Frequently the resource guarded by a binary semaphore is a memory area, the contents of which would become scrambled if they were manipulated by more than one process at a time.

Buffers When one process sends a message to another, the recipient process may not be ready to accept the message at the moment that it is sent. To prevent the sender from having to wait until the recipient is ready, we can interpose a queue called a *buffer* between the sender and the receiver. When the sender transmits a message, it is inserted at the rear of the buffer queue. When the recipient is ready to receive a message, it removes the first message from the queue. Such a buffer is sometimes referred to as the recipient's *mailbox*.

Usually only a fixed amount of memory is allocated to a buffer. When the buffer is full, the sending process must wait until a "slot" (location for a message) becomes available. We can arrange for the necessary waiting by using a semaphore to guard the buffer. The integer variable in the semaphore is initialized to the number of message slots available in the buffer. Before attempting to insert a message in the buffer, the sending process must execute *Wait*. After the receiving process has removed a message, it executes *Signal* to indicate that another message slot is available.

Buffers are also used in communicating with input and output devices. For example, most systems store characters typed on the user's keyboard in a buffer until they can be accepted by the process with which the user is communicating. Unfortunately, there is no way to get the typist to wait on a semaphore before striking each key. Some computers solve this problem by having the computer make a beeping sound if the user strikes a key when the keyboard buffer is full.

The processes that manipulate a buffer must have mutually exclusive access to its data structure. If two or more processes are allowed to manipulate the buffer simultaneously, the results may be unpredictable. For example, suppose that two processes, *P* and *Q*, try to insert values in the buffer simultaneously. To perform an insertion, each process must execute the following statements:

> *queueArray*[*rearIndex*] ← *x*
> *rearIndex* ← *rearIndex* **mod** *size* + 1

Now suppose that the two processes happen to execute the statements in the following order:

> *queueArray*[*rearIndex*] ← *x* { Executed by process *P* }
> *queueArray*[*rearIndex*] ← *x* { Executed by process *Q* }
> *rearIndex* ← *rearIndex* **mod** *size* + 1 { Executed by process *P* }
> *rearIndex* ← *rearIndex* **mod** *size* + 1 { Executed by process *Q* }

The parameter *x* holds the value to be inserted, which will be different for process *P* and process *Q*. Since process *Q* stores its value of *x* before process *P* has a chance to increment *rearIndex*, the value stored by *Q* overwrites the value stored by *P*. What's more, after *Q* stores its value, *rearIndex* is incremented twice, moving it past not only the location containing the value stored by *Q* but also past the next location, which contains garbage. Thus the effect of the two insertions is to place at the rear of the queue the value inserted by *Q* followed by a garbage value. The value inserted by *P* is lost.

To avoid this problem, we can use a binary semaphore to insure mutually exclusive access to a buffer. Each process must execute a *Wait* on this semaphore before beginning any operation on the buffer and must execute a *Signal* on the semaphore after the operation has been completed.

Review questions

1. Define and contrast the terms *abstract machine, data abstraction,* and *abstract data type*.

2. Describe two ways of visualizing a stack.

3. What is meant by the statement that a stack obeys a *last-in-first-out* discipline?

4. Define the operations *Push* and *Pop* for a stack.

5. Give the four axioms for a stack and state informally the implications of each axiom.

6. What kind of stack error is recognized by the axioms? What kind is not recognized? What is the distinction between the two kinds of error?

7. Diagram the array implementation of a stack.

8. Diagram the *Push* operation and the *Pop* operation for an array implementation of a stack.

9. Contrast the modules *IntegerStack* and *IntegerStackType*.

10. Contrast *prefix*, *infix*, and *postfix* notations. What alternate names are sometimes used for prefix and postfix notations?

11. Give a general statement that characterizes many applications of stacks.

12. Give the rule for evaluating an expression in postfix notation using a stack.

13. Give the rules for translating expressions from infix to postfix notation. Describe informally the effect of parentheses on the translation process.

14. Why are stacks useful for managing subprogram calls and returns?

15. What is a *stack frame*? What data does it contain?

16. What is a *queue*?

17. What is meant by the statement that a queue obeys a *first-in-first-out* discipline?

18. Contrast the axioms for a stack and a queue.

19. Diagram the array implementation of a queue. Why is wraparound needed? How is it implemented?

20. Diagram the *Insert* operation and the *Remove* operation for an array implementation of a queue.

21. What is a *process control block*?

22. What is a *dispatch queue*?

23. What is a *priority queue*?

24. What is a *semaphore*? Describe a simple way of visualizing a semaphore.

25. Distinguish between *ready* and *blocked* processes according to where the process control blocks for each are stored.

26. What is a *binary semaphore*? Describe an important application of binary semaphores.

27. What is a *buffer*? For what purpose is it used?

28. Describe two semaphores that may be needed to guard access to a buffer.

Exercises

1. Using the axioms for a stack, replace each sequence of operations by the simplest possible equivalent sequence. What values are returned by *Error* and *Top* after each sequence is executed?

   (a) *New*   (b) *New*
       Push(3)   *Push*(7)
       Push(2)   *Pop*
       Pop   *Pop*
       Push(6)   *Push*(5)
       Push(9)   *Push*(6)
       Pop   *Pop*

2. Express each of the following in postfix notation:
   (a) $7 + 9$
   (b) $3 * 4 + 5$
   (c) $3 * (4 + 5)$
   (d) $12 / 3 * 4$
   (e) $12 / (3 * 4)$
   (f) $3 * 4 ** 2 - 5$

3. Work through the steps of evaluating the following postfix expression using a stack:

   $2\ 3\ 4\ 5\ 6\ 7 + * + * +$

4. Work through the steps of translating each of the following infix expressions into postfix notation:

   (a) $7 * 2 - 4 * 3 + 2 * 5$
   (b) $3 * (5 * (5 - 2)) - 9$

5. Draw a set of diagrams illustrating the steps by which a stack frame is constructed when a subprogram is called and discarded when the subprogram returns. Each diagram should use arrows to show the locations pointed to by *basePointer* and *stackPointer*.

6. Using the axioms for a queue, replace each sequence of operations by the simplest possible equivalent sequence. What values are returned by *Error* and *Front* after each sequence?

(a) *New*	(b) *New*
Insert(3)	*Insert*(1)
Insert(4)	*Insert*(2)
Remove	*Remove*
Insert(5)	*Insert*(3)
Insert(6)	*Remove*

7. Modify the waiting-line simulation of Chapter 11 as described in this chapter so as to compute the average time that a customer is kept waiting.

8. Write an algorithm for the machine-repair simulation described in this chapter. Assume that all the machines are identical and are governed by the same statistics for breakdown and repair. Devise reasonable statistics for the time interval between breakdowns and the time required to repair a machine.

9. Write a module to implement a priority queue of integers. There should be five priority levels, numbered 1 through 5, with level 5 having the highest priority. A call to *Insert* has the form

$$Insert(x, p)$$

where x is the integer to be stored and p is its priority.

Hint: Use an array of queues having one component for each priority level.

10. A *deque* (pronounced "deck") is a *double-ended queue*. Values can be inserted and removed at both its front and its rear. Both the frontmost and rearmost values can be accessed. Write a module to implement a *deque*.

11. An RPN calculator pushes numbers onto a stack as they are entered. When an operator key, such as +, is pressed, the top two values are popped from the stack, the operator is applied to them, and the result of the operation is pushed onto the stack. The calculator's display always shows the top value on the stack. Write a module to implement an RPN calculator. The module should provide the procedure *Enter*(x) for entering the value of x and the procedures *Plus*, *Minus*, *Times*, and *Quotient* for carrying out arithmetical operations. The function *Display* returns the current value of the display. Initially, the stack contains the single value 0.0.

To avoid stack underflow, an RPN calculator ignores a *Pop* operation for the bottommost value on the stack. The stack behaves as if it were bottomless, with the bottommost value repeated indefinitely.

To avoid stack overflow, an RPN calculator discards the bottommost value when a new value is pushed onto a full stack. Because of this feature, we need never clear the stack of an RPN calculator. When we finish one calculation, we just start entering the data for the next calculation. Any garbage left on the stack by previous calculations will eventually be discarded. To implement this feature, wraparound must be used so that the value pushed onto a full stack can be stored in the location occupied by the bottommost value that was discarded. Pointers to both the top and the bottom of the stack will be needed.

Pascal Supplement

Figures 14.13 through 14.16 give UCSD Pascal units for *IntegerStack*, *Integer-StackType*, *IntegerQueue*, and *IntegerQueueType*. Note the use of **with** statements in the functions and procedures of *IntegerStackType* and *IntegerQueueType*.

Figure 14.13　*IntegerStack* implemented as a UCSD Pascal unit.

```
unit IntegerStack;

{ Implements a stack of integers }

interface
    function Error: Boolean;
    { Return value of and clear error flag }

    function Top: integer;
    { Return top value on stack }

    procedure New;
    { Create empty stack }

    procedure Push(x: integer);
    { Push value onto stack }

    procedure Pop;
    { Pop value off stack }

implementation
    const
        size = 100;
    var
        stackArray: array[1 . . size] of integer;
        topIndex: integer;
        errorFlag: Boolean;

    function Error;
    begin
        Error := errorFlag;
        errorFlag := false
    end; { Error }
```

```
    function Top;
    begin
        if topIndex = 0 then
            begin
                errorFlag := true;
                Top := 0
            end
        else
            begin
                errorFlag := false;
                Top := stackArray[topIndex]
            end
    end; { Top }

    procedure New;
    begin
        topIndex := 0;
        errorFlag := false
    end; { New }

    procedure Push;
    begin
        if topIndex = size then
            errorFlag := true
        else
            begin
                errorFlag := false;
                topIndex := topIndex + 1;
                stackArray[topIndex] := x
            end
    end; { Push }

    procedure Pop;
    begin
        if topIndex = 0 then
            errorFlag := true
        else
            begin
                errorFlag := false;
                topIndex := topIndex - 1
            end
    end; { Pop }

begin
    New
end. { IntegerStack }
```

Figure 14.14   *IntegerStackType* implemented as a UCSD Pascal unit. Note
the use of the **with** statement.

```
unit IntegerStackType;

{ Defines type stack and provides functions and procedures for
  manipulating stacks }

interface
    const
        size = 100;
    type
        stack = record
                    errorFlag: Boolean;
                    topIndex: integer;
                    stackArray: array[1 . . size] of integer
                end;

    function Error(var s: stack): Boolean;
    { Return value of and clear error flag }

    function Top(var s: stack): integer;
    { Return top value on stack }

    procedure New(var s: stack);
    { Create empty stack }

    procedure Push(var s: stack; x: integer);
    { Push value onto stack }

    procedure Pop(var s: stack);
    { Pop value off stack }

implementation
    function Error;
    begin
        with s Do
            begin
                Error := errorFlag;
                errorFlag := false
            end
    end; { Error }

    function Top;
```

```
begin
    with s do
        if topIndex = 0 then
            begin
                errorFlag := true;
                Top := 0
            end
        else
            begin
                errorFlag := false;
                Top := stackArray[topIndex]
            end
end; { Top }


procedure New;
begin
    with s do
        begin
            topIndex := 0;
            errorFlag := false
        end
end; { New }

procedure Push;
begin
    with s do
        if topIndex = size then
            errorFlag := true
        else
            begin
                errorFlag := false;
                topIndex := topIndex + 1;
                stackArray[topIndex] := x
            end
end; { Push }

procedure Pop;
begin
    with s do
        if topIndex = 0 then
            errorFlag := true
```

```
                else
                    begin
                        errorFlag := false;
                        topIndex := topIndex − 1
                    end
        end; { Pop }


        end. { IntegerStackType }
```

Figure 14.15   *IntegerQueue* implemented as a UCSD Pascal unit.

```
unit IntegerQueue;

{ Implements a queue of integers }

interface
    function Error: Boolean;
    { Return value of and clear error flag }

    function Front: integer;
    { Return value at front of queue }

    procedure New;
    { Create empty queue }

    procedure Insert(x: integer);
    { Insert value at end of queue }

    procedure Remove;
    { Remove value from front of queue }

implementation
    const
        size = 100;
    var
        queueArray: array[1 .. size] of integer;
        frontIndex, rearIndex: integer;
        errorFlag: Boolean;

    function Error;
```

```pascal
begin
    Error := errorFlag;
    errorFlag := false
end; { Error }

function Front;
begin
    if frontIndex = rearIndex then
        begin
            errorFlag := true;
            Front := 0
        end
    else
        begin
            errorFlag := false;
            Front := queueArray[frontIndex]
        end
end; { Front }

procedure New;
begin
    frontIndex := 1;
    rearIndex := 1;
    errorFlag := false
end; { New }

procedure Insert;
begin
    if (rearIndex mod size + 1) = frontIndex then
        errorFlag := true
    else
        begin
            errorFlag := false;
            queueArray[rearIndex] := x;
            rearIndex := rearIndex mod size + 1
        end
end; { Insert }

procedure Remove;
begin
    if frontIndex = rearIndex then
        errorFlag := true
```

```
        else
            begin
                errorFlag := false;
                frontIndex := frontIndex mod size + 1
            end
    end; { Remove }

begin
    New
end. { IntegerQueue }
```

Figure 14.16   *IntegerQueueType* implemented as a UCSD Pascal unit.

```
unit IntegerQueueType;

{ Defines type queue and proves functions and procedures for manipulating
  queues }

interface
    const
        size = 100;
    type
        queue = record
                    errorFlag: Boolean;
                    frontIndex, rearIndex: integer;
                    queueArray: array[1 . . size] of integer
                end;

    function Error(var q: queue): Boolean;
    { Return value of and clear error flag }

    function Front(var q: queue): integer;
    { Return value at front of queue }

    procedure New(var q: queue);
    { Create empty queue }

    procedure Insert(var q: queue; x: integer);
    { Insert value at end of queue }
```

```
    procedure Remove(var q: queue);
    { Remove value from front of queue }

implementation
    function Error;
    begin
        with q do
            begin
                Error := errorFlag;
                errorFlag := false
            end
    end; { Error }

    function Front;
    begin
        with q do
            if frontIndex = rearIndex then
                begin
                    errorFlag := true;
                    Front := 0
                end
            else
                begin
                    errorFlag := false;
                    Front := queueArray[frontIndex]
                end
    end; { Front }


    procedure New;
    begin
        with q do
            begin
                frontIndex := 1;
                rearIndex := 1;
                errorFlag := false
            end
    end; { New }

    procedure Insert;
```

```
      begin
         with q do
            if (rearIndex mod size + 1) = frontIndex then
               errorFlag := true
            else
               begin
                  errorFlag := false;
                  queueArray[rearIndex] := x;
                  rearIndex := rearIndex mod size + 1
               end
   end; { Insert }

   procedure Remove;
   begin
      with q do
         if frontIndex = rearIndex then
            errorFlag := true
         else
            begin
               errorFlag := false;
               frontIndex := frontIndex mod size + 1
            end
      end; { Remove }

end. { IntegerQueueType }
```

15

Strings

A *string* is a sequence of values, all of which are of the same type. Such a sequence can be stored in an array or a file. What distinguishes strings from arrays and files, however, is that we are often interested in segments of a string called *substrings*. The following are common operations with substrings:

1. Locate each occurrence of one string as a substring of another string. For example, we may wish to find every occurrence of 'the' in

    'the quick brown fox jumps over the lazy dog'

2. Delete a substring. For example, deleting 'quick' from the above string gives

    'the brown fox jumps over the lazy dog'

3. Create a substring by inserting one string at a given point within another. For example, inserting 'very' before 'lazy' in the above string gives

    'the brown fox jumps over the very lazy dog'

4. Replace a substring with a given string. The replacement can be accomplished by locating the substring to be replaced, deleting it, and inserting its replacement. For example, replacing each occurrence of 'the' with 'a' in the above string gives

    'a brown fox jumps over a very lazy dog'

Each of the last three operations changes the length of the string—the number of characters that it contains. The length of an array cannot be changed, and the length of a file can be changed only by extending it—appending values to its end. Therefore, string data types are distinct from array types and file types in their ability to allow insertions, deletions, and replacements.

The most commonly used strings are strings of characters. Indeed, when the word "string" is used without further qualification, it is assumed to refer to character strings. We will confine ourselves to character strings in this chapter. But note that strings of other types of values are often useful. For example, *bit strings*—strings of Boolean values—are important in some applications. For another example, the table implemented by the table-handling module of Chapter 13 could be considered as a string of records, since the length of the table can change as the result of the insertion and deletion of records.

String types can be classified as *fixed-length-string types* and *variable-length-string types*. All strings belonging to a fixed-length-string type have the same length; strings belonging to a variable-length-string type can have different lengths. We refer to strings belonging to a fixed-length-string type as *fixed-length strings* and to those belonging to a variable-length-string type as *variable-length strings*. Note, however, that every string value has a definite length which does not change; for example, the length of the string 'computer' is always 8. Therefore, the terms "fixed length" and "variable length" refer to the type to which a string belongs rather than to the string value itself.

Because changes in length are characteristic of string processing, only variable-length strings can truly capture the concept of a string as described above. But because fixed-length strings are widely implemented in programming languages, and because they often provide the raw material for implementing variable-length strings, we will discuss them briefly before describing the more useful variable-length strings.

15.1 Fixed-length strings

When all the strings belonging to a string type are required to have the same length, the distinction between string types and array types vanishes. Thus, fixed-length strings can be represented as arrays of characters. For example, the type of all strings of length 10 can be defined by

    type *fixedString10* = **array**[1 **to** 10] **of** *char*

and the type of all 80-character strings can be defined by

    type *fixedString80* = **array**[1 **to** 80] **of** *char*

By convention, index values for strings range from 1 through the length of the string. Index value 1 refers to the leftmost character of the string, index value 2 refers to the next to leftmost character, and so on. Thus a fixed-length-string type is any type whose description has the form

    array[1 **to** *length*] **of** *char*

where *length* is the number of characters in each string belonging to the type.

To make string processing practical, some restrictions on type equivalence need to be relaxed for string types. The simplest step is to allow structural equivalence rather than name equivalence for fixed-length-string types. That is, two fixed-length-string types are equivalent if strings belonging to the two types have the same length. For example, if *fixedString10* and *fString10* are defined by

type *fixedString10* = **array**[1 **to** 10] **of** *char*

type *fString10* = **array**[1 **to** 10] **of** *char*

then these two types are equivalent. If we declare variables *s* and *t* by

s: *fixedString10*

t: *fString10*

then *s* and *t* have equivalent types, and the assignments

s ← t

and

t ← s

are allowed. Likewise, if *u* and *v* are declared by

u: **array**[1 **to** 10] **of** *char*

v: **array**[1 **to** 10] **of** *char*

then *s*, *t*, *u*, and *v* have equivalent types, and assignments such as

s ← u

t ← v

u ← v

are all valid.

Structural equivalence paves the way for constants of fixed-length-string types. A sequence of two or more characters enclosed in single quotation marks is defined to represent a value of type

array[1 **to** *length*]

where *length* is the number of characters in the sequence. Thus,

'computer'

represents a value of type

array[1 **to** 8] **of** *char*

and

'This is a fixed-length-string constant'

represents a value of type

array[1 **to** 38] **of** *char*

Because of structural equivalence, we do not have to specify by name the type to which each constant belongs, as we do for other array types. Only the number of characters in a string constant determines whether it belongs to a given fixed-length-string type.

Constants such as 'a', '0', and '$' represent values of type *char* rather than values of type

array[1 **to** 1] **of** *char*

For fixed-length strings, this makes good sense. We would never bother to define an array type whose values are single characters; we would just use type *char* instead. When one attempts to implement variable-length strings, however, this convention becomes an annoyance, because a variable-length string containing a single character is perfectly reasonable.

Fixed-length strings can be compared with the relational operators $=$, $<$, $>$, $<=$, $>=$, and $<>$. The two strings being compared must be of equivalent types, which means that they must have the same length. Two strings are equal if they contain the same characters in the same order. One string precedes another if it comes before the other in alphabetical order. Alphabetical order is defined by the collating sequence for values of type *char*. Thus if s and t are declared by

s: **array**[1 **to** 8] **of** *char*

t: **array**[1 **to** 8] **of** *char*

then the Boolean expressions

$s < t$

$s =$ 'computer'

'operator' $>$ 'computer'

are all valid. The value of the third expression is *true*, since 'operator' follows 'computer' in alphabetical order. If the value of s is 'hardware' and the value of t is 'software', then the value of the first expression is *true* and the value of the second is *false*.

Allowing structural rather than name equivalence is as far as some languages go in relaxing type-equivalence restrictions for fixed-length-string types. For example, the type-equivalence rules just described are the ones used by Pascal. Some languages, however, will automatically convert fixed-length strings from one length to another. A string is lengthened by extending, or *padding*, it on the right with blanks. A string is shortened by truncating it on the right. For example, if the fixed-length-string variable s is declared by

s: **array**[1 **to** 6] **of** *char*

then the following assignments are valid:

$s \leftarrow$ 'pad'

$s \leftarrow$ 'truncate'

In the first case, the string 'pad' is extended on the right with three blanks to bring it up to the length of 6 required for values of s. The value assigned to s is 'pad###'

where the #s represent blanks. In the second case, two characters are discarded from the right end of 'truncate' to bring it down to the required six characters. In this case, the value assigned to *s* is

'trunca'

Padding and truncating on the right is known as *left justification,* since the first character of the string is positioned at the left of the field defined by the string variable. Some languages allow the programmer to specify *right justification,* in which the end of a string is positioned at the right of its field, and padding and truncation are performed on the left end. If right justification had been specified for the variable *s*, the values assigned to *s* by the above statements would be

'###pad'

and

'uncate'

15.2

Variable-length strings

The algorithmic language provides a variable-length-string type *string,* whose values include all one-character strings, all two-character strings, all three-character strings, and so on. Also included is the *null string*, which contains zero characters. Note that there is no such thing as a fixed-length null string. Such a string could only be represented as an array with zero components, and the algorithmic language does not allow defining an array type whose values have no components.

Suppose we declare *s* to be a string variable:

s: *string*

If *s* corresponds to a fixed area of memory, then that memory area must be large enough to hold the longest string that can be assigned to *s*. In order for the language processor to know how much memory to allocate for *s*, we must impose some upper limit on the length of strings that can be assigned to *s*. An upper limit of 80 is often used, and we will assume this limit for the algorithmic language. Thus, type *string* consists of all strings having from 0 to 80 characters.

If the strings with which we are dealing are shorter than 80 characters, we may wish to reserve less memory than would be required to hold an 80-character string. This is particularly true if a large number of strings must be stored, as in an array or file. On the other hand, we may want to allocate more than 80 characters worth of memory to store a particularly long string. To accommodate such requirements, the algorithmic language allows us to specify the maximum length of the strings belonging to a variable-length-string type. Type *string*(10) consists of all strings up to 10 characters long, type *string*(20) consists of all strings up to 20 characters long, and so on.

The integer constant in parentheses is a *parameter value.* When some aspect of a type is specified by a parameter value, we refer to the type as a *parametric type*. If the parameter value is omitted, a default value of 80 is assumed. Thus *string* and *string*(80) refer to the same type.

The types *string*(1), *string*(2), *string*(3), and so on are equivalent in every respect except in the maximum length of the strings. Thus all values of *string*(10) also belong to *string*(20), but the reverse is not true. If we declare *s* and *t* by

> *s*: *string*(10)
>
> *t*: *string*(20)

then the assignment

> *t* ← *s*

is always allowed, since every value of *string*(10) also belongs to *string*(20). But the assignment

> *s* ← *t*

is allowed only if the value of *t* belongs to *string*(10)—if it has no more than 10 characters. If the value of *t* has more than 10 characters, the attempted assignment causes an error.

To provide a uniform notation for strings, character constants and fixed-length-string constants are also used to denote variable-length strings. A constant is converted from type *char* or a fixed-length-string type to a variable-length-string type as required. For example, if *s* is a variable of type *string*, then the assignments

> *s* ← 'c'

and

> *s* ← 'computer'

are both valid. In the first example, the value of 'c' is converted from type *char* to type *string* before being assigned to *s*. In the second example, the value of 'computer' is converted from type **array**[1 **to** 8] **of** *char* to type *string* before being assigned to *s*. The null string, which contains zero characters, is denoted as follows:

> ''

This is *not* a fixed-length-string constant since, as mentioned earlier, there is no such thing as a fixed-length null string.

15.3

Operations on variable-length strings

Comparisons Variable-length strings can be compared with relational operators =, <, >, <=, >=, and <>. If the two strings being compared are the same length, the comparison is the same as for characters or for fixed-length strings. If the strings are of different lengths, they cannot be equal. As usual, alphabetical order determines which string precedes the other. Thus the value of

> 'correspondent' < 'corridor'

is *true* since 'correspondent' precedes 'corridor' in alphabetical order. If one string is equal to the initial part of another, the shorter string precedes the larger. Thus,

'compute' < 'computer'

and

'program' < 'programmer'

both have the value *true*.

Append   We can append, or join, one string to the end of another, a process sometimes called *concatenation* (literally, "chaining together"). The procedure

Append(*s1*, *s2*)

appends the value of string *s2* to the end of string *s1*. *S1* is an input-output parameter; the actual parameter must be a variable, the value of which will be changed by the append operation. *S2* is an input parameter; its value is not changed, and the actual parameter can be a constant or a variable.

For example, after the statements

s ← 'program'
Append(*s*, 'mer')

the value of *s* is 'programmer'. Likewise, after the statements

s ← ''
Append(*s*, 'to')
Append(*s*, 'get')
Append(*s*, 'her')
Append(*s*, 'ness')

the value of *s* is 'togetherness'.

Substring   A substring is a segment of a larger string. We can specify a substring by giving the position of its first character together with the number of characters in the substring. For example, in the string

'programmer'

the substring

'ram'

begins at character 5 of the larger string and is 3 characters long. An alternate method of specifying a substring is to give the positions of its first and last characters. Using this method we could say that the substring 'ram' consists of characters 5 through 7 of 'programmer'.

The procedure

Substring(*s1*, *s2*, *i*, *n*)

extracts a designated substring from string *s2* and assigns it to string variable *s1*. The value of i is the position of the first character of the substring, and the value of n is the number of characters in the substring. Thus after the procedure call

Substring(*s*, 'programmer', 5, 3)

the value of *s* is 'ram'. Likewise, after the procedure call

Substring(*s*, 'concatenate', 4, 3)

the value of *s* is 'cat', and after

Substring(*s*, 'concatenate', 8, 4)

the value of *s* is 'nate'. After the sequence

Substring(*s*, 'concatenate', 8, 4)
Substring(*s*, *s*, 2, 3)

the value of *s* is 'ate'.

Insert   The insert procedure creates a substring by inserting a given string within another string. Specifically, the procedure

Insert(*s1*, *s2*, *i*)

inserts string *s1* before the *i*th character of string *s2*. *S1* is an input parameter; its actual parameter can be a constant or a variable. *S2*, the value of which is changed by the insertion, is an input-output parameter whose actual parameter must be a variable. For example, after the statements

$s \leftarrow$ 'the lazy dog'
Insert('very ', *s*, 5)

the value of *s* is

'the very lazy dog'

If the value of i is one greater than the number of characters in the value of *s2*, the value of *s1* is appended to the end of the value of *s2*. For example, the statements

$s \leftarrow$ 'program'
Insert('mer', *s*, 8)

have the same effect as the statements

$s \leftarrow$ 'program'
Append(*s*, 'mer')

In either case, the final value of *s* is 'programmer'.

Delete   The procedure

Delete(*s*, *i*, *n*)

deletes from the value of the string variable *s* the *n*-character substring beginning at position *i*. For example, after the statements

$s \leftarrow$ 'the quick brown fox'

Delete(*s*, 11, 6)

the value of *s* is

'the quick fox'

Note that the blank following 'brown' is part of the substring to be deleted.

Delete and *Insert* can be used for the common string-processing operation of replacing a substring by another string. For example, the string

'I know, <1>, that you will be interested in our'

might occur in a form letter. Before printing the letter, the placeholder '<1>' is to be replaced by the name of the person to whom the letter is addressed. The following statements do the job:

$s \leftarrow$ 'I know, <1>, that you will be interested in our'

Delete(*s*, 9, 3)

Insert('John', *s*, 9)

After these statements have been executed, the value of *s* is as follows:

'I know, John, that you will be interested in our'

Index and length The function

Index(*s1*, *s2*, *i*)

searches the string *s1* for the first occurrence of a substring equal to string *s2*. The search begins at position *i* in *s1*. If the given substring is found, *Index* returns the position of its first character. If the given substring is not found, *Index* returns the value zero:

Expression	*Value*
Index('computer', 'ter', 1)	6
Index('computer', 'tor', 1)	0
Index('concatenate', 'ate', 1)	5
Index('concatenate', 'ate', 6)	9
Index('concatenate', 'ate', 10)	0

The function

Length(*s*)

returns the number of characters in the string *s*:

Expression	*Value*
Length('concatenate')	11
Length('computer')	8
Length('')	0

Index can be used to locate a substring that is to be replaced. For example, suppose string variables *s*, *t*, and *u* are assigned values as follows:

$s \leftarrow$ 'I know, <1>, that you will be interested in our'

$t \leftarrow$ '<1>'

$u \leftarrow$ 'John'

The following statements substitute the value of *u* for the first occurrence of the value of *t* in the value of *s*:

$i \leftarrow Index(s, t, 1)$

if $i > 0$ **then**

    $Delete(s, i, Length(t))$

    $Insert(u, s, i)$

endif

Skip   In processing a string, we may wish to skip over occurrences of a certain character. Blank spaces are the characters most commonly skipped, since blanks usually have no significance in themselves but serve only to separate significant items such as words and numbers. In the procedure call

$Skip(s, i, c)$

the value of the integer variable *i* designates a position in the string *s*. The procedure call increases the value of *i* until the character at position *i* is not equal to *c*, thus skipping any occurrences of character *c*. For example, after the execution of the statements

$i \leftarrow 4$

$Skip($'xxxyyyyyzzzyyy'$, i,$ 'y'$)$

the value *i* is 9, the position of the first occurrence of 'z'. If we think of the value of *i* as a pointer into the string, then the pointer was moved forward in the string until a character other than 'y' was encountered.

In English text, blanks separate words but are not significant in themselves. A first step in analyzing or processing the text is usually to break it down into individual words. The following statements read a line of text and print the words of which it is composed. The statements will work regardless of the number of blank spaces between the words:

output 'Text? ', **more**

input *s*

$i \leftarrow 1$

while $i <= Length(s)$

    $Skip(s, i,$ ' '$)$

    $j \leftarrow Index(s,$ ' '$, i)$

    if $j = 0$ **then**

        $j = Length(s) + 1$

    endif

if $j > i$ **then**
    $Substring(t, s, i, j - i)$
    output t
endif
$i \leftarrow j$
endwhile

The following illustrates the dialogue with the user that might occur when these statements are executed:

```
Text?    The    quick brown    fox
The
quick
brown
fox
```

The variable i serves as a pointer into the string being scanned. The call to *Skip* moves i forward in the string until the next nonblank character is encountered; i now points to the first character of a word. Variable j is set to point to the next blank following the position pointed to by i; this is the blank that terminates the word whose first character is pointed to by i. If no such blank is found, i points to the beginning of the last word of s. In that case, j is set to point one position beyond the last character of s. The word to be extracted begins at position i and contains $j - i$ characters. The substring of that description is assigned to t by the call to *Substring*; the value of t is then printed by the **output** statement. The value of i is then set to that of j, the position immediately following the word just extracted, and the scan continues.

If blanks extend all the way from position i to the end of s, *Skip* will set the value of i to $Length(s) + 1$, the position following the last character of s. In that case we assume that *Index* will return the value 0, causing j to also be set to $Length(s) + 1$. Since the values of i and j are equal, the statements for extracting and printing a word will not be executed.

Data conversion   Suppose that the value of s is the following string:

    $'$Quantity ordered: 2500$'$

We may wish to extract the number 2500 and carry out numerical processing on it; for example, we might want to multiply it by a unit price to get the total cost of the quantity ordered. The substring operation

    $Substring(t, s, 19, 4)$

extracts the string $'$2500$'$ and assigns it to t. But as far as the computer is concerned, $'$2500$'$ is a string, not a number, and no numerical operations can be carried out on it. To do numerical computations with numbers embedded in strings, we need to convert a string representing a number into the corresponding value of type *integer* or *real*.

The function *StringToInteger* takes as its argument a string representing an integer value and returns the corresponding integer. Any leading blanks—blanks preceding the first character of the integer—are ignored. It is an error if the string does not represent a value of type *integer*. The following table illustrates the function *StringToInteger*:

Expression	Value
StringToInteger('2500')	2500
StringToInteger(' + 2500')	2500
StringToInteger(' − 2500')	− 2500
StringToInteger(' 2500')	2500
StringToInteger('2y500')	error

Likewise, we may need to convert a numerical result to a string, perhaps so that the value can be inserted in the proper position in a line of a report. The procedure

> *IntegerToString*(*s*, *n*)

assigns to string variable *s* the string corresponding to integer *n*. For example, the procedure call

> *IntegerToString*(*s*, − 1000)

assigns the string ' − 1000' to *s*.

Similar procedures can be devised for real numbers. If the value of *s* is a string representing a real number, then the value of *StringToReal*(*s*) is the corresponding value of type *real*. If the value of *x* is a real number, the procedure call

> *RealToString*(*s*, *x*)

assigns the corresponding string to *s*.

Functions and procedures such as these are used to implement the statements for reading from and writing to a text file. For example, when a string representing an integer is read from a text file, *StringToInteger* must be called to convert it to the corresponding integer. When a real number is to be written to a text file, *RealToString* must be called to convert the real number to a sequence of characters that can be stored in the file.

15.4

Implementation considerations

In this section we will look at three common approaches to implementing variable-length strings. In the following section we will employ one of these approaches to write a string-handling module for use in languages such as Pascal that provide little or no support for variable-length strings.

The memory area allocated for a variable-length string will usually be larger than the actual length of the string stored there. We need, then, some way of determining the length of the string, of determining which memory locations hold characters of the string and which are unused. The most obvious way to do this is to store both the length of the string as well as the characters that comprise it. For example, a value of type *string*(10) might be stored as a record with the following form:

record

> *length*: *integer*

> *data*: **array**[1 **to** 10] **of** *char*

endrecord

The value of the *length* field gives the length of the string. If the value of the *length* field is 10, then the string is 10 characters long, and all the components of the *data* field are in use. If the value of the *length* field is 5, then the string is contained in the first five characters of the data field; the remaining five characters are unused and contain garbage. If the value of the *length* field is zero, the record represents the null string, which contains no characters. In that case all the components of the *data* field are unused. Figure 15.1 illustrates this method of representing variable-length strings.

Figure 15.1   Representing a variable-length string by a record with an integer field and an array-of-character field. The integer field holds the length of the string, and the array-of-character field holds the characters comprising the string. The shaded positions of the character array are unused.

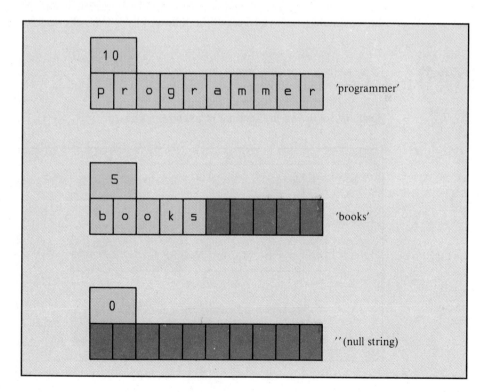

Instead of storing the length of the string as an integer, we can terminate the string with a sentinel character. The ASCII null character, the character with ASCII code zero, is usually used as the sentinel. (Don't confuse the null *character*, which has character code zero, with the null *string*, which has length zero.) With this method, values of type *string*(10) can be stored in an 11-character array of type

array[1 **to** 11] **of** *char*

Up to 10 components of the array can be used for string characters and one component is used for the sentinel. When the string 'computer' is stored, for example, components 1 through 8 of the array contain the characters of the string, component 9 contains the sentinel character, and components 10 and 11 are unused. Figure 15.2 illustrates this method of representing variable-length strings.

This method has the advantage of using a simpler data structure, since only an array is required rather than a record with an integer field and an array field. A disadvantage is that string-processing operations must scan the string for the sentinel character in order to locate the end of the string. When the length is stored as a separate field, no such scan is necessary.

Figure 15.3 illustrates a variation of this method, in which the array has only enough components to store the maximum number of characters in the string. That is, values of type *string*(10) would be stored in a 10-character array of type

array[1 **to** 10] **of** *char*

If the string has the maximum length, then all the components of the array will be used for string characters, and no sentinel will be present. If the string has less than the maximum length, then it will be followed by a sentinel character.

Figure 15.2   Representing a variable-length string by an array of characters. The end of the string is marked by a sentinel character, represented here by the symbol ϕ. The shaded positions following the sentinel character are unused.

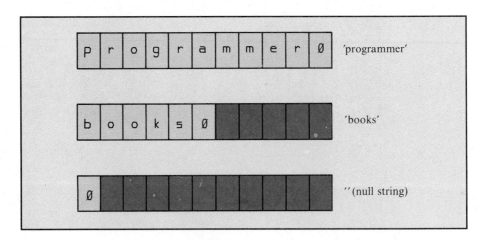

Figure 15.3   In this variation on the representation of Figure 15.2, a variable-length string that is shorter than the character array in which it is stored is terminated by a sentinel character. If the string takes up all the positions in the character array, however, no sentinel character is present.

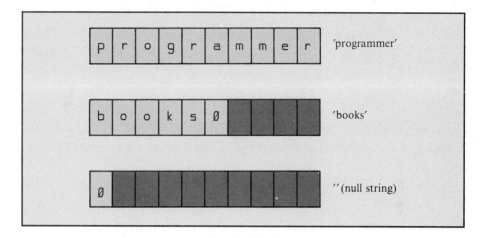

The advantage of this method, aside from saving one array component, is that it unifies fixed-length and variable-length strings. When all the array components are in use, as is always the case for fixed-length strings, then fixed-length and variable-length strings are stored in exactly the same way. When the string being stored has fewer characters than the number of array components, then (and only then) is the last character of the string followed by a sentinel character. The disadvantage of this method is that the statements for locating the end of the string become even more complex, since not only must they scan for the sentinel character, they must also make sure that they do not run off the end of the array if the sentinel character is not present.

Each of the implementation techniques discussed so far requires that enough memory be allocated for the largest possible string that can belong to a given type. In some circumstances, this can result in large amounts of memory being wasted. For example, consider an array of strings, most of which are short but a few of which are much longer than the average. Since all the components of the array must be of the same string type, the longest string will determine how much memory must be allocated to each component. Since most of the strings are short, most of this memory will be wasted.

We can avoid this waste of memory by storing all the strings used by a program in a single array of characters known as *string space*. By allowing all strings to share the same memory area, we do not have to allocate a fixed number of memory locations to each string variable. The value of a string variable is represented not by the characters of the string itself but by a *descriptor* that gives the length of the string and the index of the first character of the string. The string itself is stored in string space. Thus the value of a string variable is a record of the following form:

record

    length: *integer*

    index: *integer*

endrecord

If s is a string variable, and *stringSpace* is the character array in which all strings are stored, then the string corresponding to s is stored in components

    stringSpace[$s.index$]

through

    stringSpace[$s.index + s.length - 1$]

of the character array. Figure 15.4 illustrates this method of implementing variable-length strings.

When a string is assigned to a string variable, the string is stored in the unused area at the end of string space, and the *length* and *index* components of the string variable are modified to refer to the new string. The area of string space occupied by the previous value of the string variable becomes unused. After many assignments have taken place, string space becomes *fragmented*, with used and unused areas intermixed with one another. Although the total size of all the unused areas may be large, no one area may be large enough to hold a particular string that needs to be stored.

When string space becomes fragmented, a procedure called the *garbage collector* is invoked. The garbage collector eliminates the fragmentation by collecting all the strings into a block at the beginning of the array and collecting all the unused areas (the garbage) into another block at the end of the array. Memory for new strings can now be allocated from the block of unused locations at the end of the array. Figure 15.5 illustrates the fragmentation of string space and the effect of garbage collection.

When the garbage collector moves a string, it must appropriately modify the index component of the string variable that refers to that string. In general, the garbage collector has three tasks:

1. Determine which areas of string space are in use, that is, which areas are referred to by string variables.

2. Move each string as far as possible toward the beginning of the array so that all the strings are collected into a single block.

3. Update the index components of the string variables to refer to the new locations of the strings that were moved.

Garbage collection can be time consuming, particularly if it is poorly implemented, as it is in some microcomputer versions of BASIC.

This method of representing strings is one of the best for strings stored in main memory. It is not useful, however, for storing strings in records that are to be written to files. The fields of the records must contain the actual characters of the string,

Figure 15.4 In this representation for variable-length strings, all the strings used by a program are stored in a single character array called *stringSpace*. The value of a string variable is not the characters comprising the string but rather a descriptor giving the length of the string and a pointer to its first character.

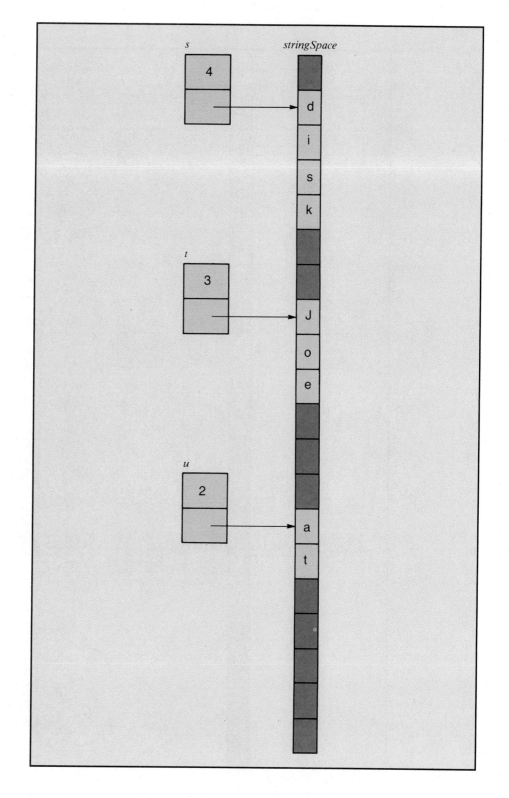

Figure 15.5   Before garbage collection, string space is fragmented; there is no block of unused space in which a 10-character string can be stored, even though the total amount of unused space exceeds 10 characters. Garbage collection collects all the strings in one block and all the unused locations in another, thus making the unused locations available for storing new strings. Note that the pointer components of the string variables must be adjusted to point to the new positions of the strings to which the variables refer.

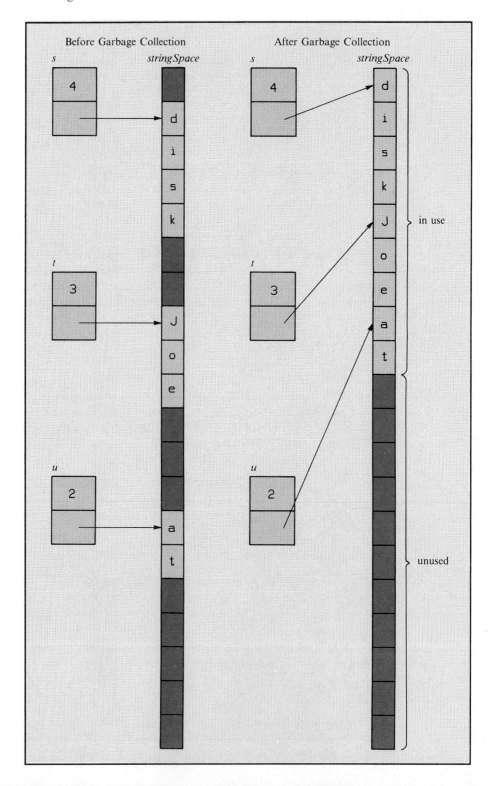

rather than references to a string space in main memory, the contents of which will be lost when the computer is turned off. Other than this, the main disadvantage of the method is the need to occasionally interrupt processing to perform a garbage collection.

15.5 A string-processing module

In this section we will look at one way of implementing variable-length strings in a language that supports only fixed-length strings. Not only does this project show us how the various string-processing operations are implemented, we can use the results to overcome one of the most important limitations of some popular programming languages, such as Pascal. Although our string-processing package will be presented as a module, the individual definitions and declarations can be incorporated individually in programs written in languages that do not provide a module construction.

We assume that the language to be used provides only fixed-length strings, which are implemented as arrays of characters. Structural equivalence is allowed for fixed-length-string types, and character and fixed-length-string constants are provided. On the other hand, no automatic padding or truncation of string values is provided. A string value can be assigned to a string variable only if the number of characters in the value is exactly equal to the number of components of the variable.

Figure 15.6 shows the module *StringType*. The **export** statement lists the constants (*vStringMax* and *fStringLen*), types (*vString*, *fString*, and *textFile*), functions (*Error*, *StringToInteger*, *Length*, *EqualTo*, and *Index*) and procedures (*ReadLine*, *WriteString*, *WriteLine*, *Append*, *Insert*, *Delete*, *Substring*, *Assign*, and *Skip*) exported by the module. Many of the functions and procedures, such as *Length*, *Index*, *Append*, and *Insert*, have already been described and illustrated in a previous section.

The string type defined by this module contains strings with a maximum length of 80 characters. In the absence of parametric types, which are not widely available in popular programming languages, there is no way to let the user select the maximum string length. The maximum string length is represented by the constant *vStringMax*, whose value is defined as 80.

Our module also provides a fixed-length-string type, which is used for small string constants. The procedure *Assign* converts the constant values from fixed-length to variable-length strings. Values of the fixed-length-string type must be long enough to hold the string constants that we are likely to need, but must not be so long that the constant strings will be cumbersome to write. We choose a length of 10 for string constants; this length is defined as the value of the integer constant *fStringLen*.

For the variable-length strings, we will use the representation of Figure 15.1, in which the length of the string is stored separately from the character array. The sentinel-character representation offers no advantages if it is not supported by the language, which we assume not to be the case here. The string-space representation is difficult to implement without support from the language processor since the garbage collector needs to know the locations of all string variables so that it can determine which parts of string space are in use and update the string variables after the strings have been moved.

Figure 15.6   The module *StringType*.

```
module StringType

[ Implement a variable-length-string type ]

declare
    export vStringMax, fStringLen, vString, fString, textFile, Error,
           StringToInteger, Length, EqualTo, Index, ReadLine,
           WriteString, WriteLine, Append, Insert, Delete, Substring,
           Assign, Skip
    const vStringMax = 80
    const fStringLen = 10
    type vString = record
                       length: integer
                       data: array[1 to vStringMax] of char
                   endrecord
    type fString = array[1 to fStringLen] of char
    type textFile = file of char
    errorFlag: Boolean


function error: Boolean

{ Return value of and clear error indicator }

execute
    Error ← errorFlag
    errorFlag ← false
end Error


function StringToInteger(s): integer

{ Convert the string s to the corresponding integer }

declare
    import maxint from system
    s: in vString
    value, limit: real
    j, sign: integer
    c: char
```

```
execute
    limit ← maxint
    value ← 0.0
    sign ← 1
    j ← 1
    Skip(s, j, ' ')
    if j <= s.length then
        c ← s.data[j]
        if c = '+' then
            j ← j + 1
        elseif c = '-' then
            sign ← -1
            j ← j + 1
        endif
    endif
    while (j <= s.length) and (not errorFlag)
        c ← s.data[j]
        if (c < '0') or (c > '9') then
            errorFlag ← true
        else
            value ← 10.0 * value + integer(c) - integer('0')
            if value > limit then
                value ← limit
                errorFlag ← true
            endif
            j ← j + 1
        endif
    endwhile
    StringToInteger ← sign * round(value)
end StringToInteger


function Length(s): integer         •

{ Return the length of string s }

declare
    s: in vString
execute
    errorFlag ← false
    Length ← s.length
end Length
```

```
function EqualTo(s1, s2): Boolean

{ Return true if the values of s1 and s2 are equal }

declare
    s1, s2: in vString
    j: integer
    equal: Boolean
execute
    errorFlag ← false
    if s1.length <> s2.length then
        equal ← false
    else
        equal ← true
        j ← 1
        while (j <= s1.length) and equal
            if s1.data[j] <> s2.data[j] then
                equal ← false
            endif
            j ← j + 1
        endwhile
    endif
    EqualTo ← equal
end EqualTo


function Index(s1, s2, i): integer

{ Return the position of the first occurrence of s2 in the part of s1
  beginning at position i. Return zero if no such occurrence is found }

declare
    s1, s2: in vString
    i: in integer
    j, k, m: integer
    found: Boolean
execute
    j ← i
    k ← s1.length − s2.length + 1
    if (j < 1) or (j > k) then
        errorFlag ← true
        Index ← 0
    else
        errorFlag ← false
```

```
        repeat
            found ← true
            m ← 1
            while (m <= s2.length) and found
                if s1.data[j + m − 1] <> s2.data[m] then
                    found ← false
                endif
                m ← m + 1
            endwhile
            j ← j + 1
        until (j > k) or found
        if found then
            Index ← j − 1
        else
            Index ← 0
        endif
    endif
end Index


procedure ReadLine(f, s)

{ Read a line from text file f and assign line read to s }

declare
    f: in out textFile
    s: out vString
    j: integer
    c: char
execute
    if EndFileP(f) then
        errorFlag ← true
        s.length ← 0
    else
        errorFlag ← false
        j ← 1
        while (j <= vStringMax) and (not EndLineP(f)) and
                (not EndFileP(f))
            input c, more from f
            s.data[j] ← c
            j ← j + 1
        endwhile
        s.length ← j − 1
    endif
```

```
            if not EndFileP(f) then
                input from f
            endif
        end ReadLine


        procedure WriteString(f, s)

        { Write string s to text file f; do not terminate line }

        declare
            f: in out textFile
            s: in vString
            j: integer
        execute
            errorFlag ← false
            for j ← 1 to s.length
                output s.data[j], more to f
            endfor
        end WriteString


        procedure Writeline(f, s)

        { Write string s to text file f; terminate line }

        declare
            f: in out textFile
            s: in vString
        execute
            WriteString(f, s)
            output to f
        end WriteLine


        procedure Append(s1, s2)

        { Append string s2 to the end of string s1 }

        declare
            s1: in out vString
            s2: in vString
            j, k: integer
```

```
execute
    if s1.length + s2.length > vStringMax then
        errorFlag ← true
    else
        errorFlag ← false
        j ← s1.length + 1
        for k ← 1 to s2.length
            s1.data[j] ← s2.data[k]
            j ← j + 1
        endfor
        s1.length ← s1.length + s2.length
    endif
end Append


procedure Insert(s1, s2, i)

{ Insert string s1 into string s2 before position i. If i equals
  Length(s2) + 1, append s1 to s2 }

declare
    s1: in vString
    s2: in out vString
    i: in integer
    j, k: integer
execute
    if (i < 1) or (i > s2.length + 1) or
       (s1.length + s2.length > vStringMax) then
        errorFlag ← true
    else
        errorFlag ← false
        j ← s2.length
        k ← s1.length + s2,length
        while j >= i
            s2.data[k] ← s2.data[j]
            j ← j - 1
            k ← k - 1
        endfor
        j ← i
        for k ← 1 to s1.length
            s2.data[j] ← s1.data[k]
            j ← j + 1
        endfor
        s2.length ← s1.length + s2.length
```

```
        endif
    end Insert


    procedure Delete(s, i, n)

    { Delete n characters from string s starting at position i }

    declare
        s: in out vString
        i, n: in integer
        j, k: integer
    execute
        if (i < 1) or (i + n − 1 > s.length) or (n < 0) then
            errorFlag ← true
        else
            errorFlag ← false
            j ← i
            k ← i + n
            while k <= s.length
                s.data[j] ← s.data[k]
                j ← j + 1
                k ← k + 1
            endwhile
            s.length ← s.length − n
        endif
    end Delete


    procedure Substring(s1, s2, i, n)

    { Assign to s1 the substring of length n beginning at position i in
      string s2 }

    declare
        s1: out vString
        s2: in vString
        i, n: in integer
        j, k: integer
    execute
        if (i < 1) or (i + n − 1 > s2.length) or (n < 0) then
            errorFlag ← true
```

```
        else
            errorFlag ← false
            s1.length ← n
            j ← i
            for k ← 1 to n
                s1.data[k] ← s2.data[j]
                j ← j + 1
            endfor
        endif
end Substring


procedure Assign(s1, s2, n)

{ Assign the first n characters of array s2 to string s1 }

declare
    s1: out vString
    s2: in fString
    n: in integer
    j: integer
execute
    if (n < 0) or (n > fStringLen) then
        errorFlag ← true
    else
        errorFlag ← false
        s1.length ← n
        for j ← 1 to n
            s1.data[j] ← s2[j]
        endfor
    endif
end Assign


procedure Skip(s, i, c)

{ Increment i while the character at position i in string s equals c }

declare
    s: in vString
    i: in out integer
    c: in char
    skipping: Boolean
```

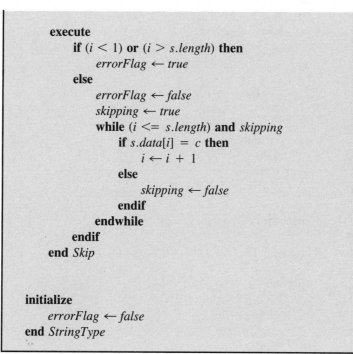

```
        execute
            if (i < 1) or (i > s.length) then
                errorFlag ← true
            else
                errorFlag ← false
                skipping ← true
                while (i <= s.length) and skipping
                    if s.data[i] = c then
                        i ← i + 1
                    else
                        skipping ← false
                    endif
                endwhile
            endif
        end Skip


initialize
    errorFlag ← false
end StringType
```

The variable-length-string type *vString* is defined as follows:

type *vString* = **record**

        length: *integer*

        data: **array**[1 **to** *vStringMax*] **of** *char*

    endrecord

The *length* field holds the length of the string; the *data* field holds the characters comprising the string.

The fixed-length-string type used for string constants is defined as follows:

type *fString* = **array**[1 **to** *fStringLen*] **of** *char*

Since the value of *fStringLen* is 10, every value of type *fString* must contain 10 characters. Thus every string constant must be 10 characters long, regardless of how many characters are actually to be used.

The type identifier *textFile* is used to assure that actual and formal file parameters have the same type:

type *textFile* = **file of** *char*

The variable *errorFlag* is set to *true* or *false* depending on whether or not the immediately preceding string operation was valid. One error flag serves for all strings; we do not incorporate a separate error flag in each string value, as we did for stacks and queues in Chapter 14. One reason for this difference is that stacks and queues are treated as *objects*; each retains its identity throughout processing. Strings, on the other hand, are treated as *values*; we are only interested in the result of a string computation, not in the individual strings that were used as data for the computation.

In the remainder of this section, we will look at each of the functions and procedures provided by module *StringType*.

Error   As usual, the function *Error* returns the value of the error flag and clears the error flag to *false*.

StringToInteger   This function converts a string to the integer value that it represents. The function call is invalid if the string does not represent an integer value. The companion procedure *IntegerToString* is left as an exercise. Ambitious students may also wish to tackle the much more complex function *StringToReal* and procedure *RealToString*.

The value represented by the string may exceed the largest permissible integer value. In that case, attempting to convert the string to an integer will lead to *integer overflow*—exceeding the largest value allowed for type *integer*. To detect integer overflow, we import from the system module the constant *maxint,* whose value is the largest permissible integer value. To prevent integer overflow from occurring unexpectedly during the computations, the value represented by the string is computed as a value of type *real* and then coverted to type *integer* if it lies in the range allowed for integer values.

The value of the input parameter *s* is the string value to be converted. During conversion, the real variable *value* holds the value of that part of the string that has already been converted. The real variable *limit* holds the real number corresponding to the largest possible integer, *maxint*. An error occurs if the value of *value* exceeds that of *limit*. The integer variable *j* is used as a pointer into the string being converted. The integer variable *sign* is set to 1 if a positive number is being converted and to -1 if a negative number is being converted. The character variable *c* holds the next string character to be processed.

To begin, *limit* is set to the largest value allowed for the result of the conversion; *value* is initialized to 0.0; *sign* is initialized to 1 (a positive number is the default if no sign character is encountered); and *j* is set to point to the first character of the string to be converted. The procedure *Skip* (defined later in the module) is called to skip any leading blanks:

> $limit \leftarrow maxint$
> $value \leftarrow 0.0$
> $sign \leftarrow 1$
> $j \leftarrow 1$
> $Skip(s, j, ' ')$

The call to *Skip* also initializes *errorFlag* to *false,* since an error cannot occur while skipping.

The variable c is set to the first nonblank character of s. If this character is a plus sign, it is skipped (*sign* has already been initialized to 1). If the character is a minus sign, it is skipped and *sign* is set to -1:

if $j <=$ *s.length* **then**
    $c \leftarrow$ *s.data*[j]
    if $c = '+'$ **then**
        $j \leftarrow j + 1$
    elseif $c = '-'$ **then**
        sign $\leftarrow -1$
        $j \leftarrow j + 1$
    endif
endif

The **while** construction scans the string to be converted as long as we have not run off the end of the string and no error has occurred. The variable c is set to the next character of the string being converted. If this character is not a digit—if it does not lie in the range $'0'$ through $'9'$—then *errorFlag* is set to *true*. Otherwise, the digit represented by the value of c is incorporated into the converted value.

In processing characters, it is often necessary to convert between the characters and their integer character codes. We will use predefined functions named *char* and *integer* for this purpose. The function *char* converts a character code to the corresponding character; the function *integer* converts a character to the corresponding integer character code. In the following examples, the ASCII character code is assumed:

Expression	Value	Expression	Value
integer($'A'$)	65	*char*(65)	$'A'$
integer($'0'$)	48	*char*(48)	$'0'$
integer($'5'$)	53	*char*(53)	$'5'$
integer($'9'$)	57	*char*(57)	$'9'$

We use the expression

integer(c) $-$ *integer*($'0'$)

to convert the digit c into the corresponding integer. For example, if the value of c is $'5'$, we have

integer($'5'$) $-$ *integer*($'0'$) $= 53 - 48 = 5$

If the value of c is $'9'$, we have

integer($'9'$) $-$ *integer*($'0'$) $= 57 - 48 = 9$

and so on.

To incorporate a new digit into the part of the number that has already been converted, we multiply *value* by 10 and add the value of the new digit:

$$value \leftarrow 10.0 * value + integer(c) - integer('0')$$

To see how this statement works, suppose that the string to be converted is $'27534'$. Assume that the digits 2, 7, and 5 have already been processed, so that the next digit to be processed is 3. The value of *value* is 275, the part of the number that has already been converted, and the value of c is $'3'$, the next digit to be processed. The above statement is executed as follows:

$$value \leftarrow 10.0 * value + integer(c) - integer('0')$$
$$value \leftarrow 10 * 275.0 + integer('3') - integer('0)$$
$$value \leftarrow 2750.0 + 51 - 48$$
$$value \leftarrow 2750.0 + 3$$
$$value \leftarrow 2753.0$$

Thus the value of the digit $'3'$ is incorporated into the converted value.

After each new digit is incorporated into the converted value, that value is checked to see if it exceeds the value of *limit*. If it does, the value being converted is too large to be represented by a value of type *integer*. *Value* is set to the value of the largest permissible integer, and *errorFlag* is set to *true*.

When the repetition terminates, we need only to change the converted value from a real number to an integer, multiply it by the value of *sign*, and return it as the value of *StringToInteger*:

$$StringToInteger \leftarrow sign * round(value)$$

As long as the maximum number of significant digits for a real number has not been exceeded, our calculations should be exact and the value of *value* should be a whole number. Thus we could, in principle, use either *trunc* or *round* to convert the real number to an integer. In practice, using *round* will help compensate for any small inaccuracies resulting from bugs in the system procedures for real-number arithmetic. If these system procedures are too inaccurate, the method described here will give incorrect results and cannot be used.

Length   The function *Length(s)* clears the error flag and returns the length of string s. Note that in the statement

$$Length \leftarrow s.length$$

the field identifier *length* cannot be confused with the function name *Length*, even if the language does not distinguish between uppercase and lowercase letters. Since *length* is preceded by a period, it must refer to the field identifier; since *Length* is not preceded by a period, it must refer to the function name.

EqualTo   The function *EqualTo(s1, s2)* returns *true* if strings *s1* and *s2* are equal and *false* otherwise. *EqualTo* plays the same role for variable-length strings as the relational operator = does for fixed-length strings. The = operator cannot be used for variable-length strings since it would compare all the array components of the string values being compared. But only the array components that are in use need agree in order for two string values to be equal. The unused array components can contain arbitrary values. It is left as an exercise to write the companion functions *LessThan* and *GreaterThan* corresponding to the relational operators < and >.

The Boolean variable *equal* is set to *false* as soon as it is discovered that the two strings are not equal. When processing has been completed, the value of *equal* is returned as the value of *EqualTo*. The function begins by comparing the lengths of strings *s1* and *s2*; if the two strings have different lengths, they cannot possibly be equal, so *equal* is set to *false*.

If the two strings have the same length, *equal* is set to *true*, the pointer *j* is set to the first character of the two strings, and the two strings are scanned from left to right. The scan continues while more characters remain to be scanned ($j <= s1.length$) and the value of *equal* remains *true*.

At each step of the scan, the values of the *j*th characters in each of the two strings are compared. If the two *j*th characters are not the same, *equal* is set to *false*, terminating the scan and causing the value *false* to be returned as the value of *EqualTo*:

> **if** $s1.data[j] <> s2.data[j]$ **then**
>> *equal* ← *false*
>
> **endif**

When processing terminates, the value of *equal* will be *true* only if no discrepancy was found between the two strings (if they have the same length and their corresponding characters are equal). Thus the final value of *equal* is returned as the value of *EqualTo*. Notice that the statements are arranged so as to terminate processing as soon as a descrepancy between the strings is found. This allows unequal strings to be detected quickly. The funtion does not waste its time completely scanning long strings that have different lengths or that differ in their first few characters.

Another approach to string comparison is to modify the procedures *ReadLine*, *Delete*, *Substring*, and *Assign* to store a given character—say the ASCII null character, *char*(0)—in all unused positions of the character array. Variable-length strings could then be compared by applying the fixed-length string operators =, <, >, <=, >=, and <> to the corresponding data arrays. That is, *s1* would be equal to *s2* only if the value of

> $s1.data = s2.data$

were *true*.

Index Starting at position *i* in *s1*, *Index* must search for a substring equal to the value of *s2*. As shown in Figure 15.7, we can think of *s2* as being laid parallel to *s1* with the first character of *s2* beneath the *i*th character of *s1*. Each character in *s2* is compared with the character immediately above it in *s1*. If all characters agree, the desired substring has been found, and the search terminates. Otherwise, *s2* is moved forward one character and the comparison is repeated. If the desired substring is not found, the search terminates when the last character of *s2* is beneath the last character of *s1*.

The index *j* points to the character in *s1* beneath which the first character in *s2* is placed. The initial value of *j* is *i*, the position in *s1* at which the search is to start.

Figure 15.7   We can think of *Index* as sliding the string *s2* along the
                    string *s1* one character at a time, checking in each position
                    whether every character in *s2* equals the corresponding
                    character in *s1*. Initially, the first character of *s2* coincides
                    with the *i*th character of *s1*. The search terminates
                    unsuccessfully if the last character of *s2* moves beyond the
                    last character of *s1*.

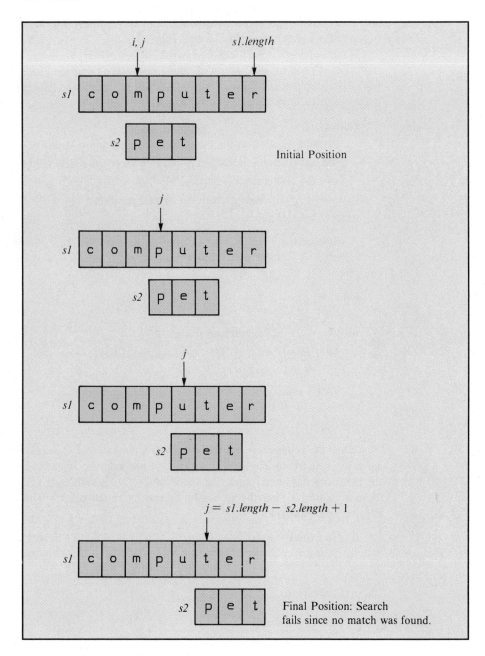

The final value of j is k, the position of the first character of *s2* when the last character of *s2* coincides with the last character of *s1* (see the bottom diagram in Figure 15.7). The value of k is set by

$$k \leftarrow s1.length - s2.length + 1$$

If the initial value of j is less than 1 or greater than the value of k, then the requested search cannot be carried out. In that case *errorFlag* is set to *true* and the value 0 is returned by *Index*. Since the value 0 corresponds to "substring not found," it will be possible in some circumstances to rely entirely on the value returned by *Index* and not check the value of *errorFlag*.

If the requested search can be carried out, *errorFlag* is set to *false* and a **repeat** statement is used to slide string *s2* along string *s1*, comparing the characters of *s2* with the corresponding characters of *s1* at each position. The flag *found* is set to *true* if the comparison is successful and *false* otherwise:

repeat
    "Compare *s2* with the substring of *s1* beginning at position j and having the same length as *s2*. Set *found* to *true* or *false* depending on whether or not the comparison is successful."
    $j \leftarrow j + 1$ { Slide *s2* forward by one position }
until $(j > k)$ **or** *found*

A **while** construction is used to compare *s2* with the corresponding substring of *s1*. Variable m is used as an index into *s2*; the character at position m in *s2* is compared with the character at position $j + m - 1$ in *s1*:

found $\leftarrow$ *true*
$m \leftarrow 1$
while $(m <= s2.length)$ **and** *found*
    if $s1.data[j + m - 1] <> s2.data[m]$ **then**
        found $\leftarrow$ *false*
    endif
    $m \leftarrow m + 1$
endwhile

When the **repeat** construction terminates, the value of *found* is *true* if the desired substring was found and *false* otherwise. If the value of *found* is *true*, the index of the substring that was found, the value of $j - 1$, is returned. (The value of j was incremented by 1 after the successful comparison took place.) If the value of *found* is *false*, 0 is returned:

if *found* **then**
    Index $\leftarrow j - 1$
else
    Index $\leftarrow 0$
endif

ReadLine *ReadLine(f, s)* reads a line from file *f* and assigns it to the string variable *s*. File *f* is of type *textFile* and is assumed to be opened in mode **text input**. We make the following assumptions about the file *f*:

1. Each line in *f* is terminated by a single end-of-line character, the value of which is immaterial.

2. If *c* is a character variable, the **input** statement

   input *c*, **more from** *f*

   reads a single character from *f* and advances the current position of *f* to the next character.

3. The **input** statement with an empty variable list

   input from *f*

   advances the current position of *f* to the beginning of the next line.

4. There is a predefined Boolean function, *EndLineP(f)*, that returns *true* when the current position of *f* is at an end-of-line character and *false* otherwise.

5. The predefined Boolean function *EndFileP(f)* returns *true* when the current position of *f* is the end-of-file position and *false* otherwise.

With these assumptions, which are consistent with our previous discussions of text files, we implement *ReadLine* as shown in Figure 15.6. If the end of file *f* has already been reached, *errorFlag* is set to *true*; otherwise, *errorFlag* is set to *false* and the next line from file *f* is read into *s*. Variable *j* is used as an index into the character array of string variable *s*. Characters are read from file *f* and stored in *s.data* as long as no more than *vStringMax* characters have been stored, the end of the line has not been reached, and the end of the file has not been reached:

$$j \leftarrow 1$$
while ($j <=$ *vStringMax*) **and** (**not** *EndLineP(f)*) **and**
    (**not** *EndFileP(f)*)
    input *c*, **more from** *f*
    $s.data[j] \leftarrow c$
    $j \leftarrow j + 1$
endwhile

When the repetition terminates, the length of the newly read string is set to the value of $j - 1$, since the value of *j* was incremented by 1 after the last character was read. If the end of the file has not been reached, the statement

input from *f*

is then executed to move the current position of file *f* to the beginning of the next line. Note that if the line read contained more than *vStringMax* characters, the excess characters were discarded.

WriteString and WriteLine.   The procedure *WriteString(f, s)* writes the characters of string *s* to the file *f*, which is assumed to be of type *textFile* and opened with mode **text output**. The current line is not terminated after the characters are written. The procedure *WriteLine(f, s)* calls *WriteString(f, s)* to write the characters of string *s* to file *f*, then executes

output to *f*

to terminate the current line. The code for the two procedures is straightforward.

Append   The procedure *Append(s1, s2)* appends string *s2* to the end of string *s1*. The value of the input-output parameter *s1* is modified by the operation; the value of the input parameter *s2* is not changed.

The length of the string resulting from the append operation is the sum of the lengths of *s1* and *s2*. If this sum exceeds *vStringMax*, *errorFlag* is set to *true*. Otherwise, *errorFlag* is set to *false* and the characters of *s2.data* are copied into *s1.data* immediately following the characters of string *s1*:

$j \leftarrow s1.length + 1$
for $k \leftarrow 1$ **to** *s2.length*
$\quad$ $s1.data[j] \leftarrow s2.data[k]$
$\quad$ $j \leftarrow j + 1$
endfor

The new length of *s1* is set to the old length of *s1* plus the length of *s2*:

$s1.length \leftarrow s1.length + s2.length$

Insert   The procedure *Insert(s1, s2, i)* inserts string *s1* into string *s2* immediately preceding the character pointed to by *i*. Only the value of the input-output parameter *s2* is changed by the operation. The value of *i* can be one greater than the length of *s2*, in which case the value of *s1* is appended to that of *s2*.

The call to *Insert* is invalid if the value of *i* is less than 1 or greater than *s2.length* + 1, or if the sum of the lengths of *s1* and *s2* is greater than *vStringMax*. If the call to *Insert* is invalid, *errorFlag* is set to *true*.

If the call to *Insert* is valid, *errorFlag* is set to *false* and the insertion is carried out. As shown in Figure 15.8, the insertion consists of two steps. First, those characters of *s2* that follow the point of insertion must be moved forward to make room for the characters to be inserted. Second, the characters of *s1* must be copied into the gap thus created in *s2*.

To move a block of values forward in an array, copying must proceed from the end to the beginning of the block of values to be moved. If we started copying at the beginning of the block, some of the moved values might overwrite values of the original block that have not yet been moved. The block of characters to be moved forward in *s2* extends from position *i* to position *s2.length*. After the block has been moved, its end will be at position *s1.length* + *s2.length*, the last position of *s2* after the insertion has been made. Index *j* points to the position from which a character

Figure 15.8   Inserting one string into another involves two steps. First, the characters following the point of insertion must be moved to the right to make room for the string to be inserted. Second, the characters of the string to be inserted must be copied into the gap thus created in the original string.

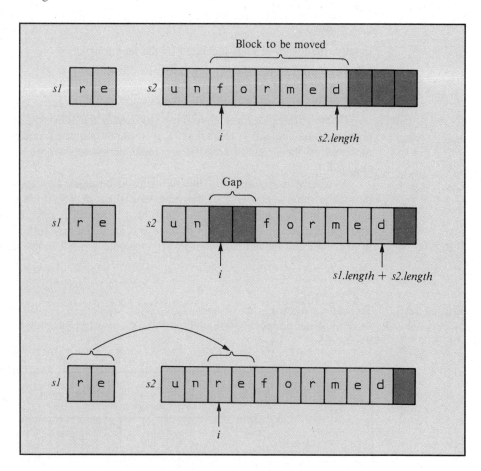

will be moved, and index k points to the position to which the character will be moved:

$$j \leftarrow s2.length$$
$$k \leftarrow s1.length + s2.length$$
while $j >= i$
    $s2.data[k] \leftarrow s2.data[j]$
    $j \leftarrow j - 1$
    $k \leftarrow k - 1$
endwhile

The characters of *s1* must now be copied into the gap created in *s2*. The gap begins at position *i* and its length is equal to *s1.length*:

$j \leftarrow i$
for $k \leftarrow 1$ **to** *s1.length*
    $s2.data[j] \leftarrow s1.data[k]$
    $j \leftarrow j + 1$
endfor

Finally, the length of *s2* is increased by the length of *s1*:

$s2.length \leftarrow s1.length + s2.length$

Delete The procedure *Delete(s, i, n)* deletes the substring of *s* that begins at position *i* and contains *n* characters. *S* is an input-output parameter whose value is modified by the deletion; *i* and *n* are input parameters whose values remain unchanged.

As shown in Figure 15.9, the substring to be deleted extends from position *i* through position $i + n - 1$. If the value of *i* is less than 1, if the value of $i + n - 1$ is greater than *s.length*, or if the value of *n* is less than zero, *errorFlag* is set to *true*. Otherwise, *errorFlag* is set to *false* and the characters following the substring to be deleted are moved backward in *s* to close the gap left by the deleted substring.

Figure 15.9   To delete a substring, the characters following the deleted substring must be moved to the left to close the gap left by the deletion.

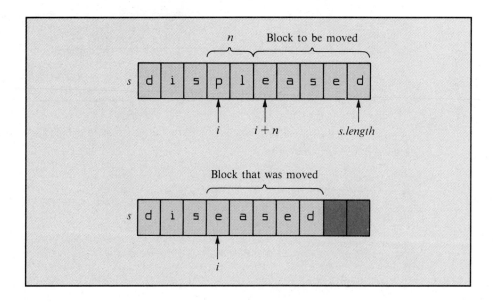

To move a block of values backward in an array, copying must proceed from the beginning to the end of the block of values to be moved. If we started copying at the end of the block, some of the moved values might overwrite values of the original block that have not yet been moved. The block of characters to be moved in *s* extends from position $i + n$ to position *s.length*. This block is to be moved so that it begins at position *i*, the beginning of the gap to be filled.

During copying, we use *j* to point to a position in which a character is to be stored and *k* to point to a position from which a character is to be obtained. Initially, *j* is set to *i*, the first position of the gap to be filled, and *k* is set to $i + n$, the position of the first character in the block to be moved. Copying continues as long as the value of *k* is less than or equal to *s.length*, the position of the last character in the block to be moved:

$j \leftarrow i$

$k \leftarrow i + n$

while $k <= s.length$

    $s.data[j] \leftarrow s.data[k]$

    $j \leftarrow j + 1$

    $k \leftarrow k + 1$

endwhile

After the copying has been completed, the length of *s* is reduced by *n*, the number of characters that were deleted:

$s.length \leftarrow s.length - n$

Substring   The procedure *Substring(s1, s2, i, n)* assigns to *s1* the substring of *s2* that begins at position *i* and contains *n* characters. The output parameter *s1* is assigned the specified substring; the values of the input parameters *s2*, *i*, and *n* are not changed.

As with *Delete*, the specified substring extends from position *i* through position $i + n - 1$ of *s2*. If the condition

$(i < 1)$ **or** $(i + n - 1 > s2.length)$ **or** $(n < 0)$

is true, the call is invalid and *errorFlag* is set to *true*. Otherwise, *errorFlag* is set to *false* and the specified substring is assigned to *s1*.

The length of *s1* is set to *n*, the number of characters to be copied. Variable *j* points to the next character of *s2* to be copied; initially *j* is set to *i*, the position of the first character of the specified substring. Variable *k* points to the next position of *s1* in which a character is to be placed; the value of *k* varies from 1 to *n*:

$s1.length \leftarrow n$

$j \leftarrow i$

for $k \leftarrow 1$ **to** n

    $s1.data[k] \leftarrow s2.data[j]$

    $j \leftarrow j + 1$

endfor

Assign   The procedure *Assign(s1, s2, n)* assigns the first *n* characters of the fixed-length string *s2* to the variable-length-string variable *s1*. The purpose of *Assign* is to convert fixed-length-string constants into variable-length strings, thus allowing the string constants built into the programming language to be used to provide data for variable-length-string operations.

Parameter *s2* is of type *fString*, the type of all fixed-length strings of length *fStringLen*. Because of structural equivalence for fixed-length-string types, any fixed-length-string constant with *fStringLen* characters can be an actual parameter corresponding to *s2*. The value of 10 was chosen for *fStringLen* so that the fixed-length-string constants would be large enough to hold most constant strings of interest yet small enough not to be burdensome to write, since each constant must contain *fStringLen* characters regardless of how many characters are to be actually used. In the following examples, number signs are used to pad each fixed-length-string constant to 10 characters; in no case are any of the number signs assigned to the string variables *s*, *t*, *u*, and *v*:

Assign(s, 'list######', 4)
Assign(t, 'Error No:#', 9)
Assign(u, 'Y#########', 1)
Assign(v, '##########', 0)

Variable *v* is assigned the null string.

Implementation of *Assign* is straightforward. If *n* is less than zero or greater than *fStringLen*, then *errorFlag* is set to *true*. Otherwise, *errorFlag* is set to *false* and the specified number of characters of *s2* is assigned to *s1*:

```
s1.length ← n
for j ← 1 to n
    s1.data[j] ← s2[j]
endfor
```

We assume that *fStringLen* is less than or equal to *vStringMax*, since a larger value for *fStringLen* would be senseless.

Skip   The procedure *Skip(s, i, c)* increments the value of *i* as long as the character of *s* pointed to by *i* is equal to *c*. The value of the input-output parameter *i* is modified as described; the values of the input parameters *s* and *c* remain unchanged.

If the initial value of *i* is less than 1 or greater than *s.length*, then *errorFlag* is set to *true*. Otherwise, *errorFlag* is set to *false* and the value of *i* is incremented until a character not equal to *c* is encountered or until the scan runs off the end of the string (the value of *i* is equal to *s.length* + 1). The Boolean variable *skipping* is initially *true* and is set to *false* when a character not equal to the value of *c* is encountered:

```
skipping ← true
while (i <= s.length) and skipping
    if s.data[j] = c then
        i ← i + 1
```

```
        else
            skipping ← false
        endif
    endwhile
```

Substitution for parameters

One of the most important and widely used applications of string processing is *substitution for parameters*. A piece of text from which copies are to be made contains placeholder symbols called *parameters*. For each copy that is made, given strings—the *parameter values*—are substituted for the parameters. A different set of parameter values can be used for each copy. Thus the original text can be customized for different purposes by substituting different strings for the parameters.

A common application of this technique is personalizing a form letter by inserting personal data pertaining to the individual to whom the letter is addressed. For example, the following master copy of a sales letter contains two parameters, denoted <1> and <2>:

Dear <1>,

As a person who needs to stay well informed, you <1>, cannot afford to be without a subscription to YESTERDAY'S NEWS. If you subscribe, then as you walk down the main street of <2> people will say, 'There goes <1>, the best informed person in <2>.' Wouldn't you like that? Please, <1>, send me your subscription to YESTERDAY'S NEWS right away.

J. S. Hardsell
Circulation Manager

In each copy of the letter, <1> is replaced by the name of the person to whom the letter is addressed, and <2> is replaced by the city in which that person resides. For example, the copy sent to John, who resides in Peoria, looks like this:

Dear John,

As a person who needs to stay well informed, you John, cannot afford to be without a subscription to YESTERDAY'S NEWS. If you subscribe, then as you walk down the main street of Peoria people will say, 'There goes John, the best informed person in Peoria.' Wouldn't you like that? Please, John, send me your subscription to YESTERDAY'S NEWS right away.

J. S. Hardsell
Circulation Manager

Parameter substitution also has applications in programming. For example, most assembly languages and some higher-level languages allow programmers to define *macroinstructions* or *macros*. Each macro is defined as a sequence of instructions. Whenever a macro is invoked, the sequence of instructions given in the macro definition is assembled or complied. The macro definition can contain parameters, the values for which are provided when the macro is invoked. This allows, for example, each invocation of a macro to refer to different memory locations and use different constant values.

For example, the following assembly-language instructions add 1 to the contents of the memory location named DATA:

```
LDA DATA
ADD 1
STA DATA
```

Suppose that instruction sequences similar to this one occur frequently in a program, but different sequences refer to different memory locations and add different constant values. We can define the macro ADDMEM as follows:

```
ADDMEM MACRO &LOC, &CONST
       LDA &LOC
       ADD &CONST
       STA &LOC
       ENDMACRO
```

Here &LOC and &CONST are the parameters; &LOC represents the memory location to be affected, and &CONST represents the constant value to be added. Whenever we invoke the macro, we specify the values to be substituted for &LOC and &CONST. For example, the assembly-language instruction

```
       ADDMEM COUNT, 5
```

causes the following code to be assembled:

```
       LDA COUNT
       ADD 5
       STA COUNT
```

Likewise, the assembly-language instruction

```
       ADDMEM SIZE, 4
```

causes the following code to be assembled:

```
       LDA SIZE
       ADD 4
       STA SIZE
```

There exist programming languages in which almost all computation is done by substituting for parameters in macros. Macros play the same role in these languages that functions and procedures play in more conventional languages. Although such macro langauges are extremely powerful, execution of programs is slow because of the large amount of string processing that must be carried out.

Many operating systems allow macro commands to be defined. For example, suppose we wish to compile, link, and execute a higher-level language source program stored in the file PROG.SRC. The first step might be to compile the program and store the resulting object program in a file PROG.OBJ, which we do with the following system command:

```
COMPILE PROG.SRC, PROG.OBJ
```

Next, the object program must be linked with functions and procedures from the program library and the resulting executable program stored in the file PROG.EXE. This is accomplished with the following system command:

```
LINK PROG.OBJ, PROG.EXE
```

Finally, we wish to run the executable program, which we do by using the name of the file containing the executable program (without the extension .EXE) as a system command:

```
PROG
```

We can define a macro command RUN to carry out these three steps:

```
COMPILE &1.SRC, &1.OBJ
LINK &1.OBJ, &1.EXE
&1
```

Here &1 is the parameter. If we issue the system command

```
RUN PROG
```

then the steps of the macro command will be carried out with PROG substituted for &1, causing the program in file PROG.SRC to be compiled, linked, and executed.

Figure 15.10 shows the algorithm *FormLetter*, which illustrates not only substitution for parameters but the use of the string-processing module described in the previous section. The program assumes that the master copy of a form letter is contained in the file *letterFile*. The master copy can contain up to 25 parameters, which are denoted $<1>$, $<2>$, $<3>$, and so on. The parameter values are contained in the file *parameterFile*. Each parameter value is on a separate line, and each set of parameters is followed by the sentinel $$END$$. Thus, the parameter file

```
John
Peoria
$$END$$
Sally
Durham
$$END$$
Larry
Austin
$$END$$
```

causes three copies of the form letter to be printed. In the first copy, John is substituted for $<1>$ and Peoria is substituted for $<2>$. In the second copy, Sally is substituted for $<1>$ and Durham is substituted for $<2>$, and so on. The copies are stored in the file *outputFile*.

Figure 15.10 The algorithm *FormLetter*.

```
algorithm FormLetter

{ Print copies of form letter in letter file. For each copy, replace
  parameters by strings from parameter file }

declare
    import textFile, vString, Assign, ReadLine, EqualTo, Index,
           Substring, StringToInteger, Error, Insert, Delete, WriteLine
           from StringType
    const maxParameter = 25
    letterFile, parameterFile, outputFile: textFile
    s, t, sentinel, leftBracket, rightBracket: vString
    pVal: array[1 to maxParameter] of vString
    i, j, k, pEnd: integer
execute
    Assign(sentinel, '$$END$$###', 7)
    Assign(leftBracket, '<#########', 1)
    Assign(rightBracket, '>#########', 1)
    open parameterFile as 'parms.text' mode text input
    open outputFile as 'copies.text' mode text output
    while not EndFileP(parameterFile)

        { Read parameter values }

        i ← 1
        ReadLine(parameterFile, s)
        while (i <= maxParameter) and
            (not EqualTo(s, sentinel))
            pVal[i] ← s
            i ← i + 1
            ReadLine(parameterFile, s)
        endwhile
        pEnd ← i - 1
        while not EqualTo(s, sentinel)
            ReadLine(parameterFile, s)
        endwhile
```

```
                { Print copy of letter }

                open letterFile as 'letter.text' mode text input
                while not EndFileP(letterFile)
                    ReadLine(letterFile, s)
                    j ← Index(s, leftBracket, 1)
                    while j > 0
                        k ← Index(s, rightBracket, j)
                        if k > 0 then
                            Substring(t, s, j + 1, k − j − 1)
                            i ← StringToInteger(t)
                            if (not Error) and (i >= 1) and
                            (i <= pEnd) then
                                Delete(s, j, k − j + 1)
                                Insert(pVal[i], s, j)
                            endif
                        endif
                        j ← Index(s, leftBracket, j + 1)
                    endwhile
                    WriteLine(outputFile, s)
                endwhile
                close letterFile
                output page to outputFile
            endwhile
            close parameterFile, outputFile
        end FormLetter
```

The algorithm *FormLetter* imports definitions, functions, and procedures from the module *StringType*:

> **import** *textFile, vString, Assign, ReadLine, EqualTo, Index, Substring,*
> *StringToInteger, Error, Insert, Delete, WriteLine* **from** *StringType*

The algorithm uses the following constant and variable declarations:

> **const** *maxParameter* = 25
> *letterFile, parameterFile, outputFile*: *textFile*
> *s, t, sentinel, leftBracket, rightBracket*: *vString*
> *pVal*: **array**[1 **to** *maxParameter*] **of** *vString*
> *i, j, k, pEnd*: *integer*

The constant *maxParameter* is the maximum number of parameters the algorithm can handle. Variables *s, t, sentinel, leftBracket,* and *rightBracket* all hold variable-length strings. The array *pVal* is used to hold parameter values; each component of *pVal* holds a variable-length string. The value of the integer variable *pEnd* is the index of the last element of *pVal* that holds a valid parameter value.

The algorithm begins by assigning the string '$$END$$' to *sentinel*, the string '<' to *leftBracket*, and the string '>' to *rightBracket*. Number signs are used for padding because they are more easily read than blanks:

> *Assign*(*sentinel*, '$$END$$###', 7)
> *Assign*(*leftBracket*, '<#########', 1)
> *Assign*(*rightBracket*, '>#########', 1)

The parameter file is opened with mode **text input** and the output file is opened with mode **text output**:

> **open** *parameterFile* **as** 'parms.text' **mode text input**
> **open** *outputFile* **as** 'copies.text' **mode text output**

Processing continues until the end of the parameter file is reached, that is, while the condition

> **not** *EndFileP*(*parameterFile*)

is true. Note that the number of sets of parameters in the parameter file determines how many copies of the form letter will be printed.

The first step in producing a copy is to read a set of parameter values from the parameter file. Each parameter value is stored in the corresponding component of *pVal*. Reading continues until the sentinel $$END$$ is encountered or until *maxParameter* parameters have been read:

> $i \leftarrow 1$
> *ReadLine*(*parameterFile*, *s*)
> **while** ($i <=$ *maxParameter*) **and**
>   (**not** *EqualTo*(*s*, *sentinel*))
> $pVal[i] \leftarrow s$
> $i \leftarrow i + 1$
>   *ReadLine*(*parameterFile*, *s*)
> **endwhile**

Variable *pEnd* is set to the index in *pVal* of the last parameter that was read (remember that the value of *i* was increased by 1 after the last parameter value was stored in *pVal*):

> $pEnd \leftarrow i - 1$

If reading parameter values was terminated because *maxParameter* values had been read, any additional parameter values in the current parameter set are read and discarded:

> **while not** *EqualTo*(*s*, *sentinel*)
>   *ReadLine*(*parameterFile*, *s*)
> **endwhile**

Having read a set of parameter values, the algorithm next reads the master copy line by line, substitutes for parameters in each line, and writes the modified line to the output file. The file containing the master copy is opened in mode **text input**:

open *letterFile* **as** 'letter.text' **mode text input**

The contents of *letterFile* are read and processed line by line. Processing continues until the end of *letterFile* is reached.

Each line read from *letterFile* is assigned to the string variable *s*:

ReadLine(letterFile, s)

Variable *j* is set to the position of the first occurrence of the symbol < in *s*:

j ← Index(s, leftBracket, 1)

Variable *k* is set to the position of the matching > symbol:

k ← Index(s, rightBracket, j)

Note that the search for the > symbol starts at the position of the < symbol, not at the beginning of the string.

If both *j* and *k* have nonzero values, indicating that a < and a matching > were found, the < and > are assumed to enclose a parameter number (see Figure 15.11). The substring containing this number begins at position $j + 1$ in *s* and is $k - j - 1$ characters long. This substring is extracted from *s* and assigned to the string variable *t*:

Substring(t, s, j + 1, k − j − 1)

Figure 15.11 The situation after a parameter has been located by the algorithm *FormLetter*. Variable *i* points to the < preceding the parameter number, and *j* points to the > following the parameter number. The substring containing the parameter number begins at position $j + 1$ and is $k - j - 1$ characters long. The entire parameter substring, including the < and >, begins at position *j* and is $k - j + 1$ characters long.

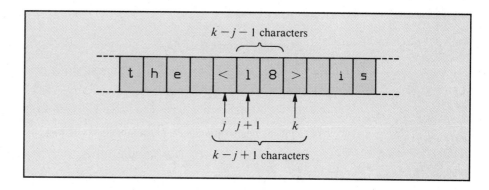

Variable i is set to the integer value represented by the substring t:

$i \leftarrow StringToInteger(t)$

This integer is the index in *pVal* of the parameter value that is to be substituted for the parameter being processed. If the string-to-integer conversion did not cause an error, and if the value of i lies in the range 1 to *pEnd*, the parameter being processed is replaced by the parameter value *pVal*[*i*]:

$Delete(s, j, k - j + 1)$
$Insert(pVal[i], s, j)$

Note that the substring to be deleted is two characters longer than the substring containing the parameter number, since the enclosing brackets < and > must also be deleted.

Variable j is set to the next occurrence in s of a < symbol, or to zero if no such occurrence exists:

$j \leftarrow Index(s, leftBracket, j + 1)$

If the value of j is not zero, the statements for replacing a parameter with the corresponding parameter value are repeated.

When all the parameters on a line have been substituted for, the line is written to the output file:

$WriteLine(outputFile, s)$

When the entire form letter has been processed (the end of *letterFile* is reached), *letterFile* is closed and the output device is sent to the top of a new page:

close *letterFile*

output page to *outputFile*

One copy of the form letter is produced for each set of parameter values in the parameter file. When the end of the parameter file is reached, processing terminates and the parameter and output files are closed:

close *parameterFile*, *outputFile*

Review questions

1. Contrast strings, arrays, and files.

2. What is a *substring*? Describe four common string-processing operations involving substrings.

3. Contrast fixed-length-string types and variable-length-string types.

4. What kind of type equivalence is usually used for fixed-length-string types?

5. What is the type of the constant 'a'? What is the type of the constant 'computer'?

6. Give the rules for comparing fixed-length strings.

7. Describe *padding* and *truncation*.

8. What is the *null* string? Is there such a thing as a fixed-length null string? Why or why not?

9. Why is it often necessary to place an upper limit on the length of the values belonging to a variable-length-string type?

10. Give the rules for comparing variable-length strings.

11. Describe the operation of the procedure *Append* and give an example of its use.

12. Describe the operation of the procedure *Substring* and give an example of its use.

13. Describe the operation of the procedures *Insert* and *Delete* and give an example of the use of each.

14. Describe the operation of the functions *Index* and *Length*. Give statements for finding the first occurrence of the value of *t* in the value of *s* and replacing that occurrence by the value of *u*.

15. Describe the operation of the procedure *Skip* and give an example of its use.

16. Describe and give examples of the operation of the data conversion function *StringToInteger* and procedure *IntegerToString*.

17. Describe three methods of implementing variable-length strings.

18. What is *garbage collection*? Which method of implementing variable-length strings requires garbage collection? What are the advantages and disadvantages of this method?

19. Describe the string-processing technique of *substitution for parameters*.

20. Describe three applications of parameter substitution.

Exercises

1. Implement Boolean functions *LessThan* and *GreaterThan* that correspond to the operators < and > in the same way that *EqualTo* corresponds to the operator =. Each function must scan the strings being compared as long as characters in corresponding positions are equal. When the first pair of unequal characters is encountered, or when the end of one of the strings is reached, the scan should terminate since at this point the value the function is to return can be determined.

2. The distinction between uppercase and lowercase letters often causes trouble when strings are compared, since humans usually ignore this distinction but

computer character codes do not. One solution is to convert all lowercase letters to uppercase (or vice versa) before making a comparison. Write a procedure *Upper(s1, s2)* that assigns to string variable *s1* a copy of string *s2* in which all lowercase letters have been converted to uppercase. Assume the ASCII character code. Note that in ASCII the code for a lowercase letter is 32 greater than the code for the corresponding uppercase letter.

3. Implement the procedure *IntegerToString* that converts an integer into the corresponding string. Note that if *n* is a positive integer, the value of

   n **mod** 10

   is the rightmost decimal digit of the integer, and the value of

   n **div** 10

   is the integer with the rightmost decimal digit removed. For example, 3245 **mod** 10 equals 5 and 3245 **div** 10 equals 324.

4. Modify the procedure *Substring* so that the user specifies the positions of the first and last character of the substring to be extracted instead of giving the position of the first character and the length of the substring.

5. Modify the procedure *Delete* so that the user specifies the positions of the first and last character of the substring to be deleted instead of giving the position of the first character and the length of the substring.

6. Modify the procedure *Skip* so that its third argument is a string rather than a character. The modified procedure increments the value of *i* as long as the character at position *i* in *s* is contained in the string given as the third argument.

7. Rewrite the string-processing module so that strings are stored using the sentinel representation illustrated in Figure 15.2. Use *char*(0) as the sentinel value.

8. A fundamental operation of string processing is *pattern matching*—locating strings or substrings that match a particular pattern. In fact, pattern matching and substituting one substring for another are the main themes of string processing. The function *Index* does a rudimentary form of pattern matching in which string *s2* is the pattern. More sophisticated pattern matching is obtained by allowing a *wildcard character* in the pattern that can match any character in the substring being sought. For example, if ? is the wildcard character, then the pattern '?ar' matches 'bar', 'car', 'far', 'jar', 'par', 'tar', and 'war'. Likewise, the pattern '?ea?' matches 'beat', 'feat', 'heat', 'heap', 'leap', 'neat', 'peat', 'seat', and 'teat'. Modify *Index* to accept patterns in which ? is used as a wildcard character.

9. In *Adventure* and similar computer games, the player explores a fictional setting such as an eerie castle. The player enters commands such as CLIMB STAIRS, OPEN DOOR, TAKE JEWELS, DRINK POTION, and ATTACK OGRE. After each command, the computer prints what happened when the

requested action was attempted. Each command consists of a verb (CLIMB, OPEN, TAKE, . . .) followed by an object (STAIRS, DOOR, JEWELS, . . .). Write a command interpreter procedure that will accept a command and translate it into two code numbers, one giving the position of the verb in the list of all possible verbs and the other giving the position of the object in the list of all possible objects. If either verb or object cannot be found on the appropriate list, the procedure should inform the player that it doesn't know the word in question.

10. Write an algorithm to do the following: (a) input lines of English text until a sentinel line consisting of a single period is encountered; (b) input the maximum number of characters that are to be printed on each line; and (c) output the text in lines that do not exceed the specified maximum length. Each line will contain as many words as possible, but no word will be broken between lines. Exception: A word that is longer than the maximum line length specified will be broken between lines.

11. A *cipher* is a method of sending secret messages that manipulates individual characters rather than entire words or phrases. The original message is the *plaintext*; the secret message is the *ciphertext*. We *encipher* the plaintext when we convert it to ciphertext; we *decipher* the latter when we convert it back to plaintext.

A *substitution cipher* uses a correspondence between a *plaintext alphabet* and a *cipher alphabet*:

> *plaintext alphabet*: ABCDEFGHIJKLMNOPQRSTUVWXYZ
> *cipher alphabet*:   VJMQDSBGKYAZPWETXCNLHORFUI

To encipher, each character in the plaintext alphabet is replaced by the corresponding character in the cipher alphabet. For the alphabets shown, A is replaced by V, B by J, C by M, and so on.

A substitution cipher is *monoalphabetic* if we use the same cipher alphabet for each character of the plaintext. For example, if we encipher AT-TACK AT NOON by monoalphabetic substitution using the alphabets above, we get VLLVMA VL WEEW as the ciphertext. If we assume that the plaintext alphabet is the normal one (A, B, C, and so on), only the cipher alphabet needs to be given. Write an algorithm to encipher and decipher messages using monoalphabetic substitution. The algorithm should obey three commands: A (accept a new cipher alphabet), E (encipher the following message), and D (decipher the following message).

12. The algorithm of Exercise 11 leaves spaces in the ciphertext where there were spaces in the plaintext. This provides too many clues for someone trying to break the cipher. Modify the algorithm of Exercise 11 to print the cipher in groups of five letters. Thus ATTACK AT NOON would be enciphered as VLLVM AVLWE EW.

13. Since cipher alphabets are difficult to remember, we would like to be able to generate a cipher alphabet from an easily remembered *key*. One approach

is to use a key word or phrase such as SCHOOL ZONE. First, write down the letters of the key, omitting any repetitions:

SCHOLZNE

Next, write down the remaining letters of the alphabet in their normal order but omit any letters already in the key:

SCHOLZNEABDFGIJKMPQRTUVWXY

This is our cipher alphabet. Modify the algorithm of Exercise 12 to accept a key and generate the cipher alphabet in the manner just explained.

14. A *polyalphabetic substitution* cipher uses more than one cipher alphabet. One type of polyalphabetic substitution uses the following 26 cipher alphabets:

ABCDEFGHIJKLMNOPQRSTUVWXYZ
BCDEFGHIJKLMNOPQRSTUVWXYZA
CDEFGHIJKLMNOPQRSTUVWXYZAB

.
.
.

XYZABCDEFGHIJKLMNOPQRSTUVW
YZABCDEFGHIJKLMNOPQRSTUVWX
ZABCDEFGHIJKLMNOPQRSTUVWXY

To encipher, a key is written repeatedly above the plaintext. If the key is CUB and the plaintext is ATTACK AT NOON, we write

repeated key: CUBCUB CU BCUB
plaintext: ATTACK AT NOON

We encipher each letter of the plaintext using the cipher alphabet that begins with the corresponding letter of the repeated key. With the key CUB, for instance, we encipher the first letter of the plaintext using the cipher alphabet that begins with C, the second letter of the plaintext using the cipher alphabet that begins with U, and so on. The ciphertext for ATTACK AT NOON is CNUCW LCNOQ IO. Write an algorithm to encipher and decipher messages using this technique. Can you think of a way to avoid having to generate and store 26 cipher alphabets?

Hint: Remember wraparound.

15. In Exercise 14, the sequence in which the different cipher alphabets are used repeats itself throughout the plaintext. This repetition provides a method of breaking the cipher. One way to avoid this problem is to use a pseudorandom number generator to determine which cipher alphabet will be used for each plaintext character. Suppose that the 26 cipher alphabets in Exercise 14 are numbered 1 through 26. If the function call *Random*(26) returns a pseudorandom integer in the range 1 to 26, we can use the value of *Ran-*

dom(26) to select the cipher alphabet. Write an algorithm to encipher and decipher in this way. Note that the initial value of the seed for the random number generator serves as a key. A message must be deciphered with the same starting value for the seed that was used when the message was enciphered.

Pascal Supplement

Pascal provides fixed-length strings essentially equivalent to those discussed in the main text. Variable-length strings are not supported, and Pascal's strong type checking hinders efforts to implement variable-length strings in the language. (Strong type checking often proves most frustrating when one is attempting to extend a langauge beyond the limits envisioned by its designers.) However, the string-processing module described in the main text can be translated into Pascal. Some of the limitations of this module, such as the need for the *Assign* procedure to handle string constants, were imposed so that a Pascal implementation would be possible.

Pascal allows a structured type to be designated as *packed* for the purpose of conserving memory space. Fixed-length strings are implemented in Pascal as packed-array-of-character types.

Packed types

Packing refers to storing a structured value with more than one component in each memory location. If a memory location has room for more than one component value, a packed value will obviously require fewer memory locations than the corresponding unpacked value. On the other hand, additional time is required to insert a component value at its proper position within a memory location and to extract the value when it is needed. Packing, therefore, conserves memory at the expense of increased access time.

We can specify an array type, record type, set type, or file type as packed by preceding the usual type description by the keywork **packed**. The following are some definitions of packed types:

```
type
    string10 = packed array[1. . 10] of char;
    flags = packed record
                    condition1,
                    condition2,
                    condition3,
                    condition4: Boolean
               end;
    numberSet = packed set of 1 . . 10;
    bitStream = packed file of Boolean;
```

Whether packing is appropriate for a particular structured type depends on the computer system on which the program is to be run. For example, many computers provide memory locations just large enough to hold one character (each location holds eight bits or one *byte* of data). On such a computer, characters are always stored one to a memory location, so specifying an array-of-character type as packed has no effect. On the other hand, some computers can store up to six characters in a memory location. For these machines a packed array of characters will require only one-sixth the storage space of the corresponding unpacked array.

Components of packed arrays can be referred to by indexed variables just as for unpacked arrays. However, it is often much faster to pack or unpack an entire array at once than it is to make repeated references to packed components.

Pascal provides predefined procedures *pack* and *unpack* for packing and unpacking an entire array. For example, suppose that a is an unpacked array variable and z is a packed array variable, both with the same component type. The procedure call

   pack(a, i, z)

packs component values of a beginning with the value of $a[i]$ and stores the packed components as the value of z. That is, if z has n components, then the values of

   $a[i]$, $a[i + 1]$, $a[i + 2]$, . . . , $a[i + n - 1]$

are packed and stored as the value of z. Likewise, the procedure call

   unpack(z, i, a)

unpacks the n component values of z and stores them in the components of a, beginning with $a[i]$. That is, the components of the value of z are stored in components $a[i]$ through $a[i + n - 1]$ of a. For both *pack* and *unpack* it is an error if all the components $a[i]$ through $a[i + n - 1]$ do not all exist, that is, if i or $i + n - 1$ lies outside the range of index values allowed for a.

The preceding discussion assumed the index types of a and z to be subranges of *integer* so that expressions such as $i + 1$ and $i + n - 1$ would be meaningful. However, the procedures *pack* and *unpack* also work in a similar manner for noninteger index types.

A component of a packed variable cannot be used as the actual parameter corresponding to a formal variable parameter. The reason is that variable parameters are referred to by their memory addresses. For a packed type, however, several component variables share each memory location, so each component variable does not have a unique memory address. For example, if s and r are declared by

   var
      s: *string10*;
      r: *flags*;

then $s[3]$ and $r.component2$ cannot be used as actual parameters corresponding to formal variable parameters.

The procedures *read* and *readln* are explicit exceptions to this restriction. Early implementations of Pascal usually considered these procedures to have variable parameters and so forbade statements such as *read*(*s*[3])

In standard Pascal, however, the parameters of *read* and *readln* are not considered to be variable parameters; therefore, component variables of packed array and record variables *can* appear in *read* and *readln* statements. You may have to determine by experiment whether this is allowed in the version of Pascal you are using.

String types

Pascal string types correspond to the fixed-length string types of the algorithmic language. The only major difference is that Pascal uses packed arrays for strings. The following statements summarize the properties of Pascal string types:

1. A *string type* is any type of the form

   packed array[1 . . *n*] **of** *char*

   where *n* is the number of characters in the strings belonging to the type.

2. Two string types are *compatible* if their values contain the same number of characters. Values of one such type are *assignment compatible* with the other type; that is, values of one type can be assigned to variables of the other type.

3. Values of compatible string types can be compared with the relational operators =, <, >, <=, >=, and <>. The relations <, >, <= and >= compare strings for alphabetical order, which is defined by the collating sequence for the character code in use.

4. A constant consisting of a single character enclosed in single quotation marks, such as 'a' or '3', has type *char*. A constant consisting of a sequence of two or more characters enclosed in single quotation marks, such as 'abc' or 'computer', has the corresponding string type. Thus the type of 'abc' is

   packed array[1 . . 3] **of** *char*

   and the type of 'computer' is

   packed array[1 . . 8] **of** *char*

5. There is no provision for padding or truncation of string values. A string value can be assigned to a string variable only if value and variable have the same number of components.

6. String values can be written by *write* and *writeln* statements but cannot be read by *read* and *readln* statements. Strings must be read character by character. Thus if *s* is declared by

   var
   　　s: **packed array**[1 . . 10] **of** *char*

then

    write(*s*)

is allowed. However, to read 10 characters and store them in the components of *s*, we must use

    for *i* := 1 **to** 10 **do**
        read(*s*[*i*])

For versions of Pascal that do not allow components of packed variables in *read* and *readln* statements, we must use

    for *i* := 1 **to** 10 **do**
        begin
            read(*c*);
            s[*i*] := *c*
        end

where *c* is a character variable.

The string-processing module

Figure 15.12 gives the Pascal version of the string-processing module *StringType*. Although the module is presented as a UCSD Pascal unit, the individual definitions and declarations can be incorporated directly into programs written in versions of Pascal that do not permit units. This will be the most usual application since extended versions of Pascal that provide units usually also provide a variable-length-string type. This is the case with UCSD Pascal itself.

The constant definitions and type declarations for the unit are as follows:

const
    vStringMax = 80;
    fStringLen = 10;
type
    vString = **record**
                length: *integer*;
                  data: **packed array**[1 .. *vStringMax*] **of** *char*;
            end;
    fString = **packed array**[1 .. *fStringLen*] **of** *char*;

Type *fString* must be packed, since it has to be compatible with the type of 10-character string constants. The *data* field of type *vString* can be either packed or unpacked, depending on which is most appropriate for a particular computer system. Type *textFile* is not defined in the Pascal unit; the Pascal predefined file type *text* is used instead.

Figure 15.12   The module *StringType* implemented as a UCSD Pascal unit.

```
unit StringType;

{ Implement a variable-length-string type }

interface
    const
        vStringMax = 80;
        fStringLen = 10;
    type
        vString = record
                        length: integer;
                        data: packed array[1 . . vStringMax] of char
                  end;
        fString = packed array[1 . . fStringLen] of char;

    function Error: Boolean;
    { Return value of and clear error indicator }

    function StringToInteger(var s: vString): integer;
    { Convert the string s to the corresponding integer }

    function Length(var s: vString): integer;
    { Return the length of string s }

    function EqualTo(var s1, s2: vString): Boolean;
    { Return true if the values of s1 and s2 are equal }

    function Index(var s1, s2: vString; i: integer): integer;
    { Return the position of the first occurrence of s2 in the part of s1
      beginning at position i. Return zero if no such occurrence is found }

    procedure ReadLine(var f: text; var s: vString);
    { Read a line from textfile f and assign line read to s }

    procedure WriteString(var f: text; var s: vString);
    { Write string s to textfile f; do not terminate line }

    procedure WriteLine(var f: text; var s: vString);
    { Write string s to textfile f; terminate line }
```

```
        procedure Append(var s1, s2: vString);
        { Append string s2 to the end of string s1 }

        procedure Insert(s1: vString; var s2: vString; i: integer);
        { Insert string s1 into string s2 before position i. If i equals
          Length(s1) + 1, append s1 to s1 }

        procedure Delete(var s: vString; i, n: integer);
        { Delete n characters from string s starting at position i }

        procedure Substring(var s1: vString; s2: vString; i, n: integer);
        { Assign to s1 the substring of length n beginning at position i in
          string s2 }

        procedure Assign(var s1: vString; s2: fString; n: integer);
        { Assign the first n characters of array s2 to string s1 }

        procedure Skip(var s: vString; var i: integer; c: char);
        { Increment i while the character at position i in string s equals c }


implementation
    var
        errorFlag: Boolean;

    function Error;
    begin
        Error := errorFlag;
        errorFlag := false
    end; { Error }

    function StringToInteger;
    var
        value, limit: real;
        j, sign: integer;
        c: char;
    begin
        limit := maxint;
        value := 0.0;
        sign := 1;
        j := 1;
        Skip(s, j, ' ');
```

```pascal
            if j <= s.length then
                begin
                    c := s.data[j];
                    if c = '+' then
                        j := j + 1
                    else if c = '-' then
                        begin
                            sign := -1;
                            j := j + 1
                        end
                end;
            while (j <= s.length) and (not errorFlag) do
                begin
                    c := s.data[j];
                    if not (c in ['0'. .'9']) then
                        errorFlag := true
                    else
                        begin
                            value := 10.0 * value + ord(c) - ord('0');
                            if value > limit then
                                begin
                                    value := limit;
                                    errorFlag := true
                                end;
                            j := j + 1
                        end;
                end;
            StringToInteger := sign * round(value)
        end; { StringToInteger }


function Length;
begin
    errorFlag := false;
    Length := s.length
end; { Length }

function EqualTo;
var
    j: integer;
    equal: Boolean;
```

```
begin
    errorFlag := false;
    if s1.length <> s2.length then
        equal := false
    else
        begin
            equal := true;
            j := 1;
            while (j <= s1.length) and equal do
                begin
                    if s1.data[j] <> s2.data[j] then
                        equal := false;
                    j := j + 1
                end;
        end;
    EqualTo := equal
end; { Equal to }

function Index;
var
    j, k, m: integer;
    found: Boolean;
begin
    j := i;
    k := s1.length - s2.length + 1;
    if (j < 1) or (j > k) then
        begin
            errorFlag := true;
            Index := 0
        end
    else
        begin
            errorFlag := false;
            repeat
                found := true;
                m := 1;
                while (m <= s2.length) and found do
                    begin
                        if s1.data[j + m - 1] <> s2.data[m] then
                        found := false;
                        m := m + 1
                    end;
                j := j + 1
            until (j > k) or found;
```

```pascal
                    if found then
                            Index := j - 1
                    else
                            Index := 0
            end
    end; { Index }


    procedure ReadLine;
    var
        j: integer;
        c: char;
    begin
        if eof(f) then
            begin
                errorFlag := true;
                s.length := 0
            end
        else
            begin
                errorFlag := false;
                j := 1;
                while (j <= vStringMax) and (not eoln(f)) and
                    (not eof(f)) do
                    begin
                        read(f, c);
                        s.data[j] := c;
                        j := j + 1
                    end;
                s.length := j - 1
            end;
        if not eof(f) then
            readln(f)
    end; { ReadLine }

    procedure WriteString;
    var
        j: integer;
    begin
        errorFlag := false;
        for j := 1 to s.length do
            write(f, s.data[j])
    end; { WriteString }
```

```
procedure WriteLine;
begin
    WriteString(f, s);
    writeln(f)
end; { WriteLine }


procedure Append;
var
    j, k: integer;
begin
    if s1.length + s2.length > vStringMax then
        errorFlag := true
    else
        begin
            errorFlag := false;
            j := s1.length + 1;
            for k := 1 to s2.length do
                begin
                    s1.data[j] := s2.data[k];
                    j := j + 1
                end;
            s1.length := s1.length + s2.length
        end
end; { Append }

procedure Insert;
var
    j, k: integer;
begin
    if (i < 1) or (i > s2.length + 1) or
       (s1.length + s2.length > vStringMax) then
        errorFlag := true
    else
        begin
            errorFlag := false;
            j := s2.length;
            k := s1.length + s2.length;
            while j >= i do
                begin
                    s2.data[k] := s2.data[j];
                    j := j - 1;
                    k := k - 1
                end;
```

```pascal
                    j := i;
                    for k := 1 to s1.length do
                        begin
                            s2.data[j] := s1.data[k];
                            j := j + 1
                        end;
                    s2.length := s1.length + s2.length
            end
end; { Insert }


procedure Delete;
var
    j, k: integer;
begin
    if (i < 1) or (i + n − 1 > s.length) or (n < 0) then
        errorFlag := true
    else
        begin
            errorFlag := false;
            j := i;
            k := i + n;
            while k <= s.length do
                begin
                    s.data[j] := s.data[k];
                    j := j + 1;
                    k := k + 1
                end;
            s.length := s.length − n
        end
end; { Delete }

procedure Substring;
var
    j, k: integer;
begin
    if (i < 1) or (i + n − 1 > s2.length) or (n < 0) then
        errorFlag := true
    else
        begin
            errorFlag := false;
            s1.length := n;
            j := i;
```

```
                    for k := 1 to n do
                        begin
                            s1.data[k] := s2.data[j];
                            j := j + 1
                        end
                end
        end; { Substring }


        procedure Assign;
        var
            j: integer;
        begin
            if (n < 0) or (n > fStringLen) then
                errorFlag := true
            else
                begin
                    errorFlag := false;
                    s1.length := n;
                    for j := 1 to n do
                        s1.data[j] := s2[j]
                end
        end; { Assign }

        procedure Skip;
        var
            skipping: Boolean;
        begin
            if (i < 1) or (i > s.length) then
                errorFlag := true
            else
                begin
                    errorFlag := false;
                    skipping := true;
                    while (i <= s.length) and skipping do
                        if s.data[i] = c then
                            i := i + 1
                        else
                            skipping := false
                end
        end; { Skip }

begin
    errorFlag := false
end. { StringType }
```

Figure 15.13   UCSD Pascal program corresponding to the module
FormLetter.

```
program FormLetter;

{ Print copies of form letter in letter file. For each copy, replace
  parameters by strings from parameter file }

uses StringType;
const
    maxParameter = 25;
var
    letterFile, parameterFile, outputFile: text;
    s, t, sentinel, leftBracket, rightBracket: vString;
    pVal: array[1 . . maxParameter] of vString;
    i, j, k, pEnd: integer;
begin
    Assign(sentinel, '$$END$$###', 7);
    Assign(leftBracket, '<#########', 1);
    Assign(rightBracket, '>#########', 1);
    reset(parameterFile, 'parms.text');
    rewrite(outputFile, 'copies.text');
    while not eof(parameterFile) do
        begin

        { Read parameter values }

            i := 1;
            ReadLine(parameterFile, s);
            while (i <= maxParameter) and
                (not EqualTo(s, sentinel)) do
                begin
                    pVal[i] := s;
                    i := i + 1;
                    ReadLine(parameterFile, s)
                end;
            pEnd := i - 1;
            while not EqualTo(s, sentinel) do
                ReadLine(parameterFile, s);

        { Print copy of letter }
```

```
                    reset(letterFile, 'letter.text');
                    while not eof(letterFile) do
                        begin
                            ReadLine(letterFile, s);
                            j := Index(s, leftBracket, 1);
                            while j > 0 do
                                begin
                                    k := Index(s, rightBracket, j);
                                    if k > 0 then
                                        begin
                                            Substring(t, s, j + 1, k − j − 1);
                                            i := StringToInteger(t);
                                            if (not Error) and (i >= 1) and
                                                (i <= pEnd) then
                                                begin
                                                    Delete(s, j, k − j + 1);
                                                    Insert(pVal[i], s, j)
                                                end
                                        end;
                                    j := Index(s, leftBracket, j + 1)
                                end;
                            WriteLine(outputFile, s);
                        end;
                    close(letterFile);
                    page(outputFile)
                end;
            close(outputFile, lock)
    end. { FormLetter }
```

The variable *errorFlag* is declared in the implementation rather than in the interface section since it is not exported but can be accessed only via the functions and procedures of the unit.

The declaration for *Skip* follows that of *StringToInteger*, even though *StringToInteger* invokes *Skip*. This is permissible in the algorithmic-language module since the algorithmic language does not require a procedure to be declared before it is referenced. The reference is also allowed in the Pascal unit since the function and procedure declarations in the interface section act as forward declarations. The identifier *Skip* is considered declared in the interface section rather than at the point where the procedure body of *Skip* occurs in the implementation section. If the individual declarations and definitions are incorporated directly in a Pascal program, however, either the entire declaration of *Skip* must precede the declaration of *StringToInteger*, or the latter must be preceded by a forward declaration for *Skip*.

Also in *StringToInteger*, note that (1) *maxint* is a predefined constant and does not have to be imported, and (2) the function *ord* in Pascal plays the some role as the function *integer* used in the algorithmic language to convert characters to their integer character codes.

To allow users to interact with their programs, UCSD Pascal follows nonstandard conventions when reading from the user's keyboard. As a result, when *ReadLine* is used to read from the user's keyboard, the blank corresponding to the end-of-line character is included at the end of the string that is read. *ReadLine* works properly with textfiles stored on disk.

Figure 15.13 shows the program *FormLetter*, which illustrates the use of the string-processing unit. The files *letterFile*, *parameterFile*, and *outputFile* are all declared as the predefined textfile type *text*. Since the unit was written in UCSD Pascal, the UCSD versions of *reset* and *rewrite* are used, and no file variables are listed in the program heading. Calls to the UCSD-Pascal procedure *close* should be omitted in standard Pascal.

16

Linked structures

pointer value is a value that designates a particular memory location. A *pointer variable* is a variable whose value is used to designate a memory location. As shown in Figure 16.1, a pointer value is usually represented by an arrow extended from the pointer variable to the designated memory location. The term "pointer" is often applied to both pointer value and pointer variable; either may be said to "point to" the designated location.

In previous chapters we have seen how array indexes can be used as pointers; the index *i* points to the array component *a*[*i*]. In addition, many programming languages provide *pointer types* whose values are specifically intended for designating memory locations. Our discussion in this chapter will be based on pointer types. Keep in mind, however, that array indexes make perfectly good pointers, so all the programs discussed in this chapter can be implemented in languages such as BASIC, FORTRAN, and COBOL that do not provide pointer types.

Pointer values can be used to link records to one another. One or more fields of each record contain pointers to locations containing other records. Such linked records represent a mathematical structure known as a *graph* (not to be confused with the graphs used to plot numerical data). Figure 16.2 shows three examples of graphs. The dots, called *nodes*, correspond to the linked records. The connecting lines, called *arcs*, correspond to the pointer values linking the records.

Figure 16.2a shows a general graph, in which the nodes are linked in an arbitrary manner. Figure 16.2b shows a *linked list*, in which arcs and nodes form a straight line. Figure 16.2c shows a *tree*, in which all paths through the graph start at the same node (called the *root*) and branch out repeatedly without forming closed loops or *cycles*. In this chapter we will be mostly concerned with linked lists and trees.

Figure 16.1   A pointer value is represented by an arrow extending from
the pointer variable to the designated memory location.
Either the pointer value or the pointer variable may be
referred to as a ''pointer'' and may be said to ''point to''
the designated location.

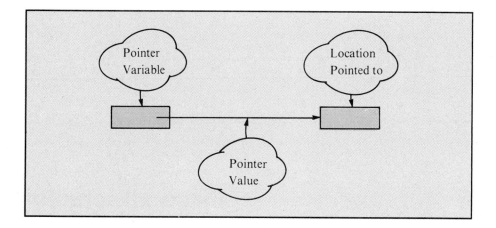

16.1

Pointer types

Pointer values are memory addresses, such as those described for the hypothetical
computer in Chapter 3. Unfortunately, different computers often use quite different
schemes for addressing memory. Some, like the computer described in Chapter 3,
use an integer value to address memory. The first memory location has address 0,
the next has address 1, the next has address 2, and so on. Other computers, however,
use two integers as a memory address; one integer designates a particular segment of
memory and the other designates a particular location within that segment. What's
more, computers may impose special restrictions on some integers used as memory
addresses, requiring that the integers be even numbers, for example, or multiples of
four. These differences present problems for using pointers in portable programs that
are to be run on many different computer systems.

To allow programs that use pointers to be independent of any particular computer
system, many higher-level languages hide all details of pointer representation from
the programmer. Pointers can be created only by the system. The programmer can
store and retrieve pointer values and can access memory locations designated by
pointers but cannot manipulate the internal representations of pointers in any way.
The programmer cannot assign specific numerical values to the integer or integers
constituting a pointer because the significance of those values would be different for
different computer systems. And the programmer cannot carry out arithmetical manipulations on those integers because, again, the effect of such manipulations would
be different for different computer systems.

Figure 16.2 Examples of graphs. The dots are called *nodes* and the lines
are called *arcs*. Part (a) shows a general graph, with
arbitrary connections between the nodes; part (b) shows a
linked list, in which the nodes and arcs lie on a straight line;
and part (c) shows a *tree*, in which paths branch out from a
common origin called the *root*.

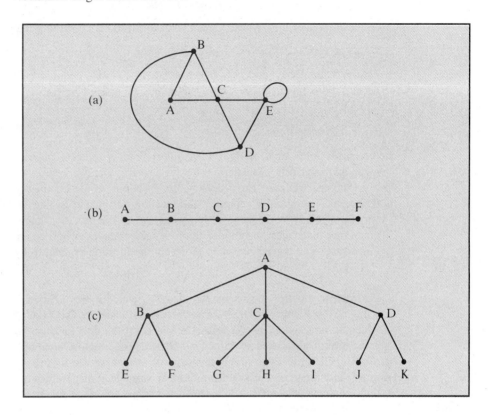

When we define a pointer type, we must state the type of values to be stored in
the locations designated by the pointers. That is, we must state whether the locations
designated by the pointers will hold characters, Boolean values, integers, real numbers, or what. There are several reasons for this. First, most computer systems provide memory locations of different sizes; the size chosen in each instance depends
on the type of data to be stored in the location. When we instruct the system to
transfer data to or from a memory location, the system must know the size of the
location in order to transfer the proper amount of data. Second, when memory locations designated by pointers appear in expressions, the system must know the type
of data stored in the location in order to evaluate the expression correctly. Finally,
specifying the type of data to be stored in each memory location—including locations
designated by pointers—allows strong type checking. The system can guard against

programmer errors by insisting that each value be manipulated only by operators, procedures, and functions that are defined for its type.

We define a pointer type in the algorithmic language with the phrase **pointer to** followed by the type of values to be stored in the memory locations designated by the pointers. For example,

> **type** *integerPointer* = **pointer to** *integer*

defines a pointer type whose values point to locations containing integers, and

> **type** *characterPointer* = **pointer to** *char*

defines a pointer type whose values point to locations containing characters. If we declare the pointer variables *p*, *q*, and *r* by

> *p*, *q*: *integerPointer*
>
> *r*: *characterPointer*

then values of *p* and *q* point to locations containing integers and values of *r* point to locations containing characters.

Pointers are used for accessing the locations to which they point. We need, therefore, a notation to represent the location designated by the value of a pointer variable such as *p*. There is little agreement on this notation among different programming languages; the following are some examples of the notations used in different programming languages to represent the location pointed to by the value of *p*:

$$p\uparrow \qquad *p \qquad .p \qquad p.\textbf{all} \qquad [p]$$

For want of a better choice, we will use $p\uparrow$, which is the notation used in Pascal.

Figure 16.3 illustrates the relation between *p* and $p\uparrow$. The value of *p* is a pointer, which is represented by an arrow in Figure 16.3. The location pointed to by the value of *p* is designated $p\uparrow$. Since $p\uparrow$ designates a memory location, it plays the role of a variable in the algorithmic language. We can assign values to $p\uparrow$ and use values of $p\uparrow$ in expressions just as for any other variable. Since values of *p* point to locations containing integers, $p\uparrow$ is an integer variable; only integers can be assigned to $p\uparrow$ and the value of $p\uparrow$ is always an integer. In Figure 16.3, the value of $p\uparrow$ is 25. After the assignment

> $p\uparrow \leftarrow 1000$

Figure 16.3   The symbol $p\uparrow$ represents the location pointed to by the pointer variable *p*.

the value of $p\uparrow$ is 1000, and the expression

$$3 * p\uparrow + 500$$

has the value 3500.

Figure 16.4 further clarifies the relation between p and $p\uparrow$ by contrasting the assignments

$$p\uparrow \leftarrow q\uparrow$$

and

$$p \leftarrow q$$

The first of these assigns the value of $q\uparrow$ to $p\uparrow$; after the assignment, $p\uparrow$ and $q\uparrow$ have the same value. Nevertheless, $p\uparrow$ and $q\uparrow$ remain distinct memory locations which at the moment just happen to contain the same value. On the other hand, the assignment

$$p \leftarrow q$$

causes p and q to point to the same location; $p\uparrow$ and $q\uparrow$ designate the same location and so have the same value. Since $p\uparrow$ and $q\uparrow$ designate the same location, assigning a new value to $p\uparrow$ also changes the value of $q\uparrow$, and vice versa.

Every pointer type contains the value *nil*, which does not point to any memory location. *Nil* is often used as a sentinel when processing linked structures. Since *nil*

Figure 16.4   The assignment $p\uparrow \leftarrow q\uparrow$ assigns the value of $q\uparrow$ to $p\uparrow$; however, $p\uparrow$ and $q\uparrow$ remain independent locations that just happen to have the same value. In contrast, the assignment $p \leftarrow q$ sets p to point to the same location as q. After this assignment, $p\uparrow$ and $q\uparrow$ represent the same location.

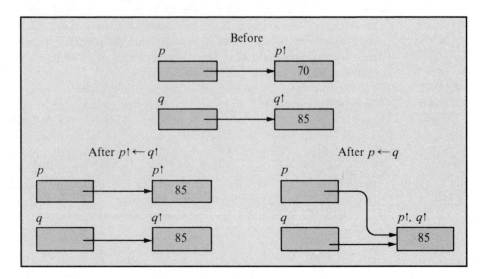

does not point to any memory location, a reference to $p\uparrow$ is illegal if the value of p is *nil*. For example, the second of the following two statements is erroneous:

$p \leftarrow nil$

$p\uparrow \leftarrow 5$

The second statement instructs the computer to store 5 in the location pointed to by p. But the value of p is *nil*, which does not designate a memory location.

Nil is the only pointer constant in the algorithmic language. As indicated earlier, we cannot represent pointers by numerical constants or obtain them as results of calculations, since the significance of such pointers would depend on a particular computer system. Aside from accessing the location designated by a pointer, the only operation we can carry out on pointers is to compare them for equality. The Boolean expression

$p = q$

has the value *true* only if the values of p and q both point to the same memory location or if both values are *nil*.

If pointer values cannot be calculated and cannot be generally represented by constants, then where do they come from? Memory locations designated by pointers are explicitly allocated (created) and deallocated (destroyed) by the programmer. This is in contrast to the memory locations corresponding to ordinary variables, which are automatically allocated when a function or procedure is called and are deallocated when the function or procedure returns. The predefined procedure *new(p)* allocates a new memory location and assigns to p a pointer to the new location. The size of the location allocated depends on the type of the pointer variable. Since the type of p is defined as **pointer to** *integer*, the procedure call *new(p)* allocates a memory location just large enough to hold an integer.

The procedure *dispose(p)* deallocates the memory location pointed to by p. After the call *dispose(p)*, the value of p is meaningless, since the location to which p formerly pointed is no longer available to the program. On most systems, *dispose* recycles memory locations; locations deallocated by *dispose* can be later allocated once again by *new*. *New* and *dispose* provide the programmer with a flexibility in memory management that is not available for memory locations that are automatically allocated and deallocated by the system.

New allocates locations from a memory area called a *heap*. The term *heap* is intended to contrast with *stack*, which refers to a memory area in which locations are always deallocated in reverse of the order in which they were allocated. (The use of a stack for allocating and deallocating memory areas for procedures and functions was described in Chapter 14). Using calls to *new* and *dispose*, memory locations in a heap can be allocated and deallocated in any order. Thus allocation and deallocation are much less ordered and structured for a heap than they are for a stack. The terms "heap" and "stack" reflect this difference.

Figure 16.5 illustrates the operation of *new* and *dispose*. After the pointer variable p has been declared,

p: *integerPointer*

Figure 16.5   The contents of a newly declared pointer variable are
undefined. The procedure call *new*(*p*) allocates a new
memory location and sets *p* to point to it. The contents of
the new location are undefined until a value is assigned to
p↑. After the location pointed to by *p* has been disposed of,
the contents of *p* are meaningless.

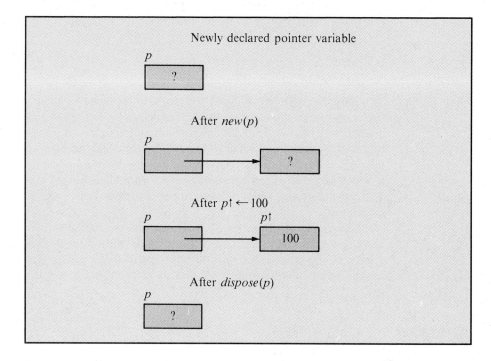

its contents, represented by a question mark in the figure, are unknown. The contents
of *p* could point to any location accessible to the program. Assigning a value to *p*↑
at this point could have disastrous consequences, since the value might be stored in
a completely inappropriate location, such as in the user's program code or in that of
the operating system.

The procedure call

   new(*p*)

allocates an integer-sized memory location and sets *p* to point to it. When the new
location is first allocated, its contents are unknown. The assignment

   p↑ ← 100

stores the integer value 100 in the new location.

The procedure call

   dispose(*p*)

deallocates the memory location pointed to by p. The value of p is once again mean-ingless since it points to a nonexistent memory location. Referring to the value of $p\uparrow$ or assigning a value to it will once again have unpredictable consequences.

The use of pointers encourages two kinds of programming errors: *uninitialized pointers* and *dangling pointers*. An uninitialized pointer is a pointer variable to which no pointer value has been assigned, either with *new* or with an assignment statement. As just discussed, attempting to refer to the location designated by an uninitialized pointer can have unpredictable consequences.

The following pair of statements create a dangling pointer:

$p \leftarrow q$
dispose(q)

The assignment statement causes p to point to the same location as q. The *dispose* statement then deallocates the location pointed to by q. Variable p is now a dangling pointer since the location to which it points no longer exists. *Dispose* might set q to *nil* or to a special error value so that the system could detect an attempt to refer to the disposed location via q. But *dispose* has no way of knowing that p also contains a pointer to the location being disposed of; hence after *dispose* has been executed, p will contain a meaningless pointer. Attempts to refer to $p\uparrow$ will have unpredictable consequences.

Because of these problems, some computer scientists have recommended that pointers themselves be disposed of, that some other means be used to implement graphs. However, because no good substitute for pointers has yet been found, they are still widely used in spite of the dangers of uninitialized and dangling pointers.

16.2
Linked lists

In Chapter 13, we saw how to represent a list of values as an array, the components of which are stored in adjacent memory locations. A list can also be stored in loca-tions scattered throughout memory, provided that each location contains a pointer to the location containing the next item on the list. A list stored in this way is called a *linked list*. Linked lists have the advantage that insertions and deletions can be made without moving existing items to make room for a new item or to close the gap left by a deleted item. A disadvantage of linked lists is that only sequential search can be used; faster search techniques such as binary search and hashing are not available. When faster search techniques are needed and linked structures are still desired, more complex linked structures such as *binary search trees* must be used.

Consider the following definitions:

type *link* = **pointer to** *cell*
type *cell* = **record**
          data: *integer*
          next: *link*
      endrecord

Values of type *link* point to memory locations containing values of type *cell*; we will call such memory locations "cells." Each cell has two fields: *data*, which contains an integer value, and *next*, which contains a pointer to another cell.

Figure 16.6 shows the list of integers

5   9   4   3   2

stored as a linked list of cells. The pointer variable *first* points to the first cell on the list, the one in which the value 5 is stored. The *data* field of each cell contains the list value stored in that cell; the *next* field of each cell contains a pointer to the next cell on the list. The *next* field of the last cell on the list contains *nil*, which is indicated in diagrams by a diagonal line drawn through the field. When processing the list, *nil* serves as a sentinel to indicate the end of the list.

Since *first* points to a cell, it must be of type *link*. Let's declare the variables *first* and *p* as follows:

first, *p*: *link*

Assume that *first* points to the first cell of the list shown in Figure 16.6. After the assignment

$p \leftarrow first$

p will also point to the first cell of the list. The value of *p*↑ is the content of the first cell. The value of *p*↑.*data* is 5, the content of the *data* field of the first cell. The value of *p*↑.*next* is the content of the *next* field of the first cell, which is a pointer to the second cell.

The assignment statement

$p \leftarrow p\uparrow.next$

sets *p* to point to the second cell on the list, the cell pointed to by the *next* field of

Figure 16.6   Linked list containing the integers 5, 9, 4, 3, and 2.

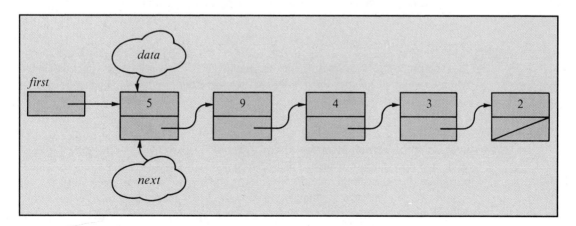

the first cell. After this assignment statement, the value of $p\uparrow.data$ is 9, the list value stored in the second cell. If

$p \leftarrow p\uparrow.next$

is executed again, p is set to point to the third cell on the list, the one pointed to by the *next* field of the second cell. Subsequent executions of the same assignment statement each sets p to point to the next cell on the list. After the assignment statement has been executed four times, p will point to the last cell on the list. Executing the assignment statement again sets p to *nil*, the content of the *next* field of the last cell. Since $p\uparrow$ is not defined when the value of p is *nil*, no further executions of the assignment statement are possible.

16.3 Applications of linked lists

In this section we will illustrate the applications of linked lists by using them to implement three modules that we previously implemented with arrays. Module *IntegerStack* maintains a stack of integers, *IntegerQueue* maintains a queue of integers, and *TableHandler* maintains a table of integer keys and real values.

IntegerStack   Figure 16.7 shows the module *IntegerStack*. Types *link* and *cell* are as defined earlier in this section. The variable *topPtr* is declared to be of type *link*. The stack is stored as a linked list as shown in Figure 16.8. The first cell on the list contains the top value on the stack; the last cell on the list contains the bottom value on the stack. The variable *topPtr* points to the first cell, the one containing the top value. The *next* field of each cell points to the cell containing the next lower value on the stack. The *next* field of the cell holding the bottom value contains *nil*. When the stack is empty, the value of *topPtr* is *nil*.

The function *Top* returns the top value on the stack. If the value of *topPtr* is *nil*, the stack is empty. *ErrorFlag* is set to *true* and *Top* returns the value zero. If the value of *topPtr* is not *nil*, then *topPtr* points to the cell containing the top value on the stack. *ErrorFlag* is set to *false* and the top value is returned:

$errorFlag \leftarrow false$
$Top \leftarrow topPtr\uparrow.data$

The procedure *NewStack* creates an empty stack. Since an empty stack is signified by a value of *nil* for *topPtr*, *topPtr* is set to *nil* and *errorFlag* is set to *false*:

$topPtr \leftarrow nil$
$errorFlag \leftarrow false$

In the original version of *IntegerStack*, given in Chapter 14, the procedure for creating an empty stack was named *New*. Since *New* conflicts with *new*, the predefined procedure for allocating memory locations, the name *New* has been changed to *NewStack*. Similar name changes have also been made in *IntegerQueue* and *TableHandler*.

Figure 16.7 The module *IntegerStack*.

```
module IntegerStack

{ Implements a stack of integers }

declare
    export Error, Top, NewStack, Push, Pop
    type link = pointer to cell
    type cell = record
                    data: integer
                    next: link
                endrecord
    topPtr: link
    errorFlag: Boolean


function Error: Boolean

{ Return value of and clear error flag }

execute
    Error ← errorFlag
    errorFlag ← false
end Error


function Top: integer

{ Retrun top value on stack }

execute
    if topPtr = nil then
        errorFlag ← true
        Top ← 0
    else
        errorFlag ← false
        Top ← topPtr↑.data
    endif
end Top
```

```
        procedure NewStack

    { Create empty stack }

    execute
        topPtr ← nil
        errorFlag ← false
    end NewStack



        procedure Push(x)

    { Push value onto stack }

    declare
        x: in integer
        p: link
    execute
        errorFlag ← false
        new(p)
        p↑.data ← x
        p↑.next ← topPtr
        topPtr ← p
    end Push



        procedure Pop

    { Pop value off stack }

    declare
        p: link
    execute
        if topPtr = nil then
            errorFlag ← true
        else
            errorFlag ← false
            p ← topPtr
            topPtr ← topPtr↑.next
            dispose(p)
        endif
    end Pop


initialize
    NewStack
end IntegerStack
```

Figure 16.8   Representation of an integer stack as a linked list. The first
cell of the list holds the top value on the stack; the last cell
holds the bottom value.

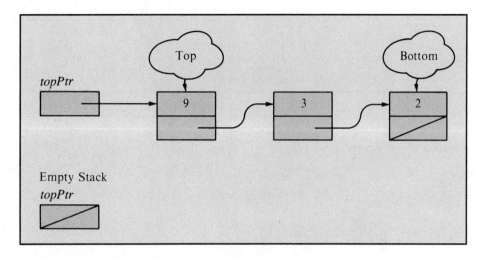

The procedure *Push* places a given value on top of the stack. *Push* starts by
setting *errorFlag* to *false*. The procedure cannot check for the possibility of stack
overflow since it has no way of knowing how much unused memory remains in the
heap. If the heap has been exhausted, the call to *new* will fail and the user will be
so informed by a system error message.

Figure 16.9 illustrates the operation of *Push*. The variable *p* is used as a temporary pointer to the cell that is to hold the value to be pushed on. The new cell is
allocated by the following procedure call:

   new(p)

The *data* field of the new cell is set to the value to be pushed onto the stack:

   $p\uparrow.data \leftarrow x$

Since the new cell is to go on top of the stack, it must be inserted just before (above)
the current top cell, the cell now pointed to by *topPtr*. Thus the *next* field of the new
cell is set to point to the current top cell:

   $p\uparrow.next \leftarrow topPtr$

Since the new cell is to become the new top of the stack, *topPtr* is set to point to the
new cell:

   $topPtr \leftarrow p$

The procedure *Pop* removes the top value from the stack by removing and dis-
posing of the top cell. If the value of *topPtr* is *nil*, the stack is empty, and *errorFlag*
is set to *true* to reflect a stack underflow error. Otherwise, *errorFlag* is set to *false*

Figure 16.9   Pushing a value onto a stack. A new cell is allocated to hold
the new top value. The new cell is linked to the current top
cell, and *topPtr* is set to point to the new cell.

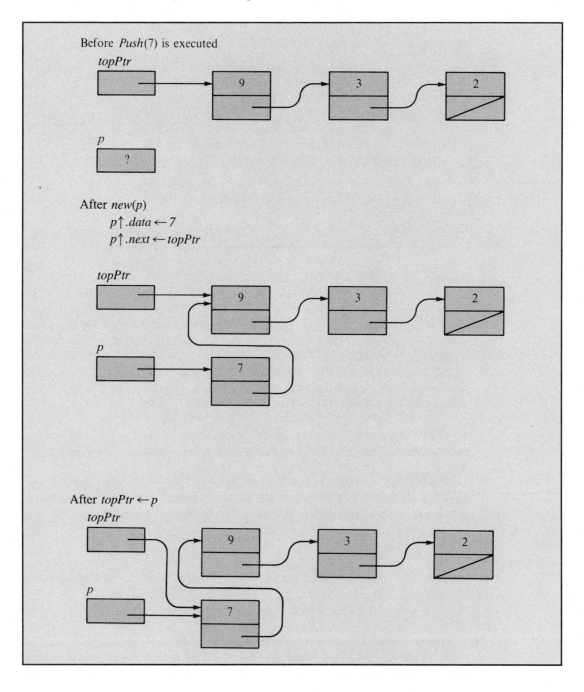

and the top cell is removed as shown in Figure 16.10. To keep from losing access to the top cell before it can be disposed of, we start by setting p to point to the top cell:

$p \leftarrow topPtr$

Next we set $topPtr$ to point to the next cell on the linked list, the one just "below" the top cell:

$topPtr \leftarrow topPtr\uparrow.next$

TopPtr now points to what was the next-to-top cell and is now the top cell. All that remains to be done is to dispose of the former top cell, which is still pointed to by p:

$dispose(p)$

IntegerQueue   Figure 16.11 shows the module *IntegerQueue*. The type declarations are the same as for *IntegerStack*. For a queue, however, we need two pointers: *frontPtr* points to the first cell of the queue and *rearPtr* points to last cell of the queue. Figure 16.12 on page 759 illustrates the linked-list representation of a queue. When the queue is empty, both *frontPtr* and *rearPtr* have the value *nil*.

Function *Front* returns the value at the front of the queue. If the value of *frontPtr* is *nil*, the queue is empty and an error is signaled. Otherwise, *frontPtr* points to the first cell of the queue, whose data field contains the value to be returned:

if $frontPtr \leftarrow nil$ **then**
    $errorFlag \leftarrow true$
    $Front \leftarrow 0$
else
    $errorFlag \leftarrow false$
    $Front \leftarrow frontPtr\uparrow.data$
endif

The procedure *NewQueue* creates an empty queue by setting *frontPtr* and *rearPtr* to *nil* and *errorFlag* to *false*.

The procedure *Insert(x)* allocates a new cell, stores the value of x in it, and inserts the new cell at the rear of the queue. (See Figure 16.13, page 760.) The variable p is used as a temporary pointer to the new cell, which is allocated by a call to *new*:

$new(p)$

The value of x is stored in the *data* field of the new cell:

$p\uparrow.data \leftarrow x$

Since the new cell is going to become the last cell of a linked list, its *next* field is set to *nil*:

$p\uparrow.next \leftarrow nil$

Figure 16.10   Popping the top value from a stack. The value of *topPtr* is "routed around" the cell that is to be removed.

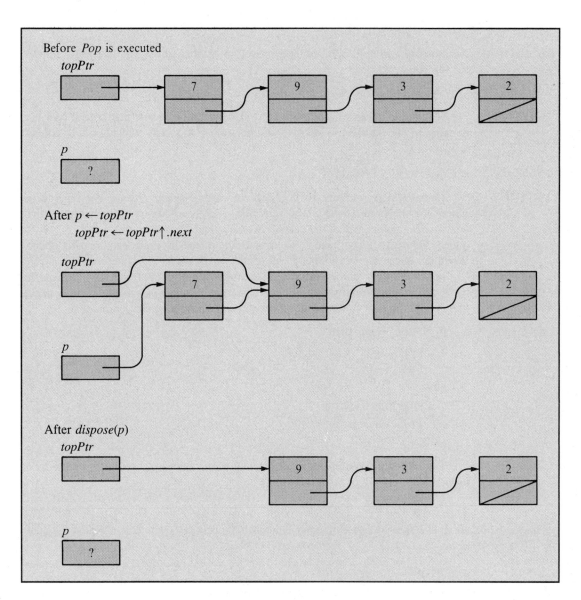

Figure 16.11   The module *IntegerQueue*.

```
module IntegerQueue

{ Implements a queue of integers }

declare
    export Error, Front, NewQueue, Insert, Remove
    type link = pointer to cell
    type cell = record
                        data: integer
                        next: link
                endrecord
    frontPtr, rearPtr: link
    errorFlag: Boolean


function Error: Boolean

{ Return value of and clear error flag }

execute
    Error ← errorFlag
    errorFlag ← false
end Error


function Front: integer

{ Return value at front of queue }

execute
    if frontPtr = nil then
        errorFlag ← true
        Front ← 0
    else
        errorFlag ← false
        Front ← frontPtr↑.data
    endif
end Front
```

```
procedure NewQueue

{ Create empty queue }

execute
    frontPtr ← nil
    rearPtr ← nil
    errorFlag ← false
end NewQueue


procedure Insert(x)

{ Insert value at end of queue }

declare
    x: in integer
    p: link
execute
    errorFlag ← false
    new(p)
    p↑.data ← x
    p↑.next ← nil
    if rearPtr = nil then
        frontPtr ← p
    else
        rearPtr↑.next ← p
    endif
    rearPtr ← p
end Insert


procedure Remove

{ Remove value from front of queue }

declare
    p: link
execute
    if frontPtr = nil then
        errorFlag ← true
```

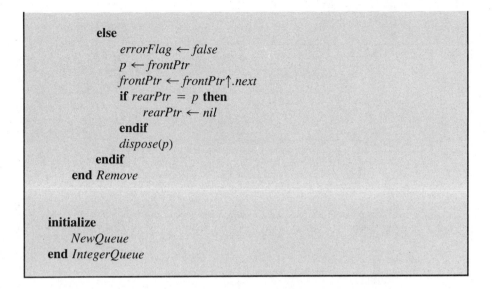

```
        else
            errorFlag ← false
            p ← frontPtr
            frontPtr ← frontPtr↑.next
            if rearPtr = p then
                rearPtr ← nil
            endif
            dispose(p)
        endif
    end Remove


initialize
    NewQueue
end IntegerQueue
```

Figure 16.12   Linked-list representation of a queue.

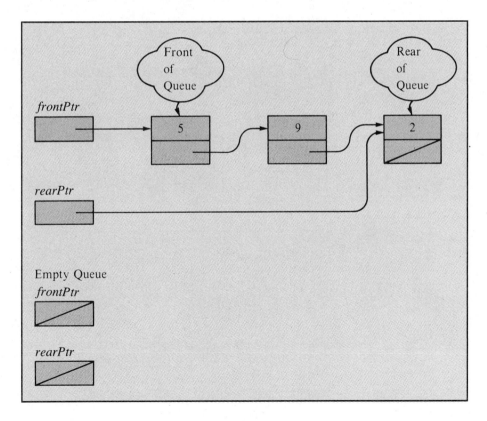

Figure 16.13 Inserting a new cell at the end of a queue. If the queue was previously empty, *frontPtr* will be set to point to the new cell, rather than to the *next* field of the preceding cell.

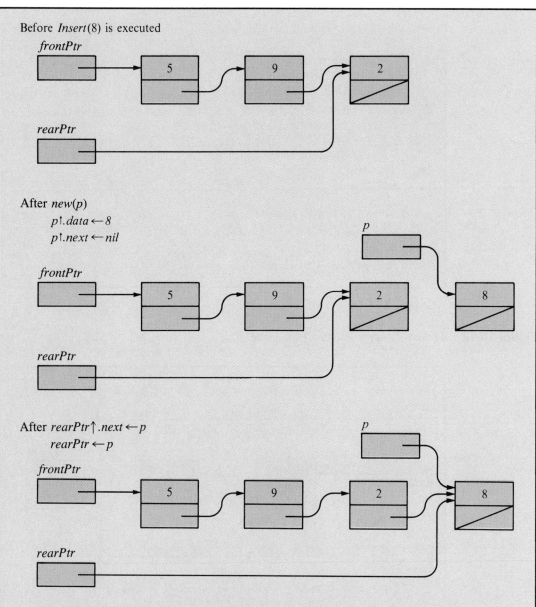

Before *Insert*(8) is executed

After *new*(p)
  p↑.*data* ← 8
  p↑.*next* ← nil

After *rearPtr*↑.*next* ← p
  rearPtr ← p

If cell is being inserted in empty queue, *front Ptr* ← p is used instead of *rear Ptr↑.next* ← p.

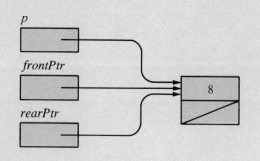

The new cell must now be linked to the end of the queue. We must consider two cases. If the queue is currently empty, the new rear cell will also become the front cell of the queue. Therefore, *frontPtr* must be set to point to the new cell:

frontPtr ← *p*

If the queue is not currently empty, the *next* field of the current rear cell, *rearPtr*↑ . *next*, must be set to point to the new rear cell:

rearPtr↑ *.next* ← *p*

The two cases can be distinguished by the value of *rearPtr*, which is *nil* for an empty queue and not *nil* for a nonempty queue:

if *rearPtr* = *nil* **then**
    frontPtr ← *p*
else
    rearPtr↑ *.next* ← *p*
endif

Regardless of which case occurred, *rearPtr* is always set to point to the new rear cell:

rearPtr ← *p*

The procedure *Remove* removes the front cell of the queue, as illustrated in Figure 16.14. If the value of *frontPtr* is *nil*, the queue is empty and an error is signaled. Otherwise, *p* is set to point to the cell that is to be removed:

p ← *frontPtr*

FrontPtr is set to point to the next cell on the linked list, the cell following the one to be removed:

frontPtr ← *frontPtr*↑ *.next*

If the cell to be removed is also the rear cell of the queue, the queue will be empty after the cell is removed, and *rearPtr* must be set to *nil*. If the cell to be removed is not the rear cell, the value of *rearPtr* is left unchanged:

if *rearPtr* = *p* **then**
    rearPtr ← *nil*
endif

Finally, the cell that has been removed is disposed of:

dispose(*p*)

TableHandler   Figure 16.15 shows the module *TableHandler*. Keys and values are stored in a linked list of data records. The pointer variable *first* points to the first record on the list. The definitions and declarations are similar to those in the other modules discussed in this section:

Figure 16.14 Removing a cell from the front of a queue. If the queue
contains only one cell, which is at both the front and the
rear of the queue, then *rearPtr* must be set to *nil* after the
cell has been removed.

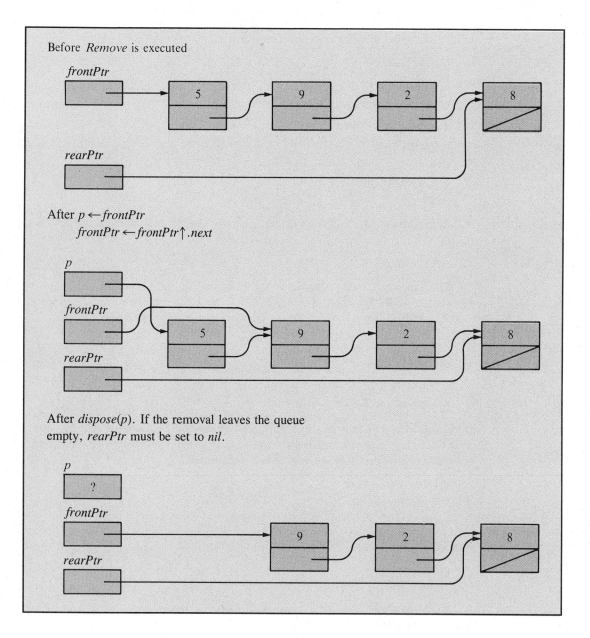

Figure 16.15 The module *TableHandler*.

---

module *TableHandler*

{ Maintain a table of data records }

declare
    export *Error*, *NewTable*, *Lookup*, *Insert*, *Delete*
    type *link* = **pointer to** *dataRecord*
    type *dataRecord* = **record**
                    key: *integer*
                    value: *real*
                    next: *link*
             endrecord
  first: *link*
  errorFlag: *Boolean*

  function *Error*: *Boolean*

  { Return value of and clear error indicator }

  execute
    error ← *errorFlag*
    errorFlag ← *false*
  end *Error*

  procedure *NewTable*

  { Initialize empty table }

  execute
    new(*first*)
    first↑.*next* ← *nil*
    errorFlag ← *false*
  end *NewTable*

  procedure *Lookup*(*searchKey*, *valueFound*)

  { Find value corresponding to given key }

```
    declare
        searchKey: in integer
        valueFound: out real
        found: Boolean
        prev, cur: link
    execute
        SequentialSearch(searchKey, found, prev, cur)
        if not found then
            errorFlag ← true
        else
            errorFlag ← false
            valueFound ← cur↑.value
        endif
    end Lookup



    procedure Insert(insertKey, insertValue)

    { Insert new record in table }

    declare
        insertKey: in integer
        insertValue: in real
        found: Boolean
        p, prev, cur: link
    execute
        SequentialSearch(insertKey, found, prev, cur)
        if found then
            errorFlag ← true
        else
            errorFlag ← false
            new(p)
            p↑.key ← insertKey
            p↑.value ← insertValue
            p↑.next ← cur
            prev↑.next ← p
        endif
    end Insert



    procedure Delete(deleteKey)

    { Delete record with given key }
```

```
declare
    deleteKey: in integer
    found: Boolean
    prev, cur: link
execute
    SequentialSearch(deleteKey, found, prev, cur)
    if not found then
        errorFlag ← true
    else
        errorFlag ← false
        prev↑.next ← cur↑.next
        dispose(cur)
    endif
end Delete


procedure SequentialSearch(searchKey, found, prev, cur)

{ Locate record with given key }

declare
    searchKey: in integer
    found: out Boolean
    prev, cur: in out link
    searching: Boolean
execute
    prev ← first
    cur ← first↑.next
    searching ← true
    while (cur <> nil) and searching
        if cur↑.key >= searchKey then
            searching ← false
        else
            prev ← cur
            cur ← cur↑.next
        endif
    endwhile
    if cur = nil then
        found ← false
    elseif cur↑.key = searchKey then
        found ← true
```

```
        else
            found ← false
        endif
    end SequentialSearch


initialize
    NewTable
end TableHandler
```

```
type link = pointer to dataRecord
type dataRecord = record
                        key: integer
                        value: real
                        next: link
                    endrecord
first: link
errorFlag: Boolean
```

The first record of a linked list differs from all other records in that it is pointed to by a pointer variable such as *first*, whereas every other record is pointed to by the *next* field of another record. This sometimes requires that the first record be treated as a special case. One way around this problem is to let the first record be a dummy record that does not contain valid data. Then every record that contains valid data is pointed to by another record, and each can be processed in the same way. The dummy record is created by the procedure *NewTable*, which initializes an empty table.

Sequential search is used for locating the record with a given key. The records on the list are maintained in ascending order according to their key values. Keeping the records in order offers no advantage in searching for a record that is on the list. It does, however, allow the search to be terminated sooner if the desired record is not on the list. The search can be terminated as soon as the point is reached where the record would be (according to the order of the keys) if it were present. If the records were not in order, a search for a nonexistent record would always have to go all the way to the end of the list.

Searching is done by a procedure

SequentialSearch(searchKey, found, prev, cur)

whose use is illustrated in Figure 16.16. The input parameter *searchKey* is the key being sought. The output parameter *found* is set to *true* if a record with the given

Figure 16.16 The pointers set by *SequentialSearch*. If the key being
sought was found, *cur* is set to point to the cell with that
key and *prev* is set to point to the preceding cell. Otherwise,
prev and *cur* are set to point to the cells between which a
cell with the given key should be inserted.

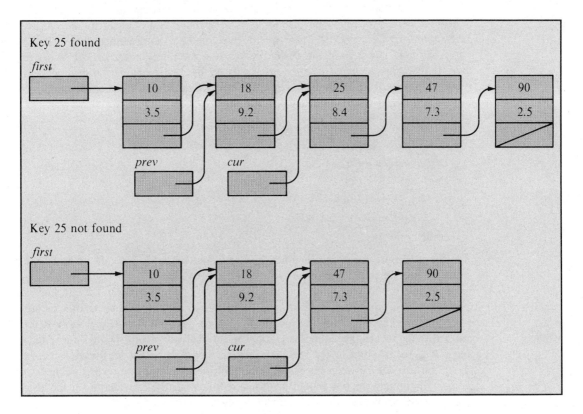

key was found and to *false* otherwise. The input-output parameters *prev* (previous)
and *cur* (current) are pointers that are set as follows. If the desired record was found,
cur points to the record that was found and *prev* points to the immediately preceding
record. If the desired record was not found, *prev* points to the record that would have
preceded the given record, had it been present, and *cur* points to the record that
would have followed it.

Note that the description of *SequentialSearch* assumes that the first record is a
dummy record that will never be pointed to by *cur*. If *cur* pointed to the first record,
then the value of *prev* would be undefined.

The procedure *NewTable* creates a list that contains no valid data records but
does contain the dummy record mentioned earlier. *NewTable* allocates the dummy
record, sets *first* to point to it, and sets the *next* field of the dummy record to *nil*.
ErrorFlag is set to *false*:

new(first)

first↑.next ← nil

errorFlag ← false

The procedure *Lookup* looks up the value of the input parameter *searchKey* and returns the corresponding value via the output parameter *valueFound*. *Lookup* calls *SequentialSearch* to search the list for a record whose key is equal to *searchKey*. *SequentialSearch* sets the values of *found*, *prev*, and *cur* as described above. If the value of *found* is not *true*, the desired key was not found, and *errorFlag* is set to *true*. If the value of *found* is *true*, *cur* points to the record having the desired key. *ErrorFlag* is set to *false*, and the content of the *value* field of the record pointed to by *cur* is returned via the parameter *valueFound*:

SequentialSearch(searchKey, found, prev, cur)

if not *found* **then**

    errorFlag ← true

else

    errorFlag ← false

    valueFound ← cur↑.value

endif

The procedure *Insert* inserts a new record whose key and value are given by the values of the input parameters *insertKey* and *insertValue*. *Insert* begins by calling *SequentialSearch* to search for a record whose key is equal to *insertKey*. If such a record is found, *errorFlag* is set to *true*, since we are not allowed to insert a record with the same key as an existing record. If no such record is found, then *prev* is set to point to the record preceding the point at which the new record should be inserted, and *cur* is set to point to the record following that point. That is, the new record should be inserted between the record pointed to by *prev* and the record pointed to by *cur*. If the new record should be inserted following the last record on the list, *prev* is set to point to the last record and *cur* is set to *nil*.

The record to be inserted is created by *new*:

new(p)

The *key* and *value* fields of the new record are set to the values of *insertKey* and *insertValue*:

p↑.key ← insertKey

p↑.value ← insertValue

The *next* field of the new record is set to point to the record that will follow the new record in the list. This record is pointed to by *cur*:

p↑.next ← cur

Prev points to the record that is to precede the new record in the list. The *next* field of this record must be set to point to the new record:

prev↑.next ← p

The procedure *Delete* deletes the record whose key field is equal to the input parameter *deleteKey*. *SequentialSearch* is called to find the record with the given key. If no such record is found, *errorFlag* is set to *true*. Otherwise, *errorFlag* is set to *false* and the record that was found is deleted.

Cur points to the record to be deleted and *prev* points to the preceding record. To delete the record pointed to by *cur*, the link from the preceding record must be "routed around" the record to be deleted and set to point to the following record. Specifically, the *next* field of the preceding record must be set to point to the record now pointed to by the *next* field of the record to be deleted:

$$prev\uparrow.next \leftarrow cur\uparrow.next$$

All that remains to be done is to dispose of the record that was removed from the list:

$$dispose(cur)$$

The procedure *SequentialSearch* scans the list for a record whose key is equal to the value of *SearchKey* and sets the values of *found*, *prev*, and *cur* as previously described. The input-output parameters *prev* and *cur* are used as pointers for scanning the list during the search. To begin, *prev* is set to point to the first record on the list (the dummy record) and *cur* is set to point to the record following the dummy record (the first record containing a valid data value). The flag *searching* is initialized to *true*:

$$prev \leftarrow first$$
$$cur \leftarrow first\uparrow.next$$
$$searching \leftarrow true$$

The search continues until it runs off the end of the list (the value of *cur* becomes *nil*) or until the flag *searching* becomes *false*. At each step of the search, the key field of the record pointed to by *cur* is compared with the value of *searchKey*. If the key field of the record equals *searchKey*, then we have found the desired record. If the key field of the record is greater than *searchKey*, then we have passed the point where the record would be if it were present. In either case, *searching* is set to *false* to terminate the search. If, however, the key field of the current record is less than the value of *searckKey*, the search should continue. Both *prev* and *cur* are moved forward one record in the list: *prev* is set to the value of *cur*, and *cur* is set to the value of the *next* field of the record it currently points to:

```
while (cur <> nil) and searching
    if cur↑.key >= searchKey then
        searching ← false
    else
        prev ← cur
        cur ← cur↑.next
    endif
endwhile
```

When the repetition terminates, we have three cases. If the value of *cur* is *nil*, the desired record was not found. If the value of *cur* is not *nil*, then *cur↑.key* is defined and can be checked. If the value of *cur↑.key* equals the value of *searchKey*, the desired record was found. If the value of *cur↑.key* is not equal to the value of *searchKey*, the desired record was not found. The following **if** construction checks for the three cases and sets the value of *found* accordingly:

> **if** *cur* = *nil* **then**
>> *found* ← *false*
>
> **elseif** *cur↑.key* = *searchKey* **then**
>> *found* ← *true*
>
> **else**
>> *found* ← *false*
>
> **endif**

16.4 Trees

A tree is a branching structure such as the one shown in Figure 16.2c. The reason for the name will be clearer if we turn the figure upside down. In computer science, we usually draw trees upside down relative to their natural counterparts.

Trees have two major applications in computer science. A tree can represent a hierarchical structure, such as the organizational chart of a corporation or the chain of command of a military unit. A tree can also represent a branching or forking path, such as all the possible paths through a maze or all the sequences of moves that can be made in solving a problem or playing a game. (The path branches because of the choice of moves available at each intersection in the maze or at each problem state or game position.)

We have already encountered both of these applications. Structure charts of algorithms represent hierarchical structures, as do the diagrams used in Chapter 2 to illustrate the recursive algorithm for solving the Towers of Hanoi problem. The decision trees used in Chapter 9 to illustrate nested **if** constructions represent both hierarchical and branching structures. Nested **if** constructions form a hierarchy, with the outermost **if** construction at the top of the hierarchy, the next outermost ones on the next level of the hierarchy, and so on. On the other hand, the sequences of tests to be made and actions to be taken in executing the nested **if** statements form a branching path. Each test of a condition has two possible outcomes and so has two branches—one to be followed if the condition is true and the other to be followed if the condition is false.

Definitions and terminology As in a general graph, the points at which lines come together in a tree are called *nodes*. (*Node* comes from a Latin word meaning *knot*.) Much of the remaining terminology for trees is borrowed from two sources: natural trees and family trees.

From natural trees, the topmost node of the tree is called the *root*, and the bottommost nodes are called *leaves*. The lines connecting the nodes are called *branches*. Figure 16.17 illustrates these terms.

From family trees, a node is said to be the *parent* of those immediately below it, which are said to be its *children*. Children of the same parent are said to be *siblings* or *twins*. Figure 16.18 illustrates these terms. The *descendants* of a node are its children, its children's children, its children's children's children, and so on. We occasionally speak of a node's *grandchildren*, *greatgrandchildren*, and so on.

Any node of a tree, together with all its descendants, is itself a tree, which is said to be a *subtree* of the original tree. Figure 16.19 illustrates subtrees. Note two extreme cases: (1) the entire tree is a subtree of itself, and (2) each leaf is a subtree consisting of only a single node.

We can use the concept of a subtree to give a formal definition of a tree: *A tree consists of a node, called its root, together with zero or more subtrees, each of which is itself a tree.* This definition is *recursive* in that the term *tree* is partially defined in terms of itself. (A tree has subtrees, which must themselves be trees, but trees are what we are defining in the first place.)

To construct an example of a tree from the definition, the definition must be applied repeatedly, as in Figure 16.20, in which triangles represent subtrees. Applying the definition once gives us a root and several subtrees. Applying the definition to each subtree expands it into a root and zero or more subtrees. We continue in this way until there are no more subtrees to which the definition can be applied. This situation can arise because a subtree can expand into a root only, with no additional subtrees to be expanded. The "root only" subtrees form the leaves of the tree being constructed.

Figure 16.17   Tree illustrating the terms *root, node, leaf,* and *branch.*

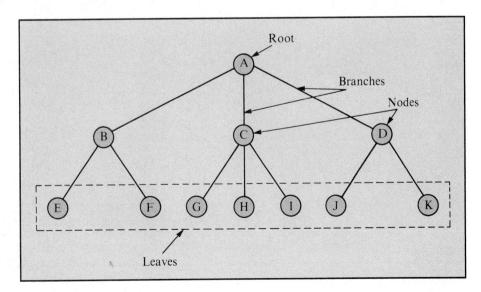

Figure 16.18   Tree illustrating the terms *parent*, *child*, *sibling*, and *twin*.

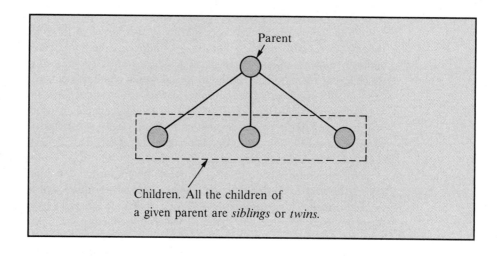

Figure 16.19   Subtrees. Note that each leaf is a subtree, and the entire tree
is a subtree of itself.

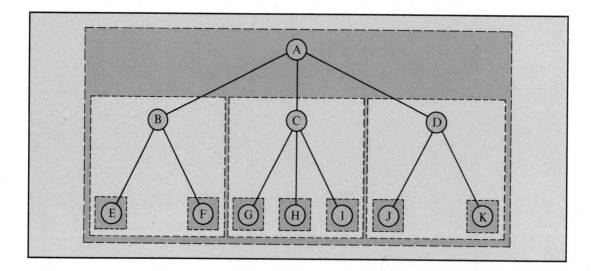

Figure 16.20 Constructing a tree according to the recursive definition of a
tree. The triangles represent subtrees.

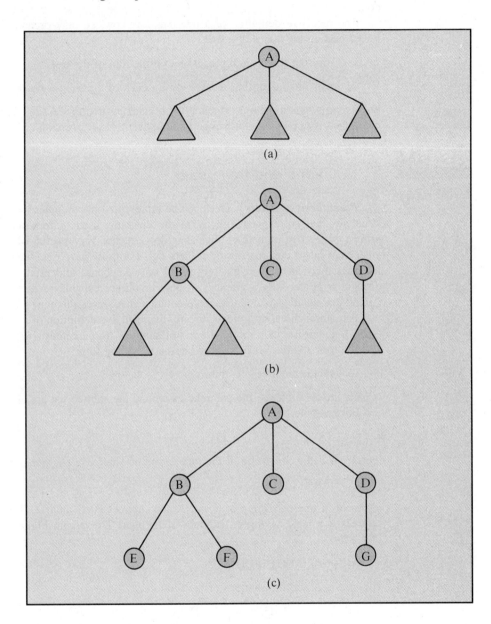

(a)

(b)

(c)

The subtrees referred to in the definition are said to be the subtrees of the root. In general, the subtrees of a node are the subtrees whose roots are the children of the node.

The recursive definition of a tree suggests how we may organize an algorithm for processing the nodes of a tree:

1. Carry out the desired processing on the root of the tree.

2. Invoke the algorithm recursively for each of the subtrees of the root.

Recursion is thus a natural principle for organizing tree-processing algorithms. Tree processing is one of the most important applications of recursion.

16.5
Notations and traversals

Parenthesis notation Trees can be represented in computer memory by linked structures that correspond directly to the diagrams used to represent trees on the printed page. Unfortunately, such diagrams are not very useful when we want to enter trees into a computer or print them out. For those purposes, we need a notation for trees that can be conveniently typed on a keyboard and printed on a standard display or printer (not a graphics display or printer capable of drawing diagrams). Parenthesis notation is one tree representation that serves this purpose.

Parenthesis notation follows directly the recursive definition of a tree, which says that a tree consists of a root and a list of subtrees. In parenthesis notation we represent the root and the list of subtrees in the following form:

root(subtree subtree . . . subtree)

If there are no subtrees, the parentheses around the subtree list are also omitted.

For example,

A

represents a tree consisting of the root A and no subtrees. The notation

A(B C D)

represents a tree consisting of a root A and subtrees B, C, and D. Each of the three subtrees is a leaf, having no subtrees of its own. The tree in Figure 16.2 is represented by

A(B(E F) C(G H I) D(J K))

The root is A and the subtrees of the root are

B(E F)   C(G H I)   D(J K)

Each subtree is itself represented in parenthesis notation. For example, the leftmost subtree has root B and subtrees E and F. The tree in Figure 16.21 is represented as follows:

A(B(C D) E(F(G)) H(I(J K) L(M N O)))

Figure 16.21   A tree, together with its representation in parenthesis notation.

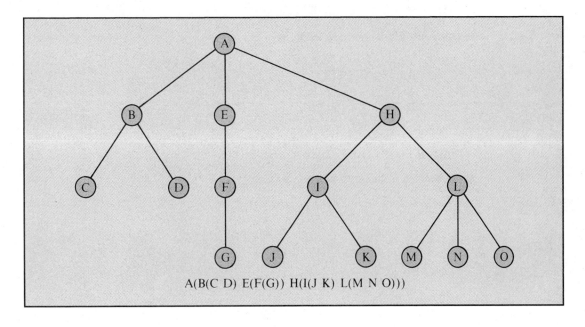

A(B(C D) E(F(G)) H(I(J K) L(M N O)))

The subtrees of the root are

    B(C D)   E(F(G))   H(I(J K) L(M N O))

The leftmost subtree has root B and subtrees C and D. The middle subtree has root E and subtree F(G). The rightmost subtree has root H and subtrees

    I(J K)   L(M N O)

We see that the nesting of parentheses provides a convenient way of representing the hierarchical structure of the tree. The root is not enclosed in parentheses, each child of the root is enclosed in one set of parentheses, each grandchild of the root in two sets of parentheses, and so on. The converse of this statement is also true: when we encounter nested parentheses, as in arithmetical expressions, we can be sure that a tree structure is at hand. There is a programming language, LISP (List Processor), in which both programs and data are represented as trees. For input and output, the trees are represented with the aid of nested parentheses.

Indented notation   Parenthesized notations can be difficult to read, an objection often raised against LISP. As an alternative, we can use indentation rather than parentheses to represent a tree structure. The correspondence between parenthesis notation and indented notation is simple. Whenever a left parenthesis is encountered in the parenthesis notation, the level of indentation is increased by one unit. Whenever a right parenthesis is encountered, the level of indentation is decreased by one unit. Thus the tree

A(B C D)

is represented in indented notation by

A
    B
    C
    D

and the tree

A(B(E F) C(G H I) D(J K))

is represented in indented notation by

A
    B
        E
        F
    C
        G
        H
        I
    D
        J
        K

Note that the root appears on the first level of indentation, the children of the root on the second level, and the grandchildren of the root on the third level.

A mixture of parentheses and indentation is often useful. Simple parenthesized structures are written on a single line, but larger structures are written on several lines with indentation used for clarity. For example, the parenthesized tree representation

A(B(C D) E(F(G)) H(I(J K) L(M N O)))

is much easier to read if written as follows:

A(
  B(C D)
  E(F(G))
  H(
    I(J K)
    L(M N O)))

LISP systems often contain a "pretty printer" routine that prints parenthesized expressions in indented form for easier reading.

As with nested parentheses, whenever multiple levels of indentation are encountered, we can be sure that a tree structure is at hand. For example, the indentation in outlines represents a tree structure, as does that used in writing algorithms and programs.

Expression trees   As suggested earlier, arithmetical expressions can be represented as trees. Such expression trees are particularly interesting because the prefix and postfix notations for arithmetical expressions correspond to important ways of traversing (passing through every node of) expression trees.

The simplest arithmetical expression consists of a single constant, such as 3. The corresponding tree, shown in Figure 16.22a, consists of a root alone with no subtrees. The next simplest kind of expression consists of two constants combined by an operator, such as

$3 + 5$

Figure 16.22b shows the corresponding tree. The root of the tree is the operator $+$, and its two subtrees are the operands 3 and 5. Finally, consider a more complex expression such as

$3 * 7 + 12 / 3$

Figure 16.22   Expression trees.

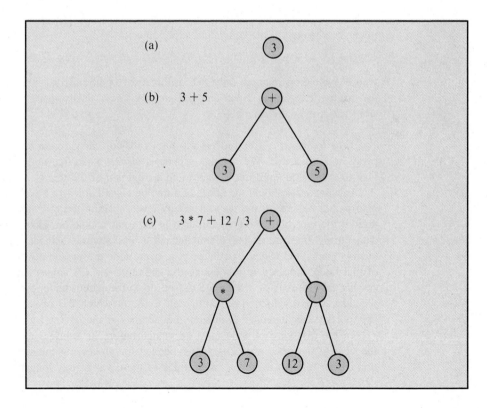

As shown in Figure 16.22c, the root of the tree is +, the operator that is applied last in evaluating the expression. The subtrees of the root are the expression trees for 3 * 7 and 12 / 3, the subexpressions that must be evaluated to compute the values that are to be added by +.

The leaves of an expression tree represent values; in our examples the leaves are always constants, although they could also be variables. Each nonleaf node is an operator that is to be applied to the values of the expressions represented by its subtrees. In evaluating the expression represented by the tree, we can think of values as starting at the leaves and moving upwards. When two values arrive at an operator node, the operator is applied to them, and the result of the operation is passed on to the parent of the operator node. Eventually, the values of the operands of the root operator reach the root of the tree, the root operator is applied to them, and the result is the value of the expression represented by the tree.

In Figure 16.22c, for example, values 3 and 7 are passed up to the * node where they are multiplied to obtain 21. Values 12 and 3 are passed up to the / node where they are divided to obtain 4. The partial results 21 and 4 are passed up to the + node where they are added to obtain 25. Since the + node is the root of the expression tree, 25 is the value of the expression represented by the tree.

Expression trees are often used by language processors. For example, some compilers, called *optimizing compilers*, try to rearrange expressions to reduce the amount of work that the computer must do. The expression

3 * 5 + 3 * 9

might be changed to the equivalent expression

3 * (5 + 9)

whose evaluation requires only two arithmetical operations as opposed to three for the original expression. Such changes are often most easily made when the expressions are represented by trees.

Tree traversal   Tree processing often calls for carrying out some operation on every node of a tree. We say that a node is *visited* when that node is processed. A visit to every node in a tree is said to be a *traversal* of the tree.

In what order should the nodes of a tree be visited during a traversal? An obvious plan would be to visit the nodes level by level, visiting the root first, then the children of the root, then the grandchildren of the root, and so on. However, the flow of data during tree processing often dictates a less obvious scheme. Two cases frequently occur: (1) values calculated at a given node are passed down to the subtrees of that node and used in processing the subtrees; and (2) values calculated by processing the subtrees of a node are passed up to the parent node. An example of the second case is evaluation of expression trees, in which the operand values for an operator are calculated by evaluating the subtrees of the operator node.

In the first case, a node must be visited before its subtrees are traversed since the visit to the node produces values needed for processing the subtrees. Since we don't want to have to store or keep track of these values any longer than necessary, we want to traverse the subtrees of a node as soon as the node has been visited. These considerations suggest a *preorder traversal*, in which each node is visited just before its subtrees are traversed.

Likewise, in the second case, the subtrees of a node must be traversed before the node is visited since values calculated during the traversals of the subtrees are needed for processing the node. Since we don't want to store or keep track of these values any longer than necessary, we want to visit a node as soon as its subtrees have been traversed. These considerations suggest a *postorder traversal*, in which each node is visited just after its subtrees have been traversed.

We can give a recursive definition of a preorder traversal as follows:

1. Visit the root of the tree.

2. Do a preorder traversal of each of the subtrees of the root, taking the subtrees in left-to-right order.

Although traversing the subtrees in left-to-right order is conventional, some other order could be used if dictated by the circumstances of a particular problem. As we will see later, it is easy to convert this recursive definition into a recursive algorithm for actually carrying out the traversal. In the same way, we can give a recursive definition of postorder traversal as follows:

1. Do a postorder traversal of each of the subtrees of the root, taking the subtrees in left-to-right order.

2. Visit the root of the tree.

Figure 16.23 illustrates a preorder traversal, and Figure 16.24 illustrates a postorder traversal. Check the figures carefully to verify that the definition of each kind of traversal is satisfied: In the preorder traversal, each node is visited immediately before its subtrees are traversed; in the postorder traversal, each node is visited immediately after its subtrees are traversed.

We can list the nodes in the order in which they are visited by a preorder or a postorder traversal. For the tree in Figures 16.21, 16.23, and 16.24, the preorder list is

A B C D E F G H I J K L M N O

and the postorder list is

C D B G F E J K I M N O L H A

These lists can serve as the basis for *linear* representations of a tree—representations based on lists of nodes rather than on linked records. To be able to recover the tree from a preorder or postorder list of nodes, information is needed as to how the nodes are grouped into subtrees. One way to provide this information is to enclose the nodes for each subtree in parentheses. If we do this for the preorder list, we get

A(B(C D) E(F(G)) H(I(J K) L(M N O)))

which is just the parenthesis notation discussed earlier. Inserting parentheses in the

Figure 16.23   A preorder traversal. To indicate where a node is visited, the line passes inside the circle representing the node.

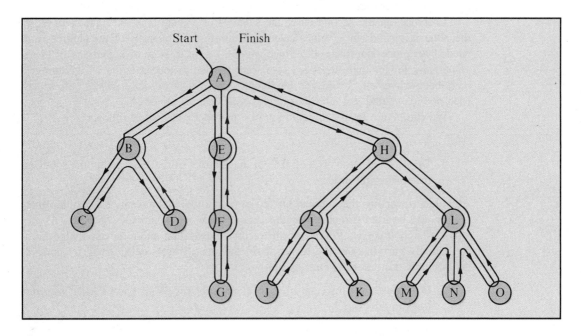

postorder list gives us a "reverse parenthesis notation" in which each node follows the list of its subtrees:

((C D)B ((G)F)E ((J K)I (M N O)L)H)A

In this notation, the subtrees of node A are

(C D)B   ((G)F)E   ((J K)I (M N O)L)H

the subtrees of node B are C and D, the subtree of node E is (G)F, the subtrees of node H are

(J K)I   (M N O)L

and so on.

Another way to provide information about subtrees is to indicate the number of children of each node. If we follow the symbol for each node by the number of its children, our preorder and postorder lists look like this:

preorder: A3 B2 C0 D0 E1 F1 G0 H2 I2 J0 K0 L3 M0 N0 O0
postorder: C0 D0 B2 G0 F1 E1 J0 K0 I2 M0 N0 O0 L3 H2 A3

We can easily recover the original tree from such a list. Using the preorder list, for example, we start by drawing node A, the first node on the list, with three

Figure 16.24   A postorder traversal. To indicate where a node is visited,
the line passes inside the circle representing the node.

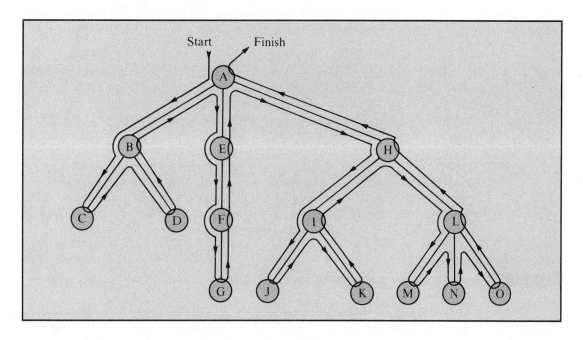

descending branches for its three children. Node B, the next node on the list, is
attached to the leftmost branch from node A, and two descending branches are drawn
from node B. Node C, the next node on the list, is attached to the leftmost branch
from node B; since node C has zero children, it is a leaf, and no branches are drawn
from it. We continue through the list in the same way, attaching each node to the
leftmost branch that does not already have a node attached to its lower end. For each
new node we draw descending branches equal in number to the node's children.

Prefix and postfix notations   Let's consider the lists of nodes produced by
preorder and postorder traversals of the expression trees in Figure 16.22. Since Figure 16.22a consists of only a single node, both the preorder and postorder lists are
the same:

   3

For Figure 16.22b, we get the following preorder and postorder lists:

   preorder: + 3 5
   postorder: 3 5 +

In the preorder list, the operator precedes its operands, and in the postorder list, the
operator follows its operands. In fact, the preorder list is just the prefix or Polish

notation for the expression, and the postorder list is the postfix or reverse Polish notation. For Figure 16.22c, the two lists are as follows:

preorder: + * 3 7 / 12 3
postorder: 3 7 * 12 3 / +

Again, the two lists are just the prefix and postfix notations for the expression.

This observation gives us some insight into why prefix notation and (particularly) postfix notation are so useful. First, given an expression tree, we can easily generate the prefix or postfix notation for the expression by doing a preorder or a postorder traversal. Second, given the prefix or postfix notation, we can reconstruct the expression tree, since we know the number of children of each node. (Operators such as +, *, and / have two children; operands such as 3, 5, 7, and 12 have no children.) Finally, since values are passed from children to parents when an expression tree is evaluated, the nodes should be visited during evaluation in the order dictated by a postorder traversal. This, however, is just the order in which the nodes appear in the postfix notation for the expression. It's no wonder, then, that an expression can be most easily evaluated while scanning its postfix notation from left to right.

16.6

Linked representation of trees

In this section we will look at one way of representing a tree as a set of records linked by pointers. To illustrate tree processing using this representation, we will look at procedures for inputting a tree in parenthesis notation and for doing preorder and postorder traversals. Figure 16.25 shows an algorithm for inputting a tree in parenthesis notation and then printing the preorder and the postorder lists of nodes for the tree. The definition of the representation and the procedures for inputting and traversing the tree are packaged in the module *TraversalRoutines*, which is included in Figure 16.25.

The following type definitions define the linked representation:

type *link* = **pointer to** *node*
type *node* = **record**
        value: *char*
        rightSib,
        leftChild: *link*
    endrecord

As shown in Figure 16.26 on page 786, each node of a tree is represented by a record of type *node*. The *value* field of the record contains the character that is used to label the node in diagrams: 'A' for node A, 'B' for node B, and so on. Each record has a field, *rightSib*, which points to its sibling to the right. The value of *rightSib* is *nil* for the rightmost sibling. Thus, all the children of a node are linked together by their *rightSib* fields. The field *leftChild* points to the leftmost child of the node. The leftmost child is the first node of the linked list containing all the children of the parent node. If a node has no children, the value of *leftChild* is *nil*.

Figure 16.25   Algorithm demonstrating parenthesis notation, linked
representations, and preorder and postorder traversal. The
needed type definitions together with the procedures for
inputting and traversing the tree are packaged in the module
TraversalRoutines.

```
algorithm TreeTraversal

{ Input tree in parenthesis notation and output results of preorder and
  postorder traversal }

declare
    import link, GetChar, ReadTree, PreorderTraversal,
             PostorderTraversal from TraversalRoutines
    p: link
execute
    output 'Tree: ', more
    GetChar
    ReadTree(p)
    output
    output 'Preorder list: ', more
    PreorderTraversal(p)
    output
    output 'Postorder list: ', more
    PostorderTraversal(p)
    output
end TreeTraversal



module TraversalRoutines

{ Provides procedures for reading in and traversing a tree }

declare
    export link, GetChar, ReadTree, PreorderTraversal,
             PostorderTraversal
    type link = pointer to node
    type node = record
                    value: char
                    rightSib,
                    leftChild: link
                endrecord
    c: char
```

```
procedure GetChar

{ Read next nonblank character into c }

execute
    repeat
        input c, more
    until c <> ' '
end GetChar



procedure ReadTree(p)

{ Read tree in parenthesis notation }

declare
    p: in out link
    q, r: link
execute
    new(p)
    p↑.value ← c
    GetChar
    q ← p
    q↑.rightSib ← nil
    if c = '(' then
        GetChar
        while c <> ')'
            ReadTree(r)
            q↑.rightSib ← r
            q ← r
        endwhile
        GetChar
    endif
    p↑.leftChild ← p↑.rightSib
    p↑.rightSib ← nil
end ReadTree



procedure PreorderTraversal(p)

{ Print preorder list of nodes }
```

```
            declare
                p: in link
                q: link
            execute
                output p↑.value, ' ', more
                q ← p↑.leftChild
                while q <> nil
                    PreorderTraversal(q)
                    q ← q↑.rightSib
                endwhile
            end PreorderTraversal


        procedure PostorderTraversal(p)

        { Print postorder list of nodes }

        declare
            p: in link
            q: link
        execute
            q ← p↑.leftChild
            while q <> nil
                PostorderTraversal(q)
                q ← q↑.rightSib
            endwhile
            output p↑.value, ' ', more
        end PostorderTraversal

    end TraversalRoutines
```

PreorderTraversal and postorderTraversal   Although a tree must be read in before it can be traversed, we will discuss the traversal routines before the routine for reading in a tree, since the traversal routines are simpler.

The procedure *PreorderTraversal(p)* does a preorder traversal of the tree whose root is pointed to by *p*. The procedure prints the value of every node it visits, so the effect of executing the procedure is to print a preorder list of nodes.

In accordance with the definition of preorder traversal, the procedure begins by visiting (printing the value of) the node pointed to by *p*:

output *p*↑.*value*, ' ', **more**

Next, the procedure must call itself recursively to do a preorder traversal of each of

Figure 16.26 Linked representation for a general tree.

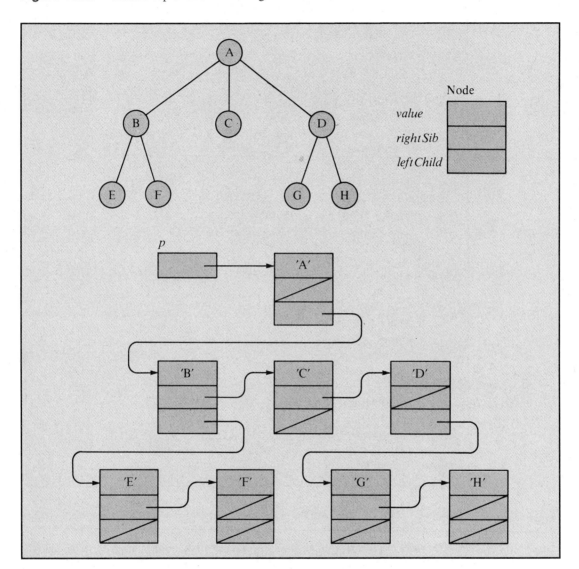

the subtrees of the node pointed to by p. The roots of these subtrees are the children of the node pointed to by p. Therefore, the procedure call

$PreorderTraversal(q)$

must be made with q pointing to each of the children of the node pointed to by p.

The children of the node pointed to by p are joined into a linked list by pointers in their *rightSib* fields. The *leftChild* field of the node pointed to by p contains a pointer to the first node on the list of children. Thus before processing of the subtrees begins, q is set to point to the first node on the list of children:

$q \leftarrow p.leftChild$

After each subtree has been traversed, q is set to point to the next child on the list:

$q \leftarrow q\uparrow.rightSib$

Processing continues until the value of q is *nil*, indicating that the end of the list of children has been reached:

$q \leftarrow p\uparrow.leftChild$
while $q <> nil$
    PreorderTraversal(q)
    $q \leftarrow q\uparrow.rightSib$
endwhile

The procedure *PostorderTraversal(p)* does a postorder traversal of the tree whose root is pointed to by p, printing the value of each cell that it visits. *Postorder-Traversal* is very similar to *PreorderTraversal* except that the node pointed to by p is visited *after* its subtrees have been traversed rather than before. Thus, *PostorderTraversal* begins by calling itself recursively to traverse each of the subtrees of the node pointed to by p:

$q \leftarrow p\uparrow.leftChild$
while $q <> nil$
    PostorderTraversal(q)
    $q \leftarrow q\uparrow.rightSib$
endwhile

After all its subtrees have been traversed, the node pointed to by p is visited:

output $p\uparrow.value$, ' ', **more**

ReadTree   The procedure *ReadTree(p)* reads in a tree in parenthesis notation, stores it in the linked representation, and returns with the value of the input-output parameter p pointing to the root of the tree that was read in. The procedure assumes that each node is represented by a single character in the parenthesis notation.

The character variable c, which is global to all the procedures of the module, is used to hold the next character of input. The procedure *GetChar* skips any blanks in the input and stores the next nonblank input character in c:

repeat
    input c, **more**
until $c <> ' '$

GetChar is called once before *ReadTree* is called; thus when *ReadTree* begins, c already contains the first input character to be processed.

The input read by *ReadTree* consists of a character representing the root of a tree possibly followed by a parenthesized list of subtrees. When *ReadTree* is invoked, the value of *c* is the character representing the root of the tree. *ReadTree* allocates a record for the root node and stores the value of *c* in the value field of the new record. *GetChar* is then called to read the next input character to be processed:

> *new*(*p*)
> *p*↑.*value* ← *c*
> *GetChar*

The node just read may be followed by a parenthesized list of subtrees, with the subtrees themselves in parenthesis notation. *ReadTree* must be called recursively to read each of these subtrees. The roots of the subtrees, which are the children of the nodes just read, must be linked by their *rightSib* fields, and the *leftChild* field of the node just read must be set to point to the first node on the list of children.

At this point we are going to do something slightly tricky. As we know, the *leftChild* field of the root should point to the first node on the list of children. The children on that list are linked together by their *rightSib* pointers. Our procedure will be simplified, however, if it has to deal with only one pointer field rather than two. For this reason, the *rightSib* (rather than the *leftChild*) field of the root will be set to point to the first child node read in, the *rightSib* field of that node will be set to point to the next child node read in, and so on. What we will end up with is a list of nodes linked by their *rightSib* fields. The first node on this list will be the root, and the remaining nodes will be its children. Before the procedure returns, the pointer to the leftmost child will be transferred from the *rightSib* field of the root to the *leftChild* field where it belongs. Figure 16.27 illustrates this approach.

Throughout processing, *q* will point to the current last node on the list just described. The only node on this list at the moment is the root, to which *q* is set to point:

> *q* ← *p*

The *rightSib* field of the root is set to *nil* so that it will contain the end-of-list sentinel in the event that no child nodes are read in:

> *q*↑.*rightSib* ← *nil*

If the next input character is a left parenthesis, there is a list of subtrees to be read. *GetChar* is called to get the next input character following the left parenthesis. Processing will continue until the next input character is a right parenthesis. *ReadTree* is called recursively to read each subtree and set *r* to point to its root. This root must be joined to the end of the list we are building. The node currently at the end of this list is pointed to by *q*; its *rightSib* field is set to point to the root of the subtree just read. The value of *q* is set to that of *r*, so that *q* will point to the new end node. After all the subtrees have been read, *GetChar* is called to pass over the right parenthesis that terminated the list of subtrees:

> **if** *c* = '(' **then**
>> *GetChar*

Figure 16.27   *ReadTree* reads a tree as a list of nodes linked by their
rightSib pointers. The first node on the list is the root of the
tree; the remaining nodes are the children of the root. Before
returning, *ReadTree* transfers the pointer to the first child
node from the *rightSib* field of the root to the *leftChild* field
of the root.

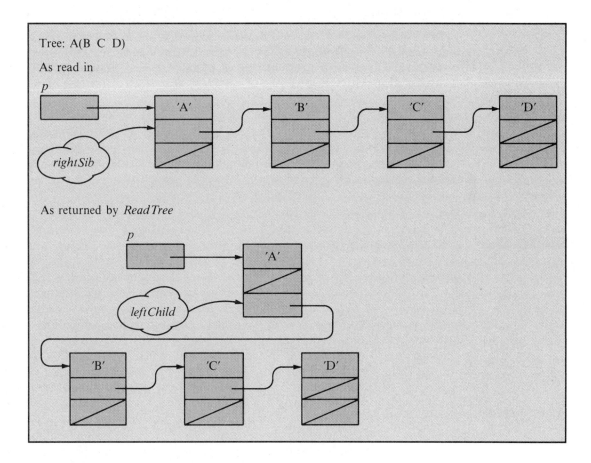

```
        while c <> ')'
            ReadTree(r)
            q↑.rightSib ← r
            q ← r
        endwhile
        GetChar
    endif
```

Finally, the pointer to the first child node must be transferred from the *rightSib* field of the root to the *leftChild* field, as illustrated in Figure 16.27:

$p\uparrow.leftChild \leftarrow p\uparrow.rightSib$

The *rightSib* field of the root is set to *nil* because (at least at this point in the processing) the root does not have a right sibling:

$p\uparrow.rightSib \leftarrow nil$

The algorithm *TreeTraversal* calls *ReadTree* to input a tree in parenthesis notation, then calls *PreorderTraversal* to output a preorder list of nodes for the tree and *PostorderTraversal* to output a postorder list of nodes. A typical dialogue with the algorithm goes like this:

```
Tree: A(B(E F) C(G H I) D(J K))
Preorder list: A B E F C G H I D J K
Postorder list: E F B G H I C J K D A
```

Note that the nodes appear in the same order in the preorder list as they do in the parenthesis notation.

16.7

Binary search trees

A drawback of linked lists is that they can be searched only by sequential search rather than the much faster binary search. Fortunately, there are linked structures called *binary search trees* that allow binary search while preserving the desirable properties of linked structures, such as the ability to make insertions and deletions without having to relocate existing records.

A *binary tree* is one in which each node has at most two children, referred to as the *left child* and *right child* of the node. The corresponding subtrees are known as the *left subtree* and the *right subtree*. If a node has only one child, it can be either a left child or a right child. In a binary search tree, records are stored in the nodes of a binary tree in such a way that all records stored in the left subtree of a node have keys less than that of the record stored in the node, and all records stored in the right subtree have keys greater than that of the record stored in the node.

Figure 16.28 illustrates a binary search tree. Only the keys of the records stored in the nodes are shown. Thus the root has key 590, its left child has key 230, its right child has key 725, and so on. Note that the node with key 610 has a right child but no left child, and the node with key 945 has a left child but no right child. Also note that the left subtree of a node contains only those keys that are less than the key of the node, and the right subtree contains only those keys that are greater than the key of the node.

To find the node having a given key, we start at the root node and compare the given key with the key stored in the node. If the given key is equal to the key of the node, we have found the node we are searching for. If the given key is less than the key of the node, we follow the left branch from the node. If the given key is greater

Figure 16.28   A binary search tree. All the keys in the left subtree of a
node are less than the key of the node, and all keys in the
right subtree of a node are greater than the key of the node.

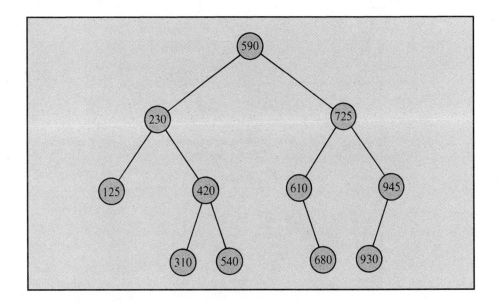

than the key of the node, we follow the right branch from the node. This step is
repeated until we find the node we are searching for or until we attempt to follow a
nonexistent branch. In the latter case, the record we are searching for is not present.

For example, let's look up the key 310 in the binary search tree of Figure 16.28.
Since 310 is less than 590, we take the left branch from the root. Since 310 is greater
than 230, we take right branch from node 230. Since 310 is less than 420, we take
the left branch from node 420, which takes us to node 310.

Now let's try to look up the key 500. We take the left branch from the root, the
right branch from node 230, the right branch from node 420, and attempt to take the
left branch from node 540. Since node 540 has no left child, however, there is no
left branch to follow, and so we conclude that there is no node with key 500. If we
wished to insert a new node with key 500, we would insert it as the left child of
node 540, as shown in Figure 16.29. If the search just described is repeated for the
tree in Figure 16.29, it will lead to the newly inserted node 500.

As in ordinary binary search, we would like each comparison in a binary tree
search to eliminate roughly half the nodes from consideration. This will be true only
if the search tree is reasonably *balanced*—if the left and right subtrees of a node
contain approximately the same number of nodes. Figure 16.30 shows two extreme
cases of unbalanced trees. In each case, there is at most one branch leaving each
node. Therefore, the comparisons made at each node cannot eliminate any nodes
from consideration, and so binary search is no more efficient than sequential search.

Figure 16.29 The binary search tree of Figure 16.28 after the insertion of a node with key 500. To determine where to attach the new node, we search for a node with key 500 and note where the search attempts to follow a nonexistent branch. That is the point at which the new node should be attached.

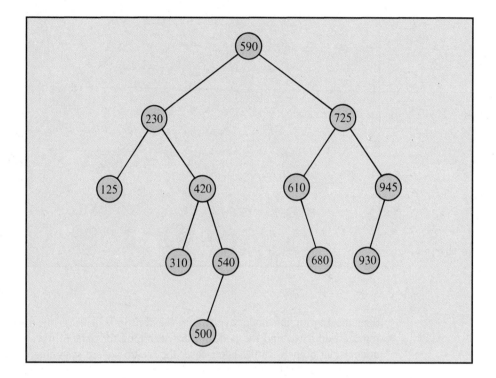

If nodes are inserted in and deleted from a binary tree in random order, the tree will probably remain reasonably balanced. To make sure, however, we can use *balancing algorithms* that restructure the tree to improve its balance. We will not go into balancing algorithms in detail here, but Figure 16.31 on page 794 illustrates their basic operation, which is called *rotation*. The rotation at the top of Figure 16.31 transfers a node from the left side to the right side of a tree or subtree; the rotation at bottom performs the reverse transformation.

TableHandler again Figure 16.32 on page 795 shows yet another version of the module *TableHandler*, one in which the records are stored as nodes of a binary tree. This version provides for only lookup and insertion of records. Deletion, which is somewhat more complicated than lookup or insertion, is discussed briefly later in the chapter. Writing a deletion procedure for *TableHandler* is left as an exercise.

The data representation is based on the following definitions:

Figure 16.30   Two extreme cases of unbalanced binary search trees. In
each case, there is at most one branch leaving each node, so
a comparison at a node cannot eliminate any nodes from
being examined by a search.

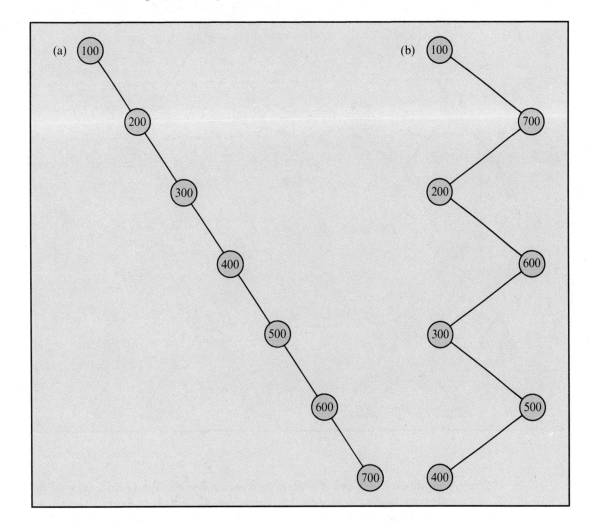

> **type** *link* = **pointer to** *dataRecord*
> **type** *dataRecord* = **record**
> > *key*: *integer*
> > *value*: *real*
> > *left*, *right*: *link*
> **endrecord**

Figure 16.31   The operation of *rotation*, which is used to balance a tree or
subtree by moving a node from one side of the tree to the
other. The triangles represent arbitrary subtrees.

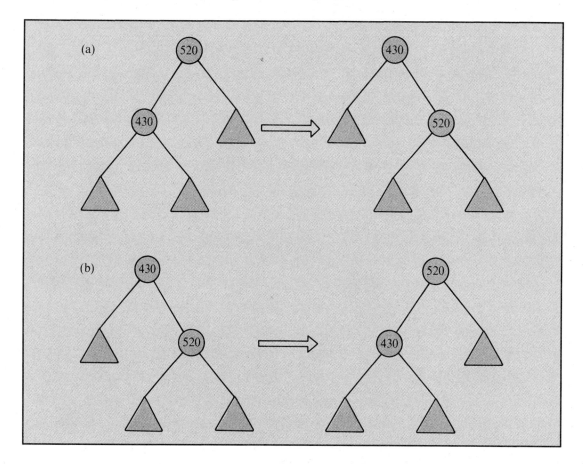

Each node of the binary tree is a record of type *dataRecord*. The *key* and *value* fields
of a node hold the data to be stored. Since each node can have at most two children,
a separate pointer field is reserved for each child. The *left* field of a node points to
the left child of the node, and the *right* field points to the right child. If a child is
not present, the value of the corresponding pointer field is *nil*.

The pointer variable *root* points to the root node. Just as we found it convenient
to use a dummy node as the first node of a linked list, we also find it convenient to
use a dummy node for the root of a binary tree. That way, every node that contains
a valid data value has a parent; none has to be treated as a special case because it is
the parentless root node. The *key* and *value* fields of the dummy root node contain
garbage; the *left* field is *nil* and the *right* field points to a node containing valid data.
(If the tree is empty, the *right* field of the dummy root node also contains *nil*). Figure

Figure 16.32 This version of the module *TableHandler* stores keys and values in the nodes of a binary search tree.

```
module TableHandler

{ Maintain a table of data records }

declare
    export Error, NewTable, Lookup, Insert
    type link = pointer to dataRecord
    type dataRecord = record
                            key: integer
                            value: real
                            left, right: link
                      endrecord
    root: link
    errorFlag: Boolean


function Error: Boolean

{ Return value of and clear error indicator }

execute
    Error ← errorFlag
    errorFlag ← false
end Error


procedure NewTable

{ Initialize empty table }

execute
    new(root)
    root↑.left ← nil
    root↑.right ← nil
    errorFlag ← false
end NewTable


procedure Lookup(searchKey, valueFound)

{ Find value corresponding to given key }
```

```
declare
    searchKey: in integer
    valueFound: out real
    found: Boolean
    prev, cur: link
execute
    BinaryTreeSearch(searchKey, found, prev, cur)
    if not found then
        errorFlag ← true
    else
        errorFlag ← false
        valueFound ← cur↑.value
    endif
end Lookup



procedure Insert(insertKey, insertValue)

{ Insert new record in table }

declare
    insertKey: in integer
    insertValue: in real
    found: Boolean
    p, prev, cur: link
execute
    BinaryTreeSearch(insertKey, found, prev, cur)
    if found then
        errorFlag ← true
    else
        errorFlag ← false
        new(p)
        p↑.key ← insertKey
        p↑.value ← insertValue
        p↑.left ← nil
        p↑.right ← nil
        if prev = root then
            prev↑.right ← p
        elseif insertKey < prev↑.key then
            prev↑.left ← p
        else
            prev↑.right ← p
        endif
    endif
end Insert
```

```
        procedure BinaryTreeSearch(searchKey, found, prev, cur)

        { Locate record with given key }

        declare
            searchKey: in integer
            found: out Boolean
            prev, cur: in out link
            searching: Boolean
        execute
            prev ← root
            cur ← root↑.right
            searching ← true
            while (cur <> nil) and searching
                if searchKey < cur↑.key then
                    prev ← cur
                    cur ← cur↑.left
                elseif searchKey > cur↑.key then
                    prev ← cur
                    cur ← cur↑.right
                else
                    searching ← false
                endif
            endwhile
            found ← (cur <> nil)
        end BinaryTreeSearch


    initialize
        NewTable
    end TableHandler
```

16.33 illustrates this representation of binary search trees. Only the *key*, *left*, and *right* fields are shown in Figure 16.33; for simplicity the value fields are omitted.

The procedure *NewTable* creates a binary search tree containing only the dummy root node. The variable *root* is set to point to a newly created node, and the *left* and *right* fields of the new node are set to *nil*:

new(*root*)

root↑.*left* ← *nil*

Figure 16.33   Linked representation for a binary search tree. For
simplicity, the *value* fields of the nodes are not shown.

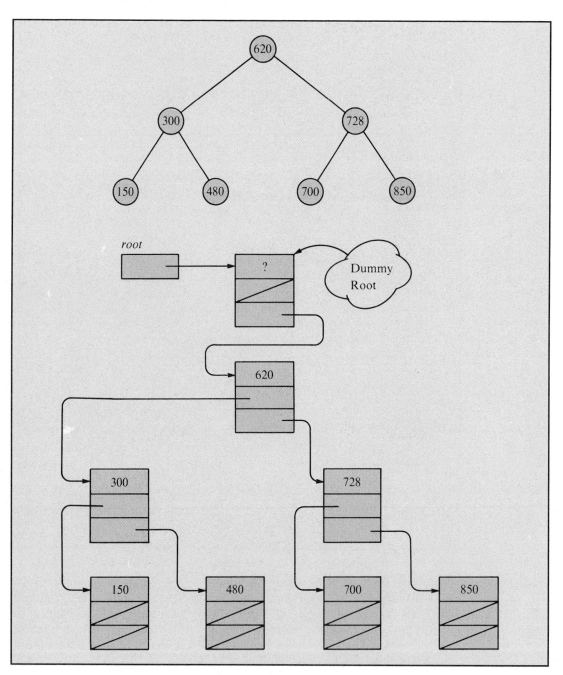

$root\uparrow.right \leftarrow nil$

$errorFlag \leftarrow false$

The procedures for lookup and insertion both call the procedure

$BinaryTreeSearch(searchKey, found, prev, cur)$

which looks up a key in the binary tree. The value of *searchKey* is the key to be looked up. The value of *found* is set to *true* or *false* depending on whether or not the desired node was found. If the desired node was found, *cur* points to that node and *prev* points to its parent. If the desired node was not found, the value of *cur* is *nil*, and *prev* points to the parent that the desired node would have had if it had been present. Put another way, if we wish to insert a new node with the key that caused the search to fail, we should insert it as a child of the node pointed to by *prev*.

The procedure *Lookup* looks up the value of *searchKey* and returns the corresponding value via *valueFound*. *BinaryTreeSearch* is called to search for the given key. If the value returned for *found* is *false*, then *errorFlag* is set to *true*. Otherwise, *errorFlag* is set to *false* and *valueFound* is set to the contents of the *value* field of the node pointed to by *cur*:

$BinaryTreeSearch(searchKey, found, prev, cur)$

if not *found* **then**

    $errorFlag \leftarrow true$

else

    $errorFlag \leftarrow false$

    $valueFound \leftarrow cur\uparrow.value$

endif

The procedure *Insert* inserts a node with a given key and value. *BinaryTree-Search* is called to find a node with the given key. If the search succeeds, *errorFlag* is set to *true*, since we cannot insert a record with the same key as an existing record. If the search fails, *errorFlag* is set to *false*, and a record with the given key and value is inserted. *Prev* points to the parent to which the new node must be attached.

To begin the insertion, a new record is created, and its *key* and *value* fields are set to the values of *insertKey* and *insertValue*:

$new(p)$

$p\uparrow.key \leftarrow insertKey$

$p\uparrow.value \leftarrow insertValue$

The newly inserted node will always be a leaf. Therefore, its *left* and *right* fields are set to *nil*:

$p\uparrow.left \leftarrow nil$

$p\uparrow.right \leftarrow nil$

Prev points to the parent to which the new node is to be attached. Unfortunately, *BinaryTreeSearch* does not tell us whether the new node should be a left child or a right child of its parent. We must consider three cases. If the parent is the dummy root node, the new node should be attached as a right child. Otherwise, if the key of the new node precedes that of its parent, the new node should be attached as a left child. If the key of the new node follows that of its parent, the new node should be attached as the right child. The following **if** construction attaches the new node to the proper branch of its parent:

> **if** *prev* $=$ *root* **then**
> > *prev*↑.*right* ← *p*
>
> **elseif** *insertKey* $<$ *prev*↑.*key* **then**
> > *prev*↑.*left* ← *p*
>
> **else**
> > *prev*↑.*right* ← *p*
>
> **endif**

The procedure *BinarySearchTree* searches for a node having a given key. Note that it is an iterative rather than a recursive algorithm. When all the nodes in a tree are to be visited, a recursive algorithm is usually indicated. But following a single path through the tree is similar to scanning a list, a job for which an iterative algorithm is best suited.

To begin, *prev* is set to point to the dummy root and *cur* is set to point to the right (and only) child of the root. The flag *searching* is set to *true*; it will remain true until the desired key is found:

> *prev* ← *root*
> *cur* ← *root*↑.*right*
> *searching* ← *true*

The search continues until *cur* has the value *nil*, indicating that the procedure attempted to follow a nonexistent branch, or until *searching* becomes *false*, indicating that the desired node has been found. If the search terminates with *cur* equal to *nil*, *prev* points to the parent that the desired node would have if it were present.

At each step of the search, the key being sought is compared with the key of the current node, the node pointed to by *cur*. If the key being sought is less than that of the current node, we follow the left branch from the current node. If the key being sought is greater than that of the current node, we follow the right branch from the current node. If neither condition holds, the key being sought must equal the key of the current node, so *searching* is set to *false* to indicate that the desired node has been found:

> **while** (*cur* $<>$ *nil*) **and** *searching*
> > **if** *searchKey* $<$ *cur*↑.*key* **then**
> > > *prev* ← *cur*
> > > *cur* ← *cur*↑.*left*
> >
> > **elseif** *searchKey* $>$ *cur*↑.*key* **then**
> > > *prev* ← *cur*
> > > *cur* ← *cur*↑.*right*

else

    searching ← false

endif

endwhile

When the search terminates, either *cur* points to the node containing the desired key or the value of *cur* is *nil*. Thus we can set *found* to *true* if the value of *cur* is not *nil*:

found ← (cur <> nil)

Deletion   Deletion from a binary tree is somewhat more complicated than lookup or insertion, so its implementation in *TableHandler* is left as an exercise. The basic ideas are as follows. There is no difficulty in deleting a leaf node. As shown in Figure 16.34a, the leaf node is simply removed and discarded. (In the representation, the field in the parent that pointed to the leaf node is set to *nil*). Nor is there any difficulty in deleting a node with only one subtree. As shown in Figure 16.34b, the subtree is attached to the branch to which the deleted node was formerly attached.

The problem arises if we try to delete a node that has both left and right subtrees. After the node is deleted, we will have two subtrees to be attached to the rest of the tree, and only one unused branch to attach them to.

Figure 16.34c illustrates a way around this problem. We locate the *next node*, the one whose key immediately follows the key of the node to be deleted. The key of the next node is greater than the key of the node to be deleted but less than the

Figure 16.34   Deleting a node from a binary search tree.

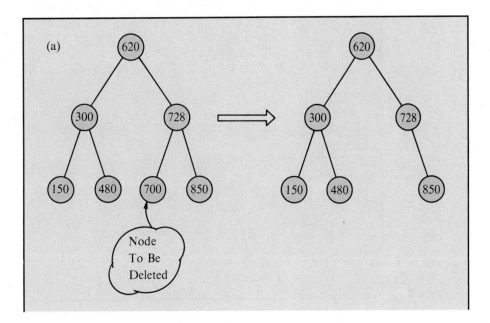

Figure 16.34
Continued   Deleting a node from a binary search tree.

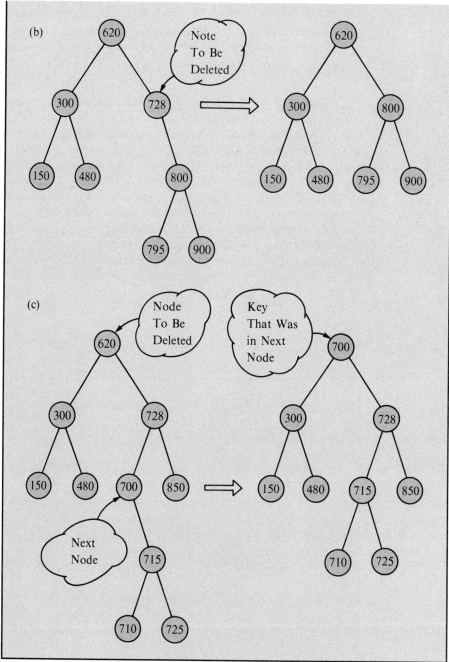

key of any other node that follows the node to be deleted. To find the next node, then, we follow the right branch from the node to be deleted and then follow left branches only until we reach a node that has no left branch. This node is the next node. And since the next node has no left branch, it has only a single child, and so it is easily deleted. Therefore, we copy the contents of the next node into the node that was originally to be deleted, and delete the next node.

Review questions

1. What is a *pointer value?* A *pointer variable?* What precisely do we mean when we say that a variable points to a certain location?

2. What are *pointer types?* What can serve as pointers in languages that do not provide pointer types?

3. What is a *graph?* What are *nodes? Arcs? Cycles?*

4. Why do many languages hide all details of pointer representation from the programmer?

5. Give three reasons why the definition of a pointer type must state the type of values to be stored in the locations pointed to.

6. What is *nil?* For what purpose is it usually used?

7. What is a *heap?*

8. Describe the predefined procedures *new* and *dispose.*

9. What are *uninitialized pointers? Dangling pointers?*

10. What is a *linked list?*

11. What are the advantages of storing a list as a linked list rather than as an array? What is a disadvantage?

12. Describe how a stack and a queue can be implemented as a linked list. Diagram the *Push* and *Pop* operations for a linked-list implementation of a stack and the *Insert* and *Remove* operations for a linked-list implementation of a queue.

13. Define the terms *root, leaf,* and *branch.*

14. Define the terms *parent, child, sibling, descendant,* and *subtree.*

15. Give the recursive definition of a tree. With the aid of diagrams, show how the definition can be applied to construct an example of a tree.

16. Describe and illustrate *parenthesis notation* and *indented notation* for trees.

17. Describe and illustrate *expression trees.*

18. Describe and illustrate a *preorder traversal* and a *postorder traversal.*

19. Give the recursive definitions for a preorder traversal and a postorder traversal.

20. Describe two ways of supplying the additional information that will allow a tree to be reconstructed from a preorder or postorder list of nodes.

21. How are prefix and postfix notation related to preorder and postorder traversal?

22. Describe the linked representation of trees used by the procedures demonstrating preorder and postorder traversal.

23. What is a *binary tree?* Describe a linked representation for binary trees.

24. What condition must be satisfied by the key values in a binary search tree?

25. Describe the method for finding a given key in a binary search tree.

26. Describe the method for inserting a node in a binary search tree.

27. What problem arises in deleting a node from a binary search tree? Describe a method for avoiding this problem.

28. What do we mean when we say that a binary search tree is *balanced?* Give two extreme cases of unbalanced binary search trees. What is the disadvantage of unbalanced binary search trees?

29. What is a *rotation?* What is it used for?

Exercises

1. Diagram the operation of the procedure *Insert* in Figure 16.15.

2. Diagram the operation of the procedure *Delete* in Figure 16.15.

3. In a *doubly linked list,* each cell contains two pointers, one to the preceding cell and one to the following cell. The pointer to the preceding cell is *nil* for the first cell on the list; the pointer to the following cell is *nil* for the last cell. Modify the table-handling module in Figure 16.15 to use a doubly linked list. Note that *SequentialSearch* need no longer return the value of *prev*, since we can always locate the cell preceding a given cell by following the appropriate link.

4. An interesting property of linked lists is that a single cell can be on more than one list at the same time. The cell needs one pointer field for each list that it is to be placed on. An application of this property arises when records must be maintained in order according to two different keys, such as names and telephone numbers. Write an algorithm to read records with two keys and insert each record on two lists, each of which is kept in order according to a different key. On request, the algorithm will print the records in key order according to either key.

5. In *hashing,* described in Chapter 13, we encountered the problem of collisions, in which the hashing function attempts to store more than one record in the same location in the hash table. One approach to handling collisions is to provide the records with a pointer field so that they can be joined into a linked list. All the records stored in a given location by the hashing function form a linked list. The first record on this list resides in the hash table; the remainder are allocated from the heap. When storing a record, if the location yielded by the hashing function is empty, the record is stored in that location and its pointer field is set to *nil.* Otherwise, the record is placed on the linked list beginning at that location. (The most convenient position at which to insert the new record is following the record stored in the hash table but preceding the other records on the linked list.) When searching for a record, if the record in the location yielded by the hashing function is not the desired one, then the linked list beginning at that location is searched. Write a version of *TableHandler* using this version of hashing.

6. Write a procedure to print a tree in parenthesis notation. The tree is stored in the linked representation illustrated in Figure 16.26. The procedure takes one parameter, which is a pointer to the root of the tree to be printed.

7. Diagram how to reconstruct a tree from a postorder list of nodes that gives the number of children of each node.

Hint: The method is similar to evaluating an expression in postfix notation except that the stack holds subtrees instead of numerical values. Scan the postorder list from left to right. When a leaf node (zero children) is encountered, push the node onto the stack. When a nonleaf node is encountered, pop the required number of subtrees off the stack, attach them to the node, and push the resulting tree back onto the stack. When the end of the postorder list is reached, the stack should contain a single tree, which is the tree represented by the postorder list.

8. Use the method described in Exercise 6 to write a procedure that reads in a postfix expression and returns a pointer to the root of the corresponding expression tree. The stack of subtrees mentioned in Exercise 6 will be implemented as a stack of pointers, with each pointer pointing to the root of the corresponding subtree. The procedure will accept postfix expressions containing the operators $+$, $-$, $/$, and $*$ and the constants 0, 1, 2, 3, 4, 5, 6, 7, 8, and 9. The procedure must distinguish between operators, which have two children, and constants, which have none. Note that the resulting trees will be binary trees; the representation for binary trees may prove more convenient than that for general trees.

9. Write a function to evaluate the expression represented by an expression tree read in by the procedure of Exercise 7. The function should take a pointer to the root of the expression tree as its argument and return the value of the expression.

Hint: The function will perform a postorder traversal of the expression tree. Like the procedure in Exercise 7, the function must distinguish between value nodes and operator nodes.

10. Show how any tree can be represented as a binary tree.

Hint: In the linked representations for both general and binary trees, each record contains two pointers.

11. Show that if the condition that must be satisfied by the keys in a binary search tree holds before an insertion is made, it will continue to hold after the new record is inserted.

12. Show that if the condition that must be satisfied by the keys in a binary search tree holds before a rotation is performed, it will continue to hold after the rotation has been performed.

13. Write a procedure for deleting a node from a binary search tree.

14. Show that if the condition that must be satisfied by the keys in a binary search tree holds before a node is deleted by the procedure in Exercise 13, it will continue to hold after the node has been deleted.

15. Write a procedure to print in key order all the records stored in a binary search tree.

Hint: This procedure must perform an *inorder traversal,* in which the root is visited after the left subtree is traversed but before the right subtree is traversed. Inorder traversal is defined only for binary trees.

Pascal Supplement

Pointer types

Pointer types in Pascal are very similar to those in the algorithmic language. In defining a pointer type, Pascal uses an upward arrow in place of the phrase **pointer to.** Thus, the types defined in the algorithmic language by

    type *integerPointer* = **pointer to** *integer*

    type *characterPointer* = **pointer to** *char*

are defined in Pascal as follows:

    type
        integerPointer = ↑*integer*;
        characterPointer = ↑*char*;

In definitions such as

type

> *link* = ↑*cell*;
>
> *cell* = **record**
>
>> *data*: *integer*;
>>
>> *next*: *link*
>
> **end**;

the definition of *link* refers to *cell* even though *cell* has not yet been defined. As an exception to its "define it before you refer to it" philosophy, Pascal allows a definition of a pointer type to refer to a type that has not yet been defined. This exception makes possible pairs of definitions such as those of *link* and *cell*, each of which refers to the other. The pointer type must always be defined before the type of the values pointed to.

Pascal also uses the upward arrow to designate the memory location referred to by a pointer. If *p, q,* and *r* are declared by

var

> *p, q*: *integerPointer*;
>
> *r*: *characterPointer*;

Then *p*↑ and *q*↑ represent the integer locations pointed to by *p* and *q*, and *r*↑ represents the character location pointed to by *r*. The assignment statement

> *p*↑ : = 5

stores 5 in the location pointed to by *p*. This is in contrast to the statement

> *p* : = *q*

which assigns a new pointer value to *p*, causing *p* to point to a different location.

Note that in a type definition, the upward arrow *precedes* the type identifier. But in a reference to a memory location designated by a pointer, the upward arrow *follows* the pointer variable.

For some reason, Pascal represents the predefined constant *nil* by a reserved word rather than an identifier. In Pascal, therefore, we must write **nil** instead of *nil*.

The predefined procedures *new* and *dispose* are the same in Pascal as in the algorithmic language. Thus,

> *new*(*p*)

allocates an integer-sized memory location and sets *p* to point to it. The statement

> *dispose*(*p*)

deallocates the location pointed to by *p*. After the call to dispose, the value of *p* is meaningless.

We recall that Pascal allows record variants, in which the structure of a record value is determined by the value of one or more tag fields. Record values having different sets of tag-field values may require different amounts of memory, even though they all belong to the same record type. Pascal allows us to specify a particular set of tag-field values when allocating a memory location. The system will allocate only enough memory for a record with the corresponding set of tag-field values. Only records having the given set of tag-field values can be stored in the location, and the tag-field values must be specified when the location is disposed of.

Let p be a pointer variable declared by

$p:$ ↑rt;

where rt is a certain record type. Suppose that $t1$, $t2$, . . . , tn are valid tag-field values for records of type rt. Then

$new(p, t1, t2, . . . , tn)$

allocates a location for a record value with tag-field values $t1$, $t2$, . . . , tn. Only record values having the given tag-field values can be assigned to p↑. When the location pointed to by p is deallocated, the tag-field values must again be specified:

$dispose(p, t1, t2, . . . , tn)$

For example, suppose that type rt is defined by

type

   · rt = **record**

               case *largeSize*: *Boolean* **of**

                   false: (*small*: **array**[1 . . 100] **of** *integer*);

                   true: (*large*: **array**[1 . . 1000] **of** *integer*)

          end;

The tag field is the Boolean field *largeSize*. The record contains an array of 100 integers when *largeSize* is *false* and an array of 1000 integers when *largeSize* is *true*. Needless to say, a record value occupies much more memory if *largeSize* is *true* than if it is *false*.

If a record of type rt is allocated with

$new(p)$

the system does not know whether the records stored in p↑ will contain 100 integers or 1000. The worst case must be assumed, so enough memory must be allocated to hold a record containing a 1000-integer array. If, however, we use

$new(p, false)$

we are assuring the system that only records for which *largeSize* is *false* will be stored in p↑. Hence, only enough memory for a record with a 100-integer array must be allocated. In contrast, the procedure call

$new(p, true)$

requests the system to allocate enough memory to hold a record with a 1000-integer array. A location allocated with $new(p, false)$ must be deallocated with $dispose(p, false)$, and a location allocated with $new(p, true)$ must be deallocated with $dispose(p, true)$.

Figures 16.35 through 16.39 show the Pascal versions of the modules and algorithms discussed in the main text. As usual, modules have been translated into UCSD-Pascal units.

Figure 16.35 UCSD-Pascal unit corresponding to the module *IntegerStack*.

```
unit IntegerStack;

{ Implements a stack of integers }

interface
    function Error: Boolean;
    { Return value of and clear error flag }

    function Top: integer;
    { Return top value on stack }

    procedure NewStack;
    { Create empty stack }

    procedure Push(x: integer);
    { Push value onto stack }

    procedure Pop;
    { Pop value off stack }

implementation
    type
        link  =  ↑cell;
        cell  =  record
                      data: integer;
                      next: link
                 end;
    var
        topPtr: link;
        errorFlag: Boolean;

    function Error;
    begin
        Error := errorFlag;
        errorFlag := false
    end; { Error }
```

```pascal
        function Top;
        begin
            if topPtr = nil then
                begin
                    errorFlag := true;
                    Top := 0
                end
            else
                begin
                    errorFlag := false;
                    Top := topPtr↑.data
                end
        end; { Top }


        procedure NewStack;
        begin
            topPtr := nil;
            errorFlag := false
        end; { NewStack }


        procedure Push;
        var
            p: link;
        begin
            errorFlag := false;
            new(p);
            p↑.data := x;
            p↑.next := topPtr;
            topPtr := p
        end; { Push }


        procedure Pop;
        var
            p: link;
        begin
            if topPtr = nil then
                errorFlag := true
            else
                begin
                    errorFlag := false;
                    p := topPtr;
                    topPtr := topPtr↑.next;
                    dispose(p)
                end
        end; { Pop }
begin
    NewStack
end. { IntegerStack }
```

Figure 16.36   UCSD-Pascal unit corresponding to the module
IntegerQueue.

```
unit IntegerQueue;

{ Implements a queue of integers }

interface
    function Error: Boolean;
    { Return value of and clear error flag }

    function Front: integer;
    { Return value at front of queue }

    procedure NewQueue;
    { Create empty queue }

    procedure Insert(x: integer);
    { Insert value at end of queue }

    procedure Remove;
    { Remove value from front of queue }

implementation
    type
        link = ↑cell;
        cell = record
                   data: integer;
                   next: link
               end;
    var
        frontPtr, rearPtr: link;
        errorFlag: Boolean;

    function Error;
    begin
        Error := errorFlag;
        errorFlag := false
    end; { Error }

    function Front;
```

```
begin
    if frontPtr = nil then
        begin
            errorFlag := true;
            Front := 0
        end
    else
        begin
            errorFlag := false;
            Front := frontPtr↑.data
        end
end; { Front }

procedure NewQueue;
begin
    frontPtr := nil;
    rearPtr := nil;
    errorFlag := false
end; { NewQueue }


procedure Insert;
var
    p: link;
begin
    errorFlag := false;
    new(p);
    p↑.data := x;
    p↑.next := nil;
    if rearPtr = nil then
        frontPtr := p
    else
        rearPtr↑.next := p;
    rearPtr := p
end; { Insert }

procedure Remove;
var
    p: link;
begin
    if frontPtr = nil then
        errorFlag := true
```

```
        else
            begin
                errorFlag := false;
                p := frontPtr;
                frontPtr := frontPtr↑.next;
                if rearPtr = p then
                    rearPtr := nil;
                dispose(p)
            end
    end; { Remove }


begin
    NewQueue
end. { IntegerQueue }
```

Figure 16.37   UCSD-Pascal unit corresponding to the version of module
TableHandler that represents the data table as a linked list.

```
unit TableHandler;

{ Maintain a table of data records }

interface
    function Error: Boolean;
    { Return value of and clear error indicator }

    procedure NewTable;
    { Initialize empty table }

    procedure Lookup(searchKey: integer;
                        var valueFound: real);
    { Find value corresponding to given key }

    procedure Insert(insertKey: integer;
                        insertValue: real);
    { Insert new record in table }

    procedure Delete(deleteKey: integer);
    { Delete record with given key }
```

```
implementation
    type
        link  =  ↑dataRecord;
        dataRecord  =  record
                            key: integer;
                            value: real;
                            next: link
                        end;
    var
        first: link;
        errorFlag: Boolean;


    procedure SequentialSearch(searchKey: integer;
                               var found: Boolean;
                               var prev, cur: link);

    { Locate record with given key }


    var
        searching: Boolean;
    begin
        prev := first;
        cur := first↑.next;
        searching := true;
        while (cur <> nil) and searching do
            if cur↑.key >= searchKey then
                searching := false
            else
                begin
                    prev := cur;
                    cur := cur↑.next
                end;
        if cur = nil then
            found := false
        else if cur↑.key = searchKey then
            found := true
        else
            found := false
    end; { SequentialSearch }
```

```pascal
function Error;
begin
    Error := errorFlag;
    errorFlag := false
end; { Error }


procedure NewTable;
begin
    new(first);
    first↑.next := nil;
    errorFlag := false
end; { NewTable }


procedure Lookup;
var
    found: Boolean;
    prev, cur: link;
begin
    SequentialSearch(searchKey, found, prev, cur);
    if not found then
        errorFlag := true
    else
        begin
            errorFlag := false;
            valueFound := cur↑.value
        end
end; { Lookup }


procedure Insert;
var
    found: Boolean;
    p, prev, cur: link;
begin
    SequentialSearch(insertKey, found, prev, cur);
    if found then
        errorFlag := true
    else
        begin
            errorFlag := false;
            new(p);
            p↑.key := insertKey;
            p↑.value := insertValue;
            p↑.next := cur;
            prev↑.next := p
        end
end; { Insert }
```

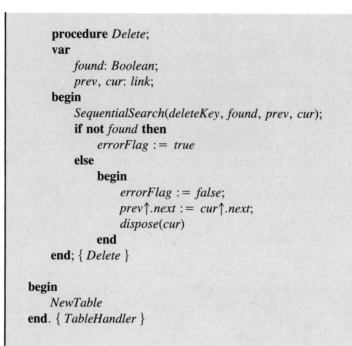

Figure 16.38 Pascal program demonstrating parenthesis notation, linked representations, and preorder and postorder traversal. Types and procedures are defined in the Pascal program rather than in a separate module as was done in the algorithmic language.

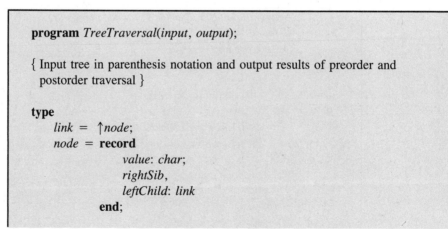

```
var
    c: char;
    p: link;


procedure GetChar;

{ Read next nonblank character into c }

begin
    repeat
        read(c)
    until c <> ' '
end; { GetChar }


procedure ReadTree(var p: link);

{ Read tree in parenthesis notation }

var
    q, r: link;
begin
    new(p);
    p↑.value := c;
    GetChar;
    q := p;
    q↑.rightSib := nil;
    if c = '(' then
        begin
            GetChar;
            while c <> ')' do
                begin
                    ReadTree(r);
                    q↑.rightSib := r;
                    q := r
                end;
            GetChar
        end;
    p↑.leftChild := p↑.rightSib;
    p↑.rightSib := nil
end; { ReadTree }
```

```pascal
procedure PreorderTraversal(p: link);

{ Print preorder list of nodes }

var
    q: link;
begin
    write(p↑.value, ' ');
    q := p↑.leftChild;
    while q <> nil do
        begin
            PreorderTraversal(q);
            q := q↑.rightSib
        end
end; { PreorderTraversal }


procedure PostorderTraversal(p: link);

{ Print postorder list of nodes }

var
    q: link;
begin
    q := p↑.leftChild;
    while q <> nil do
        begin
            PostorderTraversal(q);
            q := q↑.rightSib
        end;
    write(p↑.value, ' ')
end; { PostorderTraversal }


begin
    write('Tree: ');
    GetChar;
    ReadTree(p);
    writeln;
    write('Preorder list: ');
    PreorderTraversal(p);
    writeln;
    write('Postorder list: ');
    PostorderTraversal(p);
    writeln
end. { TreeTraversal }
```

Figure 16.39 UCSD-Pascal unit corresponding to the version of module *TableHandler* that represents the data table as a binary tree.

```
unit TableHandler;

{ Maintain a table of data records }

interface
    function Error: Boolean;
    { Return value of and clear error indicator }

    procedure NewTable;
    { Initialize empty table }

    procedure Lookup(searchKey: integer;
                        var valueFound: real);
    { Find value corresponding to given key }

    procedure Insert(insertKey: integer;
                        insertValue: real);
    { Insert new record in table }

implementation
    type
        link =  ↑dataRecord;
        dataRecord = record
                        key: integer;
                        value: real;
                        left, right: link
                     end;
    var
        root: link;
        errorFlag: Boolean;

    procedure BinaryTreeSearch(searchKey: integer;
                        var found: Boolean;
                        var prev, cur: link);

    { Locate record with given key }

    var
        searching: Boolean;
```

```
begin
    prev := root;
    cur := root↑.right;
    searching := true;
    while (cur <> nil) and searching do
        if searchKey < cur↑.key then
            begin
                prev := cur;
                cur := cur↑.left
            end
        else if searchKey > cur↑.key then
            begin
                prev := cur;
                cur := cur↑.right
            end
        else
            searching := false;
    found := (cur <> nil)
end; { BinaryTreeSearch }


function Error;
begin
    Error := errorFlag;
    errorFlag := false
end; { Error }

procedure NewTable;
begin
    new(root);
    root↑.left := nil;
    root↑.right := nil;
    errorFlag := false
end; { NewTable }

procedure Lookup;
var
    found: Boolean;
    prev, cur: link;
begin
    BinaryTreeSearch(searchKey, found, prev, cur);
    if not found then
        errorFlag := true
    else
```

```pascal
        begin
            errorFlag := false;
            valueFound := cur↑.value
        end
    end; { Lookup }


procedure Insert;
var
    found: Boolean;
    p, prev, cur: link;
begin
    BinaryTreeSearch(insertKey, found, prev, cur);
    if found then
        errorFlag := true
    else
        begin
            errorFlag := false;
            new(p);
            p↑.key := insertKey;
            p↑.value := insertValue;
            p↑.left := nil;
            p↑.right := nil;
            if prev = root then
                prev↑.right := p
            else if insertKey < prev↑.key then
                prev↑.left := p
            else
                prev↑.right := p;
        end
    end; { Insert }

begin
    NewTable
end. { TableHandler }
```

Summary of type system

Since we have now discussed all the types offered by Pascal, it is worthwhile to summarize the Pascal type system. Pascal types can be classified as follows:

1. Simple types
   1.1 Ordinal types
       1.1.1 The predefined types *integer, Boolean* and *char*
       1.1.2 Enumerated types
       1.1.3 Subrange types
   1.2 The predefined type *real*

2. Structured types
   2.1 Array types, including string types
   2.2 File types, including the predefined file type *text*
   2.3 Record types
   2.4 Set types

3. Pointer types

Pascal designates as *compatible* certain types that are subsets of some larger type. For example, the subrange types 1 . . 10 and 50 . . 100 are compatible since both are subranges of type *integer*. A related concept is that of *assignment compatibility*. A value is *assignment compatible* with a given type only if the value can be assigned to a variable of the given type. For example, the value 5 is assignment compatible with the subrange type 1 . . 10 because 5 can be assigned to a variable of type 1 . . 10.

Before stating the formal requirements for compatibility and assignment compatibility, we need two definitions:

1. A string type is an array type of the form **array**[1 . . *n*] **of** *char*

2. Special restrictions are imposed on file types and on structured types containing file types as components. Such types cannot serve as component types of file types, and assignment is not allowed for values of such types. These restricted types are defined recursively as follows. *A type is not allowed as a component type of a file type if it is a file type or if it has a component of a type not allowed as a component type of a file type.*

We can now define type compatibility as follows. Types T1 and T2 are compatible if any of the following statements hold:

1. T1 and T2 are the same type (that is, they are name equivalent).

2. T1 is a subrange of T2 or T2 is a subrange of T1 or both are subranges of the same host type.

3. T1 and T2 are set types with compatible base types. T1 and T2 must be both packed or both unpacked.

4. T1 and T2 are string types with the same number of components.

A value of type T2 is assignment compatible with a type T1 if any of the following statements hold:

1. T1 and T2 are the same type (that is, they are name equivalent) and that type is allowed as a component type of a file type. (Thus, assignment is forbidden for types not allowed as component types of file types.)

2. T1 is type *real* and T2 is type *integer*.

3. T1 and T2 are compatible ordinal types and the value of type T2 belongs to the type T1.

4. T1 and T2 are compatible set types and all members of the value of type T2 belong to the base type of type T1.

5. T1 and T2 are compatible string types.

Part V
Numerical methods

17

Errors, equations, and areas

he first computers were built to carry out the complex calculations of mathematics, science, and engineering. Nowadays, however, numerical computing is often overshadowed by more recent computer applications such as word processing, data management, and game playing. Yet numerical computation is still enormously important. Many consumer products, such as cameras and automobiles, depend on computer calculations for their design. The entire space program would be impossible without computers to design the spacecraft, control it during launch, and help the astronauts navigate it once it is in space. The most powerful computers in existence, the supercomputers, are used mainly for numerical computation.

The study of techniques for numerical computation is called *numerical analysis*. This chapter is a brief introduction to the subject. Students who expect to use computers mainly for numerical calculations should also take a separate course in numerical analysis.

17.1

Numerical errors

We are rarely able to compute numerical results exactly, although with sufficient attention to error control we can usually obtain results that are accurate enough for the application at hand. Errors arise because of the finiteness of the computation process. *Roundoff errors* occur because numbers can be represented with only a finite number of significant digits. *Truncation errors* occur because an algorithm can carry out only a finite number of steps, yet many mathematical results are defined by processes that require an infinite number of steps.

Roundoff error   Values of type *real* can be represented with only a finite number of significant digits. When two values of type *real* are added, multiplied, or divided, the exact result may contain more significant digits than allowed for a value of type *real*. The best the computer can do is return the value of type *real* that most closely approximates the exact result. In practice, this means rounding the exact result to the number of significant digits allowed for type *real*.

For example, suppose that values of type *real* are represented with six significant digits, and consider the following addition:

$$\begin{array}{r} 7.83924 \\ + \underline{6.14923} \\ 13.98847 \end{array}$$

The two numbers being added belong to type *real,* but their sum does not, since it has one too many significant digits. The best the computer can do is round the result to six significant digits and return the inexact result 13.9885.

Roundoff error is particularly troublesome when numbers that differ greatly in magnitude are added or subtracted. For example, consider the following addition:

$$\begin{array}{l} 34978.3 \\ + \underline{0.235634} \\ 34978.535634 \qquad \text{(exact result)} \\ 34978.5 \qquad\qquad \text{(rounded result)} \end{array}$$

Only the most significant digit of the smaller number contributes to the sum. The remaining five significant digits of the smaller number are lost. In the addition

$$\begin{array}{l} 764321.0 \\ + \underline{0.259613} \\ 764321.259613 \qquad \text{(exact result)} \\ 764321.0 \qquad\qquad\quad \text{(rounded result)} \end{array}$$

the smaller number makes no contribution whatever to the sum. This kind of problem frequently arises when many small numbers are added to produce a much larger sum. When the running total becomes much larger than the numbers being added, the remaining small numbers make little or no contribution to the sum.

Provided we avoid such pitfalls as adding very large and very small numbers, roundoff error is seldom a problem for short computations. Most computers can represent real numbers with at least six significant digits, and this accuracy is almost always sufficient for the needs of science and engineering. On the other hand, roundoff errors accumulate in long calculations. When a calculation involves thousands of arithmetical operations, the calculations will probably have to be done with much greater than six-digit accuracy in order to arrive at a result that is accurate to six significant digits.

Specifically, roundoff errors propagate from right to left through a number. After a few arithmetical operations have been performed on the initial data of a problem, the rightmost digit of each result may be inaccurate due to roundoff errors. After additional calculations have been performed, the rightmost two digits of each result may be inaccurate; after still more calculations, the rightmost three digits may be inaccurate, and so on. The best guard against roundoff error is to do the calculations with much greater accuracy than needed for the final result. When the results are rounded to the accuracy actually needed, the inaccurate digits will be eliminated.

For this purpose, many computer systems provide two types of real numbers, usually known as *single-precision* and *double-precision* real numbers. That is, there are two real types, say type *realSingle* and *realDouble*. Typically, values of type *realSingle* have six or seven significant digits, and values of type *realDouble* have 15 or 16 significant digits. For short calculations, type *realSingle* is almost always sufficient. But for long calculations, and particularly when the result is computed as the sum of a large number of values, the calculations should be done using values of type *realDouble*, even though far less than 15-digit accuracy may be required for the final answer.

Truncation error Many mathematical processes involve an infinite number of steps. A computer, however, can only carry out a finite number of steps of the process. Truncation error is the error that results from terminating the infinite process after only a finite number of steps.

If the results produced by the process varied wildly from one step to the next, the results obtained after a finite number of steps would give us no clue as to what the final answer should be. Processes that are computationally useful must *converge*; that is, the results produced at each step must get closer and closer to the exact answer as the number of steps increases. Such a process can be terminated after a finite number of steps with the assurance that the results obtained so far approximate the exact results.

As a simple example of truncation error, consider the problem of dividing 19 by 7. We can get a first approximation to the result as follows:

$$
\begin{array}{r}
2 \\
7\overline{)19} \\
\underline{14} \\
5
\end{array}
$$

Since the remainder is not zero, we know that the division process has not been completed. We can get another digit of accuracy by carrying out another step of the division process:

$$
\begin{array}{r}
2.7 \\
7\overline{)19.0} \\
\underline{14} \\
50 \\
\underline{49} \\
1
\end{array}
$$

The process is still not complete, but we now have two digits of accuracy. Another step of the division process gives us still another digit of accuracy:

$$
\begin{array}{r}
2.71 \\
7\overline{)19.00} \\
\underline{14} \\
50 \\
\underline{49} \\
10 \\
\underline{7} \\
3
\end{array}
$$

The successive results 2, 2.7, 2.71, and so on are better and better approximations to the exact answer, which turns out to be

2.714285714285 . . .

The division process will never yield the exact answer in a finite number of steps. But after five or six steps it will yield a very good approximation to the exact result. What's more, if we can only store our result with six-digit accuracy, it would be senseless to carry the division process beyond six or seven steps. (A seventh step would inform us that the first digit to be discarded is 5, therefore allowing us to round the six-digit result to 2.71429.)

A more typical example is provided by the following formula for approximating the square root of a number n:

$$
x' = \frac{1}{2}\left(x + \frac{n}{x}\right)
$$

If x is a reasonable approximation to the square root of n, then x' will be a better approximation. If the value obtained for x' is substituted back for x, the new value of x' will be an even better approximation to the square root of n, and so on. Let's use this formula to approximate the square root of 2. Since $1^2 = 1$ and $2^2 = 4$, the square root of 2 must lie somewhere between 1 and 2. Let's use 1.5 as our starting approximation. Substituting 2 for n and 1.5 for x gives the following:

$$
\begin{aligned}
x' &= \frac{1}{2}\left(1.5 + \frac{2}{1.5}\right) \\
&= \frac{1}{2}(1.5 + 1.33333) \\
&= 1.41667
\end{aligned}
$$

The result, 1.41667, is correct to three digits. If this value is substituted for x, the result, 1.41422, is accurate to five digits. Another iteration of the process gives us 1.41421, which is accurate to six digits, the greatest accuracy that we can use as long as we are representing our results to only six-digit accuracy.

Note that our approximations suffer from roundoff error as well as truncation error since at each step the result of evaluating the formula was rounded off to six digits. Yet in spite of the combined roundoff and truncation errors, repeated application of the formula quickly yielded a result of the desired accuracy. *Iterative methods*—those that compute successively better approximations to a result—can combat roundoff error as well as truncation error. The computation done at each step is designed to improve an existing approximation; the improvement reduces both round-off and truncation error. Methods that in principle yield exact results usually have no such error-correcting properties. Although exact methods introduce no truncation error, roundoff errors can accumulate during the course of a long calculation.

17.2 Nonlinear equations

An equation is *linear* if it contains only the first power of the unknown x. Equations that contain higher powers of the unknown, such as x^2, x^3, x^4, and so on are *nonlinear*, as are equations in which the unknown appears as the argument of a transcendental function such as the sine or cosine function.

For linear equations we can derive explicit formulas giving the unknown in terms of the coefficients in the equation. For example, the solution of any linear equation of the form

$$ax + b = 0$$

is given by the formula

$$x = -\frac{b}{a}$$

Given an example of such an equation, such as

$$4x + 3 = 0$$

we need only substitute for the values of a and b in the formula to get the solution:

$$x = -\frac{3}{4} = -0.75$$

Formulas for the solutions of nonlinear equations are either very complex or nonexistent. Consider algebraic equations for example. The *degree* of an algebraic equation is the highest power of the unknown that appears in the equation. The solutions of the general equation of the second degree

$$ax^2 + bx + c = 0$$

are given by the formula

$$x = \frac{-b \pm \sqrt{b^2 - 4ac}}{2a}$$

which is much more complex than the formula for the solution of the linear or first-degree equation. Formulas for solutions to the equations of the third and fourth degrees are so complex that few people bother learning them; such equations are usually solved numerically by iterative methods. And there are no formulas for solutions to equations of the fifth or higher degrees; such equations must be solved numerically, as must most transcendental equations such as

$$\sin(ax) + b^x + c = 0$$

In this section we will look at three of the most popular iterative methods for solving nonlinear equations. We will represent the equation to be solved in the form

$$f(x) = 0$$

where the function $f(x)$ represents the left-hand side of the equation. Thus for the algebraic equation of the second degree, $f(x)$ is given by

$$f(x) = ax^2 + bx + c$$

Our iterative methods will compute the *roots* of $f(x)$—values of x for which $f(x)$ has the value zero.

Since the methods are approximate, they will not be able to find values of x that make $f(x)$ exactly zero. We must specify how close to zero $f(x)$ must be before we will accept x as a root of $f(x)$. We do this by providing a tolerance, which we denote by the Greek letter ϵ (epsilon). If the absolute value of $f(x)$ is less than ϵ, then x is an acceptable approximation to a root of $f(x)$. Thus our iterative methods will generate successive approximations until a value of x is obtained that satisfies

$$|f(x)| < \epsilon$$

The bisection method The bisection method uses a technique similar to that of binary search to locate a root of $f(x)$. Suppose that we know two values of x, *xPlus* and *xMinus*, such that

$$f(xMinus) < 0$$

and

$$f(xPlus) > 0$$

As Figure 17.1 illustrates, the value of $f(x)$ changes from negative to positive as x goes from *xMinus* to *xPlus*. If $f(x)$ is continuous, its value must pass through zero somewhere between *xMinus* and *xPlus*. Hence, there must be a value of x in the interval *xMinus* to *xPlus* such that $f(x) = 0$. We conclude that if the value of $f(x)$ is negative at *xMinus* and positive at *xPlus*, the interval from *xMinus* to *xPlus* must contain a root of $f(x)$. Although the figure shows *xMinus* less than *xPlus*, we could also have *xMinus* greater than *xPlus*.

We begin, then, with the interval *xMinus* to *xPlus*, which we know contains at least one root of $f(x)$. We repeatedly cut the size of the interval in half while maintaining the condition that the interval contains at least one root of $f(x)$. Thus the successively smaller intervals narrow down on a root of $f(x)$. If the starting interval contained more than one root of $f(x)$, the succeeding intervals will narrow down on one of these roots, but which one is not easily predicted in advance.

Figure 17.2 shows the procedure

> *Bisection(xMinus, xPlus, xTrial, epsilon,*
>
> > *f, maxIterations, success)*

which computes roots using the method of bisection. The parameters *xMinus*, *xPlus*, and *xTrial* are input-output parameters; their values will be changed by the procedure

Figure 17.1 If the continuous function $f(x)$ is negative at *xMinus* and positive at *xPlus*, there must be a root of $f(x)$ between *xMinus* and *xPlus*.

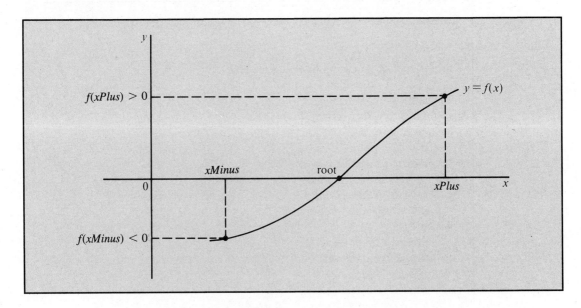

as it carries out its calculations. Before the procedure is called, *xMinus* and *xPlus* must be given initial values such that the value of $f(xMinus)$ is less than zero and that of $f(xPlus)$ is greater than zero. When the procedure returns, the value of *xTrial* is the root that was found; *xTrial* does not have to be given an initial value. Parameter *epsilon* is the limit below which the absolute value of $f(x)$ must be reduced for x to be considered a root of $f(x)$. The value specified for *epsilon* will depend on the equation to be solved and the use to which the solution is to be put.

The function f that defines the equation to be solved is passed to the procedure as a parameter. In declaring funtional parameters, we will use the mathematicians' notation for describing functions. The notation

integer → *real*

describes a function that takes one integer argument and returns a real result; the notation

integer × *real* → *Boolean*

describes a function that takes two arguments—one integer and one real—and returns a real result. Since the function f takes a real parameter and returns a real result, it is declared by

f: *real* → *real*

Figure 17.2 Procedure for solving nonlinear equations by the bisection method.

```
procedure Bisection(xMinus, xPlus, xTrial, epsilon, f, maxIterations,
                    success)

{ Find root of f(x) using bisection method }

declare
    xMinus, xPlus, xTrial: in out real
    epsilon: in real
    f: real → real
    maxIterations: in integer
    success: in out Boolean
    fMinus, fPlus, fTrial: real
    iterationCount: integer
execute
    iterationCount ← 1
    fMinus ← f(xMinus)
    fPlus ← f(xPlus)
    repeat
        xTrial ← (xMinus + xPlus) / 2.0
        fTrial ← f(xTrial)
        if fTrial < 0.0 then
            xMinus ← xTrial
            fMinus ← fTrial
        else
            xPlus ← xTrial
            fPlus ← fTrial
        endif
        success ← (abs(f(xTrial)) < epsilon)
        iterationCount ← iterationCount + 1
    until success or (iterationCount > maxIterations)
end Bisection
```

Functional parameters are always input parameters, so the type description need not be preceded by **in**. The parameter of f—that is, the x in $f(x)$—is assumed to be an input parameter.

Iterative methods will not always converge to an acceptable solution. Therefore, we must specify via the parameter *maxIterations* the maximum number of iterations that that the procedure is to perform before giving up. The procedure sets the Boolean output parameter *success* to *true* if an acceptable solution was found and to *false* if the procedure gave up after repeating the iteration process *maxIteration* times.

The variable *iterationCount* is used to keep count of the number of iterations that have been performed. The procedure begins by initializing *iterationCount* to 1. The variables *fMinus* and *fPlus* are set to the values of *f* at *xPlus* and *xMinus*:

$$iterationCount \leftarrow 1$$
$$fMinus \leftarrow f(xMinus)$$
$$fPlus \leftarrow f(xPlus)$$

At the start of each iteration, *xTrial* is set to the midpoint of the interval from *xMinus* to *xPlus*, thus dividing the interval into two equal parts. The variable *fTrial* is set to the value of *f* at *xTrial*:

$$xTrial \leftarrow (xMinus + xPlus) / 2.0$$
$$fTrial \leftarrow f(xTrial)$$

We wish to narrow the interval *xMinus* to *xPlus* to one of the two subintervals into which it is divided by *xTrial*. We wish, of course, to choose the subinterval that contains the root we are searching for. This will be the case if $f(xMinus)$ is still negative and $f(xPlus)$ is still positive after the interval has been narrowed. Thus the sign of *fTrial* determines which subinterval is chosen. If *fTrial* is negative, *xMinus* is set to *xTrial*, which corresponds to choosing the subinterval on the right. If *fTrial* is positive, *xPlus* is set to *xTrial*, which corresponds to choosing the subinterval on the left:

if *fTrial* < 0.0 **then**
    $xMinus \leftarrow xTrial$
    $fMinus \leftarrow fTrial$
else
    $xPlus \leftarrow xTrial$
    $fPlus \leftarrow fTrial$
endif

At the end of each iteration, *success* is set to *true* or *false* depending on whether or not the absolute value of $f(xTrial)$ is less than *epsilon*. The iteration count is then incremented by 1:

$$success \leftarrow (abs(f(xTrial)) < epsilon)$$
$$iterationCount \leftarrow iterationCount + 1$$

Iterations continue until a root is found or the maximum number of iterations is exceeded, that is, until the condition

$$success \ \textbf{or} \ (iterationCount > maxIterations)$$

becomes true.

Bisection is one of the most reliable of the iterative methods. If the starting values of *xMinus* and *xPlus* have been chosen properly, and if all the calculations are carried out exactly, the method is guaranteed to converge. In practice, roundoff error can prevent convergence, but this rarely occurs. On the other hand, the bisection method usually requires more iterations to find an acceptable solution than do the other two methods described in this section.

The secant method As illustrated in Figure 17.3, a *secant* is a straight line that intersects a curve at two points. If the curve does not vary too wildly, the secant can be used to approximate the curve in the vicinity of the two points. In particular, the point at which the secant intersects the *x* axis can be used as an approximation to a root of the function represented by the curve. The secant method follows this approach, which is similar to the *interpolation* technique that, before the advent of calculators, was widely used for finding values in trigonometric and logarithmic tables.

In Figure 17.3, *x1* and *x2* are the *x* values at which the secant intersects the curve $y = f(x)$. Since the *y* values for the curve and the secant line are the same at the points of intersection, the secant passes through the points $(x1, f(x1))$ and $(x2, f(x2))$. Given two points through which a straight line passes, we can write the equation of the line in the following form:

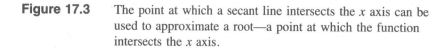

$$\frac{f(x2) - y}{x2 - x} = \frac{f(x2) - f(x1)}{x2 - x1}$$

Figure 17.3   The point at which a secant line intersects the *x* axis can be used to approximate a root—a point at which the function intersects the *x* axis.

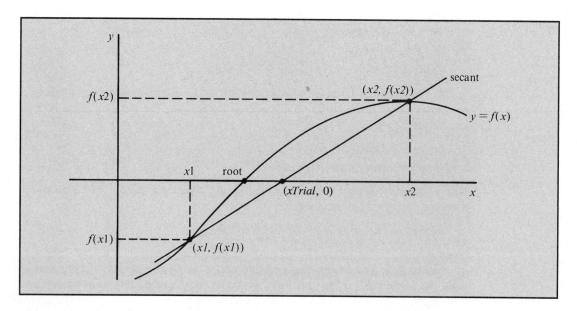

The approximate root we are seeking, *xTrial*, corresponds to the point at which the secant intersects the *x* axis, the point at which *y* is zero. Substituting *xTrial* for *x* and zero for *y* gives

$$\frac{f(x2)}{x2 - xTrial} = \frac{f(x2) - f(x1)}{x2 - x1}$$

Solving for *xTrial* gives us a formula for computing *xTrial* in terms of *x1*, *x2*, *f(x1)*, and *f(x2)*:

$$xTrial = x2 - \frac{x2 - x1}{f(x2) - fx1)} f(x2)$$

Figure 17.4 shows the procedure *Secant*. The parameters for *Secant* are the same as for *Bisection*, except that *xMinus* and *xPlus* have been replaced by *x1* and *x2*. As

Figure 17.4   Procedure for solving nonlinear equations by the secant method.

```
procedure Secant(x1, x2, xTrial, epsilon, f, maxIterations, success)

{ Find root of f(x) using secant method }

declare
    x1, x2, xTrial: in out real
    epsilon: in real
    f: real → real
    maxIterations: in integer
    success: in out Boolean
    iterationCount: integer
    f1, f2: real
execute
    iterationCount ← 1
    f1 ← f(x1)
    repeat
        f2 ← f(x2)
        xTrial ← x2 − ((x2 − x1) / (f2 − f1)) * f2
        x1 ← x2
        f1 ← f2
        x2 ← xTrial
        success ← (abs(f(xTrial)) < epsilon)
        iterationCount ← iterationCount + 1
    until success or (iterationCount > maxIterations)
end Secant
```

with *xMinus* and *xPlus*, starting values for *x1* and *x2* must be chosen before the procedure is called. Although not required, a good criterion for choosing the starting values of *x1* and *x2* is the same as was used for *xMinus* and *xPlus*: choose the values of *x1* and *x2* so that the value of $f(x)$ is negative for one of the two values and positive for the other.

The procedure begins by initializing *iterationCount* to 1 and *f1* to $f(x1)$:

$iterationCount \leftarrow 1$

$f1 \leftarrow f(x1)$

Each iteration begins by setting *f2* to $f(x2)$ and computing the value of *xTrial*:

$f2 \leftarrow f(x2)$

$xTrial \leftarrow x2 - ((x2 - x1) / (f2 - f1)) * f2$

The value of *x1* is now discarded, and the values of *x2* and *xTrial* are taken as the starting values for the next iteration. This is done by setting *x1* and *x2* to the values of *x2* and *xTrial*, respectively. We also set *f1* to the value of *f2* so that this value will not have to be recomputed on the next iteration:

$x1 \leftarrow x2$

$f1 \leftarrow f2$

$x2 \leftarrow xTrial$

As for *Bisection*, each iteration ends by setting *success* to *true* or *false* according to whether or not a root has been found and incrementing *iterationCount*:

$success \leftarrow (abs(f(xTrial)) < epsilon)$

$iterationCount \leftarrow iterationCount + 1$

Iterations continue until the condition

$success$ **or** $(iterationCount > maxIterations)$

becomes true.

When it converges, the secant method converges faster than the bisection method; that is, it requires fewer iterations to achieve a given accuracy. However, the secant method is more likely than the bisection method to fail to converge. For best results, the starting values of *x1* and *x2* should be chosen as close to a root as possible, preferably with the root bracketed between them.

Newton's method   Figure 17.5 shows what happens when one of the two points at which a secant intersects a curve moves toward the other point. The secant approaches a *tangent*, a line that touches the curve at one point and has the same direction that the curve has at the point of contact. Like a secant, a tangent can be used to approximate the curve near the point of contact. What's more, the point at which the tangent intersects the *x* axis can be taken as an approximation to a root of the function represented by the curve. This approach to approximating the root could be called the "tangent method" but is actually known as *Newton's method*, after the legendary mathematician and physicist Sir Isaac Newton.

Figure 17.5 As *x2* approaches *x1*, the secant approaches the tangent at
x1—the line that touches the curve at *x1* and has the same
direction that the curve has at the point of contact.

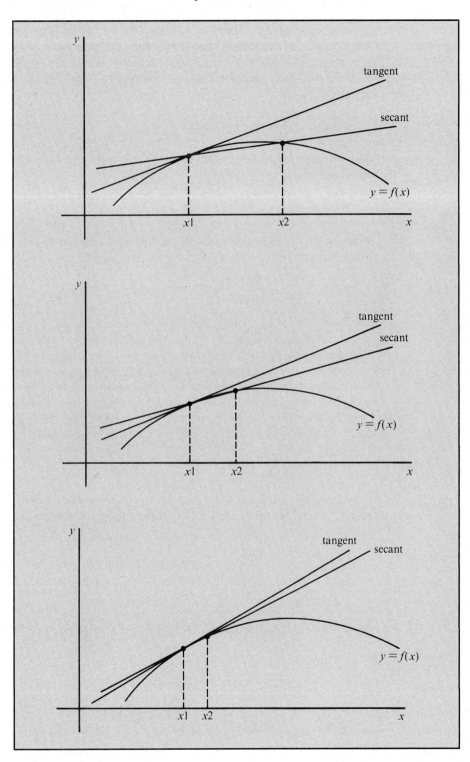

The *slope* of a straight line is defined as the change in y between two points divided by the corresponding change in x. Let's compute the slope of the secant using the two points at which the secant intersects the curve $y = f(x)$. The change in y is $f(x2) - f(x1)$, and the corresponding change in x is $x2 - x1$. Thus the slope is given by

$$\text{slope} = \frac{f(x2) - f(x1)}{x2 - x1}$$

The formula used in the secant method for computing the next approximation contains the expression

$$\frac{x2 - x1}{f(x2) - f(x1)}$$

which is just the reciprocal of the slope (that is, 1 over the slope). That formula can thus be written as follows:

$$xTrial = x2 - \frac{f(x2)}{\text{slope}}$$

When one of the points of intersection approaches the other, the slope of the secant approaches the slope of the tangent. Using methods studied in calculus courses, we can derive a function $f'(x)$ whose value at each point x is the slope of the tangent that touches the curve at that point. This function is called the *derivative* of $f(x)$. Newton's method uses essentially the same formula as the secant method for computing an approximate root; however, the slope of the secant is replaced by the slope of the tangent as given by the derivative function. Thus if x is the current approximation to the root, we compute a new approximation x' as follows:

$$x' = x - \frac{f(x)}{f'(x)}$$

The iterative method for computing square roots that we looked at earlier is a special case of Newton's method. The square root of n satisfies the following equation:

$$f(x) = x^2 - n = 0$$

Applying a rule of calculus, we find the derivative of $f(x)$ to be given by

$$f'(x) = 2x$$

Substituting for $f(x)$ and $f'(x)$ in the formula for computing a new approximate root, we get

$$x' = x - \frac{f(x)}{f'(x)}$$
$$= x - \frac{x^2 - n}{2x}$$
$$= x - \frac{1}{2}x + \frac{n}{2x}$$

$$= \frac{1}{2}x + \frac{n}{2x}$$

$$= \frac{1}{2}\left(x + \frac{n}{x}\right)$$

which is the formula that was used to demonstrate iterative methods.

Figure 17.6 shows the procedure

$Newton(xTrial, epsilon, f, fPrime, maxIterations, success)$

The input-output parameter *xTrial* is used to return the root found by the procedure. It must be given a starting value before the procedure is called. For best results, the starting value should be as close to the desired root as possible. *Newton* has two functional parameters: *f*, which is the function that defines the equation to be solved, and *fPrime*, which is the derivative of *f*. Parameters *epsilon*, *maxIterations*, and *success* play the same roles as in *Bisection* and *Secant*.

The procedure begins by initializing *iterationCount* to 1. It then repeatedly computes approximate roots until a sufficiently accurate approximation is obtained or until the maximum number of iterations has been carried out:

Figure 17.6   Procedure for solving nonlinear equations by Newton's method.

```
procedure Newton(xTrial, epsilon, f, fPrime, maxIterations, success)

{ Find root of f(x) using Newton's method }

declare
    xTrial: in out real
    epsilon: in real
    f: real → real
    fPrime: real → real
    maxIterations: in integer
    success: in out Boolean
    iterationCount: integer
execute
    iterationCount ← 1
    repeat
        xTrial ← xTrial − f(xTrial) / fPrime(xTrial)
        success ← (abs(f(xTrial)) < epsilon)
        iterationCount ← iterationCount + 1
    until success or (iterationCount > maxIterations)
end Newton
```

iterationCount ← 1

repeat

    xTrial ← *xTrial* − *f(xTrial)* / *fPrime(xTrial)*

    success ← (*abs(f(xTrial))* < *epsilon*)

    iterationCount ← *iterationCount* + 1

until *success* **or** (*iterationCount* > *maxIterations*)

Like the secant method, Newton's method may fail to converge. When it does converge, however, it does so even more rapidly than the secant method. A disadvantage of Newton's method is that one is required to compute and program the derivative function *fPrime* in addition to *f*, whereas the other two methods require only the function *f*. Another possible problem is that the tangent to a curve may not be defined at some points. If the curve has a sharp corner, for example, its direction at the corner, and hence its tangent, are undefined. Thus the derivative function may be undefined for some values of *x*.

17.3

Systems of linear equations

Systems of linear equations such as

$$3x_1 + 2x_2 + 4x_3 = 19$$
$$6x_1 + 5x_2 + 9x_3 = 43$$
$$9x_1 + 8x_2 + 13x_3 = 64$$

present another problem. Several explicit methods for solving such systems are taught in elementary mathematics courses. Unfortunately, systems of hundreds or even thousands of equations in as many unknowns are not uncommon in some applications. With so many equations, it is too laborious to do the calculations in the explicit solution by hand; a computer must be used. Because so many arithmetical operations must be performed, roundoff error becomes a problem. For this reason an iterative method may give more accurate results than an explicit solution.

One method of solving linear equations that is often taught in mathematics courses must be avoided at all costs. That is the method of determinants (Cramer's rule). Determinants are important for proving theorems and other theoretical analysis, but they are worthless for computation. To evaluate an $n \times n$ determinant requires more than $n!$ multiplications ($n!$ is the product of the first n integers; $5! = 1 \times 2 \times 3 \times 4 \times 5 = 120$, for example.) For a 10×10 determinant, more than 3,628,800 multiplications are needed; for a 50×50 determinant, the number of multiplications exceeds 3×10^{34}. This is more than any computer could accomplish within a human lifetime.

In this section we will look at one explicit method for solving linear equations, *Gauss-Jordan elimination*, and one successive-approximations method, the *Gauss-Seidel method*.

Gauss-Jordan elimination   This is the method of elimination of variables that is familiar from algebra courses. In algebra problems, it is usually left up to the student to determine which variables to eliminate from which equations. To write an algorithm that a computer can follow, however, we must specify this and all other matters explicitly. Our problem, then, is to organize the usual method into an algorithm suitable for a computer.

Consider the system of equations shown in Figure 17.7. We can use the first equation to eliminate x_1 from the second and third equations. To do this, we multiply the first equation by $6/3 = 2$ to get

$$6x_1 + 4x_2 + 8x_3 = 38$$

We then subtract this from the second equation to get

$$x_2 + x_3 = 5$$

The $6x_1$ terms cancel, eliminating x_1 from the second equation.

In the same way, we can multiply the first equation by $9/3 = 3$ and subtract it from the second equation. The $9x_1$ terms cancel, eliminating x_1 from the third equation. Figure 17.8 shows the result of using the first equation to eliminate x_1 from the second and third equations.

In exactly the same way, we can now use the second equation to eliminate x_2 from the first and third equations. Figure 17.9 shows the result of these eliminations.

Finally, we can use the third equation to eliminate x_3 from the first and second equations. Figure 17.10 shows the results of these eliminations.

Figure 17.7   A set of three simultaneous linear equations in three unknowns.

$$3x_1 + 2x_2 + 4x_3 = 19$$
$$6x_1 + 5x_2 + 9x_3 = 43$$
$$9x_1 + 8x_2 + 13x_3 = 64$$

Figure 17.8   The equations of Figure 17.7 after using the first equation to eliminate x_1 from the second and third equations.

$$3x_1 + 2x_2 + 4x_3 = 19$$
$$x_2 + x_3 = 5$$
$$2x_2 + x_3 = 7$$

Figure 17.9   The equations of Figure 17.8 after using the second equation
to eliminate x_2 from the first and third equations.

$$
\begin{aligned}
3x_1 \quad\quad + \quad 2x_3 &= \quad 9 \\
x_2 + \quad x_3 &= \quad 5 \\
-x_3 &= -3
\end{aligned}
$$

Figure 17.10   The equations of Figure 17.9 after using the third equation
to eliminate x_3 from the first and second equations. Since
each equation now contains only one unknown, the
equations are easily solved.

$$
\begin{aligned}
3x \quad\quad\quad\quad &= \quad 3 \\
x_2 \quad\quad &= \quad 2 \\
-x_3 &= -3
\end{aligned}
$$

At this point, x_1 appears only in the first equation, x_2 only in the second equation, and x_3 only in the third. We can easily solve for x_1, x_2, and x_3, getting

$$
\begin{aligned}
x_1 &= \frac{3}{3} = 1 \\
x_2 &= 2 \\
x_3 &= \frac{-3}{-1} = 3
\end{aligned}
$$

Now let's write an algorithm that will carry out this elimination for n equations in n unknowns. We assume that the coefficients on the left sides of the equations as well as the constants on the right sides are stored in an array a of n rows and $n + 1$ columns; a is called the *augmented matrix*. Figure 17.11 illustrates the augmented matrix for three equations in three unknowns. Columns 1 through n hold the left-hand-side coefficients. Column $n + 1$ holds the right-hand-side constants. Each row of a represents one equation, and any manipulation of the equations can be accomplished by manipulating the rows of a.

We will use each equation in turn to eliminate the corresponding unknown from the other equations. Equation 1 will be used to eliminate x_1 from equations 2, 3, 4,

Figure 17.11 A system of linear equations is represented inside the computer by an *augmented matrix*, which has n rows and $n + 1$ columns. Each row corresponds to an equation. The first n columns hold left-hand-side coefficients; column $n + 1$ holds right-hand-side constants.

$$a = \begin{bmatrix} 3 & 2 & 4 & 19 \\ 6 & 5 & 9 & 43 \\ 9 & 8 & 13 & 64 \end{bmatrix}$$

. . . , n; equation 2 will be used to eliminate x_2 from equations 1, 3, 4, . . . , n; and so on. Thus, we can write:

> **for** $i \leftarrow 1$ **to** n
> > "Use the ith equation to eliminate the ith unknown from the remaining equations"
>
> **endfor**

The ith equation is used to eliminate x_i from every equation except, of course, the ith one. Let j be the number of the equation from which x_i is currently being eliminated. We have:

> **for** $i \leftarrow 1$ **to** n
> > **for** $j \leftarrow 1$ **to** n
> > > **if** $j <> i$ **then**
> > > > "Use the ith equation to eliminate the ith unknown from the jth equation"
> > >
> > > **endif**
> >
> > **endfor**
>
> **endfor**

To use the ith equation to eliminate the ith unknown from the jth equation, we multiply the ith equation by $a[j, i] \, / \, a[i, i]$ and subtract the result from the jth equation. These operations on equations will actually be carried out on the rows of a:

> $f \leftarrow a[j, i] \, / \, a[i, i]$
> **for** $k \leftarrow 1$ **to** $n + 1$
> > $a[j, k] \leftarrow a[j, k] - f * a[i, k]$
>
> **endfor**

Note that for $a[j, i]$ we get

$$a[j, i] \leftarrow a[j, i] - f * a[i, i]$$
$$a[j, i] \leftarrow a[j, i] - (a[j, i] / a[i, i]) * a[i, i]$$
$$a[j, i] \leftarrow a[j, i] - a[j, i]$$
$$a[j, i] \leftarrow 0$$

We can make the elimination somewhat more efficient as follows. We know that $a[j, i]$ is going to be set to 0. Therefore, we can avoid calculating the value of $a[j, i]$ on the grounds that it is a waste of time to do a calculation for which we already know the answer. What's more, when the ith equation is used for purposes of elimination, all the coefficients $a[i, 1]$ through $a[i, i - 1]$ will already have been set to zero. Therefore, $a[i, k]$ will be zero in

$$a[j, k] \leftarrow a[j, k] - f * a[i, k]$$

for $k = 1, 2, 3, \ldots, i - 1$. Hence, $a[j, 1]$ through $a[j, i - 1]$ will not be changed by the elimination process, and we need not bother to calculate new values for them either.

In eliminating x_i from the jth equation, then, we need only calculate new values for $a[j, i + 1]$ through $a[j, n + 1]$. We can modify the elimination to read as follows:

$$f \leftarrow a[j, i] / a[i, i]$$
for $k \leftarrow i + 1$ **to** $n + 1$
$\quad a[j, k] \leftarrow a[j, k] - f * a[i, k]$
endfor

The modified calculation leaves "garbage" in the components of a that the elimination should set to zero. But since these components do not participate in any further calculations, no harm results.

The values of the unknowns are stored in one-dimensional array x, with $x[i]$ holding the value of the unknown x_i. When the eliminations have been completed, the values of the unknowns can be computed as follows:

for $i \leftarrow 1$ **to** n
$\quad x[i] \leftarrow a[i, n + 1] / a[i, i]$
endfor

Combining all these statements gives us the procedure *GaussJordan* shown in Figure 17.12. The arrays a and x are passed to the procedure as **in out** parameters; note that the components of a are modified by the procedure as it solves the equations. Parameters a and x are declared large enough to hold the largest number of equations that we might wish to solve. Parameter n gives the number of equations to be solved by a particular call to the procedure. Parameters a and x are declared by

a: **in out** *matrix*

x: **in out** *vector*

where types *matrix* and *vector* are defined by

Figure 17.12   Procedure for solving systems of linear equations by Gauss-Jordan elimination.

```
procedure GaussJordan(n, a, x)

{ Find solution to system of linear equations using Gauss-Jordan method }

declare
    n: in integer
    a: in out matrix
    x: in out vector
    i, j, k: integer
    f: real
execute
    for i ← 1 to n
        for j ← 1 to n
            if j <> i then
                f ← a[j, i] / a[i, i]
                for k ← i + 1 to n + 1
                    a[j, k] ← a[j, k] − f * a[i, k]
                endfor
            endif
        endfor
    endfor
    for i ← to n
        x[i] ← a[i, n + 1] / a[i, i]
    endfor
end GaussJordan
```

type *matrix* = **array**[1 **to** *size*, 1 **to** *size* + 1] **of** *real*
type *vector* = **array**[1 **to** *size*] **of** *real*

The constant *size* determines the maximum number of equations that can be solved; the value of *n* cannot exceed the value of *size*. The type definitions are assumed to be global to the procedure *GaussJordan*; for example, they may be included in a module of which the procedure is a part.

Unfortunately, the procedure *GaussJordan* contains a fatal flaw. Consider the step

$f ← a[j, i] / a[i, i]$

The component we divide by, $a[i, i]$, is called the *pivot*. Now what if the *pivot* is zero? Attempting to divide by zero will cause our program to be terminated with an error message.

The following system illustrates the problem:

$$x_1 + x_2 + x_3 = 6$$
$$x_1 + x_2 + 2x_3 = 9$$
$$x_1 + 2x_2 + 3x_3 = 14$$

We begin, as usual, using the first equation to eliminate x_1 from the other two equations. This gives

$$x_1 + x_2 + x_3 = 6$$
$$0x_2 + x_3 = 3$$
$$x_2 + 2x_3 = 8$$

The next step would be to use the second equation to eliminate x_2 from the other two equations. The pivot would be the coefficient of x_2 in the second equation. Unfortunately, that coefficient is zero.

The simplest way to avoid the problem is to interchange the second and third equations:

$$x_1 + x_2 + x_3 = 6$$
$$x_2 + 2x_3 = 8$$
$$0x_2 + x_3 = 3$$

Now the coefficient of x_2 in the second equation is 1. This becomes the pivot, and all is well.

Even if the pivot is not zero, we can still run into trouble. If the magnitude of $a[i, i]$ is much smaller than that of the other coefficients, then f will be very large. The statement

$$a[j, k] \leftarrow a[j, k] - f * a[i, k]$$

will subtract a very large number from a much smaller one. But we recall that adding or subtracting numbers that differ greatly in magnitude can result in severe roundoff error.

To defend against zero pivots and to help defend against roundoff error caused by small pivots, we proceed as follows. Before using $a[i, i]$ as a pivot, we search the column $a[i, i]$, $a[i + 1, i]$, . . . , $a[n, i]$ to locate the component having the largest absolute value. The equation containing the largest component is exchanged with the ith equation, so the largest component in the column becomes the pivot. (We exchange the equations by exchanging the corresponding rows of a.) Then, as before, we use the ith equation to eliminate x_i from the other equations. This technique is called *partial pivoting*.

The following statements set *maxIndex* to the row of a that contains the largest of the components $a[i, i]$, $a[i + 1, i]$, . . . , $a[n, i]$:

```
maxVal ← −1.0
for k ← i to n
    if abs(a[k, i]) > maxVal then
        maxVal ← abs(a[k, i])
        maxIndex ← k
```

endif
endfor

Now the row designated by *maxIndex* must be exchanged with the *i*th row. During the exchange, the real variable *temp* is used for temporary storage:

for $k \leftarrow i$ **to** $n + 1$
    temp $\leftarrow a[i, k]$
    $a[i, k] \leftarrow a[maxIndex, k]$
    $a[maxIndex, k] \leftarrow$ *temp*
endfor

Inserting these two sets of statements in *GaussJordan* gives us *GaussJordanPivot*, which is shown in Figure 17.13.

The Gauss-Seidel method   For large systems, the complex calculations of the Gauss-Jordan method can be time consuming. And despite such defensive strategies as partial pivoting, roundoff error can be a problem. For such large systems, an iterative method may be faster and more accurate than the explicit Gauss-Jordan method. There are many such iterative methods; we will look at one of the most straightforward, the Gauss-Seidel method.

Consider the following system of equations:

$$x_1 + x_2 = 3$$
$$x_1 + 2x_2 = 5$$

We can easily verify that the exact solution to this system is $x_1 = 1$ and $x_2 = 2$. Hereafter, we will write exact and approximate solutions in the form (x_1, x_2). Thus, the exact solution to this system is $(1, 2)$.

Now let's solve this system using the Gauss-Seidel method. We start by arbitrarily choosing $(0, 0)$ as the initial approximation to the solution. We then use the first equation to compute a new approximate value for x_1. In carrying out the computation, we replace x_2 in the first equation by its current approximate value, which is zero:

$$x_1 = 3 - x_2 = 3 - 0 = 3$$

Thus our new approximation for x_1 is 3, and our new approximate solution is $(3, 0)$. This approximate solution satisfies the first equation but not the second.

The next step is to use the second equation to compute a new approximate value for x_2. In carrying out the computation, we replace x_1 in the second equation with its current approximate value, which is 3:

$$x_2 = \frac{5 - x_1}{2} = \frac{5 - 3}{2} = 1$$

Thus our new approximation for x_2 is 1, and our new approximate solution is $(3, 1)$. This approximate solution satisfies the second equation but not the first.

We continue in this way, always using the first equation to calculate a new value

Figure 17.13 Procedure for solving systems of linear equations by Gauss-Jordan elimination with partial pivoting.

```
procedure GaussJordanPivot(n, a, x)

{ Find solution to system of linear equations using Gauss-Jordan method
  with partial pivoting }

declare
    n: in integer
    a: in out matrix
    x: in out vector
    i, j, k, maxIndex: integer
    f, maxVal, temp: real
execute
    for i ← 1 to n
        maxVal ← −1.0
        for k ← i to n
            if abs(a[k, i]) > maxVal then
                maxVal ← abs(a[k, i])
                maxIndex ← k
            endif
        endfor
        for k ← i to n + 1
            temp ← a[i, k]
            a[i, k] ← a[maxIndex, k]
            a[maxIndex, k] ← temp
        endfor
        for j ← 1 to n
            if j <> i then
                f ← a[j, i] / a[i, i]
                for k ← i + 1 to n + 1
                    a[j, k] ← a[j, k] − f * a[i, k]
                endfor
            endif
        endfor
    endfor
    for i ← 1 to n
        x[i] ← a[i, n + 1] / a[i, i]
    endfor
end GaussJordanPivot
```

for x_1 and the second equation to calculate a new value for x_2. We get the following sequence of approximation solutions:

(0, 0), (3, 0), (3, 1), (2, 1) (2, 1.5), (1.5, 1.5), (1.5, 1.75), (1.25, 1.75), (1.25, 1.88), (1.13, 1.88), (1.13, 1.94), (1.06, 1.94), (1.06, 1.97), . . .

Clearly, the successive approximations are converging toward the exact solution (1, 2). Figure 17.14 illustrates how convergence takes place. We graph each equation as a straight line; the intersection of the two lines is the exact solution. Now let's start at the point (0, 0) and generate successive approximations by the Gauss-Seidel method. Using the first equation to compute x_1 means moving along a horizontal line

Figure 17.14   The sequence of trial solutions generated by the Gauss-Seidel method. In this case the successive trial solutions get closer and closer to the exact solution, so we say that the Gauss-Seidel method *converges*.

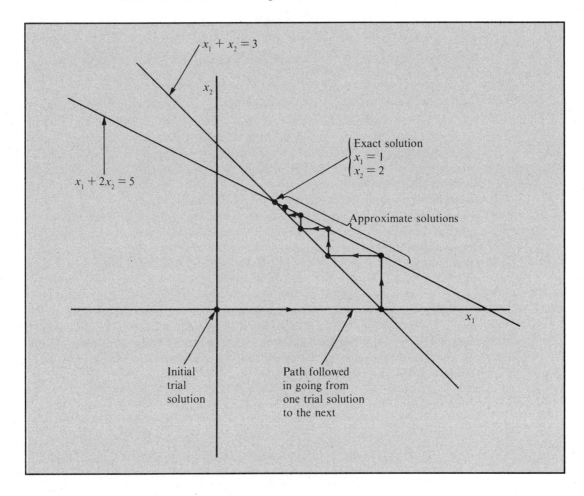

to the point where it intersects the line representing the first equation. Using the second equation to compute x_2 means following a vertical line until it intersects the line representing the second equation. If we alternate computing x_1 with the first equation and computing x_2 with the second equation, we will follow the zig-zag path shown in Figure 17.14. Following this path takes us closer and closer to the exact solution.

On the other hand, convergence cannot be guaranteed for every system of equations. Indeed, let us take the same system as before, but interchange the two equations:

$$x_1 + 2x_2 = 5$$
$$x_1 + x_2 = 3$$

We will again use the first equation to compute values of x_1 and the second to compute values of x_2, but because of the exchange, the first and second equations will not be the same ones as before. Starting with $(0, 0)$ as before, we obtain the following sequence of values for (x_1, x_2):

$(0, 0), (5, 0), (5, -2), (9, -2), (9, -6), (17, -6), (17, -14),$
$(33, -14), (33, -30), (65, -30), (65, -62)$

Obviously, are getting further and further from the exact solution $(1, 2)$ instead of closer and closer to it. The Gauss-Seidel method does not converge when the equations are written in this order.

Figure 17.15 illustrates this behavior. Using the first equation to compute x_1 means moving along a horizontal line until it intersects the line for the equation $x_1 + 2x_2 = 5$. Using the second equation to compute x_2 means following a vertical line until it intersects the line for the equation $x_1 + x_2 = 3$. Proceeding in this way, we see that our successive "approximations" are indeed moving away from the exact solution and will never get nearer to it. You can easily show that this behavior will occur for any starting point other than the exact solution, $(1, 2)$.

Clearly, then, convergence is a somewhat tricky question for the Gauss-Seidel method. Simply changing the order of the equations—which means changing which equation is solved for which unknown—can affect whether or not convergence takes place. As another example of this, the Gauss-Seidel method converges for the equations in Figure 17.7 only if the second and third equations are interchanged. It does not converge for any of the other five possible permutations of the three equations.

There is one important situation in which convergence of the Gauss-Seidel method is guaranteed. If in each equation the absolute value of the "diagonal coefficient" a_{ii} is greater than the sum of the absolute values of the other left-hand-side coefficients in that equation, the Gauss-Seidel method will always converge. Thus, convergence is guaranteed for the system

$$9x_1 + 3x_2 + 5x_3 = 30$$
$$6x_1 + 8x_2 + x_3 = 25$$
$$3x_1 + 2x_2 + 6x_3 = 25$$

because 9 is greater than $3 + 5$, 8 is greater than $6 + 1$, and 6 is greater than $3 +$

Figure 17.15   In this case, the successive trial solutions generated by the Gauss-Seidel method get further and further from the exact solution; the Gauss-Seidel method does not converge. Note that the equations are the same as in Figure 17.14; the only difference is which equation is solved for x_1 and which is solved for x_2.

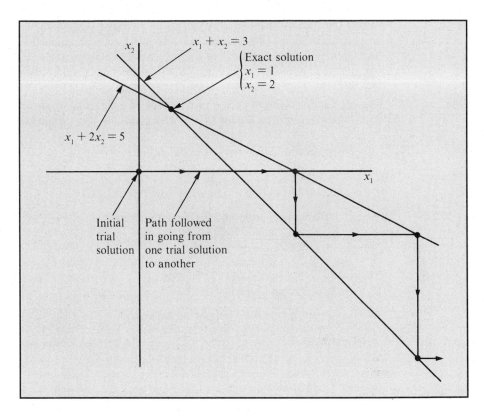

2. This condition is satisfied by many systems of equations that arise in science and engineering.

How can we tell when we have approximated the solution to the desired accuracy? We could write our system of equations as follows:

$$3 - x_1 - x_2 = 0$$
$$5 - x_1 - 2x_2 = 0$$

For an approximate solution, the right-hand sides will not be exactly zero, of course. We define the *residuals* r_1 and r_2 as follows:

$$r_1 = 3 - x_1 - x_2$$
$$r_2 = 5 - x_1 - 2x_2$$

The smaller the residuals, the more accurate the solution. We will use *maxResidual*, the largest of the absolute values of all the residuals, as our measure of the accuracy of the solution. We will continue generating successive approximations until the value of *maxResidual* is less than some given value *epsilon*. Other measures of accuracy that could be used in the same way are the sum of the absolute values of the residuals and the sum of the squares of the residuals.

Figure 17.16 shows the procedure *GaussSeidel*. As usual, parameter *n* is the number of equations to be solved; *a* holds the left-hand-side coefficients and the right-hand-side constants; and *x* holds the successive approximations as well as the final solution. Parameter *epsilon* is the value below which the absolute value of the largest residual must be reduced in order for the equations to be considered solved. Parameter *maxIterations* is the maximum number of iterations to be performed before giving up; the Boolean parameter *success* will be set to *true* if an acceptable solution was found and will be set to *false* if the procedure gave up after *maxIterations* attempts.

The procedure *GaussSeidel* can be outlined as follows:

iterationCount ← 1

repeat
  ''Do one iteration of the Gauss-Seidel method. Set *maxResidual* to the
    absolute value of the largest residual''
  success ← (*maxResidual* < *epsilon*)
  iterationCount ← *iterationCount* + 1
until *success* **or** (*iterationCount* > *maxIterations*)

We begin each iteration by initializing *maxResidual*:

maxResidual ← 0.0

We then process each equation in turn:

for *i* ← 1 **to** *n*
  ''Process one equation''
endfor

We begin the processing of the *i*th equation by calculating its residual:

residual ← *a*[*i*, *n* + 1]
for *j* ← 1 **to** *n*
  residual ← *residual* − *a*[*i*, *j*] * *x*[*j*]
endfor

If the absolute value of the residual is larger than the current value of *maxResidual*, the absolute value of the residual becomes the new value of *maxResidual*:

if *abs*(*residual*) > *maxResidual* **then**
  maxResidual ← *abs*(*residual*)
endif

Figure 17.16 Procedure for solving systems of linear equations by the
Gauss-Seidel method.

```
procedure GaussSeidel(n, a, x, epsilon, maxIterations, success)

{ Find solution to system of linear equations using Gauss-Seidel method }

declare
    n: in integer
    a: in matrix
    x: in out vector
    epsilon: in real
    maxIterations: in integer
    success: in out Boolean
    residual, maxResidual: real
    i, j, iterationCount: integer
execute
    iterationCount ← 1
    repeat
        maxResidual ← 0.0
        for i ← 1 to n
            residual ← a[i, n + 1]
            for j ← 1 to n
                residual ← residual − a[i, j] * x[j]
            endfor
            if abs(residual) > maxResidual then
                maxResidual ← abs(residual)
            endif
            x[i] ← x[i] + residual / a[i, i]
        endfor
        success ← (maxResidual < epsilon)
        iterationCount ← iterationCount + 1
    until success or (iterationCount > maxIterations)
end GaussSeidel
```

Finally, we use the ith equation to compute a new value for $x[i]$. This is easily
done using the residual we have already calculated. The residual is the amount by
which the left side of the equation falls short of the right side. If we increase $a_{ii}x_i$ by
the value of *residual*, the two sides will be equal and the new residual will be zero.
Increasing x_i by *residual* / a_{ii} does the trick:

$$x[i] \leftarrow x[i] + residual / a[i, i]$$

17.4

Numerical integration

Integration is the inverse of differentiation: given the derivative function $f'(x)$ we can use integration to compute the function $f(x)$ of which $f'(x)$ is the derivative. More generally, the function $f(x)$ may be defined by a *differential equation*, an equation involving $f(x)$, $f'(x)$, and possibly higher-order derivatives such as $f''(x)$ (the derivative of $f'(x)$) and $f'''(x)$ (the derivative of $f''(x)$). Differential equations are of enormous importance in applied mathematics, governing such diverse things as the orbits of spacecraft, the flow of air, water, heat, and electrical currents, and the growth of human and animal populations. As with other kinds of equations, it is often impossible to derive a formula for the solution of a differential equation, and we must resort to iterative numerical methods, a process known as *numerical integration*.

To avoid having to plunge deeply into the technicalities of calculus and differential equations, we will confine our discussion of numerical integration to finding the value of a *definite integral*, which has a simple geometrical interpretation as the area under a curve. As shown in Figure 17.17, we wish to compute the area bounded by the curve $y = f(x)$, the x axis, and the lines $x = a$ and $x = b$. This area is called "the definite integral from a to b of $f(x)$ with respect to x" and is denoted as follows:

$$\int_a^b f(x)dx$$

Figure 17.17 "The definite integral from a to b of $f(x)$ with respect to x" equals the area bounded by the curve $y = f(x)$, the vertical lines $x = a$ and $x = b$, and the x axis.

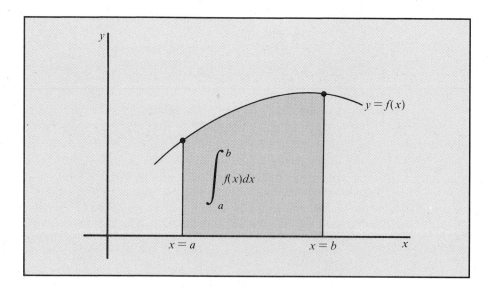

Numerical methods for evaluating definite integrals are similar in principle to those applied to more complex integration problems such as solving differential equations.

The three most popular methods for numerical computation of definite integrals are traditionally known as "rules." Two of these, the *rectangle rule* and the *trapezoid rule*, are named after the geometrical figures on which they are based. The third, *Simpson's rule*, is named after its inventor.

The rectangle rule We can approximate the area under a curve by the sum of the areas of a series of rectangles. As illustrated in Figure 17.18, we divide the interval from a to b into n subintervals, each of length

$$h = \frac{b - a}{n}$$

The points that divide a to b into subintervals are denoted $x_0, x_1, \ldots, x_n$; x_0 is equal to a, x_n is equal to b, and x_{i+1} is related to x_i by

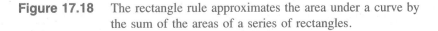

$$x_{i+1} = x_i + h$$

The first rectangle has height $f(x_0)$ and width h, and its area is $f(x_0)h$; the second rectangle has height $f(x_1)$ and width h, and its area is $f(x_1)h$; and so on. We approximate the area under the curve as the sum of the areas of the rectangles:

Figure 17.18 The rectangle rule approximates the area under a curve by the sum of the areas of a series of rectangles.

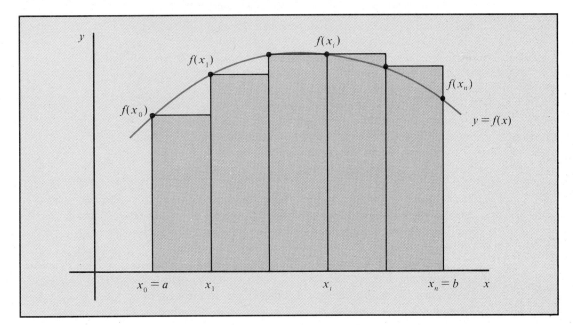

$$\int_a^b f(x)dx \approx f(x_0)h + f(x_1)h + \ldots + f(x_{n-1})h$$

$$\approx [f(x_0) + f(x_1) + \ldots + f(x_{n-1})]h$$

The sum of the areas of the rectangles is clearly only an approximation to the area under the curve since the tops of the rectangles do not exactly coincide with the curve. If we increase the number of rectangles and decrease their width correspondingly, the tops of the rectangles will more closely approximate the curve, and the sum of their areas will more closely approximate the area under the curve. Mathematicians define the definite integral as the sum of the areas of the rectangles in the limit where the number of rectangles becomes arbitrarily large and their width becomes arbitrarily small. In numerical integration, however, we can go only so far in approaching this limit. If we make n very large, we will be computing a larger quantity (the definite integral) as the sum of many much smaller quantities (the areas of the individual rectangles). We have seen that this situation is highly conducive to roundoff error. Thus making n too large and hence h too small leads to diminishing returns.

We can compute a series of successive approximations to the definite integral by computing the sum of the areas of the rectangles for n equal to 1, 2, 4, 8, and so on. For each new approximation, the number n of rectangles is doubled and the width h of the rectangles is halved. Let I_1, I_2, I_3, and so on be the successive approximations to the integral. When should we terminate the series and consider the current approximation as sufficiently accurate? As the terms in this series approach a limiting value, the difference between one term and the next will become less and less as we move further and further along in the series. When the absolute value of the difference between adjacent terms becomes less than some given tolerance ϵ, we can terminate the iterations and accept the current approximation. That is, we accept I_n as sufficiently accurate if

$$|I_n - I_{n-1}| < \epsilon$$

An even better criterion is

$$\left| \frac{I_n - I_{n-1}}{I_n} \right| < \epsilon$$

since it allows ϵ to be chosen independently of the size of I_n.

Figure 17.19 shows the procedure

Rectangle(a, b, epsilon, f, area, maxIterations, success)

Parameters a and b give the limits between which the integral is to be evaluated; f is the function to be integrated; and the value of the integral is returned via the input-output parameter *area*. Parameters *epsilon*, *maxIterations*, and *success* play the same roles as in the other iterative procedures we have studied.

On each iteration, the sum of the areas of the rectangles is computed as the value of the parameter *area*. During each iteration, the variable x takes on the values x_0, x_1, x_2, and so on. The value of n is the number of rectangles into which the area has been divided; the value of n is 1 for the first iteration and is doubled on each suc-

Figure 17.19 Procedure for evaluating a definite integral using the
rectangle rule.

```
procedure Rectangle(a, b, epsilon, f, area, maxIterations, success)

{ Find area under f(x) between x = a and x = b using rectangle rule }

declare
    a, b, epsilon: in real
    f: real → real
    area: in out real
    maxIterations: in integer
    success: in out Boolean
    prevArea, sum, h, x: real
    iterationCount, i, n: integer
execute
    iterationCount ← 1
    area ← 0.0
    n ← 1
    repeat
        prevArea ← area
        area ← 0.0
        h ← (b − a) / n
        x ← a
        for i ← 1 to n
            area ← area + f(x)
            x ← x + h
        endfor
        area ← area * h
        n ← 2 * n
        success ← (abs((area − prevArea) / area) < epsilon)
        iterationCount ← iterationCount + 1
    until success or (iterationCount > maxIterations)
end Rectangle
```

ceeding iteration. As usual, the variable *iterationCount* keeps track of the number of
iterations that have been performed. We initialize *iterationCount*, *area*, and *n* as
follows:

$$iterationCount \leftarrow 1$$
$$area \leftarrow 0.0$$
$$n \leftarrow 1$$

At the beginning of each iteration, the value of *area* computed on the previous iteration is saved in *prevArea*. This allows the current approximation to be compared to the previous one for the sake of estimating convergence. Then *area* is initialized to zero, *h* is set to the width of the rectangles for this iteration, and *x* is set to *a*, the value of x_0:

> *prevArea* ← *area*
> *area* ← 0.0
> *h* ← (*b* − *a*) / *n*
> *x* ← *a*

The sum

$$f(x_0) + f(x_1) + \ldots + f(x_{n-1})$$

is now computed as the value of *area*. The sum is then multiplied by *h* to convert it to an area:

> **for** *i* ← 1 **to** *n*
>   *area* ← *area* + *f*(*x*)
>   *x* ← *x* + *h*
> **endfor**
> *area* ← *area* * *h*

At the end of each iteration, *n* is multiplied by 2 so that twice as many rectangles will be used on the next iteration. The Boolean variable *success* is set to *true* or *false* depending on whether or not the convergence criterion is satisfied, and the iteration count is incremented by 1:

> *n* ← 2 * *n*
> *success* ← (abs((*area* − *prevArea*) / *area*) < *epsilon*)
> *iterationCount* ← *iterationCount* + 1

As usual, the iterations terminate when the convergence criterion is satisfied or the maximum number of iterations is exceeded, that is, when the following condition is true:

> *success* **or** (*iterationCount* > *maxIterations*)

The trapezoid rule   In place of rectangles we can use trapezoids as shown in Figure 17.20. Since the slanting tops of the trapezoids approximate the curve more closely than do the flat tops of the rectangles, we may expect to get a more accurate approximation to the area under the curve with a given number of trapezoids than with the same number of rectangles.

The area of the trapezoid spanning the interval x_i to x_{i+1} is given by

$$[f(x_i) + f(x_{i+1})] \frac{h}{2}$$

The definite integral is approximated by the sum of the areas of the trapezoids:

Figure 17.20   The trapezoid rule approximates the area under a curve by
the sum of the areas of a series of trapezoids.

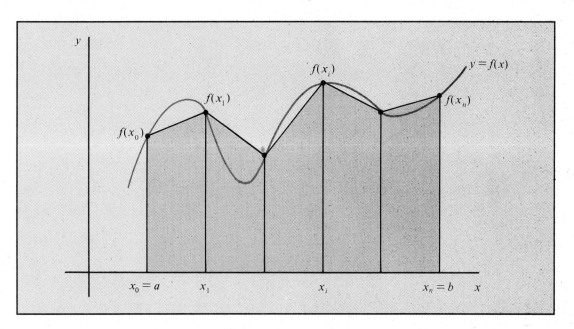

$$\int_a^b f(x)dx \approx [f(x_0) + f(x_1) + f(x_1) + \ldots + f(x_{n-1}) + f(x_{n-1}) + f(x_n)] \frac{h}{2}$$

$$\approx [f(x_0) + 2f(x_1) + \ldots + 2f(x_{n-1}) + f(x_n)] \frac{h}{2}$$

Figure 17.21 shows the procedure *Trapezoid*, which works much like the procedure *Rectangle*. The only differences are (1) $f(x_n)$ is included in the sum whereas it was not for *Rectangle*, and (2) $f(x_1)$ through $f(x_{n-1})$ are multiplied by 2 whereas $f(x_0)$ and $f(x_n)$ are not. We therefore use the **for** construction to compute the sum of $f(x_1)$ through $f(x_{n-1})$ only; this sum is then multiplied by 2 and added to the values of $f(x_0)$ and $f(x_n)$:

> *area* ← 0.0
> *h* ← (*b* − *a*) / *n*
> *x* ← *a* + *h*
> **for** *i* ← 1 **to** *n* − 1
>   *area* ← *area* + *f*(*x*)
>   *x* ← *x* + *h*
> **endfor**
> *area* ← (*f*(*a*) + 2.0 ∗ *area* + *f*(*b*)) ∗ *h* / 2.0

Simpson's rule   Simpson's rule approximates the curve $y = f(x)$ by a series of *parabolas*, curves given by equations of the following form:

Figure 17.21   Procedure for evaluating a definite integral using the
trapezoid rule.

```
procedure Trapezoid(a, b, epsilon, f, area, maxIterations, success)

{ Find area under f(x) between x = a and x = b using trapezoid rule }

declare
    a, b, epsilon: in real
    f: real → real
    area: in out real
    maxIterations: in integer
    success: in out Boolean
    prevArea, sum, h, x: real
    iterationCount, i, n: integer
execute
    iterationCount ← 1
    area ← 0.0
    n ← 1
    repeat
        prevArea ← area
        area ← 0.0
        h ← (b − a) / n
        x ← a + h
        for i ← 1 to n − 1
            area ← area + f(x)
            x ← x + h
        endfor
        area ← (f(a) + 2.0 * area + f(b)) * h / 2.0
        n ← 2 * n
        success ← (abs((area − prevArea) / area) < epsilon)
        iterationCount ← iterationCount + 1
    until success or (iterationCount > maxIterations)
end Trapezoid
```

$$y = ax^2 + bx + c$$

Since the smoothly curved parabolas can approximate the curve even better than the
flat tops of rectangles or the slanting tops of trapezoids, we expect Simpson's rule to
require fewer iterations for a given accuracy than either the rectangle rule or the
trapezoid rule.

As shown in Figure 17.22, each parabola spans two subintervals. The area under
the parabola spanning the subintervals x_{i-1} to x_i and x_i to x_{i+1} is given by

Figure 17.22   Simpson's rule approximates the area under a curve by the sum of the areas under a series of parabolas, one of which is shown here. Each parabola intersects the curve $y = f(x)$ at three points and spans two subintervals on the x axis.

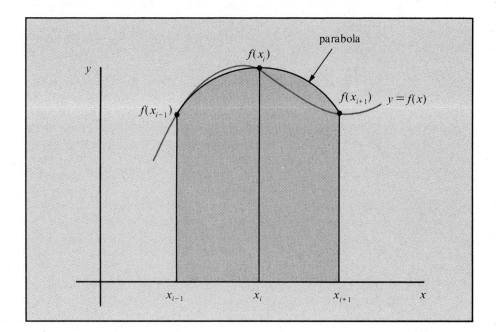

$$[f(x_{i-1}) \ + \ 4f(x_i) \ + \ f(x_{i+1})]\frac{h}{3}$$

Adding up the areas under all the parabolas gives us our approximation to the definite integral:

$$\int_a^b f(x)dx \approx [f(x_0) \ + \ 4f(x_1) \ + \ 2f(x_2) \ + \ 4f(x_3) \ + \ . \ . \ . \ + \ 2f(x_{n-2}) \ + \ 4f(x_{n-1}) \ + \ f(x_n)] \ \frac{h}{3}$$

Figure 17.23 shows the procedure *Simpson*, which is similar to *Trapezoid*. Since each parabola spans two subintervals, the number of subintervals must be even, so n is initially set to 2 instead of 1. As in *Trapezoid*, $f(x_0)$ and $f(x_n)$ are not multiplied by any coefficient. Therefore, they are not included in the sum computed by the **for** construction but are added to the sum after the **for** construction terminates. In the sum formed by the **for** construction, $f(x_i)$ must be multiplied by 4 if i is odd and by 2 if i is even. We distinguish the two cases with the predefined predicated *odd*(i), which returns *true* if i is an odd integer and *false* otherwise:

       area $\leftarrow 0.0$
       $h \leftarrow (b \ - \ a) \ / \ n$
       $x \leftarrow a + h$

Figure 17.23 Procedure for evaluating a definite integral using Simpson's rule.

```
procedure Simpson(a, b, epsilon, f, area, maxIterations, success)

{ Find area under f(x) between x = a and x = b using Simpson's rule }

declare
    a, b, epsilon: in real
    f: real → real
    area: in out real
    maxIterations: in integer
    success: in out Boolean
    prevArea, sum, h, x: real
    iterationCount, i, n: integer
execute
    iterationCount ← 1
    area ← 0.0
    n ← 2
    repeat
        prevArea ← area
        area ← 0.0
        h ← (b − a) / n
        x ← a + h
        for i ← 1 to n − 1
            if odd(i) then
                area ← a + 4.0 * f(x)
            else
                area ← area + 2.0 * f(x)
            endif
            x ← x + h
        endfor
        area ← (f(a) + area + f(b)) * h / 3.0
        n ← 2 * n
        success ← (abs((area − prevArea) / area) < epsilon)
        iterationCount ← iterationCount + 1
    until success or (iterationCount > maxIterations)
end Simpson
```

```
for i ← 1 to n − 1
    if odd(i) then
        area ← area + 4.0 * f(x)
    else
        area ← area + 2.0 * f(x)
    endif
    x ← x + h
endfor
area ← (f(a) + area + f(b)) * h / 3.0
```

In a language that does not provide the predicate *odd*, we can use a Boolean variable *odd*, whose value is initially set to *true*. Following the **if** construction, we insert a statement that negates the value of *odd*:

$$odd ← \textbf{not } odd$$

Review questions

1. What is *numerical analysis?*

2. What is *roundoff error?* Describe a situation in which roundoff error is particularly severe.

3. Why do some programming languages provide both *single-precision* and *double-precision* real numbers?

4. Define and give two examples of *truncation error.*

5. Contrast *iterative* methods with *explicit* or *exact* methods.

6. What does it mean to say that an iterative method *converges?*

7. Why are iterative methods sometimes more accurate than methods that in principle should yield exact results?

8. Distinguish between linear and nonlinear equations. Give two examples of each.

9. Describe the *bisection method* of solving nonlinear equations.

10. Contrast the bisection method with binary search.

11. Describe the *secant method* of solving nonlinear equations. If you are familiar with the procedure for interpolating in mathematical tables, compare this procedure with that for determining an approximate root in the secant method.

12. Describe *Newton's method* for solving nonlinear equations. Contrast Newton's method with the secant method. If Newton's method were named on

the same principle used for naming the secant method, what would it be called?

13. Give the respective advantages and disadvantages of the bisection method, the secant method, and Newton's method.

14. Describe the *Gauss-Jordan method* of solving systems of linear equations.

15. What is *partial pivoting?* Why does its use improve the Gauss-Jordan method?

16. Describe the *Gauss-Seidel* method of solving systems of linear equations. Why, for large systems of equations, may the approximate Gauss-Seidel method be more accurate than the exact Gauss-Jordan method? Under what circumstances is the Gauss-Seidel method guaranteed to converge?

17. What is *numerical integration?*

18. Describe a simple geometrical interpretation of a *definite integral.*

19. Describe the *rectangle rule* for computing a definite integral.

20. Describe the *trapezoid rule* for computing a definite integral. Why do we expect an iterative method based on the trapezoid rule to converge more rapidly than one based on the rectangle rule?

21. Describe *Simpson's rule* for computing a definite integral. Why do we expect an iterative method based on Simpson's rule to converge even more rapidly than one based on the trapezoid rule?

Exercises

1. With the aid of a pocket calculator, use (a) the bisection method, (b) the secant method, and (c) Newton's method to find one of the roots of the following equation:

$$f(x) = x^2 - 7x + 12 = 0$$

The derivative of $f(x)$ is given by

$$f'(x) = 2x - 7$$

The exact roots of the equation are $x = 3$ and $x = 4$.

2. The cube root of n satisfies the following equation:

$$x^3 - n = 0$$

The derivative of the left side of the equation is

$$3x^2$$

Derive an iterative formula based on Newton's method for computing the cube root of a number. Verify that the formula works by using it to compute the cube root of 8.

3. Use the Gauss-Jordan method to solve the following system of equations:

$$
\begin{aligned}
x_1 - x_2 + x_3 &= 5 \\
2x_1 + x_2 + 2x_3 &= 25 \\
3x_1 + 2x_2 - x_3 &= 16
\end{aligned}
$$

4. In the Gauss-Jordan method with partial pivoting, when searching for the largest value in the column $a[i, i]$, $a[i + 1, i]$, . . . , $a[n, i]$, we may find that all the values examined are zero. In that case, the system of equations is ill-formed and has either no solution or an infinite number of solutions. Modify *GaussJordanPivot* to check for this possibility. Provide the procedure with a Boolean input-output parameter *success* which is set to *true* if the procedure finds a solution to the system of equations and to *false* if the procedure discovers that the system is ill-formed.

5. Another approach to partial pivoting is to find the largest value in the row $a[i, i]$, $a[i, i + 1]$, . . . , $a[i, n]$ and interchange columns so that the value found becomes the pivot. When we interchange columns, we change which unknown corresponds to which column. We use a one-dimensional array *sub* to keep track of this correspondence; the value of $sub[i]$ is the subscript of the unknown corresponding to the ith column. Initially, we set $sub[i]$ to i for each i from 1 to n. Thereafter, each time we exchange two columns we also exchange the values of the corresponding components of *sub*. When the time comes to compute the values of the unknowns, the value of the unknown corresponding to the ith column is computed as follows:

$$
x[sub[i]] \leftarrow a[i, n + 1] / a[i, i]
$$

6. In *full pivoting*, we find the largest value in the subarray:

$$
\begin{array}{cccc}
a[i, i] & a[i, i + 1] & \cdots & a[i, n] \\
a[i + 1, i] & & & \\
\cdot & & & \\
\cdot & & & \\
\cdot & & & \\
a[n, i] & & & a[n, n]
\end{array}
$$

Then both two rows and two columns are interchanged to bring the largest value to the pivot position. Since columns are interchanged, the array *sub* must be used as in Exercise 5. Modify *GaussJordanPivot* to use full pivoting.

7. Investigate graphically the convergence of the Gauss-Seidel method for the following systems of equations:

$$
\begin{aligned}
\text{(a)} \quad x - y &= -1 \\
x + y &= 3
\end{aligned}
$$

(b) $2x - y = 0$
$x + y = 3$

8. For students familiar with matrix algebra: write a procedure for computing the inverse of a matrix. The inverse of a matrix is defined by the requirement that its product with the matrix yields the identity matrix. This requirement yields a system of linear equations that can be solved for the elements of the inverse matrix. You may use either Gauss-Jordan elimination or Gauss-Seidel iteration to solve the equations; for the former, it is helpful to work with an augmented matrix a having n rows and $2n$ columns. Initially, the first n columns contain the matrix to be inverted and the second n columns contain the identity matrix.

9. With the aid of a pocket calculator, use (a) the rectangle rule, (b) the trapezoid rule, and (c) Simpson's rule to compute the following definite integral:

$$\int_1^2 x^4 dx$$

The exact value of the integral is 6.2.

10. In the three integration rules, each iteration introduces new values of x at which $f(x)$ must be computed. However, the values of $f(x)$ that were used on the previous iteration are used again on the current one. We can make the rules more efficient if we can avoid recomputing $f(x)$ for the values of x at which it was computed on previous iterations. On each iteration we wish to modify the sum computed on the previous iteration to take the new values of $f(x)$ into account rather than recomputing the sum from scratch. Modify the three numerical integration procedures to use this approach. For Simpson's rule it is convenient to maintain two sums: the sum of values of $f(x_i)$ for odd values of i, and the sum of values of $f(x_i)$ for even values of i. Note that on each iteration the odd-numbered values of x_i are just the new values of x introduced on that iteration.

Pascal Supplement

In Pascal, functions and procedures are passed to subprograms as *functional* and *procedural* parameters. A functional or procedural parameter is declared by giving a complete function or procedure heading for the function or procedure to be passed. For example, the Pascal version of the procedure *Bisection* has the following procedure heading:

```
procedure Bisection(var xMinus, xPlus, xTrial: real;
                        epsilon: real;
                    function f(x: real): real;
                        maxIterations: integer;
                    var success: Boolean);
```

The functional parameter f, whose value describes the equation to be solved, is declared by means of the following function heading:

function $f(x: real): real;$

The formal parameter x is just a placeholder; it is not referred to anywhere else in the program.

Figures 17.24 through 17.32 give the Pascal versions of the procedures studied in this chapter.

Figure 17.24   Pascal version of the procedure for solving nonlinear equations by the bisection method.

```
procedure Bisection(var xMinus, xPlus, xTrial: real;
                    epsilon: real;
                    function f(x: real): real;
                    maxIterations: integer;
                    var success: Boolean);

{ Find root of f(x) using bisection method }

var
    fMinus, fPlus, fTrial: real;
    iterationCount: integer;
begin
    iterationCount := 1;
    fMinus := f(xMinus);
    fPlus := f(xPlus);
    repeat
        xTrial := (xMinus + xPlus) / 2.0;
        fTrial := f(xTrial);
        if fTrial < 0.0 then
            begin
                xMinus := xTrial;
                fMinus := fTrial
            end
        else
            begin
                xPlus := xTrial;
                fPlus := fTrial
            end;
        success := (abs(f(xTrial)) < epsilon);
        iterationCount := iterationCount + 1
    until success or (iterationCount > maxIterations)
end;
```

Figure 17.25 Pascal version of the procedure for solving nonlinear equations by the secant method.

```
procedure Secant(var x1, x2, xTrial: real;
                     epsilon: real;
                     function f(x: real): real;
                     maxIterations: integer;
                     var success: Boolean);

{ Find root of f(x) using secant method }

var
    iterationCount: integer;
    f1, f2: real;
begin
    iterationCount := 1;
    f1 := f(x1);
    repeat
        f2 := f(x2);
        xTrial := x2 − ((x2 − x1) / (f2 − f1)) * f2;
        x1 := x2;
        f1 := f2;
        x2 := xTrial;
        success := (abs(f(xTrial)) < epsilon);
        iterationCount := iterationCount + 1
    until success or (iterationCount > maxIterations)
end;
```

Figure 17.26 Pascal version of the procedure for solving nonlinear equations by Newton's method.

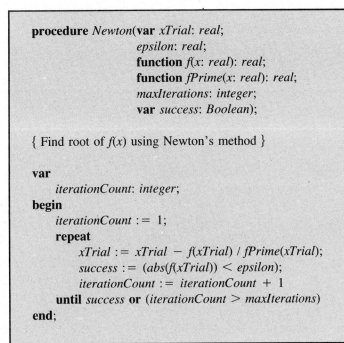

```pascal
procedure Newton(var xTrial: real;
                     epsilon: real;
                     function f(x: real): real;
                     function fPrime(x: real): real;
                     maxIterations: integer;
                     var success: Boolean);

{ Find root of f(x) using Newton's method }

var
    iterationCount: integer;
begin
    iterationCount := 1;
    repeat
        xTrial := xTrial − f(xTrial) / fPrime(xTrial);
        success := (abs(f(xTrial)) < epsilon);
        iterationCount := iterationCount + 1
    until success or (iterationCount > maxIterations)
end;
```

Figure 17.27   Pascal version of the procedure for solving systems of linear equations by Gauss-Jordan elimination.

```
procedure GaussJordan(n: integer;
                        var a: matrix;
                        var x: vector);

{ Find solution to system of linear equations using Gauss-Jordan method }

var
    i, j, k: integer;
    f: real;
begin
    for i := 1 to n do
        for j := 1 to n do
            if j <> i then
                begin
                    f := a[j, i] / a[i, i];
                    for k := i + 1 to n + 1 do
                        a[j, k] := a[j, k] − f * a[i, k]
                end;
    for i := 1 to n do
        x[i] := a[i, n + 1] / a[i, i]
end;
```

Figure 17.28   Pascal version of the procedure for solving systems of linear
equations by Gauss-Jordan elimination with partial pivoting.

```
procedure GaussJordanPivot(n: integer;
                              var a: matrix;
                              var x: vector);

{ Find solution to system of linear equations using Gauss-Jordan method
  with partial pivoting }

var
    i, j, k, maxIndex: integer;
    f, maxVal, temp: real;
begin
    for i := 1 to n do
        begin
            maxVal := -1.0;
            for k := i to n do
                if abs(a[k, i]) > maxVal then
                    begin
                        maxVal := abs(a[k, i]);
                        maxIndex := k
                    end;
            for k := i to n + 1 do
                begin
                    temp := a[i, k];
                    a[i, k] := a[maxIndex, k];
                    a[maxIndex, k] := temp
                end;
            for j := 1 to n do
                if j <> i then
                    begin
                        f := a[j, i] / a[i, i];
                        for k := i + 1 to n + 1 do
                            a[j, k] := a[j, k] - f * a[i, k]
                    end
        end;
    for i := 1 to n do
        x[i] := a[i, n + 1] / a[i, i]
end;
```

Figure 17.29   Pascal version of the procedure for solving systems of linear
equations by the Gauss-Seidel method.

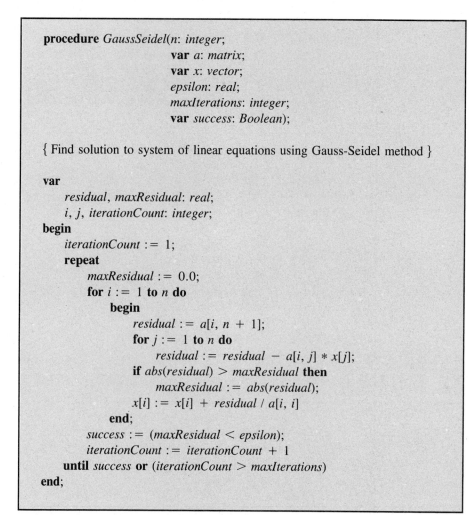

```pascal
procedure GaussSeidel(n: integer;
                      var a: matrix;
                      var x: vector;
                      epsilon: real;
                      maxIterations: integer;
                      var success: Boolean);

{ Find solution to system of linear equations using Gauss-Seidel method }

var
    residual, maxResidual: real;
    i, j, iterationCount: integer;
begin
    iterationCount := 1;
    repeat
        maxResidual := 0.0;
        for i := 1 to n do
            begin
                residual := a[i, n + 1];
                for j := 1 to n do
                    residual := residual − a[i, j] * x[j];
                if abs(residual) > maxResidual then
                    maxResidual := abs(residual);
                x[i] := x[i] + residual / a[i, i]
            end;
        success := (maxResidual < epsilon);
        iterationCount := iterationCount + 1
    until success or (iterationCount > maxIterations)
end;
```

Figure 17.30 Pascal version of the procedure for evaluating a definite
integral using the rectangle rule.

```
procedure Rectangle(a, b, epsilon: real;
                    function f(x: real): real;
                    var area: real;
                    maxIterations: integer;
                    var success: Boolean);

{ Find area under f(x) between x = a and x = b using rectangle rule }

var
    prevArea, sum, h, x: real;
    iterationCount, i, n: integer;
begin
    iterationCount := 1;
    area := 0.0;
    n := 1;
    repeat
        prevArea := area;
        area := 0.0;
        h := (b − a) / n;
        x := a;
        for i := 1 to n do
            begin
                area := a + f(x);
                x := x + h
            end;
        area := area * h;
        n := 2 * n;
        success := (abs((area − prevArea) / area) < epsilon);
        iterationCount := iterationCount + 1
    until success or (iterationCount > maxIterations)
end;
```

Figure 17.31   Pascal version of the procedure for evaluating a definite
integral using the trapezoid rule.

```
procedure Trapezoid(a, b, epsilon: real;
                    function f(x: real): real;
                    var area: real;
                    maxIterations: integer;
                    var success: Boolean);

{ Find area under f(x) between x = a and x = b using trapezoid rule }

var
    prevArea, sum, h, x: real;
    iterationCount, i, n: integer;
begin
    interationCount := 1;
    area := 0.0;
    n := 1;
    repeat
        prevArea := area;
        area := 0.0;
        h := (b − a) / n;
        x := a + h;
        for i := 1 to n − 1 do
            begin
                area := area + f(x);
                x := x + h
            end;
        area := (f(a) + 2.0 * area + f(b)) * h / 2.0;
        n := 2 * n;
        success := (abs((area − prevArea) / area) < epsilon);
        iterationCount := iterationCount + 1
    until success or (iterationCount > maxIterations)
end;
```

Figure 17.32 Pascal version of the procedure for evaluating a definite integral using Simpson's rule.

```
procedure Simpson(a, b, epsilon: real;
                  function f(x: real): real;
                  var area: real;
                  maxIterations: integer;
                  var success: Boolean);

{ Find area under f(x) between x = a and x = b using Simpson's rule }

var
    prevArea, sum, h, x: real;
    iterationCount, i, n: integer;
begin
    iterationCount := 1;
    area := 0.0;
    n := 2;
    repeat
        prevArea := area;
        area := 0.0;
        h := (b - a) / n;
        x := a + h;
        for i := 1 to n - 1 do
            begin
                if odd(i) then
                    area := area + 4.0 * f(x)
                else
                    area := area + 2.0 * f(x);
                x := x + h
            end;
        area := (f(a) + area + f(b)) * h / 3.0;
        n := 2 * n;
        success := (abs((area - prevArea) / area) < epsilon);
        iterationCount := iterationCount + 1
    until success or (iterationCount > maxIterations)
end;
```

Index

Abbreviated notation for operators, 29
abs
  (function), 156
  (Pascal function), 174
Abstract data type, 477, 615
Abstract machine, 615
Acceptance test, 455
Access arm, 72–73
Access modes, 492–495
Access to variables, 346–371
  in Pascal, 400–414
Accounting, by operating system, 128
Accumulator, 104ff
Activation record, 62, 639–643
Active process, 130ff
Actual parameter, 322ff, 393–396, 726–727
Address, 71, 101ff, 177
Add (procedure) (see *Update*)
AdvanceToNextState (procedure) (see *SimulationOfWaitingLine*)
Algorithm, 4, 9–22
  broad usage of term, 328
  characteristics of, 9–11
  effectiveness of, 10
  examples of, 12–22
  finiteness of, 10–11
  format of, 149–150
  guarantee of correctness, 9
  iterative, 12
  precision of, 9–10
  recursive, 12, 371–382
  sequential, 12
  termination of, 11
Algorithmic language, 139
Algorithmic notation, 139
algorithm (keyword), 149–150, 328
Algorithm testing, 39
Alphabetical order, 233
Alternation, 12
American Standard code for Information Interchange (see ASCII code)
Analogy, 44–45

Analytical Engine, 3
and operator, 290
  in Pascal, 317–320
Anonymous type, 481
ANSI/IEEE Pascal standard, 161
Append (procedure), 679 (see also *StringType*)
Application software, 117
Arc, 741–742
arctan (Pascal function), 174
Arguments, 322
Arithmetical expression, 151–157
  in Pascal, 173–175
Arithmetical operations, 151–156
  by arithmetic/logic unit, 69
  on binary values, 87–88
  in Pascal, 173
Arithmetic instructions, 106–107
Arithmetic/logic unit, 69–70
array
  (keyword), 548
  (Pascal reserved word), 601ff
Array processing, elements of, 550–555
Arrays, 547–614
  averaging components of, 552
  and **for** construction, 550–552
  for implementation of queues, 646–656
  input and output of, 554–555
  largest component of, 552–554
  multidimensional, 589–596
  one dimensional, 547–589
  in Pascal, 601–604
  searching of, 555–571
  sorting of, 578–589
Array types, 547–550, 589–592
  in Pascal, 601–604
Array variables, 548–550
  in Pascal, 602–603
ASCII code, 84–85, 233, 520, 686
Assembler, 120

Assembly language, 119–121
  program in, 119–120
Assertion, 14, 452–453
  final, 14
  initial, 14
  invariant, 20–22, 38, 224, 226, 229–
    230, 237–239, 326
  postcondition, 14, 38, 268–269, 382–
    384
  precondition, 14, 38, 268–269, 382–
    384
  relation to problem state, 28–29
Assignment, 180–187
  in Pascal, 207–208
  not allowed for file variables, 491
Assignment compatibility, 207–208, 813,
  819, 822–823
Assignment operator, 180
  in Pascal, 207
Assignment statement, 180–187
  in Pascal, 207–208
Assign (procedure) (see *StringType*)
AtEndP (stream function), 488–489, 497
Auxiliary memory, 67–68, 72–74
Averaging components of array, 552
Axiomatic definition
  of queue, 644–646
  of stack, 616–620

Babbage, Charles, 3
Balances
  (algorithm), 269–271
  (Pascal program), 304–305
Base-2 number system, 85–87
Base-8 number system, 92
Base-10 number system, 85
Base-16 number system, 93
Base case, 60, 371, 374
BASIC, 118, 121–122, 123, 127
BASIC machine, 127
Batch processing, 190–192
Batting averages, 194–196
begin (Pascal reserved word), 171–173,
  408
BEL (bell code), 84–85
Benchmark test, 455
Beta testing, 455
Biased exponent, 98–100
Binary AND operator, 89

Binary arithmetic, 87–88
Binary codes, 6, 81–87
Binary digits, 83ff
Binary logical operations, 88–89
Binary notation, 85–87
Binary NOT operator, 89
Binary number system, 85–87
Binary OR operator, 88–89
Binary search, 560–565
  efficiency of, 563–565
BinarySearch (see also *TableHandler*)
  (Pascal procedure), 604–606
  (procedure), 560–565
Binary search tree, 748, 790–803
Binary semaphore, 659
Binary shift operations, 88–90
Binary SHL operator, 90
Binary SHR operator, 90
BinaryTreeSearch, 797, 799–801 (see
  also *TableHandler*)
Binary XOR operator, 89
Bisection
  (Pascal procedure), 869
  (procedure), 832–836
Bisection method, 832–836
Bits, 83ff
Black box testing, 457–458
Blackjack, 294–297
Blocked process, 130ff, 658–659
Boolean
  (Pascal type), 162
  (type), 142
Boolean expression, 232ff, 290–297
  in Pascal, 251–255, 317–320
Boolean operator, 290–297
  in Pascal, 317–320
Bottom-up design, 430
Bottom-up implementation and testing,
  455–456
Boundary value analysis, 458
Branch
  of flowchart, 460–461
  of tree, 278, 771
Bubble sort, 37
Buffer, 530, 659–660
Buffer variable, 530–533, 537
Bugs, 419
Bus, 68
Bus contention, 68
Byte, 726

Calculator
 (algorithm), 283–286
 (Pascal program), 312–313
Calculator1
 (algorithm), 288–290
 (Pascal program), 315–316
Calculator simulation, 283–286, 288–290
Card punch, 76
Card reader, 76
Carriage return, 84
Carrying out a plan, 38
case
 (keyword), 287–290
 (in Pascal records), 527–528
 (Pascal statement), 314–316
Case analysis, 47–48, 268–269
Case construction, 286–290
 translation into Pascal, 314–315
Case list, 287–290
case others (keywords), 287–290, 315
Cell, of spreadsheet, 7
Census, 8
Central processing unit, 67–71
 of hypothetical computer, 103–105
Central processor (see Central processing
 unit)
Change, making of, 197–202
Change (procedure) (see *Update*)
char
 (Pascal type), 162–163
 (type), 142–144
Character codes, 84–85
Characteristics of high-quality software,
 421–423
Character literal, 143
 in Pascal, 163
Checkerboard and dominos problem, 39–
 41
Checkers, 44
CheckoutCounter (procedure) (see
 SimulationOfWaitingLine)
Chess, 9, 44
Child node, 771ff
Chip, 69, 72
chr (Pascal function), 520
Circuit board, 68
Circuits, two-state, 81–83
ClassifyAccounts
 (algorithm), 498–500
 (Pascal program), 539

Classifying triangles, 292–294
Clear (procedure) (see *Counter*)
Clock, 70
Clock cycle, 70
Clock (procedure) (see
 SimulationOfWaitingLine)
close statement, 492–494
close (UCSD Pascal procedure), 546
COBOL, 121–122
Coding, 420
Collating sequence, 233
Collision, 567ff
Comments, 149
 in Pascal, 172
common declaration, 349–352
CommonDefinitions
 (module), 504–505, 511–512
 (UCSD Pascal unit), 545–546
Compare instruction, 107
Comparisons, by arithmetic/logic unit,
 69–70
Compatability, 822–823
Compiler, 122
 error checking by, 452
Compiler generator, 455
Component type, 548
 in Pascal, 601–602
Component value
 of array, 547–550
 of record, 480
Component variable
 of array, 550–551
 of record, 480–481
Compound condition, 290–297
Compound statement, 172–173, 249–
 251, 256, 303–304
ComputeBattingAverage
 (algorithm), 194–196
 (Pascal program), 214–215
Computer portrait, 77
Computers
 characteristics of, 4
 classification of, 78–79
 concept of, 3–4
 embedded, 3, 78
 general purpose, 117–118
 hypothetical, 100–112
 main frame, 79
 micro-, 3, 78
 mini-, 78–79

Computers (continued)
  personal, 3
  special purpose, 117–118
  super, 79
Computer system, 67
Computer terminal, 75
ComputeTotal
  (algorithm), 224–226
  (Pascal program), 252
ComputeTotal1
  (algorithm), 235–238
  (Pascal program), 257
Computing science, 4
Concise notation for problem states, 36–37
Concurrent execution, 125–126, 129–134
Condition, 232ff, 251–252
  compound, 290–297
Conditional instruction, 31
Conditional jump instruction, 108
Condition-code register, 104ff
Constant definition part, 170, 207, 391, 516
Constant identifier, 148–149
Constants, 148–149
  in Pascal, 170–171
ConstantsAndOutput
  (algorithm) 149–150
  (Pascal program), 171–173
const (Pascal reserved word), 170ff
Constraints, 32ff
Continuation condition, 241
Control characters, 84–85
Control flow analysis, 452
Control key, 74–75, 84–85
Control structures, 12, 31, 192, 440, 451
Control unit, 69–71
Control variable, 221ff
Convert
  (algorithm), 195–197
  (Pascal program), 215–216
Copy, parameter passing by, 332–336, 393
Copy rule, 56n
Core memory (see Main memory)
Correlation coefficients, 8
cos (Pascal function), 174
Counter
  (module), 365–366, 380–381
  (Pascal unit), 415–416

Counters, in flowcharts, 460, 462–463
Counting, 7
CPU (see Central processing unit)
Craps
  (algorithm), 336–346, 366–371
    with **common** area, 350–351
    with nested unit definitions, 358–363
  (Pascal program), 396–400, 411–412
    with nesting, 401, 403–406
CR (carriage return code), 84–85
Ctrl key, 74–75, 84–85
Cube puzzle, 46–47, 49
Cursor, 75
Cursor control keys, 75
Cycle, 70–71, 741

Dangling pointer, 748
Data, 5–6
Data abstraction, 427, 429, 615
Data analysis, 7–8
Data bank, 8
Data base, 8
  relational, 8
Data-base management system, 8
Data conversion, 683–684
Data flow analysis, 452
Data format, for hypothetical computer, 101–102
Data management, 8–9, 124–125
Data processing, 5–6
Data representation, 81–115
Data structures, 4, 475ff
Data type (see Types)
Dead end, 43–44
Deadlock, 126
Dealer
  (algorithm), 294–297
  (Pascal program), 318–319
Debugging, 463–464
Decimal notation, 85
Decimal number system, 85–86
Decision tree, 278–282, 301
Declarations, 149–150, 179
  in Pascal, 206–207
declare (keyword), 149–150, 179
Definite integral, 856–865
Delete, (procedure) 680–681 (see also *StringType*, *TableHandler*, and *Update*)

Delete (stream function), 489–490

Deque, 663

Dereferencing, 182–187
   in Pascal, 208

Descriptor, 687–691

Design, of software, 420, 427–439

Desk checking, 450

Desktop computer, 78

Desktop metaphor, 127

Detail line, 271

Detours, 43

Device handler, 68

Devising a plan, 37–38

Difference, of sets, 522

Differential equation, 856

direct mode, 492–495

Discounts
   (algorithm), 192–194
   (Pascal program), 213–214

Disk operating system, 123

Dispatching, 132
   queue for, 658–659

Display, 74

dispose
   (Pascal procedure), 807–808
   (procedure), 746–747

Distributed processing, 133–134

div operator, 151–152
   in Pascal, 173

Document analysis, 450–452

Document inspection, 450–451

do (Pascal reserved word), 248ff, 255ff

DOS, 123

Dot-matrix printer, 77

downto
   (keyword) 220ff
   (Pascal reserved word), 248ff

Efficiency
   of binary search, 563, 565
   of hashing, 571
   of *InsertionSort*, 581–582
   of *Quicksort*, 588–589
   of sequential search, 559–560
   of software, 421–422

Elevator algorithm, 126

else
   (keyword), 266ff
   (Pascal reserved word), 303ff

elseif (keyword), 282ff

else part, 269

Embedded computer, 78

end
   (keyword), 328, 364, 149–150, 322
   (Pascal reserved word), 171–173, 408, 523

EndFilesP (function) (see *Merge*)

endfor (keyword), 220ff

endif (keyword), 265ff

End position, 487–490

endrecord (keyword), 479

endselect (keyword), 287–290

endwhile (keyword), 232ff

Entire value
   of array, 548–550
   of record, 480

Entire variable
   array, 550
   record, 480–481

Enumerated types, 516–517

eof (Pascal predicate), 258–260, 530ff

EqualTo (function) (see *StringType*)

Equations
   differential, 856
   nonlinear, 831–842
   systems of linear, 842–855

Error
   roundoff, 827–829
   truncation, 827–831

Error (function), 616–620, 643–646 (see also *IntegerQueue*, *IntegerQueueType*, *IntegerStack*, *IntegerStackType*, *StringType*, and *TableHandler*)

Evaluation function, 42–44

Exchanges, sorting by, 14

Exclusive or operation, 89

Executable program, 122

execute (keyword), 149–150

Exponent, 84, 141
   of floating-point number, 98–100

Exponential notation, 84 (see also Floating-point notation)

export (keyword), 365ff

exp (Pascal function), 174

Expression
   arithmetical, 151–157
     in Pascal, 173–175
   in assignment statement, 182–187
   Boolean, 232ff, 290–297
     in Pascal, 251–255, 317–320

Expression (continued)
  in **output** statement, 152–153, 187–
    188
  evaluation with stack, 631–636
  translation with stack, 636–639
  tree representation of, 777–778
  variables in, 182–187
Expressions
  (algorithm), 152–153
  (Pascal program), 174–175
Extended **if** construction, 282–286
extend mode, 492–495
External name, 493–495
External sorting, 578–589
Extreme cases, testing of, 39, 458

Factorial
  (function), 325–327, 374–377
  (Pascal function), 391–392, 395–396
false (Boolean value), 142
Fencepost error, 451–452
Fetch-execute cycle, 70
Fibonacci
  (algorithm), 227–230
  (function), 378–382
  (Pascal program), 254
Fibonacci1
  (algorithm), 238–241
  (Pascal program), 258
Fibonacci sequence, 378–382
Fibonacci's rabbit problem, 227–230,
    238–241
Field, 478ff
Field designator, 480–482
Field identifier, 478ff
  scope of, 482–483
Fields, of floating-point number, 98
Field-width parameters (Pascal), 209
File, 124–125, 477, 487–515
  in Pascal, 172, 208n, 528–546
file of
  (keywords), 491ff
  (Pascal reserved words), 528ff
FileUpdate
  (algorithm), 501–513
  (Pascal program), 541
File variables, 491–492
  in Pascal, 529–530

Final assertion, 14
FindRecord
  (Pascal procedure), 606–607
  (procedure), 565–571
FindUnusedRecord
  (Pascal procedure), 606–607
  (procedure), 565–571
Firmware, 72, 118
Fixed-length strings, 674–677
Fixed part, 526–528
Floating-point notation, 141–142, 162
  representation in memory, 97–100
Flowchart, 458–463
Flowgraph, 458–463
Foo (procedure), 334–336
for constructions, 220–231
  and arrays, 550–552
  nested, 222–223, 594–596
Formal parameters, 323ff, 389, 392–396
Formal proofs, 452–453
FormLetter
  (algorithm), 715–720
  (UCSD Pascal program), 737–739
for statements (Pascal), 248–255
  nested, 611
FORTRAN, 121–122
Forward declaration (Pascal), 401, 406–
    408
Four-bit group, 92–93
Fourth-generation language, 454
Fox, goose, and corn problem, 44
Front (function), 643–646 (see also
    IntegerQueue and
    IntegerQueueType)
function
  (keyword), 322–323
  (Pascal reserved word), 389ff
Functional parameters, 833ff
  in Pascal, 868–869
Functional specification, 426–428
Functional testing, 457–458
Function declaration, 322–328
  in Pascal 389–392, 516
Function heading, 323
  in Pascal 390–391
Function keys, 74–75
Functions, 389–393
  predefined, 156–157, 321
    in Pascal, 173–174
  recursive, 372, 374–382

Functions (continued)
  user defined, 322–328
    in Pascal, 389–392

Games, computer, 7–9
Garbage collection, 688–691
GaussJordan
  (Pascal procedure), 872
  (procedure), 842–847
Gauss-Jordan elimination, 842–849
  with partial pivoting, 847–849
GaussJordanPivot
  (Pascal procedure), 873
  (procedure), 847–849
GaussSeidel
  (Pascal procedure), 874
  (procedure), 849–855
Gauss-Seidel method, 849–855
General purpose computer, 117–118
GetChar (procedure) (see *TreeTraversal*)
get (Pascal procedure), 530ff
GetPlayersBet (procedure) (see *Craps*)
GetRecord (procedure) (see *Merge*)
GetStartingBankroll (procedure) (see
    Craps)
Glass box testing, 458–463
Global identifiers, 347–349
Goal state, 27ff
Graph, 741–742
Graphics display, 74
Guess
  (algorithm), 352–355
  (Pascal program), 401–402

Halt instruction, 108
Hardware, 4, 67–80
Hash
  (function), 566–568
  (Pascal function), 607
Hashing, 565–571
  efficiency of, 571
Heap, 746
Hexadecimal digit, 92–93
Hexadecimal notation, 92–93, 101ff
Higher-level languages, 121–122
Hill climbing, 42–44
How to Solve It, 35, 64
Hypothetical computer, 100–112

IBM card, 76
Icon, 128
Identifier, 147–149, 150
  field, 478ff
  global, 347–349
  local, 347–349
  in Pascal, 169–170
if constructions, 265ff
  extended, 282–286
  nested, 278–283
if statements (Pascal), 303–309
  nested, 309–312
Implementation, 420, 439–449
implementation (Pascal reserved word),
    408
import (keyword), 365ff
in
  (keyword), 322–323, 329–332
  (Pascal operator), 252, 522–523
Inactive process, 130ff
Increment (see also *Counter*)
  (Pascal procedure), 394–395
  (procedure), 331–332
Index (function), 681–682 (see also
    StringType)
Indentation, 223, 250, 311
Indented notation, 775–777
Index type, 601–603
Induction step, 60, 374
Inference, 39
Infix notation, 632ff
  translation to postfix, 636–639
Informal proofs, 452–453
Informatics, 4
Information, 3–6
  representation of, 81–115
Information hiding, 348–349, 427, 429–
    430
Information processing, 3–6, 5–6
  examples of, 6–9
Information science, 4
Initial assertion, 14
initialize (keyword), 364–365
Initial state, 27ff
Input, 188–190, 495–496
  of arrays, 554–555
  in Pascal, 209–212, 534–538
Input and output instructions, 108
Input devices, 67–68, 74–78
InputFinalize (procedure) (see *Merge*)

InputInitialize (procedure) (see *Merge*)
input mode, 492–495
Input-output bound, 71
Input/output parameters, 323, 329–332
Input-output parameters (see Input/output parameters)
Input parameters, 323ff, 329–332
input (Pascal file), 172
input statement, 188–190, 495–496
Insert, (procedure) 643–646, 680 (see also *IntegerQueue*, *IntegerQueueType*, and *TableHandler*)
InsertionSort
  (Pascal procedure), 611–612
  (procedure), 579–582
Instruction address register, 104ff
Instruction format, 101–102
Instruction set, 105–108
Integer literal, 140
  in Pascal, 161
IntegerQueue
  (module), 650–653, 755–762
  (UCSD Pascal unit), 668–670, 811–813
IntegerQueueType
  (module), 653–656
  (UCSD Pascal unit), 670–672
IntegerStack
  (module), 622–627, 750–755
  (UCSD Pascal unit), 664–665, 809–810
IntegerStackType
  (module), 627–631
  (UCSD Pascal unit), 666–668
integer type, 140
  in Pascal, 161
Integral, definite, 856–865
Integration testing, 455
Interactive processing, 190–192
interface (Pascal reserved word), 408
Intermediate goals, 48
Internal sorting, 578–589
Interpreter, 122–123
Interrupts, 132–133
  handler for, 132
Intersection, 522
Invariant assertion, 20–22, 38, 224, 226, 229–230, 237–239, 326
Inventor's request, 230–231

Investment
  (algorithm), 226–228
  (Pascal program), 253
Investment1
  (algorithm), 241–243
  (Pascal program), 262
Iteration, 12

Jump instructions, 70
  for hypothetical computer, 107–108

Kernel of operating system, 133
Keyboard, 74–75
Keypunch, 76
Keyword, 144

Language processor, 120, 122–123
Languages, programming, 118–123
Largest component of array, 552–554
LCD display, 74
Leaf node, 771ff
Left child, 790ff
Length (function), 681–682 (see also *StringType*)
Letter quality printer, 77
LF (line feed code), 84–85
Lifetime, of identifier, 346–371
Light pen, 75–76
Linear equations, systems of, 842–855
Linear search (see Sequential search)
Line feed, 84
Linked list, 741–742, 748–770
Linked representation of trees, 782–790
Linked structures, 741–823
Linker, 122
Liquid crystal display, 74
LISP, 121–122, 775–776
List, linked, 741–742, 748–770
Literal, 140ff, 150
ln (Pascal function), 174
Load and store instructions, 105–106
Local identifiers, 347–349
Local maximum or minimum, 43
Logical operations, 290–297
  by arithmetic/logic unit, 69
  binary, 88–89
  in Pascal, 317–320
Logo, 121–122
Looking back, 38–39
Lookup (procedure) (see *TableHandler*)

Machine language, 108, 118–119
Machine-language program, for
    hypothetical computer, 108–112
Macro, 45–47, 121n, 124, 713–715
Macroaction (see Macro)
Macroinstruction (see Macro)
Macrooperator (see Macro)
MagicSquare
    (algorithm), 592–596
    (Pascal program), 611, 614
Magic squares, 592–596
Magnetic bubbles, 73–74
Magnetic disks, 72–73
Magnetic tape, 72
Main frame, 79
Main memory, 67–68, 71–72
    organization of, 102–103
Maintainability, 421, 423
Maintenance, 420–421, 423, 464
MakeChange
    (algorithm), 197–202
    (Pascal program), 215–218
Mass memory (see Auxiliary memory)
Mass storage (see Auxiliary memory)
Master control program, 123
Master (procedure) (see *Update*)
Mathematical induction, 59–61, 372,
    374, 384
Maximum
    (function), 322–325
    (Pascal function), 390
maxint (Pascal constant), 170
Measures of central tendency, 8
Memory chips, 72
Memory locations, 71, 177
Memory (see Main memory, Auxiliary
    memory)
Menu, 75
Merge
    (algorithm), 500–501
    (module), 501–513
    (Pascal program), 540
    (UCSD Pascal unit), 541–542
Merge (algorithm), 18–22, 28, 45, 47–
    48
Metaphor, 127
Microcomputer, 78
Microprocessor, 69
Microprocessor revolution, 69
Minicomputer, 78–79

Missionaries and cannibals problem, 32–
    35, 44
mode (keyword), 493–495
Modeling, 7
Modem, 75
mod operator, 151–152
    in Pascal, 173
module (keyword), 364–371
Modules, 364–371, 427–439
Module specifications, 432–439
Module testing, 455
Monitor, 123
more (output command), 145–146
Mouse, 76, 128
MoveDisks (procedure) (see *Towers*)
Multidimensional arrays, 589–596
    in Pascal, 603–604
Multiprocessing, 133–134
Multiprogramming, 129–130
Multiway selection, 278–290, 309–317
Mutually exclusive access, 659–660
Mutual recursion, 406–408

Name equivalence, 486–487
Natural language interface, 8
Nested **for** constructions, 222–223, 594–
    596
Nested **for** statements, 611
Nested **if** constructions, 278–283
Nested **if** statements, 309–313
Nested records, 483–485
    in Pascal, 525
Nested scopes, 352–364
    in Pascal, 401
Nested unit definitions, 352–364
Nesting scheme, standard, 280–282,
    311–312
new
    (Pascal procedure), 807–808
    (procedure), 746–747
New (procedure), 616–620, 643–646 (see
    also *IntegerQueue*,
    IntegerQueueType,
    IntegerStack, *IntegerStackType*,
    and *TableHandler*)
NewAccount (procedure) (see *Update*)
NewQueue (procedure), 755 (see also
    IntegerQueue)

NewStack (procedure), 750 (see also
    IntegerStack)
NewTable (procedure), 766 (see also
    TableHandler)
Newton
    (Pascal procedure), 871
    (procedure), 838–842
Newton's method, 838–842
Next
    (function), 568
    (Pascal function), 607
nil (Pascal reserved word), 807
nil (predefined constant), 745–746
Node, 278, 741–742, 770ff
Nonextreme values, 458
Nonlinear equations, 831–842
Normalized floating-point number, 99–
    100
not operator, 291
    in Pascal, 317–320
Null character, 686
Null string, 678, 681, 686ff
Numerical errors, 827–831
Numerical integration, 856–865
    rectangle rule, 857–860
    Simpson's rule, 861–865
    trapezoid rule, 860–862
Numerical methods, 827–877
Numeric keypad, 74

Object program, 122
Octal digit, 91
Octal notation, 90–92
Odd numbers, generating, 40–42
Off-by-one error, 451–452
One-dimensional arrays, 547–589
    in Pascal, 601–603
One-way selection, 265–269, 303–309
O-notation, 560, 563, 565, 571, 581–
    582, 588–589
open statement, 492–495
Operating system, 123–129
    macros for, 124
    queues in, 657–660
Operation code, 101ff
Operations on binary values, 87–90
Operator priorities, 154–157, 291–292,
    317
Operators 29ff
    arithmetical, 151–156

in Pascal, 173
assignment, 180
    in Pascal, 207
Boolean, 290–297
    in Pascal, 317–320
order in which applied, 30
relational, 232–234, 678
    in Pascal, 251–255, 519, 522–523,
    727
sequence of, 29
specified by algorithm, 30–31
Optical character reader, 76–77
Ordinal types, 163, 519–520
ord (Pascal function), 520
Original equipment manufacturers, 78
or operator, 290–291
    in Pascal, 317–320
out (keyword) 329–332
Output, 144–147, 152–153, 187–188,
    485–496
    of arrays, 554–555
    in Pascal, 164–168, 208–209
Output devices, 67–68, 74–78
OutputFinalize (procedure) (see *Update*)
OutputInitialize (procedure) (see *Update*)
output mode, 492–495
Output parameter, 323, 329–332
output (Pascal file), 172
output statement, 144–147, 152–153,
    187–188, 495–496
packed (Pascal reserved word), 725ff
Packed types, 725–727
pack (Pascal procedure), 726
page (output command), 515
Page swapping, 126–127
Parameter-passing methods, 332–336
Parameters, 54–61, 393–396, 677–678
    field-width, 165–168
    functional, 833ff
    in Pascal, 868–869
    input, 323ff, 329–332
    input/output, 323, 329–332
    output, 323, 329–332
    in Pascal 164, 393–396
    procedural, 868–869
    substitution for, 713–720
Parametric type, 678
Parentheses, 155–156, 774–775
Parenthesis notation, 774–775
Partial Pivoting, 847–849

Pascal, 121–122
ANSI/IEEE standard, 161
Pascal machine, 127
PassFail
(algorithm), 276–278
(Pascal program), 305, 308–309
Path, in flowchart, 460–461
Pattern recognition, 292
Payroll
(algorithm), 272–274
(Pascal program), 304, 306
Payroll1
(algorithm), 274–276
(Pascal program), 305, 307
Period, at end of Pascal program, 171, 173
Peripheral devices, 68
control of, 124
Personal computers, 78
Personal investment, 226–228
Phonograph analogy, 4
Pitfalls of recursion, 377–382
Pivot, 847–849
Planning, 37–38, 49
for a trip, 43
PlayOneRound (procedure) (see *Craps*)
PlayRemainingRolls (procedure) (see *Craps*)
Plotter, 77
Pocket computers, 78
Pointer, 741ff
dangling, 748
in Pascal, 806–808
uninitialized, 748
pointer to (keywords), 744
Pointer types, 477, 741–748
in Pascal, 806–808
Pointing devices, 75–76
Polish notation (see Prefix notation)
Polya, G., 35
Pop (procedure), 616–620 (see also *IntegerStack* and *IntegerStackType*)
Portability, 421–422
Portable computers, 78
Position (stream function), 488
Postcondition, 14, 38, 268–269, 382–384
Postfix notation, 632–639
translation from infix, 636–639
and tree traversal, 781–782
Postorder traversal, 778–790

PostorderTraversal (procedure) (see *TreeTraversal*)
Powers of a number, 84
Precondition, 14, 38, 268–269, 382–384
Predefined constants (Pascal), 170
Predefined functions, 321
Predefined identifiers, 148
in Pascal, 169–170
Predefined types, 140, 477
in Pascal, 161
pred (Pascal function), 519
Prefix notation, 632
and tree traversal, 781–782
Preorder traversal, 778–790
PreorderTraversal (procedure) (see *TreeTraversal*)
Preprocessor, 440
Primary memory (see Main memory)
Primary storage (see Main memory)
Printer, 77
PrintFactorials
(algorithm), 326–327, 376
(Pascal program), 391–392, 414
Priorities, operator, 154–157, 291–292, 317
Priority queue, 658
Private data area, 639–643
Problem solving, 27–64
theory of, 27–35
techniques of, 39–51
Problem state, 27ff
Procedural parameters, 868–869
Procedure, 328–332, 389–393
recursive, 372
in Pascal, 164
procedure
(keyword), 328
(Pascal reserved word), 392
Procedure declaration, 391, 516
Procedure heading, 328, 391–392
Procedure statement, 164
Process, 130–133, 657–660
Processor (see Central processing unit)
Program, 4, 9
format in Pascal, 171–173
Program heading, 171–172, 207
Program loading, 124
Programming languages, 12, 118–123
Programming model, 103–105

program (Pascal reserved word), 171–172

Program synthesis, 454–455

Prompts 190–191
in Pascal, 213

Proving programs correct, 452–453

Pseudocode, 432–435

Pseudolanguage, 12, 139, 432–435

Pseudooperation, 120

Pseudorandom number generator, 340–341, 344–345

Punched card, 76

Push (procedure), 616–620 (see also *IntegerStack* and *IntegerStackType*)

put (Pascal procedure), 530ff

PutRecord (procedure) (see *Update*)

Queues, 643–660
applications of, 656–660
array implementation of, 646–656
axiomatic definition of, 644–646

Quicksort
(procedure), 582–589
(Pascal procedure) 611, 613

Quotient-remainder division, 152

RabbitProblem
(algorithm), 379–381
(Pascal program), 415–417

Radix point, 97

RAM, 72

Random-access memory, 71–72

RandomNumberGenerator, 366–371 (see also *SimulationOfWaitingLine*)
(Pascal unit), 409

Random numbers, 340–341, 344–345

Random (procedure) (see *Craps, Guess,* and *RandomNumberGenerator*)

Ranges, in case list, 288

Reading data, 235–238, 258–260

Reading (function) (see *Counter*)

ReadLine (procedure) (see *StringType*)

readln (Pascal procedure), 209–212

Read-only memory, 71–72, 118

read (Pascal procedure), 209–212, 534–538

Read (stream function), 488–489

ReadTree (procedure) (see *TreeTraversal*)

Read-write head, 73

Read-write memory, 71–72

Ready process, 130ff, 658

real
(Pascal type), 162
(type), 140–142

Real literal, 140–142
in Pascal, 162

record
(keyword), 479–487
(Pascal reserved word), 523–528

Records, 478–487
nested, in Pascal, 525

Record types, 477, 478–487
in Pascal, 523–528

Record variable, 480–482

Record variants, 526–528, 807–808

Rectangle
(Pascal procedure), 393–394, 875
(procedure), 330–331, 857–860

Rectangle rule, 857–860

Recursion, 12, 51–61, 371–382
Pascal, 413–417
pitfalls of, 377–382
requirements for, 51

Recursive algorithm, 54, 371–382
verification of, 59–61

Recursive call, 51ff

Recursive definition of tree, 771, 772–774

Reentrant program, 130

Reference, parameter passing by, 332–336, 393

Registers, 103–105

Relational operators, 232–234, 678
in Pascal, 251–255, 519, 727
for sets, 522–523

Reliability, 421

Remove (procedure), 643–646 (see also *IntegerQueue,* and *IntegerQueueType*)

repeat construction, 241–243

repeat statement (Pascal), 261–263

Repetition, 12, 31, 219–263, 440
and arithmetic/logic unit, 69–70
and control unit, 70
termination of, 20–22

Requirements analysis, 420, 423–426

Requirements definition, 423–426

Reseed (procedure) (see
      RandomNumberGenerator)
Reserved words (Pascal), 169
reset (Pascal procedure), 530ff
      in UCSD Pascal, 538–539, 546
Reset (stream function), 489–490
Reverse Polish notation (see Postfix
      notation)
rewrite (Pascal procedure), 530ff
      in UCSD Pascal, 538–539, 546
Right child, 790ff
RollDice (procedure) (see *Craps*)
ROM, 72
Root node, 278, 770ff
round
      (function), 157, 181
      (Pascal function), 174
Roundoff error, 827–829
RPN (see Postfix notation)
Running process, 130ff, 658

Scatter storage, 565
Scientific notation, 97
Scopes, 346–371
      of field identifiers, 482–483
      nested, 352–364
Searching arrays, 555–571
Secant
      (Pascal procedure), 870
      (procedure), 836–838
Secant method, 836–838
Secondary memory (see Auxiliary
      memory)
Secondary storage (see Auxiliary
      memory)
Security, 128–129
Seed, 341, 344–345
Selection, 12, 31, 265–320, 440, 451
      and arithmetic/logic unit, 69
      and control unit, 70
select (keyword), 287–290
Semantics, 256, 455
Semaphores, 658–660
Sentinel, 109, 235ff, 558ff, 686ff
Sequencing, 12, 192, 440
      and control unit, 70
Sequential access, 72
Sequential file processing, 497–498
      in Pascal, 533–546

Sequential search, 556–560
      efficiency of, 559–560
SequentialSearch (see also *TableHandler*)
      (Pascal procedure), 604–606
      (procedure), 555–560, 761–779
Set constructor, 315, 521–523
set of (Pascal reserved words), 521–523
SetPosition (stream function), 489–490
SetToEnd (stream function), 489–490
Set types, 315, 520–523
Shift left operation, 90
Shift operations, 88–90
Shift right operation, 90
ShoppingArea (procedure) (see
      SimulationOfWaitingLine)
Sibling node, 771ff
Sign, 94–95, 102
      of floating-point number, 98–100
Signal (semaphore operation), 659–660
Sign bit, 94–95, 102
Signed numbers, representation of, 94–96
Significand, 97–100
Significant digits, 141n
Sign-magnitude representation, 94–95,
      101–102
Simple types, 477
Simpson
      (Pascal procedure), 877
      (procedure), 861–875
Simpson's rule, 861–865
Simulation, 7
      in games, 9
      queues in, 656–657
      of specifications, 453–454
SimulationOfWaitingLine
      (algorithm), 424–428, 430–449
      (Pascal program), 467–474
sin (Pascal function), 174
Size (stream function), 488
Skip (procedure) 682–683 (see also
      StringType)
Slot, 68
Software, 4, 67, 117–135
Software crisis, 419
Software development life cycle, 420
Software engineering, 420–421
Software packages, statistical, 8
Sort (algorithm), 12–18
Sorting, 13
      external, 579

Sorting (continued)
  internal, 578–589
  problem of, 28–32, 37
Source program, 122
Special purpose computer, 117–118
Special values, 458
Specification, 420, 426–428
Speech recognition, 78
Speech synthesizer, 77
Spreadsheet program, 7
sqr (Pascal function), 174
sqrt
  (function), 157
  (Pascal function), 174
Stack, 615–643
  applications of, 631–643
  array implementation of, 620–631
  axiomatic definition of, 616–620
Stack frame, 639–643
Standard input file, 172, 259–260
Standard nesting scheme, 280–282
  in Pascal, 311–312
Standard output file, 172
Statement, 144ff
Statement part (Pascal), 171–173, 207
Stepwise refinement, 49, 192, 429
Storage (see Main memory and Auxiliary memory)
Stream, 487–490
  functions and procedures for, 488–489, 497
Stress testing, 458
String, 673–739
  fixed length, 674–677
  variable-length, 677–713
String literal, 143–144
  in Pascal, 163
String-processing module, 691–713
  in Pascal, 728–739
String space, 687–691
StringToInteger (function), 683–684 (see also *StringType*)
string (type), 143–144
StringType
  (module) 691–713
  (UCSD Pascal unit), 728–739
String types, in Pascal, 727–728
Strong type checking (Pascal), 207
Structural equivalence, 485–486
Structural testing, 458–463

Structure chart, 345–346
Structured programming, 440
Structured types, 477
Stub, 456
Subalgorithms, 321–417
Subgoals, 48–49, 51–61
Subproblems, 48–49, 51–61
Subprogram, 122, 321–417
  managing calls and returns, 639–643
Subrange types, 517–518
Substitution for parameters, 713–720
Substring, 673ff
Substring (procedure), 679–680 (see also *StringType*)
Subtraction, binary, 87
Subtree, 771ff
succ (Pascal function), 519
Sum (algorithm) 109–110
Supercomputer, 79
Supermini, 78
Supervisor, 123
Suspended process, 130ff
Symbol, 5–6
Symbol manipulation, 5
Syntax, 455
System command, 123, 128–129
System software, 117

TableHandler
  (module), 571–578, 761–770, 792–803
  (UCSD Pascal unit), 607–611, 813–816, 819–821
tab (output command), 145–147, 270–271
Terminating period (Pascal), 171, 173, 207
Termination
  of algorithm, 11
  of repetition, 219–220, 234, 237–241
Termination condition, 241
Testability, 421–422
Test data, choosing, 456–463
Test driver, 456
Testing, 420, 449–450, 455–464
Text display, 74
Text editor, 7
text extend mode, 493–495

Textfiles, in Pascal, 536–538
Text formatter, 7
text input mode, 493–495
text output mode, 493–495
Text processing, 7
then
    (keyword), 265ff
    (Pascal reserved word), 303ff
then part, 269
Three-bit group, 91
Time quantum, 129ff
Time sharing, 71, 78–79, 125, 133
Time slice, 129ff
to
    (keyword), 220ff, 288
    (Pascal reserved word), 248ff
Top (function), 616–620 (see also
    IntegerStack and *IntegerStackType*)
Top-down design, 341, 429–430
Top-down implementation and testing,
    455–456
Total, computing of, 223–226, 235–238
Touch pad, 76
Touch-sensitive display, 76
Towers
    (algorithm), 371–374
    (Pascal program), 413
Towers of Hanoi problem, 52–61, 371–
    374
Track, 73
Translator, 122–123
Trapezoid
    (Pascal procedure), 876
    (procedure), 860–862
Trapezoid rule, 860–862
TraversalRoutines (module), 782–790
Trees, 741–742, 770–803
    and postfix notation, 781–782
    and prefix notation, 781–782
    binary search, 748, 790–803
    decision, 278–282, 301
    expression, 777–778
    linked representation of, 782–790
    notations for, 774–782
    recursive definition of, 771, 772–774
    terminology of, 774
    traversal of, 778–782
TreeTraversal
    (algorithm), 782–790
    (Pascal program), 816–818

Triangles
    (algorithm), 292–294
    (Pascal program), 319, 321
Trivial case, 371
true (Boolean value), 142
Truncation error, 827–831
trunc
    (function), 156–157, 181
    (Pascal function), 174
Twin node, 771ff
Twos-complement operation, 96
Twos-complement representation, 95–96,
    101–102
Two-state circuits, 81–83
Two-way selection, 265–269, 303–309
type
    (keyword), 478
    (Pascal reserved word), 516
Types, 139–144
    anonymous, 481
    assignment compatibility, 822–823
    compatibility, 822–823
    component, 548
        in Pascal, 601–602
    definitions of, 478
        in Pascal, 516
    enumerated, 516–517
    equivalence of, 485–487
    file, 491–497
        in Pascal, 528–546
    index, in Pascal, 601–603
    parametric, 678
    in Pascal, 161–163
    pointer, 741–748
        in Pascal, 806–808
    predefined, 477
    record, 478–487
        in Pascal, 523–528
    set, 520–523
    subrange, 517–518
    summary of Pascal type system, 822–
        823

UCSD Pascal, 260, 408–414, 467–474,
    739
Unconditional jump instruction, 107
Underscore character, 148
    in Pascal, 169

Understanding a problem, 35–37
Uninitialized pointer, 748
Union, 522
Unit
  in algorithmic language, 328
  in UCSD Pascal, 408–414
Unit definitions, nested, 352–364
unit (Pascal reserved word), 408
Units conversion, 195–197
Unnormalized binary fraction, 100
unpack (Pascal procedure), 726
until
  (keyword), 241–243
  (Pascal reserved word), 261–262
Update
  (module), 501–513
  (UCSD Pascal unit), 542–545
UpdatePlayersBankroll (procedure) (see
  Craps)
Updating a file, 501–513
Useability, 421–422
User-friendly systems, 127–128, 422
User interface, 128
Users' Groups, 4n
uses (Pascal reserved word), 410, 474

Validation, 449–464
Value, 139–140
  array, 547–548
  component, 480
  entire, 480
  of expression, 151
  of variable, 178
  pointer, 741ff
  returned by function, 323–325, 390
Value parameter, 393–396
Variable, 177–187
  array, 548–550
    in Pascal, 602–603
  buffer, 530–533, 537
  component, 480–481, 550–551
  entire, 480–481, 550
  in expression, 182–187
  as field-width parameter (Pascal), 209
  file, 491–492
    in Pascal, 529–530
  in **input** statement, 188–190
  in Pascal, 206–207
  record 480–482

Variable declaration part (Pascal), 391,
  206–207, 516
Variable-length strings, 677–713
  implementation of, 684–691
  module for processing, 691–713
  operations on, 678–684
Variable parameters, 393–396
Variable-value table, 178
Variant part, 526–528
var (Pascal reserved word), 206, 393–
  396
Verification, 449–464
  of procedures and functions, 382–384
  of selections, 268–269
Very-high-level language, 454
Video display, 74
Video games, 9
Virtual machine, 127
Virtual memory, 126–127
Volatile memory, 71
Volume (Pascal function), 390

WaitingLine (module) (see
  SimulationOfWaitingLine)
Waiting-line simulation, 424–428, 430–
  449
Wait (semaphore operation), 659–660
Walkthrough, 451–452
Water-jar problem, 50–51
Weighing problem, 48
Wheat
  (algorithm), 230–231
  (Pascal program), 255
while construction, 231–241
while statement (Pascal), 255–260
Window, 127–128
with statement, 525–526, 666–668, 670–
  672
Word, 16 bit, 100–101
Word processor, 7
Working backward, 49–51
Working set, 126–127
WriteLine (procedure) (see *StringType*)
writeln (Pascal procedure), 164–168,
  208–209
write (Pascal procedure), 208–209, 534–
  538, 164–168
Write (stream function), 488–490
WriteString (procedure) (see *StringType*)